D0915338

By the same author

MAN AGAINST MYTH

GIANT IN CHAINS

THE ARTIST IN SOCIETY

HEROES

AND

HERETICS

Heroes & Heretics

A POLITICAL HISTORY
OF WESTERN THOUGHT

Barrows Dunham

*He that sides with a Party is adjudg'd to Hell
by the Rest; and if he declares for none, he receives
no milder Sentence from all.*

JOHN TOLAND, *Christianity Not Mysterious* [1696]

New York · Alfred A. Knopf · 1964

109
D918

ACKNOWLEDGMENT is made for permission to quote from the following:

The Dawn of Conscience by James Henry Breasted. Copyright 1933 James Henry Breasted; renewal copyright © 1961 Charles Breasted, James Breasted, Jr., and Astrid Breasted Hormann. Reprinted by permission of Charles Scribner's Sons.

The Bible: A New Translation by James Moffatt. Copyright, James Moffatt 1954. Reprinted by permission of Harper & Row, Publishers, Incorporated.

Fathers of the Church by F. A. Wright. Reprinted by permission of Routledge & Kegan Paul, Ltd.

The New English Bible: New Testament. © The Delegates of the Oxford University Press and The Syndics of the Cambridge University Press 1961.

L. C. catalog card number: 63-9141

THIS IS A BORZOI BOOK,
PUBLISHED BY ALFRED A. KNOPF, INC.

Copyright © 1963 by BARROWS DUNHAM. All rights reserved. No part of this book may be reproduced in any form without permission in writing from the publisher, except by a reviewer, who may quote brief passages in a review to be printed in a magazine or newspaper. Manufactured in the United States of America, and distributed by Random House, Inc. Published simultaneously in Toronto, Canada, by Random House of Canada, Limited.

FIRST EDITION

To My Grandsons

Richard Scott Dunham [1956]
Robert Brett Dunham [1958]
William Barrows Dunham [1963]

Aspice venturo laetentur ut omnia saeclo

218125

PREFACE

O NE OF THE THINGS a man has to do in life is to discover, so far as he can, the grounds for believing what he is asked to believe. Reason, of course, bids him believe all those assertions, and only those assertions, that seem likely to be true. Yet, so soon as he tries faithfully to follow reason, he grows aware of other grounds, or at least of pressures, which derive from the organized society around him. That is to say, he finds himself enticed or driven into beliefs he would not otherwise have held.

Belief thus attained shows the play of police power upon intellectual life. The play is ordinarily subtle, being an adroit compound of reward and punishment. Careers within one's own society are easier if one believes what the society says it believes, and those same careers may end abruptly if one ceases to hold those same beliefs. Such events have happened throughout recorded history— indeed, one may conjecture, throughout history that has not been recorded. In the early 1950's a good many Americans made personal acquaintance with the fact.

Now, science and philosophy, which presumably seek true statements and true statements alone, follow a path that cuts quite across socially established ideas. Thus the effort of some men to assert what really is the case collides with the effort of administrators to maintain unity throughout their organizations. When these crises arise, the thinker has to pit his love of truth against the administrator's authority. In the thinker's view, this is an act of simple personal integrity. To the administrator, however, it may seem rebellious and worthy of such epithets as "presumptuous" or "arrogant."

Such contrary evaluations of one and the same act characteristically occur as between members and leaders of an organization whenever a member feels himself morally bound to oppose the leadership's policy. Then the member may seem to be unduly asserting himself and thus to be guilty of arrogance. Generally speaking, therefore, "integrity" is the member's view of the case and "arrogance" the leadership's. This notion seems confirmed by the remarkable etymology of the word "heresy," which enables that word to signify an opinion personally preferred by the holder of it.

Language, accordingly, points toward the social fact (obvious enough in any event) that human opinions get themselves classified not only as true or false but as acceptable or unacceptable to organizations. These last two classes are of course political, and it is in connection with them that thinkers have been liable to punishment. The actual history of thought, however, has been a mélange, a welter, of all four—with truth, falsity, heresy, orthodoxy tumbling over one another in a style half tragic and half absurd. I think there will be some value in displaying this welter, following its course along the development of Western thought, with such shape and motion as events themselves have given it.

I have therefore undertaken a political history of philosophy, and have set it in the form of a long contest between members and leaders for control over organizational doctrine. The scale of the work had necessarily to be large. How else could one display the fact that such events, now obviously going on, have been going on since antiquity? How else could one show the repeated pattern or draw lessons for future use?

There are of course risks in this, as large as the scale itself. I cannot suppose that I understand all epochs of Western thought with equal adequacy. Few men, perhaps, are expert upon any epoch, and sensible scholars restrict themselves to portions of epochs or to portions of portions. Further, alas, there is the fact that historical writing will be damaged quite as much by ignorant (if innocent) omissions as by misconception of the material.

Some of my omissions, however, are deliberate. I have confined myself chiefly to those heretics whose notions and behavior were important to historical change. Thus, for example, I have not touched upon Savonarola, because his work was decisively done by the great Reformers rather than by himself. For the same reason I have preferred Lincoln to John Brown, and Debs to any other American socialist.

My intellectual debts are as numerous as the authors I have read and the men I have listened to. The Bibliographical Essay acknowledges some of these and at the same time exempts them from any erroneous use I may have made of their wisdom. Perhaps, however, I may here particularize so far as to thank my friend Mr. Samuel Adams Darcy, from whom directly I learned the view (held, I think, by all statesmen but by few professors) that history is the movement of human multitudes in struggle.

The title of this book I owe to the charming lyricist of *Finian's Rainbow*, Mr. E. Y. Harburg. Dissatisfied with my pedestrian efforts, he readily produced the title that the book required. And finally, I desire to thank members of the staff and administration of the Library of the University of Pennsylvania for many kindnesses and especially for giving me access to that admirable collection.

BARROWS DUNHAM

Cynwyd, Pennsylvania
September 1963

CONTENTS

HEROES
AND
HERETICS

The Criminal of Amarna

THE MAN WHO MARRIED the most beautiful woman, ever and anywhere, was also the first heretic we know of. Moreover, he was, what is unusual in heretics, a king. There was thus no trouble effecting his heresy: he simply decreed it. But the vested interests whom he thus impoverished hated him, and his people, taken too suddenly from familiar ideas, grew alarmed.

The king was Amenhotep IV, a pharaoh of the eighteenth dynasty, about 1372 to 1354 B.C. This name he changed, in celebration of his heresy, to Akhnaton. That is to say, he preferred being called "Aten is well pleased" to being called "Amon is satisfied." The reason was that the Pharaoh, having a taste for physical explanations, conceived the ruling god as a sun-disk rather than as a spirit of the sun.

The wonderful queen was Nofretete, and her name signified "Beauty is come among us." Of that beauty there can be no doubt: her portrait bust, found amid the dilapidations of an ancient studio, is sufficiently convincing. It had been intended, apparently, for use as a model, and the sculptor (Thutmose, his name may have been) omitted to furnish an iris to the left eye. Yet in art, as I suppose, nothing really can be absent when perfection is there.

One needs an historian's sobriety not to romanticize this constellation of marvels. A glance from those eyes, a word from those lips, must surely have made obedience seem like privilege. Was it

Nofretete, then, who inspired the heresy and sustained Akhnaton's zeal? There is some reason to think so. Her name has been effaced from various monuments, where, in its stead, appears the name of her daughter Meritaten. She may therefore be supposed to have suffered the same vengeance from the priesthood that erased Akhnaton's name from the calendar of kings, where he appears, when at all, as "that criminal of Amarna."

Yet one must expect a king to reign, and when a king is as nearly absolute as the pharaohs were, he must be held the genuine source of government. It seems unlikely that Akhnaton would have abolished ancient rites and old theogonies for no other purpose than to please even so lovely a queen. She agreed, no doubt, and gave him strength. She may even have sustained longer loyalty than he to the Aten cult. But the cult itself was his own notion—the concept of a dreamer and philosopher who chanced, by the rarest of chances, to be also a king.

The main facts are reasonably clear. Akhnaton outlawed the old theology, closed down the temples of the traditional gods, abolished the priesthoods, services, and profits connected with them. He built in the plain of Amarna a new shrine and capital, Akhetaten, the City of the Horizon of the Sun. Priestly wrath and consternation can hardly have been less than they would be if some modern government were to abolish, all at once and all together, Catholicism, Protestantism, Judaism, and every other religion hitherto existing. Yet the priests, thus stricken, had no alternative and no redress. The Pharaoh's will was paramount.

It is of course possible to destroy a group by destroying its functions, but this can be done only when the rest of the population desires, or at any rate supports, the change. Akhnaton, however, seems to have acted without such support and without much attempt to gather it. Perhaps some conflict with the priesthood, inherited from the previous reign, hurried him into action. At all events, he received obedience but not consent.

What were people to think and do when the gods they had worshiped, sworn by, lived by, were all at once declared nullities? One's child was perhaps ill, and one had always appealed to Amon on such occasions. One's husband had died, and it had always been necessary to settle such accounts with Osiris. But now, by decree of Akhnaton, Amon and Osiris were nowhere to be found. Their priests were scattered, their temples wasted grass. In the old days, Amon had healed and Osiris saved. Could one be sure that Aten would do these things?

The people felt, one imagines, left naked to circumstance. A trusted guard had been removed, and the new seemed no protection because untried. Thus men kept a secret faith in the old religion and the old rites; they were on the priests' side, whatever the Pharaoh might decree. And in the end, when Akhnaton had died, priests and people did to his works what he had done to some of theirs. The City of the Sun's Horizon was razed to those foundations which still linger at Amarna, and the succeeding Pharaoh, Tutankaten, changed his name to the celebrated Tutankhamon we now know.

Thus the god Aten, the divine sun-disk, lost to the god Amon, the spirit of the sun. It had happened to many gods before him, and it has happened to many gods after him. When deities engage in human politics, they must prepare to suffer the twilight and the dark.

I I

IF WE LOOK at the social structure within these events, we shall perceive why Akhnaton's views and policies were heretical. They were so because they were new and because they involved a change in the possession of power. Akhnaton had declared certain doctrines to be false and had replaced them with other doctrines that he asserted to be true. This alteration in thought had required an alteration in the political structure. Accordingly, Akhnaton had deprived an entire class of its functions and privileges—the priests of Amon, whose wealth, prestige, and power depended upon popular acceptance of the old, but now abolished, ideas. At the same time, as the episode plainly shows, ideas cannot be merely "abolished." They have a life of their own, and a larger life than is granted to governments.

Heresies are thus ideas that disrupt an existing society in such a way as to change, or to threaten to change, the distribution of power within it. It happens, however, that Akhnaton's heresy was, beyond all this, peculiarly formidable—so formidable, indeed, that in some parts of the world it still remains heresy. It had to do, and has to do, with the effort of men to become scientists—to accept the world, and to explain it, in terms of such concepts as matter and energy, space and time. These concepts are notably impersonal. They explain events without recourse to any powers conceived on analogy with human beings as having purposes or intentions. If, for example, a stone falls from a building, strikes a passer-by, and kills him, science is content to explain by the law of gravitation, the mass of the stone, and the fragility of the skull.[1] Science would never invoke the notion of a supernatural personage who produced the death by *intending* it.

Yet science, which we now glory in, has but recently attained so admired a status. The old view of the world, not radically attacked until the seventeenth century A.D., was that most happenings are intended happenings. Some deity or other, some superhuman and supernatural personage, purposed them and produced them:

> The world appears to primitive man [say the Frankforts] neither inanimate nor empty but redundant with life; and life has individuality, in man and beast and plant, and in every phenomenon which confronts man—the thunderclap, the sudden shadow, the eerie and unknown clearing in the wood, the stone which suddenly hurts him when he stumbles while on a hunting trip. Any phenomenon may at any time face him, not as "It," but as "Thou."[2]

These powers, personal but not human, the Egyptians found in animals and birds and in mere inorganic systems such as earth, sea, sky. The crocodile could powerfully bite, the falcon could greatly soar, the lion was very strong, the ibis, brooding fixedly in the water, had an air of wisdom. The world seemed full of powers excelling man's, yet joined with purposes not unlike our own.

These ideas, at some moment in their growth, disclosed political implications. For example, one reason why gods were a multitude was that there were many settled communities in the Nile Valley, each with its own tutelary deities conceived as peculiarly interested in the community itself. Consolidation of small groups into larger— ultimately into an entire kingdom—effected also a consolidation of gods. Thus Amon, sun god of the Upper Nile, and Re, sun god of the Lower Nile, were joined as Amon-Re, whose supremacy was celebrated at Thebes.

But the Egyptians seem to have preferred a plurality of gods and even a certain anarchy among them. "From time to time," says Cottrell, "the priesthood tried to organize these many gods into a

---

1) I draw this illustration, of course, from Spinoza, *Ethics,* Part I, Appendix.
2) Frankfort, Frankfort, Wilson, and Jacobsen, *Before Philosophy* (London: Penguin Books; 1949), p. 14.

single theological system, but the task was beyond them."³ Perhaps this theological anarchism reflected skillful administration. The Pharaoh's absolute authority rested on an adroit delegation of power; and local communities, which were the blocks in the great edifice, had their integrity confirmed by recognition of their favorite gods.

More impressive, however, is the pharaohs' own ascent to divinity. They seem to have begun as chief priests of some god or other, in addition, of course, to their political headship. Insensibly this status rose into that of being an incarnate god. The political advantages are obvious. A god has superhuman powers and, partly because of those powers, superhuman merit. This merit and these powers protected every pharaoh in his rule and in his life. He became remote as gods are, unapproachable except by a few consecrated persons, mostly of his own family. A stifling etiquette surrounded him. He knew, in dreadful perfection, the loneliness with which power curses the powerful.

Yet there seemed no other way to rule and be safe. One aging pharaoh, Amenemhet, warned his son:

> Hold thyself together against those subordinate (to thee), lest that should happen to whose terrors no thought has been given. Do not approach them in thy loneliness. Fill not thy heart with a brother, know not a friend, nor create for thyself intimates—that has no (happy) outcome. . . . I gave to the poor and brought up the orphan . . . (but) it was he who ate my food that raised up troops (against me) . . . and they who were clothed in my fine linen looked upon me as mere dried weeds.⁴

Divinity is, upon the whole, the most ingenious device that political theory has ever discovered. It protects the ruler in life and in power, but more particularly it protects the *office* against the human frailties of the incumbent. A mere man is too much like the governed, with all their susceptibility to error and vice. The only way, by means of theory, to equal him with lordship is to make him a god. But if this is to be done, theory must assert that gods exist: personages, that is to say, greater than human nature, greater than all nature, in respect of what they can know and choose and do. Beyond this, there must be the assertion of an order of being, of existence, of reality,

3) Leonard Cottrell, *The Anvil of Civilization* (New York: Mentor Books; 1957), p. 65. Cottrell adds, "It is, I suggest, also beyond us."
4) Quoted in Frankfort *et al.*, op. cit., p. 88.

more perfect in accomplishment and more worthy to be admired than anything we find in the physical constitution of the world.

This sort of transcendental philosophy it was the function of the priesthood to perpetuate, and from it they also drew justification of their own lofty place in the political hierarchy. Prestige, however, did not rest upon mythology alone. The Egyptian priests, the intelligentsia of those days, owed much to what they scientifically knew and to the secrecy with which they surrounded knowledge. They had learned how "to predict the time of the Nile's rising, to calculate the amount of its flooding and therefore of the eventual harvest."[5] They went on to discover, and provide, information about dams and canals, weights and measures, and the geometry required for building pyramids. Their greatest achievement was the invention of written language—that wonderful device which, as Cottrell says, permits communication without personal contact.

From all these facts we can begin to infer some of the characteristics of ideology. The ideology of a people is an assemblage of doctrines, something between a system and a flux, intended to describe the society itself and the physical environment. Ordinarily it is as scientific as the society requires or permits; sometimes it is a little more so, sometimes a little less. It preserves and perpetuates a certain number of inherited ideas, and thus attests the continuity of generations. It expresses, so far as it can, the people's control over nature and the ruler's control over people.

Ideologically, the ruler's control over people requires much more than a bare statement to the effect that it exists. It requires also justification. Nothing can be less self-evident than that a given ruler is the rightful ruler and ought to be the one to rule. Some proof is always necessary that he ought to rule and ought to rule in the way he does. We have seen how readily this "proof" can be made to follow from the idea that the ruler is a god, but the need for justification is in fact felt all up and down the ranks of hierarchy, where status, and therefore justification, are alike derivative.

Perhaps we may reconstruct, out of recorded data, a little drama of those ancient times. A poor man cries out upon the practices of courts of law: "Seizers! Robbers! Plunderers! Officials!—and yet appointed to punish evil! Officialdom is the refuge of the arrogant— and yet appointed to punish falsehood!"[6] Surely, now, "officialdom"

5) Cottrell, op. cit., pp. 42–43.
6) Quoted in Frankfort *et al.*, op. cit., p. 97.

must reply and explain itself, showing at least the rectitude of its intentions. It might say, and one vizier actually did say, "When I judged a petitioner, I showed no partiality, I did not incline my brow because of a reward . . . but I rescued the timid man from the arrogant."[7] Or, hard pressed, it might seek transcendental refuge in the just decisions of a god: "Amon judges the land with his fingers . . . He separates the unjust . . ."[8]

Thus organizational self-justification has existed since the earliest empires, and it will continue to be needed and practiced so long as human society lasts.

I I I

SELF-JUSTIFICATION is like to be a corrupt art precisely because it is *self*-justification. Suspicion rises at once, and even the lowliest observer finds himself unconvinced. He further finds, however, that he cannot pierce the explanation. The propagandist curtain shrouding the evil fact hangs thick and impenetrable. Self-justification is a mighty guard for power.

This being true, it is the more amazing that a king should ever have tried to disturb that guard, and to disturb it in a manner most likely to bring it down. In human history thus far, the ideological guard has on the whole been stronger when it involved supernatural powers and personages. By moving toward a purely scientific view of the world, Akhnaton (unknown to himself, I do not doubt) awoke all those democratic implications which lie in science. He thus may be said to have begun, very remotely, a long historical process inimical to kings.

There exists, in sizable fragments, a "Hymn to the Sun," attributed to Akhnaton himself. The "Hymn" celebrates human needs, and adores the physical sun as the great agent by which all needs are satisfied. The sun makes life possible for men and plants and animals. It makes work possible by "driving away the darkness,"[9] and it makes sleep possible by bringing the darkness again. It helps the fledgling "chirp in his shell" and the babe "live in the body of his mother." It "sets a Nile in the sky" for watering fields and towns; its rays "nourish every garden."

7) Ibid., p. 100.
8) Ibid., p. 99.
9) The quotations are in J. H. Breasted's translation, *The Dawn of Conscience* (New York: Charles Scribner's Sons; 1949), pp. 281–286.

Solar energy, beyond doubt, confers benefits on all men quite impartially. Aten might therefore be held to be an extremely democratic god. But this was not quite the inference that Akhnaton intended. On the contrary, the "Hymn" presents Akhnaton as the sun's son and only true initiate:

> *There is no other that knoweth thee*
> *Save thy son Akhnaton.*
> *Thou hast made him wise*
> *In thy designs and in thy might.*
>
> *The world subsists in thy hand,*
> *Even as thou hast made them.*
> *When thou hast risen they live,*
> *When thou settest they die;*
> *For thou art length of life of thyself,*
> *Men live through thee.*
>
> *The eyes of men see beauty*
> *Until thou settest.*
> *All labor is put away*
> *When thou settest in the west.*
> *When thou risest again*
> *[Thou] makest [every hand] to flourish for the king*
> *And [prosperity] is in every foot,*
> *Since thou didst establish the world,*
> *And raise them up for thy son,*
> *Who came forth from thy flesh,*
> *The king of Upper and Lower Egypt,*
> *Living in truth, Lord of the two Lands,*
> *Nefer-khepru-Re, Wan-Re [Akhnaton],*
> *Son of Re, living in truth, lord of diadems,*
> *Akhnaton, whose life is long;*
> *[And for] the chief royal wife, his beloved,*
> *Mistress of the Two Lands, Nefer-nefru-Aton, Nofretete,*
> *Living and flourishing for ever and ever.*

Akhnaton was no leveler. He intended to maintain society as an hierarchical order with himself in highest rank. Accordingly, it is one of the sun's fairest blessings that it causes every hand and foot to prosper for the king. There cannot often have been, in human ideology, so candid an acknowledgment of exploitation.

Yet a democratizing of the spirit, if not of the social structure, did in fact occur. Egyptian art took on a sudden realism and even informality. Akhnaton and Nofretete are shown playing with their children, fondling and kissing them as any parents might do. The son-in-law Tutankhamon and his wife (Akhnaton's third daughter) have similar treatment: the king sits relaxed in his chair, one arm over the back of it, while the queen touches his shoulder affectionately, either to adjust his collar or to give it perfume which she is holding in a vase.[1] No previous pharaohs had allowed such intimacies to be pictured. Aloofness has left the monarch; he desires his subjects to know that his affections are very like their own. He is a *père de famille* sort of king, as Louis XV and Louis XVI tried in their time to be.

The Aten disk, in portrayals of that time, stretches down many hands to help humanity. By this image, Akhnaton meant perhaps no more than that he himself was lord over all mankind. Yet, as we see, it is hard to defeat further implications of equality and brotherhood. Such implications are perhaps the heart of all heresy, whether the heretic knows it or not. It is a boon conferred even by those heresies which, otherwise, are mere folly and pride. Can it have been that the priests of old illusion, when they brought back the profitable darkness, knew, in some dim professional way, that they had saved not their own careers merely but the possibility of priestcraft in general? If they did not, then they were the only parasitic class in history to be unaware that, for parasitism to exist at all, the social opportunity for it must be maintained.

Knowledge, it is plain, does not always win, nor beauty either. Yet in the longest stretch of time, they are hard to quench. It is usual for heretics to appear in the lower ranks of society, because, in those ranks, there are fewer privileges to distort the working out of ideas. Akhnaton, however, and Nofretete took great political risks for the Aten cult, and had no reason to do so except that they believed it to be true. Perhaps, in the end, this devotion to principle has saved them. It is at any rate the case that, although the City of the Horizon of the Sun was leveled and the names of Akhnaton and Nofretete erased, we know more about that royal scientist and that royal beauty than about many others who went before them or followed them. And with them, more than with many others, we are grateful for what we know.

1) This scene, depicted on a chair back, is reproduced in Breasted, op. cit., facing p. 290.

CHAPTER

I

Man and Membership

HUMAN LIFE, from as early a time as we know, has always been social and therefore organized. There were not, except by accident, solitary Crusoes; and the notion, a favorite of our ancestors, that society derived from an agreement among previously separate persons, is a fiction about history, a *Robinsonade*.

Nor can we suppose that human life is developing toward a condition of scattered hermits. Increasing population would alone make solitude difficult, even if solitude were, as it is not, desirable. Moreover that brief segment of history which lies within written record is a kind of school for civilization—a discipline, hardly learned, by which men become *cives,* citizens, able to live together with least shock or jar and, as may be in some millennium, with love. The ant, not the mole, is our exemplar. We do our noblest works socially and in the light.

Accordingly, there are, beyond doubt, entities corresponding to the great collective nouns: "mankind," "society," "nation," "church." These are collective in respect of the fact that they are systems and display within themselves a structure of relationships which is the mode of their organization. The members of these systems are sometimes members by birth or compulsion and sometimes members by choice, but in any event their membership strongly affects their characters. If one were to subtract from the total explanation of

human behavior those parts that are socially conditioned, the remainder would perhaps be less in size and power than the part
subtracted.

There would, however, be a remainder. Human behavior shows a
certain amount of spontaneous causation, which is the striving of
each person to satisfy his needs and to gratify his wishes. This
primordial fact and, together with it, the objectivity of historical
circumstances are the two basic constants of social inquiry. That is to
say, nothing is likely to happen which will alter the nature of man
as a needy, striving animal, and nothing is likely to happen which
will turn history from the course ordained for it by the evolution of
social structures and the interplay of many billion wills.

For example, every man needs food, and this fact entails the
further fact that he will try to get it. It will not, however, determine
the manner in which he tries or the means by which he obtains.
These, rather, take their nature from the social environment in
which he lives; they follow, not from human psychology, but from
human history. No doubt, in this interaction between self and environment, certain changes occur, rather like nibbles, in the two
constants. The individual man, as his needs turn into specific wishes,
finds these wishes much shaped by all that is traditional and legalized
in his society. At the same time, the vast unfolding of history,
majestic and indomitable though it is, suffers nevertheless the dent
and pressure of his own will. Accordingly, it is perhaps the case that
men can make better history and that history can make better men.

If all social discourse proceeds within these two constants, ethics,
which is a form of social discourse, proceeds there too. Our rooted,
fundamental values seem to lie in certain desirable states of society
and of the human self. We find, moreover, that we cannot rationally
sacrifice either sort of value for the sake of the other: we cannot ask
a man to degrade himself on behalf of society or society to degrade
itself on behalf of individual men. Integrity, wholeness of conscience,
is perhaps the chief personal good; unity, harmony, the chief social.
Yet the effort after these falls often into conflict. Heretics assert their
consciences as against society, and society asserts its unity as against
heretics. It is a kind of conflict in which important values keep
getting lost, and the inference plainly is that we would do well to be
rid of the conflict altogether.

In our tradition, heretics have found much applause, if not always freedom. We tend to think of them as heroes who were badgered or destroyed by ignorant and vicious men. It is evident, however, that some heretics were no more than cantankerous oddities, and that the social order had reason to defend itself. Yet I suppose the other fact must remain more poignant and impressive: that a great many heretics were indeed liberators, thwarted and destroyed by men who would grant no liberty at all.

We shall therefore find much profit in reviewing these conflicts as they have occurred along the main development of Western thought. It is a tale of fraud and violence and heroism—of power politics, that is to say—in which the virtuous do not always suffer, the sufferers are not always virtuous, the rulers are not always evil, and the evil do not always rule. Nevertheless, government is legalized violence, and science is peaceful understanding. There is often much jostling between them.

It appears, therefore, that a veracious history of philosophy would be a political history of philosophy. It would set forth strife as well as doctrines, and it would be frank to say that every revolution in thought relates in some manner to a revolution in society. It would publicly divulge what every inquisitor has known, that theory tends to alter practice, and that, consequently, theorists are, when not carefully disciplined, God's curse upon administrators.

The human effort at understanding the world has thus occurred, and does still occur, amid the violence of contending powers. Not Socratic doctrine but Athenian government brought forth the hemlock; not inner voices but a conspiracy of French ecclesiastics and English generals cast Joan of Arc into the flames. I hope it will not be always thus. I hope that in, say, the twenty-fifth century philosophical labor will be conducted in the quiet way you would think it had always been conducted if you believed the histories of philosophy. Meanwhile, since we sing of men, we must sing of arms.

I I

BECAUSE THERE ARE FACTS to be described and values to be determined, men find it necessary to explain and justify their own conduct. It is always important for us to know what other people take to be the case and what principles they use to shape decision. If they do not tell us these things, or do not tell them truly, we shall seek the answers in their behavior, which may well be more eloquent than any words.

These conditions hold yet more strongly for human organizations. *They* are for the most part public and hence invite inspection, or, if they are in any manner secret, they are nevertheless liable to discovery, with the added interest which suspicion must give. An individual person, by practicing a quiet meekness, might escape observation; but an organization, and particularly a large organization, performs its corporate actions in the light of day. Where an individual person has his private plans and insights, an organization has programs and policies derived, or said to be derived, from certain assumptions about facts and values. These assumptions, verbally expressed, constitute what may be called its "ideology."

Organizations have a special need to explain and justify their actions. They must do this for their own members, who, otherwise, might doubt the value of membership. They must do it also for non-members, with a view to recruiting or to being tolerated. And nation-states have the most need of all, because they are very large and powerful, because they administer so many important affairs, and because, in administering these, they cannot help intruding upon the member's conduct of his own life.

The size of an organization bears no proportion to the size of its ideology. Small organizations may chance to assert, officially, a great many things. On the other hand, nations like France, Great Britain, and the United States of America, all of which have flowered under capitalism, make remarkably economical use of official doctrine. They concentrate upon a few principles, and leave extensive description of the world to their scientists and philosophers. By contrast, the socialist nations have established as official the whole world-view of Karl Marx. Their ideology is thus as extensive in range, if not in detail, as that of any of the churches. It wears, indeed, a scholastic look, which intellectuals of the West have not been slow to deride.

Organizational ideology, whatever its size, will usually contain three types of assertion. There will be, first, a group of sentences describing the objective circumstances in which the organization acts and stating the moral values which the organization regards as ultimate. So far as the United States of America is concerned, this group of sentences will be found in the second paragraph of the Declaration of Independence. They were put there, no doubt, to explain the single act of separation, but they have been traditionally used in justification of policy. Here are the sentences:

> We hold these truths to be self-evident, that all men are created equal, that they are endowed by their Creator with certain inalienable Rights, that among these are Life, Liberty and the pursuit of Happiness. That to secure these rights, Governments are instituted among Men, deriving their just powers from the consent of the governed. That whenever any Form of Government becomes destructive of these ends, it is the Right of the People to alter or abolish it, and to institute new Government, laying its foundations on such principles and organizing its powers in such form, as to them shall seem most likely to effect their Safety and Happiness.

The second group of sentences will contain those which state the purpose of the organization and its structure. Sentences of this sort will be found, for example, in the Preamble to the Constitution of the United States:

> We the people of the United States, in order to form a more perfect union, establish justice, insure domestic tranquility, provide for the common defence, promote the general welfare, and secure the blessings of liberty to ourselves and our posterity, do ordain and establish this Constitution for the United States of America.

After which, the Articles proceed to describe what the United States of America is, at any rate in respect of its fundamental law.

The third group of sentences will contain those which state how the purposes of the organization are to be achieved in the given objective circumstances. These sentences follow as inferences from the first two groups. They are, accordingly, programmatic: they state policies, set forth plans, establish guidance. If, for example, the purpose be "the general welfare," and if the objective circumstances be an industrial society of the mid-twentieth century, it may be held to follow that there ought to be public programs for education, for medical care, and for the solace of citizens in old age.

It is plain that an organization which, in its ideology, lacked any of these three groups of sentences would be unable to explain or justify its existence and actions. Without a description of objective circumstances, nothing can be explained; without a demonstrable system of values, nothing can be justified. Without a statement of purposes, it cannot be known what the organization intends; without a program, it cannot be known how the purposes are to be attained.

Because of their use in explanation and justification, the sentences thus composed into an ideology are an important source of unity within the organization. They bind the members to the organization and to one another in respect of the fact that they assert, presumably, what each member takes to be the case. In reality, one may suppose, this presumption is no more than a presumption. Probably the individual members do not all understand the sentences in quite the same sense. It may even be that some of the members do not understand any of the sentences, and that there are some sentences which none of the members understands.

For example, the members, let us say, of a Protestant congregation would be hard put to it to explain the Apostles' Creed, which from time to time they recite in unison, and they would perhaps be surprised to learn how much they differed among themselves upon the doctrine of the Trinity which is there laid down. Nevertheless their recitation in unison expresses the *intent* to agree. So long as this intent exists, unity will follow. What organizations fear is loss of the intent.

Now, it happens that human beings have all sorts of limitations, and are therefore prone to error. Their senses, which connect them with the environing world, are not inclusive enough nor penetrating enough, even when helped with scientific apparatus, to present the world accurately in any single moment or series of moments. Men are therefore thrown back upon ratiocination to amend the incurable defects of the senses. "Science," said Fontenelle, "originates from curiosity and weak eyes."[1] But, alas, the intellect is brief in attention, prone to illogic, and subvertible by prejudice. Thus we sometimes assert what we do not know, and we sometimes do not know what we assert.

Human organizations are founded and built by human beings, and their ideologies have precisely the same human source. It follows that into the ideologies of organizations there creep errors, which

---

1) *"Toute la philosophie n'est fondée que sur deux choses: sur ce qu'on a l'esprit curieux et les yeux mauvais."* Entretiens sur la pluralité des mondes, Premier Soir.

may on occasion be gross. Once these errors imbed themselves in doctrine, they are beyond the reach of easy correction. They have become part of the source of unity. Their removal is not a mere scientific adjustment but a dislocation of the corporate body.

Now a sentence, simply as a sentence, is (if unambiguous) either true or false. It remains so when it becomes part of an organization's doctrine, but it now takes on certain new and striking attributes. After it has become an object of assent by the members and part of their ground of agreement with one another, it is involved with the whole psychology of belief, with the ebb and flow of institutional loyalty, and with the policymaking of the leadership. When a number of people believe a certain sentence to be true, when that belief helps to make them content in the organization and loyal to it and willing to pay dues to it, neither they nor the leaders are prepared to be told that the sentence is false. For unless they are to voice a *credo quia absurdum,* they must accept the rule of reason that a false sentence is to be disbelieved. From that moment on, the bonds of unity begin to loosen, for if it turns out that the organization has been professing one false doctrine, there is surely some reason to think that it may be professing others.

Conceivably there might be—and perhaps, indeed, there have been —organizations so flexible in unity and so skilled in leadership that erroneous doctrines could be expelled from the ideology with very little shock. A great deal depends, however, on the importance of the doctrine which is said to be false. If it is basic to the ideological system, as the doctrine of the incarnation is to Christian theology, then its falsity would engulf the entire system in disbelief. The organization would then lose the means—or, at any rate, the traditional means—of explaining and justifying itself. This result no leadership willingly permits. It is therefore part of the strategy of leadership and part of the politics of organizational life to regard doctrines not merely as true or false but as conducive to unity or disruptive of it. In this second pair of alternatives lies the distinction between orthodoxy and heresy. For a doctrine is orthodox if it helps unite the organization; it is heretical if it divides.

The question whether a sentence is true or false is a question in science, in logic, and in philosophy. But the question whether a sentence is orthodox or heretical is an organizational question, as simply and thoroughly as are matters of dues payment, attendance at meetings, or mode of selecting officers. A man, let us say, is honest or less than honest, and it is desirable that an officer in an organization be an honest man. Nevertheless, so far as the organization goes, an officer is a man in office, whether he is honest or not. Similarly, a sentence is true or false, and it is desirable that the sentences in an organization's ideology be true. Nevertheless the sentences in the ideology are the ones that are there, whether they are true or not.

Truth-falsity and orthodoxy-heresy are thus two different questions. Furthermore there is between them an active political strife. The question of truth and falsity evokes within the membership, and not infrequently within the leadership, an effort to correct when correction seems necessary. The question of orthodoxy and heresy evokes within the leadership and also within part of the membership an effort to preserve unity by keeping the ideology as it was. Since the apparent motive of the innovators is truth, even when they are in error, the general tenor of their conduct seems honorable and humane. Since the apparent motive of the leaders is organizational unity, the tenor of their conduct, whether right or wrong, seems rigid and reactionary.

The fact that the word "reactionary" is now an opprobrious epithet bears quiet witness to struggles which were not quiet at all. There was a long epoch, which ended only some three hundred years ago, when the more ancient an ideology could claim to be, the more credible it was held to be. In his *Commonitorium* of 434 A.D., Vincent of Lerins had defined orthodoxy as "that which has been believed everywhere, always, and by all."[2] *Ubique, semper, et ab omnibus creditum est:* that is bold enough, and it expresses the strategist's ideal of founding leadership on as broad a base as possible. But no less striking is the tense of the verb. Vincent's backward glance lasted into the seventeenth century as the approved posture of intellectuals. Even the Reformation looked back in order to advance.

Since the seventeenth century (philosophically, since Descartes; sociologically, since the rise of capitalism) the approved glance has been toward the future—so much so that a truly philistine contempt developed toward the past. Yet, despite such excesses, the forward glance has made life more difficult for the leaders of organizations, who can no longer appeal to mere antiquity of doctrine. A radical suspicion has now developed that the older an idea is, the wronger

2) See *infra,* Interlude: On Nets and Fishes.

it is. In respect of the sciences, natural and social, this suspicion is obviously well founded. It is less so in philosophy and perhaps not at all in ethics and the fine arts.

I will leave for later contemplation the paradoxes which thus ensue: for example, that although men understood decent behavior before they understood physics, they have achieved a great deal more in the understanding of physics than in the prevalence of decent behavior. I here suggest, as a small sign of progress, that the question of truth has noticeably gained upon the question of orthodoxy, in respect of what is important for a man to believe. Consequently, the leaders of organizations have rather less control than formerly over the human mind.

I I I

So INEVITABLE IS IT that men must live in organized groups, and so intimate are the bonds which thus unite them, that one cannot without some distortion consider what men are like apart from these milieux. Nevertheless, there is a highly personal experience which goes by the name of "making up one's own mind." Many social influences no doubt play upon the process, but the culminating and decisive act is performed by the person himself.

This act, or the possibility of doing it, has traditionally been called "free will." For my part, I think the possibility is a fact observable by introspection. If, however, some philosophical generalization is needed to sustain it, then I would say that free will is part of the spontaneity in all causation. Every event is genuinely new and has powers of its own. Accordingly, in the behavior of every entity there is always something that is not the effect of other causes.

This "something," which is not mere effect and therefore not mere passivity, has always had for human beings a singular value. It stands at the very center of the self and is suffused with that love with which one loves oneself. The failure of plans, the defeat of intentions, are painful and hard to bear; yet one can suffer them and still feel that some values remain to be cherished. But if the making up of one's own mind, the self-determination of one's own behavior, is taken away, is lost, then there does seem "nothing left remarkable beneath the visiting moon."

Now, deciding for oneself what opinions are true is ordinarily an important part of self-determination. No man of mature intelligence likes to accept an idea as true merely for having been told that it is so; still less will he accept it under command. Indeed, he is often so eager for his ideas to be truly his own that he will make them as much as possible unlike those of anyone else. He has, that is to say, some tendency to be a crank. No doubt there is folly in this, but at least he thereby escapes intellectual passivity.

It happens that this desire for independence of mind is laid down in the Greek root of our word "heresy." The noun came from a verb ($\alpha\iota\rho\epsilon\omega$) which originally meant "to take by the hand," and which afterward, pursuing the metaphor, came to mean "personally to choose." Whatever a heresy may otherwise be, it is at any rate an opinion which some person chooses as his view of the case. It represents his making up of his own mind. This act the leaders of organizations often fear and usually deprecate, and precisely to this fear is owing the sense of wilfulness and insubordination which the word "heresy" still conveys. *Superbia mater omnium haereticorum,* cried Augustine, who espoused some heresies while suppressing others: "Pride is the mother of all heretics."

Unless self-determination has been lost by psychological manipulations of which the man himself is unaware, or by a surrender to coercion of which he is very much aware, it remains and thrives as a subjective limit upon the power of organizations. It is like a fortress which can only be yielded up, not taken. Organizations may seize a man's body or destroy his life, but they cannot possess his will unless he lets them. If, however, they do possess his will, what is it they then have? A will-less member is not more useful than a mere thing or instrument. He cannot be as valuable as he would be if he acted from full consent.

Musing upon this theme, amid the struggles within seventeenth-century England, Jeremy Taylor wrote an eloquent passage in one of his sermons:

> Any zeal is proper for religion, but the zeal of the sword, and the zeal of anger . . . for if the sword turns preacher, and dictates propositions by empire instead of arguments, and engraves them in men's hearts with a poignard, that it shall be death to believe what I innocently and ignorantly am persuaded of, it must needs be unsafe to *try the spirits, to try all things,* to make inquiry . . . This may ruin souls by making hypocrites, or careless and com-

pliant against conscience or without it; but it does not save souls, though peradventure it should force them to a good opinion.[3]

Coercion, that is to say, cannot make a man hold "good opinions" in the way in which good opinions ought to be held, by simple awareness of their truth and value. Yet Taylor, after he became bishop of Down and Connor in 1661, found among his clergy an assortment of Calvinists ("Scotch spiders," as he called them) whose subversive activities included a plan for declaring the Bishop himself heretical. He thereupon vacated thirty-six pastorates, and thus expelled from their livings those clerics whom he could not convince. As for the Irish Catholics in his diocese, who spoke only Gaelic, he obliged them to attend services in a language they did not understand, expressive of a ritual and a theology which, if they had understood, they would have repudiated.

A hypocrite, shall one think? Quite to the contrary, Jeremy Taylor was one of the honestest men who has ever lived. The majesty of his prose style had proper foundation in a certain majesty of character. What happened was that a member of an organization, who said one sort of thing as member, became a high official of that organization, who had thereupon to say and to do another sort of thing. It is a fact of organizational life that certain virtues (tolerance, for example) are much more available to members than to leaders. An administrator may wish to be tolerant, and may in fact be personally so; but if he pursues tolerance to the point of ceasing to administer, he has in effect resigned. One may regret, but one must expect, that an administrator will undertake to manage the affairs which come before him, and that he will follow procedures laid down as basic by the organization.

Thus when one praises, as it seems natural to do, the individual man defending his own integrity, one must at least respect the administrator defending the life and unity of his organization. He has cares which the mere member has not, and problems far more formidable. If he happens to be the head of a powerful nation-state, his burdens are so vast and the risks so desperate that it is amazing men can be found to undertake them. As Shakespeare makes Henry V say on the eve of Agincourt,

3) Excerpted, e.g., in *English Prose*, edited by W. Peacock, (Oxford: Oxford University Press; World's Classics Series; 1925), Vol. II, pp. 56–57. Italics Taylor's. "To try" means, of course, "to test."

Upon the king! let us our lives, our souls,
Our debts, our careful wives,
Our children and our sins lay on the king!
We must bear all. O hard condition,
Twin-born with greatness, subject to the breath
Of every fool, whose sense no more can feel
But his own wringing! What infinite heart's-ease
Must kings neglect, that private men enjoy!

In what I shall subsequently say, therefore, I shall not be holding the view that all leadership is wrong because it involves coercion. I have no doubt that, as against certain heretics, orthodoxy has been rightly defended. Nor do I doubt that the violence used against heresy has sometimes issued, not from a leadership's brutality, but from its ignorance of any way to do the thing better. It is always well, before casting blame, to put oneself in the offender's place and to guess imaginatively what one's own decisions might have been.

Nevertheless it is the case that orthodoxy has from time to time been defended by men who sought, not organizational unity, but profit for the leadership—or who sought, not the professed humanitarian aims, but social advantage for the organization. Such leaders knew what they were doing, and may therefore be called rogues. Their historical damnation lies in their having destroyed the best men of an age. Their vices fatally evoked in other men the exactly contrary virtues, and were therefore doomed.

Finally, I may say that I do not seek to establish a balance between the claims of personal integrity and of organizational unity. This problem has produced, through the ages, a mass of casuistical discourse, to which can be added nothing new. It seems better, and may prove more practicable, to reduce the anarchy among organizations, even as organizations have reduced the anarchy among individual men. To the extent that this is accomplished, leaderships will feel less need to abandon tolerance, and members will be less exposed to the choice between being honest and being safe.

The present age seems not very fit for such attainments. Yet the present age, precisely because it is visibly unfit, gives us the knowledge of what we need to do. Social change we cannot escape, and its whole dynamic is that of the lowly inheriting the earth. At the same time, conflicts are so sharp and armaments so deadly that human life upon our planet may come to an end. We are moved, therefore, by instinct as by reason, toward a peaceful solution of disputes, and, in this, a knowledge of past contests will have value. For our hope must be to establish throughout the world a social order such that, though there remains lively disputation, there will be no orthodoxy and no heresy at all. Then we shall behave in politics as we now behave in science, and we shall have peace.

CHAPTER

2

Exile and the Hemlock

WHEN THINKERS of the eighteenth century A.D. bestowed upon their age the proud name of "Enlightenment," they were celebrating an emancipation from theology.[1] They were sloughing off as untrue and dangerous the notion that happenings in the physical world issue from the decisions of supernatural personages. Instead of propitiating higher powers, therefore, men were to control nature by their knowledge of it. They would, when sick, rely on medical science rather than on prayer. They would, when in peril, seek escape by mastering the peril itself.

The feeling of liberation which accompanies this view derives from the fact that people, when they understand a given state of affairs, can usually do something about it. I think we all know from our experience of governments the helplessness of depending, in great matters, upon purposes and decisions not our own. Thus, when physical nature began to come under extensive human control, men could feel (because they really were) less dependent and therefore more free.

It is very remarkable that an intellectual event of comparable size and kind happened in the Greek world in the sixth century B.C. The place was Ionia, a tract of land along the eastern shores of the Aegean Sea. Consequently, the event itself is known to us as the Ionian

1) See *infra*, Chapter 13.

Enlightenment. As one looks back, the event seems sudden: we know almost nothing of its antecedents. But the enlightenment was there, in the cities of Ionia, brilliantly and with the usual flames of satire and analysis. These cities—Miletus, which produced Thales, Anaximander, Anaximenes; Clazomenae, which produced Anaxagoras—were connected by trade routes with the most flourishing areas: overland, with Sardis; by sea, with the Pontus and with Egypt. Their language and culture were Greek, and they had inherited the view of the world, then already archaic, which appears in Homer and in Hesiod.

I think that commerce accounts for much in the Ionian Enlightenment. Ideas always follow existing trade routes, and travel indeed more readily than goods. Moreover, commerce displays in itself some mastery of the physical world. It moves upon a cool appraisal of reality, to which magic and things supernatural are alike irrelevant. A man who accumulates wealth knows at any rate his own part in the achievement and is less disposed to think it the work of any god.

Thus, in the culture of commercial societies, gods tend to be displaced, the true idols being more obviously just those riches that make the commonwealth thrive and the culture flourish. Descriptions of the world grow naturalistic. Acts of the imagination are more readily recognized to be—acts of the imagination, and the mistaking of these for science appears at last as superstition.

This kind of development went far in Ionia. From the records we possess, which are persuasive, if fragmentary, we can hardly doubt the fact. There was, first, a rejection of the supernatural world and of the great poets who had described it. The rejection began rather solemnly, but by the end of the sixth century it attained a truly Voltairean scorn. Heraclitus of Ephesus, a city dedicated to Diana, was heard to growl that Homer ought to be expelled from the games and flogged, and that an acquaintance with many subjects evidently does not give understanding or else Hesiod would have been a more sensible man.[2] And Xenophanes, the most thorough of the old iconoclasts, wrote, in five devastating hexameters, his classical account of the origins of anthropomorphism:

2) Cf. Diogenes Laertius, *Lives and Opinions of Eminent Philosophers*, Book 9, § 2. Diogenes wrote in the second century A.D., and his information had already passed through the hands of several doxographers. But he had a fine flair for gossip and a taste for epigram.

If cattle and horses—or lions as well—had hands,
Could draw with those hands and do all the things men do,
Horses would picture their gods as horses, cattle
As cattle: each would delineate bodies
Such as they had themselves.[3]

And he knew the anthropological evidence:

Ethiopians say their gods are snub-nosed and black;
Thracians, that *theirs* are blue-eyed and red-haired.[4]

Morality went hand in hand with common sense. The Greek
gods were, and were often recognized to be, a deplorable lot: Zeus,
the parricide, the henpecked and adulterous husband; Hera, the
henpecking, ineffective wife; Ganymede, the boy cup-bearer, exciting
the gods to pederasty; Aphrodite, married to Hephaistos and
cuckolding him with Ares;[5] Hephaistos, laughed at by the gods
because he limps; tedious exploits of murder, theft, and fornication—
of which the last provided certain select families of Greece with
extremely eminent ancestors.

Greek theology (as perhaps it ought not to be called) was a
perpetual holiday for human appetites.[6] If the gods escaped doubt as
to their existence, they could scarcely escape doubt as to their dignity.
Given the hair-raising narratives, Xenophanes' rebuke seems rather
mild, though it is sufficient:

Homer and Hesiod ascribe to the gods all things
Which, among men, are shameful and reproached.[7]

To this skepticism about gods the Ionian enlightenment added,
characteristically, an explanation of the world in physical terms. The
notion was that things had developed, or had been developed, by the
exertion of force upon some common and primordial stuff, as a

3) Quoted by Clement of Alexandria, *Stromateis* ("The Carpets"—a genre title
of the second century A.D.), V, 109, 3. My translation.
4) Ibid., VII, 22, 1.
5) I.e., Love, married to Technology and betraying him with War—a remarkably profound idea, which we may well meditate.
6) In the Judaeo-Christian tradition, what is deified is sometimes the human
conscience and sometimes the authority of a religious organization. There are
no moral holidays here. I suppose this is what caused Swinburne's lament, in
the "Hymn to Proserpine," "Thou hast conquered, O pale Galilean; the world
has grown grey from thy breath . . ."
7) Quoted by Sextus Empiricus, *Adversus Mathematicos* ("Against the Astrol-
ogers"), IX, 193.

potter would shape clay. The earliest guesses as to what the "stuff" might be were fixed by an inherited doctrine of earth, air, fire, and water as basic elements. In the search for a common stuff, it seemed necessary either to choose one of these elements or to abandon them all. Accordingly, Thales conjectured water, Anaximenes air, and Heraclitus fire (which gave him matter and energy united). Anaximander, dismissing the four elements as superficial, assumed the existence of a stuff not otherwise describable than as neutral and unlimited.

These notions were more sophisticated than they seem. The whole idea that the parts of the universe are united by a process of derivation—united genetically, that is to say—has been highly fruitful and (it would appear) highly accurate. All the sciences are now founded upon it, and even in those early days it enabled Anaximander to make his remarkable guess that men derived from fish: "Anaximander said that the first living creatures were born in moisture, enclosed in thorny barks; and that as their age increased they came forth on to the drier part and, when the bark had broken off, they lived a different life for a short time."[8]

Though the thought was sophisticated in view of its richness of implication, the language seems, in retrospect, naïve. As general terms, "matter" and "energy" are much more scientific than "fire," which signifies only a limited occasion of them both. But the naïvety of the language lets us see what a more sophisticated speech might have blurred—namely, the thoroughness of Ionian materialism. The men who talked of water or fire were obviously not talking of supernatural entities. If they had wished to do so, they would have named Poseidon, who had the seas in charge, or Hephaistos, who controlled fire, or perhaps the demi-god Prometheus, who stole some of it as a surreptitious gift to mankind.

Pleasing as corporeal explanations were to the great Ionians, confident as was their belief that the world is body and no more, the city-states of the Greek peninsula had quite other ideas. Gods, when tutelary, are very precious: they maintain the strength and safety of the people whose guardians they are. Consequently, to doubt their existence or deny it is to remove, or seem to remove, an essential

---

8) Quoted from Aetius, and translated, by G. S. Kirk and J. E. Raven, *The Pre-Socratic Philosophers* (Cambridge: Cambridge University Press; 1957), p. 141.

protection. It may even seem to be a kind of treason against the community.

Such a view, no doubt, was somewhat fanciful. If the national gods really did exist, and if they really did defend the city, neither fact would have been altered by being denied. The case would merely have been that the skeptic was mistaken. Logic, however, has a trick of sliding off the supernatural, and is not quite the base on which organizations defend their ideology. The fear, endemic among rulers, that disunity waits upon discussion translates itself into a religious fear that gods are displeased when their existence is denied.

Moreover, if every thread and tissue of myth be stripped from politics, it is difficult to endure what then remains to be seen: the naked fact that every government has come to birth by violence and has by violence maintained its life. No god of mercy, justice, wisdom would have anything to do with such activities—though Greek gods might, being masters of chicane.

Myths survive in politics because, with them, governments survive and populations are tractable. The stuff which composes these myths is not necessarily itself mythical: myths can be made of science, if the data are misconstrued or distorted.[9] But political myths have rather greater power if they derive from legendary material, from ideas so ancient and so generally diffused that they appear to be notions one has always had, a natural way (indeed, the natural way) of looking at things.

Persuading people to give up traditional (though erroneous) ideas is rather like persuading people to undergo surgery. They will do it if an authoritative person, thus advising, points to the perils of continuing in the old way. But if we imagine a supreme authority, armed with police power, advising to the contrary, it will not be difficult to suppose that people will reject enlightenment or surgery with equal rigor. Thus, although the gods of Olympus may seem scoundrels to us, they were no doubt objects of awe and veneration to their devotees, who therefore were likely to see in skepticism a poignant personal threat.

The Greek pantheon was very populous. There were gods, or half-gods, for all sorts of phenomena, including those we would call "celestial." The moon was the goddess Selene, who, in a moment of

9) E.g., the quasi-Darwinian doctrine of "fitness to survive," which, in our own time, has been used to justify the rich as against the poor.

charming aberration, lay with the shepherd Endymion. The sun was the god Phoebus (or Helios), who daily drove his chariot across the sky, as even now he does, in fragments, upon a pediment of the Parthenon. These lovely images kept the Greeks on good terms with the cosmos. Accordingly, when Anaxagoras let it transpire that, in his view, the sun was no Phoebus but a red-hot mass of metal (a *mudrós*), he publicly abolished a god in favor of a scientific object. One could worship Phoebus, but only with some difficulty could one worship a red-hot mass.

Now, Anaxagoras of Clazomenae was a late Ionian, born in perhaps the year 500 B.C., who emigrated to Athens as a young man. Educated under the enlightenment's full noon, he thus came to a greater city, which the enlightenment was only just reaching and, in respect of materialist philosophy, never did conquer. There he became a friend of Pericles and a teacher of Euripedes, either of which achievements might reasonably be considered a career in itself. We are not told, but we may conjecture that his critical powers and his scientific prepossessions marked him from the first as a somewhat "dangerous" man.

In due course he became the Athenian equivalent of a heretic and was prosecuted. The doxographers, if we take them all together, appear to mention two trials for heresy: one when the prosecutor was Cleon and the charge impiety, another when the prosecutor was Thucydides and the charge not only impiety but "Medism"—that is, sympathizing with a foreign power.[1] It is possible that we have here one single event given two different contexts, but the charge of Medism would have had greater aptness and force if it was made during the generation after 480 B.C.—a time before Cleon was eminent. On this view of the case, we can imagine Anaxagoras first prosecuted about 455 B.C., amnestied about 445, prosecuted again about 430, and exiled to Lampsacus, where he died in 427. And we shall thus see the portrait of a resolute materialist, whose beliefs suffered no dent from political pressure. It would be pleasant to accept the story that, upon his second condemnation, Anaxagoras remarked, very dryly, "Nature has long condemned me—and my judges too."

---

1) According to Diogenes Laertius, op. cit., II, ¶ 7, Sotion asserts the first, Satyrus the second. "Medism" signified a favorable view of Persia, Athens' defeated but memorable enemy. The Thucydides in question is not the celebrated historian.

The charges that prompted these trials, and the results that issued from them, have long become classical—not simply because they happened in Greece. Political attack upon dissenters, once they seem to have grown schismatic and therefore dangerous, begins at a point where they can be isolated from their fellows. This point is always something moral. The victim must be displayed as speaking and acting contrary to ultimate values, as behaving in such a way as to cause the commonwealth grievous risks. The charge of Medism, for example, laid down the dark calumny that Anaxagoras had some wish to serve Persia at the expense of Athens.

Thus the strategy of isolation proceeds by attributing to the dissenter purposes and values hostile to those of the body politic. He is thrown at once on the defensive, and, instead of arguing for the truth of his actual views, he exhausts himself in explaining that they are not what the government says they are. He finds himself in a personal crisis founded upon an irrelevance, while the citizens are made to rehearse their devotion to values not imperiled at all. This brings us to the question of Greek patriotism in general and of Athenian patriotism in particular.

I I

THE MOST STRIKING TRAITS of an ancient Greek city were its smallness, its exclusiveness, and its resolute independence. Athens at her most populous had perhaps three hundred thousand inhabitants, of which a third were slaves. Sparta, the great example of a nuisance-state, had a population very much less; but, since that population was wholly organized for war, its effect upon history is conspicuous, if almost entirely destructive. Utopian thinkers like Plato planned ideal communities of about five thousand persons. It is astonishing that minds which embraced the whole cosmos very snugly should have accepted such narrow limits upon social theory, and should, despite those limits, have produced some of the richest social ideas. But intellectually the old Greeks could do anything.

The chief reason was, perhaps, geography. The Greek peninsula is a succession of heights and depths, surrounded by sea. After twenty-five hundred years of poetry, Arcadia seems to us a warm, quiet, gentle land; but the actual Arcadia is, and ever was, a rugged boisterous terrain, fit for sheep and goats and herdsmen, where few poets would care to dwell. Sparta lay, and its ruins lie, within a bowl of bleak, horrendous mountains. Attica sloped, with not a few eminences, toward the sea. If people were to live on land they could till, their communities had to be small. Greek topography is as different as can be from that of the Nile Valley, the Mesopotamian plain, or those amplitudes of flat arable land where, in due order and succession, the Assyrian empire, the Babylonian, the Lydian, and the Persian effectuated rule.

The Greek communities were organized primarily for defense— or, as Aristotle said with an eloquence he rarely indulged, they "came into existence for the sake of life."[2] Under invasion or threat of it, the citizens could take refuge upon a fortified hill, within easy distance of the fields they worked in. Such events were frequent enough, for not only did these communities war with one another but they were subject to attack from Persians, from Cretans, and from tribes of the northern wilderness. Survival meant that the community had proved self-sufficient, and in such a fact there was much confidence and pride.

The glories—and the defects—of individualism are everywhere displayed in the history of Greek city-states. Strength against enemies and prosperity within the group, these immense values the city-state seemed abundantly to supply—until Alexander and, after him, the Romans taught a new lesson, that size makes a big difference. But precisely while Alexander was teaching this lesson, his old tutor Aristotle, still charmed by the familiar smallness, completed his remarks on the city-state with the words ". . . and it keeps on existing for the sake of the good life."[3] Defense, that is to say, isn't all one wants from social living. One wants also growth and flowering and attainment to philosophy.

It is important to realize how natural such phenomena seemed to an ancient Greek. Aristotle himself, who had in full measure the human frailty of mistaking the familiar for the essential, defined man as *politikòn zóon,* an animal suited to life in a city-state. By translating this phrase as "political animal" or "social animal," we have been able to squeeze into it our vastly larger idea that, everywhere, men need to live together. But Aristotle probably wanted only to say that life in a city-state is normal social life and that other forms are deviations. In the light of this, one can understand why Socrates pre-

2) *Politics,* A, 2.
3) Ibid., loc. cit.

ferred death to exile and why he could no more leave Athens for Megara (a city thirty miles to the west) than he could have left Athens for the antipodes.[4]

By comparison with the old empires, and even by standards of modern liberalism, political life in the Greek city-state was reasonably democratic, except for the slaves. Chattel slavery, an institution which the Greeks cultivated with a mixture of greed and guilt, was of course the supreme social defect. Aside from its damage to the slaves themselves, it discouraged invention, slave labor being always cheaper than machinery. It disconnected theory from practice, theory being the delight of leisured gentlemen and manipulation the work of slaves. It even evoked from so majestic a mind as Aristotle's a theoretical defense of the odious doctrine of biological inferiority.[5]

Greek democracy was therefore as democratic as slavery allowed, and it existed as a means of settling inner conflicts peaceably. Such conflicts were never absent, for, superimposed upon the slaves, there were no less than three classes, whose rivalries sometimes exceeded constitutional bounds. There was the "aristocracy," composed of rich hereditary landowners; there was the "oligarchy," composed of commercial magnates; there was the "democracy," composed of artisans and shopkeepers, the class of all persons who were free but not rich.[6] Among these the struggle for political power was ceaseless

4) In Plato's *Phaedo*, 99a, Socrates is made to say, ". . . these muscles and bones of mine would have gone off long ago to Megara or Boeotia . . . if I had not chosen the better and nobler part . . ." Jowett's translation. It is the famous autobiographical passage in which Socrates attacks Anaxagoras's materialism as having ignored the influence of ethics upon human behavior. *Phaedo*, 97c–99c.

5) *Politics*, A 5: ". . . the lower sort are *by nature* slaves [italics mine], and it is better for them as for all inferiors that they should be under the rule of a master." In a sentence just prior to this we are informed that "the male is by nature superior, and the female inferior; and the one rules, and the other is ruled; this principle, of necessity, extends to all mankind." Jowett's translation, as edited by Sir David Ross. Surely there are some ideas a man cannot be excused for holding, no matter how mighty his intellect or how long ago he lived.

6) The Greeks themselves assigned these names to the various classes: "aristocracy" = "rule by the best men," "oligarchy" = "rule by a few men," "democracy" = "rule by the people." This nomenclature would appear to have been invented by aristocrats, and Plato, himself an aristocrat (a descendant, in fact, of the god Apollo), uses it throughout the *Republic*. Our present feeling about

and acute. Each class ruled at the expense of the others, and all ruled at the expense of the slaves.

As happens in such circumstances, the interests of class sometimes exceeded the national interest. Classes were known to intrigue with foreign governments against domestic rivals, even to the point of surrendering the whole community. For example, when, toward the beginning of the Peloponnesian War, the Athenians blockaded Mitylene, on the island of Lesbos, the following events occurred, according to Thucydides' description:

> The commons [i.e., the "democracy"] no sooner found itself possessed of arms than they refused any longer to obey their officers, and, forming in knots together, told the authorities to bring out in public the provisions and divide them amongst them all, or they would themselves come to terms with the Athenians and surrender the city. The government, aware of their inability to prevent this, and of the danger they would be in, if left out of the capitulation, publicly agreed with Paches [the Athenian commander] and the army to surrender Mitylene at discretion and to admit the troops into the town . . .[7]

Loyalty to the city-state was thus much modified by loyalty to class, and, in the often unscrupulous maneuverings of politics, the suspiciousness of governments would be high. What, then, was an Athenian government to think of Anaxagoras, who came from a land rather near Persia? What was an Athenian government in the hands of the democracy to think of Socrates, who left the artisan class he was born in, to consort with aristocrats like Plato and magnates like Cephalus?[8]

As a political system, Athenian democracy had noble ideals, nobly set forth by Pericles in his oration over the city's warrior dead:

> Our constitution is named a democracy, because it is in the hand not of a few but of the many. But our laws secure equal justice for all in their private disputes, and our public opinion welcomes and

---

the words has been set by the revolutions of the seventeenth and eighteenth centuries, in which, according to official legend, "democracy" overthrew "aristocracy."

7) Thucydides, *The Peloponnesian War*, III, 27–28. Cowley's translation, as edited by Sir Arthur Livingstone (Oxford: World's Classics Series; 1943).

8) Plato's *Republic* purports to be the account of a long *conversazione* at the house of Cephalus at the Piraeus.

honors talent in every branch of achievement. . . . And as we give free play to all in our public life, so we carry the same spirit into our daily relations with one another. We have no black looks or angry words for our neighbor if he enjoys himself in his own way, and we abstain from the little acts of churlishness which, though they leave no mark, yet cause annoyance to whoso notes them.[9]

No doubt Pericles was, in a manner now familiar, covering over a commercial war with democratic ideals. But the ideals were genuine enough, and had practices corresponding to them. For example, in order to insure a general participation in government, some offices were filled not by vote but by lot. The judges at Socrates' trial were chosen in this way, and the narrowness of the vote by which they condemned him shows that accusers had need to veil their class interests with a show of public concern, and that even then they might fail of success.[1] To choose by lot was to choose without preference: social status (except, of course, for slavery) could not enter in. Justice would be assisted, if not always served, by the undoubted impartiality of chance.

Also there was the practice of ostracism, wasteful and unfair yet also strangely sagacious. Any man, however eminent—and, indeed, the more eminent the more vulnerable—could be sent into exile by simple majority vote. Visitors to the American Museum at Athens can see, this very day, some of the sherd fragments (the *óstraka*) that bear the names of men whom ancient Athenians chose to be rid of. Among these sherd fragments are several with the name of Aristides, who, having let himself be popularly called "The Just Man," grew in time tedious to his fellow citizens. It is evident that Athenians feared the power of prestige, and that the practice of ostracism did much to mitigate the strife of classes by occasional sacrifice of eminent victims.

Thus Greek democracy encouraged, and even demanded, participation in public affairs, while at the same time putting limits on careerism. Amid so great opportunities for service and so constant change in the staffing of government, there seems not to have been

9) Thucydides, op. cit., II, 37. Sir Alfred Zimmern's translation, which Livingstone has incorporated into his edition.
1) There were at the trial 501 "judges" (i.e., jurors). Socrates points out (*Apology*, 36a) that a shift of 30 votes would have acquitted him. Hence the final vote had been 280 to 221.

in Greece the immovable bureaucratic burden that hung upon ancient empires. There were, for example, priests, but there was no priesthood. A priest was, so to say, a priest in his spare time.

Since the citizens were caught up in political activity, and since a Greek could give you a theory before he gave you anything else, the problems of citizenship, of public and private behavior, were swiftly stated and swiftly solved—not, perhaps, permanently. Other ancient cultures have left us codes of law; the Greeks have left us political theory. Everyone else has told us what we ought to do; the Greeks have told us why we ought to do it. The convincing verisimilitude of debate in Plato's dialogues—indeed, the fact that they are *dialogues*—leaves no doubt (in my mind, at any rate) that this is how the Greeks actually did talk and what they did actually talk about: Virtue with the capital *V*, the virtues in detail (courage, justice, and the like), social harmony, and that ultimate goal of human striving which they liked to call "The Good." "The unexamined life," Socrates told his judges, "is not worth living." There were indeed very few Greeks who left life unexamined—or, at any rate, undiscussed.

I I I

It MUST BE ADMITTED that the Greeks made of all this a lordly, magnanimous enterprise. There was nothing servile or diffident about their philosophizing, nor anything leaden. Even their pomposities had wings. For philosophers were to be "in love with all existence, surrendering no part of it."[2] They were to explain what Virtue is, and they could give you a definition of it even if they failed to give you the quality itself.

These philosophical debates were in great part given over to rationalizing class interests. The effect of social status is everywhere visible. Aristocrats like Plato tend to think in terms of broad permanent principles, and democrats like Protagoras in terms of convenience and improvisation. The Athenian democracy, indeed, produced an entire philosophical school, the Sophists, whose dictum that "man is the measure of all things" meant, apparently, that human knowledge is highly personal, that it is in fact no more than the opinion of any one man at any one moment. This anarchist

2) *Republic*, 485b. My translation.

view, implicitly rebellious, dissolved the traditional ethics in the same way that American pragmatism dissolved nineteenth-century systems, but the Sophists were more candid about their opportunism than pragmatists have been. The first generation of Sophists (Protagoras, Gorgias) were honorable men; the second generation, whom these men reared, were professing scoundrels. It was possible to think that the teachers had corrupted the pupils, though the fact seems to have been, if anything, just the reverse. Nevertheless, Sophistic principles did lend themselves to pursuit of the main chance. What else could they do, as a small-business philosophy?

It was in such theorizing and in the internecine strife which had produced it that Socrates seems to have been entangled. Anaxagoras may have been so too, but what we are told of him suggests merely the offense of challenging the national theology. Socrates, however, could be thought to have "betrayed" his class—or at least to have deserted it. He had been born into the democracy: his father, Sophroniscus, was a journeyman-sculptor, and his mother, Phaenarete, was a midwife. But money-grubbing was repugnant to him, and the reduction of all concern to self-concern violated his moral sense. He had an acute awareness of tendentious argument—and, less admirably, much skill in it also. But, on the whole, he far preferred getting beyond parties and classes to a study of the great principles themselves.

In the culture of the aristocracy Socrates found his spiritual home. These leisured gentlemen, having time to talk and being of a speculative turn, pursued philosophy and the arts with great elegance. There was about it, to be sure, something of the dilettantish air which surrounds "first families." Yet I think we have to suppose that occasions of extempore rhetoric and true philosophizing, such as we find in Plato's *Symposium,* were what Socrates most loved. In that wonderful dialogue, he survives the tediousness of other speakers, the blandishments of Alcibiades, the wine and the food and the dancing girls; and, at the end, as dawn breaks and all other guests but two have fallen asleep, he is still arguing a literary question.

A tangle of contradictions, Socrates; no man was ever more so. The presence of these contradictions in Plato's portrait of the great man, all undiminished and unexcused, is what makes that portrait so convincing. Socrates is sober, but no one can drink him down. He is chaste, but extremely flirtatious with young men. He loves truth and honest argument, but he must win all arguments, no matter how. He is highly rational, but he is subject to cataleptic trances, which may have been hysterical in origin. The one trait of character to which no opposite appears is self-display. Socrates is never reticent nor, except out of mockery, humble. Indeed, a humble Socrates would be an absurdity.

Let us be glad these things were so, for they made his triumph the greater. Other philosophers with similar defects, but without the comparable virtues, have lamented the tragedy of existence. Socrates set about mastering all that welter of conflict within, and he so far succeeded that, martyred or not, he would have survived to posterity as an ideal of the rational man. It is wisdom he is famed for, not passion; temperance, not profligacy. Of this success the inward sweat and agony must have been prodigious: was it this that made him look on death as liberation?[3]

Nor can we regret the unintermitted self-display. Socrates was well worth seeing. His contemporaries, however, though no less fascinated, were less pleased. He seemed to them guilty of *húbris,* "arrogance," that massive vice. He associated with enemies of his own social class. He gave instruction to the young, though he took no pay for it. This fact distinguished him from the Sophists, who took a great deal of pay; but otherwise he seemed rather like them by virtue of his taste for unscrupulous argumentation. Worst of all, perhaps, he liked to point out the singular fact that famous and virtuous fathers seldom have sons of any virtue at all. "I want to warn you," said Anytus to him on one occasion, "not to talk in this way about our great men."[4]

The fact was that Socrates acknowledged loyalty to Athens but to no one class within it. His contempt for the Sophists and their mercenary pedagogy showed that he was no sound tradesman. His faith in philosophical criticism alarmed the conservatives. Thus he arrived at old age with some disciples, many listeners, and no general

---

3) Perhaps the most exquisite image in literature is to be found in Socrates' dying words (*Phaedo*, 118a): "Crito, I owe a cock to Esclapius: will you remember to pay the debt?" Esclapius was the god of healing, and it was customary to sacrifice to him when one had recovered from an illness. The meaning of the image is, then, that Socrates, by death, is recovering from a long disease which was life.

4) *Meno*, 94e. The translation is mine and is rather free.

support. He had all the requirements of a target at a time when the government wanted one.

The long disastrous war between Athens and Sparta had drawn to a close. The Athenians had staved off defeat in the year 406 by a sudden naval victory at Arginusae, where, however, the generals had neglected to bury the bodies of the slain. The democracy, then in power, wanted to try the generals collectively, with a view to executing them all. This procedure happened to be illegal, and Socrates, a member of the executive committee of the Senate, declined his support. His fellow members, who had at first taken his view of the case, were terrified out of it by a threat to include their own names in the indictment. The old sage, however, stood firm.

In 404 Athens surrendered to the Spartan general Lysander, who replaced the democracy's government with an oligarchical regime known as the Thirty Tyrants. Their rule was brief but bloody, and in the course of it Socrates again had the chance to prove his allegiance to the constitution by refusing to make an illegal arrest. This fact he pointed out during his trial,[5] but without much impressing the judges.

The oligarchical Terror ended in 403 in a revolt of the democracy. There was a search for scapegoats and a disposition to pay off old scores. Although we know who brought the formal accusations in 399, it is not clear who originated the idea of prosecuting Socrates. He had, as he acknowledged,[6] many enemies; and to the dim, revengeful minds of the democracy it may well have seemed attractive to assault the loftiest intellect in Greece. They would show him that thought is no master of power; in one purgative act they would wash out the guilts which their own rapacity had long made sore. In these two efforts they astoundingly failed, and, instead, have come down to us as little wicked men and unexampled fools.[7]

The three accusers were Anytus, a politician, Meletus, a poet (more probably a poetaster), and Lycon, a public orator. These men are nowhere described except by implication, but I have the feeling I know what they were like and even how they looked. Anytus was

---

5) *Apology*, 32 c–d.
6) Ibid., 18a–19d.
7) Socrates warned them of this (ibid., 35b), but he cannot, of course, have foreknown how great the obloquy would be. For an effect of this magnitude a man needs not only his own greatness but a biographer like Plato.

a respectable fuddyduddy, a muddled moderate, unsure of his ideas and insecure in holding them: the perfect liberal front. Meletus was a young man, not very bright, with political ambition and no scruples. Lycon was—well, an orator. These two hounded the sage to death. Old Anytus stood by and mumbled righteousness.

There were two charges: subversion of the national theology, and corruption of the Athenian youth. Such charges have the singular power that, although they are incredible, they produce conviction. No one man can overturn a doctrine socially held; no one man can corrupt generations. For either purpose an organized movement is required. As for corrupting the youth, that occurs year by year in institutions of great age and variety, which, taken all together, constitute the educational system.

The charges being contemptible, Socrates treated them with contempt, even with flashes of his old skill at talking for victory. There was a delicious moment when, playing on Meletus's fear of offending judges and audience, he brought him to state, very roundly, that Socrates was the *only* man in Athens who corrupted the youth.[8] This wild improbability no doubt damaged the accusation; but the great confession of faith which followed, if it ruined the accusation forever, also destroyed the physical Socrates. For in that supreme passage, in which he laid down the duty of philosophers, the issue of the case was made plain:

> I do nothing [said Socrates] but go about persuading you all, old and young alike, not to take thought for your persons or your properties, but first and chiefly to care about the greatest improvement of the soul. I tell you that virtue is not given by money, but that from virtue comes money and every other good of man, public as well as private. This is my teaching, and if this is the doctrine which corrupts the youth, I am a mischievous person. But if anyone says that this is not my teaching, he is speaking an untruth. Wherefore, O men of Athens, I say to you, do as Anytus bids or not as Anytus bids, and either acquit me or not; but whichever you do, understand that I shall never alter my ways, not even if I have to die many times.[9]

8) Ibid., 24c–25b.
9) Ibid., 30b. Jowett has allowed himself, in translating this passage, some liberties and one mistake. ("Another howler, Master!" Swinburne used to say to him while correcting the proofs.) "I am a mischievous person" ought to be "my doctrines are mischievous indeed."

At this declaration, which seemed to the audience quintessential arrogance, the court room was in uproar, and Socrates had to cry, "Don't interrupt me, Athenians, but hear me a little longer!" The case, however, was settled, the doom, the hemlock made sure. Judges and audience might perhaps have tolerated his self-display, his carelessness of their power, and even the subtle insults with which he showered them,[1] but they were not prepared to forgive his moral superiority. On this rock, at last, the collision occurred. The survivors perished in immortal disgrace, and the victim lived on to enlighten centuries.

The accusers, shrewd little men, had miscalculated grossly. They had studied their man, they had gauged his responses; they knew everything except the man himself. The Socrates they did not know and were not competent to know, the Socrates who burst upon them with such sudden light in that Athenian transfiguration, was the man of wanton appetite vanquished by conscience, by "a knowledge of the best." Within that riot of feeling there had always been a central calm, which, during seventy years, had spread outward until it grasped and silenced the whole. The Socrates of the last days was serene.

He was no man's man but an independent spirit, and this was what the court condemned him for. Yet in prison he showed another side, no less endearing. His friend Crito, a wealthy man, had bribed the jailers to permit escape. Escape in such cases was usual, and the government on the whole preferred it. But Socrates, the strict constitutionalist, the loyal Athenian, desired the law to take its course. Moreover, what on earth would he do in Megara?

The choice was perhaps a little extravagant and tainted by a wish to squeeze his foes in their own iniquity. But I am not sure that a rational heretic could have done otherwise. The rational heretic must show—and in this, Socrates is his exemplar—that he means what he says and that he is at the same time loyal to his community. Between these actions there is no necessary conflict, but it is the strategy of oppressive governments to produce one. Their word to the dissenter is, "If you want to show loyalty, agree with us." On such terms, the dissenter, if he is to be accounted loyal, must be

1) E.g., he admitted being the wisest man in Greece, as the Delphic oracle had called him—but only because every other Greek was so ignorant. Ibid., 20c–24b.

submissive—must be, that is to say, not quite himself. But if he declines to be submissive and resolves to be himself, then he must let loyalty appear in his acceptance of penalties, until his fellow men, in their varying degrees of wisdom, learn to honor his value and his name.

To know such things is some sort of gift—by birth perhaps, or labor, or circumstance. Yet the knowledge comes to us rather more readily two thousand four hundred years after the man who made it the substance of his speech and of his life. He thought (among many notions—some mistaken, some very wise) that virtue, integrity, the habit of knowing what one is doing, place a man beyond the reach of harm.[2] Thus received, pains are painful but not damaging; death is deadly but not bad.

Is it really so? I have pondered the notion for years, have doubted it and surrendered it. And yet I think that in some exquisite sense, not easily rendered, it is almost certainly true.

2) "No evil can happen to a good man, either in life or after death." Ibid., 41d.

CHAPTER

3

The Kingdom of God

Mᴀʀᴛʏʀs, as the famous etymology tells us, are "witnesses." By sacrificing themselves, they instruct others. After this manner, Socrates may be said to have taught the value of personal integrity, of being loyal to one's own best self. It is a lesson that philosophers are peculiarly fitted, when they will, to teach.

Yet there are other kinds of martyrdom, and therefore other lessons, which display not so much what the martyr himself is as what he desires human society to be. It is a social ideal he is after, not a personal. He finds existing arrangements to be foolish or evil, and he proposes to change them in some significant way.

Such proposals arise whenever the will of a governing class collides with the will of a subject majority. Then the subjects begin to dream, to conjecture, to plan—and possibly to act. Their dreams, conjectures, plans are all heretical, as contrary to the reigning ideology; and their actions are of course schismatic, as aimed at breaking up and reconstituting the establishment. Thus, where societies are exploitative,[1] social ideals will be more or less heretical, and troubles must always attend the concept of a kingdom of God.

In respect of human attainment, the kingdom of God has seemed to lie in the future, near or remote as the particular prophet foresees.

---

1) I.e., societies in which one class appropriates, without full compensation, economic values created by another.

Even if God is held to be reigning now and to have reigned always, it is clear that the perfections of his kingdom are not immediately accessible to men. Rather, we must work and hope, in a probationary state; then perhaps—but only perhaps—we shall arrive.

The seat and style of the heavenly kingdom are now vague and getting vaguer. There is, to be sure, a sense that the kingdom (which ought by now to have become a democracy) somehow administers the ultimate affairs of the moral order, adjusting happiness to virtue and suffering to vice. But no one seems to know any longer what the rewards and penalties may be, or how administered, or to whom. Perhaps it is as well. Men know little enough how to conduct such affairs within their own societies.

The first users of the phrase "kingdom of God" had, however, quite precise ideas. The kingdom was to have a definite geographical site: Palestine. Its inhabitants were to be living men of identifiable nationality, namely Jewish—though the kingdom might eventually contain other groups as these decided to adhere. The kingdom, in any event, was to be an harmonious society of righteous men; and if there were classes within it, these would treat one another with all honesty and fair dealing. Historically, this concept served as the ideal of various movements for national liberation—movements often defeated, but, until the year A.D. 135, never hopeless and never destroyed.

The men who conceived this ideal lived at the southwestern end of the "fertile crescent"—that storied arc of land which bounds the Arabian Desert and stretches from Egypt to the Persian Gulf. For long centuries this district was a footpath for the great predatory powers: Egypt, Assyria, Babylonia, Persia, Macedonia. Tribes like the Hebrews who settled in the area and grew into kingdoms not only jostled one another but were likely to be swept aside by these monsters on the march. The author of the Book of Daniel, writing in the second century B.C. at the time of the Maccabean revolt against Antiochus IV, describes a phenomenon which had been occurring for almost a thousand years:

The king [of the north] shall do as he pleases, he shall uplift himself and exalt himself above every god, uttering amazing vaunts against the God of gods; he shall prosper till the wrath divine has run its course. . . . For his strong forts he shall procure soldiers who worship a foreign god; his favorites he shall advance to high honor and make them rulers over the masses, selling land to them for a bribe. When the end arrives, the king of the South shall butt at him, but the king of the North shall attack him like a whirlwind. . . . He shall also invade the fair land of Palestine, and myriads shall be killed . . . the land of Egypt shall not escape, but he shall lay hands on the treasures of gold and silver and all the valuables of Egypt, the Libyans and Ethiopians following in his train. Then rumors from the east and the north shall alarm him, till he retires in great fury to inflict doom and destruction on many, pitching his royal pavilion between the Mediterranean and the sacred hill so fair. So shall he come to his end, with none to help him.[2]

We may note especially Verse 39, which says, ". . . his favorites he shall advance to high honor and make them rulers over the masses, selling land to them for a bribe." It is policy characteristic of big exploitative societies in their relations with small exploitative societies. The big control the small by confirming in the small society the power of its own ruling class. We shall see that this was the heart and essence of Roman administration, but it had been going on a long time before that. Since a foreign power was likely to rule you through your own rulers, it followed that national liberation required you to separate those rulers from their rule. National liberation involved social revolution.

The ancient Jews met and suffered every variation upon this basic theme. Sometimes their cities were occupied or laid waste, sometimes allowed to stand without fortification, sometimes (when the foreign potentate, like Artaxerxes, needed border defense) refortified. Sometimes the people were led off into captivity—though the famous Babylonian one was by no means severe: the captives were not enslaved, but were allowed to live and even to prosper as free citizens. Always, however, there was the incurable seditiousness of the ruling class, particularly of the priests. They corrupted reform after reform, until the outraged prophet Ezekiel began to regard Nebuchadnezzar's destruction of Jerusalem (597 B.C.) as a good thing, as the only possible good thing. "You have played the harlot," cried Ezekiel to Jerusalem,

2) Daniel II: 36–45. The translation is by James Moffat, The Holy Bible (New York: Harper and Brothers; 1926), p. 970. Events of the sort described had already happened to the Assyrians and the Babylonians, and were then threatening the Seleucid dynasty.

You have played the harlot with your neighbors, the sensual Egyptians. . . . You have played the harlot with the Assyrians, so insatiable was your lust; and even then you were not satisfied. You repeated your harlotry over and again with Chaldaea, the traders' land; but even that left you unsatisfied.[3]

In the Judaic tradition, on the whole, the prophets are revolutionary and the priests reactionary. The priests, ideological spokesmen for the governing class, were in daily administration both of public affairs and of private behavior. The prophets sprang from lower social ranks, especially from the peasantry, and won leadership by the eloquence with which they proclaimed existing social facts and mandatory moral values.[4] To them we owe the gallant and ineradicable habit of protest that informs our whole cultural tradition. It is doubtful how far we would have advanced, if we had possessed only the philosophical analysis of the Greeks, unmixed with the prophetic passion of the Jews.

But, beyond this, the prophets had certain victories of their own. The greatest of these was the abolition, not easily achieved, of human sacrifice. The original Jahweh (or Jahu) had been a rain god, really quite "pagan," equipped with female consorts and worshiped with rites which included human sacrifice.[5] It will be remembered that, according to legend, Jephthah thus sacrificed his daughter, Abraham was quite willing to sacrifice his son Isaac, and the priest Samuel "hewed Agag in pieces before the Lord."[6] It took a lot to civilize

3) Ezekiel 16: 26–29 Moffat.
4) "To prophesy" meant, originally, "to announce"—not necessarily "to foretell the future."
5) See Archibald Robertson, *The Origins of Christianity* (New York: International Publishers; 1954), p. 21. My debt to this wonderfully persuasive book is great, and will unfold as we proceed. Robertson, who died in 1961, was the son of a Bishop of Exeter, and had his career in the Admiralty. He was thus a scholarly amateur of the subject rather than a professional. There is an advantage in this, namely, that the attractiveness of his view rests solely upon the cogency of his argument.
6) These episodes appear, respectively, in Judges 11: 31–40, Genesis 22: 1–19, and I Samuel 15: 32–33. The quotation is from the Authorized Version. The third episode is very pitiful. Saul has defeated Agag in battle but has spared his life. The priest Samuel then reads Saul a typical ruling-class lecture on the need for punishment. "Rebellion," he says (in Moffat's translation), "is as bad as the sin of divination [i.e., competing with the priesthood], and self-will as bad as the iniquity of idols." Thereupon Samuel summons Agag to execution. "Agag came to him with tottering steps" (the AV says that he came "delicately"). " 'Death is a bitter thing,' said Agag. But Samuel said, 'As your sword

a deity in those days, and every step was a step in the civilizing of man.

The earliest prophet whose writings we may suppose ourselves to possess is Amos, the peasant poet. He saw and denounced the crimes of exploiters—and surely it must have been an extreme convenience, now lost to us, to put denunciation in the mouth of Jahweh himself. "Listen to this," cries Amos through Jahweh:

> ... you men who crush the humble,
> and oppress the poor,
> muttering, "When will the new moon be over,
> that we may sell our grain?
> When will the Sabbath be done,
> that our corn may be on sale?"
> (small you make your measures, large your weights,
> you cheat by tampering with the scales)—
> and all to buy up innocent folk,
> to buy the needy for a pair of shoes,
> to sell the very refuse of your grain ...[7]

Nor does gallantry limit his indignation. The wives of the rich, as anyone could see, were fat and bovine:

> Listen to this, you cows of Bashan,
> you women in high Samaria,
> you who defraud the poor and are hard on the needy,
> who tell your husbands, "Let us have wine to drink!"
> As sure as I am God, the Lord Eternal swears,
> your day is coming,
> when you will be dragged out with prongs,
> the last of you with fish-hooks;
> out you go, through breaches in the walls,
> each of you headlong ...[8]

So sang the first of the prophets in a time when priestly frauds had begun to seem intolerable. We are told in I Samuel 2 that the sons of Eli were "depraved creatures," who, when people came to make burnt offerings, took the best part of the meat for themselves. We are also told in I Samuel 8 that the sons of Samuel "turned aside for money, they took bribes and tampered with justice." It is an inclination of officials, whether priestly or not.

---

has bereaved women, so shall your mother be most bitterly bereaved'; and Samuel hacked Agag to pieces before the Eternal at Gilgal."

7) Amos 8: 4–6. Moffat.
8) Amos 4: 1–3. Moffat.

Thus the two sequences of events continued parallel, the prophets denouncing evil and the priests committing it, until some fifty years before the descent of Nebuchadnezzar. By then a series of invasions by Assyrians and Scythians had shaken the community, and a time came when the people could at last deal faithfully with their ruling class. The priesthood saved itself by a judicious compromise, which accepted into the Law a good part of the prophetic program. These additions will be found, notably, in the Decalogue and in the injunctions (Exodus 22: 21-27) against usury, against mistreatment of aliens, widows, and orphans.[9] "The Decalogue," says Robertson, "was the notice to quit served by eighth and seventh century prophets on rulers whose cults of fertility-gods and fertility-goddesses, with human sacrifices thrown in for good measure, had signally failed to stave off calamity from their country."[1]

The notice, however, was as usual ignored, and the old pattern of domestic strife, conquest by foreign powers, occasional captivity and occasional rebirth lasted until Roman arms and Roman government finally removed the Jewish state from the ancient world.

In its own time, the Roman Empire was, I suppose, the most remarkable administrative success that had yet occurred. Before its appearance, empires seldom lasted more than a century, and sometimes less. The prophets, therefore, could confidently predict the fall of every oppressor; the Jewish people could keep alive the hope of national liberation and social reform. Geography, the play of international politics, and a certain endemic love of freedom made them the most difficult of ancient peoples to govern. The jest that the modern state of Israel has a president attempting to govern three million other presidents has lively corroboration in old historical fact.

A successful movement toward ends so vast and valuable would require a leadership adequate to its success. One man would suffice if he were great enough, and, if he did suffice, he might seem to have been consecrated to his mission from the beginning of the world. He would be the Messiah, "the anointed one." Surely a just

9) "You must not injure or maltreat an alien among you, for you were aliens yourselves in the land of Egypt. You must not oppress a widow or orphan. . . . If you lend money to any poor man of my people, you must not treat him as his creditor, nor must you exact interest from him . . ." (Moffat). The reforming zeal of the prophets is evident not only in the injunctions themselves but in the appeal to the Jews' own experience of oppression.
1) Robertson, op. cit., p. 29.

and merciful God, having in mind the salvation of his people, would in due time and at the historically right moment supply such a leader. This leader, having freed the commonwealth from foreign oppression and domestic iniquity, would be seen as savior and redeemer; and the glory of his mission, crowned with an ineffable glory of success, would show that his human nature had all along shared the nature of the divine.

Thus, toward the end of the sixth century B.C., when the Persian Empire seemed falling into that death which had already swallowed Assyria and Babylon, the Second Isaiah sang a celebrated hymn of hope:

> For unto us a child is born, unto us a son is given: and the government shall be upon his shoulder: and his name shall be called Wonderful, Counsellor, The mighty God, The everlasting Father, The Prince of Peace. Of the increase of his government and peace there shall be no end, upon the throne of David, and upon his kingdom, to order it, and to establish it forever. The zeal of the Lord of Hosts will perform this.[2]

The Persian Empire survived to fall before Alexander, whose imperial legacy slowly wasted away amid the quarrels of inheriting dynasts and the growing power of Rome. The Maccabean interlude, a great Jewish revolutionary success (168 B.C.), seemed for a time to be the promised fulfillment: "He [Simon Maccabeus] made peace in the land, and Israel rejoiced with great joy: and they sat each man under his vine and his fig tree; and there was none to make them afraid."[3] Yet, after some seventy years, the misbehavior of the priesthood revived the social struggles within. A series of military defeats brought on a six years' civil war, at the end of which Alexander Janneus, Simon's grandson, "crucified eight hundred Pharisees and slew their wives and children before their eyes."[4]

---

2) Isaiah 9: 6–7. Authorized Version. I use the AV here because, though it is less clear than Moffat's, it is more grand. Moreover it is the passage which Handel set (how wonderfully he caught the rhythms of Jacobean prose!). Moffat's version shows, more lucidly, that the Messiah was to be "a wonder of a counselor, a divine hero, a father for all time, a peaceful prince." The little hymn, as Robertson points out (op. cit., p. 36n), has been interpolated between two passages of "undiluted gloom" and fierce denunciation, and does not belong to the original Isaiah.
3) I Maccabees 14:12. Quoted by Robertson, op. cit., p. 49.
4) Ibid., p. 50.

Thus the Maccabean experiment closed in ruin and despair. A group of revolutionary purists, the Essenes, exchanging national for personal redemption, constituted themselves a brotherhood practicing the common ownership of goods. They endured some persecution, in the course of which they lost a leader, whose miraculous return, however, they confidently expected. In them, in a section of the Pharisees, and in the lonely laborious multitudes the revolutionary ardor lived on, never wholly quenched, through the vicissitudes of Roman civil strife, into the Augustan peace and the Tiberian expansion. All still awaited the predestinate Messiah, the son of David, the redeemer and judge who was to cast the mighty from their seats and avenge so long and so grievous a slaughter of saints.

And then in Judaea, in the reign of Tiberius, there appeared a man of lowly origin, a carpenter's son, who, having labored to save his people, was posthumously believed to have saved mankind, and who, instead of being (like the Caesars) a man enlarged into a god, was held in the end to have been a god diminished into a man.

I I

THERE ARE SOME STORIES so charming, so perfectly at ease with human wishes, that their beauty seems persuasive of their truth. One at first accepts them, then rejects; then, if one has grown wise enough, one lets the fable thrive—as fable. There cannot be, I think, a lovelier story than that of the child, the manger, the crowded caravanserai, the astounded shepherds, the adoring kings, the sudden singing glory of an heavenly host. If mankind were to have among its progeny one single efficacious redeemer, this, one feels, is how he would be born.

But songs are not science, and poetry is not literal description. The historian, therefore, whose task is to seek out what has actually been the case, must be guided not by metaphor but by probabilities. If he knows a good story when he sees one, he may also hope to know when a story is too good to be true. From what I have said in previous pages it will be evident that the view I take of history allows me no belief in supernatural personages who direct the world, or influence it, according to their own supernatural intent. The view which Christian orthodoxy takes of the person of Jesus is therefore denied me. I have to regard that view as a poem, a sublime poem indeed, but not as science. I have to regard the historical Jesus as man only and no god, in precisely the same sense in which you and I are men only and not gods.

I think this view of the case is almost certainly true, but I do not insist upon its acceptance, nor have I any zeal for the conversion of people to it. Too many hopes and fears, too many strivings after righteousness, are now mingled with that central poem for me to urge on any man a reading he finds repugnant.

Yet whether the orthodox account be taken as science or as poetry, it is plain that the historical Jesus was in his time and place a heretic. In this book, therefore, I am required to state, with due foundation of argument, what kind of heretic I think he was. Let me say at once, then, that I believe the historical Jesus to have been the leader of an armed movement for national liberation. The movement, betrayed on the eve of insurrection, was crushed, and the leader was executed. These events happened in perhaps A.D. 30—at any rate, before Pontius Pilate's recall to Rome in the year 36.

I am aware that it may seem alarming, and even horrifying, to think of Jesus as an active revolutionist. There is in the Gospels, however, some direct evidence for this view—evidence which is the stronger because it cannot be suspected of tendentiousness and may therefore be thought to record a tradition of fact. Moreover, the view will go far to explain what really is tendentious in the Gospels; and, beyond that, it will help explain (as I did not expect when I began this study) why Christian theology is the sort it is, and, more particularly, why the Christian God is, and had to be, trinitarian.

This account of the historical Jesus, accordingly, I find convincing; that is to say, I think it has a greater probability of being true than any other account I know of. Yet, along with all the other accounts, it suffers from being, on the whole, less probable than an historian would like. We know rather less of the historical Jesus than we do, for example, of the historical Socrates. Three different writers—Plato in the dialogues, Xenophon in the *Memorabilia,* and Aristophanes in *The Clouds*—have left reports of Socrates, who is visibly the same person in them all. But the four evangelists (by no means the persons they purport to be) were not separate observers of one man's life. They were men reworking a tradition, partly oral and partly written, forty to seventy years after the events described.[5]

5) Papias, the Bishop of Hierapolis, writing circa A.D. 130, says that "Mark became the interpreter of Peter and wrote down accurately all that he remem-

This reworking they did with an eye on current politics. They wished to assure the Roman government that, whatever the Jews might be, the Christians were not subversive, and that the Master had not intended his kingdom to be "of this world." They were the more eager to give this assurance, after Nero's totally unexpected persecution in the year A.D. 64.

The pro-Roman, anti-Jewish tone of the Gospels is sufficiently discernible, and appears most strikingly in portions of the narrative that are hard to believe. The disciples, for example, are portrayed as stupid and cowardly: they seldom understand the Master's apothegms, they run away at the crucial moment of arrest, and Peter, their chief, when asked "Are you now or have you ever been a follower of Jesus?" replies, "I don't know whom you mean."[6] The Roman procurator, Pilate, a tough imperialist, is described as humane and sympathetic toward Jesus, while the Jews howl for his death; and we are asked to believe that Pilate, whose prime duty was to put down insurrection, was willing, under Jewish pressure, to release an imprisoned revolutionary, Barabbas, so that Jesus might die.[7]

As we have seen, the Jewish people had earned, with much gallantry, a reputation for rebelliousness. The first Christians were a sect within the synagogue, and the first Christian missionaries were Jews with a special message. It was natural enough for Roman officials to regard the new movement as potentially subversive. The movement had therefore to disclaim rebellion, though in this it never did convince the Romans. Perhaps the Romans knew its origins better than we, and were aware that the messiahship of Jesus had been precisely that of John the Baptist and of Judas Maccabeus before him—namely,

---

bered without, however, recording in order the things said or done by the Lord." Papias' work, *An Exegesis of the Lord's Sayings*, has been lost, but this quotation is preserved in Eusebius's *Ecclesiastical History*, 3, 39, 15. I have taken it from Johannes Quasten, *Patrology* (Brussels: Spectrum Publishers; n.d.), Vol. I, p. 83. The reason for dating the Gospels after A.D. 70 is that they contain accounts of the destruction of Jerusalem, which occurred in that year, by a Roman army under Titus. The accounts are, to be sure, put into Jesus' mouth as prophecy, but we must follow the rule that all prophecy which is both detailed and accurate has been written after the event. Moreover, some of the details match Josephus's account, in *The Jewish War*, Book V, Chapters 10–13.

6) Cf. Matthew 26: 69–75; Mark 14: 66–72; Luke 22: 54–62; John 18: 25–27.

7) Matthew 27: 15–26; Mark 15: 6–15; Luke 23: 18–23; John 18: 39–40.

the liberation of the land and the establishment of an ideal commonwealth.

Let us now examine the evidence for this view. We have said that the evangelists have left traces of original facts, rather like geological remnants which show what the ancient topography was. For example:

Ever since the coming of John the Baptist the kingdom of Heaven has been subjected to violence and violent men are seizing it.[8]

Again, a parallel passage in Luke:

Until John, it was the Law and the prophets: since then, there is the good news of the kingdom of God, and everyone forces his way in.[9]

These are strange passages to find in narratives that purport to describe a man of non-revolutionary aims and otherworldly intentions. If they are metaphorical and only mean to say that one has to work hard to get into the kingdom of God, they are remarkably hyperbolical. If they are later interpolations, we should have to suppose (what seems contrary to the evidence) that the apostolic missions had some revolutionary intent after all. My guess is that the passages assert a fact which a thousand years of experience had demonstrated—namely, that the liberation of the country required armed effort, and that thus only could one attain "the kingdom of God."

Further, Luke's Gospel has a remarkable twenty-second chapter, in which, among passages apparently put in later to validate the Eucharist, we get the picture of a band of revolutionaries, a sort of executive committee or general staff, supping together on the eve of insurrection. The leader announces, what he has surmised or been

8) Matthew 11:12. The translation is that of The New English Bible (Oxford and Cambridge University Presses; 1961), p. 20. Though far from expert in this field, I have the impression that the tone of this translation is nearer than others to that of the original Greek. At any rate, this passage is rendered somewhat less vigorously than, e.g. in the Revised Standard Version, which has, ". . . the kingdom of heaven has suffered violence, and violent men take it by force." The key words in the Greek are βιάζεται (= "subjected to violence"), βιασταί (= "violent men"), and ἁρπάζουσιν (= "seizing it"—like the Harpies, who did just that).

9) Luke 16: 16. NEB. "Forces his way in" is our old friend Βιάζεται.

told, that one of them is a police agent. The little band is amazed and horrified; the police agent brazens it out. A quarrel begins over who is to have the best appointments in the new order. The leader points out that honest revolutionaries do not seek personal advancement but only service to the whole community.[1] Nevertheless these lieutenants of insurrection will "eat and drink at my table in my kingdom and sit on thrones as judges of the twelve tribes of Israel."[2]

Then, suddenly, the leader says,

> "When I sent you out barefoot without purse or pack, were you ever short of anything?" "No," they answered. "It is different now," he said; "whoever has a purse had better take it with him, and his pack too; and if he has no sword, let him sell his cloak to buy one. For Scripture says, 'And he was counted among the outlaws,' and these words, I tell you, must find fulfillment in me; indeed, all that is written of me is being fulfilled." "Look, Lord," they said, "we have two swords here." "Enough, enough!" he replied.[3]

It sounds like insurrection, does it not? If that is what it was, then Judas's treason becomes for the first time intelligible. In the Gospels, his act of betrayal consists in identifying Jesus to the arresting officers. But neither they nor the Sanhedrin needed such help. Jesus was by that time a notable public figure, who had been greeted at the city gates by a throng shouting the insurrectionary cry "Hosanna!" (= "Deliver us!"). But if Judas brought word that the insurrection was about to begin, that was news well worth thirty pieces of silver.

Finally, that insurrection was the order of the day may be seen from two passages concerning Barabbas. Mark says (15: 7), "As it happened, the man known as Barabbas was then in custody with the rebels who had committed murder in the rising" (NEB). Luke says (23: 19), "This man had been put in prison for a rising that had taken place in the city, and for murder" (NEB). Those were tumultuous times, and only the rich were safely pro-Roman.

1) Verses 26–27: ". . . the highest among you must bear himself like the youngest, the chief of you like a servant. For who is greater—the one who sits at table or the servant who waits on him? Surely the one who sits at table. Yet here I am among you like a servant." NEB.
2) Verse 30. NEB.
3) Verses 35–38. NEB. From a government point of view, "outlaws" (ἀνόμων) is an apt term for revolutionaries.

If the historical Jesus was a social revolutionary, we can more readily appreciate the considerable body of radical doctrine which the Gospels contain. The Golden Rule suffices of itself to outlaw exploitation, but, besides this, there are many doctrines which envisage a precise reversal of the social order. The last are to be first; the lowly are to inherit the earth. Where the movement is concerned, there is to be no "business as usual"—the moneychangers are driven from the Temple. The upperclass collaborators with Rome are "whited sepulchres full of dead men's bones." The legalists "strain at [out] a gnat and swallow a camel."[4] On being asked a treacherous question whether the Roman tax ought to be paid, Jesus asks to see the sort of coin that usually serves for payment. One of his interlocutors produces a *denarius,* and then stands self-confuted, self-betrayed— for who would be so likely to have a *denarius* as a man in the pay of Roman officials?[5] The would-be ensnarers are then silenced with a curt "Give Caesar what belongs to him, but give our country's freedom what belongs to it."

Most striking of all, in many ways, is the encounter with the rich young man—a charming fellow, apparently, since Jesus is attracted to him at once. The young man, who has lived irreproachably, wants to know what more is needed for eternal life. "Sell all your property," says Jesus, "and come join the movement." But the fine young fellow, like many another since, cannot change his class allegiance, cannot give up security for a doubtful, if gallant, effort at social reform. He goes away sadly, and Jesus observes that rich men will always have great difficulty getting themselves into the ideal commonwealth: it is easier to get a camel through a narrow gate.[6]

At this the disciples, goggling as the evangelists like to have them do, cry out, "Well, if the rich can't be saved, who can?" To which Jesus replies, "The truth is that no one can do this for himself, but if you join sides with history, all things become possible." This accurate generalization is a long time sinking in. Meanwhile the disciples, reminded how much they have themselves given up, begin to worry about future rewards. According to Mark, the answer is:

4) The preposition "at" is a famous misprint in the original text of the Authorized Version (1611). "Out" was the word intended.

5) I owe this insight to Professor J. Spencer Kennard.

6) The Needle's Eye was, I have been told, the jocular name for a particularly narrow gate into Jerusalem.

I tell you this: there is no one who has given up home, brothers or sisters, mother, father or children, or land, for my sake and for the Gospel, who will not receive *in this age* a hundred times as much—houses, brothers and sisters, mothers and children, and land—and persecutions besides; and in the age to come eternal life. But many who are first will be last and the last first.[7]

In this age! The rewards, then, are not all transcendental and postponed to some other order of existence. Some of them, at least, are to be enjoyed in the same historical continuum in which they were striven for. These will consist in economic prosperity ("houses" and "lands") and in a wider, more intimate brotherhood.

If the Master's aim was national liberation, how skilled a leader, how good a judge of the historical moment may we suppose him to have been? Looking back, as we do, upon the long life, the brute stability, of the Roman Empire, we may think that he miscalculated badly. But he did not so. Palestine was always on the Empire's fringe. One might reasonably expect that a great popular movement, devotedly and intelligently led, would be able by force of arms to break away from that fringe and establish an independent state. Others thought so during those years. It had been John the Baptist's idea—and, perhaps, Barabbas's.

Nor do I think that Jesus was mistaken in his "general staff," the disciples. Their alleged stupidity is an incredible fiction. They knew perfectly well what the movement was about, and, when it had failed and there was plainly no chance for similar enterprises, they preserved and disseminated what they could of it—the great ethical doctrines, the broad social ideals. They did this, indeed, so well that in the twentieth century A.D. Christianity still keeps its revolutionary ardor, and all the commentaries of all the theologians cannot quench it.

Lastly, there is no doubt that the movement had won the people. We have the priests' word for that: they told Pilate, "His teaching is causing disaffection among the people all through Judaea. It started from Galilee and has spread as far as this city."[8] There is some reason to think, indeed, that the Romans and their collaborators struck at the last possible moment, and that further delay would have been perilous. For Jesus had understood the law of all such

7) Mark 10: 29–31. NEB. Italics mine.
8) Luke 23: 5. NEB.

movements, that people must be enlightened about their true social interests and then organized to attain them: "Ye shall know the truth, and the truth shall make you free."

The burden of leadership is heavy even in the midst of hope. Jesus, gathering his courage in Gethsemane, wished what every true leader wishes, that he might not have to be the one to lead—knowing, the while, that the mission with all its risks was his. It was, however, the moment before catastrophe. Officers came up with soldiers and a mob, and arrested him. Then unfolded the familiar sequence: the rump trials, the defamatory questions received with silence or with irony, the scourging, the mock regalia, the crown of thorns, the cross he was by then too weak to carry, and at the last the awful death itself. As he hung there, seeing the oppressed used to maintain oppression, he cried, "Father, forgive them, for they know not what they do."

On the way thither, there had been a moment when for the first time he realized that all was over, that the movement, so green with promise, was doomed. If he thus failed, who should succeed? He paused for a moment in the ghastly march, and said, "If they can do this when the wood is green, what will they do when the wood is dry?"[9]

He was crucified beneath a legend which ran: THIS IS THE KING OF THE JEWS. The words were satiric but not mistaken: it was precisely what he had intended to be. And because he had so intended, and perhaps even because he failed, he remains to this day the inspirer of revolution, the herald of human brotherhood, the immortal bringer-in of the kingdom of God.

I I I

So ENDED AN EPISODE which changed the world. Pilate, quite unaware of anything unusual, went on to other business, and his wife to other dreams. The Sanhedrin resumed its watch against further insurrection. The disciples, surviving defeat, reknit their unity as a sect within the synagogue, and confidently awaited the leader's miraculous return. They reminded one another of all the things he had said—those preternatural insights, those astounding profundities: how he could sharpen even the prophets' wisdom, how

9) Luke 23: 31. My translation.

he could make a story like that of the Gadarene swine convey the lesson that the Roman pigs must be driven into the sea.[1]

Then, suddenly, about the year A.D. 35, there occurred, in a quite different culture and under quite different skies, a psychotherapeutical event of which the last echoes have not yet been heard. A certain Jew of the Dispersion, named Paul, found unexpected release from emotional tension, conceived that the crucified Messiah had been the cause of it, surmised (very accurately) that other people needed such release, and set about providing them with it. He had not approved, and indeed had opposed, the effort at national liberation—perhaps because he understood its political impossibility. But so pure a spectacle of benevolence and self-sacrifice infected his opposition with feelings of intolerable guilt. He was prone to such feelings in any case, and now the provocation was extreme. He would wash out the guilt of opposition by surrendering to the movement, and he would redirect the movement toward success. It occurred to him that very probably this had all along been his mission.[2]

This remarkable man was rather less attractive than the putative Founder, whom (it appears) he knew almost nothing of. Nevertheless he established throughout the Roman Empire, at much risk of life and limb, a movement which eventually mastered the Empire itself and, afterward, the Huns, Goths, Vandals, and every other barbarian invader of the West. "Are you not aware that we are to judge angels?" said Paul to the Corinthians. "How much more, mere matters of business!"[3] And so it proved—though, of course, he was not foreseeing so grand an historical result.

What, now, was this organization which Paul had to do with, and what were its *biotiká*, its "matters of business"? Well, these were rather different from anything the Founder had in mind. The Founder's intent, if we have identified it correctly, was to establish a free, utopian, Jewish state in Palestine; and in that Cause he had died.

1) Matthew 8: 28–32.
2) Galatians 1: 15–16: "But then in his good pleasure God, who had set me apart from birth and called me through his grace, chose to reveal his Son to me and through me, in order that I might proclaim him among the Gentiles." NEB. Galatians is either by Paul or by a close associate of Paul; it seems a reliable source.
3) I Corinthians 6: 3. NEB. The actual intent of the remark was to encourage Christians to settle their disputes with one another without going to law in the "pagan" courts.

But Paul was a hellenized Jew, born (it is said) at Tarsus in Cilicia, of a tentmaking family which may have supplied the Roman quartermaster. There was, therefore, as much Hellenism in his culture as Judaism, and rather more of it in his thought. Indeed, the intellectual atmosphere of the Pauline letters is strikingly different from that of the Gospels, and is so in the way that Greek culture differs from the Judaic. Rabbi Sandmel suggests, very persuasively, that the Jews of the Dispersion stood to the Palestinian Jews as present-day Jews in the United States stand to their immigrant ancestors.[4] There is a common tradition, much modified, however, by the new and vast environment. It is unavoidably so, whatever one may wish, because problems have to be solved in the place where one lives, and in the circumstances there existing.

And Paul had problems—chiefly psychological ones, which, with remarkable astuteness, he had analyzed to their foundation. He felt, acutely and lucidly, the desperate inward struggle which is known to us all as conscience against appetite. The universality of this struggle, its presence in every normal person, supplied the ground for the evangelical triumphs of Christianity, and put that movement (for such it was) beyond the power of government to suppress.

This striking circumstance lets us see, on a very large scale, the interplay of personal problems with social, and shows that any solutions attained in the one are likely to have interesting effects in the other. Generally speaking, people solve what problems they can under the circumstances. If a movement toward social reform collapses, if for a time there is no chance of solving problems by a reconstruction of society, attention turns toward psychological problems, which social injustice has itself made more acute. The very evil underlying public relationships makes life harder for everyone, particularly in respect of decent behavior.

Now, the problem to which the Roman Empire addressed itself was the maintenance of chattel slavery. This inglorious task it had inherited from rivals or from predecessors, once formidable but brought down by their own inability to solve the problem. The Macedonian Empire, which had destroyed with equal finality the independence of Greek city-states and the dominance of Persia, had offered the most impressive previous solution. But Macedonian con-

4) Samuel Sandmel, *The Genius of Paul* (New York: Farrar, Straus, and Cudahy; 1959), p. 16.

trol had not been wide enough. Nothing less than an organizing of the whole Mediterranean world under one supreme authority could suffice. While the great thieves were at war, the plundered masses could always find allies.

The Roman Empire, from Augustus's founding of it to Alaric's assault on it, a period of four hundred years, resembled a vast and powerful stomach engaged upon the digestion of indigestible material. There were, to be sure, periods of calm, and Gibbon was perhaps not wrong to admire the apparent serenity of the Antonine Age. But chattel slavery, indigestible in itself, produced yet other disorders. Slave labor undercut the labor of free men; it hurled peasants from their farms and artisans from their shops. Floating multitudes of "free" men, absorbable in no trade or even in the army, drifted across the Empire or congregated in cities, where (if we borrow Tacitus's description of Rome) "from all sides every possible horror and shame met and found exercise."[5] The grossest superstitions, the most debilitating vices, a drowning sea of violence and lust—such things these men were diurnally acquainted with. And it may be that worse than the peril of death—though that was never absent—was the difficulty or (as it must often have seemed) the impossibility of being human.

So majestic a social edifice set upon so iniquitous a base cried out for rehabilitation. Yet the years went by, and the decades, and everything was much the same. From time to time the landscape grew hideous with the bodies of rebellious and crucified slaves, the legions marched and slaughtered and were slain, and in the subject provinces the ruling classes continued their intrigues with the Roman imperium. Events put off, and again put off, the Messiah's triumphant return, until at last that climax was removed to an entirely different order of phenomena. Meanwhile there remained the sheer hopelessness and indecency of life. One had to do something about that, and if one could not alter "conditions," perhaps one could alter oneself.

About the year 35, Paul's personal problems reached—or seemed to him to reach—sudden resolution. He had heard (no one knows how or in what form)[6] of Jesus' crucifixion, of a subsequent resur-

---

5) *Annals*, XV, 44: *"cuncta undique atrocia aut pudenda confluunt cele-branturque."*

6) The celebrated conversion story, well worthy of Luke's narrative skill, is told three times in Acts (9: 1–9, 22: 6–11, 26: 12–18), the third time with

rection, and of an expected return. This was all that Paul knew, or in the end cared to know, about the matter: in the authentically Pauline parts of the Epistles there is only one reference to any of the sayings attributed to Jesus.[7] Paul had little faith in social reform, still less in social revolution. Perhaps his political acumen told him such things were impossible to achieve. His first feeling about the Jerusalem Christians was that they were a visionary, and therefore dangerous, sect. Throughout his life, he never did come to like them.

But the news of a crucified and resurrected Messiah was striking indeed. Suppose one were to read this event allegorically, as one did with so much else in Hebrew lore. Suppose that what had happened was not the execution of a rebel but an astounding cosmic event in which the *Logos,* the ruling principle of the universe, entered human form, suffered human afflictions, and, issuing from all these unimpaired, established the certainty that sin and death, the ultimate destroyers, are themselves to be destroyed. If one could suppose so stupendous a thing, one could draw the inference, half-empirical and half-mystical, that the essential work of salvation was already done, and that what was required of men was not activity in politics but activity in belief.

This remarkable idea has been so much battered by middle-class radicalism, or by what the Roman Church calls "secularism," that intellectuals of our day cannot imagine how anyone has thought such things. They reject the whole concept, not perceiving that in their rejection they show themselves as oblivious of the nature and presence of poetry as any true believer. Pauline theology, so far as we can recover it from the Epistles, is a drama conceived with Aeschylean magnificence. It describes, not realistically but imaginatively, the state men must inevitably be in so long as the wealth and power of a few derive from poverty and impotence among many. It tells us, perhaps, rather less than human redemption requires, but what it tells is necessary.

The Pauline drama breaks some of the rules of good theater, and

---

embellishments confirming the "mission to the Gentiles." The story is, however, an invention, and is so not only because it relates a miracle. Galatians 1: 13–17 tells no such story, and moreover says that Paul did not go to Jerusalem until three years after his conversion, whereas Acts sets the time at a certain number of days.

7) I Corinthians 7: 10, which repeats Jesus' declaration against divorce.

is the more effective on that account. The climax has come and gone before the play opens. Everything essential, having already happened, is reserved to what dramatists call "the exposition." The Christ has died and risen, the atonement has been accomplished, the means of reconciliation have been made sure. We settle down to enjoy the "catharsis" issuing from a previous play. Thereupon Paul proceeds to show that dramatic catharsis is a more complicated affair than Aristotle had supposed. It is a drama, though a lesser drama, in itself.

The events accomplished, which are set forth in the exposition, reveal symbolically the fact that, wherever the social order is iniquitous, no great benefit can be conferred upon men without sacrifice of the best and noblest among them. These sacrifices, however, are not in vain: they set the course of history toward a perfect commonwealth. Moreover they help a man to adapt to present circumstances, however stubborn and difficult those circumstances may be. They teach him nobility of motive, steadfastness of character, and a primal love for the disinherited. They make him able to replace the "fleshly" lusts after power, wealth, and copulation with gentler appetites (no less fleshly, I dare say) for self-mastery, for a competence, and for love humanized by respect. In short, they "reconcile" him to the world by helping him to live decently in it; they redeem his faults by blunting them; and they assure him of his own worth by connecting him with values which are beyond damage and beyond doubt.

Disordered societies exhale pessimism like a mist, and the mist veils these truths from more than one sophisticate. They are, however, evident to not a few common folk, whose life experience, shrewdly interpreted, offers the verification. Sophisticates are often hangers-on of power, and therefore it may be that sophistication lies in finding apt excuses for servility. Which fact, it seems possible, Paul had in mind when he said, in language so metrical that the illiterate could commit it to memory:

> To shame the wise,
>   God has chosen what the world counts folly,
> and to shame what is strong,
>   God has chosen what the world counts weakness. . . .[8]

This insight sustained Paul in his encounters with pundits and pedants. Every innovator in ideology has to meet these and bear their

8) I Corinthians 1: 27. NEB.

scorn. There were, for example, if Acts is correct, certain mocking intellectuals at Athens.[9] There were the emissaries from the Jerusalem Christians, who followed his trail, undoing his organizational work by imposing dietary restraints and circumcision. These matters being both irrelevances and obstacles to recruiting, Paul felt an organizer's rage against pedantry. In the great debate over circumcision he cried out at last, "I wish they would go ahead and cut the whole thing off!"[1] For the heart of Pauline ideology was simple and unpedantic: it held just those truths which the drama of "Christ crucified" may be said to suggest. No doubt the new and strange dramatization was "a stumbling-block to the Jews and folly to the Greeks,"[2] but people who really understood, whether they were Jews or Greeks, grew aware of a highly effective wisdom.

In the seventh chapter of Romans, Paul presents his own inner struggle as a typical case:

> We know that the law is spiritual; but I am not: I am unspiritual, the purchased slave of sin. I do not even acknowledge my own actions as mine, for what I do is not what I want to do, but what I detest. . . . I discover this principle, then: that when I want to do the right, only the wrong is within my reach. In my inmost self I delight in the law of God, but I perceive that there is in my bodily members a different law, fighting against the law that my reason approves . . .[3]

He has, he thinks, the wish for righteousness but not the power; something not himself—strength of appetite or compulsiveness—intervenes to corrupt decision. This experience, bitter and comical at the same time, is surely everyone's portion. Three hundred years after Paul, the great Augustine was heard to cry out in his *Confessions,* "O Lord, make me chaste—but not just yet!"

It is by such unconscious self-satire we recognize our humanity. Conscience becomes an adversary whose commands, with seditious acumen, we try to circumvent. With Paul, as I suppose with many others who belong to the Judaic tradition, conscience had public

9) Acts 17: 32—"When they heard about the raising of the dead, some scoffed; and others said, 'We will hear you on this subject some other time.' " NEB.
1) Galatians 5: 12. A free but I think accurate reading, which is my own.
2) I Corinthians 1: 23. NEB.
3) Romans 7: 14–16 and 21–23. NEB. Compare Ovid's celebrated complaint: *Video meliora proboque/ Deteriora sequor. Metamorphoses,* VII, 17.

manifestation in the Law, the code of Israel—so much so, indeed, that he was willing to share the belief, common among ancient peoples, that nothing is wrong until some authority pronounces it so: "where there is no law there can be no breach of law."[4] This naïve notion, which is far from explicating the moral life, is, however, candid psychology.

The psychotherapeutical problem is how to resolve the tension between appetite and conscience, or, as Paul would say, between appetite and the Law. Until his time, tradition had been satisfied with simple obedience: you were a good man if you did what the Law required. Paul's astuteness lay in perceiving that you would be a much better man if you got beyond the tension altogether, if you did the right thing readily and (so to say) naturally, without needing threats from the Law. Precisely this had been Aristotle's idea of the virtuous man,[5] but Paul was, I believe, the first to ground it in accurate psychology.

Thus Paul intended to lift the moral life (especially among ordinary people) to a new level, to introduce a certain ease into righteousness and familiarity into virtue—to do, in short, a number of amiable things, which his dour Protestant descendants have largely forgot. The common folk in the Roman Empire, and some of their superiors too, welcomed the new enlightenment for what it was. They were quite willing to be "reborn," to settle accounts with their consciences, to postpone paradise to whatever order of existence seemed possible, and meanwhile to live in decent, friendly relations with one another.

They had had enough of sin and the miseries of trespass. They were well aware that brief and casual satisfactions of appetite, with no concern for related effects, demoralize the doer rather more than they please him. And so, when Paul gave to the Corinthians his characteristic list of malefactors—idolators, adulterers, homosexuals, thieves, alcoholics, and common scolds[6]—they were quite prepared to believe such persons unfit for any ideal commonwealth. "Some of you," Paul went on to say, prodding their memories where the prodding hurt, "some of you were once like that, but you have washed yourselves clean." Devoutly they hoped they had.

4) Romans 4: 16. NEB.
5) *Nicomachean Ethics*, 1107a.
6) I Corinthians 6: 9–10.

The kinds of behavior thus specified are, in our day, the familiar material of psychiatrists. I imagine that these "physicians of the soul" would not approve some of Paul's doctrine—for example, his preference for celibacy.[7] But Paul is in fact friendlier to human wishes than the clergy allows us to suspect. He is quite willing to concede that everybody needs some satisfaction. If one cannot be comfortable in celibate life, why, "better be married than burn with vain desire."[8] And if there is marriage, then "Do not deny yourselves to one another, except when you agree upon a temporary abstinence in order to devote yourselves to prayer; afterwards you may come together again."[9]

Paul is similarly relaxed about dietary laws, about meat offered to idols, about circumcision or the absence of it.[1] Part of this issued from a therapist's sense of making the patient comfortable, but most of it, I fancy, came from his genius as an organizer. From the Greek and Jewish traditions alike he cut away all that might discourage recruitment—high-toned intellectuality from the Greek, legalistic tabus from the Judaic. He reduced to a minimum the required ideology, and this he endowed with an almost irresistible charm. God (or the *Logos*) had so arranged the world that you could be rescued from demoralization and from death. This was all the doctrine you had to accept in order to become a Christian.

By way of making belief even easier (as if the idea were not already captivating), Paul supplied a few further images by which you might conceive it. You might, for example, regard the Christ as a Second Adam who had canceled out the sin of the first, or you might think that the *Logos* had adopted you as a foster-parent adopts a son and as the Christ himself was said to have been adopted, or, best of all perhaps, you might think that by joining the Christian community

7) I Corinthians 7: 1—"It is a good thing for a man to have nothing to do with a woman." NEB.
8) Ibid., verse 9. NEB.
9) Ibid., verse 5. NEB.
1) See I Corinthians 8, *passim.* It is worth noting that the illiberal injunctions are evidently later interpolations. The famous ban upon preaching by women (I Corinthians 14: 34–35), which has played such havoc in Christian churches since, is one of these interpolations. I Corinthians 11: 2–16 specifies that women who pray or prophesy must wear veils. This was the original practice, "corrected" by some later hand.

you became in some mystical but convincing manner a part of the Christ himself.[2]

The result is plain in the various groups which Paul founded. Their customs, their strayings, and their affectionate fellowship may be read in the eleventh to fourteenth chapters of I Corinthians. It is a touching and enchanting picture. Here was a little band of converts, mostly ordinary people but with some men of status among them, set down in the most voluptuous city of the age, trying to be comfortable with conscience and to observe their founder's maxim, "Let all be done decently and in order."[3]

It wasn't easy. They had brought to the movement all sorts of ideas, all sorts of talents, all sorts of preferences. Some liked to "speak in the tongues," some liked to utter prophecy, some liked merely to preach. Since they all participated, there was much argument over the validity of these modes. But what said the master organizer? He said that their several skills were all useful, that their differences need not disrupt but might rather confirm their unity:

> There are varieties of gifts,
>   but the same spirit.
> There are varieties of service,
>   but the same Lord.[4]

Paul was the opposite of sectarian. It is one of several lessons his followers have lost.

On Sundays the members had a common meal, which served to celebrate their fellowship and also to feed the poorer brethren. It was a true meal, not the present Eucharistic ritual, and the diners sometimes wolfed their food. "If you are that hungry," admonished the astute organizer, "you can eat at home; meanwhile, try to show better manners."[5]

2) The relevant passages are, respectively, I Corinthians 15: 21–22 and 45–49; Romans 8: 15; Mark 1: 11; and I Corinthians 12: 12–27. This last passage, a brilliant short discourse on political theory, ends with the words, "Now you are Christ's body, and each of you a limb or organ of it." NEB.

3) I Corinthians 14: 40. NEB.

4) Ibid. 12: 4–5. NEB.

5) Ibid. 11: 33–34—"Therefore, my brothers, when you meet for a meal, wait for one another. If you are hungry, eat at home, so that in meeting together you may not fall under judgement." NEB.

There were cliques also,[6] and ideological differences, particularly concerning the essential doctrine of resurrection.[7] The Greeks were generally materialist enough to doubt the doctrine, and early converts must have retained their doubts. Paul could not really prove the case, but he bestowed upon it some of the most eloquent prose which has ever been written. The Authorized Version does it ample justice:

> Behold, I shew you a mystery: We shall not all sleep, but we shall all be changed, in a moment, in the twinkling of an eye, at the last trump: for the trumpet shall sound, and the dead shall be raised incorruptible, and we shall be changed. For this corruptible must put on incorruption, and this mortal must put on immortality. So when this corruption shall have put on incorruption, and this mortal shall have put on immortality, then shall be brought to pass the saying that is written, Death is swallowed up in victory. O death, where is thy sting? O grave, where is thy victory?[8]

Doubts shriveled in the flame of this rhetoric, and even today it takes some effort not to be consumed.

But the great thing was the fact of fellowship, the sweet unspeakable communion which went by the name of *agapē*. You might have a gift of tongues or of prophecy, you might understand mysteries and sciences, you might impoverish yourself to feed the poor or martyr yourself to save the brotherhood, but everyone knew that if you had not also *agapē* (love, charity, comradeliness), and if *agapē* were not the motive of all these other wonders, then you were in fact nothing and of no profit. For it had been learned that love is patient and kind, free of envy or of boasting, happy to find goodness, reluctant to think evil, hopeful always, and expectant of the best. Through dimnesses and immaturities it had grown clear that people need, for their own health, some faith in men and things, some hope of future benefit, some intimate joy in one another. And everyone knew which was the most important of these.

Such were the folk who, in A.D. 64, were convicted (says Tacitus)

6) Ibid. 11: 18—"I am told that when you meet as a congregation you fall into sharply divided groups; and I believe there is some truth in it (for dissensions are necessary if only to show which of your members are sound.)" NEB. How much organizer's wisdom there is in that parenthesis!

7) Ibid. 15: 12—"Now if this is what we proclaim, that Christ was raised from the dead, how can some of you say there is no resurrection of the dead?" NEB.

8) Ibid. 15: 51–55.

"not so much of setting fire to the city as of hating the human race."[9] It was not the first time, nor has it been the last, for a group of people to suffer ascription of views precisely contrary to those they hold. But in those days the Christians were a small minority, a defenseless target. Nero had no trouble blaming upon them the arson he had committed himself. And no one could guess—least of all the imperial lunatic—what strength was growing in the charity that seeketh not her own, in the charity that is not easily provoked.

Paul died, it is generally believed, in the Neronian blood bath, by decapitation. It was a cruel but expectable end to a lifetime of controversy. He left to the world a heresy that became orthodox, a psychology that became a science, a scattering of societies that became a church, a church that became an empire. It has been a remarkable inheritance, but it has also been not quite the kingdom of God.

9) *Annals,* XV, 44: "... *haud perinde in crimine incendii, quam odio humani generis, convicti sunt.*"

CHAPTER
4

The Making of an Orthodoxy

I F THE EMPEROR CONSTANTINE, when he accepted Christianity as the state religion, thought of the text "My kingdom is not of this world," he must have allowed himself a wry smile. Rulers ordinarily know what they are doing and are not inclined to develop policies contrary to current interests. Constantine recognized the Church because he had to, because the Empire contained no other unifying power at once so general and so cohesive. His acceptance (as it doubtless seemed to himself), his surrender (as it may have seemed to the Christians), was the definitive political triumph of *agapē*.

Philosophers who delight to see in history the play of dialectics, the turning of all tendencies into their opposites, may marvel, enchanted, at the extraordinary result. The crucified Messiah had sought political power and failed of it. The tormented Apostle had ignored political power, and in the end his successors acquired it. The movement collapsed which was to have brought heaven upon earth in Palestine. The movement which was to have brought heaven in heaven took sudden rise to power upon earth. Every intended glory escaped, and every unintended glory pressed in to be received.

In retrospect (such being the nature of retrospection) the development seems as sure as it was astounding. All errors, all opposition, alike assisted the one result. "If the Christians had peace," says Jeremy Taylor, "they brought in converts; if they had no peace, but

persecution, the converts came in to them."[1] The Church grew by
love while the Empire decayed by harshness, until there came to pass
that remarkable blend of harshness and love, of temporal politics
and eternal designs, the Papacy—"no other than the ghost of the
Roman Empire, sitting crowned upon the grave thereof."[2]

This vast alteration, in which everything was unexpected and
everything planned, displays to us, as in a laboratory, the opposite
but kindred natures of heresy and orthodoxy. During its first three
centuries of life, Christianity was heretical: its doctrines had not been
authorized by any organization then socially acceptable, and some of
them were contrary to doctrines which had been thus authorized.
For example, imperial orthodoxy required that the reigning emperor
be worshiped as a god, and punished refusal as treason. The Christians, however, were political realists: in their view, God was God,
and the Emperor merely an emperor. They suffered death in thousands because they would not grant him more status than he
actually had.

One can understand their feelings. Half the emperors were
rogues, and all were of necessity warriors, men of blood. But the
Christians' God was the work of their consciences, a projection of
their better selves. One could not hesitate over the choice as to which
god was the more worshipable. Nevertheless, it was also Christian
doctrine to obey constituted authority, however gross and venal the
person in whom it was embodied. Although the Messiah, with
insurrectionary zeal, had proclaimed that the last would one day be
the first, the cautious and unsubversive Paul had asserted twice in
the same passage, "Every man should remain in the condition in
which he was called"[3]—that is to say, every man should keep the
same social status he had when he became a Christian. As for civic
duty, "Every person must submit to the supreme authorities. There
is no authority but by act of God, and the existing authorities are
instituted by him; consequently anyone who rebels against authority
is resisting a divine institution, and those who resist have themselves
to thank for the punishment they will receive."[4] It is evident that
Jesus and Paul had very different views of human government.

These contrary views form the true content of Christian ortho-

1) Sermon preached at the funeral of the Lord Primate.
2) Hobbes, *Leviathan,* Part IV, Chapter 47.
3) I Corinthians 7: 20 and 24. NEB.
4) Romans 13: 1–2. NEB.

doxy; they are its historical life blood. Despite the labors of theologians, Christianity is not a single body of doctrine supernaturally revealed and logically self-consistent. It is, rather, a perpetuated struggle between doctrines of compromise and doctrines of decisive change. Its long life and present liveliness are due precisely to this struggle, which goes on and seems never to resolve itself. For the truth perhaps is that one must accommodate to the world in order to change it, and that one cannot accommodate to the world without altering it by the accommodation.

Ordinarily one would expect a social problem to be solved by means of a social program aimed directly at it; hence reformers in general, and revolutionaries in particular, have little faith in tinkering with psychology. They are right about this, so far as the solution of a social problem must in the end be social. But as for the play of tactics within strategy, it is very possible to underestimate the power of psychological change. There are indispositions of character, even diseases of it, which prevent people from discerning faults in the social system and from applying to those faults the appropriate remedy. Presumably, an abatement of these neurotic ills would somewhat assist, perhaps considerably assist, the whole social advance. There is something philistine in the notion that history occurs as if there were no people in it or as if these people had no motivation. Such philistinism the growth of Christianity refutes, and shows, on the contrary, that small groups of people whose rather limited aim is to live decently with one another may become, under certain circumstances, a great social force.

The occasion of this remarkable change we have now to describe. Let us, by way of preliminary, lay out as on a map the pairs of opposites that mark, with more than usual accuracy, the origin and the result. Between the time of the apostolic missions and the time of Constantine's surrender, Christianity passed from a democratic doctrine (in which the embers of revolution still glowed) to an authoritarian doctrine, from popular self-government to hierarchical rule, from discontent with "this" world to control of "this" world's power, from persecution to patronage,[5] from an expectation of millennial glories to a prosperous enjoyment of things as they are. And here are specific evidences of the change:

(1) In Luke's Gospel, Mary, the maiden, having learned from

5) This telling phrase is Professor F. A. Wright's, *Fathers of the Church* (London: George Routledge and Sons; 1928), p. 12.

the angel Gabriel that she is to bear a royal and holy son, breaks into a triumphant song, the *Magnificat:* "My soul doth magnify the Lord."[6] This song is substantially the one that Hannah had sung, centuries before, when, after years of barrenness, she conceived and bore the priest Samuel.[7] A good deal of Mary's *Magnificat* (verses 51–53), and of Hannah's too, is highly subversive in sentiment:

> ... the arrogant of heart and mind he has put to rout,
> he has torn imperial powers from their thrones,
>   but the humble have been lifted high.
> The hungry he has satisfied with good things,
>   the rich sent empty away. NEB.

It is what a mother might sing who wanted her son to emancipate his people.

But Saint Jerome, writing in the early fifth century, about the time of Alaric's sack of Rome, offers us a quite different Mary, with the subversive sentiments entirely expelled. His version of the annunciation scene is this:

> ... the blessed Mary, whose purity was such that she earned the reward of being the mother of the Lord. When the angel Gabriel came down to her in man's form and said, "Hail thou that art highly favored; the Lord is with thee," she was filled with terror and consternation, and could not reply; for she had never been greeted by a man before. Soon, however, she learned who the messenger was, and spoke to him: she who had been afraid of a man conversed fearlessly with an angel.[8]

This Mary is the "Theotókos" or "God-bearer." She is no longer, and has not been since, the mother of an insurrectionary hero. Her son having been proclaimed part of the Godhead, she is "the Mother of God."

(2) We remember the unflattering description the evangelists gave of the disciples as cowards, dunces, oafs. In the *Epistle of Barnabas* (circa 120), those of the twelve who had become apostles are described as "sinners above every sin."[9] Yet even before that early

6) Luke 1: 46–55.
7) I Samuel 2: 1–10.
8) From Jerome's letter to Eustochium, a high-born Roman girl whom he was trying to recruit, and did successfully recruit, into the monastic life. The translation is Wright's, op. cit., p. 263.
9) V, 9.: . . . ὄντας ὑπὲρ πᾶσαν ἁμαρτίαν ἀνομωτέρους.

date, these same "sinners" attained elevated rank. Clement's *Epistle to the Corinthians,* written shortly after Domitian's persecution in A.D. 96, lays down for the first time a doctrine of hierarchical status:

The Apostles received the Gospel for us from the Lord Jesus Christ; Jesus Christ was sent forth from God. So then Christ is from God, and the Apostles are from Christ. Both therefore came of the will of God in the appointed order. . . . So preaching everywhere in country and town, they appointed their first-fruits, when they had proved them by the Spirit, to be bishops and deacons unto them that should believe.[1]

By the year 250, when the Church's size and power were fully manifest, and when its leaders could foresee a great political rôle, Cyprian, the Bishop of Carthage, embellished this doctrine with the notion of Peter as *primus inter pares:*

The other Apostles were, to be sure, what Peter was, but primacy is given to Peter, and the Church and the throne are shown to be one. And all are pastors, but one flock is indicated, which is fed by all the Apostles with unanimous consent.[2]

Whence one may infer that

the invariable source of heresies and schisms is in refusal to obey the priest of God [the bishop], the failure to have one in the church who is looked upon as the temporal representative of Christ as priest and judge.[3]

The cowards and dunces, the sinners above every sin, have achieved lofty rank in the downward transmission of authority.

(3) The earliest Christian communities had no clergy. Their meetings were an anarchist's ideal of free participation. Contributions were small, finances were administered with the utmost economy, and the leaders took as little in the way of fees as possible.

By the year 366, when Damasus was elected Bishop of Rome,

1) § 42. The translation is Bishop Lightfoot's, *The Apostolic Fathers* (London: Macmillan and Company; 1898), p. 75. The word "appointed" is highly significant, as indicating a superior source of authority. Originally, bishops and deacons had been chosen by the membership.

2) *On the Unity of the Catholic Church,* Chapter 4. Translated and excerpted by Henry Bettenson, *The Early Christian Fathers* (Oxford: Oxford University Press; 1956), p. 364.

3) Ibid., p. 370.

the revenues of that see and the contributions of wealthy ladies had grown so large, and the election was in consequence so hotly contested, that one hundred thirty-seven corpses were counted at the end of the day.[4] Damasus himself acquired the nickname *auriscalpius matronarum,* "the matron's ear-tickler," so great was his skill at eliciting donations.

Much more impressively, after 375, Ambrose, the Bishop of Milan, simply by threatening to withhold the sacraments, gained constant obedience from the Emperor Gratian, and forced Theodosius to do penance for a committed massacre.

A long way in a short time, from group therapy to world empire!

I I

IN THEORY and practice, Christianity is, we have said, a tension between opposites—specifically, between a wish to improve the general human lot and a wish not to disturb existing constituted authority. The source of this tension, we also have said, lies in the two traditions from which Christianity sprang: the Palestinian, which was to yield a paradise here and now by force of arms, and the Pauline, which aimed at personal rehabilitation through psychotherapy and small economic adjustments. People who were attached to the Palestinian tradition (like the Christians at Jerusalem) bided their time, awaiting further chance for insurrection, or, more mystically, the consummatory day of wrath when the Messiah should return. These folk were as conscious of being Jews as of being also Christians. They were nationalists, who held with some rigor to dietary laws and circumcision, and who viewed with distaste any "mission to the Gentiles." But the Paulinists, engaged upon self-improvement, desired a social peace in which self-improvement could more expeditiously occur, and they were eager to share their psychiatric discoveries with all nations whatever.

It is wrong, I think, to derogate either party. The devoted insurrectionaries were not mere subversives; they had aims which the human race is still ambitious to achieve. Nor were the Paulinists mere compromisers; they had a sober sense of the political possibilities. A very real question was at issue: how might the dispossessed multitudes end the evils they suffered from? It was a nice decision,

4) Wright, op. cit., pp. 12–13.

whether one should try to contract the bounds of empire by revolution or to construct little colonies of goodness within the empire's wide expanse.

The Church solved this problem, on the whole, in favor of the Pauline tradition, and thus attained, quite unexpectedly, political lordship upon earth. It is a great lesson in what can be done by feeling one's way. No matter what one thinks of religion, and particularly of organized religion, in present times, it is obvious that the Fathers of the Church were no dunces. Beneath the skin of their theology, now dry as is a mummy's, lay muscles of wonderful dexterity, and within that now sightless skull a most attentive brain. That brain measured, and those muscles moved, plans of desperate contrariety, of which the issue, less foreseeable to them than the issue of our plans is to us, determined, rather for the better than the worse, the lives of all who have come after.

Let us consider now some of the basic contradictions of early Christian politics. Their resolution issued in a celebrated orthodoxy, which in its turn gave rise to celebrated heresies—all of which, orthodoxy and heresies alike, will teach us how human affairs may be more sensibly conducted.

There was, first, the problem how to detach the movement from Judaism while at the same time appropriating large portions of Judaism. The motives for attempting both these opposites are quite clear. In the eyes of the Roman imperium, Judaism had acquired a permanent insurrectionary taint. The priests, to be sure, remained servile and alert against rebellion, but neither their servility nor their watchfulness sufficed. The revolt of A.D. 70, crushed by Titus, was followed by a revolt in 116, which Trajan died before crushing. The final revolt, in 135, provoked Hadrian to definitive action. The revolt collapsed in torrents of blood. Its leader, Simon Barocheba, was executed, and the Rabbi Akiba was flayed alive. Hadrian built upon the ruins of Jerusalem a new Roman city, Aelia Capitolina, and replaced the old Temple with a temple to Jupiter. An imperial edict banished all Jews from the city and made their return thither punishable by death.

This catastrophe confirmed the alienation of Christians from Jews which has been so great a catastrophe in itself. No organized movement, whatever its announced purposes, could hope to survive with such associations. Moreover, a good many things had happened which disposed the Christians toward such a view. The Neronian massacre had come on them as a surprise. Perhaps Nero himself delighted in the novelty. But how had he chosen the new victims? Was it because the Roman Christians had developed out of the Jewish community at Rome, and were therefore suspect?

Domitian's persecution in 96 made things rather more plain. During it, Domitian executed Flavius Clemens, his own cousin, and banished Clemens' wife Domitilla, on a charge of "atheism and Jewish practices."[5] Now, Domitilla was a Christian; one of the catacombs lies in ground she once owned. It seems probable, then, that, in respect of the Jews, the Christians suffered the familiar taint of guilt by association.

Moreover, since the imperial government was by no means inhospitable to religions other than its own, since the Emperor's pantheon elastically received alien deities whenever that was politically desirable, and since Rome itself teemed with soothsayers, cranks, and celebrants of obscure mysteries, Christians were bound to think it strange that they, along with Jews, should be reserved as staples of persecution. Punishment for revolt they would have understood, but they were never rebels. Why was it, they were bound to ask, that, despite their vow and habit of obedience, they nevertheless periodically suffered? It must have been, they then thought, that the authorities confounded them with Jews.

In this atmosphere of developing estrangement, the Pauline version of Christianity gained notably upon the old tradition of revolt. In the corpus of the New Testament, only one book, the fiery tract called Revelations, is anti-Roman.[6] The rest assert, with varying degrees of emphasis, an opposition between Judaism and Christianity. Yet the fact that Revelations was a great popular success and was early admitted into the Canon, shows how much the Christians still desired political remedies of a more immediate sort.

5) Dio Cassius, *History of Rome,* LXVII, 14, 1; Robertson, op. cit., p. 159. Robertson goes on to say, "Eight months later Domitian was assassinated in his bedchamber by the steward of Domitilla, Stephanus, and some accomplices. One Christian at least—and she a woman—was no non-resister!"

6) In Revelations 13: 18, the Emperor Nero appears as Beast N. 666—a cipher which, rendered in the Hebrew language, spells out NERO. The text invites the reader to work out the cipher for himself. The scarlet whore Babylon is Rome. She rides a beast with seven heads, and we are told (17: 9) that "the seven heads are seven hills on which the woman sits." NEB.

Taken as a whole, however, the books within the Canon and without suggest that there was a warm and even bitter struggle between Paul with his mystery-god (the Christ) and the Jerusalem Christians with their liberationist Messiah. Paul's very disconnection from the original movement must have made him appear an upstart, a claimant to leadership with no title thereto. He had not been among the original warriors; he had not borne the heat and burthen of the calamitous times. In fact, the Jerusalem Christians thought of him as a persecutor, whether he ever had been one or not. Nevertheless, from the beginning, he showed himself a remarkable organizer and propagandist. His services were clearly too valuable to lose.

The compromise came, ideologically, with more ease than one might think—though, in truth, anything can be done with ideology, the most plastic of human inventions. The Book of Acts puts an end to the cold war, establishes coexistence, writes a treaty of cooperation. It does so by assimilating the chief antagonists, Peter and Paul, in respect of their behavior and experiences. Paul is described as suffering the hostility of the non-Christian Jews exactly as the disciples had suffered it, and Peter baptizes an uncircumcised Roman, Cornelius, and, for that matter, those of Cornelius's household who happened to be there.[7] According to the narrative, Peter had been predisposed to this much deviation from the Jewish Law (he ought not even to have associated with uncircumcised persons) by a dream the night before, the message of which was, "It is not for you to call profane what God counts clean." In Cornelius's presence, Peter readily decides that "God has no favorites, but that in every nation the man who is godfearing and does what is right is acceptable to him." This internationalism is speedily confirmed by a descent of the Holy Ghost upon all present. As Peter later says (Acts 11: 15), it was just like Pentecost.

This little episode validates the mission to the Gentiles, which was the Paulinists' main idea. As if to clinch the concession, Acts goes on to describe the ensuing debate between Peter and his own associates, the "circumcision party," whom he wins to the Pauline

7) In Acts 9: 23, Paul risks assassination by the Damascan Jews; in 21: 27–31, the Jews in Jerusalem try to kill him. He is rescued, this time, by a detachment of Roman soldiery, rather as in our folklore the United States Cavalry rescues beleaguered virtue. The story is clearly anti-Jewish and pro-Roman. Peter's baptism of Cornelius will be found in Acts 10: 1–48.

view with truly remarkable ease. Rabbi Sandmel, playing on a famous phrase of Paul's, says that Acts gives us, not Paul, but "Paul neutralized."[8] No doubt this is partly the case, but the neutralization of Paul is nothing compared to the metamorphosis of Peter into a sound Paulinist. This man had been Jesus' chief lieutenant in the insurrectionary movement. He now undergoes a fate similar to his Leader's: the Leader became a mystery-god, and the lieutenant the putative head of a mystery religion.

Acts also records a double Pauline victory, over reactionaries and radicals alike. The tedious controversy about circumcision and the dietary laws ends in Paul's favor, and the extraordinary complex of inherited prohibitions resolves itself at last into three: not to eat food offered to idols, not to taste animal blood or the flesh of strangled animals, not to engage in sexual vice.[9] At the same time, the radical wing of Judaism is invited to reconsider its utopian schemes and to replace them with a present peace of mind and the expectation of personal immortality. Such proposals did not go unchallenged. In Acts, as in other New Testament books, the Jews are made to seem a stubborn lot, and Paul and Barnabas, outside the synagogue at Antioch, symbolically shaking the dust from their feet, cry out, "It was necessary that the word of God should be declared to you first. But since you reject it and thus condemn yourselves as unworthy of eternal life, we now turn to the Gentiles."[1]

But Judaism was rejected only to be seized again. This part of the ideological compromise is the one which held, like a risky but well-loved secret, the old revolutionary tradition. And the reason was that much of the movement's ground, much of its mass appeal, lay precisely there. The slaves, freedmen, and freemen, all alike impoverished and all candidates for conversion, demanded that there be at least some meaning in the promise that the last shall be first. Accordingly, the organizers of the early Church faced a kind of dilemma. To the extent that they diluted the old tradition, they pleased the Roman authorities; but to that extent also they tended to lose members. This kind of loss the Church has never been willing to incur,

8) Op. cit., p. 161.

9) Acts 15: 20. The same list is repeated in 15: 29 and 21: 25.

1) Acts 13: 46. NEB. It is, of course, part of our narrator's bias to say that "when the Gentiles heard this, they were overjoyed and thankfully acclaimed the word of the Lord" (v. 48, NEB).

and we shall find that the effort to avoid it explains a good deal in Christian theology.

The refusal to abandon Judaism appears most remarkably in the affair of the Docetic and Marcionite heresies. These were the first deviations to be successfully pronounced heretical by the young and growing Church—or, at any rate, by its leaders. The Docetic heresy takes its name from the Greek word *dokéo* (= "seem" or "appear"), and the notion was that the Christ had only seemed to be the sufferer in the crucifixion. Actually, so the notion ran, the sufferer had been an entirely different person; and Basilides, the Gnostic philosopher, ingeniously suggested that it had been Simon of Cyrene, who, according to the Synoptic Gospels, helped Jesus carry the cross.

The effect of Docetism was to abolish the Christ as an historical personage and thus to cancel the validity of just those events in space and time that, in theory, had redeemed the world. If such a doctrine had ever grown orthodox, the historical Jesus would have vanished from theology, and with him the last trace of the revolutionary tradition. One may imagine the effect upon the membership. Accordingly, the author of the Epistle to the Trallians (supposedly St. Ignatius) thunders:

> Turn a deaf ear therefore when anyone speaks to you apart from Jesus Christ who was of the family of David, the child of Mary, who was truly born, who ate and drank, who was truly persecuted under Pontius Pilate, was truly crucified and truly died.... But if, as some godless men, that is, unbelievers, say, he suffered in mere appearance (being themselves mere appearances), why am I in bonds?[2]

The Marcionite heresy is even more interesting because it directly reveals the influence of economic status. Marcion was a well-to-do shipowner of Sinope, in the Pontus, an entrepreneur therefore who had extremely familiar reasons for emptying Christianity of its revolutionary content. If, as would appear, he was also anti-Jewish, he was so in the way that commerce has made classical. The Gnostic philosophy, to which he was addicted and which was in itself a fantastic debilitating mélange, contained the view (not altogether un-

2) Excerpted and translated by Bettenson, *Documents of the Christian Church,* (Oxford: Oxford University Press; 1947) pp. 49–50.

convincing) that the created world was no great credit to its creator and revealed him indeed to be of very inferior stuff. Gnosticism assumed, however, a hierarchy of deities, called by the pregnant if baffling name of *aeons,* who approached perfection in the degree that they disappeared from fact. In this hierarchy, the god-creator of our world was plainly a lesser being, and this god-creator Marcion proceeded to identify with the god of the Jews. He then went on to say that it was not this god who had sent Jesus into the world, but rather the Supreme Aeon. Like a whirlwind from without, Jesus had come to sweep away the Law and the Prophets—a signal cosmic supervention, which was to cut Christianity once for all from its Jewish origins.

Marcion did succeed in founding some churches, and so became schismatic. He also edited Luke's Gospel and Paul's Epistles, taking care to remove every subversive utterance and everything suggestive of Jewish origins.[3] His works are lost or have been destroyed, but we know his views from the extensive attacks upon them by Irenaeus and Tertullian. Tertullian, as usual, whips the victim with anything he can lay his hands on, beginning with the population, topography, and climate of Marcion's home town: *Gentes ferocissimae . . . sedes incerta . . . vita cruda . . . libido promiscua . . . dies nunquam patens . . . sol nunquam lucens . . . omnia torpent . . . omnia rigent (Adversus Marcionem,* § 1). This is worth Englishing: "Wild population . . . insecure home . . . crude sort of life . . . promiscuous lust . . . day never dawning . . . sun never shining . . . everything numb and stiff." It is clear that Tertullian little understood the climate of the Black Sea.

Irenaeus tells two anecdotes which, whether factual or not, amply show the horror with which some leaders of the early Church regarded the Gnostic deviations:

> . . . John, the Lord's disciple, went to the baths at Ephesus; and rushed out, without taking a bath, when he saw Cerinthus [an eminent Gnostic] inside, exclaiming, "Let us get away before the baths fall in; for Cerinthus is in there, the enemy of truth." . . . Polycarp [Bishop of Smyrna] once was confronted by Marcion, who said: "Do you know who I am?" To which Polycarp replied, "I know you for Satan's eldest son." Such dread of heresy had the

3) Robertson, op. cit., p. 186.

Apostles and their disciples that they shunned even verbal communication with those who had perverted the truth.[4]

The doctrinal deviations of Marcion were matched by deviations of ritual and practice. He proposed to his fellow Christians an extremely ascetic life, the rule of which was to be an avoidance of all bodily pleasures. Marriage was to be eschewed, and the eating of flesh also. The weekly common meal, which had simultaneously fed the poor and commemorated the Founder, he reduced to a regimen of bread and water. In short, Marcion's proposals exceeded the bounds where spiritual blessings are any adequate compensation for earthly ills. It is reasonable to conjecture that, if Marcion had triumphed, the membership would speedily have dwindled to such few as were capable of ascetic living. Christianity would then have been never more than a sect, and the rise to empire would have been impossible.

In Marcion's bread-and-water communion one may also see, a little speculatively, some further attack upon the revolutionary tradition. People made wine in those days, and some make it now, by trampling on grapes. Moreover, the color of some wines is the color of blood. Thus it was possible for wine to symbolize the people's tread upon their oppressors—and also the blood of revolutionary sacrifice. Americans, having as their greatest anthem the "Battle Hymn of the Republic," will remember the Lord "trampling out the vintage," thus bringing chattel slavery to an end. Accordingly, it may have been the case that, to some Christians, the ceremonial wine celebrated and sanctified social revolution. What these Christians thought of Marcion's bread and water is not difficult to guess.

In any event, the Gnostic ideology was wholly inadequate to a mass organization or a mass movement. It was hopelessly contrary to human wishes, to human habits, and, in large measure, to human intelligence. Like all such ideologies, the toys of an intelligentsia, it proliferated divisions within itself, until the forms of Gnosticism that might be held equaled in number the *aeons* that might be worshiped. The author of I Timothy, in the New Testament, shows excellent organizational sense when he warns against those who "forbid mar-

4) *Adversus Haereses*, III, 3. The translation is Bettenson's, *Documents*, p. 126. The John of this anecdote has been shown to be, not the Lord's disciple, but John of Ephesus, the presbyter and perhaps the actual author of the Fourth Gospel.

riage and inculcate abstinence from certain foods, though God created them to be enjoyed with thanksgiving by believers who have inward knowledge of the truth."[5] And at the end of the letter he tells exactly whom he means: those, namely, who urge "the antitheses of the *gnosis* falsely so called."[6] *Antitheses* was the title of one of Marcion's works, and the *"gnosis* falsely so called" is, of course, the philosophy known to us as Gnosticism. Marcion was an able man, but no match for the talented administrators who opposed him.

Such, then, was the compromise by which Christianity accepted and repudiated Judaism at one and the same time. The effects are visible to this day. Everyone understands that Christians are not Jews nor Jews Christians, but also everyone knows, if he is knowledgeable at all, that the tradition itself must be called "Judaeo-Christian." In Christian churches the Old Testament is invoked as reverently as the New; indeed, there have been times, as among the Puritans, when it had rather greater eminence. The Ten Commandments are beyond doubt Judaic, but every Christian learns them and some Christians even obey them. And in times of social crisis, Christian congregations hear again the wrath of the prophets, and the crucified Messiah once more proclaims that the lowly shall inherit the earth. For the revolution is always dead and always being born, and Christianity, to its great unease, is of old time a bearer of it.

I I I

WE TURN NOW to consider the development of Christianity "from persecution to patronage," from democratic to hierarchical forms of organization. There was here no such degree of compromise as there had been between accepting and rejecting Judaism. For, in the end, the Church patterned itself upon the Empire, and people who wished to recover the innocent life of early Christianity had to seek it in the simplicity of monastic or eremite orders.

In the beginning an almost pure democracy prevailed. The members were folk for whom the slave system had no place or had place only as slaves. The consequent dependence of multitudes upon decisions not their own, upon the bread and circuses which alternately

5) I Timothy 4: 3. NEB.
6) Ibid., 6: 20–21. The translation is Robertson's (op. cit., p. 181), and it has the special merit, which other translations have not, of making plain the allusion to Marcion and to Gnostic theory.

fed and cajoled them, produced the characteristic psychological ills: passiveness, spite, debauchery, and self-contempt. These "sins," which only showed that the victims were victims, an odious social system could beget and multiply without, however, preventing all recovery. It was still possible to educate such folk into a measure of self-control and into the rudimentary amenities of social life. Paul's genius lay in recognizing this possibility and in providing, by a kind of inspiration, the necessary means.

Following his theory, then, the early Christian communities aimed at bestowing upon their members the virtues and graces which Roman society had intercepted, thus to exchange the beast for the man. The guiding principles were to be fellowship and a sense of mission. Instead of the fears which low estate engenders, there would be the security of equal comradeship; and in place of an aimless, trivial life, dependent upon chance or upon the caprice of superiors, there would be dedication to a cause—and not to a cause merely, but to the greatest of causes.

This psychological insight was exquisitely just. There is, I dare say, no joy in life—not the joy of fame or conquest or satiety—comparable to the joy of fellowship in a lofty cause. For then one loves and is loved, not indulgently (or, at any rate, not merely so), but as giving value to the common effort and as gaining value from the common success. And everyone who has possessed this joy knows its glories.

So the first Christians met in candid, intimate communion. They told one another their hopes, their guilts, their fears. They were encouraged to express rancor if they had it, so that it would no longer fester, as it had done, unseen. Thus cleansed of negative feeling and in harmony with all, they shared the weekly meal, made arrangements for the poorer brethren (preferably by employment rather than alms), sermonized, prophesied, and "spoke in the tongues."[7] They had no clergy, for those were the days of the universal priesthood of all believers. Thus the faithful were equally blessed, and it was yet to be discovered that any of them had been set apart, by special unction, for the clerical life.

A little work which circulated in Egypt and Syria about A.D. 100, and which was recovered, interleaved with other manuscripts, in

7) I.e., incoherent babbling, which was believed, though not by Paul, to be particularly inspired.

1875, is *The Teaching of the Twelve Apostles,* known more briefly as the *Didachē*. It offers advice on a number of pastoral questions, and thus illuminates much early practice. It leaves no doubt, for example, that the common meal was a *meal:* "after you have eaten your fill," says the text, "then give thanks thus. . . ."[8] Nothing in the text suggests that the bread and wine symbolize the body and the blood of Christ; on the contrary, the bread is specifically said (§ 9) to symbolize the unity of membership within the organization. The symbolism of the wine is left unstated—perhaps, as Robertson suggests, because it was too dangerous.[9]

The *Didachē* gives some prominence to itinerant preachers, who were to be welcomed, but not allowed to stay more than two days— preferably only one. The same rule held for every other visiting Christian. If any one of them wished to settle down, he had to take a job. There would be no difficulty if he chanced to be a craftsman, "but if he has no craft, according to your wisdom provide how he shall live as a Christian among you, but not in idleness."[1]

The reason for so much caution is plain. Some of the itinerants were frauds, mere careerists seeking easy money. "When he departeth," says the *Didachē*, "let the apostle [i.e., the itinerant] receive nothing save bread, until he findeth shelter; but if he ask money, he is a false prophet."[2] And the text continues, "From his ways therefore the false prophet and the prophet shall be recognized. . . . And every prophet teaching the truth, if he doeth not what he preaches, is a false prophet."

These lines affirm the disputed, and rather un-Pauline, doctrine of "justification by works." It is a doctrine usually associated with popular movements, because it states the rule by which the lowly judge the platitudes of their masters. The New Testament Epistle of James, for example, contains the celebrated maxim, "Faith without works is dead" (2: 20). This maxim occurs at the end of a longish passage concerning inequalities within some of the churches. Class distinctions common to the surrounding world have somehow turned up among Christians: the rich are getting the best seats at service; the

---

8) *Didachē,* § 10. My translation. The verb is ἐμπλησθῆναι (= "have been filled to the full").

9) Op. cit., pp. 146–47.

1) § 12. Lightfoot's translation, *The Apostolic Fathers* (London: Macmillan and Company; 1898).

2) § 11. Lightfoot.

poor are left to stand or sit on the floor. The practical principle of all religion seems to have been forgotten, namely, that "pure religion and undefiled before God and the Father is this, To visit the father-less and widows in their affliction, and to keep himself unspotted from the world" (1: 27—AV).

I suppose it is not surprising that the vast imperial society should have begun to corrupt Christian practice during the early years of the second century. If anything can be attributed to human nature as such, it is that men will respond to the largest social pressures. The Emperor Hadrian has left an alarming and perhaps exaggerated account how far such corruption might go. In the year 130 he visited Alexandria and from there reported to Servianus, his brother-in-law, that the inhabitants "have but one god, money. This is he whom Christians, Jews, and the whole world revere."[3] An emperor's weary cynicism—but there was doubtless truth in the charge. The craftsmen in the Christian movement were surely subject to the laws of com-modity exchange and temptible toward those deceits which effect shrewd bargains. Indeed, in the *Shepherd of Hermas,* a charming popular work of the Antonine age, the author is found lamenting, with guilty tears, the lies he has told in the course of business. The Shepherd assures him that a reformation into truthfulness and fair dealing will save him morally and will even cast some credit back-ward upon his *pragmateíais,* his commercial affairs.[4] The whole narrative is extremely hopeful: the Shepherd seems to say that there is nothing repentance cannot do, and that, except for renegades, the actually damned are just those who happen to be unrepentant at the moment of death. The main thing is not to lie, not to covet, not to steal; it is economic vices that are chiefly to be avoided. "Do your own work and you shall be saved."[5]

But movements, of whatever sort, need leadership. Unless the members are to spend their whole time on organizational affairs, they must delegate some of their tasks and powers to certain people who act as their representatives. In this unavoidable fact lies the be-

---

3) Quoted by Robertson, op. cit., p. 179.
4) Mandate 3. Hermas is the author's name, apparently authentic: he was an emigrant from Greece (possibly Arcadia) to Rome. Historians of American philosophy will be interested to note Hermas's use of the Greek word *pragmateíai* (= "business dealings").
5) Parable 1, § 11. My translation. In the section just before this parable, Hermas quotes a verse from James 4: 12. These two works are joined by a common democratic interest.

ginning of bureaucracy and of its evils. The trouble is not so much the delegation of powers as the division of labor, in which most of the members go about their usual daily tasks and the representatives go about running the organization. Once a membership establishes this arrangement of its affairs, the organization has begun to pass out of the membership's control. No amount of electing, however frequent, will restore to the members the control they had before they chose representatives.

The early Christians seem to have approached this structural change with a good deal of caution. "Appoint for yourselves," says the *Didachē,* "bishops and deacons worthy of the Lord, men who are meek and not lovers of money, and true and approved."[6] I Timothy says the same thing, in much greater detail:

> Our leader, therefore, or bishop, must be above reproach, faithful to his one wife, sober, temperate, courteous, hospitable, and a good teacher; he must not be given to drink, or a brawler, but of a forbearing disposition, avoiding quarrels, and no lover of money. He must be one who manages his own household well and wins obedience from his children, and a man of the highest principles.[7]

That the churches sometimes failed in such choices, though not for lack of trying, is evident from a passage in the *Shepherd of Hermas,* which tells of "deacons that exercised their office ill, and plundered the livelihood of widows and orphans, and made gain for themselves from the ministrations which they had received to perform."[8]

A little etymology will now be useful. "Presbyter," a transliteration from the Greek, means "an elder." "Bishop," from the Greek *epíscopos,* means "an overseer." "Deacon," from *diákonos,* means "a server" or "a servant." "Clergy," comes from *klêros,* which meant "an allotment of land" or "an estate." Thus the clergy, when they developed, probably took their name from the fact that they handled the church finances.[9]

These etymologies silently suggest the democratic intent of their

6) § 15. Lightfoot.

7) 3: 2–4. The same goes for deacons (verses 8–13), whose wives, moreover, must be "women of high principle, who will not talk scandal." NEB.

8) Parable 9, § 26. Lightfoot.

9) See Wright, op. cit., p. 12. Wright's judgment is the more impartial because (p. 2) he shows little taste for the economic interpretation of history.

original use. Men are thought to grow wiser as they grow older; hence the community would benefit by giving over to elders (presbyters) the conduct of its affairs. A bishop would superintend or manage. A deacon would be at the service of the community. A cleric would be a sort of treasurer. There would be a certain status about these groups, but in serving or overseeing or simply being old there is no hint of special appointment from on high. Yet precisely this concept of appointment from on high is the one which ultimately triumphed, and which, in its triumph, almost obliterated the democratic spirit of primitive Christianity. That spirit, though it never died, did not soar again until the Reformation.

Cynicism might lead us to suppose that these results followed because such results always follow when a man is given an office. The low view of human nature expects that every office has enough emoluments to corrupt the holder: he likes them as they are, and he seeks to enlarge them. There is, as we have seen, evidence of such cupidity at work in the early churches.

But self-aggrandizement will not really explain the trend towards hierarchy. Bishops of the second century would have repudiated such a charge with indignation, and would have asserted, with much truth, that the hierarchical principle was necessary to hold the Church together. Any organization that has life in it will, when it comes under attack, replace spontaneity with discipline, will gather round its leaders and urge those leaders to wield authority. This is what happened during the several persecutions. The attacks were fierce, the torments diabolical. Many members could not bear the strain and recanted or fled. Yet, as Engels ironically observed of the last persecution under Diocletian, "It was so effective that seventeen years later the army consisted overwhelmingly of Christians, and the succeeding autocrat of the whole Roman Empire, Constantine, called the Great by the priests, proclaimed Christianity as the state religion."[1]

It is incredible that such a result could have issued from hesitant, weak, or inauthoritative leadership. On the contrary, the result is proof that the bishops, deacons, presbyters had done wonders with the membership's morale—such wonders indeed that, after each persecution, Christian doctrine and life in the Christian community

---

1) Introduction to Marx's *Class Struggles in France*.

seemed more attractive than ever. Converts came in by scores, and many of the *lapsi,* the recanters, begged to return.

This last phenomenon raised problems which had a certain charm. What was one to do with the *lapsi* when they wanted to come back? And what was one to do with people whom the *lapsi* or other heretics had baptized? These matters Cyprian discussed, the Bishop of Carthage from 248 to 258. Cyprian was rigorous on both questions: the *lapsi* would have to give convincing guarantees of a restored faith, and the doubtfully baptized would have to be rebaptized. Organizational loyalty was paramount: "No man can have God as his Father unless he has the Church as his Mother."[2]

These views, to Cyprian's embarrassment, were very like those of Novatian, who in the year 251 became schismatic and a kind of anti-pope. For, although Cyprian's cautiousness with the *lapsi* seemed sensible and was so, his rigor with the heretically baptized tended to depopulate the Church. Accordingly, Stephen, the Bishop of Rome, held that rebaptism was not necessary, and went so far as to excommunicate those who thought it was. "Cyprian," wrote Jeremy Taylor in *The Liberty of Prophesying,* "did right in a wrong cause . . . and Stephen did ill in a good cause." Meanwhile the Church overlooked no chance to grow as large as possible.

What the leaders did for organizational morale was to found it upon doctrines most widely held among the membership, purging away deviationists like Marcion and the Docetics. Further, they asserted a glory in martyrdom, and at last accepted it for themselves when that was necessary. Without crediting the almost psychotic taste for martyrdom which the spurious epistles attribute to Ignatius, we may believe that he faced the lions with sufficient joy. Polycarp, at eighty-seven, was sensibly reluctant: he offered every required form of obedience except that of swearing by the Emperor and reviling the Christ. "Fourscore and six years have I been His servant," said the old man, "and He hath done me no wrong. How then can I blaspheme my King who saved me?"[3] And so they burned him to ashes.

Justin Martyr (he acquired the surname by earning it) was the ideologist who had done the most to connect Christian doctrine with Greek philosophy. He thus paved for non-Christians a road he had

2) Quoted by Bettenson, *Early Christian Fathers,* p. 32.
3) *Letter of the Smyrneans,* § 9. Lightfoot.

himself already trod, and the persecutors were not pleased. At Rome, the Prefect Rusticus said to him and to six of his followers, "Let us come to the pressing matter in hand. Agree together and sacrifice with one accord to the gods." And Justin said, "No right-minded man turns from true belief to false."[4] Whereupon Justin and the six were beheaded.

In due course it happened to Cyprian also. On the fourteenth of September, in the year 258, occurred the following official interrogation by Galerius Maximus, the Roman proconsul at Carthage:

—Are you Thascius Cyprianus?
—I am.
—The most sacred Emperors have commanded you to perform the rite [i.e., of worshiping them].
—I refuse.
—Consider your own interest.

. . . .
—Do as you have been ordered. In so clear a case there is no need for pondering.[5]

There was a large field outside the city, near a river; and in that field, before a multitude, they cut off his head. Cyprian left twenty-five gold pieces to the executioner.

There was, I believe, no example of ignominious panic to be found among the leaders of the Church. Retreat, though not retreat from principle, there sometimes was: Cyprian went into hiding during the Decian persecution in 250, and the great scholar Origen had fled Alexandria, in 215, during a massacre known as the "Fury of Caracalla." Such evasions were generally thought wise, for the Church was far too shrewd to sacrifice its leadership collectively. In any event, Cyprian's martyrdom was atonement enough, and Origen ultimately died of tortures suffered under Decian. Even without this seal of integrity, he would have been a great man. His pupil Gregory Thaumaturgus has left a description of his pedagogy which remains the definitive account of any true teacher:

No subject was barred, nothing was kept from us. . . . We were allowed to make ourselves familiar with all kinds of doctrine,

4) *A Treasury of Early Christianity,* edited by Anne Freemantle (New York: Mentor Books; 1960), pp. 171–72.
5) Ibid., p. 199. I have somewhat altered the translation for brevity's sake.

from Greek and Eastern sources, on spiritual or secular subjects, ranging freely over the whole field of learning. [The master taught] in words which inspired us as well by their humility as by their confidence that, as the eye seeks light, and the body craves food, so our mind is informed by nature with a longing to know the truth of God and the causes of phenomena.[6]

Thus it was by their own labor, ingenuity, and sacrifice the leaders of the Church successfully established the hierarchical principle. They won power by deserving it, by constantly resolving organizational problems in favor of growth and unity in the membership. They were masters in the art of accommodating ideology to political needs, and their performance in this regard is the more extraordinary because a great deal of it had to be improvisational. There were few precedents for what they did.

Yet so skillful were they in controversy, in the conduct and resolution of their disputes, that success grew upon them, and, as it grew, seemed to confirm their own divine appointment and the divine foundation of the Church itself. By the year 200, everyone was aware that there existed, side by side with the Roman imperium, a parallel power, which had acquired the singular attribute of indestructibility. Tertullian darkly reminded the Alexandrians what Christians could do if it were not for Christian charity: "One night, with a few little torches, could work an ample revenge."[7] And he continued, proudly and truly, "We are but of yesterday, and we have filled everything you have—cities, islands, forts, towns, exchanges, yes! and camps, tribes, decuries, palace, senate, forum. All we have left to you is the temples!"[8] Nowadays, the newspapers would call this "infiltration."

Between the second and the fifth centuries, the Church passed from parallel power to equal power to superior power. During this process of change, the Church patterned itself more and more upon the Empire, and thus thought in terms of a chain of command. The origins of this notion may be found in Clement's *Epistle to the Corinthians,* A.D. 96, which offers to settle certain quarrels within the Corinthian Church. The author proposes as model the legendary discipline of the Roman army:

6) Quoted by Bettenson, *Early Christian Fathers,* pp. 26–27.
7) *Apologeticus,* XXXVII, 3: *"una nox pauculis faculis largiter ultionis posset operari."* My translation.
8) Ibid., XXXVII, 4. Translation by Glover, in the Loeb Classical Library.

Let us therefore enlist ourselves, brethren, with all earnestness in His faultless ordinances. Let us mark the soldiers that are enlisted under our rulers, how exactly, how readily, how submissively, they execute the orders given them. All are not prefects, nor rulers of thousands, nor rulers of hundreds, nor rulers of fifties, and so forth; but each man in his own rank executeth the orders given by the king and the governors.[9]

Such discipline was the response to Domitian's persecution, and it put the movement beyond possibility of harm.

What, then, were the effects on basic doctrine, what the resulting orthodoxy and its attendant heresies? If primitive democracy in the Church derived from the insurrectionary Jesus, the hierarchical system derived from the supernatural and Pauline Christ. It had, as we know, become clear that neither of these sources could be abandoned without sundering the unity of the Church. Loss of the historical Jesus would have abolished the human kinship which Christians felt with their Founder. Loss of the supernatural Christ would have abolished their connection with divinity.

From all this, two difficult problems arose. What was the relation of the historical Jesus to the transcendental Christ—or, to put it in theological language, what was the relation between divinity and humanity in the person of Jesus Christ? And what was the relation between Christ the Son and God the Father? The official resolution of these questions belongs to the fourth and fifth centuries, and we shall consider it in the next chapter. Meanwhile let us observe what direction the argument took.

I may say at once that I have no doubt the Fathers believed themselves to be dealing with matters of knowledge, with "the truth of God and the causes of phenomena." They did nothing so vulgar as to inquire what doctrine would unite the most people, and then declare that doctrine true. They were not mere spokesmen, apologetical hacks, supplying arguments for a predetermined policy. They were men who undertook to combine the assertion of ultimate truth with the conduct of an organization. The truth they supposed themselves qualified to assert had to do with no less a thing than human salvation, and of this salvation the organization they presided over was the means, the vehicle, the sole and exemplary instrument. We shall

9) § 38. Lightfoot.

never understand how great a burden the Fathers carried until we are aware that they believed themselves to be carrying all burdens whatever.

Nevertheless, it is very striking that in every one of the great questions the resolution was such as to convince and unite the greatest number of Christians. Some Christians loved more the man Jesus, others the God Christ; orthodoxy told them to think of Him as man and God. Some Christians were more struck with His sonship, others with His entire divinity; orthodoxy told them that He was both Son of the Father and Sharer in the Godhead. Some feared that the sacraments would be void if administered by heretics, others that the validity of such sacraments would validate the heretics; orthodoxy told them that the sacraments remained sacraments and the heretics heretics.[1] I think there is no doubt that beneath the consciousness of the Fathers there moved a potent talent, a genius indeed, for organization. Never did they choose a partial view or a sectarian. Always they chose doctrines which combined maximum unity with maximum membership. It may be that this would never have happened if they had not chanced to mistake politics for science and accommodation for truth.

The doctrinal compromise was, as we shall see, so subtle that it could scarcely be expressed in words. Assuming, as then seemed obvious, that men could not effect their own salvation, there would have to be a God to do it if it were to be done at all. There did exist (so the doctrine ran) such a God, who, in his efforts to rescue mankind, was confronted with the fact that human damnation is the consequence of human sin. It had long been the practice to atone for sin by an acceptance of sacrifice. Accordingly, God sent a part of himself, His Son, into the world to inhabit the body of the historical Jesus, to suffer and to die, though all the while innocent of any sin, and thus to effect in one supreme atonement the cancellation of all sins.

In the course of this life and these sufferings, the incarnate Christ had founded an organization whose "only commonwealth is the universe,"[2] and whose aim is the bringing of men more certainly to salvation. From this act of establishment the authority of bishops,

1) This compromise took care of the heresies of Novatian and Donatus.
2) Tertullian, *Apologeticus*, XXXVIII, 3: *Unam omnium rempublicam agnoscimus mundum.* Robertson's translation, op. cit., p. 208.

presbyters, deacons, and indeed of the whole Church flowed. The institution was divine and therefore the authority was complete.

No other organization in history has made so grand a claim. Islam is a powerful community, but its founder never described himself as more than a prophet. Buddhism has more adherents than Christianity, but Gautama, so far from being a god, tended to dethrone what gods there were.[3] Most human organizations acknowledge men as their founders, and Communists are quite content to have descended from Marx.

But the Fathers of the Church most astonishingly combined a gift for compromise with a search for ultimates. *Their* Founder was not to be a mere man or prophet or secondary deity. He had to be, and was, coeval with the Father, only begotten and unbegotten, Very God of Very God. Any lesser status would have impaired his authority and consequently the authority of the bishops and of the Church. And so, whenever a clergyman acts *in nomine Patris, et Filii, et Spiritus Sancti,* what he means to say is, "Nothing can be done which is more authoritative than this."

If consistency within the compromise was difficult to express, comparison with objective fact baffled the imagination. One can compare, say, the verbal definition of a mountain with any of various mountains, and thus see that there really is something which corresponds to the definition. But how can one determine whether there is anything at all which corresponds to the definition of the Trinity? And, more painfully yet, what can be done with a description some elements of which contradict our experience of the world? So far as we *see,* the dead don't rise, the lame don't walk after a mere touch of hands, and men are not born of virgins.

Over areas like these the Fathers scudded on wings of faith, and nowhere else is their shrewdness more amply shown. They knew the limits and encumbrances of their world; they understood that what men cannot do, magic must somehow be made to do. Without that there would be no hope, and without hope no Christian Church. Faced with this choice of all or nothing, they found in themselves, every one of them, something of Tertullian's defiance. For Tertullian, stung by the taunts of his moral inferiors and laboring to prove what

3) See John B. Noss, *Man's Religions* (New York: The Macmillan Company; 1949), p. 171.

cannot be proved, had asserted the contradictions in all their purity and had made a virtue of contradiction itself:

> The Son of God was born like any child: there's no shame
>   in that, precisely because the fact is shameful.
> The Son of God died like any man: the fact is wholly
>   believable, because it is absurd.
> And he rose from the dead: the fact is certain,
>   because it is impossible.[4]

This blaze of paradox historians of philosophy, even reputable ones, are accustomed to reduce to the bare *credo quia absurdum,* which they attribute to Tertullian and which Tertullian never quite said. Nor can he be made to say it. For the paradoxes with which he showered his enemies, and in which any fool can detect the presence of contrary ideas, had their source in the political contradictions within the movement, in the ceaseless resolve to join the dead revolutionary with the living God. The more difficult this concept became in logic, the more adequately it expressed the needs and triumph of the organization. Paradoxical the concept was and is, but without those paradoxes the Church would have perished.[5]

Accordingly, we will leave skeptics to their skepticism, in which, in respect of theory, they will be right. But ordinarily they are not

4) *De Carne Christi,* § 5: *Natus est dei filius; non pudet, quia pudendum est: et mortuus est dei filius; prorsus credibile est, quia ineptum est; et sepultus resurrexit; certum est, quia impossibile.* The translation is mine: I have been at some pains to show that the verbs *natus est* and *mortuus est* are used of the Son of God in precisely the same sense in which they would be used of people. The force of the contradictions depended on this.

5) I here elaborate politically one of Pascal's insights. In that part of the *Pensées* subtitled *Pensées chrétiennes,* he writes: "There are many truths, both of faith and of morals, which seem mutually exclusive and contradictory, yet which subsist, all of them, in an excellent system. The source of all heresies is the exclusion of some of these truths. Further, the source of all the objections which heretics make to us is simply ignorance of some of our truths. And ordinarily it happens that, not being able to see the connection between two opposed truths, and believing that acceptance of the one requires rejection of the other, they hold fast to the one and reject the other. The Nestorians wanted there to be two persons in Jesus Christ because there are two natures, and the Eutychians, on the contrary, wanted there to be one nature because there is one person. The Catholics, however, are orthodox because they join the two truths together, namely, the two natures and the one single person." My translation. Pascal did not apply this insight to his own espousal of the Jansenist heresy.

heads of organizations or primary makers of policy. Hence they are less likely to understand that every program is a marriage of contradictions, and that no organization can survive without some accommodation among Father and Son and Holy Ghost.

CHAPTER

5

The Making of Heresies

THE Fathers of the Church had lovely names. There was Theodore of Mopsuestia, who regrettably inclined to the Nestorian heresy. There was Shenoutē of Atripē, who, in the Theban Desert, ruled over twenty-two hundred monks and eighteen hundred nuns, and lived to an age of one hundred eighteen years. There were Serapion of Thmuis, Nonnus of Panopolis, Severian of Gabala, Isidore of Pelusium, and Didymus the Blind.

These names cannot have had in their own time the quaint enchantment they now possess. To be sure, if you were named Theodore, the assertion was (and, for that matter, is) that you were a gift of God. The name "Severian" connected you, at whatever distance, with personal sobriety. "Didymus" would only indicate that you were a twin. Yet the Didymus here in question, though blind from the age of four and consequently unlettered, acquired so vast an erudition that he became the teacher of the great Jerome, and Jerome always called him *magister*.

I mean to suggest that the Fathers were worthy of their names, and that they matched the grandeur of polysyllables with a certain grandeur of achievement. These were no timid, retiring intellectuals, even when monkish or eremite. In society they fought a thousand foes; in solitude they fought a thousand appetites. The human foes were imperial bureaucrats, or rival religionists, or sectarians within the faith—all difficult to repel. The appetites were, as it seemed, lusts—all alarmingly compulsive and difficult to control. Against men and appetites, both equally hostile, one set the strength of personal integrity and the doctrines of redemptive faith.

There was, moreover, a connection between the desired health of character and the desired clarity of doctrine. "People weary of what is extraordinary and incoherent," says Guignebert; "the faith of most ordinary men naturally aims at stability, which is a synonym to them for truth."[1] I suppose we have all, from time to time, mistaken a stable opinion for a true; if so, it is because truth does in fact give stability. At the same time, stability can come from other sources—for example, organizational support—and hence we are left confusing an attribute of truth with truth's essence.

During the second and third centuries, the Fathers labored over a mass of accumulated and contrary doctrines, with a view to rendering each doctrine clear and the totality consistent. Their individual results were such as would fail of orthodoxy if measured strictly by the Nicene canon (A.D. 325), but they led toward that canon and were indeed contributions to it. It is doubtful, for example, whether Origen's doctrine of the "subordination of the Son"[2] would have passed muster in the fourth century but, despite the implications of this view, Origen was disposed to accept the unity of the Godhead. Justin Martyr and Clement of Alexandria, rather too much Hellenized, were more interested in the philosophical *Logos* than in a religious God; and, in any case, Clement was less a theologian than a puritanical critic of contemporary morals.[3] Tertullian actually did wander into an organized heresy, the Montanist, which prescribed absolute celibacy and practiced "speaking in the tongues."[4] Yet these

1) Charles Guignebert, *Christianity, Past and Present* (New York: The Macmillan Company; 1927), p. 131.

2) *De Principiis* 3: 6.

3) See, e.g., *The Instructor*, excerpted in Freemantle, op. cit., pp. 52–61. Clement's remarkable maxim that "shame disappears with the underclothing" has been quoted on occasions of a sort he did not intend. In Casanova's *Mémoires* (*Bibliothèque de la Pléiade*, Vol. II, p. 944) we are told, "*Hedvige, en rougissant, peut-être craignant de perdre à mes yeux avec plus de retenue, laissa tomber le dernier voile de la pudeur, en citant Clément d'Alexandrie, qui dit que la honte ne gît que dans la chemise.*"

4) Named after its founder, Montanus, early in the third century. As Guignebert says (op. cit., p. 140), "Montanus had, in truth, committed an anachronism." That is to say, by his time it was too late to obey literally the more detailed injunctions of Saint Paul.

three were far too mighty to be cast aside or even rebuked. Justin had died a martyr; he and Clement had made doctrine attractive to the "Gentiles," and Christianity has never had an advocate (in the legal sense, at least) more potent than Tertullian. Thus the same effort at uniting a large membership, which produced in the fourth century a series of carefully stated creeds, preserved the earlier Fathers, if not from the taint, then at any rate from the blame, of heresy.

I I

WHILE THE FATHERS thus labored, the Empire sank intermittently toward ultimate decay. Domitian's calculated reign of terror (A.D. 95-97), when compared with Caligula's imbecility and Nero's mindless brutality, seems, to be sure, almost intelligent. Yet Domitian, while appearing as savior of the state from subversive activities by Christians and Jews, and thus as defender of the exploiting classes generally, fell into a bitter contest with the Senate. Now, the Senate was, in the main, an organ of the great Italian landowners, who formed a powerful part of the ruling class. Their sudden subjection to imperial tyranny gave them common cause for a time with the usual popular victims. It is probable that some of the upper-class conversions to Christianity occurred as a result of this new, if temporary, political alignment.

Domitian's terror ended with his assassination. Under the succeeding emperors—Nerva, Trajan, Hadrian—the Empire took on some of the aspects of a welfare state. It was, as Robertson suggests, "the reformist phase which so often immediately precedes the final breakdown of imperialism."[5] The oppressed classes had suddenly become valuable to their oppressors in other ways than as a source of profitable labor power.

For one thing, the Empire, by Hadrian's time (117-138), had ceased to grow and was in fact on the defensive. The slave class could no longer be recruited by further conquests, and thus its existing members became, through relative scarcity, rather more valuable. So also did the impoverished freedmen and freemen. The Italian peninsula felt these effects with peculiar severity: as the Empire wore on, and wore down, prosperity (such as it was) and political power passed to the provinces. Accordingly, Nerva established, and

5) Op. cit., p. 170.

Hadrian increased, a public fund for the children of the poor in Italy, with a view to their education and general support.

Further, defense of the Empire required stability within the Empire itself: internal struggles had to be eased and the peoples given some inducement toward loyalty. Hadrian's reforms, which have made him seem a singularly enlightened ruler, cancelled unpaid taxes, replaced tax farming with direct taxation,[6] and abolished the power of life and death that slave owners had long exercised over their slaves. These things accomplished, the imperial masters could perhaps say to their subjects, "You would be worse off under the barbarians."

And in fact this is precisely what they did say. Between the years 177 and 180, the philosopher Celsus produced a series of attacks on Christianity.[7] He very ably probed the theoretical weaknesses, and some of his criticisms will be found, sixteen centuries later, in Voltaire. But the heart of his argument was that Christian dissent from the state religion seriously weakened the whole imperial defense. Celsus invited the Christians to consider that they too would collapse under a barbarian triumph. This prediction proved, in the event, exactly wrong. The Christians took pains to convert the barbarians before victory, and Alaric, in his sack of Rome, largely spared Christian monuments and possessions.

The Roman Empire, we have said, was a vast political device for the support of chattel slavery. In view of the odiousness of its purpose, the brutality of its means, and the extravagance of its upkeep, it must be admitted to have survived for a remarkably long time. Colonial imperialisms of the nineteenth century, quite unable to endure the wars and civil strife they have engendered, are collapsing before our eyes after a mere hundred or one hundred fifty years. If one wished to rewrite history, speculatively, in a series of statements contrary to fact, one might show that a rebellion of the dispossessed would sooner or later have brought down the Empire—or, equally perhaps, that Roman administration, by virtue of its enormous skill, would have

6) Tax farming (i.e., allowing the collectors a percentage of their collections) has been, throughout history, a peculiarly hateful method, because it adds to the exactions of governments the exactions of personal cupidity.

7) Celsus's works were destroyed by the Church triumphant, but his doctrines have survived in an extensive and fair-minded rebuttal by Origen.

survived revolt. But before either of these things could happen, the waves of "barbarian"[8] invasion made them alike impossible.

The barbarians were migratory tribes from the east, who had, so to say, driven one another westward until they reached the outer defenses of the Empire along the Danube and the Rhine. Thence they made forays into imperial territory, but the defenses themselves generally held firm. Pressure from the east, however, continued. In A.D. 376, during the reign of Valens, the Visigoths, hounded by the Huns, sought and obtained admission into the Empire.

But the Empire was now too frail and its population too hopeless for longer defense. In the year 408, Alaric led his Goths to the out-skirts of Rome and cut the route to the seaport of Ostia, on which Roman economy depended. The city offered to ransom itself. Alaric accepted the offer with some magnanimity, and waited long months for the ransom to be paid. When, by the year 410, it had become clear that the Romans and Italians were sliding out of their bargain, the sack began.[9] Large areas of Rome were committed to the flames, and large numbers of people to the sword; but, according to ecclesi-astical accounts, Christians, their property, and their chastity were very generally preserved by the piety of Alaric and the intervention of saints. It was, by Roman calculation, the eleven hundred and sixty-third year *ab urbe condita*.

Toward the end of his account of these events, Gibbon remarks, very levelly, that "there exists in human nature a strong propensity to depreciate the advantages, and to magnify the evils, of the present times."[1] No doubt there does, and I must myself be candid enough to confess that I share it. Nevertheless, one cannot fail to hear, across the ages, the thunderous ruin of a city that had stood so long and had so vastly governed. Indeed, the city's fall was a true symbol of the

---

8) The Romans used this word to describe any cultural phenomenon that was neither Roman nor Greek. The Greeks had used it to signify, depreciatively, anything "foreign" or "alien." One suggested etymology is that, to Greek ears, the speech of the Persians sounded like repetitions of the syllable "bar." Hence a "barbarian" would be someone who kept saying "bar-bar."

9) Gibbon observes, in a pregnant comment, that the Roman defenders "were unable to guard against the secret conspiracy of their slaves and domestics; who, either from birth or interest, were attached to the cause of the enemy." *Decline and Fall of the Roman Empire,* Chapter XXXI. In short, imperialism had at last become, in the eyes of its victims, the main enemy.

1) Ibid., loc. cit.

greater historical event. A whole social order—that of chattel slavery —lying, iniquitous, and cruel, passed finally into wreckage; and here and there, within the shattered bulk, sprang up those new, strange, vertical, treelike growths which in the end composed the local and anarchic powers of the feudal system.

Imperial collapse, effected by the barbarians, had been prepared by many miseries. The fourth century, which in this chapter mainly concerns us, endured a decrease of population and a spread of infanticide. There were therefore fewer people to pay taxes and to fill the legions. Towns grew less prosperous; lands were more and more left waste, their owners having sought escape from tax collection. Riots broke out among starving peasants in Gaul and among city populations, as at Antioch in 387. And always there were the civil wars for control of the Empire, and the rapacity of the despots who conquered.

Through these vicissitudes, as through many before, the gods of the Romans followed their remote but perilous path. The pantheon they were enshrined in opened itself to many strange deities, none stranger, perhaps, than the *manes* of successive emperors. The augurs studied, with what perspicacity they could, the flight of birds and the entrails of sheep; but there never came a time when they, sad augurs, could mock their own presage. Jupiter, Mars, Vulcan, with all their consorts and mistresses, had found in the Christian God an adversary who repelled their acquaintance, who would not give up lordship for equality nor the government of earth and heaven for a place in the pantheon. These transactions among deities expressed the fact that, by the end of the third century, the Christian Church knew its own power, and knew the time to be at hand when an emperor, in order to govern at all, would have to profess Christianity.

The Roman gods had never been challenged so forcefully, but they had been challenged. From the time (about 300 B.C.) when Epicurus founded his community at Athens upon the principles of friendship, self-discipline, and science, the tradition that bears his name spread throughout the Mediterranean world. His doctrine, which regarded the universe as composed of atoms in movement, was singularly free of superstition. It asserted the existence of gods, but these gods had nothing whatever to do with the world. Inhabitants of some remote and blissful sphere, they enjoyed the life of virtue and the fruits of perfection. On this view, official deities—the gods of states and empires—were political fictions, and the effect of such fictions was lamentable. The great Lucretius (96–55 B.C.), a prophet of Epicureanism to the Romans, paused, in Book I of the *De Rerum Natura,* to contemplate the folly of Iphigenia's sacrifice. *Casta inceste,* "stainless maid mid the stain of blood," she had been slain by her father on behalf of favorable winds for the voyage to Troy. *Tantum,* says Lucretius with a bitterness that still drips gall, *tantum religio potuit suadere malorum.*²

The Epicureans had thus detected in official religion something anti-humanist and, indeed, inhumane. It imposed evils and imposed them by illusion. The greatest of these evils was a certain permanent terror of mind, from which, however, a man could free himself (so Lucretius said), not by "the sun's rays or the clear shafts of day," but by "nature's aspect and reasonableness."³ Science was to be the consolation of man; through knowledge, earth would become for the first time habitable.

These doctrines, born of old Ionian materialism, struck at the incurable weakness of official ideology. The gods had in fact been inventions, first of the fancy and then of the state. In this second phase they served the uses of government, adorning rulers with supernatural attributes and cowing the ruled even more than force could do. But the Epicureans were no revolutionists. They simply offered in their communities a haven for men of poverty and good temper, and in their doctrine a calm acceptance of the world. The state, however, eyed them doubtfully; they were less than respectable, and only in his letters did Cicero admit that he had ever read *De Rerum Natura.*

Epicureanism had only that latent threat which will be found in ideas divorced from action. Christianity was a somewhat different matter. That the Roman imperium partly believed and partly disbelieved the Christian denial of revolutionary intent may be inferred from the fact that the persecutions came suddenly after longish intervals of tolerance and peace. Moreover, the persecutions sometimes

2) Line 102: "So great the evils to which religion could prompt." The translation here, and before, is Munro's.
3) Book I, ll. 172–74. My translation. The Latin is:
> *Hunc igitur terrorem animi, tenebrasque necesse est*
> *Non radii solis, neque lucida tela diei*
> *Discutiant, sed naturae species, ratioque.*

Lucretius liked these lines so well that he repeated them several times in the poem.

occurred in new places, under the conduct of men unfamiliar with the task. The younger Pliny, for example, the Procurator of Bithynia in A.D. 112, groped at a policy between respect for his duty and distaste for the consequences. In the end, he wrote to his emperor, Trajan, for advice.[4] Pliny was frank and honorable, he had in no way the inquisitor's temperament, and he gave the most convincing account we have of the day-to-day impact of Christianity upon the Empire.

The problem in Bithynia was not insurrection nor the wish for it: Pliny could not find the smallest trace of either. The problem was strictly, crassly, almost trivially economic. Christianity had had much success there. A great many converts had adhered, and, to the extent that they did so, the ancient temples lost attendance, the ancient rites grew disused, and (plainly worst of all) the sale of sacrificial victims fell almost to nothing. Christianity, as a poor man's religion, was necessarily inexpensive: it offered upon the market the ideal perfection of a commodity, enormous value at hardly any cost. What you got was nothing less than personal salvation. This you got partly by your own act of belief, partly by gift from the crucified Savior. As for money, you gave (not paid) what you could.

We are not told, but we can well imagine, the wrath of sellers of images, lambs, and fowl at this unfair competition. They saw a whole market disappearing before them: there can be no greater impiety. The old gods, it was clear, were imperiled by a new God, of whom no image could be made, and to whom no sacrifice could be offered except that of a broken and a contrite heart.

Then followed those events which customarily follow when vice plays inquisitor to virtue. There are people who so hate their own consciences that a chance to harm their nobler brethren offers an exquisite and irresistible relief. So libels abounded, informers multiplied, and Pliny knew very well that much of it was lies and all of it prompted by hostility. *Ut fieri solet,* he wrote in some embarrassment, "the usual result followed: the very fact of my dealing with the question led to a wider spread of the charge."[5] He interrogated firmly, he demanded sacrifice to the Emperor, he put two deaconesses to torture, and he executed those who, after a third trial, remained unmoved. But all he ever found out about the Christians was

4) This celebrated letter is No. XCVI (or, by some tallies, XCVII) of Book X of the *Epistolae.*
5) Ibid., § 4. Translation Bettenson's, *Documents,* p. 6.

that on an appointed day they had been accustomed to meet before daybreak, and to recite a hymn antiphonally to Christ, as to a god, and to bind themselves by an oath, not for the commission of any crime but to abstain from theft, robbery, adultery, and breach of faith, and not to deny a deposit when it was claimed. After the conclusion of this ceremony it was their custom to depart and meet again to take food; but it was ordinary and harmless food. . . .[6]

The oath and the food having proved harmless, and the tenor of Christian conduct benign, Pliny was left at a stand. The two deaconesses, under torture, revealed nothing more than *superstitionem pravam et immodicam,* "a depraved and extravagant superstition." By executing only the firmest, Pliny had removed from Bithynian life just those persons most likely to adorn it. Nevertheless, the desired economic results were indeed forthcoming. "There is no shadow of doubt," wrote Pliny, "that the temples, which have been almost deserted, are beginning to be frequented once more, that the sacred rites, which have been long neglected, are being renewed, and that sacrificial victims are for sale everywhere, whereas, till recently, a buyer was scarcely to be found."[7] From which effect Pliny concluded that "a host of men could be set right, were they given a chance of recantation." It is hard to think of Pliny as naïf; yet has there ever been a more candid identification of religion with economics?

Trajan replied that Pliny had done just the right thing. He added, a little hopefully, that, as for the flood of anonymous libels, *nec nostri saeculi est*—"it is contrary to the spirit of our age."[8] But there can, alas, be few ages when people will not do ignominious things out of fear; and freedom from such ignomiy still awaits a brighter day when governments will no longer terrorize. In those early, dreadful times when superstition, feeding upon human impotence, unseasonably abounded, the same minds which entertained extravagant hopes and fears could also entertain extravagant suspicions. Christians said that (symbolically or otherwise) they ate the flesh and drank the blood of their risen Savior; it was thereupon alleged that Christians were cannibals. They called one another

6) Ibid., § 7. Bettenson.
7) Ibid., § 10. Bettenson.
8) Trajan to Pliny, *Epistolae,* X, XCVII [XCVIII], 2.

brother and sister, and asserted an intimate love for each; it was thereupon alleged that they practiced incest. The weekly meal was a love feast, a celebration of *agapē;* it was thereupon alleged that these weekly gatherings were orgies. "The dogs," cried Tertullian with transcendent irony, "are our pimps in the dark, forsooth, and make a sort of decency for guilty lusts by overturning the lamps. That, at all events, is what you always say about us."[9]

It is evident that the Roman public of the second and third centuries understood Christianity as little as the American public of the twentieth century understands socialism. Faced with a historical phenomenon which grew in proportion as it was attacked, and lamed by mythology for the explication of such events, the Romans and the "Gentiles" generally could only conclude that witches were at work —malevolent powers which somehow escaped the usual axioms of defense, which prospered upon adversity, and which seemed likely to enthrone themselves upon the enfeebled gods. But these witches and powers were in fact no other than a growing congregation of men in search of righteousness. Their efficacy was an efficacy of virtue, the most underrated of human talents and at the same time the most unifying. Administered with a skillful eye on current politics, this talent is always irresistible. The emperor Constantine perhaps did not need that vision in the sky over the Milvian Bridge, though by it he was edified and (it is said) made victorious. But there is no doubt that he needed the Christian Church, and hence that, like any sensible monarch, he embraced it.

I I I

DURING THE RISE of Christianity toward supreme power, the innocence and purity of its original conceptions grew much modified by political needs.[1] A certain unity of doctrine had always been

9) *Apologeticus,* VII, 1. Translation by Glover.
1) Gibbon observes (op. cit., Chapter XVI) of Christianity in the reign of Diocletian: "Prosperity had relaxed the nerves of discipline. Fraud, envy, and malice prevailed in every congregation. The presbyters aspired to the episcopal office, which every day became an object more worthy of their ambition. The bishops, who contended with each other for ecclesiastical pre-eminence, appeared by their conduct to claim a secular and tyrannical power in the church; and the lively faith which still distinguished the Christians from the Gentiles was shown much less in their lives than in their controversial writings."

desirable as expressing the unity of the growing Church; but there could at the same time be, as in fact there was, a surge of various interpretation around the central core. When, however, Christianity triumphed as the Empire's "official" faith, it ceased to be what it had thus far been: an heretical theology. It became, in the fact of triumph, orthodoxy, and for the first time an exact statement of its doctrines took on supreme political importance.

Worshipers who recite the Apostles' Creed as a compendium of Christian ideology are aware that they express belief in an entity called "the Holy Catholic Church." In this phrase the word "catholic" means, of course, "universal," and Protestants, when they use it, are not referring to Rome. Now, from the assertion that the Church is holy we can infer an intimate connection with Deity. From the assertion that it is Christian we can infer an exclusiveness of doctrine. From the assertion that it is universal we can infer that in some manner it comprehends mankind. These three assertions, with their attendant inferences, will explain the extraordinary concept which, with much elevation and no little mystery, crowns the great edifice of Christian doctrine.

This extraordinary concept is the concept of the Trinity—of three Persons who are in the most intimate sense one Person, and of the one Person who is most distinctly three. It will be well to discuss the notion before we describe the struggles which marked its definitive formulation. About it, indeed, there yet hangs a veil, not of unreason, but of something like distance, as of an object conjecturably real but too remote to be accurately discerned. Gibbon remarks, in language faintly touched with his habitual skepticism, that "the incomprehensible mystery which excites our adoration eludes our inquiry."[2] And Newman, who was, in respect of religious belief, as far from skepticism as may be, observes, "There the inquisitiveness of a pious mind rests, viz., when it has pursued the subject into the mystery which is its limit."[3]

I am aware that there must be some brashness in setting aside the counsels of so grand an historian and so lucid a theologian, but the fact is that I think I understand the Trinity. Moreover, the mystery which does no doubt intellectually suffuse the concept is in itself a

2) Gibbon. op. cit., Chapter XXI.
3) John Henry Newman: *Arians of the Fourth Century* (London: Longmans; 1833), Book II, Chapter I, § 1.

means of understanding. For the fact of mystery, which I think all theologians attest, obliges us to infer that this particular concept was not chosen on grounds of self-evidence or clarity or even probability. It was, indeed, not chosen on intellectual grounds at all. It was chosen because it, and it alone, could organize three hundred years of speculation into a single, coherent proof that the Christian Church was supremely authoritative, was exclusively authoritative, and was authoritative for all.

If the concept of the Trinity were in fact irrational, as many people have thought, then no object corresponding to the concept could exist, and Christianity would be left asserting the impossible. This would have been a stupendous defect, which must, long before now, have brought doctrine down in ruin. For myself, I do not think that ideology has upon human events any effect so powerful as reactionaries always fear it has; but I do think it unlikely that demonstrable nonsense could have supported a great institution for some two thousand years. Inspection of the concept itself will show that it signifies nothing impossible, even though what it does signify is, in respect of existence, rather hard to believe.

The first difficulty which people feel is this: how can three entities be one entity, or one entity three? Well, one might say, nothing is simpler, and indeed the requirement is very modest. Every sane man has a lively sense of the oneness of his body, which remains itself even though the hairs whiten and the skin wrinkles and organs decay. Yet this body is composed, not of three, but of billions of entities. If we could hear, and respect, the lamentations of our molecules, we would perhaps have a soberer sense of what we really are. Yet the molecules, though speechless, are nonetheless distinct; they are not lost in the totality they compose. Compared with this much intricacy of union and independence, the Trinity is easy traffic indeed.

But there is more. The *pattern* of relation that lies in the concept of the Trinity is not only possible; it is also an ideal pattern of what we must consider human brotherhood. People in the capitalist world, for example, fear that socialism will submerge their personal identity; people in the socialist world know from past experience that capitalism tends to sunder social unity. Plainly, an ideal brotherhood would simultaneously preserve personal identity and social unity, so as to possess the goods of each. Wholeness without loss of individuality: this is what the Trinity symbolizes. It is what our molecules have already achieved within us, and, one may hope, what we shall some-day achieve with one another. If we wished to take the concept as metaphor, and to risk what in our time would be egregious heresy, we might regard the Trinity as an early experiment in socialism.

In respect of reason, there is no more mystery in the Trinity than there is in the notion, familiar enough in mathematics, of a limit. A limit, we are told, is "a fixed value or form which a varying value or form may approach indefinitely but cannot reach."[4] One can con-ceive and express these limits on the basis of what one knows from more immediate experience. After this manner, the relation which is said to hold within the Trinity (wholeness without loss of indi-viduality) may be regarded as the ultimate, limiting case of a series of well-known cases. Our experience of relations amply shows that every relation unites distinct entities. If their distinctness disappears, so does the relation, as having nothing any longer to unite. But if, on the other hand, the distinctness of the elements is total, then the elements cannot be related at all. What we familiarly find is that elements exist quite distinctly in their various relations with one another. Hence, in order to conceive of the Trinity, all that is re-quired of us is to imagine a limiting case in which the unity of the relation and the distinctness of the elements are simultaneously complete.

So much is less than difficult. It is, however, harder to compose into unity the three specific Persons with whom Christian doctrine has basically to do. The problem has been much complicated by metaphor, on which, indeed, turned the Arian controversy we are now to describe. Extracting the literal sense (or senses) of a meta-phor is never easy, because one seldom knows where the metaphor leaves off and the imageless meaning begins. What, for example, is meant by calling God a father and Christ His son? The expected meaning would be that God stands to Christ in the relation of be-getter to begotten, of creator to creature, of maker to thing made. There would be a precedence in time and perhaps also a superiority in prestige. Especially in the ancient world, where patriarchal habits and notions had long given fathers lordship over family and property, this crucial and perplexing metaphor must have suggested inferior status for Christ the son.

Biologically and socially, what other inference could there be?

4) Webster's Collegiate Dictionary, fifth edition, 1936, p. 582.

Across the intervening ages we can hear the Arian protest: how can the Son be as old as the Father? how can he be part of the Father's identity?[5] As we shall see, Arius just missed political success, and hence his views just missed establishment as orthodoxy. If he had won, we Christians would all be unitarians, like Mohammedans and Buddhists and Jews, and trinitarians would perhaps have survived as a stubborn sect *in partibus infidelium.*

But (as historical novels say) that was not to be. The orthodox Fathers—orthodox they are, since they made their doctrine stick— were as cunning as serpents, though not perhaps as harmless as doves. Harmless as doves, indeed, they could not be: no dove would have survived that climactic contest. For the contest, as we know, had to do with control of an organization essential to the Empire's security, an organization which became the Empire's heir.

The extraordinary thing about the Fathers is the immeasurable grandeur of their intent. Mired as we are in the mid-twentieth century, where drowning seems as probable as breath, we can scarcely imagine—or, imagining, endure—the sight of a human organization urging ultimate claims. We, who can convince one another of nothing, who suppose (alas, from fond experience) that every argument is tendentiously set forth, what can we comprehend of men who thought they were God's ministers, ruling and healing with the moral law, inspiring emperors with reverence, people with holiness, and the mournful present with a future joy?

Moreover, three hundred years of democratic political theory have exactly reversed the jurisprudence[6] on which the concept of the Trinity is based. For example, that great libertarian document, the Encyclopedia that Diderot edited between 1751 and 1765, asserts, under the heading *Autorité Politique,* "The Prince holds from his subjects themselves the authority he has over them."[7] No patriarch

5) Arius himself (256–336) put these protests in very careful prose, both for accuracy's sake and for protection against his adversaries: "We are persecuted because we say that the Son has a beginning, but God is without beginning." Letter to Eusebius, Bishop of Nicomedia, circa 321, excerpted in Bettenson, *Documents,* p. 55.
6) I.e., the theory of the nature and function of law.
7) *"Le prince tient de ses sujets mêmes l'autorité qu'il a sur eux."* The article is by Diderot himself. It will be found, excerpted, in John Lough, *The Encyclopedie of Diderot and D'Alembert* (Cambridge: Cambridge University Press; 1954), pp. 6–15.

or emperor of old time would have held such a view. Such rulers would never have thought—or would never have said—that authority, sovereignty, the legal title to power, derived from the "consent of the governed." Sovereignty did not ascend from the people; it descended upon them from a yet higher power unchallengeably supreme. It was bound up either with the rulers' own divinity or with some special relation they stood in to divinity.

The imperial solution will seem, I think, a little improvisational. It consisted in deifying each successive emperor as he became emperor. These sudden metamorphoses, translations as they always were of violent men into worshipable gods, put an appalling tax upon credulity. By contrast, how stable and safe and well ordered was the Christian account of the universal economy! There was a Creator, who had made everything. There was an Offspring of that Creator, who had rescued everything (or at least everything worth rescue). There was a sort of Spirit-Messenger, who appeared on suitable occasions to confirm, by the beatitude of his presence, divinely miraculous events. In the course of these labors, the Son and only Offspring had founded an institution named after himself, had appointed a fisherman to be the first head of it, and had given both head and institution complete authority over human affairs.[8] These appointments and this authority the Spirit-Messenger confirmed by sudden descents upon the appointees, as on the Day of Pentecost.[9]

In the Christian doctrine that became orthodox, authority moves *down* and salvation moves *up;* and, indeed, salvation will not move up unless authority has first moved down. In the posture of the membership, therefore, obedience is more obvious than spontaneity; and it will be by following orders, as these descend the chain of command, that the member himself will ascend to ultimate and eternal bliss. And if, in the mind of the member, the question arises, as surely it may, what validity the orders really have, the answer will be that they have issued, one and all, from an original Source in which creativity and righteousness are permanently combined.

8) Matthew 16: 18–19. This celebrated passage (a late interpolation, since the early Church knew no such claims) runs as follows: "And I say also unto thee, That thou art Peter, and upon this rock I will build my church; and the gates of hell shall not prevail against it. And I will give unto thee the keys of the kingdom of heaven: and whatsoever thou shalt bind on earth shall be bound in heaven: and whatsoever thou shalt loose on earth shall be loosed in heaven." AV.
9) Acts 2: 1–4.

In hierarchical theory, obedience to God requires obedience to God's appointees: the general's orders are no less binding because they chance to have been transmitted by a sergeant. The question would then be, not whether the orders are useful or effective, but whether they are the general's—and, further, whether the general truly holds supreme command. This last question the Fathers undertook to settle, without any compromise whatever, in terms of ultimates. The Founder of *their* Church was to be, not a man merely, nor a prophet, nor an emissary, nor a demi-god, nor a hemi-demi-god, but an inseparable part of the Godhead itself. He would have, not derivative authority, but original and supreme authority; he would be part of, and identical with, that Source from which all authority flows. Kings might claim, as in early modern times they still did, to govern by "divine right" (i.e., God had conferred on them the legal title to rule); but Christ the Son, like God the Father, ruled by Right itself, by being that Being in whom all Right is lodged as part of the divine essence. If, as you perceive, I am driven to use capitals in the expression of this view, that is because capitals are necessary to the proclamation of ultimates.

At its base and ground, the doctrine of the Trinity does not belong to theology or metaphysics or morals, though it shares in these. It belongs to *jurisprudence,* because it is the effort—most extraordinary and even sublime—to justify one specific organization as the ruler, governor, and final arbiter of all human affairs whatsoever. This jurisprudential intent is fully manifest in the use which successive popes have made of the doctrine.

For example, the first Boniface, since canonized, writing at a time (422) when the See of Rome was still contending for the leadership of Christendom, told the bishops of Thessaly that

> the universal ordering of the Church at its birth took its origin from the office of blessed Peter, in which is found both its directing power and its supreme authority . . . So it is clear that this church [i.e., the Roman See] is to all churches throughout the world as the head is to the members. . . .[1]

In the year 1302, a successor and namesake, Boniface VIII, issued a celebrated bull, *Unam Sanctam,* asserting the supremacy of the

---

1) *The Papal Encyclicals,* edited by Anne Fremantle (New York: Mentor Books; 1956), p. 49.

Church over all secular powers. His argument was one we should by now find familiar:

> Therefore if the earthly power err it shall be judged by the spiritual power; but if the lesser spiritual power err, by the greater. ... This authority, moreover, even though it is given to man and exercised through man, is not human but rather divine, being given by divine lips to Peter and founded on a rock for him and his successors through Christ Himself whom he has confessed; the Lord Himself saying to Peter: "Whatsoever thou shalt bind," etc. Whoever, therefore, resists this power thus ordained by God, resists the ordination of God, unless he makes believe, like the Manichean, that there are two beginnings. This we consider false and heretical, since by the testimony of Moses, not "in the beginnings," but "in the beginning" God created the heavens and the earth. Indeed we declare, announce, and define that it is altogether necessary for every human creature to be subject to the Roman pontiff. The Lateran, November 14, in our eighth year. As a perpetual memorial of this matter.[2]

The secular powers remaining unconvinced, there came a time when Pius V was faced with a queen, Elizabeth of Britain, who was at once virginal, heretical, and intransigent. Armed with trinitarian jurisprudence, Pius did not hesitate: he excommunicated and deposed her, in a scarcely less celebrated bull entitled *Regnans in Excelsis* (February 25, 1570):

> He who reigns on high, to Whom is given all power in Heaven and on earth, has entrusted His holy Catholic and Apostolic Church, outside which there is no salvation, to one person alone on earth, namely to Peter the Prince of the Apostles, and to Peter's successor, the Roman Pontiff, to be governed by him with plenitude of power. Him alone He has appointed Prince over all nations and kingdoms, to root up, pull down, waste, destroy, plant and build, so that he might preserve his faithful people linked together by the bond of mutual charity in the unity of the Spirit, and might present them, saved and blameless, to their Savior.

> ... But being strengthened by the authority of Him, Who willed to place us on the supreme throne of justice though unequal to so great a burden, out of the plenitude of our Apostolic power we

2) *The Portable Medieval Reader,* edited by Ross and McLaughlin (New York: The Viking Press; 1949), pp. 235–36.

declare the aforesaid Elizabeth to be heretic and an abetter of heretics, and we declare her, together with her supporters in the aforesaid matters, to have incurred the sentence of excommunication and to be cut off from the unity of the Body of Christ.

Furthermore we declare her to be deprived of her pretended claim to the aforesaid kingdom and of all lordship, dignity and privilege whatsoever.[3]

In view of the motives which prompted its first formulation, and in view of the uses it has been put to since, the concept of the Trinity belongs, as we have said, to jurisprudence: it assumes that legal authority is acquired by descent—is *conferred,* that is to say, by some "higher" power and ultimately by some "highest" power. This assumption still seems natural, so little are we removed, ideologically, from feudal times; and, when united with the legend of the Church's founding, it required that the Founder be taken into the Godhead without loss of his identity or his humanity. Thus the Founder had to be at one and the same time completely human and completely divine, as the name "Jesus Christ" signifies. If he were not so, his founding of the Church and his redemption of mankind would have been of less effect or of no effect at all.

One may think, a little skeptically, that an omnipotent God could found the Church and redeem mankind in any of various ways, of which the asserted way might not have been the actual one. Yet there is probably some truth in the notion that it takes a man to redeem Man; and, in any event, the Fathers could not dismiss accumulated tradition. Ideologically, they labored within a vineyard which had proved fruitful, and the grapes would yield only a certain kind of wine.

Although jurisprudence makes the Trinity plain, we must not suppose that the Fathers vulgarly sacrificed theology to politics. They were as far as may be from the practices we associate with Madison Avenue, where, with pragmatic cynicism, the commodity to be sold is chief concern and ideology is but the means of sale. The Fathers honorably believed, and by comparison with anything else extant accurately believed, that they possessed the ultimate answers, and that they veritably could effect for mankind something deserving the name "salvation." They sought, not power alone, but righteous-

3) Fremantle, *Papal Encyclicals,* pp. 83–84.

ness supported and attained by power. No doubt, in the course of centuries, the zeal for righteousness dropped away, while the zeal for power survived; but that was not Athanasius's fault, nor Ambrose's, nor Augustine's.

The members of the Church, who were the immediate objects of ministry, had, however, far less interest in political power—a possession they were accustomed to find in other people's hands. Their purpose remained what for three centuries it had been, to escape demoralization. Now, demoralization is the odious paralyzing sense that one can do nothing for one's own welfare, that one is as helpless before one's appetites as before the demands of government or of exploiters. Demoralization is passive drift—drift toward mere automatic response, in which action answers stimulus without any intervention of rational choice. Why choose, the demoralized man might say, when choice effects nothing and events occur as if no choice had touched them?

Moreover, every demoralized man knows, or dimly feels, contempt for his own condition. He grows angry with himself, with the guilts that arise, not only from deeds done, but from simple passivity under appetite. He has lost, for lack of exercise, the habit of solving problems, and then the problems solve themselves, contemptibly, upon his flesh. He has lied, thieved, whored; but the worst is that he did all these out of sheer inability to do the contrary.

Plainly such a man needs help, and when he finds it he responds to it. In particular, he needs some rock on which to rest his conscience, some safe and permanent haven for his ideals. If he fails to get this by scientific self-knowledge, he can still get it, obscurely but powerfully, by metaphor. Let him imagine in the world a power supreme, august, benign, whose commands have the same clear excellence he remembers in those of his human father, and he will see how obedience becomes a means of being valued, and acceptance of principle a sign of worth.

If the *pattern* of Christian doctrine is attributable to jurisprudence, the *concepts* in that pattern have a different source. They derive from the human family, most obviously as metaphor but also as a reworking of patriarchal ideas. The relations existing within the Trinity and between the Trinity and the Church suffice (or may be thought to suffice) to justify ecclesiastical government; and the content of the Trinity, the great supernatural personages, are as universally attractive as they are readily understood. For who needs metaphysics to tell him what a father is, or a son, or a mother, or a messenger of good tidings, an ever available friend?

The family has long been, and still remains, on the whole the most intimate of social relationships. It is, as people experience it, by no means free from shocks and antagonisms, and the resulting traumas are well known to psychiatry. Yet when the family attains, or approaches, the perfection it is capable of, the members of it know that they are enjoying the best of human existence. Then they feel secure, useful, valued, and understood.

Now, suppose we project upon the cosmos this image of the perfect family. Suppose we say that all human affairs—and indeed all affairs whatever—are under the conduct of a supremely wise and lovingly paternal intelligence, that through an act of filial sacrifice the ground of all guilt has been removed and guilt itself separated from disaster, that an agency exists which can dispose men toward right decisions, and that there is, last, a maternal personage[4] who can intercede for even the basest of men. Why, then everyone knows, as children would know, that goodness will be acclaimed and rewarded, that faults will be pardoned when the doer admits them to be faults, and that frailty will in any event be expected and understood.

These circumstances remove from the moral life that strange desperation with which it is often practiced, and which issues from two tragic defects: good actions going unappreciated or even punished, and hostility venting itself under pretense of morality.[5] For I do not well know which is the more repellent: the sufferings of the righteous, or sinners' sufferings hypocritically imposed by greater sinners than themselves. Such extreme aberrations the Christian view proscribed, by making the cosmic economy a moral economy and the moral economy livable by man. No doubt it would have been better if Christianity had made the social economy a moral economy; then mankind would have found the moral life not only tolerable but easy, and there would have been no need to await those climactic storms which, with judicial violence, were expected to usher in the millennium.

4) The "Theotókos"—the "God-Bearer" or "Mother of God."
5) For example, the psychotic folk who nowadays advocate the castration of sexual offenders.

Yet there is always some merit in surrogate satisfactions, even if they are necessarily not satisfaction entire. They keep alive the purpose and the hope. For myself, I have no doubt that in perhaps the twenty-fifth century of our era, when mankind will have ascended the planets, the universe will seem as just and as friendly as Christians have long imagined it to be, and that human relations upon this earth, at last civilized, will bear full resemblance to all that is meant by membership "in the body of Christ." Then the church (which is to say, mankind in peace and concord) will truly be catholic and holy; the saints will have permanent communion; sins will be forgiven as having no malice; and (for aught one knows) the resurrection of the body and the life everlasting will be scientific facts—namely, the prolongation of physical life into a deathless age.

To say, in the fourth century, that all this had already happened was erroneous and premature. But to say that it had already happened was also to say that it *can* happen, and in this the Fathers were quite correct. They were correct also in their appreciation of its value and in their belief that the salvation of people is the necessary ground of authority over people. In short, the Fathers produced a doctrine which inspired loyalty and hope in the membership as surely as it gave justification by jurisprudence. This has not often happened in human affairs, and to it is due at least some of the awe which still surrounds the concept of the Trinity.

I V

"THE CHRISTIAN CHURCH," wrote Cardinal Newman, "as being a visible society, is necessarily a political power or party. It may be a party triumphant, or a party under persecution; but a party it always must be, prior in existence to the civil institutions with which it is surrounded, and from its latent divinity formidable and influential, even to the end of time."[6]

The phrase "latent divinity" expresses, with wonderful exactness, the jurisprudence of the Church's claim, as modified for a British public by a clergyman who lived some three centuries after Henry VIII. From this basic view, Newman went on to suggest how far doctrinal questions are organizational questions in disguise. "Christians depart from their duty, or become in an offensive sense political, not when they act as members of one community, but when they do

6) Op. cit., pp. 257–58. Newman wrote this in 1833, when he was still a clergyman of the Church of England.

so for temporal ends or in an illegal manner; not when they assume the attitude of a party, but when they split into many."[7]

In other words, Christians will err politically either when they act against the ideals of the movement or when they break the movement up into sects. Two principles, then, supremely guide: that the organization always be bent upon its authentic purposes, and that the unity of the organization be always maintained.

As we know, such principles are easier to acknowledge than to practice, and departures from either one provoke departures from the other. That is to say, if the organization begins to shirk its ideals, something very like schismatic behavior will be required for amendment: a minority loyal to the ideals will have to correct the leadership. And if the organization breaks into parts, the ideals are not well served and may even be defeated. In the fourth century, the Fathers of the Church, seeking to unite grandeur of mission with grandeur of authority, faced both these difficulties—but, more painfully and particularly, the danger of schism.

In March of the year 313, the Emperors Constantine and Licinius issued a joint edict of universal religious toleration. "We decided," ran the text, "that of the things that are of profit to mankind, the worship of God ought rightly to be our first and chiefest care, and that it was right that Christians and all others should have freedom to follow the kind of religion they favored; so that the God who dwells in heaven might be propitious to us and to all under our rule."[8] This edict was followed, in the same year, by further edicts restoring Church property, subsidizing the clergy, and exempting the clergy from public duties. In 319 Constantine suppressed those itinerant prophets known as soothsayers, and in 321 established Sunday as the weekly day of rest, suitable for the manumission of slaves.

The Church which thus rose to official recognition was, however, far from the desired state of inner concord. Indeed, Newman is able to say, with almost Gibbonian irony, that Constantine's "conquest of the East (A.D. 323) did but enlarge his prospect of the distractions of Christendom."[9] The unhappy Emperor, who had embraced Chris-

7) Ibid., p. 258. I suppose that in the last clause there is a suppressed noun, and that the reading is "many parties."
8) Bettenson's translation, *Documents*, p. 23. Constantine and Licinius were plainly "hedging their bets."
9) Op. cit., p. 247.

tianity because of its organizational prowess, thought for a time that he had only increased the number and intensity of his conflicts.

That part of the Roman Empire known as the Procuratorship of the East included the north coast of Egypt (notably the city of Alexandria), the Greek peninsula, the Mediterranean shores of Asia Minor and Palestine. We have already observed that, by the fourth century, economic prosperity had very largely passed from west to east. Intellectual liveliness and the clash of ideas had passed thither also, partly because they ordinarily go with commercial activity, and partly because the cultures of the east were so heterogeneous. Thus, while Christianity at Rome remained the disciplined, soldierlike organization which the author of Clement's Epistle had wanted it to be, Christianity in the east teemed with factions. Most of the great heresiarchs came from there: Arius of Alexandria, Meletius of Antioch, Sabellius of Libya, Nestorius of Constantinople, Apollinaris of Laodicea, Paul of Samosata, Donatus of Carthage. There was, to be sure, the Novatian schism at Rome in 251, but this turned on a purely organizational question, the readmission of renegades. The Romans had never been much given to theorizing, and readily maintained the trinitarian doctrine as the best ground of ecclesiastical unity.

The great struggles were fought out in Alexandria, where, in those years, the intellectual life of the Empire centered. They were fought out with every mode of violence and defamation: the antagonists were titanic, the rhetoric savage, the intrigues inconceivably complex. Troops of bishops flitted, on foot or on horseback, from synod to synod and council to council, where, says Professor Krüger, they "cursed one another turn by turn."[1] All imaginable vices (and some unprintable) were charged of the contestants. At the Council of Caesarea (333), the great Athanasius was confronted with a severed hand alleged to be that of Bishop Arsenius, whom he stood accused of having mutilated and slain. To the consternation of the Arian party, however, Athanasius, who had meanwhile gained Arsenius' friendship, was able to produce him in the midst of the assembly, alive, in sound health, and with members whole. Whose the severed hand was has never transpired.

Something more than a generation in age separated the chief antagonists: Arius (256–336) and Athanasius (296–373). They were both members of the Alexandrian Church, in which Arius was for

1) *Encyclopaedia Britannica*, eleventh edition, Vol. II, p. 544.

many years a presbyter, and of which Athanasius became Bishop in 326. His long reign, which ended only with his death, was interrupted by five depositions from office and by as many departures into exile. The sum of these enforced absences amounted to seventeen years, so that Athanasius spent almost a third of his reign apart from that Chair which was the seat and symbol of his authority. During those years when the intermittent tides of politics flowed strongly against him, he was the now legendary Athanasius, *Athanasius contra mundum,* "Athanasius against the world."

Arius, for his part, was of a patience and an assiduity no less profound. If not the ultimate statesman that Athanasius seems, he was nevertheless an extremely skillful leader, with much popular appeal. Theologians still recount, in tones of scandal, how Arius turned his doctrines into songs for the people to sing, how he gave over the most sacred subjects to be the themes of street-corner disputation. At the imperial court in Constantinople, says Newman, "the eunuchs and slaves of the palace (strange to say) embraced the tenets of Arianism; and all the most light-minded and frivolous of mankind allowed themselves to pervert the solemn subject in controversy into matter for fashionable conversation or literary amusement."[2] The actual event was perhaps just the reverse: namely, that the subject, being politically contested, was not yet "solemn" and did not become so until the Athanasian view was fully established as orthodox.

Such accounts, at any rate, suggest that Arius was something of a people's leader. Moreover, he seems to have had the motley following which gathers round a man of dissident but popular ideas. For, as Gibbon says, "he reckoned among his immediate followers two bishops of Egypt, seven presbyters, twelve deacons, and (what may appear almost incredible) seven hundred virgins."[3] If we knew what the seven hundred virgins were in search of, we would know more about Arius, about his heresy, and perhaps also about the concept of the Trinity.

At any rate, Arius generated his doctrines during the decade before 319, the year in which he published them. It is fair to say that he had felt scandalized by what he took to be the doctrinal impiety of his own Bishop, Alexander of Alexandria. Alexander's view,

2) Op. cit., p. 264.
3) Op. cit., Chap. XXI.

which shortly became orthodox and which had the invincible support of Athanasius, was that "as God is eternal, so is his Son,—when the Father, then the Son,—the Son is present in God without birth (ἀγεννήτως), ever-begotten (ἀειγενής), and unbegotten-begotten (ἀγεννητογενής)."[4] These paradoxes were too strong for Arius: the unbegotten-begotten, the Son as old as the Father. To be sure, the paradoxes could have been resolved, ingeniously, by a doctrine to the effect that every father-to-be in some sense "contains" his offspring—a doctrine which yields the pleasant inference that all generations are contemporaneous.

Arius did not hit on this view, nor was the view, I dare say, Alexander's. Arius was sure that a father must precede his son in some manner. Human fathers precede their sons in time, but chronology would not hold of the two great Persons, both of whom were, by definition, out of time. Arius's argument, as recorded by the historian Socrates in that bare, stubborn Greek (so characteristic of Greek philosophical writing), which is untranslatable into English idiom, was this: "If the Father begat the Son, he that was begotten had a beginning of existence; hence it is clear that there was when the Son was not. It follows then of necessity that he had his existence from the non-existent."[5]

Now, anything which came out of non-existence has clearly not existed eternally. Hence, though the Father had existed eternally, the Son had not done so, and this fact would point to an inferiority of status. Thus detached from ultimate divinity, the whole concept of the Son begins to shrink back toward the historical Jesus, losing more and more of the Pauline mystery-god on the way. Presumably Arius and his followers intended no such shrinkage, but administrators who are also ideologists understand very readily that a direction not necessary in logic may nevertheless be traversed in psychology. Alexander replied by excommunicating his presbyter and the whole Arian party so far as it came under his jurisdiction.

The struggle was now joined, and it proceeded, with vast but

4) *Encyclopaedia Britannica,* eleventh edition, Vol. II, p. 543.
5) Translation by Bettenson, *Documents,* p. 56. "There was when he was not" exactly reproduces the original ἦν ὅτε οὐκ ἦν, but the clause perhaps makes no sense in any language. One cannot say "There was a time when. . .," because the whole affair is beyond chronology. Socrates was writing about A.D. 440, *Historia Ecclesiae,* I, v.

diminishing convulsions, until the Council of Chalcedon (451) settled the main questions once and for all. By that time Arius and Athanasius were long dead; and Ambrose, Jerome, and Augustine —who, with Gregory the Great, constitute the Four Doctors of the Church—were dead also. It cannot be said that the ferocity of the struggle much shortened life. Arius was eighty when he died, Athanasius seventy-seven, Jerome eighty, Augustine seventy-six. Ambrose was only fifty-seven, to be sure; but the astonishing Hosius, Bishop of Cordova (*obit* 357), was a centenarian and had reigned sixty-one years.

Constantine's first response to the controversy was an effort at compromising it. In his role of statesman or at least politician, and in almost complete ignorance of the subject under dispute, he generously announced that each side had its merits and defects. Yet the ideology of an official religion could not be suffered to remain doubtful or contested. It would be necessary to determine what the ideology precisely was. To that end, Constantine summoned representatives of the Church to assemble at Nicea, in Bithynia, in 325.

All told, two thousand and forty-eight persons attended, of whom three hundred eighteen were bishops. On occasion, Constantine himself sat in their midst on a low stool, having the air of a school-boy among teachers—an air perhaps as honest as any other there displayed. In two months the Council settled little but formulated a good deal. With remarkable linguistic refinement, it pared down the trinitarian controversy to a choice between two words, and one of these it was able to select as satisfactory expression of the orthodox view.

These words, which I here transliterate from the Greek and hyphenate for greater clarity, were *"homo-ousios"* and *"homoi-ousios."* You will note that, in respect of spelling, a single *i* (or *iota*) marks the difference. The difference seems sufficiently pedantic, and there have been many jests about the breaking of heads and maiming of bodies over a single *iota*. The fact was, of course, that the head-breaking belonged to politics and would have happened anyway. The *iota* belonged to ideology, and represented the effort of two rival parties to capture a common tradition. The tradition, that is to say, was so well fixed after three hundred years that the one solitary *iota* shows how little the rivals dared depart from it.

Gibbon observes in a footnote that "the difference between the

Homoousion and *Homoiousion* is almost invisible to the nicest theological eye."[6] I am sorry to say (since I usually take Gibbon as an oracle) that this is simply not the case. The difference is, in point of fact, familiar and clear. The Greek adjective *homoousios* means "the same as" or "identical with." The adjective *homoiousios* (the one with the *iota*) means "like" or "similar" or "having resemblance to." You will observe the difference clearly and familiarly, if you compare the following two sentences: "These are the very same gloves I wore yesterday," and, "These gloves are like the ones I wore yesterday." Or let us imagine a man who has married one of twin sisters (and let the sisters be, if you like, "identical" twins). I speak here not of romance but of ethics and legality: it will make quite a difference whether he cohabits with the *same* sister or with the *similar* sister.

"Same" and "similar" represent our English-speaking effort to express differing degrees of unity. When we say "same," we mean the unity to be complete or almost so; when we say "similar," we mean the unity to be noticeably less than the separation. Transpose, now, these rules of usage into the concept of the Trinity, and you will perceive that it is one thing to say, "The Son is the same as the Father," and quite another thing to say, "The Son is similar to the Father." For if the Son is only "similar," the resemblance may lie in some relatively minor trait; but if the Son is "the same as" or "identical with" the Father, then there can be no difference of *status,* whatever differences of detail there may be.

Accordingly, I think there can be no doubt that when the Church wished to deify its Founder and therefore to make the Son equal in divinity with the Father, it had to prefer, and thenceforth to require, the adjective *homoousios.* Identity alone could have achieved the intended purpose. Mere resemblance would have released the Son to slide imperceptibly down all the degrees that separate divinity from humanity, until he became once again the historical Jesus, the crucified revolutionary. This view would seem very credible to a modern historian, but, in the fourth century, it would have wrecked the Church by dissipating the membership. And so the Creed of Nicea, in addition to the doctrine it asserts, has also a list of doctrines which it rejects, thus:

6) Op. cit., Chap. XXI, note 75.

And those that say "There was when he was not,"
        and "Before he was begotten he was not,"
    and that "He came into being from what-is-not,"
    or those that allege that the Son of God is
            "Of another substance or essence,"
        or "created,"
        or "changeable,"
        or "alterable,"
these the Catholic and Apostolic Church anathematizes.[7]

There remained, ideologically, a further and related problem. Just as it seemed wrong to dislocate the Son from the Father within the Godhead, so it seemed wrong to dislocate the divine from the human within the person of Jesus. The idea of two natures in one Person was difficult, but not more difficult than the idea of three Persons in one Godhead. The question was this: When the Incarnation occurred, when the Word was made flesh, did the divine mind replace the human mind in Jesus, or the divine will the human will? The Fathers, with customary tenacity, declined to surrender any doctrines they could possibly retain, and therefore said, No. Jesus, in his life on earth, had both a divine mind and a human mind, a divine will and a human will. If you said he had only one mind and that a divine one, you were a "Monophysite" and heretical. If you said he had only one will and that a divine one, you were a "Monothelite" and heretical. As in the Trinity you were not to "confound the Persons or divide the Substance," so in the Christ you were not to confound the natures or divide the Person. Nothing was to be surrendered; everything was to be retained; and by a judicious use of dialectical logic the whole doctrine was to be harmonized.

In just this state the doctrine has remained. Expositors can do little more than repeat it carefully, for the ancient formula is so precise that every new version risks deviance, and every proof risks heresy. The desirous believer will do well to take the doctrine as it stands, reflecting that, all things considered, this is how the world really is. If he cannot do this, then he must resign himself to unbelief on this particular subject.

All attempts to rationalize the doctrine or assimilate it to common sense have failed, and will be found within the list of heresies

7) Translation by Bettenson, *Documents,* p. 36. "Changeable" and "alterable" mean "morally changeable."

long identified and named. For example, if you think it more sensible to regard God as a single Being and the three Persons as "aspects" of that single Being, then you are a Sabellian[8] and a heretic. If you think it was God the Father who entered into the physical Jesus and thus suffered in his sufferings, you are a Patripassian[9] and a heretic. If you think that, spiritually, Jesus was all *Logos* and no man, you are an Apollinarian[1] and a heretic. If you think that Mary can have been mother only of what was human in Jesus, then you are a Nestorian[2] and a heretic. You may try the thing yourself, if you like—and as long as you like—but I think you will never hit upon a restatement which is not a deviation, nor upon a deviation which is new.

It seems clear that, in the contest between Arius and Athanasius, victory would lie with him who possessed the whole tradition and therefore eventually the whole membership. Any mere faction, however large, was doomed; it would be hopelessly inadequate to the mission, suddenly bestowed, of organizing and sustaining terrestrial empire. From every place of exile, where he had variously lived among the intellectuals of Gaul or the monks and hermits of the Theban Desert, Athanasius infallibly returned, and thus put beyond doubt the political acuteness of his doctrine. He only seemed to be *contra mundum;* in fact he was always *cum mundo,* and had the world on his side.

As for Arius, his were the illusory joys of a skilled leader who does not perceive the deeper course of history. He was bound to mistake successes for victory, and there is something appropriate in the manner of his death. In the year 336, after Athanasius had departed into the first of his terms of exile, Arius entered Alexandria in a triumphant procession. Turning aside (it is said) "to satisfy a natural need," he was struck at that moment with apoplexy. He died imagining a victory that could never be won.

8) After Sabellius of Ptolemais (*floruit* A.D. 250), who held that God is, so to say, "concealed" behind the three manifestations of himself to men.
9) *Pater* plus *passus est*—i.e., "The Father suffered." This romantic view was that of Praxeas, a contemporary target of Tertullian.
1) After Apollinarius, Bishop of Laodicea (*obit* 392).
2) After Nestorius, Bishop of Constantinople, 428–431. His doctrine that Mary cannot be called "Theotókos" ("God-Bearer") was anathematized at the Council of Ephesus in 431.

The death was, indeed, singularly apt; and Newman, contemplating it, could not withstand the sense of magic. "Under the circumstances," he wrote, "a thoughtful mind cannot but account this as one of those remarkable interpositions of power, by which Divine Providence urges on the consciousness of men in the natural course of things, what their reason from the first acknowledges, that He is not indifferent to human conduct."[3]

All this is as may be. But whatever one thinks of providential interpositions, it remains the case that no doctrine can become orthodox unless it is first politically successful, and that it cannot be politically successful unless, by metaphor or by science, it explicates for large masses of mankind their true condition and destiny. Such things, in the fourth century, the trinitarian doctrine did. Consequently it prevailed, while the heresies which deviated from it proved as drifting and insubstantial as clouds.

3) Op. cit., p. 269.

CHAPTER

6

Free Will and
Organizational Destiny

About the year a.d. 416—six years, that is to say, after the fall of Rome—Rutilius Claudius Namatianus, a Gallic lord and a poet who still possessed the classic power, thus apostrophized the city:

> *Exaudi, nutrix hominum genetrixque deorum*
> *(Non procul a caelo per tua templa sumus):*
> *Te canimus semperque, sinent dum fata, canemus. . . .*[1]

But the nurse of men and mother of gods, though she might hearken, could not longer reply. Barbarians had seized her temporal power, and Christians her spiritual. She was gathered into the limbo of lost cities, whither she had sent many another before her; and even the Christian Jerome, the mightiest scholar of the age, felt that somehow "the whole human race is included in the ruins."[2]

In that same year, the young Spanish presbyter Orosius, who, like other Spaniards since, was zealous against heresy, brought back from Palestine to Aurelius Augustinus, Bishop of Hippo in North Africa, news concerning the amiable heresiarch Pelagius. Pelagius, it transpired, had really meant what he seemed to have said: namely,

---

1) "Hear my prayer, O nurse of men and mother of gods (for, at thy temples, we are not far from heaven)! We sing thee, and shall always sing thee while the fates permit. . . ." This excerpt will be found as selection 373 in the *Oxford Book of Latin Verse*.
2) Quoted by H. F. Stewart, *Cambridge Medieval History* (1911), Vol. I, p. 574.

that it is possible for men to achieve salvation by their own efforts, and that if in this enterprise they need divine help, they must nevertheless cooperate with divinity to render the help effective. These views and their author had undergone scrutiny at Jerusalem, during which Pelagius yielded some ground, as men do under inquisition. But he had yielded nothing essential; and Augustine, who himself became a saint some centuries before his own doctrines became heretical, resolved upon the political defeat of a reluctant adversary.

By the year 416, also, Nestorius, then a presbyter at Antioch, was already preaching those persuasive sermons in which he held that Mary, the human mother of Jesus, could in no wise have been *genetrix* of what was divine in the Christ. He thus seemed to make the Second Person of the Trinity more of a man than a god—by contrast with Apollinarius, Bishop of Laodicea, who, thirty years before, had seemed to make the Second Person of the Trinity more of a god than a man. Thus do heresies, inevitably if oddly, beget one another by opposition.

One year before these events—that is to say, the year 415—occurred in Alexandria the lynching of Hypatia, a mathematician and neo-Platonist, whose chastity subdued the loves which her beauty inspired. This was, I suppose, not the first instance of wanton cruelty by Christians, who, especially in Alexandria, had long assisted the persecution of Jews. It is, however, the first instance to attain permanent celebrity. The victim was innocent and wise, learned and pure; the inciter, still hidden behind the manipulated riot of a mob, was the first of a dismal series of *éminences grises*: Cyril, Bishop of Alexandria. A man of immense intelligence and skill, he allowed no morals to modify the play of power politics. Yet the blood which sprang from that fair and naked body, as bigots scraped its flesh with oystershells, has left a lasting blush upon the cheek of Christianity.[3]

Rutilius' poem, Hypatia's martyrdom, Augustine's controversial zeal, and Cyril's ruthless diplomacy illustrate the kinds of event that define the violent and muddy conflicts of the fifth century. From

3) Gibbon decides (op. cit., Chapter XLVII, note 20) in favor of oystershells as against tiles, and this is good enough for me. The "lasting blush" may be seen, e.g., in the contemporary patrologist J. Quasten, who describes Hypatia as "cruelly torn to pieces on the steps of a Church by a mob of Christians in March 415." *Patrology*, Vol. III, p. 117. He, however, exculpates Cyril. The church in question was the Caesarium.

these conflicts (one of them at least—the Pelagian—still unresolved) the Church issued, hardened in doctrine and practice. It systematized such doctrines as could be systematized; other doctrines which it felt the need of, but which even an ingenious dialectic could not embrace, it nevertheless retained. The Church, as before, aimed at possessing the whole Christian tradition, and it rejected as heretical any doctrine which, if accepted, would have produced the smallest splinter.

I I

"WE SING THEE, and shall always sing thee while the fates permit." From this age on through many an age thereafter, as regards the city of Rome, singing was all the fates permitted. The Empire, in its heyday, had been a world market, united by excellent roads and sustained by copious supplies of capital and credit. In those halcyon years (halcyon at least for the ruling classes) economic forces and political forces matched each other and worked toward a general stability.

Yet that world market which was the Empire, by its very success, evoked creativity within the provinces. These speedily became so productive as to be self-sufficient while at the same time offering specialties for export. The *Exposition of the Whole World and of Nations,* translated from Greek into Latin about A.D. 345, gives an interesting list of these specialties.[4] Ascalon and Gaza exported wines to Egypt; Scythopolis, Laodicea, Byblis and Tyre, linens to all the world. From Caesarea, Tyre, Sarapta, and Neapolis came purple-dyed tissues. Egypt, which had a monopoly of papyrus, also shipped wheat to Constantinople and the eastern provinces. Cappadocia supplied furs; Galatia, various sorts of clothing; the Hellespontine area, wheat, wine, and oil; Macedonia and Dalmatia, iron and lead; Illyria, bacon and cheese; Epirus, fish; Numidia, cattle; Spain, bacon, oil, and mules; and Pannonia and Mauretania, slaves.

The provinces, as they grew self-sufficient, grew independent; and their bartering of surplus goods took on the usual character of commercial rivalry. I think we can suppose that this sort of competition had a great deal to do with the chief disputes about doctrine. The disputants did in fact align themselves geographically, and each

4) *Cambridge Medieval History,* Vol. I, p. 548. How evocative the place names are!

drew political support from the organizations within its own territory. Thus, in the fifth century, Alexandria was generally at odds with Constantinople and Antioch, while Rome shifted support from side to side. And in the last of these conflicts, Alexandria and Constantinople undertook a reconciliation on terms that Rome disapproved.

The areas in question were no longer merely episcopal sees; they had risen to the dignity of patriarchates—a name which signifies that their size, their affluence, and their degree of organization had been much enlarged. Thus the old Empire, already divided secularly between two emperors, was splitting further toward its original and (as one may say) its "natural" components. This process, in its beginnings, had helped make the barbarian invasions successful, and was in turn further stimulated by their success.

All this while, the emperors of East and West tried to defend the unity of empire by measures aimed at freezing the status quo. These measures met varying degrees of ill success, and were in any case burdensome; but they did impose on historical change that peculiar kind of delay which ordinarily lies within the power of rulers.

For example, toward the end of the third century, the Emperor Diocletian, whose own soldiers suffered from extortionate prices as they moved about the Empire, undertook a general control of the price system. He threatened, and sometimes exacted, capital punishment. Blood flowed, but the tradesmen, moved by one of the mightiest if not one of the worthiest of human wishes, declined to be terrorized. Prices survived around that norm which is the union of scarcity with rapacity, and original sin continued to manifest itself in a form not quite envisaged by Augustine.[5]

Again: there was the attempt, by no means unsuccessful, to freeze all citizens within their professions and businesses, to impose on them a rigidity of status such as had always been the lot of slaves. Corporations and trade guilds had to retain their members for life: if, for example, you were a shipowner (*navicularius*), you were forbid-

5) In the fourth century, a piece of purple linen used for ornamental stripes and weighing six ounces might sell at (roughly) 80 to 120 dollars in our present currency. See *Cambridge Medieval History*, Vol. I, p. 549. Augustine thought of "original sin" in terms which are political or sexual—i.e., as insubordination or as lust. The profit motive seems not to be, even by inference, a part of his concept.

den to be anything else. In 395, the Emperors Arcadius and Honorius decreed fines in gold against anyone protecting or harboring a fugitive from a corporation, the fines being levied at so much per fugitive head. It thus appears that evasions of the law were not uncommon, and it seems likely that the corporations themselves approved the levy, since otherwise they would be liable to the state for their missing members.

Indeed, imperial control over commerce had always been necessary. The victualing of Rome, for example, could not be left to the whims of private enterprise. Was such a population to starve because entrepreneurs in Egypt or the Hellespont found it profitable to withhold grain? Accordingly, the rule was that every shipowner had to send his ships to sea at least once in two years, and if any grain ship was delayed in port en route, the local authorities had to send it promptly on its way. In the not uncommon event of shipwreck, there would be an official investigation, the surviving sailors would be questioned under torture, and the owner would have to make good the loss. On precisely these grounds, Augustine, as Bishop of Hippo, declined a bequest from a certain shipowner, Bonifacius, who, having disinherited his son, desired to leave his business to the Church. Capital, thus in pawn to the state, had become too plainly risk capital.

The growing difficulties of empire appeared most strikingly in the agonies of the middle-class townsmen, the *curiales,* who were made to bear, willy-nilly, certain painful functions of government. Specifically, they had to assist the collection of taxes, to make good any arrears in the same, and to inspect the public stores. From burdens so gratuitous many a *curialis* sought escape, but none could depart the city without a leave-of-absence from the governor. In time the condition of this class grew so deplorable that convicts were forcibly enrolled into it as a form of punishment: "sons of veterans, e.g., who, by chopping off their fingers, had rendered themselves unfit to serve in the army, were stuck into the *curia,* and the same fate awaited unworthy ecclesiastics."[6]

As not infrequently happens in the dissolution of societies, a loss of privileges by possessing classes is matched by gains in privilege among those who had none. The Empire, for all its commerce, had rested upon agriculture as the solid, ultimate base, and, in more

6) Ibid., p. 557.

prosperous times, agriculture had consisted of great estates cultivated by slaves. We have already noted the increasing scarcity of slaves and the consequent rise in their market value. To this we may now add the fact that the captured barbarians—Germans, Slavs, Huns—proved extremely inept at agricultural labor and hence unprofitable as slaves. The solution was to settle them on the land as small but independent farmers.

Moreover, agriculture, the economic base of empire, had been the great source of tax revenue, and the government was obliged to treat it carefully. There was already some diminution of it, as owners abandoned their estates in order to escape taxation, and, in any event, the *latifundia* were breaking up for lack of cheap labor. Tillers of the soil had therefore to be encouraged or coerced into continuing their occupations. A kind of sharecropping system, mingled with independent farming, began to replace the large estates. The effect was to lift the former slaves toward the status of free farmers (*coloni*). A series of imperial edicts removed from the masters the nearly absolute control they had once exercised, but at the same time bound them all—masters, slaves, and farmers of all degrees—to the land they owned and tilled. The landowner could not sell a portion of his land without also conveying to the buyer the farmers who worked it, nor could he sell tracts of fertile soil or of less fertile soil independently of each other.

It seems, in retrospect at least, quite apparent that slavery, as the established system of exploiting human labor, was by this time inefficient economically and difficult politically. Thus, though the Empire's purpose had been to maintain chattel slavery, the ultimate issue, effected through the slow labors of armies and bureaucracies, was a new system, the feudal, which the dying Empire established upon its own grave.

During those decades of wrath, when Rome fell and classicism vanished into literature, when the Empire shook apart into its elements, when barbarians possessed France and Spain and Germany and Italy and laid siege to Hippo at the very moment of Augustine's death, the bishops and clergy of the Christian Church were engaged upon stupendous labors. Consider, for example, a bishop:

Not only did he [says Professor Wright] baptize, receive confessions, preach, prescribe penances, issue anathemas, and lift excommunications, he visited the sick, ministered to the dying, buried the dead, and gave relief to widows and orphans. He built churches, founded hospitals, ransomed captives, administered the revenues of the church, adjudicated as justice of the peace in private suits, and arbitrated quarrels between different cities. At the same time he wrote treatises on doctrinal theology, combated heresy and paganism, corresponded with churches and bishops, monks and hermits, and sat on innumerable councils and synods. Finally, he was in many cases called in by the Emperor to advise on questions of foreign policy, and sent as ambassador to usurpers and barbarian potentates.[7]

Those treatises, that correspondence! Where, amid so multitudinous labors, did these bishops find the time for composition? Cyril's works occupy ten volumes in Migne's *Patrologia*. There exist four hundred authentic sermons of Augustine, besides his copious controversial writings and his two celebrated masterpieces, the *Confessions* and the *City of God*. John Chrysostom ("John the Golden-Mouthed"), Bishop of Constantinople, left an astonishing corpus (still extant) of sermons, homilies, baptismal catechisms, discourses, letters. Ambrose crowned all his other achievements with a series of magnificent hymns, which still live in the literature and which gave new poetic forms to the Latin language:

> *Splendor paternae gloriae,*
> *de luce lucem proferens,*
> *lux lucis et fons luminis,*
> *diem dies illuminans.*[8]

The light in those lines is dazzling but endurable; not always so, the light in the bishops. Yet one may judge how formidable they were, in their multifarious ecstasies of creation, by a colloquy between the Prefect Modestus and Basil the Great, Bishop of Caesarea. Basil was an orthodox Athanasian, and the Emperor Valens, an Arian, sent Modestus to him, threatening exile and confiscation of goods. Basil replied, very levelly, that a man who had no goods could not

7) Op. cit., p. 14.
8) See Wright, op. cit., pp. 188–89:
          O splendor of God's glory bright,
          O thou that bringest light from light,
          O Light of light, light's living spring,
          O Day, all days illumining. Wright's translation.

fear confiscation, nor a man without a home, exile. As for death, that would be "an act of kindness for it will bring me nearer to God."[9] Modestus remarked that no one had ever spoken to him so roundly. "Perhaps," said Basil, "you have never met a bishop before."

Under men like these, churches became sanctuaries, within which —and within fifty yards of which—all men of misery, folly, or crime might take refuge. A bishop conducted the affairs of his office surrounded by these wretches, whom dislocation from society had brought low. Such folk, after all, the revolutionary Jesus had taken into his movement; such folk the Pauline mystery-Christ had specifically come to save. This daily ecclesiastical touch between the miserable and the mighty gave to the writings of the Fathers a poignant humanity, possible only to men who somehow contrived to live with all other men. Augustine, for example, is one of the clearest thinkers we have, but he comes to us bronzed and sweating from the heat of actual life.

Paganism was doomed before such adversaries. Its economic base in agricultural slavery had crumbled; its philosophies—even the enlightened materialist ones—had somehow never lit the invincible flame. There was a brief recovery under the Emperor Julian, who reigned only from 360 to 363. The altar of Victory, symbol of the old Roman power, was restored to the Forum; the Olympic games and Eleusinian mysteries continued; and that rational calm that Gibbon so much admired prevailed once more over the administration of events.

But this calm was the calm of extreme and torpid age amid the vigor of things new. Rome the city lost its dignity as administrative center of the Western Empire, first to Milan during the fourth century and then to Ravenna[1] after 402. It was to Milan that Aurelius Symmachus went in 384—a pagan prefect of Rome, who sought from the Emperor Valentinian II another restoration of the altar of Victory. The old religion, he said in effect, had made Rome great and would again make great the inherited empire; he desired that young Romans, by worshiping Victory, might be strengthened to achieve it. Yet, despite Symmachus's rhetorical gifts (and he was the premier orator of the age), Ambrose had no trouble persuading Valentinian that the proposal was in fact impious and that the security of empire

9) Quoted by Quasten, op. cit., Vol. III, p. 206.
1) Now a small town with glorious mosaics, near Venice.

must thenceforth rest on Christian doctrine and Christian practice. Accordingly, the altar of Victory remained in oblivion, the Olympic games ceased in 394, and the Eleusinian mysteries in 396. The temples, already much disused, were now generally shut up or even razed, and sacrifices to the old gods were prohibited.

The Christian triumph was, by the end of the fourth century, formally complete. Yet ideas survive where practices fail, and penetrate areas forbidden them. Jerome never ceased to be a considerable classicist, and Augustine never quite lost, despite his pious horror of them, the neo-Platonic and Manichaean notions in which he had, at one time or another, ardently believed. Indeed, the word "paganism" is itself wonderfully instructive. It refers, of course, to those beliefs held by the *pagani,* the peasants,[2] the farmers, the bucolic folk. In rural areas ideas are very commonly laggard—a phenomenon which Marx described as "bucolic idiocy," and which is still evident in an age of nuclear physicists and cosmonauts.

What the *pagani* of A.D. 400 believed was the old magic, the power of familiar demons and local divinities. All this it had been the intent and striving of Christianity to supersede; but one may doubt whether, in the process of accommodation, paganism did not leave more imprint upon Christianity than Christianity upon paganism. In time the saints and their relics came to do what demons had long done, but perhaps on this level they behaved more like demons than like saints. Magic falsifies the actual causality in nature, and has its effects, not in the objective world, but in the mind of the believer. Consequently, there cannot have been much difference between a pagan thaumaturge and a Christian miracle worker in respect of science or even of intent.

On the high level of doctrinal formulation there were, however, struggles enough, some surviving from the fourth century into the fifth, and one at least newly arising, as portentous as unexpected. The basic trinitarian formula was, to be sure, firmly established; but there remained much doubt how the human Jesus was related to the divine Christ. There remained further doubt (it was the Donatist controversy) whether sacraments[3] administered by recusant or heretical clerics were at all valid. Since orthodoxy was still unsettled, since

2) From late Latin *pagensis,* which is in turn from *pagus* ("a country district") where, naturally enough, the inhabitants would be *pagani* ("pagans").
3) Officially there are seven of these: baptism, confirmation, marriage, penance, holy orders (i.e., the ministry), the Eucharist, and extreme unction.

bishops had a deplorable habit of excommunicating one another, and since all clergy nevertheless administered sacraments, it was a painfully uncertain question whether one had got properly confirmed or married or shriven. For if the relevant sacrament had in fact failed, one would find oneself adulterous instead of married, unpardoned instead of shriven, and, instead of membership in Christ's body, cut off and consequently damned.

Then, quite suddenly, there came into dispute a genuine problem—a problem, that is to say, which was more than one of composing doctrines into unity. It was a problem which, rather strangely, had never perplexed the ancients nor been much noticed by them, a problem lying nevertheless at the heart of all problems whatever. It was the problem not so much of the effect of human behavior upon events as of the effect of human decision upon human behavior. It was the problem of free will.

Christianity may claim as one of its achievements the discovery that this problem exists. The discovery occurred precisely because Christianity had interested itself in *all* men and their possible salvation, and was therefore supremely concerned to know the essential nature of those beings who were to be saved. At the heart of this nature stands the fact, and the act, of choice. All men are choosers, and their salvation depends upon how they choose. Yet, although they all have the faculty of choice, they on occasion seem to have it rather weakly. Some decisions require great strength, and the man who confronts them wonders whence that strength is to come. Has he it already? Can he summon by act of will the strength his own will needs? Or does that strength have a source other than himself, and must he therefore await its arrival from elsewhere?

I think it is fair to say that no one yet possesses indisputable answers. Sides have been taken and battle lines drawn: the libertarians against the determinists. Yet certain doctrines of each side most oddly imply certain doctrines of the other, and extremist frenzies tend to reverse the very positions that were to be maintained. There are versions of free will (notably William James's) which put the world quite out of human control, and there are versions of determinism (notably Spinoza's) which set the will free.[4] Neverthe-

4) James's universe—a universe, as he said, "with the lid off"—has so much uncertainty in it as to render planning, and hence control, impossible. Spinoza's determinism, however, makes the world knowable and hence subject to human planning.

less, Augustine and his adversary Pelagius put the question clearly and said the essential things that are to be said about it. To their views, accordingly, we now turn.

III

AMERICANS, more than others, may be interested to know that the name "Pelagius" (from *pélagos* = "sea") is the rendering into Greek of the Welsh name "Morgan" (= "seaman"). Possibly it was that the Greek offered more dignity, but I conjecture that Pelagius, a modest man, only wanted to make himself clear. He was a British monk, of Irish origin, who came to Rome in A.D. 400, and he cannot have expected the Romans to make anything of the name "Morgan."

It chanced that the year in which Pelagius came to Rome was also the year in which Augustine published his *Confessions*—one of the greatest of autobiographies, written undoubtedly for the edification of the reader but also addressed to the information of God.[5] Pelagius, reading it, came upon and stumbled over a now celebrated plea: *Da quod iubes, et iube quod vis*—"Give what you command, and command what you will."[6] This was one of Augustine's many invocations to the Deity, and the meaning was, "Make it possible for me to do whatever you bid me to do, and then bid me to do whatever you wish." On its face, this seems the plea of a servant to be made easy in servitude, or, less extremely, of an inferior to be made comfortable in discipline.

The obvious meaning is genuine enough: Augustine really intended it. And yet Augustine was no more a servant or an inferior than lightnings are, or winds, or halcyon fair weather, or any other massive fact in nature. Is it inconsistency then, of the sort that makes robust characters so attractive? Possibly, but I think that in fact the

5) The narrative is thickly interspersed with explanations to the Deity of the workings of the Deity's own providence. Augustine writes sometimes like a schoolboy showing how well he has learned the lesson, but also, it is pleasant to observe, sometimes as man to man.

6) *Confessions,* Book X, Chapter 29, § 40. The translation is Monsignor John K. Ryan's, *The Confessions of Saint Augustine* (Garden City, N.Y.: Doubleday & Co., Image Books; 1960), p. 256. The whole passage, in Monsignor Ryan's translation, is: "O Love, who are forever aflame and are never extinguished, O Charity, my God, set me aflame! You enjoin continence: give what you command, and command what you will." I may observe that Ryan's translation is preferable to Pusey's, whose attempt at Jacobean prose is painfully mawkish.

inconsistency can be removed. The social relations of inferior to superior are, in Augustine's use, but metaphor and drama. He is actually addressing himself to his conscience, his "higher nature," and he is asking it to give him, along with its commands, the power to obey them. That power being given, he says, let conscience command what it will.

Now, Augustine was, to be sure, a man, a bishop, a saint, but he was more than these. Like Rabelais, Shakespeare, and Tolstoy, he was a force of nature. Everything that can be found in nature—and particularly in human nature—can be found in him: guilt and purity, zeal and prudence, lust and discipline, anger and generosity, violence and love. He was a troubled man, and said so. He hid nothing and uttered everything; he had the candor not so much of courage as of sublime self-confidence.

Augustine's faults, abundantly confessed, were mild enough. As a boy, he once stole pears from a neighboring orchard, and he lamented that he had enjoyed the act of stealing even more than he had enjoyed the pears.[7] That is to say, he was a rebellious adolescent, selecting as target a small portion of the system of private property. As a youth, he was amorous, but not more amorous than youths healthily are. He truly and faithfully loved the mistress who bore him his son Adeodatus, and he loved the son as a father should. He mourned the mistress when he put her away, at his mother's bidding, on behalf of an advantageous engagement to marry.[8] His life with that mistress had been, in effect, a marriage—and so successful a marriage that the mistress, departing, vowed "she would never know another man."

The mother, Monica the mother—she was the moving power! In the great portrait (*Confessions*, IX, 8–9 and 17–22) Augustine's habitual candor so far triumphs over his conscious love as to show us a woman pious, pliable, victorious, and appalling. There have

---

7) Ibid., II, 4, 9: "For I stole a thing of which I had plenty of my own and of much better quality. Nor did I wish to enjoy that thing which I desired to gain by theft, but rather to enjoy the actual theft and sin of theft."

8) Ibid., VI, 15, 25: "The woman with whom I was wont to share my bed was torn from my side as an impediment to my marriage. My heart still clung to her: it was pierced and wounded within me, and the wound drew blood from it." Augustine never married the fiancée. She was then too young to marry, and before she grew old enough Augustine became Christian and celibate. But he did, meanwhile, take another mistress.

been many women like her, and in their presence men would do well to leave off struggling and surrender at once. She had always been a Christian. Her husband Patricius was pagan most of his life; she converted him. Her son Augustine was pagan for thirty-two years; she converted him. Deferential, patient, permissive of all aberrancies in husband and son, she made the husband at last monogamous and the son celibate. Monica conferred the appearance of free choice, and then things always turned out her way.

From such evidence what was Augustine to conclude? He had loved his mother entirely; he had identified his conscience with her will. His appetites, quite normal, had collided, quite normally, with her wishes; and he had felt, throughout, the expectable guilt. When he was thirty-two, the struggle, plainly sexual in origin and content, suddenly resolved itself. On an afternoon in a garden near Milan, at the extraordinary juxtaposition of Paul's Epistle to the Romans with the seeming cry of a child, Augustine found he could be celibate.[9] Monica had dismissed all rivals and fully possessed her son.

One cannot doubt the power of such a mother upon any son. The final conversion in the garden was the cumulative effect of her will, adroitly manipulating the guilts of thirty-two years. So massive a weight has either to slide away or crush the carrier. It slid away. To Augustine, who was well aware that such workings and their consequences were independent of his own will, this seemed a transcendental deliverance, an unmistakable act of God. He had always wanted to obey, he had always resisted obedience, and suddenly obedience (in sexual behavior at least) actually occurred. He was reconciled with mother and with God—amid tears and agony, to be sure, but without one quiver of the will. There was therefore, he

---

9) Ibid., VIII, 12, 29. This is the famous *Tolle, lege* scene: "And lo, I heard from a nearby house a voice like that of a boy or a girl, I know not which, chanting and repeating over and over, 'Take up and read. Take up and read.' . . . So I hurried back to the spot where Alypius was sitting, for I had put there the volume of the apostle when I got up and left him. I snatched it up, opened it, and read in silence the chapter on which my eyes first fell: 'Not in rioting and drunkenness, not in chambering and impurities, not in strife and envying; but put you on the Lord Jesus Christ, and make not provision for the flesh in its concupiscences.' . . . Instantly, in truth, at the end of this sentence, as if before a peaceful light streaming into my heart, all the dark shadows of doubt fled away." The text that produced this remarkable effect is Romans 13: 13–14; the translation is the Douay.

could not but think, a power not ourselves that makes us righteous, that seizes the human will as one might seize a lash, to whip the appetites out of their riot and anarchy. When such a power operates, it is irresistible; and, unless it operates, the man is lost.

So Augustine many times said,[1] and so undoubtedly he thought. But he also thought other and quite opposite things. The black pall that ought to cover a man who believes himself powerless to do good is simply not there; it does not darken even the appropriate passages. On the contrary, a supernal gaiety sweeps all before it, and we are told, "The very fact of existing is by some natural spell so pleasant, that even the wretched are, for no other reason, unwilling to perish."[2] This is Augustine in his role as force of nature—alive, in love with life, the personification itself of irresistible grace. "And how much human nature loves the knowledge of its existence, and how it shrinks from being deceived, will be sufficiently understood from the fact that every man prefers to grieve in a sane mind, rather than to be glad in madness." This love of existence and of knowing that one exists Augustine deemed peculiar to human beings, their special glory. And the reason? "We have another and far superior sense, belonging to the inner man, by which we perceive what things are just, and what unjust. . . . By it I am assured both that I am, and that I know this; and these two I love, and in the same manner I am assured that I love them."[3]

Nothing dour can be made of this. Soaring now upon wings which defense of Christianity had given him,[4] Augustine proceeded to show that men, so far from being powerless, can in fact do many

---

1) E.g., in *On Nature and Grace*, Chapter 11: ". . . without the grace of God a man cannot be without sin"; and in *On the Grace of Christ*, Book I, Chapter 13: ". . . by such grace it is effected, not only that we discover what ought to be done, but also that we do what we have discovered." The translations are by Peter Holmes and Robert Wallis, in *A Select Library of the Nicene and Post-Nicene Fathers of the Christian Church*, edited by Philip Schaff (New York: The Christian Literature Company; 1887), Vol. V, pp. 124 and 222, respectively.
2) *The City of God*, Book XI, Chapter 27. The translation is by Marcus Dods, in the Modern Library edition of the work (New York: Random House Inc.; 1950), p. 371.
3) Ibid., loc. cit.
4) Augustine wrote the *City of God* between the years 413 and 427, with a view to proving (1) that the fall of Rome had not been the Christians' fault, (2) that Christianity was not a program for social disaster, and (3) that, on the contrary, Christianity possessed and expounded the ultimate, saving social ideal.

more things than they imagine. The following passage I take to be, on the whole, the most remarkable in the history of philosophy:

> We know, too, that some men are differently constituted from others, and have some rare and remarkable faculty of doing with their body what other men can by no effort do, and, indeed, can scarcely believe when they hear of others doing. There are persons who can move their ears, either one at a time, or both together. There are some who, without moving the head, can bring the hair down upon the forehead, and move the whole scalp backwards and forewards at pleasure. Some, by lightly pressing their stomach, bring up an incredible quantity and variety of things they have swallowed, and produce whatever they please, quite whole, as if out of a bag. Some so accurately mimic the voices of birds and beasts and other men, that, unless they are seen, the difference cannot be told. Some have such command of their bowels, that they can break wind continuously at pleasure, so as to produce the effect of singing. . . .[5]

Such facts (for facts they doubtless were) Augustine took to show, not what men might be in the future, but what Adam had been in the past. The ancients very generally regarded human history as a decline from an original perfection.[6] On this view, existing skills would be vestiges of greater skills now lost, and exceptional skills would tend to prove that there had once been skill complete. And what is skill complete? It is perfect control of behavior in purpose, in choice, and in execution.

This perfect control (so Augustine thought) Adam had been created with and had therefore possessed. All his actions were originally voluntary; he had not a nerve of which the functioning was merely reflex. If, in Eden before the Fall, he had wished (as apparently he did not) to beget a child upon Eve, he could have produced the necessary glandular rigidity by simple act of will.[7] He would

5) Ibid., XIV, 24.
6) See Dean Inge's celebrated remark, "The ancient pagans, we are told, put their Golden Age in the past; we put ours in the future. The Greeks prided themselves on being the degenerate descendants of gods, we on being the very creditable descendants of monkeys." From "The Idea of Progress," first paragraph, in *Outspoken Essays: Second Series* (London: Longmans, Green and Company; 1922).
7) Augustine was fascinated by this idea, which is, it must be confessed, fascinating. Plainly, his guilt feelings clustered around the *enjoyment* of lovemak-

have needed no excitation, no adventitious stirring of desire, none of those nasty-lovely pruriences that attend the propagation of our race. And thus he would have approached the modern ideal of artificial insemination.

The consequent anthropology (for so theologians still call it) is as charming as it is naïve. Adam's original sin had been disobedience to a divine command, and the sin had issued from a flaw in Adam's own nature. How such a flaw, so fatal in effect, came into a nature created perfect we are baffled to know. God cannot have put it there; but why did he allow it there, particularly when he foresaw the dreadful consequences? At this point Augustine, like most other theologians, retreats into the doctrine that God's purpose is ultimately inscrutable—which is a way of saying that nobody knows.[8]

This failure of theory is perhaps not calamitous: origins are always lost in mist. Not so the inferences from the postulates. Adam's sin had necessitated punishment, and the punishment had been to suffer strife within his own character: "the law in my members warring against the law of my mind."[9] In this contest the "members" are always wrong and the "mind" always right, so that if a man did only what he really wanted to do, his acts would be gross and unrelieved in sin. This inward degeneracy, this deplorable strife, Adam communicated to his descendants without exception. It was the first

---

ing, and I have no doubt that Monica put them there, being motivated (as mothers often secretly are) by the wish that her son should delight in no other woman. For example, Augustine writes (*On Marriage and Concupiscence,* Chapter 17) that ". . . if sin had not preceded, man would have been begotten by means of the organs of generation, not less obedient than the other members to a quiet and normal will." And in *The City of God,* XIV, 23 and 24: "The field of generation should have been sown by the organ created for this purpose, as the earth is sown by the hand. . . . The man, then, would have sown the seed, and the woman received it, as need required, the generative organs being moved by the will, not excited by lust."

8) E.g., this passage, from *Nature and Grace,* Chapter 35: "But I would indeed so treat these topics, as to confess myself ignorant of God's deeper counsel. . . ."

9) Romans 7: 23 (AV). In Freudian terms this is, of course, id against superego. Augustine says, for example, in the treatise *On Marriage and Concupiscence,* Book II, Chapter 22: "[Shame] . . . is the rebellion against our own selves, proceeding from our own selves, which by a most righteous retribution is rendered us by our disobedient members." The translation is by Holmes and Wallis, in op. cit., p. 291. Freud, by the way, is extremely Augustinian, even to the point of projecting his psychology as "anthropology."

time an acquired characteristic had been inherited, and it was a disaster.

In respect of righteousness, therefore, human beings need help as cripples need crutches and blind men need to be led. Virtuous resource, the power of righteous action, is simply not in them; it has to be supplied from moment to moment, as time and decision require. God supplies it, so far as it is supplied at all; and what he supplies is "grace," the ability to prefer right to wrong. One cannot even pray for the gift of it unless God has previously disposed one's mind so to pray.

This moral inadequacy, of which some evidences are all too plain, Augustine enlarged into a primal cosmic fact. Salvation was in any case outside human influence. God had created all souls simultaneously: some of them he elected to be saved; others to be damned. The candidates would live out their lives never knowing the ultimate issue; they would learn it only when, entering upon eternity, they found themselves permanently saved or permanently damned. A life of virtue might suggest, but could not guarantee, salvation; a life of sin might suggest, but would not necessitate, damnation. It was all God's great drama, and there would be many surprises in the last act.

This ferocious doctrine is, by reason of its ferocity, easier to disbelieve than to believe. But the ferocity lies in the metaphor (which Augustine read literally) and not in the fact described. A God, a Supreme Person, who would trifle thus with human souls would be odious and contemptible, and a heaven which was His Presence would very probably be hell. But if we remove the metaphor in order to see the fact, we do find that some differentiation among human "souls" has primitively occurred in their physiological and psychological equipment. Some people are genetically incapable of morality, just as some people are genetically color blind. Others are blunted toward morality, as men are made blind, by forces they cannot control. In short, there really is a determinism that affects, and sometimes decisively affects, how righteous we can be or indeed whether we can be righteous at all.

But this determinism seems not of a sort which needs renewal from moment to moment as decisions occur. Rather it seems that the moral man has from nature (or, if you like, from "God") the ability to be so. The exercise of this ability is the man's own exercise, and he is therefore sufficiently accountable for the results. This was Pelagius's view, in a passage which Augustine quotes in the *De Gratia Christi*:

We distinguish three things and arrange them in a definite order. We put in the first place *"posse"* [ability, possibility]; in the second, *"velle"* [volition]; in the third, *"esse"* [existence, actuality]. The *posse* we assign to nature, the *velle* to will, the *esse* to actual realization. The first of these, *posse,* is properly ascribed to God, who conferred it on his creatures; while the other two, *velle* and *esse,* are to be referred to the human agent, since they have their source in his will. . . .[1]

And again:

Everything good and everything evil, in respect of which we are either worthy of praise or of blame, is *done by us,* not *born with us.* We are not born in our full development, but with a capacity for good and evil; we are begotten as well without virtue as without vice, and before the activity of our own personal will there is nothing in man but what God has stored in him. . . .[2]

This humane, as well as humanist, doctrine yields certain inferences which Pelagius and his pupil Coelestius went on to draw. Once it is granted that nature (or "God") gives to some men at any rate the ability to be righteous, less anxiety attends the taint of Adam's sin. There will be no need to think that infants are born depraved or that, dying unbaptized, they must suffer damnation.[3] Quite to the contrary, infants may be accurately judged to be as innocent as they seem, and when they grow into maturity, they will yet have the chance to be sinless, or nearly sinless, men. Indeed, on this last point, Pelagius, a patient man, turned impatient. Amid the sloth and licence of Rome he often heard men excuse their vices on grounds of simple human helplessness: "What else can I do? After

1) *On Christ's Grace,* Chapter 5. Translated by Bettenson, *Documents,* p. 75. Augustine always quotes accurately and copiously so that we are well supplied with Pelagian *ipsissima verba.* These particular words come from Pelagius's work *Pro Libero Arbitrio* (*On Behalf of Free Will*).

2) Quoted also from *Pro Libero Arbitrio,* in Augustine's *On Original Sin,* Chapter 14. Translated by Bettenson, *Documents, loc. cit.* The italics are Bettenson's.

3) This absurd, extraordinary doctrine (which Professor Warfield, a devout Christian scholar, called "terrible and incredible") has done more damage to Christianity, and particularly to Protestantism, than any other doctrine in the corpus. I think it really does follow from Paul's theory about redemption by the Second Adam, but Paul was far too sensible a man to draw nonsensical inferences even when logically entailed.

all, I'm only human." To these Pelagius gave a blunt reply: "Make the effort!"

> . . . we cry out at God [he wrote] in the scornful sloth of our hearts, and say, "This is too hard and difficult. We cannot do it. We are only human and hindered by the weakness of the flesh." Blind folly and presumptuous blasphemy! . . . [God] has not willed to command anything impossible, for he is righteous; and he will not condemn a man for what he could not help, for he is holy.[4]

On all these points Pelagius seems as accurate as he is clear. His concept of free will prospers in a scientific age, and I would doubt that the abundant empirical evidence yet to be discovered will require much alteration in the view. To liberal theologians he is the saint and Augustine the heretic, but the Church's *via media* (not so *media*, after all—and perhaps not much of a *via*) lies closer to Augustine than to him. The reason is not far to seek, and it characteristically has to do with retention of membership. The Church and the churches depend in great measure upon the guilt feelings of their members. "There is no health in us," says one of the most famous of prayers, and those who murmur the words imagine more sins in themselves, I dare say, than ever they have committed.

Whatever may be judged of ultimate redemption and the power to grant it, the fact is that Christian churches do, week by week and even day by day, ease the burdens of guilt and anxiety. Without this function they might find it difficult to survive. They are therefore unlikely to entertain a doctrine which, by removing guilts altogether, would leave no burden to be eased. Pelagian theory does just this, and, in doing it, cancels (ideologically at least) one of the closest bonds between any church and its membership. Augustine the bishop had no difficulty recognizing this fact, from an administrative point of view as well as a theological. He was prompt to say—and he said it often—that Pelagius "rendered the cross of Christ of none effect:"[5] in other words, if men can be righteous by their own efforts, then they don't need either Christ's sacrifice or his Church for the purpose.

This implication Pelagius himself perceived, and, under pressure,

---

4) *Letter to Demetrias,* 16. Translated by Bettenson, *Documents,* p. 74.
5) E.g., in *On Nature and Grace,* Chapters 10 and 21. This work belongs to the year 415. The passage in Chapter 10 continues: ". . . then is Christ dead in vain, forasmuch as all might accomplish so much as this, even if he had never died." Translated by Holmes and Wallis, op. cit., p. 124.

renounced. His pupil Coelestius, however, was more staunch, and so was his follower Julian of Eclanum, one of the nineteen Pelagian bishops banished by imperial edict in 418. But I think that Pelagius never knew, or only dimly knew, the naturalistic bent of his philosophy. He did in fact regard man as an animal species more than as a child of God, and if he were living in the twentieth century, he would doubtless prefer psychiatry to religion. This tendency, this preference, the much more penetrating intellect of Augustine readily perceived and, in a series of remarkable treatises, made plain to his fellow Christians.

The consequent political struggle lasted some seven years. Pelagius left Rome shortly after its fall, stopped briefly in Hippo, which he left without accepting Augustine's invitation to discuss theology. From this, Augustine inferred a certain timidity, which, very probably, Pelagius did feel. Augustine was surely formidable in controversy; moreover, Pelagius seems to have been the sort of intellectual who, avoiding political struggle, hopes that his ideas will work as well in his absence as in his presence. An appeal to reason very often hides a distaste for personal involvement.

From North Africa, Pelagius went to Palestine, where his purity of manners and clarity of thought quickly won prestige. But in Palestine also lived the great Jerome, and Jerome was on Augustine's side in the dispute. In 415, at Jerome's insistence, John the Bishop of Jerusalem summoned Pelagius for questioning. John made no headway against Pelagius's skill, and in December of the same year a synod of fourteen bishops met at Diospolis (Lydda) to pursue the investigation. The proceedings were wildly ineffectual. The bishops shared a common language neither with the defendant nor with one another. Assertions that are difficult to state in any language were thus left to the mercies of an interpreter, and Pelagius maneuvered brilliantly amid the confusion of tongues. Whenever the bishops wanted him to anathematize a certain doctrine, he did so, preserving unscathed his own private version of it.[6] There was nothing to do but acquit him.

6) So says Augustine *passim* in *The Proceedings of Pelagius,* written in A.D. 417, and in the treatise *On Original Sin,* Chapters 11–13, written in A.D. 418. These treatises, translated by Holmes and Wallis, will be found op. cit., pp. 183–212 and 237–55. I find the account very credible. Such behavior has appeared in many intellectuals, who, though in possession of truth, were politically on the defensive.

News of this result reached North Africa some months before the authentic records of the synod. Regional rivalry was, as we know, easily whetted, and accordingly the African bishops rallied to denounce the laxity of their brethren in Palestine. Both sides appealed to Innocent I, the Bishop of Rome, who, for his part, was as much surprised as pleased to find himself holding the balance of decision.[7] He sided with the Africans, and pronounced Pelagius and Coelestius excommunicate until they should recant. Then, suddenly, he died. His successor Zosimus was a man who believed wavering to be a policy. Letters came to him from Pelagius, and Coelestius appeared in person at Rome—all with assurances of fidelity to orthodox doctrine as the Roman see defined it. Thereupon Zosimus pronounced both Pelagius and Coelestius free of heretical taint, and berated the Africans for a too hasty zeal.

It was a fatal error. The great Augustine, who knew politics as well as he knew the human heart, who also knew the exquisite touch of ideology upon politics, had, during the year 417, exhaustively searched the synodic record. In treatises, sermons, letters he laid bare all the implications of Pelagian doctrine, and showed what must be their effect if members of the Church came to believe them. Administrators, of whatever rank, could not fail to see the threat of schism, and accordingly two hundred bishops, meeting at Carthage, rejected with great vigor all that Zosimus had pronounced.

Zosimus wavered again, and, while he wavered, the blow fell. It seems not to be known how much Augustine had to do with this (though the brilliance of the stroke was worthy of him), but at any rate on the thirtieth of April, 418, the Emperor Honorius, at Ravenna, issued an edict banishing all Pelagians and confiscating their property. Someone in the Church (for myself, I suspect Augustine) had appealed to the secular power for aid against heresy, and had thus set the precedent for a long and lamentable series of martyrdoms in which the Church was instigator and the State executioner. It is known that Augustine favored this practice, and I fear that, to this extent, he fell short of his own maxim, "He who loves to govern rather than to do good is no bishop."[8]

Zosimus had now to yield or be banished. He yielded, and then

---

7) Rome was not yet the premier see in Christendom, and Innocent perceived, with much joy, that events were beginning to make it so.
8) *The City of God,* XIX, 19.

he died. By the year 420, Pelagius had disappeared from history. Coelestius turned up in Constantinople in 428, trying to convert Nestorius, who, however, had a heresy of his own. Augustine went on governing and writing. In 427, after thirteen years, he finished the *City of God,* and then proceeded to discuss, in separate treatises, the gift of perseverance and the predestination of saints. Then Vandals laid siege to his city, and in the midst of the siege, exhausted with zeal and creativity, he died.

The Vandals took Hippo and, afterward, Carthage. They have vanished long since and have left no more than an ugly name, easily ignored. But Pelagius lives in every Marxist and Augustine in every Freudian and both in many more than these. For Pelagian views and Augustinian views are complementary to each other: free will makes determinism useful, and determinism makes free will possible. Together they can, though perhaps they will not, lead us to that perfection of social life which Pelagius thought possible on earth and Augustine only in heaven: "There we shall rest and see, see and love, love and praise."[9]

I V

In 482 the Eastern Emperor was Zeno, whose original name had been Tarasicodissa, son of Rusumbladestus. He came from Isauria, a district on the Asiatic mainland just north of the island of Cyprus. He had been son-in-law of the Emperor Leo I, and had, rather oddly, succeeded his own infant son Leo II in 474.[1] There was a shortish interval, during which his brother-in-law Basiliscus squeezed him from the throne, but by a timely conquest Zeno justified those adjectives—at least in part—with which he described himself in the *Henoticon:* "pious, victorious, supreme, ever-worshipful."[2]

The *Henoticon,* or *Proposal for Unity,* was Zeno's effort at establishing peace in the Church. There had been none throughout the century. Quite to the contrary, "murders innumerable [so the *Henoticon* said] have been committed, and not the earth only but the very air has been polluted by the abundance of bloodshed."[3] The public

9) Ibid., XXII, 30.
1) This was possible through the system of "colleagues." Leo I took Zeno's son as colleague, and then, after Leo's death, Zeno got himself made colleague of the infant Leo II.
2) Bettenson, *Documents,* p. 125.
3) Ibid., p. 126.

utterances of emperors and bishops were not notable for absence of hyperbole, but this particular statement, though it exaggerates, exaggerates little. There had been murders and many other crimes, all done on behalf of ecclesiastical unity, and at the end the Church was still less unified than before. "Who would not pray," asks the *Henoticon,* "for the transformation of this state of things into good?"

During the fifth century, three successive struggles convulsed the Church on the problem of the nature of Christ (the subject known as Christology). Throughout these struggles, the chief contestants were Alexandria and Constantinople, and the episodes can therefore be designated by names of the rival bishops: Theophilus versus Chrysostom, Cyril versus Nestorius, Dioscorus versus Flavian. In all these contests Alexandria appeared the immediate victor, but in fact she sank beneath the weight of so many triumphs and in the end left Christendom to be ruled—schismatically, alas—by Constantinople and by Rome.

Let us now restate what we have already said about Christology. There was (it seems) in the first century A.D. a young insurrectionary leader in Palestine who sought to liberate his country by expelling the Roman colonial government together with its agents, the Jewish ruling class. He failed and was executed. Some years later, a certain Jew of the Diaspora, Paul of Tarsus, hearing the story, interpreted it to mean that the apparent insurrectionary had in fact been a god incarnate, who had aimed, not at historically liberating Palestine, but at transcendentally rescuing the whole human race.

The Christian Church had grown by possession of these two personages, the historical Jesus and the mystery-Christ. Further, it had grown by an assurance that the two personages were somehow one. But how was this unity to be expressed? Human nature is sinful, being caught in Adam's sin; yet the Christ, the god-man, was surely sinless in both natures. The man Jesus had had a human mother; was she also mother of the incarnate *Logos,* the Second Person of the Trinity? And who had suffered on the Cross—the man or the God or both?

These were minor points, though much disputed. The heart of the controversy was the question of union itself. How was the union to be described? Did the divine nature swallow up or (less extremely) dominate the human? Perhaps it was that the *Logos,* as divine intellect, simply replaced the human intellect, or, alternatively, the divine will the human will. If so, one could understand how the god-man came to be sinless. Yet both these versions proved heretical.

Then there was the question of unequal age. The Second Person of the Trinity, being coeternal with the Father, was infinitely old. The human Jesus, however, had been begotten in time, born in time, reared in time: he had been an embryo, a babe, a boy, and a man. It was difficult to correlate these ages. "I cannot," said Nestorius sadly, "speak of God as being two or three months old."[4]

Altogether the problem was troublesome. Its subtleties were so much ice on which one easily slid away from the true path, drawn by one's tastes or the unconscious power of one's point of view. The Alexandrians, after years of interpreting by allegory, were less given to emphasizing the divine. The School of Antioch, however, which dominated thought in Asia Minor, took all references to divinity quite literally, and was much more sensitive to the differences between humanity and divinity than to that union of them which every Christian believed to be somehow or other the fact. Theodore of Mopsuestia (*obit.* 428), the prime intellect of the Antiochene School, got no nearer the proper unity than to compare it with marriage, in which husband and wife form "one flesh" while remaining separate persons.[5] And Nestorius, his pupil, never could believe that Mary, the human mother, had been the bearer of God. "Anyhow," he once cried out in the disgust that follows futile argument, "don't make the Virgin a Goddess!"[6] The Church never has—not quite; but it drove out Nestorius, whose name and doctrines adorn a sect of Christians still flourishing in our time.

The problems of Christology had just those attributes which would serve as an occasion of quarrel: they were important, they were subtle, and they were unresolved. By themselves they could scarcely excite bloodshed, but then they did not exist by themselves. On the contrary, their resolution would affect the destiny of Church and Empire and would express the relative importance of sees and bishops within both. Treasuries of wealth and panoplies of power would attend the issue. The classic inducements to organizational

---

4) Quoted in the *Cambridge Medieval History,* Vol. I, p. 497.
5) Bettenson, *Documents,* p. 65. Theodore was much admired in his day, but was pronounced heretical a century or so after his death.
6) *Cambridge Medieval History,* loc. cit.

scurrility were all there, and subsequent events attested their presence.

Egypt, of which the chief city was Alexandria, was a singularly disorganized province. It had no well-established institutions. Greek culture had settled upon the earlier Egyptian, Roman upon the Greek, and Christian upon all. Alexandria itself was rife with factions: pagans, Jews, Christians theorized, proselytized, and collided. In the deserts, where thousands of monks and nuns lived as hermits or cenobites, there developed a tempestuous mingling of anarchy with fanaticism. For all their solitude and seeming rejection of society, the monks were a political force, which bishops had to reckon with but could not master. The monks were given to strong, if unenlightened, views upon theology: it was one of these who complained, when anthropomorphism was condemned, that "they had taken away his God."[7]

Over this congeries, and amid such factions, Theophilus presided as Bishop of Alexandria at the beginning of the fifth century. He was cultivated to the point of enjoying even those books that he condemned,[8] and he was scientist enough to calculate the Easter cycle. He had shown talent as a peacemaker among churches and talent also as a destroyer of churches by razing the ancient and famous temple of Serapis. Once a follower of Origen's theology, he turned against it with much violence but with reasons that were far from clear. At his instigation the Alexandrian prefect ordered an assault by night upon a community of Origenist monks at Nitria. The monks were scattered, and their four leaders, known to history as the Tall Brethren, fled to Constantinople.

There they had courteous reception from the Bishop, John Chrysostom, who had all Theophilus's administrative difficulties along with a difficulty much more acute: he had to deal, daily and almost hourly, with the Emperor Arcadius and the Empress Eudoxia. Chrysostom, a great orator and rigorous ascetic, fell to denouncing that love of pleasure which was as dear to the populace as to the throne, and he took upon himself the thankless task of extirpating corruption wherever possible. He had been doing this at Ephesus, with various dismissals of clergymen, just before the Tall Brethren arrived.

7) *Cambridge Medieval History,* Vol. I, p. 490.
8) I here borrow Alice Gardner's epigram, *Cambridge Medieval History,* loc. cit.

Yet Chrysostom's zeal retained a certain self-discipline. He did not court trouble with Theophilus. Observing this, the Tall Brethren one day stopped the Empress as she rode in her chariot through the streets of Constantinople, and begged her help in the evils which had befallen them. The secular rulers of those days were dilettantes in theology—perhaps they could not avoid being so—and the result was that Theophilus found himself summoned to answer charges of persecution.

This summons proved, in the event, an invitation to attack. Theophilus began by practicing infiltration and by establishing as the central issue a subject quite other than his own past behavior. He sent out Epiphanius, the Bishop of Constantia, with a considerable entourage of other bishops and clergy, whose first act upon arriving at Constantinople was to ordain a deacon in obvious violation of Chrysostom's authority. Epiphanius was a shrewd choice. An old man of eighty-six years and as venerable as old, he had produced, amid a considerable corpus, a work entitled *Panarion* ("Medicine Chest"). This Chest, says Quasten, was intended to "furnish an antidote to those who have been bitten by the serpent of heresy and to protect those who have remained sound in the faith."[9] It was in fact the most extensive compilation of heresies that had ever been made: it listed no less than eighty of them, including twenty that antedated Christianity itself. So knowledgeable a smeller-out of heresy could not have failed to notice the deviations of Origen, who had been, as we know, the most scholarly and high-minded of the early fathers.[1]

Arrived in Constantinople with his troop of clergy, Epiphanius began a hunt for Origenists. There were indeed some to be found, but these had never until then supposed themselves to be heretics. Chrysostom, for his part, held aloof and declined to condemn Origen. Epiphanius retired apparently baffled, but he had set up the lever with which Theophilus was to move the world. The issue was no longer whether Theophilus had abused the Tall Brethren but whether Chrysostom himself was orthodox.

At this decisive moment Theophilus appeared with thirty-six bishops, and more in reserve. Chrysostom had forty. Expert intrigue

9) Op. cit., III, p. 387.
1) *Supra,* Chapter 5. In the fifth century, Origen was thought to have under-valued the humanity of the Christ.

had gained Theophilus the Emperor's support, but even so, he took care not to give battle in Constantinople itself. Instead he convoked a synod near Chalcedon, over which he himself presided. The accused, thus taking on the functions of a judge, four times summoned Chrysostom to appear. Chrysostom as often refused. The Synod of the Oak (as it came to be called) thereupon deposed Chrysostom and ordered him into exile. And what of the Tall Brethren? Why, of the four, two had died and the other two made no protest.

Chrysostom was three days gone upon his journey into exile when the earth shook beneath Constantinople, and many supposed that God had given a sign. Chrysostom was summoned back, and once more entered upon his episcopal duties. But the renewal did not last. Smarting perhaps under the Empress's unreliability, he preached a sermon in which he alluded to her as a Jezebel; and when a second sermon was interrupted by music and dancing attendant upon the erection nearby of a statue to the Empress, he broadened the scriptural analogy to include Herodias. "Again Herodias raves; again she rages; again she dances; again she asks for the head of John upon a charger."[2]

Argument by analogy is always risky: the Empress Eudoxia, now fully angered, did not meet the fate of Jezebel, but something not unlike the fate of John did happen to his namesake. John the Golden-mouthed was definitively banished, first to Cucusus on the Armenian frontier, then to Pityus on the Black Sea, not far from what is now Sochi, a resort for Soviet proletarians. But before he could reach those salubrious climes he died, on the fourteenth of September, 407. Theophilus lingered in triumph until 412; then, dying, made way for a yet more terrible successor.

The second episode of the Christological drama was a repetition of the first, but on a grander scale. The contending bishops were Cyril and Nestorius, the Emperor was Theodosius II, and there were now two imperial ladies, Pulcheria, the Emperor's elder sister and Eudocia, the Emperor's wife. The ladies were, like the preceding Empress, amateurs of theology and thus susceptible to Alexandrian influence.

Crises in ideology often occur upon subsidiary questions, because

2) Quoted by Quasten, op. cit., III, p. 427, from Socrates, *Historia Ecclesiae,* 6, 18, and from Sozomen, *Historia Ecclesiae,* 8, 20.

in these the theoretical differences are most finely drawn. If, for example, the union of humanity and divinity in the Christ were absolute, then it seemed that the Virgin must have been mother to both. If, however, she were regarded as mother only to the human Jesus, then the union would be noticeably less secure. And the more the two natures separated ideologically, the more the Church itself tended toward schism.

As in the trinitarian dispute, the issue came to turn upon a word: *Theotókos* (Θεοτόκος). This word, as Bettenson suggests, meant nothing quite so startling as "Mother of God," but rather "God-bearer," a less disturbing term. If you could call the Virgin "Theotókos," you could keep the two traditions, and with them the membership, united. Precisely this Cyril proposed to do. He then collided with a variety of views which held, or tended toward holding, that the Second Person of the Trinity had only one nature—since common sense suggests that a person cannot have two.

Such views were called "monophysite" (i.e., "one-natured"), and their contraries can be called, if one likes, "dyophysite." Monophysite views had the advantage of simplicity. Just as a unitarian God is somewhat more credible than a trinitarian, so a single nature is somewhat more credible than a dual. Even compromises tended to be monophysite: as we shall see, the version of Eutyches was that the Christ had had two natures before union but only one nature afterward.

The second struggle began during the Christmas festival of 428, when Proclus, the Bishop of Cyzicus, preached a sermon in Constantinople advocating the doctrine of *Theotókos*. Nestorius replied with a sermon of his own, cautioning discreetly against so extreme a view. There followed a brief correspondence with Cyril, in which Nestorius's orthodoxy came under attack. Alexandrians always began by throwing the adversary off balance.

Cyril prepared his offensive carefully. In a series of letters to the imperial court he addressed Theodosius as "the image of God on earth" and Pulcheria and Eudocia as "most pious princesses." These flattering appellations were prelude to a feast of theological exposition, which did not fail of effect. There was, said Cyril, a new heresy abroad in Christendom, which sought to establish two Christs instead of one and to undo the work of the Atonement by sundering the God from the man. There was no mention of Nestorius. The theological ladies were ingeniously, but disingenuously, left to draw their own inferences.

At the same time, Cyril sent word of all these matters to the Bishop of Rome, Celestine I. Now, Celestine had already collided with the see of Constantinople over what may be called a "boundary dispute" in Illyria. He therefore had no trouble in recognizing the heretical bent of Nestorian Christology, and in 430 he convoked a synod at Rome, which condemned Nestorius. A synod at Alexandria confirmed this sentence immediately thereafter, and Cyril dispatched a letter to Constantinople announcing the fact and adding his celebrated "twelve anathemas."[3] Nestorius replied, as the custom was, with a list of counter-anathemas.

Theodosius now stepped forth to resolve the conflict. He summoned eastern and western bishops to a synod to meet at Ephesus in 431 at the time of Pentecost, fifty days after Easter. Cyril lost not a moment. Disregarding what might be thought the needs of the flock at Eastertide, he left Alexandria with a large following, and arrived at Ephesus before Nestorius could gather all his forces. In particular, John, the Bishop of Antioch, with twoscore other bishops, all on Nestorius's side, somewhat ambiguously delayed arrival at Ephesus, alleging the duties of Easter.

Theophilus, it will be remembered, had been a defendant turned judge. Cyril acted as a judge turned prosecutor. As president, he opened the synod, after a decent but highly advantageous delay of sixteen days, John still not having appeared. Nestorius declined to attend in the absence of John. It was but one day's work to procure the condemnation of Nestorius and his removal from his see. Five days later John arrived, and he and Nestorius set up a synod of their own, satirically called the "Little Council" (*Conciliabulum*). There they excommunicated Cyril and Memnon of Ephesus, and deposed

3) The anathematized doctrines were in part: (1) that the Virgin was not "Theotókos"; (2) that the Word was not joined with the flesh; (3) that the two natures were merely conjoined, not united; (4) that the expressions used of Christ in the Gospels apply, some to the man, and some to the God; (5) that Christ can be called a "God-bearing man"; (6) that the Word can be called the God or Lord of Christ; (7) that Jesus as man was energized by the Word; (8) that the Word merely "assumed" the flesh; (9) that Jesus exercised a divine power alien to himself . . . (12) that the Word did not suffer in the flesh and was not crucified in the flesh. Bettenson, *Documents,* pp. 65–66.

them from office. The original synod replied by excommunicating John.

Affairs had now reached a point where all the participants were in one way or another heretical. Theodosius decided to bring order out of chaos by putting the leaders in jail. Accordingly, Cyril and Memnon were imprisoned, and Nestorius escaped by retiring to a monastery. Meanwhile the lavish bribes and eloquent propaganda of Cyril were doing their slower but more effective work. Under such pressures the Nestorian party steadily lost ground. By the time Cyril and Memnon were released, an accord had sprung up between Egyptians and Asiatics on the formula "two natures united into one." There remained only to add the word "Person" to this phrase, as was done, after a third struggle, at the Council of Chalcedon in 451.

Cyril returned to Alexandria in triumph, and reigned there as Bishop for another twelve years. When he died, in 444, Theodoret, the ablest theologian of that time and the only one to have had a sense of humor, proposed that a large stone be laid over the grave "to keep the disturber quiet." In 435 Nestorius suffered banishment, in the course of which, mischance following upon mischance, he died (some say) a violent death at the hands of Shenoutē, the abbot-monk who lived to be one hundred eighteen years.

The third struggle was history caricaturing itself. The new *personae dramatis* were, with one exception,[4] lesser men, and some were outright comedians. One will look far to find personages more preposterous than Peter the Fuller, Peter the Stammerer, and Timothy the Cat. These men were all bishops, and their merit was answerable to their names.

Dioscorus, who succeeded Cyril at Alexandria, had Cyril's unscrupulousness without his stature. Flavian, at Constantinople, had Chrysostom's piety without his massive worth. Leo the Great alone showed himself deserving of the epithet, and in the ensuing struggle established, if not the dominance, at any rate the impregnability of the Roman see.

Now, in Constantinople or in its environs there lived an abbot of monks named Eutyches (ironically enough, "the fortunate one"). Eutyches was old but ardent, and, as Bettenson says, his "anti-

4) Leo I (Leo the Great), Bishop of Rome—not to be confused with the eastern emperor of that name.

Nestorian zeal far outran his imperceptible theological discretion."[5] In his eagerness to show that the Virgin really could be called "God-bearer," he played down the humanity of her historical son. He thus committed the error, frequent among heretics, of supposing that you can be orthodox by merely contradicting some established heresy.

In 448, Eutyches, to his surprise, found himself called before the local council of bishops. There, under pressure from Flavian and other bishops, he yielded ground so far as to say that, since the Virgin was consubstantial with us human beings, her son must have been consubstantial with us also. But he would not pass over into the notion of a dual nature in the Christ. "I follow," he said, "the doctrine of the blessed Cyril and the holy fathers and the holy Athanasius. They speak of two natures before the union, but after the union and incarnation they speak of one nature not two."[6]

Eutyches, having been condemned, appealed to Leo and to Theodosius, who was still Eastern emperor. Leo decided against Eutyches, and took occasion to reassert Roman supremacy in deciding matters of faith. On the premise that "Peter has spoken through Leo," he composed and issued what has come to be called the *Tome of Leo,* and therein he laid down the doctrine that in Christ Jesus "the properties of each nature and substance were preserved entire, and came together to form one person."[7]

One purpose of the *Tome* was to head off a general council, but Theodosius had already decided that a council should be called. It met at Ephesus on August 1, 449; and Dioscorus, whom the Eutychian party had gathered to itself, presided, as Cyril and Theophilus had done before him. The subsequent proceedings were so scandalous that the council has never lost the name of *Latrocinium* ("Robber Council") with which Leo dubbed it.

For one thing, the *Tome of Leo* was not only not discussed but not read. Important dignitaries had stayed away, and in their stead came fanatical monks from the deserts of Syria. Terrorism, both of

5) Bettenson, *Documents,* p. 68. Bettenson's judgment is a little harsh. Eutyches at least showed himself a man willing to defend what he believed to be the case. If this is "indiscretion," then perhaps, as Lincoln said of Grant's whiskey, we "ought to send some of it to the other generals."
6) Ibid., p. 69.
7) Ibid., p. 70.

body and mind, produced the intended effect. Eutyches was declared orthodox and restored to his rank. The wise and gentle Theodoret was deposed *in absentia*. Flavian was likewise deposed, and was treated so roughly that he died soon thereafter. Hilary, a deacon from Rome, cast the sole negative vote, the one *contradicitur,* and fled for his life.

It was, in some sort, a victory for Dioscorus; it was also his last and the last for Alexandria. Such antics, worthy of ward politicians, could not possibly settle the affairs of an international body like the Church. The results of the *Latrocinium* were largely ignored, and Leo proceeded to arrange, with the new Eastern emperor, Marcian,[8] a further council for the year 451. Nicaea was first chosen as the site, since it was hallowed by a famous and most successful council. But this was inconvenient for the Emperor, and, ultimately, the council met at Chalcedon, in the Church of Saint Euphemia.

It was a lively affair, and it avenged the wrongs inflicted by the *Latrocinium.* Two sessions were given over to the case of Dioscorus, whose behavior at Ephesus had brought down a general odium. He was deprived of his see. His associates likewise suffered, except so far as they earned, by timely recantation, a generous pardon. Three sessions sufficed to determine dogma, and the council declared that the Second Person of the Trinity was

. . . one and the same Christ, Son, Lord, Only-begotten, recognized IN TWO NATURES, WITHOUT CONFUSION, WITHOUT CHANGE, WITHOUT DIVISION, WITHOUT SEPARATION; the distinction of natures being in no way annulled by the union, but rather the characteristics of each nature being preserved and coming together to form one person and subsistence.[9]

The sessions, which had been punctuated with shouts of "throw him out!" "kill him!" and with groans of penitential sorrow, did rather better with doctrine than with the thirty canons it laid down as guide to future policy. For the Twenty-eighth Canon announced, with due solemnity, that the see of Constantinople was thenceforth to be held equal to the see of Rome and supreme over all the other sees in Asia. This result Leo had by no means desired: a New Rome

8) Pulcheria's husband.
9) Bettenson, *Documents,* pp. 72–73. The capitals are at least Bettenson's.

level with the Old Rome. His gains at Chalcedon had been considerable, but they were now matched by the emergence of a new power, contrary and never to be mastered. From then on, neither union nor dominance was possible, but only separation and schism.

Alexandria, which, after two triumphs, had tripped over the third, sank into a state yet more disorganized. Proterius succeeded Dioscorus, but had no flair for popularity. Amid the general distaste, a certain Timothy went by stealth and by night to the bedsides of electors, and "told them, as they lay between sleep and waking, that he was an angel, sent to bid them provide themselves with a bishop and, in particular, to choose Timothy."[1] It was perhaps the first authenticated use of subliminal advertising, and it worked. This Timothy was a Teuton, whose tribal name *Herul* was turned, by satiric anagram, into *Aelurus* ("The Cat"). And so it came to pass that Timothy the Cat, who had perhaps effected the murder of his predecessor, sat upon the throne of Cyril, of Theophilus, and of Athanasius. There he reigned intermittently and, all told, not very long. He was followed by Peter the Stammerer, whose reign and whose wit were briefer still, though he did help Zeno with the *Henoticon.*

The Monophysites had by no means been crushed at Chalcedon. Throughout Asia they recurrently displayed spasms of strength, like waves that never quite disappear. In one of these spasms, Peter the Fuller, Bishop of Antioch, inserted into the *Trisagion* of the Mass (the *Tersanctus,* the *Holy, Holy, Holy*) the scandalous phrase "Who was crucified for us." Since, in the Mass, it is the Lord God of Hosts who is said to be holy, the Father would thus be crucified along with the Son. Peter's emendation threw Christianity back two hundred years into Patripassianism.

But these things vanished with the usurper Basiliscus, who had brought Peter the Fuller to power; and Zeno, the pious, the everworshipful, specifically reprobated, in the *Henoticon,* all such heresies. Yet Zeno's *Henoticon,* a proclamation from the East, effected no more unity than Leo's *Tome,* a proclamation from the West. The new pope, Simplicius, excommunicated Acacius, the Patriarch of Constantinople; and an emissary pinned notification of the fact to Acacius's mantle while he was celebrating Mass. Simplicius was no

1) *Cambridge Medieval History*, Vol. I, p. 513.

respecter of persons: he excommunicated Peter the Fuller and the Emperor Zeno too.

"The alienation of churches," says Alice Gardner, "seems in many cases to be at bottom the alienation of peoples and nations, the religious difference supplying pretext rather than cause."[2] It is very true. And that is why the Christ could, with equal orthodoxy or equal heresy, have one nature in some regions and in others two, though all the while his Church, seeking growth and unity, desired him to have two natures in one person, always and everywhere.

2) Ibid., p. 519.

ON NETS AND FISHES

AUGUSTINE ONCE WROTE a psalm against the Donatists—the heretics whose notion had been that corrupt clerics corrupt the sacraments. In this psalm he called attention to the fact that fishermen, having cast their nets and then drawn in the catch, separate upon the shore the good fish from the bad. The good they put into baskets; the bad they throw back into the sea. Some fish, indeed, thrash so violently that they break through the net. These of course never reach the baskets, and have not the honor to be selected.

Now, let the fish represent all types of human being, the net represent the Church, the shore the end of the age (*saeculi finis*), and the separation the Last Judgment. Then the sea is the world, which rebels delight in; and the baskets are *sedes sanctorum,* the seats of the holy, which rebels will never reach. The analogy is extensive and, like all analogies, treacherous. For clearly the salvation of a fish lies in not being caught—in breaking the net and escaping the ultimate basket. One could erect an argument for heresy upon just this image, with equal worth and perhaps with greater wit.

But there is no need to quarrel with a poet's imagery, even though the poet be a bishop and a controversialist. Let us allow him, instead, to draw his intended moral:

An attentive listener may want to know who those were that broke the net. They were very self-assured people, who claimed to be righteous. In fact, however, they were factionalists, and set altar against altar. They delivered themselves over to the devil when they got into conflict with tradition, and they wanted to attribute their own crime to other people.[1]

They were factionalists and they fought against tradition: that was their crime. But what is tradition, and what can be criminal about fighting it? The answer to these questions was given by a certain Vincent, who wrote a celebrated but much expurgated book some four years after Augustine's death, and who, as it chanced, regarded Augustine himself as heretical.

In the Mediterranean, not far from Cannes, there is a sunny little island called St. Honorat, known in Roman times as Lerinum and later as Lerins or Lérins.[2] On this island there was a monastery, the monks of which, mostly Gallic in origin, maintained a civilized, semi-Pelagian belief in free will and in the persistence of God's image in man. Thither Vincent came, after an unsatisfactory life in secular society.[3] In the charm of that island and the peace of that monastery Vincent proposed to "propitiate God by the sacrifice of Christian humility and thus avoid not only the shipwrecks of the present life, but also the flames of the world to come."[4]

The Council of Ephesus, which had condemned both Nestorian and Pelagian views, was not long ended. Thirty years ahead (how discouraging it would have been to have known it!) lay the venal antics of Peter the Stammerer and Timothy the Cat. The strife among doctrines, which was the strife among factions, did not cease,

---

1) This psalm will be found excerpted in *The Oxford Book of Medieval Latin Verse*, edited by F. J. E. Raby, C.B. (Oxford: Oxford University Press; 1959), § 23. My translation. The relevant text is:

> *Bonus auditor fortasse quaerit, qui ruperunt rete.*
> *homines multum superbi, qui iustos se dicunt esse.*
> *sic fecerunt et scissuram et altare contra altare.*
> *diabolo se tradiderunt, cum pugnant de traditione*
> *et crimen quod commiserunt in alios volunt transferre.*

2) Scholars sometimes use the accent and sometimes not. Presumably the pronunciation varies accordingly. The present name, St. Honorat, derives from Honoratus, Bishop of Arles, who founded the monastery on Lerinum.
3) He has a telling phrase for it: ... *"tristibus saecularis militiae turbinibus"*— "in the sad, whirling confusions of secular strife." *Commonitorium*, Chapter I.
4) Ibid. The translation is by Rudolph E. Morris, J.U.D., *Fathers of the Church* (New York: Fathers of the Church, Inc.; 1949), Vol. 7, p. 268.

because the factions themselves were not seriously weakened. Successive compromises at successive councils fell apart and required later compromises at later councils. It was time for a man to sit down in peace and seclusion to inquire, What after all *is* orthodoxy?

Vincent's purpose was to get beyond the strife of factions, to come at the meaning of the term as that meaning must indubitably be. In this he succeeded wonderfully well; he had a magisterial grasp of the relevant sociology. The result, indeed, is rather too illuminating, for it brings into broad daylight the connection between orthodoxy and organizational success. When you have read Vincent, you know all that needs knowing about the puzzling questions why some doctrines win praise and others defamation, some thinkers earn reward and others punishment.

Vincent wrote his book probably in the year 434. Its full title is sufficiently revealing: *Commonitorium adversus profanas omnium haereticorum novitates,* "A Warning against the Profane Innovations of All Heretics." The word "innovations" (*novitates*) is very striking: it suggests an alarm at new doctrines just because they are new.[5] Yet such is the irony of historical circumstances that the *Commonitorium* itself exists only in truncated form, the missing parts having apparently been excised and destroyed. Were they destroyed as dangerous? It seems very probable. For there is an orthodox view of what orthodoxy is, and Vincent, more bent on truth than on accommodation, may have exceeded the limits.

But no matter: he tells us enough and to spare. The problem was how to distinguish "the truth of the Catholic faith from the falsity of heretical corruption."[6] This problem had troubled him a long time. He had, as a layman, appealed to certain ecclesiastical leaders, whose advice was to judge by the divine law and the Church's tradition.

The answer had been impressive but not quite satisfactory. The divine law was set forth in Scripture, and it was surely adequate. Why did there need to be tradition—"the authority," as Vincent said, "of ecclesiastical interpretation"? Well, the fact was that, al-

---

5) Contrast this with the present fact that, in American advertising, "new" is nearly synonymous with "good" (e.g., "Get *new* Lifebuoy"). In the ancient world nothing whatever could have been sold under such a slogan. On the contrary, you would have had to say that the commodity in question had been used in the Garden of Eden.

6) *Commonitorium,* Chapter II. Morris, p. 269.

though the text of Scripture was perfectly public, it seemed to yield as many meanings as there were readers. Arius could appeal to it as well as Athanasius, Pelagius as well as Augustine. There had therefore to be a canon of scriptural interpretation along with the canon of scriptural text, so that the believing Christian might be assured which of the various suggested meanings he was to believe.

Now, a canon is, of course, a rule of procedure, and all such rules need not only their own content but some guarantee of their own validity. What then is the rule, or canon, which distinguishes those doctrines which a Christian believes, by virtue of being a Christian, from those other doctrines which, by virtue of being a Christian, he is to disbelieve? And what would be the ground of such a rule, the source and origin of its validity?

Vincent's answer deserves the celebrity which has attended it. "In the catholic Church itself," he said, "we take the greatest care to hold that which has been believed everywhere, always, and by all."[7] Or, turning these adverbs into nouns, we can say that the content of Christian belief is properly determined by "universality, antiquity, and consent." The adverbs, perhaps, are rather clearer. At any rate, if it can be said of a doctrine that Christians in all parts of the world have believed it, that in all times they have believed it, and that every one of them has believed it, then that doctrine, Vincent persuasively suggests, must be in fact part of the Christian faith. Sociologically speaking, the conclusion is irresistible. So far as an organization can be defined by its ideology, this is precisely the kind of definition there would have to be.

But, as a matter of historical fact, are there really any doctrines which all Christians, in all times and places, have believed? The proliferation of dissent, the hurrying of bishops from council to council, the riot of mobs and the imprecations of adversaries, make this very doubtful. Indeed, a cynic might be led to feel that struggle, bribery, and coercion were more nearly *ubique, semper, et ab omnibus*. There was more purity of belief before the Church had political power, but there was not more unity. As for the Apostles, Paul's own letters record how little they agreed. And the disciples, the most

---

7) Ibid., Chapter II. Bettenson's translation, *Documents*, p. 118. Let us give the original of this famous passage: *In ipsa item catholica ecclesia magnopere curandum est, ut id teneamus, quod ubique, quod semper, quod ab omnibus creditum est.*

primitive Christians of all? Well, the Gospel narratives (which we have suspected of error on this point)[8] assert that the disciples, so far from agreeing on the Master's doctrine, understood very little of it.

Vincent was well aware of this problem—as how should he not be in the year 434? His solution was that, whenever any of the three criteria is rendered doubtful in application, the others are to be employed. Thus, if some new doctrine makes inroads upon general consent (the *quod ab omnibus*), the doctrine can still be tested against antiquity. This happened, Vincent thinks, with the Donatist heresy, which won a good deal of support in its own time but was found contrary to the old established view of the case.

Or again, if antiquity itself is found to have been divided on a certain question, one can confidently employ the decrees of General Councils, which, since they officially represented the whole Church, supply the criterion of universality (the *quod ubique*). This was, specifically, the ground for rejecting Arianism. Lastly, if we remain in doubt about the "always" and the "everywhere," we can still cleave to that doctrine which is most likely to elicit present consent. Vincent thought, not quite accurately, that this criterion had sufficed to dispose of Nestorius.

But what if all three criteria chance to leave the result in doubt? Vincent, who very honorably faced up to all contingencies, had a further answer here—an answer, to be sure, somewhat pragmatic and improvisational. In such a case, he said, it will be necessary to consult and compare the writings of the Fathers, "teachers approved and outstanding,"[9] whose membership in the Church was continuous and unimpeached. Beyond all this it was scarcely possible to go. For Vincent had no trust whatever in the validity of private insight. Private insight, personal inspiration, is the very opposite of anything organizational; it can no more constitute orthodoxy than anarchy can constitute order.

I I

Such is the main content of the *Commonitorium*. Let us now see what it has to teach us concerning the sociology of belief.

8) *Supra,* Chapter 3.
9) . . . *qui* . . . *magistri probabiles extiterunt,* "men who have stood out as approved teachers." *Commonitorium,* Chapter III. Bettenson's translation in the main text, *Documents,* p. 119.

Vincent's criteria appeal, not to facts, but to persons; they claim their validity, not from any correspondence with reality, but from an agreement with certain human opinions. The opinions, to be sure, are made credible by being, or being thought to be, authoritative— that is to say, they are those of unanimity, or of long standing, or of men with enormous prestige. Vincent has nowhere any appeal to the rules of scientific method, as these have been refined from Plato's day to the present.

Now, the whole point of scientific method is to get beyond human opinion, because, to the extent that one gets beyond human opinion, one gets beyond error. If a scientist wants to know, say, the physiological behavior of a cell's surrounding wall, he sets up experiments, with appropriate apparatus, such as will (he hopes) cause that behavior to be evident. The findings of previous investigators are of course useful, but our scientist wouldn't think of basing himself on his predecessors alone. Indeed, if truth could be determined by authority only, we could get along with libraries and we wouldn't need laboratories at all.

It is quite clear why science is and must be non-authoritarian. Men live in the world, and observe it, and describe it as best they can. Meanwhile the world goes on being just what it is. If any description happens to state what actually is the case, then that description can be said to be true: it "corresponds," as the saying is, with reality. But in order to know that the description corresponds, we have to look at reality as well as the description. And when we look at reality, we are by no means looking at some authority's description of reality. Hence, to the essential act authority is irrelevant.

Accordingly, if you want really to know whether the Godhead is triune, or whether the Christ is God-Man, you can't merely look into Scripture; you must look at the phenomenon itself. But, alas, "looking" is precisely what you cannot do with these phenomena. No eyes can see them; no senses can grasp them; no instruments can bring them within reach. They remain as *possible* explanations of observed events, but no experiment can test whether such explanations really explain. This state of affairs holds not only for Christian theology —or Mohammedan or Buddhist—but for all ideologies whatever that deal with things supernatural.

The supernatural, being "above" or "beyond" nature, is a world that science simply cannot get at. Probably its contents are imaginative projections of needs, hopes, wishes in the natural world, which science really can get at. But, except as such a projection, supernature remains impenetrable. Scientific criteria of truth and falsity will not even enable us to know whether there is such a world, though they strongly suggest that a world to which they cannot apply is a world which itself cannot exist.

This peculiar detachment of the supernatural from anything we would ordinarily describe as knowledge probably explains why scientists are more concerned with truth than with tradition, and theologians more concerned with tradition than with truth. No doubt in either area the truth of a sentence will seem to depend on whether or not the sentence corresponds with reality. But since supernatural reality (if there is any) never gets directly perceived,[1] and since thus comparison fails, tradition or authority or general consent tend to replace correspondence as the test of truth. Accordingly, Vincent's criteria suit the supernatural order as aptly as scientific method suits the natural order.

It is one of the blessings of life, and also an evidence of our rationality, that when we believe, we feel it necessary to have grounds for our belief. We do not make belief a matter of accident or whim. There have been, to be sure, various rebels who proclaimed their private insight as being true and as being their own; but even these judge the insight by its intensity, and hence have a criterion and a ground. The consequence has been that as beliefs come to be disputed, so also do the grounds of belief. The solidity of grounds and the validity of criteria thus constitute, to the present day, the chief problems of philosophy.

Very well: we can see why Vincent's criteria had to be, as a matter of theory, the criteria they were. It is useless to complain that he did not give us a discourse on scientific method in an area to which scientific method is irrelevant. On the contrary, we can learn a great deal from the fact that the criteria he did use, the scientific being set aside, were one and all organizational. For what importance do universality, antiquity, and consent have except as they define the long life, the unity, and the prosperity of an organization? Why should anyone surrender his own view before other views held "everywhere, always, and by all," unless he thinks that peace within

1) Mystics would say that they directly perceive such a reality, but I think they are mistaken about this—and so, for that matter, do the Churches.

the organization deserves to prevail over private dissent? Thus orthodoxy is that corpus of beliefs which will unite the most members for the longest time and consequently make the organization formidable against antagonists.

That this was Vincent's notion, every page of the *Commonitorium* makes plain. His praise of the confessors of the Church turns on their having defended the old tradition, "not as regards a particular group but as regards the whole body."[2] More remarkably yet, he cites the fact that Cyprian, whose view on the rebaptism of heretics did not prevail, continued to be regarded as a member in good standing, while later men who held the identical view were pronounced heretical.[3] And the reason was that Cyprian, though in disagreement, was never schismatical, but remained amicably in communion with his opponents. Thus heresy is not mere disagreement; it is, rather, active dissent "tending toward schism."[4]

The line between disagreement and schismatical dissent is not easy to draw, and Vincent comes near to thinking that any new notion is heretical just because, being new, it is strange to canonical doctrine. "Antiquity was retained," he said of the rebaptismal controversy, "novelty, repulsed."[5] Over and over he charges heretics with introducing new ideas, although some at least of these "new" ideas were in fact as old as Christianity itself. It is the backward gaze that Vincent trusts to, the look toward the past, in which loom the mighty Fathers, and, behind them, the yet mightier Apostles, and, behind them, the Messiah and Redeemer himself. The only allowable novelty will be a reworking of the tradition in more contemporary terms:

The Church of Christ, zealous and cautious guardian of the dogmas deposited with it, never changes any phase of them. It does not diminish them or add to them; it neither gives up its own nor usurps what does not belong to it. But it devotes all its diligence to one aim: to treat tradition faithfully and wisely; to nurse

---

2) *Commonitorium*, Chapter V: . . . *non partis alicuius sed universitatis* (my translation). The "confessors" were those men who had most forcefully attested their faith in Christian doctrine.

3) Ibid., Chapter VI. See *supra*, Chapter 4.

4) Most dictionaries, quite correctly, include this phrase in their definitions of the word "heresy."

5) *Commonitorium*, Chapter VI: *Retenta est scilicet antiquitas, explosa novitas.*

and polish what from old times may have remained unshaped and unfinished; to consolidate and strengthen what already was clear and plain; and to guard what already was confirmed and defined.[6]

This posture is the stance of an organization, in a competitive environment, defending itself.

But the thing that most reveals the connection between orthodoxy and organizational politics is the assumption, never proved nor even attempted to be proved, that heresy issues from malicious intent. There is never the smallest admission that the heretic may honestly believe what he is saying and may honestly desire, in saying it, to promote the welfare of the organization. On the contrary, the heretic is said to be a man of pride and malice—a wolf among sheep, a serpent in the garden, Satan's secret emissary upon earth.

Such epithets will be found *passim* throughout the *Commonitorium,* but they are by no means confined to that work. They teem of course in controversial writing, and they appear by no means infrequently in the encyclicals of popes. For example, in 1758, the French philosopher Helvétius was horrified to find himself described, in a bull of Clement XIII, as doing Satan's work and as opening "the broadest possible path to lead souls to perdition."[7] And advanced thinkers of 1870 were, according to Pius IX in the encyclical *Quanta Cura,* "evil men, who . . . endeavored by their fallacious opinions and most wicked writings to subvert the foundations of Religion and of Civil Society, to remove from our midst all virtue and justice, to deprave the hearts and minds of all,"[8] and so on and so on.

All such abuse is organization talk. It has nothing to do with describing the heretic accurately. Its intent is to cut him off from his fellow members, and thus to prepare their approval of penalties later to be imposed. If the heresy is in fact defeated, the opprobrious description may remain for a long time the standard view of affairs. Whether the disputed subjects be religious or secular, such has been the mode of struggle among factions and organizations, from a time long before the Apostles and the Fathers, down through Trotsky

6) Ibid., Chapter XXIII. Morris's translation, p. 312.
7) My translation, from a printed copy of the original bull.
8) Fremantle, *The Papal Encyclicals,* p. 136.

and Stalin and Khrushchev. Orthodoxy is sometimes merely the view of the winning side; heresy, that of the defeated.

These last observations are not quite Vincent's, but he gives the hints for them. It is perhaps not too much to say that he is as basic to the science of orthodoxy as Darwin is to evolution. He defined all relations between the nets and the fishes, and it is pleasant to know that he has been made a saint.

CHAPTER
7

The Little Foxes
That Spoil the Vines

Sometime about the year 1140, when Abelard was condemned at the Council of Sens, Peter the Venerable, Abbot of Cluny, wrote to Bernard of Clairvaux these following few and devastating words: "You perform all the difficult religious duties: you fast, you watch, you suffer; but you will not endure the easy ones—you do not love."[1]

Ease of duty depends upon the doer. Peter, the most amiable man of his time, found loving easy; Bernard, a less amiable man, found it hard. Yet Bernard loved nevertheless, and even wrote a book about it, the *De Diligendo Deo*. He loved as administrators love—that is to say, he loved the organization, which in this instance was the Church. And organizational love, as it appears in administrators, has the singular property that, in proportion as the whole body is cherished, the individual member is suspect of fault.

Bernard's organizational love worked many wonders. It has been observed, for example, that from the large group of his disciples there issued, in time, one pope, six cardinals, and thirty bishops.[2]

1) *Non vis levia ferre, ut diligas.* The translation is Henry Adams's, *Mont Saint Michel and Chartres,* Chapter XIV.
2) *The Age of Belief,* edited by Anne Fremantle (New York: Mentor Books; 1954), p. 101. Bernard's great rival, Abelard, produced one pope, nineteen cardinals, and more than fifty bishops. Pierre Gaxotte, *Histoire des Français* (Paris: Flammarion; 1957), p. 152.

In one of the recurrent papal schisms, 1130–1138, he effectively sustained Innocent II against the "anti-pope" Anacletus II, whose father had been a banker in Rome, and whose election had been singularly corrupt. In 1145, Bernard, at the request of Pope Eugenius III, began preaching the Second Crusade, which, undertaken two years later, achieved even less than the First Crusade had done.

Altogether, Bernard was a leader—and of an austere, devoted sort. The purity of his faith, his purpose, his morals was ever unimpeached and unimpeachable. That emaciated man, with the flashing dark eyes and the stupendous eloquence, moved serfs as well as lords, parsons as well as prelates. His abbey at Clairvaux, austerely disciplined, stood forth in steadfast rebuke of the wildness of some monastics, the laxity of others. And if, as Peter the Venerable said, he did not know how to love, he nevertheless (in my view at least) solved the vexed problem of free will, by postulating in the human will a spontaneity that could cooperate with the spontaneity of divine grace.[3]

Although, as he thought, the human will had spontaneity, Bernard did not always, or even often, approve the ends toward which the spontaneous wills around him visibly exerted themselves. In an administrative view, there is no spontaneity so striking as the effort of members to do what the organization forbids. The Church asked devotion, and carelessness was everywhere. The Church asked self-discipline, and self-indulgence was everywhere. The Church asked faith, and everywhere there was disputation. Particularly there was disputation wherever Abelard was. It was perhaps unfair of history to confront Bernard with the beginnings of a renaissance.

A renaissance, indeed, it may be properly called, though it was not of course *the* Renaissance. Between Vincent's time and Bernard's there had passed some seven centuries of wrath, disintegration, and decline. The schism between East and West, both in Church and Empire, grew permanent. Mohammedanism spread over Asia Minor, North Africa, and Spain, bringing much culture with it but also destroying much. The old, pleasant Gallic civilization sank toward barbarism under Merovingian kings. The Bishops of Rome clung

3) ". . . consent is spontaneous assent of the will. . . . The will can no more be deprived of its freedom than it can be deprived of itself." *De Gratia et Libero Arbitrio,* translated by Watkin Williams and excerpted in Anne Fremantle, *The Age of Belief,* pp. 104–05.

desperately to the chief remaining see in western Christendom. Even Charlemagne's enormous organizing skill gave dubious strength to the Papacy and to that Holy Roman Empire which was, in Bryce's famous phrase, "neither holy nor Roman nor an empire."

Those were the Dark Ages, when builders ransacked the ruins of antiquity for architectural materials they no longer knew how to construct. It is now fashionable to say that the Dark Ages were not dark and that the name is a libel set upon them by the modernizing zeal of later times. This view, like most other views of history, can be supported by evidence: certainly the mosaics at Ravenna (sixth-century works) are sufficiently astonishing, and men of the ninth century like Alcuin and that lovely philosophical intellect John the Scot would have adorned any epoch. Yet if the Dark Ages were not dark, they were also not very bright. It is difficult to imagine that any modern man, however romantic, would wish to go back to *them*.

A good many people, however, have wished to go back to the twelfth century, because the things you would lose in so doing can seem less important than the things you would gain. You would lose much science and technology, of course; but the sea of ignorance and violence into which you would fall is perhaps not worse than the sea of knowledge and violence in which you now swim. By way of compensation, you would share in Abelard's disputes, where every received idea got turned into its contrary; you would be ravished with Bernard's eloquence; you would sing Adam of Saint Victor's enchanting hymns; you would glitter, it might be, in the courts of love; and, best of all, you would watch Our Lady's crown rise stone by stone at Chartres, with those windows and that glass, that glass! And if you survived into the thirteenth century, you would perhaps know Saint Francis of Assisi, a spirit amorous of all created beings, the adorable pure summation of the age.

Feudalism was then not new, and, as we are aware, can be traced to Diocletian. Yet its flowering was a new fact. Arrived at by a series of subtle transitions from slave society, feudalism for a time adequately answered two questions: how to get the soil tilled, and how to protect the tillers. A great lord, perhaps a king, was the ultimate owner of the land, which he administered through an hierarchy of subtenants founded on a base of farming serfs, who generally owned nothing and labored over everything. What the lord owed his inferiors was protection. What the inferiors owed the lord was obedience. What the serfs owed everyone else was a large, fixed portion of the products of their labor. It will be seen that the lord had the better of these arrangements; the inequality indeed always disturbed and at last unhinged the feudal system.

Nevertheless, as a system, feudalism had certain graces which commercial society has never been able to supply. Chief of these was the sense it gave its members of belonging to the whole and of performing a useful function—indeed, an appointed function—within it. You could know almost *a priori,* and in any case you could infer from status of birth, what your function was to be, and you could know that your function, whether or not brilliant, was essential. According to John of Salisbury,[4] the husbandmen were the feet of the body politic—nearest the ground and needing guidance, but essential alike to movement and repose. Medieval society had many miseries, but "alienation" was not one of them.

Thus the little feudal structures were well composed within, however anarchic they might be toward one another. No doubt they were in fact not all the things they claimed to be in law: they had not all the unity which their favorite comparison with organic bodies would suggest. But medieval man felt the universe to be friendly as a family is friendly—to be, that is to say, a moral as well as a material order, in which the inevitable righting of wrongs and punishing of vices seldom entailed total rejection of the evildoer. You had to commit treason to the cosmos before you were definitively cast out. Dante's three ultimate scoundrels, in the iciest depths of hell, each chewed eternally by a separate Satanic mouth, were not thieves or whoremongers or even tyrants; they were traitors.

Another medieval trait, which certainly had its disadvantages, was a general indistinction between matters of poetry and matters of fact. One must understand that when John of Salisbury described husbandmen as the feet of the body politic, he thought there really was such a body with precisely such feet. After the same manner, the assertion that the Church is the body of Christ was intended quite literally. The assertion is still made, but now it can scarcely be entertained even as poetry. In that remarkable blend of science and imagination which was the medieval mind, all powers, yearnings, ideals grew personified in beings celestial or demoniac, and these personages were every man's familiar companions.

This fusion of fact with poetry around the concept of a friendly

4) In the *Policraticus.* See the excerpt in *The Portable Medieval Reader,* pp. 47–48.

universe came near to throwing European Christendom into heresy. I think, indeed, that it did so throw it, and that the event, at once so awful and so enchanting, was simply never named. For over twelfth-century Europe there presided the loveliest personage that super-nature has ever known: Our Lady, the Virgin, Saint Cyril's *Theotókos* grown fully sublime. "Don't make the Virgin a goddess!" Nestorius had cried in his contest with Cyril. Yet how could one not, especially when the way one felt about her was the way one felt about the cosmos? A God-bearer, she was superior to the Trinity as mother is to child, as creator to creature, as cause to event. Surely she was the ultimate object of adoration—the more surely so, indeed, because she in her turn would love the adorer. This was why the guilds of furriers, glaziers, and other craftsmen gave her those jewels which shine undimmed at Chartres, and this was what they wanted to say.

It was also what Adam many times sang, among the mystics at Saint Victor:

> *Salve, mater salvatoris,*
> *vas electum, vas honoris,*
> *vas caelestis gratiae;*
> *ab aeterno vas provisum*
> *vas insigne, vas excisum*
> *manu sapientiae.*[5]

Adam intended more than to show how many metaphors there can be for a womb. He had his eye on the importance of *origin*. The story is that, as Adam wrote these lines, the Virgin appeared smil-ingly before him and bowed acknowledgement.

Such were the two great mysticisms of the twelfth century: at Saint Victor, the calm adoration of a gracious universe; at Clairvaux, the militant, disciplined devotion to a ruling Church. But mysticism

---

5) *The Oxford Book of Medieval Latin Verse,* § 163. This is singularly hard to render, but the following version, which is my own, will give a little of the meaning and the melody:

> Greet we now the Savior's mother,
> Chosen vessel and of honor,
> Vessel of the heaven's grace;
> From eternity forethought us,
> By the hand of wisdom wrought us,
> Vessel of our risen race.

by itself does not ordinarily make a renaissance; there needs also to be a soaring of the speculative reason. This soaring—or, at any rate, a flitting—we may observe in the swift, tormented intellect of Abelard.

Abelard was not the earliest of the scholastics—an honor usually reserved for his first teacher, Roscelin. But Abelard was a gadfly in the Socratic style, and he stung so deeply the medieval mind that for two centuries thereafter, all the way through Duns Scotus and William of Ockham, the schoolmen labored to give a reasoned, encyclopedic exposition of the Christian faith.

If the founder of psychoanalysis, Sigmund Freud, had wished one single case on which to ground his theories, Abelard would have sufficiently served. It is not often, I fancy, that so much of a man's lifelong activity can be attributed to rivalry with the father, suppressed sexuality toward the mother, and an undercurrent of guilts attending both. This brilliant, passionate man, talented and eager to display his talents, lived in a society that liked to limit the talents it admired. In the end, after physical and spiritual wanderings so various that they may well be called picaresque, he died in faithful communion with the Church and even in some faint odor of sanctity. He typified the intellectual, familiar enough to us now, who knows how much the organization limits him, but who cannot bear to give up membership. That is to say, he had enough of the heretic in him to tinker with doctrine, but not enough to fight for corrections. And so he ended by being no heretic at all.

Nevertheless, few celebrities have contrived to be so fascinating or to endow themselves with such permanent historical life. The twelfth century has not left abundant personal records of its famous men, but of Abelard there remain the autobiography and the correspondence with Héloïse. The autobiography, irresistibly entitled *Historia Calamitatum,* is persuasive without being altogether credible; and the letters—well, they have produced an entire literature and have even called forth amorous couplets from Alexander Pope.

Abelard's father was a formidable, though doubtless unintending, rival. A knight of the minor nobility, with a chateau in Brittany near Nantes, he desired his sons to learn letters before they learned arms. This pedagogy was an instant success with Abelard, who gave up his rights as eldest son and set himself to conquer the whole realm of intellect as that realm then was. Nominalism,[6] which he learned from Roscelin, equipped him with destructive weapons for the war of words, and with these weapons he went on to assault his later teachers.

It seems improbable that very many professors would now accept to teach under conditions which prevailed in the twelfth century. In those days if you felt a vocation to instruct the youth you set up at an intellectual center (say, Paris), satisfied certain requirements, announced a series of lectures on such and such a subject, and hoped for an audience. The audience, if it came, would listen and then dispute with you, and the chances were that it came less to listen than to dispute. You had the constant risk of being overturned in argument by an upstart but brilliant pupil. When you encountered one of these, you were truly caught. You could not, without disgrace, retreat from further trials; yet further trials might bring only further defeats.

Perhaps we had better say what the word "defeat" would mean in a context like this. It would not necessarily mean that you were found to be mistaken; it would only mean that something you said in one part of your lecture was discovered to *seem* to contradict something you said in another part or something the bright pupil induced you to say during the question period. Now, since the world itself is full of contrariety, any faithful description of the world will be full of contrariety too. Hence, the more honest your intention and the more accurate your account, the more exposed you are to the charge of self-contradiction. The bright pupil has a signal advantage, which he seldom fails to exploit.

Abelard was the brightest of bright pupils, and, at the age of twenty, swept through his master William of Champeaux as a whirlwind scatters chaff and grain indiscriminately around. He did not do much damage to William's theoretical position, which has in fact remained indestructible; but William himself collapsed under the pressure. After further years of rivalry, not as between teacher and pupil but as between competing lecturers, William withdrew into a monastery, and Abelard was left, triumphant and full of discourse, upon the Mont Sainte Geneviève.

6) Generally speaking (which in fact no nominalist can do), this philosophy asserts that individual things are real but that classes and systems are "abstractions" or even merely names (*nomina*). Thus, for example, your pet dog is real, but dogs in general (i.e., the class of dogs) is not.

It was now the year 1117. There was a canon of Notre Dame named Fulbert, whose niece, aged seventeen, was already renowned for learning and for beauty. She knew Greek and Latin and theology, but she was by no means a *précieuse*. Abelard, at forty, had survived (it appears) untouched the blandishments of aristocratic ladies and bourgeois matrons, who, in his Parisian environment, were particularly light and charming. He determined, as he tells us,[7] having philosophically reviewed the general nature of sexual attraction, to make the niece his pupil first and then his mistress. "I thought I could easily do it," he said: *me id facillime credidi posse.*

He was never more right. Fulbert, vain though jealous, was delighted to have as tutor to his niece the premier intellectual of the age. Abelard came to live in Fulbert's house, and there, night and day, he instructed Héloïse and himself too in more things than are theological, though not more than are philosophical. Amid these varied ecstasies the pupil, who acquired everything without difficulty, conceived and bore, in secret solitude, their son Astrolabe. There followed a secret marriage, which, like the secret birth, was very generally known. Then Fulbert, his dim wit further dimmed by scandal, visited upon Abelard a revenge such as other men too have wished for their successful rivals. At his urging, certain "kinsmen" fell upon Abelard in sleep and did to him what, nine centuries before, the learned Origen, misunderstanding Matthew 19: 12,[8] had done to himself.

There was general horror, in which Abelard shared. Two of the perpetrators, being caught, were similarly mutilated—and blinded to boot. Yet Abelard, whose ample feelings of guilt were somewhat eased by suffering, was ready to accept certain blessings in disguise. He would henceforth have Origen's serenity without having committed Origen's crime; moreover, the dreadful event having occurred in sleep, there had been little pain.[9] He would retire into the

7) *Historia Calamitatum,* 4b: *Hanc igitur, omnibus circunspectis que amantes allicere solent, commodiorem censui in amorem mihi copulare, et me id facillime credidi posse.* Henry Adams Bellows translates thus: "It was this young girl whom I, after carefully considering all those qualities which are wont to attract lovers, determined to unite with myself in the bonds of love, and indeed the thing seemed to me very easy to be done."

8) ". . . and there be eunuchs, which have made themselves eunuchs for the kingdom of heaven's sake." AV.

9) *Historia,* 15d.

monastery at Saint Denis, whilst Héloïse pursued a cloistered life among the Benedictines at Argenteuil.

At Saint Denis, from the very first, things went badly. The implacable logician, who had driven William to cover and had overturned that "barren fig-tree" Anselm of Laon,[1] fell upon the monks like a hawk on field mice. He denounced them for laziness and immorality, and went on to prove that their Saint Denis had by no means been the Dionysius whom Paul was thought to have converted on the Athenian Areopagus. It of course availed nothing that all these allegations were perfectly true.

The inevitable break came. In 1122, Abelard sought isolation and obtained it. In the environs of Nogent-sur-Seine he built with his own hands a hut of reeds, where he might settle down to solitary meditation. But a man like Abelard is seldom left alone. Disciples thronged to him, built their own huts, and discovered, as M. de Gandillac says, "the combined delights of solitude and vegetarianism."[2] At length it became necessary to build an oratory of durable stone. Much consoled by the number of disciples, Abelard dedicated his oratory to the spirit itself of consolation, the Holy Ghost, the Paraclete. Hither, in 1128, when he had already abandoned the place for some years, he brought Héloïse with all her nuns, and gave it them in perpetuity. The faithful wife, the immortal mistress, received at last some measure of reward. She had never ceased loving Abelard; she had never withdrawn the gift of herself. Other men have other men as rivals. Abelard, it seems somehow fitting to say, had in his lady's affections no other rival but God.

A life like Abelard's can make scandals, but it does not necessarily make heretics. To discover Abelard's flirtation with heresy we must look at certain of his doctrines; and, first of all, we must touch upon a very thorny problem, which has never been thornier than in the dense and prickly language of the scholastics. This is the problem of universals.

If we consult our immediate experience, we are vividly aware of objects that seem unmistakably individual and not to be confused

---

1) Ibid., 3a: . . . *ficulneam cui maledixit Dominus.* This Anselm is not to be confused with the great Anselm of Canterbury, inventor of the "ontological argument" for the existence of God.

2) *Oeuvres choisies d'Abélard,* textes présentés et traduits par Maurice de Gandillac (Paris: Aubier; 1945), p. 16.

with any other objects. We have this particular father or mother, this particular brother or sister, this particular husband or wife, this particular suit or dress, this particular pair of gloves, and so on. Yet words like "father," "mother," "suit," "dress" are by themselves so general in import that we have to add the adjectival phrase "this particular" in order to restrict the meaning to one object and one alone. Presumably this is because only one person can be this particular husband or this particular wife, whereas a great many people can be wives or husbands.

Further, it seems that whenever people are husbands or wives, they are so in precisely the same respect. If you say that the Duke of Edinburgh is the husband of Elizabeth II and that President Kennedy is the husband of Jacqueline Bouvier Kennedy, you surely mean that the relation between the members of each pair is one and the same. It is, in fact, the relation of being married, and that relation is general in the sense that it can occur in an indefinite number of instances.

It seems quite clear that particulars are somehow or other imbedded in universals, and that universals are somehow or other revealed in particulars. Yet, after twenty-five centuries of speculation, there is still no account of the relationship so satisfactory as to have defeated all rival accounts. One difficulty is linguistic: we don't yet have the vocabulary for a solution, and, as you see, I was driven to use metaphors like "imbedded" and "revealed." Another difficulty is that science, although it begins with the exploration of particulars, indubitably ends in the proclamation of universals: somewhere in the course of its activity it somehow negates its origin.

If what impresses you is the result of science, you will (like Plato) regard universals as more important and perhaps also as more real. If what impresses you is science grappling with facts, then (like Aristotle) you may regard particulars as more important and perhaps also as more real. Plainly, it is possible to regard both as equally real and equally important, but it is surprising how few thinkers have been able to maintain the equilibrium.

In medieval times, the views upon this question ranged from extreme to extreme.[3] Extreme realists ("realist" signified anyone

3) Nowadays they do not. No extreme realists will be found, though there are moderate realists. But there are plenty of extreme nominalists (the semantics people, for example), and they have a good deal of prestige.

who believed in the objective reality of universals) held that universals existed from eternity as patterns in the mind of God: *universalia ante res,* as the Latin tag had it. Extreme nominalists held that universals were hardly even names, but mere sounds, mere exhalations of breath: *universalia post res.* In between, there was the view of universals as existing "in" things: *universalia in rebus.* But this view, though very sensible, was one you tended to slide away from in either of the two directions.

Consider, now, the effect of these philosophies upon the notion of the Trinity, the three Persons in one Person. From extreme realism, the doctrine that the universal is more real than the particular, it would follow that, in God, oneness is more real than threeness. In other words, realism led straight to unitarianism, and the ghost of Arius walked again. More than that, realism tended to cancel out the distinction between God and the world, and thus proceeded, alarmingly, toward pantheism. It was precisely these implications that Abelard had used against William of Champeaux. What extinguished William was not so much Abelard's logic as the fear of his own conclusions.

On the other hand, nominalism led no less straight toward heresy. If particulars are more real than universals, then the three Persons are more real than the one God. In that event there are three Gods really—a kind of polytheism—and the ghost of Sabellius walks again. William seems not to have used this argument against Abelard, but the point did not escape Bernard of Clairvaux. In the bill of particulars which confronted Abelard at the Council of Sens, the very first item charged him with having said that "the Father has perfect power, the Son a certain amount, and the Holy Ghost none at all."[4] This differentiation among the Persons of the Godhead in respect of their efficacy is just the sort of result that nominalism yields. Abelard seems never to have said exactly this, but the Church is always sensitive to possible implications in a general philosophical view.

Evidently the trinitarian doctrine can be maintained only upon an assumption of *universalia in rebus,* such as will assert that universals and particulars are equally real and that their union is of the most intimate sort. It is interesting to note that, if this intimateness is to be fully expressed, Aristotelian logic (and, with it, most modern logic)

4) De Gandillac, op. cit., p. 333.

will have to be abandoned and dialectical logic put in its place. But if this is done, then there will be the risk of Hegelian pantheism on the one hand or of Marxist materialism on the other. One sees why it is sometimes necessary to prefer faith to reason.

Nominalism is a tremendous intellectual disintegrator, and will unglue anything. It thus has the curious effect, not of solving problems, but of making them disappear. For part of any problem whatever consists in identifying certain elements as elements and then in seeing how they are related to a whole. But if there are no wholes, the elements cannot be related; and then, strangely but inevitably, the elements themselves begin to vanish from sight. The trend of Abelard's nominalism, as he himself came to observe with some horror,[5] would have sloughed off not only the unitary God but the three Persons as well.

More than all this, however, the Church faintly but correctly discerned the prophecy of a new epoch, in which men would frankly concern themselves more with things temporal than with things eternal, in which they would trust to scientific method and let authority announce itself unheard. For nominalism, despite its incompetence to explain, does, as we have said, direct attention to the place where science starts; and in that place, which is immediate sense experience, there are simply no supernatural agents to be found.

The individualism that inspires nominalist logic inspired also Abelard's view of ethics. His chief work on this subject was significantly entitled *Scito Teipsum* ("Know Thyself"), and in it he asserted that "what makes an action good is good intention."[6] Accordingly, sin lies in "consenting to do evil." This view is very arguable and has much nobility, but it leaves us short of knowing what we are to think of actions that, though excellently motivated, have disastrous consequences. What, for example, of the crucifixion of Jesus? A case can be made (and Abelard makes it) for innocent

5) E.g., in his "Profession of Faith," when under attack at Sens: "It has been maliciously said that I have written, 'The Father has complete power, the Son a certain degree of power, and the Holy Ghost no power at all.' Such words are more diabolical than heretical. I am in full conformity with justice in detesting them, abhorring them, condemning them as I would condemn anyone who wrote them. If perchance they can be found in my writings, then I admit I am indeed a favorer of heresy." Ibid., p. 336. My translation.

6) Ibid., p. 164. The next quotation is from page 167.

ignorance in the Romans and Jews who committed that crime: "their ignorance exculpated them from any fault."[7] Abelard thinks, indeed, that this was Jesus' meaning in the celebrated pardon, "Father, forgive them, for they know not what they do."

The Church, however, was not inclined to be so indulgent toward the murderers of its Founder. So great a crime seemed to cover the perpetrators with guilt, however ignorant (and to that extent innocent) they might have been. And if a man were to be so generous toward the murderers of the Founder, what would he be like to be toward temporary and contemporary enemies of the Church? Such a man might say that Moslems were innocent because ignorant—Waldensian heretics likewise, and Albigensian, and . . . and . . . pardon would grow universal. Accordingly, in the bill of particulars which we have already mentioned, the tenth item charged Abelard with having said that "those who crucified the Christ without knowing what they were doing committed no sin, and, in general, nothing done in ignorance ought to be imputed as a fault."[8]

Abelard had already encountered authority in 1121, at the Council of Soissons. His punishment, there decreed, was perpetual retirement into monastic life. The punishment entirely failed. Abelard, though condemned, came back in public triumph, and continued for twenty years more his picaresque career. But, by 1140, Bernard of Clairvaux had acquired such hold upon the Pope and the people as gave him confidence that he might at last end the gadfly's sting. The Council at Sens was rigged to perfection, the result absolutely foreordained. The judges, all of them prelates of the Church, slept throughout the tedious proceedings, but roused now and then to mutter, "*Damnamus—namus.*"[9] Bernard, who knew that Abelard had admirers at the papal Curia, took care to enlighten Innocent II. Innocent thereupon confirmed the Council's verdict, and superintended a burning of Abelard's works outside St. Peter's.

Abelard, now turned sixty, was beginning a journey to Rome when the news reached him. He had already issued his *Profession of Faith,* in which he denied ever having said various things he certainly had said and various other things his doctrines perhaps

7) Ibid., p. 170.
8) Ibid., p. 333.
9) Henry Adams, op. cit., Chapter XIV. A pun can be made of *"–namus"* (= "we swim").

implied. "It is proverbial [so the *Profession* begins] that nothing is ever put so accurately that its meaning cannot be distorted."[1] His own doctrines, Abelard thought, had been similarly misrepresented, perhaps by malice. Yet there were—were there not?—the possible implications and the plain verbatim text.

Finding authority impregnable, Abelard gave up his journey at Cluny, where Peter the Venerable was abbot. This remarkable man, the healer that every organization needs and seldom finds, not only sheltered Abelard but shortly thereafter produced a reconcilation with Bernard of Clairvaux. Abelard, in truth, was now exhausted; but what can have abated the flame of Bernard's bottomless fuel? Nothing else, I fancy, than Peter's inconsumable love, which embraced persons rather than organizations, and which proclaimed that all men, however they differentiate themselves by membership or interest, are one.

Abelard died on the twelfth of April, 1142, and Peter, with exquisite tact, wrote Héloïse to report that the death had been as noble and as redemptive as one could wish. For Peter understood Héloïse as Héloïse understood herself, and rather more than Abelard had done. He had conveyed Abelard, he says, to the more healthful climate of Châlons, to be "near the city indeed, but yet near where the Saône flows."[2] There Abelard resumed his creative meditations, with due perseverance and prayer. "In these holy exercises, the coming of that angelic visitor found him, and discovered him not sleeping, like many, but vigilant. It found him truly watchful, and summoned him, not as the foolish, but as the wise virgin, to the marriage feast of eternity."[3] It is pleasant to be assured that these things were so.

Strange to say, love, the ultimate unifier, is seldom to be found within the ligaments of organizations. If it were there it would, and when it is there it does, make orthodoxy less stubborn and heresy less sharp. But the lesson of the twelfth century is, I suppose, that love is slow to be begotten, and, being begotten, may be misplaced. Bernard, it is plain, loved the Church. Héloïse loved Abelard. Peter the Venerable loved everyone, to the entire benefit of all. And

1) De Gandillac, op. cit., p. 334.
2) *The Portable Medieval Reader*, p. 337. Translated by Mary Martin McLaughlin.
3) Ibid., loc. cit.

Abelard? Well, it seems to have been his burden, his blight of genius, his bent toward a certain ineffectuality, that, when all was said and done, what he loved was himself. His intellectual progeny abound, using their gifts to display themselves; other men they do not greatly bless, because them they scarcely know. But Peter the Venerable knew in many men, and Héloïse in one, when it is that one can say:

> Hic amor ardet dulciter,
> dulcescit mirabiliter,
> sapit delectabiliter,
> delectat et feliciter.[4]

I I

IN OUR ACCOUNT of Christian heresies we have thus far dealt with such as arose from collisions among the rival sees of the Church and areas of the Empire. Now, in the twelfth century, we meet a swarm of heresies, with a proliferation of names—all amounting, however, to one and the same thing. They are, in substance, the heresy of the underprivileged, and this heresy consists in the assertion that the underprivileged are to have, and by right ought to have, the privilege of living their lives in harmony with their best ideals.

Among these heretics the most eminent was Arnold of Brescia.[5] He was born, it would appear, shortly before 1100. According to Otto of Freising, he studied under Abelard at Paris in the year 1115; and this event, though subject to some doubt, is very probable. But there is no doubt of a relation at some time between Arnold and Abelard. They were both condemned at the Council of Sens in 1140,

4) *The Oxford Book of Medieval Latin Verse*, § 233. Anonymous: this poem was once attributed to Bernard of Clairvaux, but has been proved to be the work of an English Cistercian. I supply to this verse the following effortful translation:

> A love like this with sweetness glows,
> And marvelously sweet it grows,
> And with delight knows all it knows,
> And in delight and fortune goes.

5) Brescia, in the Lombard region of north Italy, is the ancient Roman Brixia, mentioned, e.g., in Virgil's poem about the muleteer, which he wrote in amused imitation of Catullus:

> . . . *sive Mantuam*
> *opus foret volare sive Brixiam.*

("Whether the business had to do with rattling away to Mantua or to Brixia.")

and Bernard, in a subsequent letter to the Pope, observed, with scriptural vigor, that "the bee of France has hissed to the Italian bee and together they have advanced against the Lord and against his Christ."[6] Which was to say, they had "advanced" against the ruling hierarchy of the Church.

Here we have the classic pattern: Bernard, whose love of the Church made him hostile to change in ideology or structure, was the reactionary; Abelard, who loved ideas and disputation, was the liberal; Arnold, who loved common folk and hated princes, was the radical. Bernard, one may surmise, saw in Arnold the social consequences of Abelard's liberalism: this is always the reality which exposes liberals to "guilt by association." In any event, it tied Abelard's rebellious speculations to a precise political ground, such as the Pope and the Curia could scarcely ignore.

One would like to know, as unfortunately one cannot, what exactly it was that Arnold learned from Abelard. Arnold's convictions were already formed when his discipleship began; he had got them at Brescia from the Patarini, who, in their zeal against the hierarchical system, sought a return to the egalitarianism of early Christianity.[8] Abelard, for his part, had no such intense interest in social questions. Perhaps the relation was that Arnold delightedly found a certain unreasonableness in medieval theology, and that Abelard found (with possibly less delight) a social basis for his own skepticism.

Abelard's surrender and reconciliation were not, I think, the mere weariness of age; he would in any case have surrendered. But Arnold, fully committed from his youth to the welfare of the lowly, could not abandon their cause without abandoning himself. He must have known, throughout, the risks of such a struggle; and an admirer of the early Christians would scarcely retreat from martyrdom. It is possible that Abelard, differently situated, would have

6. *Siquidem sibilavit apis quae erat in Francia, api de Italia: et venerunt in unum adversus Dominem et adversus Christum eius*—Epistle 189; translated by George William Greenaway, in *Arnold of Brescia* (Cambridge: Cambridge University Press; 1931), p. 76. Bernard's metaphor is an allusion to Isaiah 7: 18 —"And it shall come to pass in that day that the Lord shall hiss for the fly that is in the uttermost part of the rivers of Egypt, and for the bee that is in the land of Assyria. . . ." AV.

8) They were named from the fact that their center at Milan was in the rag-pickers' quarter. *Pates* was the provincial term for a rag.

displayed Arnold's heroism; but an intellectual who relies only on other intellectuals and seeks no allies among the future inheritors of the earth will have little else to do but waver and repent. Arnold, however, had begun with the basic choice and had made it right.

It was just the sort of choice the historical Jesus had made, except that it seems not to have contemplated any armed seizure of power. It got no farther than armed defense of the people's interests. Arnold would have been content with an hierarchy purged of avarice and ostentation, restrained in its exercise of administrative duties, and modest toward the membership. These graces, however, the hierarchy was unwilling to grant—less perhaps from personal greed than from a fear that not to display power soon becomes not to possess it.

Thus at a very early stage Arnold had taken sides in the class conflict that long disturbed and at last abolished the feudal system. Specifically, the conflict was between wealth based on commerce and wealth based on the exploitation of agricultural labor. By the year 1050 commerce had begun to flourish again in the cities of Lombardy. "Old, disused trade routes were reopened," says Professor Greenaway, "and increased intercourse between town and town was fostered by the survival of the great Roman military roads traversing the Lombard plain."[8] With the rise of commerce went that kind of cultural development which the Church, to the present day, calls "secular." That is to say, just as there came to be a new form of wealth, so there came to be a new form of learning, of ideology, of interpreting the world.[9] Erudition, the arts, and (more impressively) politics ceased to be a monopoly of the Church. Over the notion of an appointed status for every man there grew the notion that a man could make something of himself. The moral requirements of life would no longer be satisfied by docility of membership; a man's own conscience had now to be appeased.

Meanwhile, the Church, as one human organization among

8) Op. cit., p. 16.
9) Otto of Freising complained of the Lombards that "they do not disdain to raise to the badge of knighthood, and to all grades of authority, young men of low condition, and even workmen of contemptible mechanical arts, such as other people drive away like the plague from more honorable and liberal pursuits. From which it happens that they are pre-eminent among the other countries of the world for riches and power. And to this they are helped also, as has been said, by their own industrious habits. . . ." Translated by U. Balzani and excerpted in *The Portable Medieval Reader*, p. 282.

others, had taken on the attributes of a feudal power. Writers of the twelfth century (including the Barbarossa himself) customarily refer to Pontifex Maximus as "the Lord Pope." Cardinals, bishops, and other hierarchs stood to the Lord Pope as, in secular society, the lesser nobles stood to their kings; and elections to the Papacy involved the same political maneuverings as elections to headship of the Holy Roman Empire. The lawless anarchism that now prevails among nations prevailed then among the tiny units of the feudal system, and self-defense required an exercise of naked force together with the less violent vices of intrigue and mendacity.

Now, it happens that Christian thought, as the Gospels ordain it, is singularly opposed to every conceivable procedure in power politics. The pure in heart, who are to see God, must, in order to be pure, avoid and reject all those devices that have enabled other men, not to see God, but to rule empires. In any contest, if the conduct of it is to be Christian, both sides must act upon identical principles; otherwise, because power has no necessary connection with morality, a side that uses power will always defeat a side that does not. One cannot expect that administrators, whose prime duty is to defend the organization, will let ethics in general and Christian ethics in particular weaken their use of power. There is no need to regard such administrators as depraved, though depraved they may be or may become. One need only recognize that the exercise of power is precisely what makes an administrator an administrator.

The paradox, exquisitely painful, of organized Christianity is that the clergy, and especially the hierarchy, in conducting the Church's affairs, must do certain things which their ideology expressly forbids. If they do them, they are self-condemned; if they don't do them, they have no Church. In this particular agony, however, they are not alone: the very same paradox has perplexed liberals and socialists. It is, at bottom, the paradox of attempting to realize ideals in a world of power.

When people are disposed by the circumstances of their lives to question the policies of their superiors, it strikes them very forcibly what antagonism there is between those policies and the organization's professed ideals. A Lombard merchant of, say, the eleventh century, just beginning to be prosperous, would discover in this regard the wildest incongruity. What resemblance could there possibly be between a feudal magnate and any member of that original group of fishermen, tax gatherers, and other outcasts along the shores of Galilee?

Moreover, no matter how much authority the popes might claim to have derived, through Peter the fisherman, from the Second Person of the Trinity, the other (and secular) feudal magnates acknowledged that authority only insofar as the popes enforced it. The doctrine of a divine right of kings developed as counterpoise to the doctrine of a divine appointment of popes,[1] and was in its turn enforced so far as kings could enforce it. More than one pope learned, like his first predecessor, the pains of exile and defeat. Churchmen are understandably fond of recounting how the great Hildebrand (Pope Gregory VII) made Henry IV, the Holy Roman Emperor, stand for three days barefoot in the snow at Canossa in 1177; but the fact is that, three years later, Henry was able to depose Gregory, who died (1185) a captive of the Normans at Salerno.

Thus the Church, always embattled, could not tolerate disunity within. Yet at just this moment, when its behavior least agreed with the maxims of its Founder, there came into being a new social ground for disunity. Tradesmen, artisans, and laborers may need religion, or think that they need it; but, in this regard, what they chiefly need is a religion that is inexpensive. Their wishes upon this point they have, through many centuries, made abundantly plain. Especially they do not need, and have often proclaimed that they do not want, a large ecclesiastical bureaucracy expending vast sums in self-maintenance and in idle repetitions of ritual. One could approach God directly, it has seemed, with less expense and with the same effect. What else did one do in prayer? And success of approach would manifest itself in the sobriety, purity, modesty of the worshiper's own life.

---

1) In 1157, Frederick Barbarossa, the Holy Roman Emperor, had this to say to certain legates of Pope Adrian IV: "Inasmuch as the kingdom, together with the empire, is ours by the election of the princes from God alone, who, by the passion of His Son Christ subjected the world to the rule of the two necessary swords [State and Church]; and since the apostle Peter informed the world with this teaching, 'Fear God, honor the king': whoever shall say that we received the imperial crown as a benefice from the lord pope, contradicts the divine institutions and the teaching of Peter, and shall be guilty of a lie." Translated by E. F. Henderson, *The Portable Medieval Reader*, p. 261.

This, as one recognizes, is the authentic voice of Protestantism, already to be heard in the twelfth century. It was the voice that spoke through Arnold, and with an eloquence equal to Bernard's own. For, as John of Salisbury said, Arnold "was seditious and a fomenter of schism, and wherever he lived he did not allow the laity to have peace with the clergy."[2] At Brescia he succeeded so well that the people opposed the return of their absent bishop.

Exiled by Innocent II on this account, from Lombardy into France, Arnold began the long, if intermittent, discipleship with Abelard; and, after the defeat at Sens, he even took Abelard's place as lecturer upon the Mont Sainte Geneviève. There, says John of Salisbury, "he had no auditors except poor ones, and those who begged alms publicly from door to door, while they spent their life with the master. . . . He did not spare the bishops, attacking them because of their avarice and shameful money-grubbing, and because of their so frequently blemished lives, and because they strove to build the Church of God by the shedding of blood."[3]

The unwearying Bernard next achieved his expulsion from France. He took refuge for a time in Switzerland with sympathizers among the lesser nobility. Meanwhile Eugenius III, Bernard's old pupil, became Pope. There then occurred, very strangely, a reconciliation, the grounds of which are not only unclear but unknown. Arnold promised obedience and in fact did penance;[4] but nothing in his subsequent behavior suggests, what is in any case almost incredible, that he compromised his lifelong principles. Eugenius, perhaps, gained some pacification of Arnold's followers.

In the midst of this new unity, Arnold appeared at Rome, where there was very little unity to be found. Rome was in those days ruled by an oligarchy of rich families, who had popular support as against the Papacy. The Pope himself had retired to Viterbo, whence he came forth to Rome and whither he again withdrew, as the shifting tides of conflict required. Arnold was at once a tribune of the people, his favorite and familiar role, which he was now to play for

2) *Historia Pontificalis.* This excerpt has been translated by Mary Martin McLaughlin, *The Portable Medieval Reader,* p. 339.
3) Ibid., loc. cit.
4) So John of Salisbury says (ibid., p. 340), who, however, does not state the terms of the agreement.

the last time. The four powers at work—the Roman people, the Roman oligarchy, the Pope, and the Holy Roman Emperor—reached, in the year 1155, the particular balance (or imbalance) that crushed him.

The Pope was now Adrian IV: Nicholas Breakspear, the only Englishman ever to be Pontiff. The Emperor was Frederick Barbarossa, who descended into Italy to be crowned at Rome, acquiring the iron crown of Lombardy on the way. There was a contretemps at Campo Grasso, when Frederick declined to hold the stirrup for Adrian to dismount, and this traditional ceremony had to be repeated next day. The episode was most suggestive: the four powers were as likely to turn out enemies as friends, and no one knew what pattern might appear.

Arnold's fate was the one certainty. Adrian had already procured his expulsion from Rome, and Frederick flushed him from his Tuscan refuge by seizing one of his protectors as hostage. In an armed struggle following the coronation, imperial troops defeated the citizens of Rome, and Roman independence vanished. Arnold, his followers scattered and his allies stricken, had now to face the inevitable doom. There was a trial, a condemnation, a hanging, a burning of the corpse, a scattering of the ashes into Tiber. On the scaffold, Arnold was fearless and self-reliant (*mirabile dictu,* says the anonymous chronicler), and proclaimed that his doctrines still seemed to him sound, having nothing in them either noxious or unreasonable. He was, he said, quite willing to die for them, and thus he accepted the noose.

O learned Arnold [says the chronicler, moved to rhetoric, if not to sympathy] what did so much learning profit you—so much fasting, so much toil, so straitened a life that scorned leisure and fleshly joys? What made you turn a slanderous tooth upon the Church, that you should thus come, wretched man, to the mournful noose? See now the fate of the doctrine you have suffered for: all doctrine passes away, and yours will soon pass also. It has been consumed in the flames and reduced with you to a little ash, lest by some chance there be anything left for men to honor.[5]

5) *Gesta di Federico,* by the Bergamasque Poet, lines 851–60. My translation. The hexameters are worth recording:

> *Docte quid Arnaldi profecit litteratura*
> *tanta tibi? Quid tot ieiunia totque labores?*

That *dogma perit* is the hopeful belief of all administrators who regard ideology as a nuisance.[6] Yet in fact doctrine never does pass away until it has become useless. Arnold's survived to carry the Reformation to triumph, and there is still much work for it to do. As for the *quid profecit tibi?*—the "what did it profit thee?"—well, this is a question of which the asker would never understand the answer. Men like Arnold, who seek to liberate the lowly, have no other wish for themselves than to be seekers of just that sort. They come into the world already rewarded; their gain lies in constant sight of their ideal.

Strange notions beset alike the possessors and the sycophants of power. Excellence, when punished, is still excellence. A true assertion is still true when it is consumed by flames, and a false assertion is still false when it escapes them. It is no doubt possible to determine, by faggot or rope, how many men will attain excellence and profess truth, but it is certainly not possible, by any such means or indeed by any means at all, to change the essential nature of the values themselves. These exist as limits upon administration, and rulers who ignore them or think to make play with them take rather greater risks than they appear to suppose.

I I I

BERNARD OF CLAIRVAUX, whose zeal sometimes gave way to amiability, once described heretics as "the little foxes that spoil the vines."[7] He here referred, I fancy, not to the eminent men whose originality and influence had made them heresiarchs, but to the little folk who, by reason of multitude, were yet more dangerous. And

---

> *Vita quid arta nimis, que semper segnia sprevit*
> *otia, nec ullis voluit carnalibus uti?*
> *Heu quid in ecclesiam mordacem vertere dentem*
> *suasit? Ut ad tristem laqueum, miserande, venires!*
> *Ecce tuum pro quo penam, dampnate, tulisti,*
> *dogma perit, nec erit tua mox doctrina superstes!*
> *Arsit, et in tenuem tecum est resoluta favillam*
> *Ne cui reliquie superent fortasse colende.*

This passage is excerpted in Greenaway, op. cit., Appendix III.

6) "What gets into philosophers?" cried a university vice president to me on one occasion.

7) *Encyclopaedia Britannica*, eleventh edition, Vol. III, p. 797. Bernard was quoting the Song of Solomon 2:15.

(if we may explore the image) it is noticeable that Bernard was more interested in the vines than in the grapes. A few grapes or many would be a loss but not a disaster. But if the vines are damaged, there will be no further grapes at all.

The vines are, of course, the organization. A great fox, a chief of foxes, is dangerous in that he starts something and leads something, but he cannot by himself spoil many vines. A large company of foxes, however, stealing forth with all the reputed slyness of their species, could ruin the vineyard once for all. Precisely thus can a multiplicity of dissenters ruin an organization.

In other ways too, the fox image eloquently expresses the administrative point of view. The reality is that members of an organization, when they begin upon dissent, ordinarily (though not always) do so with a certain gravity. They value the organization; they wish only to purge it of what they take to be error and vice. To an administrator all such efforts come as a surprise. There seems something sly about them: he did not observe their beginning or their first movement—yet, suddenly, the foxes are at the vines!

By the twelfth century, there were such foxes by the thousands. As is usual in such circumstances, it would have been possible to distract their attention upon other food, granting thus their right to eat. But, as is also usual in such circumstances, the lords of the vineyard did not wish to be at so much expense. It was preferable, they thought, to exterminate the foxes, and they so far succeeded in this endeavor as to delay human advance by at least four hundred years.

The little foxes had many groupings. There were the Bogomili ("God-prayers") in Bosnia, the Patarini in Lombardy, the Tisserands ("weavers") and Waldenses (followers of Peter Waldo) at Lyon, and those celebrated martyrs, the Albigenses, who inhabited Languedoc in the south of France.[8] Among these groups there were certain variations of doctrine—obscure, however, because the doctrines are known to us chiefly through hostile accounts. Thus when a given

8) In the development of the French language from the Latin, France was divided, linguistically, into two parts, according to the manner in which one said "yes." In the northern part one said *oïl* (from *hoc ille*); a further derivative was the ultimately triumphant *oui*. In the south one said *oc* (from *hoc* without the *ille*). Thus there were the Languedoïl and the Languedoc. The geographical line of division ran, roughly, from Bordeaux, through Limoges, Montluçon, Clermont-Ferrand and Tournon, to Grenoble.

doctrine is attributed to one group rather than another, there is always the chance that a special animus motivated the attribution.

It has become customary to place all these groups under the common title of Cathari ("the purified ones"), and this title does admirably express the striking fact that the human beings thus named were engaged in a great moral effort; indeed, they considered religion to be primarily and almost exclusively a form of personal ethics. They were interested in establishing the purity of their own lives, and they cared rather less about the fate of the Church as an organization. They had, in a way, a highly practical view of human excellence: they desired virtue in the here and now, and the due rewards of virtue in the hereafter.

It was an ethics suited to hardworking, thrifty, sober, and earnest men. The Cathari were quite willing to have their actions measured against their principles, and to be themselves judged by the degree of correspondence. They were—and in this, of course, they gave great sociological offense—the opposite of organization men. An organization man can have only one virtue—namely, obedience to the commands of his superiors; and organization men of those days (as since) were engaged in climbing, by means of obedience, the not very wide ladder (for the ladder never is very wide) of hierarchical status. But the Cathari, so far from seeking status, did not even care for affluence. They desired just to be what conscience told them they ought to be, and upon this sort of success, peculiarly moral, they bent an inexhaustible zeal.

The working of ethics within human history is a theme to excite mockery or platitude; yet it is one of the most instructive themes there can be. It deserves neither the derision nor the rhetoric which, in equal measures, it has evoked. What fascinates and appalls in the persecution of the Cathari is the contest between high authority in a leadership and high morality in a membership. The effect had necessarily to be that the victims suffered because of their virtue, whilst the persecutors prevailed because of their power.

The doctrines of the Cathari spread along the trade routes westward from a common source in the Balkans. By the twelfth century these doctrines had covered northern Italy and southern France, and had even penetrated the Lowlands. At Antwerp, for example, there appeared the remarkable prophet Tanchelyn, a man certainly mad, who one day announced his forthcoming marriage to the Virgin

Mary. Since, already, "all Antwerp was his harem,"[9] this consummation seemed not impossible, and disciples thronged about the prophet as he bore through the streets an image of his affianced bride.

In general, the Cathari were as sober as Tanchelyn himself was mad. They did, however, share with him what was rational in his madness—namely, a resolve that their beliefs were to be truly their own. The movement was anti-sacerdotal; indeed, so far from showing respect to priests, the Cathari believed them to be the probable appointees of Satan, and could point to various visible corruptions as proof. If, for example, a wealthy man bought himself a bishopric, it was difficult to think that his new status had anything to do with an alleged apostolic succession. The Albigensian part of the movement, inheriting (as it seems) the old Manichean view that good and evil are equally potent forces in the world, judged the Church, by reason of its political behavior, to be closer to Satan than to God. For their part, they wished no such proximity.

Thus the Cathari were a membership in constant repudiation of an official leadership, and, in their thousands, they threatened to produce, intentionally or not, a situation in which the leaders could no longer lead. By the end of the twelfth century the organizational crisis was real and immediate: this early Protestantism, if left to grow, would soon have achieved without violence what later Protestantism achieved amid infinite smoke and flame. It would, that is to say, have abolished the feudal structure of the Church and very likely also the structure of the feudal system.

The crisis developed rather slowly during the eleventh and twelfth centuries. The not infrequent persecutions of Cathari served only to spread the doctrines and to rally the believers. Bernard's attacks were more eloquent than effective, and even as late as 1165, at the Synod of Lombers, orthodox theologians had to discuss the issues peacefully with Catharist doctors. Meanwhile Languedoc had become the most civilized part of Europe, with a rare and happy blend of feudal graces and business enterprise. Here flourished the troubadours (*trovères*, they were in the north), and flourished also the courts of love, where a knight could find elaborate judgment upon the propriety of his own behavior. The guiding principle of these decisions, as ingenious as ultimate, was that any lady worthy to be adored was

9) John Lothrop Motley, *Rise of the Dutch Republic* (New York: A. L. Burt, n.d.), Vol. I, p. 59.

by definition a perfect being; the knight had therefore to make himself perfect and to show in elegance of behavior that he was so. This remarkable idea, which has not survived the satire of Cervantes, translated religious devotion into secular terms. Sacred and profane love, adoration of the Virgin and of one's lady, grew nearly the same thing. Perhaps their union expressed the felicity of all who lived in Languedoc.

Within this bower of exquisite and aristocratic grace, the Albigensian Cathari, not at all unwilling to be called heretics, set about the various tasks of personal salvation. A few of them reached the eminence of being *perfecti* ("the perfect ones"), ascetics who foreswore marriage and practiced a communism of goods. The rest, *credentes* ("believers"), were allowed to make what spiritual advance they might. They were not expected to go far in asceticism nor even to believe all the Catharist doctrines, but they were required to agree that before their death, or in the moment of it, they would receive the *consolamentum,* a baptism of the Holy Spirit, which should convey them, saved and ennobled, into eternal life.

It is affecting how the Cathari sought to temper the wind to the shorn lamb. Let those be righteous who can, the doctrine seemed to say; let the rest be as nearly righteous as their strength of appetite permits, and, in any event, let them have at the last a means of salvation. There has not been, I fancy, a more genial principle at work in human affairs: it is what one would hope to find in some distant and enchanting social order.

Such graces the Albigenses already possessed, and the Church could not suffer them to do so. Itself condemned to the desperate corruptions of power politics, where to survive is to be made brutal, the Church looked with mingled shame and horror upon a pleasant civilization in which, somehow or other, the historic benefits of Christianity were readily available. The Cathari were rebellious or at least stubborn. They were vulnerable upon points of doctrine, and they even retained Augustine's lifelong (though suppressed) taste for the Manichean heresy. Pope Innocent III (1198–1216) considered these matters briefly, and then resolved to act.

The first maneuvers were exploratory but rigorous. The papal legate, Peter of Castelnau, went into Languedoc, demanding the exposure and surrender of all heretics. Since this amounted to a surrender of the population, Raymond VI, Count of Toulouse, an amiable if weak monarch, declined. Peter thereupon excommunicated him. The consequent, retaliatory anger produced Peter's assassination by one of Raymond's vassals. It was, in effect, a declaration of war.

Innocent was not the pleasantest of popes, but he was surely one of the ablest. By the year 1208 there had been four Crusades against Moslem territory in Palestine and Egypt. They had gained for their participants very little more than tons of relics (saints' bones and the like),[1] and Innocent himself had excommunicated the Fourth Crusade for following, not his orders, but Venetian cupidity. The Moslems had proved disappointingly staunch. Yet the crusading spirit was still rife. Suppose one were to turn it, nearer home, against the Albigenses?

The notion was irresistible in attraction and in success. Knights who "took the Cross" had certain astounding benefits and had them immediately. Their sins, past, present, and to come, were all forgiven; they had the certainty of Paradise, regardless of any deed whatever upon earth. But absolution from blame would not by itself have drawn many feudal lords into crusading. Crusades were extremely expensive, and there needed to be the prospect of economic and political gain. Fiefs taken from Moslems were a form of this; but the fiefs, when taken, were not long held. Moslems were an obdurate and powerful foe, able to recoup all losses. It would surely be different—and indeed it proved to be very different—with the neighboring Albigenses, who, having obduracy but not enough power, could be attacked with less expense and with more probability of success.

Accordingly, Innocent, through the Cistercian Order, called upon the lords of northern France to take the Cross against the heretics of Languedoc. The property of heretics, being in any case forfeit, would fall to him who could take it; and the northern lords had no difficulty perceiving how a successful extirpation of heresy would add to their domains. There has never been, I dare say, an ideological

1) After the looting of Constantinople in 1204, one Martin, Abbot of Pairis, in Alsace, reported that he had acquired an arm of Saint James and "a not inconsiderable piece" of Saint John the Baptist—Charles Homer Haskins, *The Renaissance of the Twelfth Century* (New York: Meridian Books; 1957), p. 234.

justification of plunder at once so compendious and so convincing. It whetted appetites for satisfaction, and it pronounced all methods free of blame.

The Crusade began in the spring of 1209. Count Raymond collapsed at its approach, and gave up his rule, his dignity, and many castles. Warmed with these easy conquests, the Crusaders appeared before Béziers, a walled town between Marseilles and Carcassonne. Here the Albigenses had drawn in their forces for a resolute stand; but a foray into the besiegers' camp miscarried, and in their retreat they allowed the enemy to enter the town. The ruin was complete. The Crusaders, not quite comprehending how far morality had been intermitted, and supposing that in the slaughter they were to distinguish between heretic and orthodox, asked the papal legate, Arnold Amalric, how they were to know whom to kill. "Kill them all!" cried this astounding bigot: "God will recognize his own!"[2]

And so they killed them all, to a number not less than fifteen thousand. And they killed many, many more throughout Languedoc during subsequent months and years—in battle, by treachery, and by inquisition. Simon de Montfort had his brief and pestilential eminence. Innocent died, having seen, along with these triumphs, the work of the Fourth Lateran Council (1215), which decreed the sacraments to be the necessary channel of grace and condemned the Cathari once again for thinking otherwise. In 1226 a last campaign by Louis VIII ended the brilliant civilization of the south. Three years later, the son, Louis IX, Saint Louis, fifteen years old, officially acquired the County of Toulouse; and thus the saint saw his dominions stretch, with reputable orthodoxy, from Paris to the Mediterranean shore.

Amid these horrors, the Albigenses in effect vanished from history, though there are still Frenchmen, good Catholics all, who make a yearly pilgrimage to Monségur in the Gironde, there to commemorate the martyrs of an inquisition seven hundred years past. Of other Catharan sects, the Waldenses (the *Vaudois*) have, in much diminished numbers, survived and retained an organization. Their good fortune was that during those years they possessed nothing in the way of castles and fiefs which could excite the rapacity

---

2) *Tuez-les tous! Dieu reconnaîtra les siens!*—so runs, according to tradition, the celebrated cry, the ultimate word of embattled orthodoxy.

of feudal lords. In their regard, accordingly, the Church could with less ease defend orthodoxy by a timely appeal to economics.

These heretics, who styled themselves, very quaintly, *Li Poure de Lyod*,[3] were originally recruited by Peter Waldo, a rich merchant. Waldo had made a study of the Scriptures, and had discovered that their message—or at least some of it—was plain to any intelligent and attentive mind. For example, the injunction, delivered in all three Synoptic Gospels, "Sell that thou hast and give to the poor,"[4] was surely basic, since it was asserted to be Jesus' own answer to the question, "What good thing shall I do, that I may have eternal life?" Very little in the behavior of the organized Church suggested accord with the principle: the prelates were conspicuously acquisitive, and the poor were conspicuously—poor.

The Cathari, however, in all their varieties, had, as we have seen, the endearing desire to show forth, in every moment of behavior, the ideals that presumably make a Christian a Christian. Accordingly, Waldo one day offered his wife a choice between his landed property and his movable effects. She chose the landed property; the rest he sold. Part of the proceeds he portioned upon his two daughters, whom he thereupon placed in the nunnery of Fontevraud. The rest he distributed among the poor. Then he gave himself over to teaching and to the propagation of his faith.

Three of Waldo's doctrines are striking because of their effect on organized social life. The first of these was a revival of the old Donatist heresy, that sacraments cannot be validly administered by a clergyman corrupt in morals. Waldo in fact drew the extreme converse inference also, that the sacraments *can* be validly administered by any morally sound Christian whatever. The right to preach and to conduct all other religious activities followed therefore, not the structure of an organization, but the requirements of ethics. It is easy to see what would be the fate of any human organization of hierarchical form in which the members could accept or reject policies and obey or not obey commands according as the leaders seemed righteous or unrighteous. The hierarchical form would soon be much modified or even lost and the organization itself be turned into a loose congeries of self-determining units.

3) "The poor men of Lyon" (now France's third city, 512 kilometers southeast of Paris). The Roman name for the city had been Lugdunum.
4) Matthew 19:21; Mark 10:21; Luke 18:22.

Something of this sort did happen when Protestant sects pro-liferated after the Reformation. Nevertheless, when one has listed all the imaginable perils of anarchism, there remains in the hierarchical scheme an ineradicable clash between authority and decency. The corruption of leaders *does* soil the acts which, by established ritual, the leaders perform; and the feeling must be that neither grace nor virtue can pass uncontaminated through a contaminated medium. Moreover, since righteousness and wisdom are as available to mem-bers as to leaders (rather more so, indeed), and since righteousness and wisdom are (in the Catharan view) enshrined in the definitive expositions of Scripture, we are led insensibly toward the celebrated Protestant doctrine of "the universal priesthood of all believers." And this was Waldo's second important idea.

The third, of a similarly anarchist sort, was the incurable im-morality of oaths, particularly of test oaths. For this view there was excellent scriptural support in Matthew 5: 33-37—

> Again, ye have heard that it hath been said by them of old time, Thou shalt not forswear thyself, but shalt perform unto the Lord thine oaths: But I say unto you, Swear not at all; neither by heaven; for it is God's throne: Nor by the earth; for it is his foot-stool: neither by Jerusalem; for it is the city of the great King. Neither shalt thou swear by thy head, because thou canst not make one hair white or black. But let your communication be, Yea, yea; Nay, nay: for whatsoever is more than these cometh of evil. AV.

Now, if the historical Jesus, the insurrectionary leader, did actu-ally say these words, there may well have been profound political insight in the injunction. Test oaths (the kind in which one swears never to do such and such) have long been an instrument of tyranny. Their purpose, as Erasmus once very shrewdly remarked, is "that want of submission may be punished as perjury."[5] In this manner, the law can penalize a great many acts that otherwise would be quite legal. It is the "shortest way with dissenters," whose activities cannot without gross exaggeration be thought seditious.

Suppose, for example, you take an oath never to join a "subversive organization." Years pass, and then an organization which you do belong to and which has never dreamed of subversion falls foul of

5) Quoted and translated by J. A. Froude, *Life and Letters of Erasmus* (New York: Charles Scribner's Sons; 1894), p. 68.

another organization possessing state power. Your ancient oath, which from sheer habit of observance you had forgotten, now opens you to a charge of perjury, if the dominant organization succeeds in describing its opponents as subversive. Politics being what it tends to be, your safety will lie either in belonging to no organizations or in taking no oaths.

The second of these alternatives became a basic principle with Waldo and with the Cathari generally, and is perhaps an example how an honest political need transforms itself into a moral imperative. It is still thus maintained by the Quakers and other groups of what might be called "left-wing Protestantism." The Inquisition had no end of trouble with it, because the witness, by thus introducing a wholly new issue, could maneuver for a long time without ever doing the essential thing—namely, to *swear* that his views were not heretical. In the early fourteenth century, Bernard Gui, a shrewd inquisitor and by no means the worst of an odious lot, wrote a manual of inquisition, called the *Practica,* in which he described this sort of colloquy (*I* is the inquisitor, and *A* is the witness):

I. Will you then swear that you have never learned anything contrary to the faith which we hold to be true?

A. (growing pale). If I ought to swear, I will willingly swear.

I. I don't ask whether you ought, but whether you will swear.

A. If you order me to swear, I will swear.

I. I don't force you to swear, because as you believe oaths to be unlawful, you will transfer the sin to me who forced you; but if you will swear, I will hear it.

A. Why should I swear if you do not order me to?

I. So that you may remove the suspicion of being a heretic.

A. Sir, I do not know how unless you teach me.

I. If I had to swear, I would raise my hand and spread my fingers and say, "So help me God, I have never learned heresy or believed what is contrary to the true faith."

Then, trembling as if he cannot repeat the form, he will stumble along as though speaking for himself or for another, so that there is not an absolute form of oath and yet he may be thought to have sworn.[6]

Though the Waldenses, acting on these principles, were never

6) Quoted and translated by Henry C. Lea, *The Inquisition of the Middle Ages,* abridged by Margaret Nicholson (New York: the Macmillan Company; 1961), p. 192.

exterminated, they were often persecuted. As Europe moved into its Protestant era, the attacks grew weaker, and in the Piedmont the Waldenses acquired territory and towns which they were able to defend. A massacre they suffered in this area in 1655 brought forth effective diplomatic pressure from Cromwell and the splendid thunder of Milton's sonnet, "Avenge, O Lord, thy slaughtered saints . . ." The saints, if never quite avenged, have persevered, and may teach lessons to the twentieth century. For test oaths and inquisition are by no means dead, and consequently Matthew 5: 33-37 is much alive.

The Cathari did not regenerate the Church, but they forced some changes within it. Their appeal to primitive Christianity, to the agreement of conduct with ideals, could not be merely suppressed; it had also to be imitated. From it there arose, within the Church, the mendicant orders, Dominican and Franciscan, which undertook to make orthodox doctrine more persuasive by the practice of poverty. The Dominicans (named after Domingo de Guzman, their founder, 1170-1221) abandoned their purer insights rather too soon; it was they to whom the Inquisition was entrusted, so that they acquired the satiric, punning title of *Domini Canes,* "hounds of the Lord."

The Franciscans, too, in time degenerated, but at least they had for founder as lovely a human personage as the Virgin had been a divine. If we are to think that Francis of Assisi was not quite sane, then we are also to desire that his madness may infect the world. For Francis loved all creatures—human, animal, elemental—with the same love with which he loved God. In him the medieval *fabliaux* (the animal stories) became a sort of science to live by: he preached, as we know, to swallows and other birds; he spoke amicably to Brother Fire, which (or who) burned away at his sleeve; he made a good citizen of the wolf of Gubbio.

> "Promise [said he to the wolf] thou wilt never play me, thy bondsman, false." Then the wolf, lifting up his right paw, placed it in the hand of Saint Francis. Whereat . . . there was such marvel and rejoicing among all the people—not only at the strangeness of the miracle, but because of the peace made with the wolf —that they all began to cry aloud to heaven. . . .[7]

7) *The Little Flowers of Saint Francis,* translated (wonderfully well!) by Thomas Okey, Everyman's Library (London: J. M. Dent and Sons; 1910), pp. 40-41.

The peace made with the wolf! That was indeed a lesson to remember and to praise. We think of the world, physical and social, as reluctant to part with its treasures; we fancy to grapple with it, to wrest, and to seize. Francis thought of the world as a generous giver, and of harmony as needing only gentleness to be achieved. No one before his time, and none after him, has so clearly and sweetly conceived what it would be like for men to be at home in their world. He has been said to be the first modern mind; but this is boasting—we are still short of his vision. We follow him in time, but more in moral distance; and not until we have made peace with the wolf—which is to say, among ourselves—will we be his peers.

Now, Francis was a kind of heretic, and would in fact have been one if the Church had allowed. He was a pantheist, the divinity of nature and the divinity of God being for him nearly identical. He trusted to private insight, as mystics do, and he had the mystic's habit of ignoring human commands. He liked doctrine little and rationalizing of doctrine still less; at just this point his otherwise boundless love gave out. At a meeting of his Order in 1218, eight years before his death, and in the presence of Saint Dominic, he uttered a remarkable cry:

". . . I want you to talk of no Rule to me, neither Saint Benedict nor Saint Augustine nor Saint Bernard, nor any way or form of Life whatever except that which God has mercifully pointed out and granted to me. And God said that he wanted me to be a pauper and an idiot—a great fool—in this world, and would not lead us by any other path of science than this. But by your science and syllogisms God will confound you, and I trust in God's warders, the devils, that through them God shall punish you, and you will yet come back to your proper station with shame, whether you will or no.[8]

The Cathari might have said as much; yet they were heretics, and Francis, in the year 1228, became a saint. What made the difference? The astuteness, I would surmise, of the Church. As with Augustine, the Church resolved to absorb what it could not digest; and Francis, for his own part, had never been habitually defiant. So the Church adorned itself with a true saint, with that saint's good works, and with the infinite allure which Francis, like the Virgin, could cast

8) Quoted and translated by Henry Adams, op. cit., Chapter XV.

across all human wishing. It was statesmanship of the first order.

But the little foxes—cannot they be saints or at least be saved? They could and they can, but it is not yet known how to manage their relations with the vines.

CHAPTER

8

Piers and His Plows

"I F THERE WERE a hundred popes," cried John Wyclif in 1382, "and if all the friars were turned into cardinals, their opinions on matters of faith ought not to be believed except in so far as they have been founded upon Scripture."[1] Popes, cardinals, friars, Scripture: what were the relations among them?

The friars were those mendicant orders, Dominican and Franciscan, which arose to prove that the Church itself, or sections of it, could practice holy poverty as well as the Cathari had done. Yet within a hundred years of their foundation they began to show the effects of being an institution and a political force. Begging they turned into an extraordinary art.[2] Confession, which they were empowered to hear, and absolution, which they were empowered to

---

1) *Trialogus*, 266, quoted in Herbert B. Workman, *John Wyclif* (Oxford: Oxford University Press; 1926), Vol. II, p. 3: *Ideo si essent centum papae, et omnes fratres essent versi in cardinales, non deberent credi sententiae suae in materia fidei, nisi de quanto se fundaverint in scriptura.* My translation.
2) E.g., Chaucer's friar, who was "the beste beggere in his hous:"

>   For thogh a widwe hadde noght a sho,
>   So plesaunt was his 'In principio,'
>   Yet wolde he have a ferthing er he wente.

Canterbury Tales, Prologue, ll. 253–55. Chaucer's geniality makes his character types somewhat better than perhaps they were. For the popular resentment against suffering, one must turn to *Piers Plowman*.

grant,[3] admitted them into the secrets of the lowly and the high, and gave them influence over the conduct of very many people. Their itinerant life dispersed them, in continual movement, throughout the population; they were, as one may say, a finger upon the decisions of every man, pressing, pressing.

This power they had not easily won. Their first efforts, within the lifetime of Francis and Dominic, brought them into collision with other parts of the ecclesiastical establishment. For example, the friars in their peregrinations had portable altars, which they set up at need for the saying of mass. They heard confessions; they remitted sins. All these important offices had belonged theretofore to the parish clergy, who, being situated at great distances from Rome and at considerable distances from one another, had attained an independence they much prized. More than this, they had long grown accustomed to collecting the fees that all these services required.

Christianity, indeed, had moved a long way from Saint Paul's liberality: salvation in exchange for faith. You could now acquire salvation only in exchange for faith plus fees. There was in fact a fee for every important transaction in life, from birth to burial. Beyond burial, there were fees for the repose of your soul and of as many other souls as were dear to you. In our own time, a devout man of commerce will pay for nothing more perpetual than the perpetual care of his place of interment.

The parish clergy, and the bishops also in their sees, felt competition from the friars in two very sensitive places: their purses and their prestige. Moreover, they suffered the characteristic ills of long establishment: they were well and indeed tediously known to their parishioners, and they had flaunted authority perhaps too much. The friars came, offering the same attractive services, and asking (originally) no money at all, just a frugal meal and a night's lodging. Salvation had suddenly grown inexpensive—and not salvation only, but the recovery of physical health. Francis himself had touched the sores of lepers, and it was a maxim with his followers to treat all human diseases, however horrible. In that great medieval catastrophe the Black Death (1348–1350), the friars went faithfully nursing while many a priest fled.

The Roman Church was a union of rival parts and powers, in which respect it resembled every other human organization of large

3) By Pope Gregory IX, in 1227.

size. The priests and bishops—also, indeed, the other monastic orders—resented and rebuffed the mendicants, who moved among the populace, the ultimate source of profit, with a deadly infiltration. What seemed worst was that the populace welcomed them. The extraordinary mixture of novelty, devotion, and economy was irresistible. And so priests and bishops, archbishops and cardinals, appealed to the Vicar of Christ for a surcease of mendicant activity.

The response from some of these vicars was all that could be hoped, but the response from heaven was shattering. Events of miraculous convenience attested the fact that the Trinity was so far on the side of the friars that the Second Person was willing to remove his Vicar to make all plain. For example, in 1254, when the friars had got into a fierce struggle with the University of Paris, William of Saint Amour, the head of the faculty, procured from the then pope Innocent IV a bull, *Etsi Animarum,* closely limiting the activities of the friars. The Dominicans thereupon ordered their members into special prayers. On December seventh, sixteen days after promulgation of the bull, Innocent suddenly died; and, not long after, the Cardinal of Albano, who had urged the bull, fell in his home, a beam having given way, and broke his neck.[4]

Innocent's successor found for the friars, and revoked the bull. But in 1287, nine popes later, the friars chanced to fall foul of the whole Gallican Church. Honorius IV determined upon a further bull depriving them of the right to preach and to hear confessions. He chose Good Friday as the day for issuing the bull, and on the night of Maundy Thursday he died.[5] The verdict of heaven was now clear. It was also confirmed by the political acumen of men, for the leaders of the Church grew aware that they possessed in the friars "an instrument more efficient than had yet been devised to bring the power of the Holy See to bear directly upon the Church and the people in every corner of Christendom . . . and to lead the people into direct relations with the successors of Saint Peter."[6]

From the Dominicans came, very early, the Inquisition. From all the mendicants came a system of espionage, blackmail, and betrayal that brought it to pass that mere simple villagers would flee the sight

4) Lea, op. cit., pp. 132–33.
5) Ibid., p. 136.
6) Ibid., pp. 128–29.

of a friar entering town.[7] What God seemed to have ordained, men were at last driven, out of self-protection, to destroy. William Langland, in *Piers Plowman* (greatest, perhaps, of people's poems), tells us, speaking of personified Charity:

> In a friar's frock he was found once,
> But that was afar back in Saint Francis' lifetime:
> In that sect since he has been too seldom witnessed.[8]

Great as were these scandals, the scandals in other parts of the Church grew even greater. The use of religion for the extraction of money had been well known to the priests of ancient Egypt, and, as we have seen, traces of it in early Christianity are recorded in the *Didachē*. But even Pope Damasus, the "matrons' ear-tickler," would have been astounded at the skill and thoroughness of his medieval imitators. By the fourteenth century the great institution founded for the saving of souls had become a vast engine of exploitation. No part of life was exempt from its intrusive claims. For example, priests, bishops, friars, searching out the degrees of consanguinity, could pronounce marriages lawful or unlawful as authority might determine.[9] Couples who for many years had supposed themselves married could be told, suddenly, that they were in fact living in fornication, that their children were bastards, and that inheritance of property was thus compromised. But fees would set all right: upon sufficient payment, the marriage would be validated, the children legitimatized, and the inheritance (now somewhat reduced) made secure.

All this plundering of the people's wealth and labor excited the keenest competition, and the Church was rent upon the division of the spoils. The difficulties and perils of travel sundered Europe far more than the entire globe is sundered nowadays. Factions could proliferate geographically, hostile to one another and to the ever-

7) Erasmus reported as much—James Anthony Froude, *Lectures on the Council of Trent* (New York: Charles Scribner's Sons; 1896), p. 12.

8) Excerpted in *The Portable Medieval Reader,* p. 201. Translated by H. W. Wells.

9) The canon law on this point was, and still is, as follows: "If anyone says that the degrees of consanguinity and affinity mentioned in Leviticus [18: 6 ff.] can, of themselves alone, prevent the contracting of marriage or render null a marriage already contracted, that the Church cannot set aside some of those degrees or decide that yet others may be cause of impediment or nullity, let him be anathema." Excerpted in Gervais Dumeige, *La Foi Catholique* (Paris: Éditions de l'Orante; 1961), p. 498. My translation.

invading friars. The stupendous Ecclesia, bride and body of Christ, was torn with mutiny; and there were times when humble, devout Christians, seeking only to adore, knew not what human authority to accept. The popes, beset from within by rivalry among the orders and from without by rivalry with secular powers, could sometimes scarce maintain their eminence or know whether they were in fact popes. During the seventy-odd years between 1305 and 1378, the popes, under French control, deserted Rome for Avignon, whence they returned only to enter upon the Great Schism. When John Hus went to the stake in 1415, there were no less than three claimant popes; and John XXIII, the one pope recognized by the council which condemned Hus, fled that council for his life, was brought back and deposed.[1] The conciliar movement, then in its heyday, threatened to turn the Church from a monarchy into an oligarchy.

Feudal society had in fact entered upon its epoch of self-destruction. For a hundred years, to Joan of Arc's time, the lords of England and the lords of France slew one another. That done, they fell to slaughter among themselves, until (gunpowder assisting) their castles gave way to country mansions, and barons were reduced to courtiers within the presence of a king. Meanwhile the men of commerce, congregating in towns, grew rich and virtuous: it was evident that they understood the proper conduct of society much more than did the lords, and that they had a new, if heretical, religion for the purpose. And behind them rose the potential majesty of common men, laborers and tillers of the soil, who were all along, as Jesus and Paul had said, the objects of wise administration, and who might one day discover that they were so.

Some such discovery, indeed, had begun with a revolt of peasants in France (1358, the *Jacquerie*) and in England (1381). This latter, a great event, Richard II crushed with contemptible treachery. Yet the power of people acting in their own interests had not been felt for many a long year. It was now to be felt, with ever briefer interruptions, down into our own times and into the times beyond us. In the fourteenth century, however, what to us is knowledge could be no more than hope. The poet of *Piers Plowman,* having desired that conscience be with the king and grace with all the clergy, adds thereto his highest wish:

1) John's deposition has made it possible for the late pope to assume his name.

... that Piers with his plows, the newer and the older,
Were emperor of the world, and all men Christian!²

I I

THUS the point of Wyclif's sentence becomes plain. He was looking for certainty in a time when little was certain. Rival popes and
contentious clerics had blurred the image of authority. Corruption
of all sorts and of all intensities had torn the institution from its
divine and evangelical purpose. Surely God could not have been so
baffling as to leave unclear the descent of sovereignty or to leave
degenerate the exercise of it. There must somewhere be the unbreak-
able, unshakable rock. There was such a rock, indeed, and the rock
was Scripture.

The vicissitudes which have befallen that assemblage of writings
known to Christians as the Holy Bible offer an unexampled lesson in
the social use, life, and fate of ideology. However inspirational they
may be, the writings seem by no means equally inspired. Some are
folk poems (like Genesis); some are love poems (like the Song of
Songs); some are chronicles of variable authenticity. Taken as a
whole, the writings display no clear and settled doctrine but, on the
contrary, extensive and even bitter disagreement. Appeals to rectitude
and mercy alternate with tales of remarkable savagery, and the same
volume which bids us love our enemies rejoices that Saul has slain
his thousands and David his tens of thousands.

No man in his senses and able to choose would attempt to unite
under one canon writings of so extravagant variety. But the canon of
Scripture was a developing affair, and the men who in successive
generations presided over it were not free to choose. The refusal of
the early Church to break with Judaism opened the canon to all
those books that constitute the Old Testament. The New Testament
contains works which the experience of the early Church had shown
to be most useful for propagating and sustaining the faith.

In short, the canon of Scripture was set by political convenience
and historical necessity. In their love of unity and abhorrence of
schism, the Fathers acted shrewdly on the principle that a book, in
order to be canonical, ought first to have a following. Inconsistency
of doctrine (the bane of abstract thinkers) had, as we have seen, no

2) *The Portable Medieval Reader,* p. 199. Translated by H. W. Wells. The
"plows" are the two Testaments.

terrors for them. They smoothed out each inconsistency as it demanded notice, or defiantly (and sometimes rightly) asserted both contraries to be true.

Their successors have practiced the same art with ever-increasing refinement, until Christian doctrine presents a flawless surface, and few can guess the explosive contradictions within. The contradictions, however, are there, and they happen to be peculiarly volatile. In origin, and hence in possible application, they relate directly to the struggles of the weak against the mighty. No ingenuities of doctrine can alter, and no power long suppress, the fact that Jesus sought to make men masters of their social order, and that Paul sought to make men masters of themselves. The democratic content of Christianity is ineradicable. Democracy was in fact the evangel, the "good news," and on no other doctrine have the churches survived.

When therefore the churches behave autocratically, they at once collide with the doctrine that most sustains them. They are seen to do those things which it was the essence of their creed never to do. Every tyrannical act assimilates them to Nero, to Herod, to Caiaphas the High Priest. The membership finds itself walking with Jesus, while the leadership moves with his executioners. In a new but now familiar way the Incarnation repeats itself, and the God whom clerics had hopefully kept in the sky appears upon earth to confound the powerful.

In the development of the Church from its beginning to the Middle Ages, the Scriptures never had the supremacy that Protestants later accorded them. They were really a part of the general tradition. Separated from this by application of the canon, they then held equal rank with what was left—namely, Tradition with the capital T. Interpretation by the councils had obvious importance; so also the commentaries of the Fathers and the pronouncements of popes. It is most clear that, from an administrative point of view, an organization acts with greater unity when its doctrines can be officially defined to yield new applications as the need occurs. If the members have nothing but a book and a moment of application, they tend to fall into dispute concerning what text is applicable and what interpretation of the text is authentic. This is incipient anarchy. A leadership is therefore likely to feel that it can best maintain unity by asserting its own interpretation to be as authoritative as the traditional ground.

Accordingly, the Roman Church has preferred, and still prefers, to decide the content of doctrine by more than one criterion: by Scripture, by Tradition, by the findings of councils, and by those exceptional papal pronouncements that are said to be infallible.[3] When, therefore, some signal occasion arises for interpretation of doctrine, the whole vast enginery goes into operation, settling the question (if possible) on some lower level, but in any case drawing the entire membership in unity toward the final decision. The procedure is political and therefore pragmatic; one would not expect to develop a science in this way. But one would be hard pressed to say in what other manner there can be extensive unity and extensive ideology at one and the same time.

Yet there is, it seems, no gain without loss. The method of determining doctrine by manipulation of various criteria suffers from its own efficiency. All goes fairly well if circumstances are such that the manipulation can be honest. But when the evils in exploitative societies have grown acute, any formulation of doctrine in favor of the rich and powerful will seem obvious special pleading. This is especially the case, as we know, with Christianity. A social order founded upon spoliation and suffused with vice is visibly unchristian, and those who lead and those who profit will inevitably seem to lose whatever Christian authority they had been deemed to possess. Their pronouncements are invalidated by their iniquities. Men cannot willingly obey authority which they know to be corrupt, for obedience enlists them in the general banditry.

Now, feudal wealth derived from a plundering of the labor of serfs. The Church, possessing much land and many serfs, was one of the chief exploiters. As a feudal power, its class position was with the lords against the serfs and the commercial townsmen. The Church therefore shared the fundamental iniquities of its class, and to those iniquities it added others: the sale of its offices, the sale of indulgences, nepotism, and the permission (if not actually the encouragement) of vice. It is clear, for example, that Chaucer regards his poor parson as an exception—a man who did not abandon his flock to seek sinecures in London, who was always loath "to cursen

3) The dogma of papal infallibility renders the hierarchical determination of doctrine parallel to the hierarchical administration of the Church. Its whole purpose is organizational. Once this is understood, the apparent absurdity of having a pope (Pius IX) announce his own infallibility disappears.

for his tythes" (i.e., to excommunicate members for not paying dues), who would, quite to the contrary, relieve their poverty by gifts of his own:

> But Cristes lore, and his apostles twelve,
> He taughte, and first he folwed it himselve.[4]

It appears that not many others did.

The horrors of class rule and of power politics, the corruptions that (issuing thence) soiled the private lives and public behavior of ecclesiastical functionaries, drove most observers and all sufferers into the belief that they confronted not Christ but the antichrist, not God but Satan. The prestige of organizational pronouncements having fallen away, what was there left to turn to? The writings of the Fathers showed much the same contentiousness, and besides, the Fathers were only the Fathers. Tradition itself had sprung from the canonical Scriptures, long held to be divinely inspired. The Scriptures, moreover, were complete and definitive; they were also objective, in the sense that their message had been delivered once for all, independent of the play of later politics. You could measure popes and priests against Scripture, and they could not tinker with the plain public text to invite favorable judgment.

Something fixed and therefore incorruptible, something authoritative and therefore to be obeyed: that would be the doom of scoundrels, the salvation of sufferers, the cleansing of the Church. Such a thing was Scripture, "a Charter written by God," "the marrow of all laws." These phrases are Wyclif's, and to them he added the pungent remark that "Science of God feedeth men well; other science is meet for hogs, and maketh men fat here but not after doomsday."[5]

While these remarkable changes were going forward, other changes no less remarkable appeared in scholastic philosophy. Although Wyclif was himself the last of the great scholastics,[6] it is probable that he had scholasticism in mind as part at least of that "other science" which is "meet for hogs." The purpose of scholasti-

---

4) *Canterbury Tales,* Prologue, ll. 527–28. Compare Wyclif: "The priest that lives better sings better mass." Workman, op. cit., Vol. II, p. 13.
5) Ibid., pp. 150–51.
6) He was the *Doctor Evangelicus.* Aquinas had been the *Doctor Angelicus,* Albertus Magnus the *Doctor Universalis,* and Duns Scotus the *Doctor Subtilis.* There was the pleasant custom of awarding illustrious thinkers sobriquets descriptive of their special talents.

cism, as we may now recall, was to give a systematic account of the whole range of Christian doctrine, such that in the complete rendering no assertion should contradict any other assertion. None of the scholastics—except perhaps Abelard, and he not finally—thought of this vast enterprise as any substitute for faith and revelation. It was rather the sort of thing you would do if you were debating with an Arabian philosopher or a Talmudist, both sides accepting the principles of logic as procedural rules. There would be an establishing of definitions and axioms, and then an advance to theorems inferable from these. The result was impressive, if often unreadable, and the scholastics felt themselves to be potent defenders of the faith. Roger Bacon (1210?-1294), the most empirical of the scholastics and a very sensitive observer, felt likewise, but he also understood that philosophy occurs in a political context:

> And when Christians confer with pagans . . . they [the pagans] yield easily and see that they are held by errors. The proof of this is that they wished most willingly to be made Christians if the Church were willing to permit them to retain their freedom and to enjoy their goods in peace. But the Christian princes who labor for their conversion, and most of all the brothers of the Teutonic house, wish to reduce them to servitude, as is known to the Dominicans and Franciscans and other good men throughout Germany and Poland. And therefore they offer opposition; whence, they stand against oppression, not against the arguments of a better religion.[7]

I fancy that Bacon's notion of the ease with which pagans "yielded" to argument is somewhat overdrawn, and that his keenness of observation has been modified by his loyalty. If, however, we take the picture as he gives it, the pagans were arguing from politics to philosophy, from the intended enslavement to a rejection of the doctrine. The Christian masses, exploited and suffering, did not reject basic doctrine but only believed that it had been distorted by error and vice. The pagans did not want to join, but the Christians

7) *Opus Maius,* Moral Philosophy, Part IV. Translated by Richard McKeon, *Selections from Medieval Philosophy* (New York: Charles Scribner's Sons; 1930), Vol. II, p. 106. I have recapitalized the proper names, which McKeon, following a fashion once avant-garde, reduced to lower-case—yet he left capitalized the words "Church" and "Teutonic"—one wonders why.

wanted to remain members. It is a true measure of decay and desperation in the leadership of the medieval Church that, toward the end, it could neither recruit nor retain.

The scholastics, whatever their faults, did possess and exercise a kind of critical intelligence, which somewhat increased the tempo of general dissolution. Their goal in any case had been unattainable. The amplitude and contrariety of Christian thought could not be expressed in one coherent system; and even if that had been possible, no one man, by his own efforts, could do it. Knowledge of the universe, of man's place in it, of the duties men have toward one another and the privileges they may enjoy with one another—all this, so far as it exists, is an achievement of the whole race, and, even so, must always remain somewhat incomplete. Despite these impossibilities, however, each great scholastic has left his monument, "his tale of the weal and woe," in mighty tomes of demonstration, learning, and logic chopping. The life of these systems was brief indeed. Albertus Magnus vanished before his pupil Aquinas. Aquinas, who died in 1274, was outmoded by the end of the century, and did not become the Church's authoritative philosopher until the time of the Counter-Reformation.

And his successor? Well, that was Duns Scotus, who died in 1308 at an age (it is believed) of less than forty years, having produced more than a dozen magisterial volumes. During his brief maturity, the *Doctor Subtilis,* consonantly with his name, had cut the ground from under his predecessors in somewhat the way that Immanuel Kant, later on in 1781, cut the ground from under "rational theology." He showed that those arguments are defective which move from data in science to conclusions in theology, that scientific knowledge is in any case uncertain, and that absolute certainty belongs to supernatural revelation alone. To the self-posed question "whether any sure and pure truth can be known naturally by the understanding of the wayfarer without the special illumination of the uncreated light," he answered very roundly, "I argue that it cannot."[8]

The disconnection thus revealed between science and theology has one or other of two effects: it makes theology dubious or science disappointing. More painfully still, it establishes two radically different procedures for the determination of truth: one, the method

8) Ibid., Vol. II, p. 313.

we now regard as scientific; the other, acceptance of revelation. At the same time, it does liberate the sciences from any obligation to theology: the sciences cannot be required to do what *ex hypothesi* they are unable to do—namely, yield theological conclusions. Their gaze may therefore play, without distraction, upon the observable world of nature and of men. This shift in philosophical view, occurring about the year 1300, follows closely upon Bacon's brilliant analysis of the "rainbow effect" as he had observed it in certain stones, in dew, in rain drippings, in spray from water mills and oars, and in the rainbow itself.[9] As Abelard foretold the Renaissance, so Bacon and Scotus foretold the nineteenth and twentieth centuries.

This being the case, the fate of Scotus is remarkable. After his death he fell not so much into disuse as into ridicule. He had been a staunch churchman without taint of heresy; indeed, his views, if followed, would have brought philosophers to vent their quibbles upon matters of fact rather than matters of faith. Yet his very name "Duns" became the common noun "dunce," and his favorite conical cap the symbol of stupidity. In the year 1535, one of Thomas Cromwell's correspondents wrote that at Oxford, Scotus's writings were "fast nailed up upon posts in all houses of common easement *id quod oculis meis vidi.*"[1] One reason was that Scotus, like Aristotle, had been unlucky in his followers, who tried, two centuries after him, to prevent the urbane Erasmian glories of the English Renaissance.

But further, as I suspect, the tedium of logic chopping had grown dense by the mid-fourteenth century. As happens from time to time with the philosophical enterprise, scholasticism lost relevance to the crises of medieval society. How were the pains of men and their struggles against organized power to be represented in those dry, clipped, impenetrable definitions, in those quiddities, hecceities, susceptions?[2] How, for that matter, was the natural world itself to be so represented—the world in which, as was hoped, the struggle

9) Ibid., Vol. II, p. 80.
1) Workman, op. cit., Vol. I, p. 109. The Latin is ironical, not only in its meaning but in its very use. The correspondent is burlesquing scholasticism by setting a bit of erudite language amid the vernaculer context: "as I have seen with my own eyes."
2) "Quiddity" = "what the thing (any thing) is"; "hecceity" (Scotus's own word) = "the fact that a thing is *this* rather than *that*"; "susception" = "the taking on of an attribute" (e.g., my automobile is now painted blue).

would be resolved and the pains removed? Scholasticism had perhaps some answers to some questions, but none as yet to those great questions which bore the ache and body of the age. This, Wyclif knew, the last of the schoolmen. And he found answers.

I I I

THE ANSWERS, like all the chief Protestant answers, derived from Saint Augustine. The event is one of the most remarkable in intellectual history, because the borrowed doctrines seem so unsuited to the function they actually served. For how could men make a great revolution upon the view that God had already settled all questions in advance, and how could they make a good revolution upon the view that all men are naturally depraved? Each view negates the behavior alleged to be based upon it.

Yet this is how it is with ideologies. They don't always logically entail the behavior they seek to justify. They often give but a kind of oblique support, and, with Protestantism, the support proceeds around an arc of one hundred eighty degrees, from one opposite to another. The reason for these apparent oddities is that an ideology on behalf of social change cannot be a mere construct; it has to be discovered, in whole or part, among the then current and familiar notions. Otherwise it will attract no followers: possible adherents will, through sheer lack of acquaintance, remain unconvinced. Moreover, the ideologists themselves are tied to the notions of their era, and are capable of nothing absolutely new.

Something familiar, then, something available, something provocative: these are what an ideologist requires when he wants to lead his fellow men toward a reconstitution of the social order. We have seen that the Church had very shrewdly made Augustine a saint, although some of his doctrines were certainly heretical. As a saint— and, more probably, as an intellect of the first order—he had retained his eminence throughout the Middle Ages. The schoolmen never set down any assertion without a list of authorities behind it, and in such lists Augustine's name very often appears. His views were therefore well known and were part of the tradition. They were, that is to say, familiar and available.

We have now to see (what is puzzling) why they were provocative. Well, in the first place, we have already observed[3] that, if they

3) *Supra,* Chapter 6.

were true, the Church was unnecessary. For if, as Augustine held, God had chosen some souls as saved and some as damned from the very moment when he created them, there was nothing whatever the Church could do to alter the fate of either. Augustine had therefore robbed the Church of its function and the members of the chief reason for paying dues. He had thus committed an egregious heresy: indeed, there can be no greater heresy than for a member to assert or imply that the organization has no reason for existence. Augustine, of course, asserted no such thing, and would no doubt have been horrified by the implication. The institution swallowed him as a savory, if difficult, morsel, and set about the process of digestion.

After a thousand years, Augustine himself proved digestible, his doctrines not. They rent the body, in fact, in a way that overstrains my metaphor. The irrelevance of the Church to human salvation was by no means the inference that Wyclif and the later reformers wished to draw; it belongs to the eighteenth century and after. But the reformers did have the idea that the authentic and genuine Church was, in Wyclif's phrase, *congregatio omnium predestina-torum,*[4] the assembly of those predestined to salvation. Such would have to be the case, or else the Church would permanently include a certain number of the damned. But these unfortunates (or, in a severer view, villains) are surely much more, as John Hus said, "like dung which in the Day of Judgment are to be separated from the body of Christ."[5]

So God had made his original, all-powerful, and definitive choice between the saved and the damned. These souls were, accordingly, predestined to election or damnation: God had determined which they were to be. There was, however, the difficulty (for human beings, at any rate) that both the fact of choice and the grounds of choice were equally inscrutable. No man (said Wyclif), whether pope, priest, or serf, "wots whether he be of the Church, or whether he be a limb of the fiend."[6] Augustine himself, the most candid of

4) *De Ecclesia,* II, 5.

5) *Commentary on the Lombard,* quoted in Schaff's translation of Hus's *De Ecclesia*—an almost verbatim transcript of Wyclif's work (New York: Charles Scribner's Sons; 1915), p. 10n. The "Lombard" was Peter Lombard (*obit* 1164), Abelard's pupil, whose book of *Sentences* was a favorite theological compendium in the Middle Ages.

6) Quoted by Workman, op. cit., Vol. II, p. 9. In true medieval style, Satan has a body also, and people can be members of it.

thinkers and the most aware of objections, had faced the difficulty and had asserted that inscrutability was the fact nevertheless:

> But of two pious men, why to the one should be given perseverance unto the end [i.e., survival into salvation], and to the other it should not be given, God's judgments are even more unsearchable. Yet to believers it ought to be a most certain fact that the former is of the predestinated, the latter is not.[7]

The Augustinian argument, thus far, established the *possibility* that this or that churchman, from pope to lay member, was in fact not a member of the authentic Church, the *congregatio omnium predestinatorum,* no matter how much he appeared to belong to the visible institution. This possibility at once suggested another—namely, that some of these churchmen who did not really belong although they seemed to belong were imposters. An infiltration of the visible Church by imposters is exactly what one would expect of Satan, and Satan would surely choose for the purpose the most cunning among the "limbs of the fiend."

How was one to distinguish? The basic and divine choice no doubt remained inscrutable, but there might yet be external signs suggestive of the difference. Augustine himself had dropped a hint or two: "He who falls, falls by his own will, and he who stands, stands by God's will."[8] That is to say, sinners have only themselves to blame; the righteous, however, may attribute their righteousness to God. It follows that righteous behavior, being due to God, is some sign (though not definitive) of election; whereas sinful behavior, being not due to God, is some sign (rather indeed a potent one) of damnation. Generally speaking, it makes sense to suppose that the saved will act in a manner which suggests that they deserve to be saved, and that the damned will exhibit on earth the marks of their future damnation. This is why Presbyterians are the way they are.

Once the righteousness of visibly committed acts was taken as proof (though not final proof) of ultimate sanctity, and therefore as proof (though not final proof) of membership in the authentic Church, Wyclif and Hus and then Luther and Calvin had all the doctrine they needed. For, as we know, the behavior of popes and

7) *De Dono Perseverantiae* ("On the Gift of Perseverance"—Augustine's last work), Chapter 21. Translated by R. E. Wallis, op. cit., p. 532.
8) Ibid., Chapter 19, loc. cit.

prelates and functionaries of all degrees was wildly iniquitous, harmful to the visible Church itself and to society in general. The subtlest apologetics collapsed beneath political absurdities. For example, Richard FitzRalph, Archbishop of Armagh in Ireland, undertook, in his *Summa in Questionibus Armenorum,* to prove that the churchmen in Rome had the right to select the successors to Saint Peter (i.e., the popes). The reason was, he said, that Rome is the capital of Christendom.[9] He said this, unfortunately, during precisely the period when the popes were in France at Avignon—a fact which Wyclif pointed out to him with no trouble and much joy. The argument was the more remarkable because FitzRalph himself had several times journeyed to Avignon on ecclesiastical business.

The doubts thus morally aroused concerning churchmen's title to their various offices had soon to turn upon a central sacrament, the Eucharist. Wherever and whenever Mass was celebrated, there occurred the climactic moment at which the two "species," the bread and the wine, became, by sacerdotal efficacy, the body and the blood of Christ. This miracle the ordained clergy, and only the ordained clergy, could effect. It was, furthermore, the most precious act in the whole range of Christian ceremony. It supplied to the worshiper the veritable body and blood of "the Lamb for sinners slain"; and thus it offered, not the symbol of salvation, but the reality. The unexpressed premise, very old and very primitive, was that a man grows to be like what he eats.

It is not hard to imagine what men of sensitive conscience must have felt at seeing the Eucharist administered by known and obvious scoundrels. The said scoundrels were presumed able to work this miracle, though laymen of blameless life could not. But could the scoundrels really do so? Can a bad man effect a good miracle, and a very bad man the best miracle of all? A suspicion opened in the mind that perhaps there occurred in fact no transubstantiation, no change of bread into body or of wine into blood. The important thing, in any event, was Christ's presence. Perhaps the case was that Christ was there before, during, and after the elevation of the host—present—that is to say, along with the elements (this was Luther's doctrine of consubstantiation) and surviving when all had been accomplished (this was Wyclif's doctrine of remanence). If such things could be supposed, then priests and other clergy were mere celebrants

9) Workman, op. cit., Vol. II, p. 77.

and not workers of the central miracle. They would stand at one remove from the great event, unconnected with its causality; and thus their sinfulness could not soil, because it could not even touch, the sacrament.

From the leadership's point of view, however, the precisely contrary doctrine had to be required. The power to work that particular miracle—a power descending through ages by the laying on of consecrated hands—was the one mark which distinguished the clergy from every other group. Without that power, they might be teachers or philosophers or physicians or social workers or mere dues collectors, but they would not be what, in theory, they had been supernaturally ordained to be. Their loss of power would induce a yet greater loss of power by the whole institution, which would be left to draw smaller revenues from less impressive services.

This is perhaps the supreme example of how an organization gets entangled in its own ideology. Protestants, and non-Catholics generally, have long maintained that the doctrine of transubstantiation is not only false but unnecessary to religion. That may be so. Nevertheless the doctrine of transubstantiation is absolutely necessary to the Roman Catholic Church, because that Church has a special ideological history. Once the organization based itself on a core of doctrine to the effect that God's Son had died for human salvation, that members could be strengthened toward salvation "as often as ye eat my flesh and drink my blood," and that the organization maintained a group of men especially prepared to work the miracle, there plainly could be no alteration of view. These doctrines had not been developed all at once, with foresight into the future. They had grown, rather slowly indeed, as the organization grew; they had grown round it like vines and under it like petrifactions. Supportive and constrictive at the same time, they confronted the Church at last with a dreadful choice between radical change and loss of leadership. There is a certain gallantry in the fact that the Church declined the first alternative.

At any rate, we can understand why transubstantiation, apparently so remote and even so eschatological a question, has caused in its day the shedding of tears and blood. For really the question had little to do with wafers and wine and the presence or absence of a risen Lord. What was at issue was the power of an hierarchy of functionaries and therefore of the organization which they controlled. The question, that is to say, was political and organizational; it had to do with highly practical matters of wealth, dominance, and survival. It is a privilege of the twentieth century to see these truths bodied forth beneath the garments that once concealed them. We may rejoice in the privilege, and rejoice also to perceive that morality has made a difference in human affairs.

The moral requirements which Wyclif made the ground for holding membership and office in the Church were extremely strict. Leaders and members alike were to live in the same poverty and with the same humility that had distinguished the Founder and his disciples. Also, like the Founder, they were to forswear temporal dominion and devote themselves entirely to things spiritual. Plainly, the Church could not do all this without ceasing to be a feudal power, or indeed a power of any kind in the political sense. Nor could the leadership practice poverty without forgoing that ostentation which is the public display of power possessed. Some of the medieval popes were not careerists but devoted servants of the Church; yet, the more devoted they were, the greater the impulse to accept, on behalf of the institution, the violences and corruptions of power politics. The decisions of critics are ordinarily less onerous than those of administrators; and a historian may perhaps sympathetically imagine more than one pope, otherwise willing enough to be righteous, saying to himself, "But if I do *this,* the whole thing may be lost." Did such popes long for the vanished days of primitive Christianity, when there was no more at issue than worship and rehabilitation and the Sunday meal? I would not be surprised to learn that some of them did.

In any event, corruption worsened. Whether it arose from the social system or whether it was rather the effect of careerist avarice, corruption was the general fact, and caused Wyclif to visit upon the reigning pope a series of thunderous epithets: "leader of the army of the devil," "limb of Lucifer," "head vicar of the fiend," "simple idiot who might be a damned devil in hell."[1] The pope was, moreover, a "detestable fugitive," having, like his immediate predecessors, kept away from Rome in the safety of Avignon. There, about the year 1330, when Wyclif was but a boy, John XXII had given, among many other feasts, one that offered the banqueters eight oxen, fifty-five sheep, four boars, eight pigs, six hundred and ninety fowl, five

1) Ibid., Vol. II, p. 81.

hundred eighty partridges, three thousand eggs, and various un-numbered quantities of fruit, vegetables, and bread. Events like this Wyclif had in mind when he wrote, some thirty years later, "If anyone saith, Lo here at Avignon is the Christ, believe them not, for the deeds shall show who is the antichrist."[2]

It followed that disobedience, legalized by the illegality of the leadership, became also a virtue as the sole means of rescuing the Church. Wyclif's development followed the usual path of heresy toward schism: first, the identification of gross evils; then the wish to correct them; then the search for help among the membership. He was Master of Balliol College at Oxford—the first eminent master of a distinguished line—and Oxford remained loyal to him throughout his career. There he recruited, and thence he sent out, his Poor Preachers, whose vocation, modeled upon that of St. Francis, was to spread the authentic gospel of the authentic Church among the common people. "Mute prelates," said Wyclif, "are the ruin of the Church," while evangelical preaching, since it can persuade people from sin, is "more precious than the administration of any sacrament."[3] This function, indeed, had fallen, if not into disuse, at least into triviality: parish priests were more expert at hunting down hares than case endings in the Latin, and the friars "would preach more for a bushel of wheat than to bring a soul from hell."[4] Professor Workman reminds us that volumes of ready-made sermons were available to the lazy cleric—the title of one of which, *Dormi Secure* ("Sleep Soundly"), referred, not to the repose of the congregation, but to the preacher's peace of mind.[5]

The Poor Preachers spoke in the vernacular, not in Latin, and thus their words entered the lives and hearts of the humblest men. Wyclif, himself a vastly learned scholar, had that grace which crowns all scholarship: the wish to share its truths and glories with every human being on earth. The wish drew with it a genial faith that people were susceptible of instruction, that, in order to learn, they had only to be taught. A love went with it also, the kind of love which, in *Piers Plowman,* the fair lady, interpretress of Christianity, explained to the poet while he dreamed of the field full of folk:

2) Ibid., Vol. II, p. 78.
3) Ibid., Vol. II, p. 209.
4) Ibid., Vol. II, p. 215.
5) Ibid., loc. cit.

Heaven could not hold love, it was so heavy in itself. But when it had eaten its fill of earth, and taken flesh and blood, then it was lighter than a leaf on a linden-tree, more subtle and piercing than the point of a needle. The strongest armor was not proof against it, the tallest ramparts could not keep it out.[6]

It was soon evident that more than sermons were needed in the vernacular. If Scripture was in fact the inerrant repository and rule of faith, if, further, Scripture offered the sole sure criteria of righteousness, then the salvation of common men lay in their knowing what Scripture said. They would have to acquaint themselves with it in their own tongue; translation was therefore necessary.

There were many obstacles—chiefly official reluctance, which in time became official hostility. The clergy, jealous of its own control over doctrine, was not eager for the laity to form unguided opinions —any more than a newscaster is nowadays eager to have people judge events for themselves.[7] Moreover, Latin (along with Greek and Hebrew) was one of the three sacred languages; translation would destroy the sanctity of the text. Moreover, as Thomas Palmer, a Dominican, said, the English tongue sounded "like the grunting of pigs or the roaring of lions."[8] It is a strange fact in history that there never has been a great social advance which was not objected to on esthetic grounds.

Wyclif's energy overrode all difficulties, and he became the sponsor and inspirer of the first Bible in a tongue which can be called "English." We should, I suppose, call this Bible only "Wyclif-fite," since it has not been established, and apparently cannot be established, whether any of the translation is Wyclif's own. The work seems mainly to have been done by his close associates Nicholas of Hereford and John Purvey. Hereford, it is known, did the books from Genesis to Baruch in the Apocrypha. He stopped at Baruch

6) Passus I. This is J. F. Goodridge's translation (Baltimore: Penguin Classics; p. 74), more successful and poetic in its prose than many versified translations.
7) The "continuator" of Henry Knighton's *Chronicon* wrote (early fifteenth century), "This master John Wyclif translated into English (not, alas, into the tongue of angels [a pun on *Angles*]) the gospel which Christ gave to doctors and clerks of the Church, in order that they might sweetly minister it to lay-men and weaker men. . . . Thus the pearl of the gospel is scattered abroad and trodden under foot of swine. . . ." Quoted by James Baikie, *The English Bible and Its Story* (London: Seeley, Service and Company; 1928), p. 127.
8) Workman, op. cit., Vol. II, p. 193.

3:20, because he was obliged at that point to flee arrest on a charge of heresy. It is possible that Wyclif carried on from there to the end of the Gospels, but the style is less noble and vivid than that of the scriptural quotations which stud his sermons and treatises (there are no less than seven hundred of these in the *Trialogus* alone). Despite these uncertainties, Wyclif was in some sense the father of that Bible. Contemporaries, and later men too, attributed it to him—as, for example, Arundel, Archbishop of Canterbury, a great hunter of heretics, in 1412: "That wretched and pestilent fellow John Wyclif, of damnable memory, that son of the old serpent, the very herald and child of antichrist, [in order] to fill up the measure of his malice, devised the expedient of a new translation of the Scriptures into the mother tongue."[9]

The Poor Preachers founded a movement, the members of which, mostly common folk, were nicknamed "Lollards"(from the verb *"lollen"* = "to mumble"). These folk undertook to display in their own lives the simplicity and sobriety which had adorned the lives of the early Christians and which are known to us under the adjective "puritanical." The charming episode that Chaucer imagines in his little prologue to the Shipman's Tale seems accurately descriptive. The poor parson, being invited (with many oaths) by the host to tell a story, rebukes the host for profanity. "I smell a Loller in the wind," cries the host; "this Loller he wol preche us somewhat." "Nay, by my fader's soule!" breaks in the shipman, "that shall he nat!" And then the shipman gives his reason: "He wolde sowen som difficulte, or springen cokkel in our clene corn [weeds amid our wheat]." In the reigning view, that is to say, the Lollards were disruptive, being "radicals." And so, to fend this off, the shipman hastens on to tell a story which, as he says, will have nothing in it of philosophy or erudition. The parson, the saintly radical, does not get his chance until the very end of the *Tales*.

The Lollard movement survived Wyclif's death in 1384, and survived prosperously. Its strength issued from just those people who were "the feet of the body politic," and who thus bore, with unquiet suffering, the exactions of the higher orders. Rulers are always alarmed when masses of the governed begin to stir, and grow more alarmed as the stirring increases. By the turn of the century, the Lollards had passed well beyond Wyclif's more modest doctrine,

9) Quoted by Baikie, op. cit.

and were denouncing a great deal of religious practice as wasteful, auricular confession as unnecessary and dangerous, images and saints' relics and even the Eucharist itself as superstitious magic. "We think truly," says a Lollard document of 1394, "that the holy water used in church would be the best medicine for all kinds of illnesses—sores, for instance; whereas we experience the contrary day by day."[1]

So much hardheaded empiricism among the masses offered the beginnings of a threat. Parliament responded with the Act known as *De Haeretico Comburendo* ("On the Desirability of Burning Heretics"). Observing that "the said false and perverse people go from diocese to diocese . . . to the utter destruction of all order and rule of right and reason," the Act prescribed that convicted heretics were to be burned in some prominent place, "that such punishment may strike fear to the minds of others."[2] It was the year 1401: legislators were candid in those days.

The Act was repealed under Henry VIII (himself, as we shall see, something of a heretic), was renewed under Mary, and was repealed once for all under Elizabeth (the daughter of her father's heretical days). The Act sufficed, however, to scatter the Lollards. Hereford and Purvey had already been driven down various degrees of recantation. A Lollard uprising in 1414, led by Sir John Oldcastle, had as its aim the kidnapping of Sir John's youthful chum, Henry IV, with a view to winning Henry to the Lollard side. The uprising failed. Oldcastle survived for three more years, a fugitive but still an agitator, for he did not yield easily. Then he was captured, brought sorely wounded to London, and at last hanged and burned— "gallows [says the chronicler] and all." His special immortality, however, is totally unexpectable. For he was the original, much altered in adaptation, of "a goodly portly man, i' faith, and a corpulent; of a cheerful look, a pleasing eye and a most noble carriage"— Jack Falstaff!

Wyclif had never contemplated any change in the social structure; he intended to reform society by persuading its members to act justly and decently. He stood aloof from the Peasants' Revolt of 1381, in which not a few Lollards took part; and it is possible, as some say, that he was opposed to it. In earlier years he maintained relations

1) Bettenson, *Documents,* p. 250.
2) Ibid., pp. 255–56 and p. 258.

with John of Gaunt that are unclear and may perhaps have been equivocal; at any rate, John's men broke up two of his trials for heresy. Edward III regarded him with favor, by reason of a well-argued treatise explaining why Edward need not pay certain monies that Pope Gregory XI claimed. "England," he wrote on one occasion, "is not bound to obey the pope except in so far as obedience can be deduced from Scripture."[3] We may believe that he seldom found it thus deducible, for he went on to assert that foreign priests ought to take oaths of allegiance to the English Crown.

Thus Wyclif, with much political acumen, based himself on the nascent nationalism of his time. He perceived (or so we may conjecture) that this nationalism would develop around the king, that it would therefore take a secular form, and that it would find support in the great masses of Englishmen. Thus allied with the might of king and people, he proved invincible. He was never long out of controversy and hence never long out of danger, but he died peacefully at the last, after a second stroke of apoplexy, on the thirty-first of December, 1384. Thirty-four years later, pursuant to an edict of the Council of Constance (which had found Wyclif guilty of some two hundred sixty heretical assertions), his bones were disinterred, burned, and the ashes cast into the little river Swift.[4] "His vile corpse," said an attendant bigot, "they consigned to hell, and the river absorbed his ashes."[5] But not, it is obvious, the memory of the man.

There is something spiteful and futile about physically abusing the dead. The like abuse of the living is no less spiteful, but, at least in the view of the perpetrators, it will silence an enemy. Such, at all events, is the hope. But the death and agony of John Hus cry out, through the subsequent centuries, that this hope is futile too. For here a man of entire sweetness and candor collided with a leadership that was neither candid nor sweet. The man was resolved to make ideals prevail; the leadership was resolved to maintain unity around itself throughout the organization. No other episode in history more

3) Workman, op. cit., Vol. II, p. 24.
4) This vengeance upon dead (and hence victorious) heretics has not been unusual, and is due to struggles persisting after the heretic's time. Cromwell's corpse was removed from Westminster Abbey and hanged at Tyburn in the early part of Charles II's reign. By contrast, the Emperor Charles V, when urged to scatter Luther's bones, replied, "I do not make war on the dead."
5) Workman, op. cit., Vol. II, p. 320.

strikingly shows how powerless a pure man is in the face of power, and how certain is his doom when ideals throw him into conflict with authority.

The reason is quite plain, and we need not be Machiavellis to see it. In any contest for power, the issue is decided by superior *power*. Righteousness as such has no political power at all, though it can acquire it if it chances to evoke popular support. Unfortunately, power as such is often increased by the abandonment of righteousness; and, worse still, the habit of abandoning it can become the settled practice of an organization. In the Middle Ages, for example, simony (the sale of church offices to the highest bidders) was an important source of papal revenue. I imagine that many a pope would have been glad to abolish the practice, but from what other source could he raise equal funds? He might also think that at least, with simony, the funds came from those who could most afford the expense; and, as regards administrative capacity, the purchasers were by no means incompetent. Thus power fed on vice and vice on power, and, as we see, the feeding still goes on.

The marriage of Richard II to Anne of Bohemia in 1382 established a channel for the transmission of Wyclif's writings into Prague. They were carried thither by courtiers and by scholars like Jerome, who, visiting Oxford, copied out the *Trialogus* with his own hand. Though hemmed round by opposing forces, Bohemian nationalism was already far advanced, and the teachings of Wyclif found quick acceptance among the people. Most of all, they found a gifted expositor in John Hus, whom a blameless life and a charming character had made the ideal of a popular leader. What Hus believed, he believed devoutly; and so he followed a path, without swerving or faltering, from principle to the stake.[6]

At this time the organization of the Church was in extreme disarray. Between 1378 and 1409 there were two claimant popes, Gregory XII (representing the Roman line) and Benedict XIII (representing the Avignon line). After 1409 there were three claimant popes, the number having been increased by one Alexander V. Alexander had been elected by a council that met at Pisa, and the

6) For example, the remarkable little scene which Lea describes (op. cit., p. 509): "One learned doctor urged his submission [to the Council of Constance], saying, 'If the council told me I had but one eye, I would confess it to be so, though I know I have two,' but Hus was impervious to such example."

hope was that the other two contenders would thereupon disappear. Nothing of the sort happened, but within ten months Alexander was dead. His successor in the doubtful rank was John XXIII, a man of torturous diplomatic skill and (as was later charged) of unmentionable vices. His maneuverings were more swift than successful, and at last, in 1415, the growing conciliar movement exacted from him the summoning of a council at Constance.

To this council John Hus was called, to acquit himself of heresy. He went thither under a safe-conduct granted by the Emperor Sigismund, who, when the struggle grew difficult, ingloriously withdrew his protection. That Hus was aware of danger may be inferred from the fact that he disposed of all his personal possessions before leaving Prague. One wonders, indeed, why he went: he would have been safe in Bohemia. The psychology of authentic martyrs is not well understood, but let us suppose him simply a man firm and clear in conviction, fearless before consequences, able to assert truth and confound rogues, and not despairing of doing both.

Such hopes were soon disappointed: he had entered a lair of wild, if ceremonious, beasts. The agony was protracted, as the description of it need not be. Two elements of the scene, however, are full of instruction: the behavior of Stephen Palecz and the behavior of John XXIII.

Stephen Palecz had been a friend and disciple of Hus. A brief imprisonment by John XXIII had filled him with mortal terror and made of him an informer, an accuser, and a general inquisitorial drudge. There are always such dogs around such banquets. Stephen was prepared to assert, and did assert, "that since the birth of Christ there had been no more dangerous heretics than Wycliff and Hus."[7] The fact was that since the arrest of Christ there had been no such Judas.

When the day of death approached, Hus expressed the surprising wish to have Stephen as his confessor. Stephen, arriving at the cell, urged him to recant. "What would you do," asked Hus, "if you knew for certain that you did not hold the errors imputed to you? Would you abjure?" Stephen had not lost quite all his virtue, and answered, with tears, "It is difficult."[8] He wept again when Hus begged pardon for insults uttered in the heat of controversy. He wept, but,

7) Ibid., p. 501.
8) Ibid., p. 509.

within a year's time after Hus's death, he went on to destroy the next noblest reformer, Jerome of Prague. Organizations impose many calamities upon many men, but the worst of these, I fancy, is the habit of cowardice.

The proceedings against Hus lasted, all told, some seven months, from November 28, 1414 (the date of his arrest) to July 6, 1415 (the date of his execution). Midway, in March of 1415, John XXIII, whose difficulties with the Council had become acute, fled Constance in the clothing of a commoner, with a crossbow at his side. He was apprehended, returned to Constance, and lodged in the same prison with Hus, the Castle of Gottlieben. There ensued a little drama that sufficiently distinguished the fate of a man of integrity from the fate of an organizational hack. John Hus, certain of being right, would confess to no doctrinal errors, and so was doomed. John XXIII admitted all that was charged against him and yielded entirely to the Council's will. Hus ended his days amid the smoke and flames of an execution site near the river Rhine. John XXIII ended his days as Dean of the Sacred College under Pope Martin V.

Snuggling within the bosom of a strong organization, men are almost always safe. But the chill of danger will never leave those other men whom righteousness requires to stand alone.

I V

THE POLITICAL INTENT of an organization, and the view it takes of its membership, may be accurately judged from the writings it encourages the members to read or discourages from reading. Tolerance in this regard is, in principle, better than intolerance, and there must always be something presumptuous in deciding for other people what shall be available to them as satisfactions of their tastes and of their need for knowledge. Such graces, however, belong to periods of stability, when the organization is under no great stress. They begin to disappear as the organization begins to be embattled, and perhaps vanish altogether if the organization fears for its life. Similarly, new victorious revolutionary organizations make short shrift of writings that defend the old order and even of some that have survived from it.

Every organization, we have said, needs an ideology, and leaderships have therefore to foster one. But as for the members' acquaintance with that ideology, the extent and intimacy vary over a wide range. On the whole, the more intimate and extensive the acquaintance, the more probable it is that members will want to tinker with the ideology. They have become, in an unprofessional way, theoreticians. No doubt it is desirable for them to be so, but leaderships are likely to prefer a quieter intellectual life within the organization. Moreover, in social affairs, the course of events is often so changeful, so sudden in shifts from opposite to opposite, that a prolonged and general debate over strategy might entail the loss of opportunities.

During the Middle Ages (and, indeed, throughout all previous history) the great mass of human population could neither read nor write. Even for those who were literate there were not many books or manuscripts. Wealth determined, in some measure, whether a private person, unconnected with a monastic library, had anything to read at all. In 1380, Richard II laid out twenty-eight pounds as part payment for a Bible "written in the French language," a copy of the *Roman de la Rose,* and a copy of *Percevall and Gawayne.*"⁹ It will be seen that, once upon a time, a royal personage had but a tiny portion of what is now available (in modern societies, at least) to the humblest person.

The general illiteracy and lack of books, the restriction of both literacy and books to groups who held rank in the medieval establishment, offered ideal conditions for a conservative policy. They were impediments, upon enlightenment certainly, but also upon change in general. Common folk in the Middle Ages learned their ideology from sermons, from ritual, from windows of stained glass, and from those charming sculptures which still adorn, more eloquent than any text, the churches of the age. Such "visual education" has perhaps never been equaled. The Last Judgment stands across many a portal, enacting the old drama of eternal loss and gain; one had only to look in order to see the ultimate questions and the fate that would ultimately follow the various answers. I would conjecture that some part of Protestant image smashing was an attempt to suppress these proclamations in stone of doctrines held to be outmoded and pernicious.

The case differs with organizations in movement or movements becoming organized. With them, discipline and efficacy require a much more knowledgeable membership. Every member,

9) Workman, op. cit., Vol. II, p. 193.

indeed, is a kind of missionary, and the movement grows from his successful teaching of others. We have seen that this was the office of Wycliff's Poor Preachers; it was an office assumed also by various laymen, particularly by those with good memories. For, books being scarce (though less scarce than they had been), recitation supplied the lack of text. In England of the early fifteenth century, quite a few people were, for these public recitations, brought before clerical tribunals. One Thomas Chase, for example, had been heard to recite the Epistle of St. James and the first chapter of Luke's Gospel.[1] These he had learned from a woman, Agnes Ashford, whose memory embraced yet larger portions of Scripture. The bishops commanded her to teach such lessons no more, especially not to her children.

We of the twentieth century, who have seen, and do still see, much larger populations emerge into literacy, culture, and the conduct of their own affairs, may, more than our immediate ancestors, appreciate the charm of all such efforts. Devotion to Scripture as the supreme source of enlightenment took on that sanctity which only common folk can grant and then only when they are engaged upon a great social regeneration. People sometimes sat up all night to hear, by reading or recitation, the inspired words. They sometimes paid five marks, or a load of hay, for copies of a few chapters in James or Paul. John Foxe, who reports these facts, goes on to say, "To see their travails, their earnest seekings, their burning zeal, their readings, their watchings, their sweet assemblies, their love and concord, their godly living, their faithful demeaning with the faithful, may make us now, in these our days of free profession, to blush with shame."[2]

Foxe was writing in Elizabeth's time, when English Protestantism had triumphed; his description goes back, with suitable accuracy, over the previous two hundred years. Yet another generation passed before the English Bible attained, in the Authorized Version of 1611, its perfection of phrase and power. There is no other work, except perhaps Luther's German Bible, which so incomparably unites the spirit of a language with the spirit of them that use the language.

---

1) Raikie, op. cit., p. 144. It will be remembered that the Epistle of Saint James is the great democratic tract of the New Testament and that the first chapter of Luke contains (verses 46–55) Mary's highly subversive Magnificat.

2) Quoted by Raikie, ibid., p. 145.

Bereft of their classics, other languages might yet stammer on; bereft of our King James Bible, we English-speaking persons would be mute.

Three extraordinary events coincided, during a space of two centuries, to effect this result: (1) the consolidation of English as the national speech, used by all classes; (2) the invention of printing; and (3) the development and triumph of a revolutionary movement. Without the first, there would be no *English* Bible; without the second, no Bible in manifold copies; without the third, no prose of anything like the pure celestial passion which a century of translators, refining one another's work, did in the end achieve.

(1) In the year 1300 it would have been hard to guess that, before the century was out, English would displace French as the national language. Robert of Gloucester, in a rhyming *Chronicle* of about that time, observed that "unless a man knows French, he is of little account; but common people hold to English and to their own speech yet." Robert actually wrote this observation as follows:

Vor bote a man conne Frenss, men telthe of him lute;
ac lowe men holdeth to Engliss and to hor owe speche yute.[3]

This is what English looked like about the year 1300, and Robert, by using it, contributed his bit toward the coming change. The Hundred Years' War, which began in 1338, between the feudal lords of England and those of France, helped to make the French language seem unpatriotic for Englishmen. Political stirrings among the people evoked so eloquent a work in the vernacular as *Piers Plowman,* and Chaucer, one of our greatest poets, gave literary sanctity to the English tongue simply by writing in it. John of Trevisa says, about 1385, that "in al the gramerscoles of Engelond childern leveth Frensch, and construeth and lurneth in Englysche. . . . Also gentil men habbeth now moche yleft for to teche here children Frensch."[4] This English is a good deal nearer ours: you will, at most, only need to be told that "gentlemen have now generally given up teaching their children French."

3) Quoted by Charles C. Butterworth, *The Literary Lineage of the King James Bible* (Philadelphia: University of Pennsylvania Press; 1941), p. 35. I have quoted Butterworth's modernization; the reader may, with a little ingenuity, find its equivalent in the original.
4) Ibid., p. 37.

A century later, Caxton, who had brought the first printing press to England, remarked how much the language had changed during his own lifetime, and complained that it still differed shire by shire. A group of merchants, he said, traveling through Kent, stopped at a house, where one of them "axyd after eggys." The housewife replied that she "coude speke no frensche." Another member of the party, however, asked for "eyren" and got them. "Loo," wrote Caxton, "what sholde a man in thyse dayes now wryte?"[5]

(2) Printing, a German invention of the mid-fifteenth century, came to England about the year 1474. It was, of course, one of the great achievements of the human race, one of the most democratic; and its power to lift multitudes toward control of their own destiny is by no means spent. This effect, indeed, was its first as it will be its last. Except for Bibles, the early printed books had nothing particularly heretical about them, but, as Mr. Myers says, printing "helped to form a lay public opinion not dependent for its information on the pulpit and the cloister."[6] Next to the revolutionary movement itself (of which it has steadily been the faithful ally), printing has done the most to make society "secular"—i.e., independent of control by clerics. This transformation, illimitable in growth and irreversible in direction, began with the "Open Bible," the Bible wrested from the hands of a bureaucracy and offered to every man who could read. Without this transformation, anything in the nature of freedom of thought would be most difficult; with it, freedom of thought, despite the mistrust of governments, becomes very nearly inevitable.

(3) Between the time of Wycliff and the time of James I, popular acquaintance with Scripture passes from being more or less forbidden to being more or less obligatory. In resisting the change, the Roman Church consulted its fears more than its wisdom, as is the wont of declining institutions. The indescribable folly (as it now seems) of hounding people because they could recite the first chapter of Luke came from fear founded upon an accurate expectation. The expectation was that when people read a certain work, they form their own ideas of it. They do indeed, and they did. The folly lay in fearing the result. No doubt the result would have been changes in the

5) Ibid., p. 38.
6) A. R. Myers, *England in the Late Middle Ages* (Baltimore: Penguin Books; 1952), p. 224.

Church and in the feudal system; the Middle Ages would have become Modern Times. But this happened anyway. It seems to be universally the case that ruling groups and governing classes develop a psychotic dread of being "modernized." Why this is so, I have long wondered and cannot tell. Even psychiatrists, ordinarily so knowledgeable about human motives, provide as yet no persuasive explanation.

The hero of the struggle for the Open Bible was William Tyndale, who was born near Wales about 1484 and who perished by strangulation and the flame near Antwerp in 1536. At Oxford, where he took his degree in 1515, Tyndale acquired the necessary languages and erudition for his life's task, the rendering of the Bible into English, not from the Latin Vulgate as Wyclif's associates had done, but from the original Hebrew and Greek. In 1516 there appeared a new and stupendous aid to scholarship, Erasmus' edition of the New Testament in Greek, with a commentary that still remains the fount of learning upon that subject.[7]

Tyndale began his work in England, and for a time even had hopes of doing it within the household of the Bishop of London. Repression, however, drove him to Germany and, in Germany, from Hamburg to Cologne to Worms, where the strong Lutheran movement offered a haven. By 1526 his first version of the New Testament was in print, was smuggled into England,[8] and was there distributed by devoted colleagues. Froude, in his picturesque way, describes the London scene:

> . . . poor men, poor cobblers, weavers, carpenters, trade apprentices, and humble artizans, men of low birth and low estate, who might be seen at night stealing along the lanes and alleys of London, carrying with them some precious load of books which it was death to possess; and giving their lives gladly, if it must be so, for the brief tenure of so dear a treasure. These men, for the present, were likely to fare ill from the new ministry. They were the disturbers of order, the anarchists, the men disfigured *pravitate hereticâ* [by heretical depravity], by monstrous doctrines,

7) Erasmus was the first of the "higher critics"—men who treated the original manuscripts of the New Testament in the same way that scholarship would treat any other ancient manuscript, namely, as secular rather than sacred phenomena.

8) Mostly by merchants, the rising bourgeoisie!

and consequently by monstrous lives—who railed at authorities, and dared to read New Testaments with their own eyes. . . .[9]

There followed a preposterous ceremony outside the north transept of old Saint Paul's, where, in the presence of Cardinal Wolsey, eighteen bishops, and thirty-six lesser functionaries, as many copies of Tyndale's New Testament were burned as had been seized, and some six penitent distributors confessed their sorrow unharmed. Then, having thus abolished the future, the Cardinal "departed under a canopy with all his mitred men till he came to the second gate of Paul's, and then he took his mule."[1]

Sadder still is it to find, in later days, the great Thomas More, that bifurcated man—half humanist, half reactionary—assailing with gutter talk the herald of the new age. Tyndale, said More, was "a beast discharging a filthy foam of blasphemies out of his brutish beastly mouth." He was also one of the "hellhounds that the devil hath in his kennel."[2]

This vituperation was aimed perhaps less at Tyndale's text than at his occasional glosses upon it. There are some engaging ones in his subsequent translation of the Old Testament. On Exodus 32:35, for example, "And the Lord plagued the people because they made the calf, which Aaron made," Tyndale remarked, "The Pope's Bull slayeth more than Aaron's calf." And on Exodus 36: 5-6, where Moses restrains the people from bringing offerings, Tyndale cries out, "When will the Pope say Hoo! [Hold!] and forbid an offering for the building of Saint Peter's Church? And when will our spirituality[clergy] say Hoo! and forbid to give them more lands? Never until they have all."

Thus economics was then, as ever, the leaven of social change. Wealth and power being at issue, any threatened subversion evoked the usual penalties, and translation of the Bible into the vernacular became a capital offense. Yet in the safety of Antwerp, a trading city, Tyndale pursued his perilous task. There was a ludicrous episode when, in order to get money for the printing of a revised edition, he

9) James Anthony Froude, *History of England* (London: Longmans, Green, and Company; 1870), Vol. I, pp. 170–71. This great work, very controversial in its day, has become a classic.
1) Quoted by Raikie, op. cit., p. 172.
2) Quoted from More's *Confutation,* by Raikie, ibid., p. 175.

sold a stack of New Testaments to an agent of the Bishop of London, who took them back to be burned. Then there came a spy to Antwerp, one Henry Philips, who lured Tyndale outside the city and the city's protection, and there betrayed him to the arresting officers. At the stake, Tyndale was strangled before being burned. "Lord, open the King of England's eyes!" he was heard to cry as the cord cut off further utterance.

Remarkable to say, the Lord did, and indeed had already done so. In the year 1535 the first complete Bible to be printed in English, by Miles Coverdale, appeared in London. Like all its successors, it was founded on Tyndale's work, and it was produced under the powerful protection of Thomas Cromwell. Coverdale dedicated it to the King himself (whom he compared, not unjustly, with "that most vertuous kynge Iosias") and to Anne Boleyn, Henry's second queen. Coverdale's claims were as modest as his prose was mellifluous, for in the Preface he presented himself "not as a reprover or despyser of other mens translacyons (for amonge many as yet I have founde none without occasyon of greate thankesgevynge unto god) but lowly and faythfully have I folowed myne interpreters, and that under correccyon."[3]

To Coverdale we owe some of our Bible's sweetness. If we wish to hear this genial and devoted spirit expatiate upon a theme especially suited to its talents, we may turn to an epicurean passage from Ecclesiasticus:

> For oure tyme is a very shadow that passeth awaye, and after oure ende there is no returnynge, for it is fast sealed, so that no man commeth agayne. Come on therfore, let us enjoye the pleasures that there are, and let us soone use the creature like as in youth. We wil fyll oure selves with good wyne and ointment, there shal no floure of the tyme go by us. We wil crowne oure selves with roses afore they be wythered. There shal be no fayre medowe, but oure lust shal go thorow it. Let every one of you be partaker of oure volupteousnes. Let us leave some token of oure pleasure in every place, for that is oure porcion, els gett we nothinge....[4]

There were several Bibles in English after Coverdale's: the Matthew, the Taverner, the Great, the Geneva, the Bishops', the

3) Butterworth, op. cit., p. 95.
4) *The Oxford Book of English Prose*, § 34.

King James. None appeared during the reign of Mary, that sad queen, more blind than bloody, to whom history denied every wish and blotted out every hope. The counter-revolution lasted but five years, and all men know what came in with Elizabeth. One thing, less known, which came in, in 1582, was a New Testament in English by Catholics and for Catholics, the work of refugees from Elizabeth in the French university town of Douai. The Church had decided to practice what it could not prevent.

The most celebrated English Bible—and in some ways the definitive—is, of course, the Authorized Version of 1611, which we call the King James. Forty-seven translators labored over it during a space, as the Preface says, of "twice seven times seventy-two days." Miles Smith, the Orientalist who wrote the Preface, explained that the purpose had been not "to make a new translation, nor yet to make of a bad one a good one . . . but to make a good one better, or out of many good ones, one principal good one, not justly to be excepted against."

With what success indeed! The Authorized Version, the Open Bible made eternally sure, is a monument *aere perennius* to the effect of social revolution upon the language of a people. The glories of that version are cumulative: they belong, not to the forty-seven translators only, but to their predecessors into the time of Wyclif. Some of those men wrote in peril of their lives, and all wrote in the awareness of sublimity. By a circumstance happy but not fortuitous, the language lay ready to their hands, new, fresh, eloquent, as the people of England fashioned it from their struggles to become a nation. There is, indeed, a loftiness that is, I fancy, not always matched in the Greek and Hebrew originals. The Authorized Version (like Jowett's Plato) is an English classic. What else it is seems, sometimes, not very much to matter.

Let two celebrated verses, Matthew 6: 28–29, serve to illustrate this growth of genius upon genius. The felicitous order of words in the opening sentence may be attributed to the original Greek, which has precisely this sequence.[5] The remaining wonders are the work of the translators, whom I shall indicate phrase by phrase, as their contributions accumulate. But I suppose the palm must go to the King James translators, whose ear for melody and rhythm chose from out so many versions the elements of this incomparable pas-

5) καταμάθετε τὰ κρίνα τοῦ ἀγροῦ πῶς αὐξάνουσιν.

sage, and who crowned all else by changing the verb "labor" to the verb "toil":

Consider the lilies of the field,
>   [Tyndale's revised New Testament, 1534]
how they grow;
>   [Tyndale's New Testament, 1525]
they toil not
>   [Authorized Version, 1611]
neither do they spin:
>   [Coverdale's Latin–English New Testament, 1538]
And yet I say unto you,
>   [Great Bible, 1539]
That even Solomon in all his glory
>   [Geneva Bible, 1560]
Was not arrayed like one of these.
>   [Great Bible, with Cranmer's prologue, 1540]

The literary moral of all this is, I suppose: Find yourself geniuses to write with, and write in the midst of revolution.

During one of his many contests, Tyndale turned upon a learned antagonist and said, "If God spare my life, ere many years I will cause the boy that driveth the plow shall know more of the Scripture than thou doest." This bold remark was heresy then, and I have the sense that it is heresy still. The boy that drove the plow now drives tractors and machines, and it is not impossible that he will one day be "emperor of the world."

CHAPTER
9

The Nationalist Heresy

IN SCENE IV of Bernard Shaw's *Saint Joan,* the Earl of Warwick and the Bishop of Beauvais are brought to discuss the historical meaning of the Maid. The two high functionaries—one clerical, one lay—bait each other for a time, and we are made aware of sharp competition within feudal society. Then they agree that the Maid represents two rebellious and heretical movements, which are at bottom one and the same. The Earl, twitting the Bishop, calls it "Protestantism"; the Bishop, warning the Earl, calls it "Nationalism."

One movement, then, in two forms. The attempt to cure the vices and to lift the stifling weight of ecclesiastical bureaucracy gathered support along national lines. The English, for example, and the Germans disliked to see large portions of their wealth moving across borders in the direction of Rome. And, equally, the effort at independence and self-sufficiency brought the emerging nations into conflict with the Church, which, international in structure and purposes, asserted supremacy over all peoples, even to the appointment or deposition of their sovereign lords. Thus there could be no reformation of the Church without a growth in nationalism, and no growth in nationalism without a diminution of the Church.

Vast and subtle were the ideologies which guided this change; yet one single doctrine, well known to the Maid, lay beneath them all. It was the doctrine that there is direct, immediate, and inseparable communion between each human being and the ultimate source of moral authority. If that source were conceived as God, then every man could know God and God's will without intermediaries: the clergy would be in any case unnecessary, and might be obtrusive. If the source were conceived as the king, the people might approach him directly; their fealty would go at once to him, and the intervening ranks of peerage would be socially superfluous. Most remarkable of all, if the ultimate source of moral authority were identified as the private conscience, then every man—every honest man, at any rate—would be able to decide matters for himself and act accordingly.

Faith in one's own decisions as honest and enlightened and faith in one's own decisions as in accord with God's will are, generally speaking, the same. The one description is literal, the other metaphorical. Either expresses the essential anarchist integrity, without which men cannot be men. Precisely this had been the faith of the Albigenses, the Waldenses, the followers of Wyclif and Hus. It became the Protestant doctrine of the "universal priesthood of all believers"—or, every man his own cleric. It became the "social-contract" theory of popular sovereignty vested in a king, and, later, the ground of doing without kings altogether.

It was Joan's faith when, speaking of her "voices," she told her inquisitors, with a poetry which horrified them, "Before the raising of the siege of Orléans and every day thereafter, when they spoke to me, they many times called me 'Joan the Maid, daughter of God.' "[1] The new world which, five centuries later, we still live in and have not yet built arrived with more flame and mystery than would attend a collision of comets or sudden perturbations among the stars. For the whole new world, the modern world, existed, in concept, in the mind of an illiterate, teen-age peasant girl, who, in the year 1429, knew, though no one else knew, what was necessary to be known.

When they burned this same peasant girl in 1431, a participant, so the story runs, terrified with guilt, cried out, "We are lost; we have burned a saint!" He little knew a saint's powers. Quite to the contrary, they had burned a saint, and they were saved.

1) *Les procès de Jeanne d'Arc*, traduits, présentés et annotés par Raymond Oursel (Paris: Éditions Denoël; 1959), p. 66: *"Avant la levée du siège d'Orléans, et tous les jours depuis, quand elles me parlent, elles m'ont plusieurs fois appelée 'Jeanne la Pucelle, fille de Dieu.' "* My translation.

I I

BEFORE WE TELL the oft-told story of Joan of Arc, it will be necessary to describe that remarkable engine of conformity, the Inquisition, of which Joan was herself the purest and perhaps the most distinguished victim. The peculiar purpose of this engine, its efficiency, and its final failure set it quite apart as an historical phenomenon. There has been nothing else so destructive and at the same time so futile, and the human race, having survived it, may be expected to survive most other evils that may appear.

It is probable that few of my readers have ever seen or (one may hope) ever will see an inquisitor. The chief common characteristic is a hatred of human beings, together with a gift for concentrating it upon one person at a time. The hatred is at once so deep and so uninhibited as to constitute the overruling motive of all behavior. The hatred may attach itself to some justifying principle, or it may seek enjoyment without any disguise of morality. That is to say, the inquisitor may be a bigot or, more candidly, a rogue; but, whichever of these he is, he is quintessentially sadist. What attracts him is the doing of harm to human beings, in such a way that he can watch the harm shatter the victim.

This psychotic delight allows an odious and sinister embroidery. Inquisitors find an especial charm in reversing the moral order, in assaulting just those persons whom it would normally be a privilege to help or to admire. The sight of weakness, of purity, of affectionate zeal for the welfare of mankind, arouses in inquisitors a strange and special fury, as if, unable to endure excellence, they made haste to banish it from their sight and from the sight of all. What to other men would be recognizable blessing they perceive, accurately enough, to be a condemnation of themselves. With the cunning of old, envenomed serpents, such as have sloughed off a thousand separate skins, they set about accomplishing, down infinite degrees of torment and defamation, the ruin of the best.

Their garb proclaims the social institution in apparent defense of which they exercise their hostilities. The medieval inquisitor, a member probably of the Dominican order or the Franciscan, wore black garments and, over the head, a black cowl, from within which his eyes looked out with voluptuous anger. He had also, perhaps, a crucifix, where hung, in semblance, the divine inquisitorial victim;

and never once did it occur to him that this crucifix confuted and damned the whole career he had embarked upon.

The modern inquisitor wears a business suit, unless, seeking greater dignity, he happens to choose striped trousers and a coat of funerary black. He has no cowl, but spectacles will enhance the gimlet of the eyes. If he sits, as he sometimes does, at an elevation of two or three feet, while the victim sits at floor level, he can give the impression of a bird of prey about to swoop upon carrion.

Even in dress, the difference between a medieval inquisitor and a modern inquisitor is plain enough. The medieval looked as sinister as he was powerful. The modern looks less sinister and is less powerful. He looks, to be sure, as sinister as he can: the bitter petrifaction of his face records a lifelong tedium of evildoing. Yet the modern world differs from the medieval precisely in this: that inquisitors cannot, within constitutional limitations, do all the evil they would wish. If any man thinks this difference is slight, he is simply unacquainted with inquisitors.

To come at the purpose of the medieval Inquisition—and of all like enterprises—we shall have to understand the meaning of the term "belief." Belief is a poise of the body; it is action latent or about to be begun. A man "believes" the world or his immediate circumstances to be such and such, and proceeds to act accordingly. A man "believes" that certain types of decision are preferable to other types (candor, let us say, to duplicity), and proceeds to act accordingly. All human decision turns upon what the world and values are thought to be. Rulers therefore incline to think that if they can control the notion of the world and of values, and particularly if they can control the joining of these two at the crucial moment of decision, they can control the behavior of every person upon earth.

When decision (i.e., the passage into action) occurs in human beings, as from moment to moment it customarily does, there is something spontaneous about it. The man has made up his own mind; he has juxtaposed a view of the world to a view of values; and has made a choice. This spontaneity is just what escapes external control; indeed, if it does not escape it, it ceases to be spontaneity. There then arises in the minds of administrators a notion to the effect that this spontaneity itself, resistant to outward control, is precisely what must be extirpated.

The Inquisition's purpose, then, was to reach into that most intimate center of human life, the place where fact and value are united in decision, the precise point at which theory joins practice, and to make that joining, that union, such as it would have been if only the administrator, and not the man himself, had had anything to do with it. The member's will was to be annihilated; what was to remain was his body and a quiet consent of behavior. Loyalty would be ensured by a general abolition of brains, and thus the organization would prosper.

Imagine yourself to be living in a medieval town of five hundred or a thousand inhabitants. One day, without warning, there arrive an inquisitor and his staff. The inhabitants are summoned to report any heretics they may know of, or any persons they may suspect of heresy, under pain of being themselves thought heretical if they are silent. This proclamation is, in itself, a shattering blow to the public peace. There ensues a first panic, a *sauve-qui-peut,* in which the timid babble names—any names at all—in order to display their own orthodoxy and to save their own skins.

To panic succeeds the venting of hostilities. Now is the time for settling old scores: one man has hurt you; another has slighted you; still another you simply have never liked. In go their names to the inquisitor's list, and home you go, warmed with a vengeance that a powerful organization has made possible, has made legal, and has made blameless. Family contentions are now released: wives accuse husbands; husbands, wives; parents, children; children, parents. And the accused will never be told who the accusers are or what the specific accusations.

At Carcassonne, for example, in 1254, a certain Bernard Pons shrewdly guessed that his wife was among the delators.[2] He had caught her in adultery, had beaten her (wife beating was standard medieval practice), and, later on, had heard her say that she wished him dead so that she might marry her lover. These were all true facts, but they did not save him.[3] Again: in 1312, a certain Pons Arnaud charged that, during a serious illness, his son had tried to convert him to Catharism. The son was able to prove that his father

2) I.e., informers, those who made charges or supplied "information."
3) Lea, op. cit., p. 213. The next incident will be found, ibid., p. 209. Lea remarks, loc. cit., upon the temptation offered all witnesses "to gratify malice by reckless perjury."

had not been ill at the alleged time and that there were no Cathari in the alleged place. For once the inquisitor scrupled at a lying accusation and dropped the charge against the son. Thus there were, though rarely, inquisitors who did respect the rules of evidence and who even sent false witnesses to the stake. Regularly, however, the procedure was that spouses could not testify *in favor of* their spouses, nor members of households in favor of an accused member; but derogatory testimony from such sources carried greater weight than testimony from outside the household. An extension of this principle was acceptance of testimony from "excommunicates, perjurers, infamous persons, usurers, harlots, and all those who, in the ordinary criminal jurisprudence of the age, were regarded as incapable of bearing witness."[4]

But if you gave names and "evidence" purely out of panic or hostility, you had but superficially explored the opportunities for corruption. The property of heretics was confiscate, and one quarter of it was set aside for the compensation of delators. The inquisitor in the case got a third, and the rest fell to the Church or to some relevant section of it. This process of seizure began with the victim's arrest, when his property was at once sequestered and inventoried, and his family was "turned out-of-doors to starve or to depend upon the precarious charity of others—a charity chilled by the fact that any manifestation of sympathy was dangerous."[5] In this way, wealthy burghers and members of the *petite noblesse* became prime targets. Poor people were persecuted because they were potential revolutionaries. The very rich were rather too strong to be attacked, but they could be, and were, threatened. They could, however, purchase pardon from the pope, either before or after accusation, and even after conviction.

The whole inquisitorial process turned upon "the erection of suspicion into a crime."[6] No doubt, as Lea says, this morally absurd practice arose from the general state of law in the Middle Ages, when an accused man had to prove himself innocent rather than the government's having to prove him guilty. But it arose much more from organizational pathology. Disease in organizations, as we know, takes two forms: either the members grow so hostile to one another

4) Ibid., p. 205.
5) Ibid., p. 247.
6) Ibid., p. 217.

and to the leadership that unity vanishes, or the leaders grow so authoritarian that liberty vanishes. In medieval society, the hierarchical structure sufficed, of itself, to determine that the second of these diseases would be the one to prevail; and so the Inquisition set about removing dissent by paralyzing the very faculty that could exercise it. If to be suspected of an offense is equivalent to being known to have committed it, then safety can lie only in avoiding the entire area of behavior.

But in those days avoidance was quite impossible, for the area into which the Inquisition probed covered the whole range of valuation and of opinion concerning the nature of the world. To be empty of these, one would have had to be a vegetable. The trap, therefore, was set for any and every person, of either sex, to a minimum age of fourteen years for males and twelve for females. These virtual children could be embroiled as witnesses if not as defendants, and indeed there was one case in which a ten-year-old boy, Arnaud Olivier, gave evidence against his father, his mother, and some sixty-five other persons. This "evidence" was recorded and accepted—and used, it appears, to the destruction of all.[7]

After the Inquisition had entered a town and fastened upon it, all human choices sank to an astonishing simplicity. There were, in fact, just two pairs of choices: (1) you could fend off attack by turning informer, or you could risk attack by declining to inform; and (2) once accused, you could surrender utterly the conduct of your own life, or you could try to protect your integrity, through increasing degrees of torment, to the final sacrifice at the stake. This last choice was fraught with peculiar difficulty, because the torments were of such a sort as to make surrender almost an automatic response. Sometimes, indeed, the surrender was entirely so:

A heretic priest [says Lea], thrown into prison by his bishop, proved obstinate, and the most eminent theologians who labored for his conversion found him their match in disputation. Believing that vexation brings understanding, they at length ordered him to be bound tightly to a pillar. The cords eating into the swelling flesh caused such torture that when they visited him the next day he begged piteously to be taken out and burned. Coldly

7) Ibid., p. 206. Lea remarks upon "the wonderful exercise of so young a memory."

refusing, they left him for another 24 hours, by which time physical pain and exhaustion had broken his spirit. He humbly recanted, retired to a Paulite monastery, and lived an exemplary life.[8]

Integrity, however, if hard to maintain, is also hard to kill. People who are emotionally mature do not readily yield up the attribute that defines their maturity. More than one martyr survived the thumbscrew and the rack, to reach at last the only value left him: defense of his true selfhood in the midst of flame. More than one hero, quailing before the fire, recanted; then, gathering his courage again, recanted his recantation, and went on to die. These occasions of "relapse" the inquisitors especially abhorred, because then the victim, contrary to expectation, suddenly withdrew his will from captivity to the leadership, and renewed, though in death, its pressure upon events.

From the very nature of the case it follows that inquisition, wherever practiced, will destroy only the best. Every man of lesser strength and talent escapes. Thus the medieval Inquisition, the most thorough of these enterprises, was in intent most foul and in every part abominable. And yet, as if its accumulated crimes were not enough, it swathed them all in the rank wool of hypocrisy. It took as official name "The Holy Office"—although even its own bigoted intellects could perhaps not conceive what could possibly be holy about destroying the best. Each holocaust of victims came to be known by the Spanish phrase *auto da fé,* an "act of the faith." The inquisitorial process itself went by the name of "The Question," until the phrase "being put to the question" grew synonymous with being tortured. For the whole nature of inquisition lies in the fact that questions are asked, not in order that the answer may enlighten, but in order that the answerer may be destroyed.

Further there was the myth that the Church was a non-violent organization. It did not seek the death of its errant members and did not impose it. Rather, it delivered its victims over to the "secular arm," the police power of feudal princes, which, uninhibited by religious ideals and a sacred calling, might slay with lesser guilt. In exactly this manner the victims of congressional committees have been turned over to the "secular arm," their employers, to be pun-

8) Ibid., p. 195.

ished with loss of livelihood—the committees all the while maintaining that their sacred and special vocation was the gathering of data for legislative purposes.

But worst and most treacherous of the hypocrisies was the assertion that the Inquisition desired to rescue the victim—"from the devil," which was to say, from himself. Some, perhaps most, inquisitors appear to have believed this nonsense, which quieted their own guilts so far as those guilts had being. Inquisitors, indeed, pursued their victims into the very flames, seeking, to the last, possession of the victim's will. And there, while the faggots began to burn and the limbs to be scorched, they continued to offer, in exchange for recantation, the redemptive offices of the Church.

During the years 1452 to 1456, when proceedings for the rehabilitation of Joan were under conduct, the Grand Inquisitor of France, Jean Bréhal, observed, "To act against conscience is to prepare for hell; there is no need to abdicate, at the demand of a prelate, a well formed conscience founded on a well tested faith."[9] It was very true, but it came too late, too late. In history as in schooling, the pupil cannot precede the master: Jean Bréhal had necessarily to come after Jeanne d'Arc. But let us here assert the great truth so that, knowing it now, we may prevent martyrs hereafter:

No man can surrender his power of rational decision without ceasing to be a man. Consequently no leadership may, in law or in morality, require him to do so.

Citizens of the United States of America may recall with pride that their basic law rests upon precisely this principle. When the founders of the Republic had sketched, in the main body of the Constitution, the structure they wished the government to have, they added at once a series of ten amendments, of which the purpose was to define, with remarkable clarity, what that government might *not* do. At least half the specified limitations arose from mankind's experience of inquisitorial practices and of the medieval Inquisition itself. I list here those portions of the first ten amendments that are relevant:

First Amendment: Congress shall make no law respecting an

9) Quoted by the R. P. Michel Riquet, S.J., Preface to *Les Procès de Jeanne d'Arc*, p. 15: "*Agir contre sa conscience, c'est édifier pour l'enfer . . . Il ne faut pas à la voix d'un prélat déposer une conscience bien formée, fondée sur une créance bien éprouvée.*" My translation.

establishment of religion or prohibiting the free exercise
thereof; or abridging the freedom of speech or of the press ...

Fourth Amendment: The right of the people to be secure in their
persons, houses, papers, and effects, against unreasonable
searches and seizures, shall not be violated and no warrant
shall issue but upon probable cause, supported by oath or
affirmation ...

Fifth Amendment: No person shall be held to answer for a capital or other infamous crime unless on a presentment or indictment of a grand jury ... nor shall any person be subject for
the same offense to be twice put in jeopardy of life or limb;
nor shall be compelled in any criminal case to be a witness
against himself, nor be deprived of life, liberty, or property,
without due process of law ...

Sixth Amendment: In all criminal prosecutions, the accused shall
enjoy the right to a speedy and public trial, by an impartial
jury of the State and district wherein the crime shall have
been committed ... and to be informed of the nature and
cause of the accusation; to be confronted with the witnesses
against him; to have compulsory process for obtaining witnesses in his favor, and to have the assistance of counsel for
his defense.

Eighth Amendment: Excessive bail shall not be required, nor
excessive fines imposed, nor cruel and unusual punishments
inflicted.

Every one of these forbidden practices was, not the occasional,
but the habitual usage of the Inquisition, its ordinary rule of life.
Since, however, questioning was (and is) the heart of inquisitorial
procedure, that clause in the Fifth Amendment which exempts a
witness from imperiling himself by answers remains the supreme,
and thus far nearly impregnable, bulwark against governmental
malevolence. That single phrase, wonderfully brief and wonderfully
exact, "compelled . . . to be a witness against himself," precisely
defines the essence of inquisition; and exemption from all that the
phrase signifies defines, no less precisely, freedom from inquisition.

I I I

I AM NOW to tell that story which is, of all historical episodes, the
most astounding, the most pitiful, and the most instructive. It is
astounding, because, against all probabilities, it really happened. It is
pitiful, because, in it, men destroyed what they ought to have adored.

It is instructive, because it teaches us to doubt everything we believe —everything except the supremacy of essential values. The life and martyrdom of Joan of Arc offer all the proof there need be that, though facts may be doubted, values are sure.

It will have appeared by now that I am not a man to construe theological assertions literally. Yet I think that if there were a God who interested Himself in the welfare of the humblest, and if, by consequence, He desired to confound the mighty (they being always in need of confounding), He could hardly have done other than produce Joan upon earth in the first half of the fifteenth century. *Jeanne, fille de Dieu:* one can almost believe it! If she was not quite that, she was something very like it: she was history's corrosive comment upon organizations.

In every social organization of large size, the members have varying degrees of culture and enlightenment. The "lowliest" have perhaps little of either, and the leadership is on the whole content that this should be so. By contrast, organizational myth always asserts that the bureaucratic hierarchy is occupied by men of superior knowledge and talent. This has sometimes chanced to be the case; but if one were to define the single talent which distinguishes the members of a bureaucratic hierarchy, one would have to say that it is *adhesiveness*. They get there and they stick.

Ordinarily, the true state of organizations is that leaders are not as knowledgeable as they seem nor members as ignorant as they are thought. The things that leaders know are limited by a fear of knowing other things disadvantageous to the organization. This fear is less lively among the membership, and therefore a member may go on to explore the real world, which reveals to him its true nature by experience if not by formal education. These facts being assumed, superior insight in the members and inferior awareness in the leaders become not only possible but even likely.

Such facts assure that Joan's history can have happened without magic or supernatural intervention, but they will scarcely reduce our astonishment. We are all tied to the usual expectations, which are the seductive offspring of organizational myth. Wisdom in the membership, and in the lowest order of membership, is precisely what a higher wisdom would teach us to expect. Psalmist and evangelist have told us as much, apparently in vain: "The stone which the builders rejected, the same is become the head of the corner."[1]

1) Matthew 21: 42, Psalms 118: 22. AV.

Consequently Joan, though five hundred years dead, still comes over us with wonder, and we would be as blank as Charles VII if a second Joan were to confront us now.

Suppose—for we desperately need the supposition—an illiterate, teen-age peasant girl were to appear before the present governments of earth with a message comparably new and comparably accurate. Suppose that, just as the first Joan had asserted nations to be necessary, the new Joan asserts them to be relics of a bloody and barbarous past. Suppose, further, she were to say that social conflicts (and in particular class conflicts) have become too dangerous to be endured. What does one fancy would be her reception? Would it differ, and in what way would it differ, from that of the first Joan? I hope, though I do not know, that it would differ in the fate of the prophetess herself.

The Meuse River takes its source in France, in the Department of the Haute Marne, and empties into the North Sea near Rotterdam. It flows through celebrated places of defense or catastrophe, like Verdun and Sedan; but, near its source, it flows through Domremy, birthplace of Joan of Arc. The village has long been known as Domremy-la-Pucelle, the Maid's Domremy, because among her amazing attributes virginity seemed the most impressive of all. It was in itself an exceptional fact, for village girls married early or gave to some first and fortunate lover what was called, by a pleasant euphemism, *la rose*. But Joan's maidenhood was far more than a sociological rarity. Joined with the sense of mission which she ardently proclaimed, it assimilated her, in a way she did not intend (being humble), to the Virgin Mother of God. There is ample testimony that, among the soldiers, she not only canceled out any appetite for herself, though she was charming, but lifted them for a time beyond appetite for any woman whatever. Twenty-five years after her death, Dunois, her old comrade-in-arms, asserted at the proceedings of rehabilitation that he and others, "when we were with the Maid, felt no wish or desire to have commerce with a woman." And he added, convincingly, "It seemed to me that this was truly miraculous."[2]

2) Oursel, op. cit., p. 249: *"J'atteste pareillement que moi-même, et d'autres, quand nous étions avec la Pucelle, nous ne nourissions aucune volonté ou désir d'avoir commerce avec une femme ou d'en fréquenter: il me paraît que c'était réellement un miracle."* My translation.

Virtue, indeed, seldom hides itself, and even the sufferings it incurs are the result of its publicity. In all her acts Joan had a moral candor that made her virtue emphatically clear and emphatically without pretense. She went to Mass oftener than most, made confession oftener than most; "it annoyed her," reported a girlhood friend, "to hear people say she was too devout."[3] She was faithful also in the household tasks, the *besognes ménagères:* she spun, looked after the kitchen and the cattle, and sometimes followed the plow. So acutely, indeed, did conscience touch her that it took, quite early, the imaginative form of a personal presence—an hallucination partly visual but mostly auditory. Conscience spoke to her as Saint Michael or (more usually) as Saints Catherine[4] and Margaret; and, although she is rather vague as to how the three saints looked, she is always clear as to what they said.

Within this nevrosity and proneness to hallucination there worked an intellect of the very first rank. When conscience in the form of the three saints delivered imperatives to Joan, it always prescribed specific, concrete actions, and at the same time predicted their success. It did not speak in vague generalities; it told her to go lift the siege of Orléans and to get her Dauphin crowned at Reims. Her intellect, that is to say, was so intimately joined with her conscience, and both of these with her extraordinary sense of the practical, that in her there was no laborious dragging of the particular case beneath a relevant principle, as formal ethics might seem to require. She knew what was at once righteous and practicable, and she knew this so far instantaneously that the insight seemed to come like voices from heaven.

The nearest her saints approached mere generality was when they counseled boldness, as they often did. But this counsel always fell so entirely within a context that Joan was able to express it as an adverb (*hardiment*) modifying the specific act. "Saint Catherine and Saint Margaret told me to take my banner and carry it boldly."[5] At the third session of her trial (Saturday, February 24, 1431), she

3) Havriette, wife of Gérard Guillemette, Oursel, op. cit., p. 220.
4) If this Saint Catherine was, as I suppose, Catherine of Siena (1347–1380), Joan's imagination had fastened upon a personage singularly apt. For Catherine of Siena had been a girl very much like Joan, and had sustained, through many trials, the flagging spirits of Pope Gregory XI.
5) Oursel, op. cit., p. 61: "*Sainte Catherine et sainte Marguerite me dirent de le prendre, de le porter hardiment. . . .*"

told her alarmed inquisitors that she had but yesterday heard the voice saying, *"Réponds hardiment, Dieu t'aidera."*[6] Then, turning upon the pig Cauchon, Bishop of Beauvais and chief inquisitor, she cried, "Take care, you who call yourself my judge! Take care what you do. For the truth is that I have my mission from God, and you put yourself in great danger!" He did indeed. And Cauchon dimly perceived (for no man becomes a bishop without some measure of wit) that he stood at a disadvantage with destiny.

According to her own account, Joan was thirteen years old when she grew aware what was politically necessary to be done and what her own mission was to be.[7] This was the year 1425, toward the end of a century of war. The territory of France was almost entirely possessed by the English in alliance with the Burgundians. Peasants sowed their crops not knowing whether there would be a harvest: soldiers might arrive to pillage and destroy. Joan and her family had themselves fled Domremy before just such a raid. These threats to the economic basis of existence explain why common folk rallied to Joan and understood, as she did, that they and their crops and their cattle would never be secure until the French had recovered France and made a nation of it. Joan's special insight was that the time had arrived when this could be done.

A nation, to be built, must be built around a center, and in the late Middle Ages that center would have to be a king. Joan's judgment guided her swiftly and inerrantly. If there were a throne of France and a king to sit upon it, that king would have to be the Dauphin Charles. The Duke of Burgundy was hopelessly compromised by his alliance with "the foreigner." Meanwhile Charles, "l'Indolent," was engaged in "gaily losing his realm."[8] Fouquet's wonderful portrait of him is persuasive because so little flattering. Yet behind that vapid countenance lurked possibilities of grandeur, which Joan with her preternatural insight perceived. She made a king of him, and he lived to see the English driven from all French soil except Calais. In the course of these triumphs he acquired two further nicknames, which sufficiently describe his reign: he was "Charles le Victorieux" because he was also "Charles le Bien Servi."

6) Ibid., p. 34.

7) Ibid., p. 30: *"La voix me disait de venir en France, et je ne pouvais plus durer où j'étais! La voix me disait de lever le siège d'Orléans."*

8) Nouveau Petit Larousse (Paris; 1925), p. 1273.

In 1429, however, Charles lay at the Château de Chinon while the last of his large cities came under siege. He had sunk to the lowest tide of fortune, and a popular song of those days, still sung in France, put the pitying question:

> Mon ami, que reste-t-il
> A ce Dauphin si gentil?
> Orléans, Beaugency,
> Notre Dame de Cléry . . .

He had not much left in the way of fortified places, and the best of these was about to fall.

In this crisis, Joan arrived at Chinon. The Château is now a grassy ruin, but a great fireplace aloft upon one wall designates the hall where she met him and, contrary to all expectation, recognized him. Charles was interested at once, as a man must be who is told that he need not be defeated. It was necessary, however, to consult the *clercs,* the professors, the local intelligentsia. Rulers have a strange dependence upon these creatures, whose only possession is intelligence, and whose low pay reflects a low esteem for low services. At Poitiers, for a month, these learned mice harassed the Maid with questions. A Dominican tried the pacifist tack: "Joan, you say that God wants to liberate the people of France. If that is his wish, he has no need of soldiers." To which Joan replied with her invincible common sense, "Why, the soldiers will fight, and God will give the victory."[9] A certain Friar Séguin, professor of theology at the University of Poitiers, "a very bitter man," inquired in his Limousin dialect what language Joan's voices spoke. "Better than yours," said the redoubtable Maid.

The professors opined, as it had been determined they should, that Joan was genuine, her mission authentic, and the expectation favorable. Charles assigned her some ten thousand soldiers—more than the besiegers had—and by early May, Orléans was free. Before undertaking military action, however, Joan had sent the English a letter, which, later on, they introduced, with solemn official horror, at her trial. It was addressed to the King of England (then the child Henry VI), to the Duke of Bedford, and to Sir John Talbot, who commanded the siege. Joan invited these worthies to leave France

9) Jules Michelet, *Jeanne d'Arc,* édition critique par G. Rudler (Paris: Librairie Hachette; 1925), p. 28. My translation.

peaceably or be expelled. "I have come here by God's grace," she said, *"pour vous bouter hors de toute France,* to drive you right out of the country." "If," she continued, "you refuse to believe this notice which God sends you through the Maid, why then, wherever we find you, we will bash your heads in, and we will kick up a greater rumpus than there has been in France these thousand years. ... You had better take it for certain that the King of Heaven will reveal more power in the Maid and in her good soldiers than you could bring against her in all your assaults. Thus we shall see which will have the better right, Heaven's God or you."[1]

One can imagine wrath rattling the armor within which those veteran butchers stood fortified. The insolence, the arrogance, of a little country girl! Pride was one of the seven deadly sins, and this was a prime case of it. They had their revenge, which was also their ruin, exactly two years later. On the first of March 1431, the letter was read aloud to Joan at her trial, and the presiding inquisitor asked, as inquisitors do on such occasions, "Do you recognize this letter?" Joan coolly pointed out that they had somewhat falsified the text by three interpolations, and then she said, "Nobody else dictated that letter; I dictated it myself."[2]

The letter's prophecy was, as we know, confirmed—so amply confirmed, indeed, that both prediction and demonstration seemed miraculous. It was the first time that a scientific insight into history had scientifically brought success, and everyone, including the Maid herself, supposed that divine governance rather than human knowledge had been at work. After liberating Orléans, Joan drew her cautious Dauphin toward a coronation at Reims. Charles liked to loiter, but it was imperative that he be crowned King of France before the English pretender could claim the title. On the way to Reims, at a little place called Patay, Joan came upon the retreating English army, and scattered it in rout. Charles was duly crowned at Reims on Sunday, the seventeenth of July, 1429. He had first met Joan in February, and on the ninth of May she had raised an altar in a field outside

1) Oursel, op. cit., p. 47. Joan's language is wonderfully racy: *"Si vous ne voulez croire les nouvelles de par Dieu de la Pucelle, en quelque lieu que nous vous trouverons, nous frapperons dedans à l'horions, et nous ferons un si gros hahaye, qu'il y a mil ans qu'en France ne fut fait si grand. ... Et croyez fermement que le Roi du Ciel trouvera plus de force à la Pucelle que vous ne lui sauriez mener de tous assauts, à elle et à ses bonnes gens d'armes; et alors on verra qui aura meilleur droit, de Dieu du Ciel ou de vous."* My translation.
2) Ibid.

Orléans to celebrate the liberation. Five months, then, from near captive to anointed king! Even in our hasty years such speed of change would be remarkable.

After the holy oil had touched him and he was truly king, Charles went forth to heal, as kings could do, the sufferers from scrofula. Joan looked at the rejoicing crowd, and said, with the air of one whose life's work is over, "What good, decent people! If I have to die, I would be very happy to be buried here." "Joan," said the archbishop, "where do you think you will die?" "I know nothing about that—wherever it shall please God. But I'd like it also to please him that I go tend sheep with my sister and my brothers. They would be so happy to see me again."[3]

Politics seldom allows a pastoral conclusion—especially international politics, which Joan had brought into being. The English were still in France; the Burgundians were still collaborators. Joan could not retire from the contest. She led an abortive attack on Paris; she was herself besieged by the Burgundians in Compiègne, and, in a sally beyond the fortifications, taken prisoner. This tremendous event seemed like the capture of a secret and absolute weapon. The English wanted her, and, after long negotiation, got her for the sum of ten thousand francs—in literal truth, a king's ransom. They had, however, added to the bribe some judicious economic pressure, by interrupting the exchange of English wool for Burgundian cloth. One trader understands another, and the Burgundians replied according to English expectations.

Joan was captured on May 23, 1430. Some weeks later, she leaped from her tower cell at Beaurepair—a height of sixty feet—was stunned by the fall and retaken. She had hoped to rescue the besieged at Compiègne,[4] and more especially to escape the English, who, as she well understood, intended her death. She was kept in irons thereafter, and when, at Rouen at the opening of her trial, she complained of the fact to Cauchon, he replied, not unreasonably, "It's because you have tried to escape from the other prisons." "Well," said Joan, "It's very true that I wanted to escape from those other places and that I'd like to do so now. Every prisoner has the right to escape."[5] She was an uncompromising libertarian, Joan.

The drama so brief in time, so rich in import, entered its last and

3) Michelet, op. cit., p. 48. My translation.
4) They freed themselves shortly thereafter.
5) Oursel, op. cit., p. 28: *"Tout prisonnier a bien le droit de s'évader."*

dreadful weeks. The Maid, who had known vision and victory, had now to acquaint herself with the disciplined cunning of human hate. Cauchon, the Bishop of Beauvais, had always been a creature of the English; for that reason, indeed, his fellow townsmen had driven him out. He had spent some time in England, and he was available for inquisitorial purposes when the English resolved to try the Maid at Rouen. There was some problem of jurisdiction, how a Bishop of Beauvais could rightly function at Rouen; but the faculty of the University of Rouen, being applied to, gave, as faculties do, the desired justification. And so it came to pass that on Wednesday, February 21, 1431, Cauchon looked out upon a nineteen-year-old girl, the founder of the modern age, whom he proposed to question "as suspect of heresy."[6] *"Quant à Nous,"* he had written in the *Ordonnance Solennelle d'Ouverture,* "as for Ourself, Bishop, faithful to the duty of our pastoral charge and earnest to protect the Christian faith at all costs, we have thought it proper to seek basic information on these matters, and then to proceed with due deliberation as law and reason shall have persuaded us."[7]

Law had perhaps something to do with what followed; reason, nothing at all. Joan defended herself with wonderful skill, closing traps as they opened, overleaping snares, and yielding never the moral initiative. The inexperienced will perhaps not realize how hard this is to do. Mere intelligence, for example, is more of a curse than a boon. If the victim is by training a theoretician, he will almost certainly be a feast for inquisitors. He is accustomed to giving reasons for acts and reasons for reasons, and the inquisitors will press him from one assertion to another until he has spun the web in which he is to look ridiculous and die. But Joan, who saw everything rational as practicable and everything practicable as rational, was not to be so used. She would not answer questions irrelevant to the subject of inquiry, nor let inquisitors probe her roots of honesty. *"Passez outre!"* she burst out on such occasions.[8] She understood our Fifth

6) Ibid., p. 23.
7) Ibid., p. 24: *"Quant à Nous, Evêque, fidèle au devoir de notre charge pastorale et soucieux de fortifier coûte que coûte la foi chrétienne, nous avons pensé qu'il convenait d'instruire à fond sur ces faits, et de procéder mûrement ensuite selon ce que le droit et la raison nous auraient persuadé."* My translation.
8) Ibid., e.g., pp. 29, 30, 31, 32.

Amendment, without possessing its power of defense: "Would you have me speak against myself?" she cried, during the sixth of her hearings.[9]

Those traps! Was she sure, asked Maître Beaupère, substituting for Cauchon, that she was in a state of grace? "If I am not in it," said the Maid, "may God put me there; and if I am in it, may God keep me there."[1] Another inquisitor, lucky enough to have survived nameless, tried exploring the sexual content of her visions. "What did Saint Michael look like when he appeared to you?" "I didn't see any crown on him, and I don't know anything about his garments." "Was he naked?" "Do you think Our Lord had nothing to clothe him with?" Dense and undaunted, the inquisitor went on: "Did he have hair?" "And why, pray, would they have cut it off?"[2]

They tried to prove that she sought wealth. "Have you ever had other bounties from your king than these horses?" "I asked nothing of the King except good arms, good horses, and money to pay the men of my establishment."[3] They tried to prove that she sought personal renown—most foolish effort, in view of her obvious dedication to a cause. "Why was your banner carried to the coronation at Reims rather than those of the other captains?" "It had shared the suffering; it deserved to share the glory!"[4] They tried to prove that she had practiced sorcery, because she allowed women of the populace to kiss her ring and her jewelry. "Many women have touched my rings, but I don't know what were their ideas or intentions."[5] They tried to prove her blasphemous. "Did you not say, before the walls of Paris, 'Surrender the city, by command of Jesus'?" "No, I said, 'Surrender it to the King of France!'"[6]

They did, however, reveal two weaknesses, of which the second was in fact her strength and her ruin. The first was her constant use of man's apparel. To this subject they returned over and over like clucking, gossipy hens. Why had she worn it? Why did she still wear it? Had her saints ordered it? Would she give it up? Yes, she would give it up if they would set her free. No, the saints had not

---

9) Ibid., p. 53.
1) Ibid., p. 36: *"Si je n'y suis, Dieu m'y mette; si j'y suis, Dieu m'y tienne!"*
2) Ibid., p. 51.
3) Ibid., p. 62.
4) Ibid., p. 86: *"Il avait été à la peine, c'était bien raison qu'il fût à l'honneur!"*
5) Ibid., p. 57.
6) Ibid., p. 71.

yet told her to change. She would report something definite later on. She never did. And never once did that wonderfully practical girl say, with her customary simplicity, that man's apparel is plainly the costume in which to fight a war. It was an acutely tender spot with her, the one place where she seems to show some feeling of guilt; and the cause is still mysterious, after five hundred years.

The second "weakness," which was (as I say) an essential strength, was her absolute faith in her own convictions. This was what the imagery of the saints, the hallucinatory sense of their presence, had always signified. This brilliant public exercise of private judgment the inquisitors of course seized upon, and it delivered her into their hands. She claimed to have contact with the Church Triumphant—the angels and saints and redeemed souls in Paradise; she had been, in fact, simply carrying out their orders. But how did she stand, asked the inquisitors, toward the Church Militant here on earth, the organization with the living, breathing membership? On March seventeenth she told them, "As for submitting to the Church Militant, I won't answer anything more for the time being."[7] On May second she said, "I do indeed believe in the Church here below. But as for my acts and assertions, as I've said before, I fall back on God. I do believe that the Church Militant can neither err nor fail; but, as for my acts and assertions, these I refer to God, who made me do them. Myself I submit to Him; I rest upon Him, on His own person."[8]

It was obvious that she would never yield up her independence of mind. It was likewise obvious that this was a case of purest heresy, the member defying (though respectfully) the leadership. The inquisitors discussed a possible application of torture, and even had the instruments exhibited. Then they decided against it, perhaps because they had all the evidence necessary. Accordingly, in the "Last Charitable Warning Before Imposition of Sentence," Article 12 charged, "You [tu] have said that if the Church ordered you to do the opposite of what you claim to hold from God, you would not obey for

7) Ibid., p. 82.
8) Ibid., p. 105: *"Je crois bien à l'Église d'ici-bas. Mais de mes faits et de mes dires, ainsi que je l'ai déclaré autrefois, je me rapporte à Dieu. Je crois bien que l'Église militante ne peut errer ni faillir; mais quant à mes faits et mes dires, je les rapporte à Dieu qui me les a fait faire; et moi aussi, je me soumets à Lui; je m'en rapporte à Lui, à Sa personne propre."* My translation.

anything in the world. . . . On this point the learned intelligentsia [*les doctes clercs*] deems that you are schismatic, evil-thinking toward the unity and authority of the Church, apostate, and up to the present moment heretical toward the faith with an inveterate obstinacy—*hucusque pertinaciter errans in fide.*"[9]

They sentenced her—these sixteen doctors, six bachelors of theology, the Venerable Chapter of the Cathedral of Rouen, two licentiates in canon law, eleven lawyers of the Court of Rouen, two Reverend Fathers in Christ, two abbés, one treasurer, and four more bachelors of theology—they sentenced her to be delivered over to the secular arm, to be used as that arm chose. It meant, of course, death by fire, and before that awful prospect Joan collapsed. She recanted, to the delight of her inquisitors, who ought by that time to have known her better. One of the Inquisition's minor faults was that it did not make recantation sufficiently attractive. So supreme was its hatred of dissent that it punished with life imprisonment those persons who said they would not dissent any longer.

Joan could not accept a lifetime in prison, face to face with a conscience she had (though only once) denied. Better integrity in the flame than survival in recantation of the truth. She therefore became a relapsed heretic, the worst of all. "I have done nothing against God or the faith," she told her inquisitors at the final session, May 28, 1431; "I will, if you wish, wear women's clothes again, but as for the rest I will not change!" And the pig Cauchon, President of the Ecclesiastical Tribunal, said, "We will draw the necessary conclusions from that!"[1]

They did. On the thirtieth of May, Joan went to the stake in the old market place of Rouen. On the way thither, the procession paused to hear a sermon, by one Maître Nicolas Midy, upon the theme, "When one member of the Church is sick, the whole Church is sick." There was no doubt that the Church was sick, but what of the member? As the flames rose around her, she was heard to cry, "Yes, my voices *were* from God; they have not deceived me!" She and her conscience were, as they always had been, one. There followed a last moment of pure illumined pain. "Jesu!" she sighed, and was free forever.

In the sad great contests of our clumsy world, Joan is the mem-

9) Ibid., p. 116.
1) Ibid., p. 123.

ber's member. She has proved, once for all, that the least of these our brethren are to be cherished, not because they are least, but because they are enlightened. Wisdom comes to them on wings of life, not clipped and tamed by any tricks of policy. The lordly of this earth, mere bureaucratic erections, gather to themselves the news and hints and guesses of the globe; yet there is not one of them who can assure survival, let alone prosperity, to the globe's inhabitants.

Joan's spirit is gentle with these folk, perhaps because she also knew the agonies of leadership. She says to them, "Why do you not listen to the people's wish and wisdom? It sounds in the ear like the voices of saints, of archangels, and of God." And we billions of the earth, who may die for no better cause than folly, repeat after her, in tears and exaltation, "Why not, why not indeed?"

CHAPTER

10

The Earth Exults

A<small>T THE VERY BEGINNING</small> of Henry VIII's reign—that is to say, the year 1509—William Blount, the fourth Earl Mountjoy, wrote to Erasmus a letter descriptive of the new glories. "If you could see," he said, "how all the world here is rejoicing in the possession of so great a Prince, how his life is all their desire, you could not contain your tears for joy. The heavens laugh, the earth exults, all things are full of milk, of honey, of nectar!"[1]

It was very true, and, after four hundred years, enough remains of Henry's work and of the whole great European rebirth for us ourselves to feel the joy if we so wish. Henry, like Joan, was the founder of a modern state. Indeed, my intention had been to include him in the previous chapter; but there is still something about Joan that forbids, as in her own time it forbade, companionship. I think it is her purity, beside which mere practical statesmanship, however skilled and however beneficent, must seem an exercise of animal cunning.

Nevertheless the young Henry, who, like Joan, was seventeen years old when he entered upon high politics, did at first bear to her some moral resemblance. His motives were pure, his purpose lofty; and he had rather more faith in the honor of rulers than Joan's

1) F. M. Nichols, *Epistles of Erasmus,* Vol. I, p. 457; quoted by A. F. Pollard, *Henry VIII* (London: Longmans, Green and Company; 1934), p. 40.

shrewdness allowed her to have. It is as instructive as painful to see how Henry's innocence evaporated in the dire need to control events, whereas Joan's led swiftly through triumph to the state. Nations get born in many ways, and from the travail of those births only a few leaders have issued without soil.

Henry's innocence (for such it seems at first to have been) met soon enough the kind of trial that must shatter innocence: a contest with duplicity. He had married his older brother's widow, Catherine, the daughter of Ferdinand, King of Aragon. A month after the marriage, Catherine wrote to Ferdinand that she valued his confidence more than any other thing in life; and she acted as ambassador after the official ambassador was withdrawn. She was in fact a Spanish agent highly placed in the British realm, and her loyalty was not to the husband but to the father. One of her letters home contains the remarkable assertion, "These kingdoms of *your* highness are in great tranquillity."[2]

While Henry was thus bedded with a subversive power, the father-in-law set about accomplishing the ruin of the son-in-law. Henry was in those days a loyal Catholic. He was so for many years thereafter: his little treatise attacking Luther won for him a title that British monarchs still assert, *Defensor Fidei*. On pretext of defending the Papacy, Ferdinand lured Henry into a joint attack upon France—or into an attack which would have been joint, except that Ferdinand had no notion of engaging in it. The result was a military fiasco, which Henry redeemed one year later with the first English victories upon French soil since the time of Joan of Arc. He never trusted monarchs again. The brilliant open-hearted prince, who could joust, wrestle, and shoot arrows with the best, who could write poetry, discuss theology, and compose music, who in fact did set one of the great English anthems,[3] became as shrewd, as devious, as free of scruple as politics could require. In this remarkable change he was much assisted by a conscience in its way as robust as Joan's. All that he did, however worthy of self-reproach, he did without the smallest feeling of it. He was, rather early for northern Europe, a complete, self-reliant, Renaissance man.

England had long been, perhaps had always been, independent in the Catholic world and jealous of its independence. The Statute of

2) Ibid., p. 51. Italics Pollard's.
3) "O Lord, the Maker of All Thyng."

Praemunire, in 1353, had forbidden the English clergy to appeal to the pope without the king's consent. We have seen that Wyclif proposed loyalty oaths for foreign priests serving in England. The logic of nationalism would no doubt have wrought a breach with Rome in some way or other, if not in the way it actually did. We must therefore regard the events that did happen as the occasion rather than the cause of the breach. They were clouded by feudal practice and by some taint of personal immorality, but these merely suffused a social change which was scarcely avoidable.

In those days, the internal security of a state—particularly of an emerging one—depended upon security of dynastic succession. The heir to the throne needed a clear title, and a plurality of doubtful claimants was a source of civil strife. Accordingly, the heir ought, if possible, to be male, and ought in any event to be the child of the reigning monarch. The feudal system was thus exposed to the vicissitudes of biology. It happened that, in this regard, the Tudors had some sort of congenital weakness: their children tended to be born dead or to die young. Elizabeth, who died at seventy, was very old for a Tudor.

Catherine's first four children, of whom three were sons, were either stillborn or died within days. Then, in 1516, came Mary, who lived to be forty-two, and who herself bore no child, though, as wife of Philip II, she had fantasies and even symptoms of pregnancy. Then came more stillbirths and miscarriages, uncertain in number since the mounting disappointments were concealed. After 1525, when Catherine was forty, Henry gave up hope of male issue by her.

Then began a series of wild, calamitous maneuvers, all directed to the production and legitimation of a male heir, whose eventual marriage would not involve the fearful dynastic uncertainties attendant upon the marriage of a female heir. In 1533, a lady of the court, Anne Boleyn, found herself pregnant by Henry. Part of the problem (namely, production) was now solved; the rest of the problem could be solved by legitimation of Anne's child. Few events in history more amply reveal the human skill of making legal what the laws forbid. The easiest solution was for Henry to get rid of Catherine either by invalidating the marriage as incestuous (she having been his brother's wife) or by an act of divorce. When Catherine proved stubborn on both counts, there was a proposal, from Pope Clement VII himself, for the permission of bigamy: precedent existed for it where dynasties were at stake. One potent ground for dissolving the marriage—namely, that Catherine all along had been a Spanish agent —seems never to have been suggested. Perhaps international politics rendered it unusable.

If Henry and Pope Clement could have consulted merely their personal wishes, the affair would easily have been compromised. Clement had no moral objections to divorce or to bigamy or indeed to much of anything else, and he did not wish to lose England from the Church's authority and revenues. But Clement had become a creature, and for a time a physical captive, of Charles V, King of Spain and Holy Roman Emperor. Catherine was Charles's aunt. Consanguinity forbade the insult, and policy forbade the surrender of Spanish influence. Charles allowed Clement to grant neither divorce nor bigamous marriage. There was nothing left for Henry but to hand down his own law on the question.

Accordingly, on the twenty-third of May 1533, Thomas Cranmer, the Archbishop of Canterbury, pronounced that the pope had had no power to legalize the marriage of a man with his brother's widow, and that consequently Henry and Catherine had never been lawfully wed. Five days later, he declared Henry and Anne to be man and wife, and Anne received the crown on June first. On September seventh, the great Elizabeth was born.

Systems of law belong, of course, to the ideology of the establishment they serve. I suppose that nothing shows so spectacularly the power of politics over ideology as the constant transformation of law under press of circumstance. One ordinarily thinks of law as robust and supreme, able and entitled to bring circumstance under its own sway. No doubt it often does so—with weaker members of the body politic. But where high policy is concerned, the law accommodates itself to "great and present" need. Within three years of the time when Cranmer pronounced Henry and Catherine not married and Henry and Anne married, he found himself pronouncing Henry and Anne not married—a little late, to be sure, since Anne's head had been already struck off. Cranmer, a considerable man, was acting as the establishment required; he could not have shown more organizational propriety. Yet his own fate was to be burned as heretic and marytr during Mary's reign. And Mary and Elizabeth, each of whom had been in one way or another made bastard, alike ruled as lawful queens—lawful, it would appear, because none could overthrow them. Politics has its own sense, and has no other.

Quite promptly, in 1534, the new condition of political affairs recorded itself in law and social doctrine. A convocation of clergy at Canterbury, being asked the question "Whether the Roman pontiff has any greater jurisdiction bestowed on him by God in the Holy Scriptures in this realm of England than any other foreign bishop," gave in answer thirty-four nays, four ayes, and one vote of no opinion.[4] Two months later, a similar convocation at York, "after careful discussion . . . and mature deliberation" upon precisely the same question, reached precisely the same result, this time unanimously. The wind that blew from Canterbury swept all doubt and dissidence from York.

Parliament, with which Henry carefully kept on good terms (he was perhaps the first "constitutional monarch" of England), followed the same line. A Dispensations Act prescribed that "no person or persons of this your realm shall from henceforth pay any pensions, censes, portions, Peter-pence or any other impositions, to the use of the said bishop or the see of Rome, like as heretofore they have used, by usurpation of the said Bishop of Rome and his predecessors, and sufferance of your highness and your most noble progenitors, to do."[5] A Supremacy Act made it law that "the king our sovereign lord, his heirs and successors, kings of this realm, shall be taken, accepted, and reputed the only supreme head in earth of the Church of England, called *Ecclesia Anglicana*."[6] This same act laid down that part of the King's religious labor would be "to repress and extirp all errors, heresies, and other enormities and abuses." Thus we may perceive that revolutions, which replace the power of one organization with the power of another, do not (or do not necessarily) abolish the contest between orthodoxy and heresy. They make orthodox what was previously heretical, but at the same time they open up new spheres of heresy, of doctrines inimical to themselves.

To all these acts the new pope, Paul III, replied with a bull, *Eius Qui Immobilis,* excommunicating Henry, Henry's heirs and descendants, his "accomplices and abettors," and absolving his subjects from allegiance to him. But one of the good things in life is that it is useless to utter what you cannot effect. The language of *Eius Qui Im-*

4) Bettenson, *Documents,* p. 323. I surmise that the man who voted "doubtful" could not decide between the ideology he had learned and the state power that threatened him.
5) Ibid., pp. 317–18.
6) Ibid., p. 322.

mobilis, like the language of *Regnans In Excelsis* (which excommunicated and deposed Elizabeth), remains to this day, what then in fact it was, pompous and empty.

Meanwhile Henry, the theologian,[7] who could formulate doctrine as readily as any doctor of the Church, made it plain that, so far as his intentions went, the English Reformation was to have strict limits. Royal supremacy over the English Church was the heart of it and almost the only doctrinal change, a change indeed easily made since the headship of the Bishop of Rome had been no part of early Christian theology. There were, to be sure, certain Royal Injunctions of 1536, which forbade the worship of images and relics and the collection of fees therefore, and which required the clergy to "provoke, stir, and exhort every person to read" the Bible in English.[8] All this was clearly social advance. But a series of Six Articles, in 1539, "the bloody whip with six strings," reasserted transubstantiation, celibacy for the clergy (Cranmer had to put away his wife), and auricular confession. Henry's religion was Catholicism with himself and his heirs supreme in England.

There had been, in 1533, shortly after Anne's coronation, a sad little episode, presaging this result. A certain man named Frith and a second man named Andrew, a tailor of London, were burned at the stake for denying transubstantiation. In the Tower, Frith was left unfettered; and Walsingham, writing to Cranmer, reported, "Although he lacketh irons, he lacketh not wit nor pleasant tongue. . . . It were a great pity to lose him."[9] Andrew the tailor, if less in wit, was not less in courage. They duly suffered in flames. But it also chanced that Frith's writings converted Cranmer, who had sat in judgment upon him and who later introduced into the Communion Service Frith's doctrine and even his very words:

The natural body and blood of our Savior Christ are in Heaven, and not here, it being against the truth of Christ's natural body to be at one time in more places than one.

Sanguis martyrum semen Ecclesiae!

7) Some historians have expressed regret over Henry's interest in theology. For myself, I think it is a merit, or at least an interesting talent, in a ruler that he is able to handle the ideology by which he rules.
8) Bettenson, *Documents,* p. 328.
9) Froude, *History of England,* Vol. I, p. 487n.

I I

BETWEEN THE BIRTH of that enchanting painter Botticelli, which occurred in perhaps the year 1447, and the Peace of Westphalia, which in 1648 ended the Thirty Years' War, the human race—or at any rate the European part of it—passed through such convulsive struggles as are equaled only by those of our own present time. Two great epochs, each named for a separate and spectacular change, coincided and were in fact one: the Renaissance and the Reformation. The Renaissance began somewhat earlier, and is customarily dated from 1453, when the Turkish capture of Constantinople drove scholars with their Greek manuscripts to Italy, there to reconstitute within philosophy the lovely, untormented Platonic view of things. By similar custom, the Reformation is held to have begun in 1517 with Luther's ninety-five theses upon the church door at Wittenberg. Such dates are perhaps more precise than accurate, but their precision sheds a kind of piercing light (one knows where one is), and their possible inaccuracy allows historians to write other, and corrective, works.

If one compares in the mind's eye Botticelli with any of those grim and weary veterans who made the Peace of Westphalia, the difference between Renaissance and Reformation will be clear enough. Botticelli was not the whole of the Renaissance, but he was the whole, and uniquely, of its essence. A new fantasy had shimmered down upon the world, Greek in birth, Italianate in rebirth; and for the first time in fifteen hundred years Europeans could look at one another and at nature without considering either the penitence of Saint Paul or the self-sacrifice of Jesus. In the Renaissance view, the world, a place of beauty and delight, needed not to be changed but only to be embraced; and the world's people, free of guilt, might be simply and candidly loved.

It was not realism which the Renaissance achieved, only a different and more fruitful fantasy. Botticelli's maidens at springtime, the Venus upon the shell and waves, the Madonna who sits within her circular frame above a Gospel open to the Magnificat, are far too lovely for human verisimilitude, and they are engaged upon enterprises which the purest human deeds can only approximate. They are, that is to say, idealized—cast forth by his brush as visual signs of perfection, which, once seen, would live (as indeed they do) in imagination forever. This much, to be sure, ecclesiastical art had always done. The difference was that perfection now ceased to be exclusively divine; it became human and therefore attainable within our world.

On the other hand, the Peace of Westphalia confirmed the Peace of Augsburg (1555), which had confirmed the Confession of Augsburg (1530). And what had the Confession of Augsburg said? (Remember, as you now read, the Botticelli "Primavera," the "Venus," the "Madonna of the Magnificat.") The Confession of Augsburg asserted that "after the fall of Adam, all men born according to nature are born with sin," that this sin brings "condemnation and also eternal death to those who are not reborn through baptism and the Holy Spirit," that "men cannot be justified in the sight of God by their own strength, merits, or works, but that they are justified freely on account of Christ through faith."[1] This is Melanchthon's statement of the Lutheran view.[2] Plainly it casts us back into our ancient troubles, into dark forebodings and inspissate guilts. Try, if you can, to think of these things when you look at Botticelli, and you will feel with a wild incongruity the difference between the Reformation and the Renaissance.

Yet these two epochs occurred together and were joined together by the painful interpenetration of opposites gnawing upon opposites. The theoretical ground of their unity was that they had both rediscovered the value of human beings as individual persons. The social ground of their unity was that they both assisted the rise of the merchant class and the disintegration of feudalism.

They have, I think, a more general unity, in respect of the fact that they are both required if one is adequately to describe what may be called the human condition. Paradise, we now know, is possible, is available, not celestially but terrestrially. At the same time, so long as men do evil things, there will be feelings of guilt, of anger, and of guilt at feeling angry. Perhaps it may be found that the ideology of any epoch has much to say about the world and its possibilities, about the attainment or recovery of good character, about happiness and justice in relations among men. These are the three great themes, and there really isn't much else to talk about.

1) Bettenson, *Documents*, p. 297.
2) Melanchthon was Philip Schwartzerde (="Black Earth"). The scholarly fashion of rendering one's name into Greek yielded "Melanchthon" (*melan*= "black"; *chthonos*="earth"). Thus also Erasmus (*Desiderius*="loved one"), and Oecolampadius (*Hausschein*="house lamp").

The three themes, however, occur, epoch by epoch, in varying patterns and with variable light and shade. The ancient Greeks made so much of poise, of the suitable (Tò ικανόν), and of moderation, none of which they very successfully practiced, that they have left an impression of untroubled urbanity; yet a people who invented the Furies were surely well acquainted with guilt. Medieval Europeans made so much of celestial government and celestial destiny that they seem hopeless about terrestrial affairs; yet their love of the world and of one another is set forth, often tenderly and sometimes satirically, in illuminations, in wood carvings beneath the seats of choir stalls, in stone carvings that hide near the capitals of columns in a church nave. It is *emphasis* which betrays the spirit of an age. Your Greek was as guilt-ridden as any other man, but he thought it best to attempt serenity. Your medieval loved his neighbor and his life, but he thought it best to accept trouble first and blessedness thereafter. And we? We want beauty, virtue, abundance, blessedness, here and now, in a crowded present upon a crowded globe. This our wish will be our monument, and since ideals do shape achievement, the legacy we leave may be extraordinary.

The Renaissance was a shift from gloom to light, from eschatology to science, from remoteness of adoration to immediacy of love, from prostration in guilt to dignity in achievement. What God had done assimilated itself subtly to what men could do. The celestial hierarchy, a projection of ancient hopes and fears and social structures, slowly withdrew from beyond sky and cloud, to seek the human soil of its origin. In respect of doctrine, all this was highly heretical. Yet no men of the time were more fully Renaissance men than the popes, the cardinals, the higher clergy inhabiting Rome: patrons, or in any case admirers, of Raphael and Michelangelo. When Giovanni de' Medici became pope as Leo X, he was heard to say, "Let us enjoy this Papacy which God has given us." It was a Renaissance remark, and it would not have been uttered by Gregory the Great.

So for a time the hierarchy dreamed in voluptuous enchantment, broken at intervals by spasms of energy in administration or in war. There were the paintings, the buildings, the music, the poetry ancient and new—delights of eye and ear; there were the "brown Greek manuscripts, and mistresses with great smooth marbly limbs." Erasmus visited Rome in perhaps 1504 and again in 1507; he loved the cultivation, especially the worldly wit of cardinals. Luther was there in 1512, and left it horrified. At first sight of the city from a distance, he had exclaimed, with lifted hands, "I greet thee, thou Holy Rome, thrice holy from the blood of the martyrs."[3] Rome, which during two thousand years had received many distinguished visitors, did not perhaps require this salutation. In any event, the sight of Renaissance living and the sound of Renaissance talk were a great deal more than this innocent Teuton, troubled and mystical, could endure. Nothing in life effects more disillusion than a member's discovery of how the leadership behaves.

Such discoveries were unavailable to Erasmus: he had always known the true facts. Orphaned in boyhood, he had been lured, like many other such youths, into a monastery, while guardians spent (or, in any case, lost) the property he was to inherit. In his monastery there was more drunkenness and debauchery than learning, and, having little taste for either, he chafed and fidgeted until, at the age of twenty, he escaped to become secretary to the Bishop of Cambrai. There followed student years at the University of Paris—years of poverty but of joy—during which he came to know Lorenzo Valla, the brilliant ecclesiastic whose classical learning had exposed the forgery of the *Donation of Constantine*.[4] Erasmus already had taught himself Greek; he had been a voracious reader and a prolific writer, and he remained both. He embraced the new learning as a man would embrace salvation; and salvation, of a by no means contemptible sort, it surely was.

During the first decade of the sixteenth century, Erasmus became a famous man. An extended visit in England earned him the acquaintance and respect of the most eminent persons, including the king, Henry VII, and the young prince who was to be Henry VIII. The Archbishop of Canterbury, William Warham, granted him a yearly stipend. Wonderful to say, he liked the weather: "The air," he wrote, "is soft and delicious."[5] Less surprisingly, he liked the girls and their habit (now, alas, disused) of ceremonial kissing:

3) *Cambridge Modern History*, 1934, Vol. II, p. 117.
4) A document of the eighth century purporting to be the Emperor Constantine's bequest (in the fourth century) of the Roman Empire to the Christian Church. The forgery stood revealed in the document's odd vocabulary—in words like "satrap," which Constantine almost certainly would not have used.
5) Epistle XIV: J. A. Froude, *Life and Letters of Erasmus* (New York: Charles Scribner's Sons; 1894), p. 39. All my quotations from Erasmus's letters are in translations by Froude, who does them wonderfully well.

. . . the English girls are divinely pretty. Soft, pleasant, gentle, charming as the Muses. They have one custom which cannot be too much admired. When you go anywhere on a visit the girls all kiss you. They kiss you when you arrive. They kiss you when you go away; and they kiss you again when you return. Go where you will, it is all kisses.[6]

This witty and flirtatious elegance, which Erasmus could not exclude from his soberest writings, made him, very recognizably, a prototype of Voltaire. Accordingly, his satirical works, like the *Adagia* and the *Praise of Folly*,[7] had rather more social effect than the scholarly works. They cannot now be read with the delight, still less the glee, they once aroused; their appositeness is almost gone, and they seem labored. But once upon a time they lashed the monks and other orders and ranks of clergy till all those clerics howled.

In 1514 there occurred in Germany an example of the ceaseless *odium theologicum,* in a pattern not yet vanished out of history. The newborn love of Greek, already a force for the elucidation of Christian origins, passed over into concern with Hebrew—the third, as we remember, of the "sacred languages." This concern had infected a man named Reuchlin, who became the founder of Hebraic studies for modern Christian scholars. He had caught the infection from Pico della Mirandola in Italy. Pico was a Renaissance charmer, who, at twenty-one, in an incomparable bloom of brilliance and beauty, had publicly offered some nine hundred theses for debate. Some of these proving heretical, debate was forbidden, and Pico withdrew, with undiminished loveliness, into solitude and mysticism. In due course he came to know that mystical Jewish work, the Cabala, and at this moment Reuchlin met him.

Reuchlin was a mystic too, but the Cabala, instead of miring him in contemplation, called forth his enormous powers of scholarship. He studied Hebrew under a Jewish physician, and then labored so scientifically over the Old Testament that, ever afterward, it could be interpreted "as little through the Cabala as through the Roman associations of the Vulgate."[8] It was, in short, ready for use by the Protestant movement.

6) Ibid., p. 45.
7) *Encomium Moriae*: the title is a genial, if robust, pun on the name of Sir Thomas More, a lifelong and intimate friend of Erasmus.
8) *Cambridge Modern History,* Vol. II, p. 696.

Meanwhile the monks, and in particular the Dominicans, had long taken refuge in that hostility toward knowledge with which reactionaries always surround themselves, defensively, like the cuttle-fish with its ink. They desired enlightenment neither by Reuchlin nor by anyone else. The weapon of anti-Semitism lay ready, as so often happens, to hand: the monks could denounce all study of a language used by Jesus' executioners.[9] Moreover, as so often happens, there appeared a Jew to assist the anti-Semitism, one Johann Pfeffer-korn, a late convert to Catholicism. All converts like to attack the organization they have abandoned, and not a few converts, who perhaps always lived nearer to fantasy than to fact, give accounts in which very little fact can be found. Pfefferkorn could speak as one who had been a Jew; he could profess himself "purified"; he could squeeze out the last bitter nonsense from that dreary, oft-repeated, and mendacious routine. It was Pfefferkorn's fancy that all Hebrew books except the Bible ought to be destroyed.

Reuchlin lay in prison for a year, while the Inquisition, unable to do all that Pfefferkorn fancied, burned Reuchlin's books only. It was only the books they burned. Every scholar in Europe rallied to Reuchlin, and Leo X, who had determined to enjoy his pontificate and who was (as we know) a Renaissance man, set the prisoner free. Erasmus assisted the cause, with such loathing of Pfefferkorn that he would not mention the Pfefferkorn name: it would "pollute my papers!"[1] "I believe the creature," Erasmus went on, still not naming him, "was only baptized that he might the better poison people's minds—a veritable Satan, Diabolus, slanderer, going among foolish women and canting about heresy and the need of defending the faith."

Leo had been generous: scholarship was saved, and the Renaissance prospered. Early in 1517, Erasmus, being fifty-one years old, thought it worthwhile to keep on living, in prospect of a golden age. "We have," he wrote, "a Leo X for Pope; a French king content to make peace for the sake of religion when he had means to continue the war; a Maximilian for emperor, old and eager for peace; Henry VIII, king of England, also on the side of peace. . . . Learning is springing up all around out of the soil; languages, physics, mathe-

9) By Jesus too, of course, along with the Aramaic.
1) Froude, *Erasmus,* p. 184.

matics, each department thriving. Even theology is showing signs of improvement."[2]

Most of us have written such prognostics. Within a few months of this delighted augury, the ninety-five theses stood nailed upon their door, the market for indulgences vanished out of Germany, and Leo X, that man of the Renaissance, could no longer conceive how to finance the completion of Saint Peter's Church. Amid the languor of his enjoyments, Leo was at first not wrathful. It was well known that Germans were drunkards, and it appeared, from information received, that Luther was a German. "When he has slept off his wine," said Leo patiently, "he will know better."

I I I

LUTHER was indeed drunk, not with wine, but with what he took to be the Holy Spirit. The intoxication grew upon him until his death, and has accompanied his posthumous fame. Not many heroes of the twentieth century, perhaps, have cared to display it in Luther's style, but what they have displayed is nevertheless very like it. It exists in a certain stance of members toward leaders in an organization. It is a stance of invulnerability: there is something in the member that the leadership cannot seize, cannot wound, cannot even touch. "To act against our conscience is neither safe for us nor open to us," runs Luther's celebrated peroration at Worms. "On this I take my stand. I can do no other. God help me. Amen."[3]

Now, Luther was no political anarchist. He granted power in the secular state to be desirable and necessary: "The civil sword shall and must be red and bloody."[4] Luther's anarchism had to do with that special relation which obtains between a man and his conscience— or, if one likes so to say, between all else there is in a man and the one pregnant power that effects decision. In such a relation there is a notable and peculiar privacy. The sense of Lutheran doctrine—of all Protestantism, indeed, and of individualism generally—has been

2) Ibid., p. 186.
3) Bettenson' translation, in *Documents*, p. 285. Luther uttered the last sentences in his native German: *Hier stehe ich. Ich kann nicht anders. Gott helff mir. Amen.*
4) Quoted from Luther's treatise "On Commerce and Usury" (*Von Kaufshandlung und Wuchen*) by R. H. Tawney, *Religion and the Rise of Capitalism* (New York: Harcourt, Brace and Company; 1926), p. 102.

that, on the whole, what happens between a man and his conscience is more important in itself and more fruitful in result than what happens between man and man in social organizations or organized society. It is certainly difficult to be a heretic without entertaining some such notion as this.

The notion itself will be brilliantly clear if we set beside it the extreme opposite. When Loyola founded the Society of Jesus in 1534, he laid down in his *Spiritual Exercises* an ultimate rigor of obedience. Number 13 of the "Rules for Thinking within the Church" asserts that "if she [the Church] shall have defined anything to be black which to our eyes appears to be white, we ought in like manner to pronounce it to be black."[5] Elsewhere appeared the following exhortation: "Let each one persuade himself that they that live under obedience ought to allow themselves to be borne and ruled by divine providence working through their superiors exactly as if they were a corpse which suffers itself to be borne and handled in any way whatsoever."[6]

Exactly like a corpse! This wondrous simile describes to perfection the organization man.

These opposite views of organizational life, the Lutheran and the Jesuit, reproduce themselves as theological doctrine, in the very conception of God. The Protestant God is a projection of the human conscience, a God who defines the separation of right from wrong, gives moral commands, and, like conscience, is immediately accessible to the worshiper. Disobedience to his commands, as to those of a human father, at once evokes feelings of guilt and fear of punishment. The Catholic God, however is a projection not so much of personal conscience as of organizational unity.[7] He is a head of state, and His commands come down to the worshiper, not with immediacy, but through a series of vicars and vicars' vicars. The relation of a worshiper to this God is the relation of a private to the GHQ: "theirs not to reason why."

What you have in the Catholic God, then, is the policy and program of the Catholic Church considered as authoritative. What you have in the Protestant God is a moral code, or set of codes, con-

---

5) Bettenson, *Documents,* p. 365.
6) Ibid., p. 366.
7) See Tawney's pregnant remark that the Church "aspired to be, not a sect, but a civilization," op. cit., p. 19.

sidered as authoritative, the contents being disclosed to the believer directly upon inquiry. Since the struggles of the sixteenth century rose from the vices of feudal society, and since these vices in turn rose from incurable defects in the social structure, every reform, however slight, assisted the decomposition of the old order. The God who presided over feudalism had to give way, and did give way, to a God who expressed and magnified the conscience of reformers; and the reformers, lacking any sanction from the old order, had to present all the proposed gains and remedies as their own idea. Thus the Catholic God was, and remains, an image of organizational authority; the Protestant God was, and remains, an image of personal, self-determining choice.

Such facts the contending parties have been pointing out to each other these past four hundred years, the Protestants warning against oppression, the Catholics against anarchy. In 1520 Luther inquired, rather tartly, "If God spoke by an ass against a prophet [Balaam], why should he not speak by a holy man against the pope?"[8] In 1534, Loyola deprecated all attacks upon superiors as tending to "scandal and disorder." "Such attacks set the people against their princes and pastors; we must avoid such reproaches and never attack superiors before inferiors."[9] Yet both Gods, both images, survive among us and do even prosper. Perhaps it is because we all of us, of whatever religion or of none, have equal need for unity and dissent.

Nothing is gained scientifically, and indeed much is lost, by lifting authority on wings of metaphor beyond the clouds; but a good deal seems sometimes to be gained emotionally. It is one way of handling great events and, in particular, great crises. The signers of our Declaration of Independence were men of the Age of Reason, not much given to supernatural imaginings. Yet, since they risked their lives, their fortunes, and their sacred honor, they allowed themselves references to "Nature's God," to the "Creator," and to "Divine Providence." It is not easy to make momentous choices on the frail and suspect base of private insight and personal responsibility; in fact it is so difficult that many men cannot make such choices at all. There is a need to feel that the choice is amply justified and that it is

8) In his Address to the Christian Nobility, excerpted in *Great Voices of the Reformation*, edited by Harry Emerson Fosdick, (New York: The Modern Library; 1954), p. 104.
9) Bettenson, *Documents*, p. 364.

supported, not by ethics alone, but by the majesty of historical events. The historical events are clearly objective, the ethics can be held to be so; and thus, by an act of poetry, the two phenomena (one moral, one factual) unite in the image of a divine person administering salvation. If it ever befalls you to set your own integrity against some evil demand of government, you will feel what the founders of Catholicism and of Protestantism alike felt: a hope, amounting to a conviction, that history on the whole favors righteousness, and that virtue has, in the very nature of the case, armor for its nakedness and a stronghold for its home:

> *Ein' feste burg ist unser Gott,*
> *Ein' gute Wehr und Waffen.*

These celebrated lines, which introduce Luther's own poem of the year 1529—the battle hymn of Protestantism—give way immediately to comment upon Satan, the Enemy, the evil one, *der alte böse Feind*. Satan has got two weapons in his armory, great power and great cunning; and no other personage so formidable is to be found upon earth. What Luther had known theoretically before 1517 the twelve succeeding years confirmed in terrifying fact. Satan's scheme was to interpose between men and their consciences with a thousand skillful arguments and threats. Had it not been thus with Adam? And was it not also thus with the poor Augustinian monk, Luther himself? He had sought to rectify a small evil, to wipe away a trifling blot, only to find himself suddenly an heresiarch, an excommunicate, the leader of a revolution. All this, we may suppose, is what comes of defying the Fiend.

Nothing in the world can be more familiar than devices for raising money. They are so familiar indeed that historians can usually ignore them, though they are of the essence of history. Some attempts of the sort, however, have brought down the whole organizational structure; it is the failures that are notable. Among these, none is more notable than Pope Leo's attempt to finance the completion of Saint Peter's Church through the sale of indulgences. The Papal agent in Germany was Archbishop Tetzl, a man who has acquired (as Froude says) a "forlorn notoriety."[1] Tetzl moved from town to town with a train of assistants—salesmen, they actually were—who made the specific deals. The whole party entered a town in proces-

1) "Times of Luther and Erasmus," Part II, in *Short Studies on Great Subjects*, World's Classics Series (Oxford: Oxford University Press; 1924), p. 67.

sion, set up the papal arms in a church, and proceeded to the business (for such it was) of selling to sinners the remission of their sins and degrees of escape from purgatory for the sinners themselves and their deceased parents.[2]

In theory, the Son of God had died in order to remit human sins, and had, before dying, appointed Peter the first temporal head of an organization that would do the same thing in later ages. Remission of sins was thus a unique talent in the Church. Like transubstantiation, it was a miracle to be worked only by the consecrated clergy. If the Church used its monopoly of grace for the raising of funds, why, organizations must be expected to profit from the blessings they exclusively confer. It was disappointing, perhaps, to find that one's membership in the organization had produced, not the benefits, but only the chance to buy them. Was this merely good business, or was it, just possibly, the cunning of the Fiend?

The Archbishop Albert of Mainz prepared Tetzl's arrival with a series of pastoral instructions. There was to be, he announced, a graduated scale of rates, based on the principle of ability to pay. Thus kings and bishops would pay twenty-five Rhenish gold guilders; abbots, counts, barons, ten; lesser notables, six; ordinary folk, one; and the poor, one half.[3] Since religion demanded that "the kingdom of heaven would be as open to the poor as to the rich," the poor were to be allowed the privilege of paying for the remission of their sins also. The effect of this communal contribution, the Archbishop said, would be that "help will surely come to departed souls, and the construction of the Church of Saint Peter will be abundantly promoted at the same time."[4] Thus blessings would simultaneously descend upon the members as individuals and upon the organization as a whole.

The singular fact about this enterprise was that it depended, for

2) Protestantism has always denied the real existence of purgatory (anteroom to heaven or to hell), plainly because a belief in it was altogether too expensive. It is pleasant to hear the amiable thunders of King James I of England on this point: "As for Purgatory, and all the trash depending thereon, it is not worth the talking of." *A Premonition to All Most Mighty Monarchs, Kings, Free Princes, and States of Christendom,* excerpted in More and Cross, *Anglicanism,* (London: Society for the Promotion of Christian Knowledge; 1951), p. 5. If economic interest leads often to error, it leads, not less often perhaps, to truth.

3) Bettenson, *Documents,* p. 261.

4) Ibid., p. 263.

success, entirely upon what the members *believed*. The alleged benefits, for which the money was paid, were beyond empirical verification: you could not know, with any immediate awareness, whether your deceased parents were in fact getting early release from purgatory or indeed whether they had been in it. Nor could you know whether you yourself would ever be in purgatory, needing release. The "value" you were paying for when you bought an indulgence depended essentially upon what you took to be the case. If that "value" were to exist at all, you had to believe the following: (1) that you had sinned; (2) that sin ordinarily entails punishment; (3) that punishment is something you want to avoid; (4) that sin can be disconnected from punishment; (5) that the Church, through its consecrated clergy, can so disconnect it; (6) that the written certificate of indulgence does validly and truly assert that the disconnection has been effected. If any of these propositions is false—and none of them is demonstrable—you have bought a gold brick.

Doubtless Luther was the last man in the world to regard himself as free of sin, or sin as free of punishment. Quite to the contrary, with true Protestant masochism, he welcomed punishment for sin. It was the fifth and sixth propositions that Luther denied, and, in denying, expressed the sense of almost the entire German people and of many others in Christendom.

The ideological difficulty was in fact extreme. Suppose, for example, that some human male had raped the Virgin Mary during her lifetime upon earth. Could a papal pardon, bought at whatever cost, absolve him?[5] If so, there is no magnitude in crime; if not, there are limits on papal power. More generally, can there be pardon of any sort without some evidence that the sinner knows his sin to be a sin, is sorry for it, seeks its correction and his own improvement? No such penitence is guaranteed by any purchase of pardon; on the contrary, purchase suggests avoidance of the proper change of heart.[6] Christians show their morality best, not by buying pardons,

5) This is Number 75 of Luther's ninety-five theses: "To hold that papal pardons are of such power that they could absolve even a man who (to assume the impossible) had violated the mother of God is to rave like a lunatic." Ibid., p. 269.

6) Number 40: "True contrition asks for penance and accepts it with love; but the bounty of indulgences relaxes the penalty and induces hatred of it." Ibid., p. 266.

but by giving to the poor.[7] Accordingly, "Christians are to be taught that in dispensing pardons the pope has more desire (as he has more need) for devout prayer on his behalf than for ready money."[8] And further, "Christians must be taught that if the pope knew the exactions of the preachers of indulgences, he would rather have Saint Peter's basilica reduced to ashes than built with the skin, flesh, and bones of his sheep."[9]

These last two theses seem profoundly and winningly naïve, but they were surely less naïve than they seem. Luther had been to Rome, had observed the papacy at work, and had cried out at his departure, "Everything is permitted in Rome except to be an honest man!" He was as little disposed as Leo himself to imagine that the Pope preferred prayers to ready money or the prosperity of the poor to the completion of Saint Peter's. The difference could only have been that Leo would have received the idea with Renaissance laughter, whilst Luther received the true facts with anguish and rage. The attribution of a more sensitive morality to the Pope was, rather, a shrewd political device, aimed at detaching the highest functionary from the organization's side and inviting him (if not actually gaining him) to the side of reform. The device might have worked with Leo's successor, Adrian VI, a much less worldly pope, but to Leo it suggested drunkenness and things German.

When a membership can no longer endure the exactions of a leadership, there always comes the moment of refusal—often on apparently trivial questions. We have observed (what is for our purposes essential) that, as regards the Reformation, the moment came when the Church, the all-embracing organization, had outstripped everything but ideology. If you bought ecclesiastical office— a cardinalate, let us say—you could grow exquisitely aware in your daily life of the revenues and delights attendant upon the purchase. If you bought divorce from a repellent spouse, you could feel, with the same exquisite awareness, the pleasures of release. But what that you could be aware of did you buy when you bought an indulgence? Words only, only words. Reality behind those words you had to supply for yourself, out of faith. There was no such reality thrusting itself upon you.

7) Numbers 42–45. Ibid., p. 267.
8) Number 48. Loc. cit.
9) Number 50. Loc. cit.

The indiscretion thus committed by the leadership—an indiscretion which became a disaster—was that of overstraining the frailest part of organizations: the theory, the ideology. This most plastic of human inventions (as we have called it) is by no means the strongest. There arrived, accordingly, the dreadful climactic time, the *dies irae,* when it was obvious to all that, so far from the leadership's following the ideology, the ideology was following the leadership. Nothing makes a proposition more doubtful than the sight of an economic motive for it. Accordingly, there was nothing left for the membership but to assert true belief and honest conviction as the immediate values. The Church, having in this regard no works by which to win justification, made inevitable the Lutheran doctrine that justification cannot be by works but only by faith.

When Luther walked into the Diet at Worms, where the Fiend had assembled his forces rank on rank—the clergy in their robes, the knights in their armor—a baron tapped him on the shoulder with his gauntlet. "Pluck up thy spirit, little monk," said the baron; "some of us here have seen warm work in our time, but, by my troth, nor I nor any knight in this company ever needed a stout heart more than thou needst it now. If thou hast faith in those doctrines of thine, little monk, go on, in the name of God."[1]

It is not often that a man of ideas gets this kind of tribute from a man of action, and we have here some proof that there are times when ideology is the decisive thing in organizational life. Luther's celebrated dictum that faith is more important than works records the fact that he lived and wrote at just such a moment. "The soul can do without everything except the word of God," and, "the word of God cannot be received and honored by any works but by faith alone."[2] That is to say, the one thing altogether necessary to a man is a true view of the nature of things and of the proper ground for making choices. This view he would need even though he were never to act upon it, for it is what distinguishes him from the beasts of the field.

It is expected, however, that the man will act. Luther's magnification of "faith" was not intended to depreciate "works," but only to

1) J. A. Froude, *Short Studies on Great Subjects,* First Series (Oxford: Oxford University Press, World's Classics Series; 1924), p. 76.
2) "Concerning Christian Liberty," in Fosdick, *Great Voices of the Reformation,* pp. 83 and 84.

state where the main value lay. "It is thus impossible," he wrote in his Preface to St. Paul's Epistle to the Romans, "to separate works from faith—yea, just as impossible as to separate burning and shining from fire."[3] Given sincerity of conviction (that much abused phrase!) and purity of motive, good works would inevitably follow. But sincerity of conviction and purity of motive were precisely the qualities that a purchased pardon rendered valueless, while at the same time they lay open to punishment by the serried might of the ecclesiastical orders. Their intrinsic value was what the "little monk" went to Worms, at risk of life, to assert. For myself, I would not read his shade a lecture on the indissoluble unity of theory and practice. He knew that unity perfectly well. The more one understands the social environment of philosophic utterance, the more one sees why it is that thinkers, and in particular great thinkers, seldom mean just what they appear to say.

But there are two ways of judging ideology to be important, and they differ as excuse differs from justification. You can invent a doctrine as a public cover for policy, the policy and its motives being of main concern; or, having accepted doctrine as true, you can deduce policy from it. In the first case, doctrine is something specious and *ad hoc:* the normal relation of theory and practice is reversed, and instead of theory's giving rise to practice, practice gives rise to theory in the form of apologetics. In the second case, doctrine behaves honestly: it is theory enlightening practice by supplying the means to know and the wisdom to choose. Such was the whole intent of Luther's extraordinary effort. He proposed to re-establish the true relation between theory and practice, to silence doctrine as mere excuse and to give it tongue as justification. Without his gallant labors, the Western world might have lingered long in the mere pragmatism of a ruling order. The founders of the Christian Church had deduced policy from ideals; the hierarchy of Luther's day used ideals to embellish policy. It was high time to turn back toward the purer origins.

This turning back was more of a turning forward. By asserting theory as supreme, as supremely discoverable in the canonical scriptures, and as the pronouncement of the human conscience deified, Luther far exceeded the bounds which leaderships ordinarily allow to memberships. He appealed to an authority above the leadership,

3) Ibid., p. 122.

and at the same time asserted that the members had direct access to that authority. This ideological device put the leadership in a squeeze. Since the supreme authority, God, was in fact Luther's conscience, the leadership could not resist Luther without resisting God, nor could it obey God without obeying Luther. There was plainly nothing to do but kill the man.

It had happened, as we know, to many others; but with Luther it proved difficult and at last impossible. Protectors intervened: the Elector Frederick of Saxony,[4] and indeed the entire German people. The Emperor Charles V, very young and very skillful, shied away from direct attack; moreover, he had too many other troubles in too many other domains. Luther, who had learned politics like a genius, united against the hierarchy all the social ranks in Germany: the feudal lords, the merchant townsmen, and the peasants (until he turned upon these during the Peasants' War of 1524). Heresy passed, in the classic manner, into schism. A new Church arose, the Lutheran, with a new catechism and a new clergy. Hundreds of men and women, released from monastic life, learned the secular delights of trade and wedlock. Luther himself married a former nun, Catherine Baron; and we have charming glimpses of a household in which Katie (as he always called her), a good *hausfrau,* addressed him as "Herr Doktor," and, in awe of his eruptive intellect, asked unprovocative questions, like, "Is not the master of the ceremonies in Prussia the brother of the Margrave?"[5]

One time at least Katie ventured near the heart of ideology. "Herr Doktor," she said, "how is it that under Popery we prayed so often and so earnestly, and now our prayers are cold and seldom?" "Ah," replied Luther, "here begins the weariness of the word of God. One day new lights will rise up, and the Scriptures will be despised and flung away into the corner."[6] If he had said nothing else in his life, he would nevertheless have been a true prophet.

The age that was to come and was then beginning—the age of commerce, banking, industry—needed religion (in fact, several religions) for its rise to power; then, for a time, it almost did without religion, until at the last, prone upon its tedious and anguished death

4) On one occasion Frederick was heard to say, "There is much in the Bible about Christ, but not much about Rome." Froude, *Short Studies,* p. 71.
5) Ibid., p. 104.
6) Ibid., loc. cit.

bed, it called back the clergy to sweeten its demise. But in truth the Christian clergy have not been altogether kind to it, though they have often been obedient. Henry of Ghent gave the characteristic medieval view: "the business of buying and selling is perilous in the extreme"[7] —he meant, perilous to the human soul. The feudal lords, not infrequently in debt, denounced as usurious the taking of interest on money. The Church's view was that you lent money, not in order to make money, but to help someone in need. "Usurers"—that is, any men taking interest on loans—were denied absolution and Christian burial, and the Council of Vienne, in 1311, stigmatized as heretical the assertion that usury is not a sin.

Luther's view upon this question was wholly traditional; he even denounced the Church itself for having sunk to the level of a business enterprise. As for the Fuggers, the great bankers of the age, who held debts from the papacy and various European monarchs, and who paid their investors as much as fifty per cent—why, said Luther, it is "time to put a bit in the mouth of that holy company."[8] But he had no extensive theory on social questions. His comments, as Tawney says, were "the occasional explosions of a capricious volcano,"[9] and, when pressed on specific issues, he retreated into vagueness. The rising merchants had to be content, and for a time were content, with his defense of the right of private judgment, which they construed as the right to commercial negotiation.

This point being reached, the Reformation (even as extended by Calvin) began to give way again to the Renaissance, and Luther to Erasmus. The relations between these men were never happy. Erasmus had in some manner prepared the way for Luther, and Luther, finally embattled, awaited him as ally. The ally never joined. Erasmus understood the social issue profoundly: "Luther," he said, "has committed two sins: he has touched the Pope's crown and the monks' bellies."[1] But Erasmus liked neither schism nor the tendency of the movement. He had, he said quite candidly, no taste for martyrdom. He took no stand at all, for Luther or against him; and,

---

7) *Summe periculosa est venditionis et emptionis negotiatio.* Quoted by Tawney, op. cit., p. 34, from the *Aurea Quodlibeta.*

8) Ibid., p. 82: *"Hier müsste man . . . der geistlichen Gesellschaft einen Zaum ins Maul legen."*

9) Ibid., p. 88.

1) Froude, *Short Studies,* p. 72.

to protect his detachment, he made a point of not reading Luther's books. Thus, whenever he was urged to write against Luther, he could always say that one cannot attack what one has not read.

This failure to join battle has somewhat blemished Erasmus' fame. Luther, in exasperation, called him "the worst enemy that Christ has had for a thousand years."[2] It is true that Erasmus shunned this particular conflict, and that he thus can seem, or can be made to seem, a mere intellectual floating timidly near the edge of great events. He was, however, no coward, and moreover he was wise. If he had joined Luther, the limitations of Lutheranism would have swallowed him up. By remaining a man of the Renaissance rather than of the Reformation, he survives into our time like a neighbor. We can ask him many questions and get answers. From Luther we can get an answer only to one.

Yet that answer is useful enough: candor and honesty of belief. No doubt social problems require for their solution a social theory. And yet—may not the good works follow (as Luther thought) from the good faith? May it not be that—somehow, somewhere, sometime —the triumph will wait upon the intent, and that, because our conscience was in fact a fortress, *Das Reich muss uns doch bleiben?*

I V

THAT *doch* in the *doch bleiben:* "nevertheless," "for all that," "in spite of everything"! God's kingdom, the Christian commonwealth, will remain ours, regardless of other losses (and Luther named them) like goods, family, even life itself. The struggle, that is to say, was inevitable; it was also worth the undertaking, because triumph was sure to crown it. Such is the sense of embattled righteousness whenever and wherever it appears in history—most often in the rise toward power of classes which have as their "mission" the purification of society. A certain sternness inhabits this shrine as *genius loci,* and, to later and relaxed ages, dims the first wonders of achievement. In proportion as capitalism gave affluence to its beneficiaries, the chief motive for thrift, accumulation, dropped away, and expenditure became both enjoyable in itself and significant of status. To spenders reveling in the gains of ancestral struggles, Luther and Calvin, Zwingli and Knox, seemed (and still seem) dour disciplinarians. Thus did the Restoration wits feel about the Puritans, the

2) Ibid., p. 105.

Edwardians about their Victorian grandfathers, and Americans of the twentieth century about the godly giants who colonized New England.

It is a striking attribute of all middle-class revolutions—the ones which replaced landed wealth and power with commercial wealth and power—that they embraced more radical possibilities then they ever allowed to be made actual. They took leadership over society with the aid of forces they thereupon suppressed. Thus, for example, Luther and the German peasants were allies as against the papacy, Cromwell and the levelers as against Charles I, the French bourgeoisie and proletariat as against Louis XVI. Yet Luther helped suppress the peasants in 1525, and Cromwell the levelers throughout the 1650's. As for the French Revolution, the majority of *guillotinés* were at the beginning aristocrats and at the end proletarians. The blade that severed Louis' head, severed also Babeuf's.

The reason is not obscure. Every political contest is, at bottom, a contest for the assent of a majority. Ultimate strength lies, not in arms or coercion, not even in nuclear arms and nuclear coercion, but in what the human multitude decides to do. Every politician knows this, and consequently, in the effort to win assent from multitudes, each party to the struggle displays itself as representing the general social good. There follows much maneuvering (hopefully masterful), in the course of which each party identifies its main enemy and constructs such alliances as will bring the greatest weight to bear.

Thus, if we attend to the spread of political opinion in a society, we shall find that the maneuvering occurs chiefly around the center, the place where most people are usually to be found. The right wing tries to persuade the center that the main enemy is the left, the left wing that the main enemy is the right; and the center, if what it wants is stability, falls to denouncing "extremes." In Germany under Hitler, the right wing succeeded in its effort. In the Russia of 1917 and the China of 1949, the center was so far compromised by unpopular (and indeed unpatriotic) policies that the left could take power in its own name. In the United States of America after the Second World War, the right wing drove the center into an attack upon the left, and the result almost was that the center became a captive of the right. By effecting the fall of McCarthy, however, the center recovered, for a time at least, its independence and leadership.

In the sixteenth century, Erasmus's position was at the precise center: reform of behavior without change in the organizational structure. Everyone wished something of the sort, except the few whose privileges would have been limited. Just to the left of this position stood the moderate schismatics, Henry VIII and Luther, who created two national churches and made some changes in ideology. To their left stood Zwingli and Calvin, who expressed with great clarity the social intent of Swiss merchants. To their left stood the Anabaptists and a confusion of other sects, who expressed the hopes of the disinherited—the impoverished peasants, laborers, artisans. These groups, seeing some reform accomplished and further change possible, resolved to attempt in various parts of Europe a true millennium, the coming of the old messianic and revolutionary kingdom of God.

It is interesting to observe, and I believe a moral can be drawn from it, that the whole of modern history (which we may date from Erasmus's youth, as being also the time of Columbus's discoveries) is a record of catastrophic defeat for right-wing politics. The popes lost, the peers lost, the kings lost, the emperors, czars, and kaisers lost, the führers and duces lost, the Asian warlords lost, the imperialists are losing. Almost five hundred years of strife—stubborn, constant, and decisive—proclaims the fact that, short of the maiming or annihilation of our race, the members of it are to be supreme upon the planet, with none to molest them and none to rule.

The human future is thus extremely bright and would rejoice us all except for the rigors, indeed perhaps the horrors, of the journey thither. Yet it is something to be able to look, with genuine apprehension of fact, upon an historical prospect here (if not quite now) where the globe turns and the sun shines and the stars circle. We at least, men of the twentieth century, have no longer need of a transcendental paradise, a "kingdom not of this world." An ideal society—or, at any rate, a society almost ideal—is, we now know, quite attainable: if we do the right things, our descendants will possess it.

But the men of the sixteenth century had only faint and occasional glimmerings of assurance that paradise might be terrestrial. One such glimmering was More's *Utopia;* a second, Campanella's *City of the Sun.* There was also Rabelais' description of the Abbey of Thélème, where the gate bore the motto (not licentiously intended) "Do What You Like." But Machiavelli's sadly accurate account of power politics discouraged much temporal hope. Accordingly, the ultimate realm of bliss appeared to remain in heaven, and the question of arrival there lay in God's hands, either largely (as in the Catholic view) or wholly (as in the Protestant).

The Reformers, if they let heaven's life be heaven's, were by no means slothful about things to be done on earth. They understood that righteousness, though rising from a state of soul, would be manifest in social behavior. It therefore seemed desirable that society be arranged in such form as would make righteousness more readily manifest, or even (and this was Calvin's addition) enforceable in every detail by law. All things, if they survive long enough, turn into their opposites: the tradition which Saint Paul founded with a view to rendering law unnecessary fell at last into the hands of a professing Paulinist who legislated upon the entire range of human behavior, in gross and in detail. He was that stern moralist, that stupendous intellect, that man of little mercy and no compromise, John Calvin.

It is startling to think that Calvin began as a man of the Renaissance, but this was generally true of French Protestants. One of the early martyrs of the movement, Louis de Berquin, had been a pupil of Erasmus. The movement itself was led and staffed by laymen, and it sprang rather more from the New Learning than from the inner politics of the Church. Renaissance inspiration thus led two ways. Either (as with Rabelais) you could blow down the old order with astounding gusts of obscene imagery, or, taking the sword of faith and the helmet of salvation, you could crush the old order beneath superior self-discipline. Change so complete and so definitive required, and received, both methods. I think there cannot have been elsewhere in history a more public and more powerful alliance between superego and id.

French politics, however, was such as to evoke more attention to discipline than to indulgence. The Curé of Meudon and (later) the Sieur de Montaigne found their way to tolerance and laughter, but only by means of a timely skepticism on religious subjects. Any man, however, who took religion seriously had then to accept strife and the rigors of strife. The King of France, Francis I, was, for all his cynical charm, a persecutor, and his successors prolonged the policy beyond the dreadful massacre of Saint Bartholomew. The first Protestant martyrdoms in France occurred at Meaux, near Paris, in 1523. They grew steadily more frequent. In 1534–35, twenty-seven persons suffered at the stake in Paris. In 1568, more than ten thousand were slain throughout France. In 1572, the Saint Bartholomew affair slaughtered perhaps fifty thousand. A Protestant estimate of the year 1581 put the total number of victims during the century at two hundred thousand and more. To all this may be added a like butchery, during the same years, in the Low Countries, provinces then of Spain, where the bigoted Philip II and the murderous Duke of Alva destroyed, with orthodox violence, some fifty thousand persons. These victims were not combatants; they were simply people executed for heretical opinions.

If, therefore, Calvin seems harsh and his Genevan rule tyrannical, the chief reason will be found in the violence—always prompt and always malignant—with which the old order defended itself. When you have defeated such an adversary, you are not disposed to let him revive upon mercies of your own granting. Revolutions in their first triumphs are still insecure, and need to retain after victory the same rigor and discipline that made the victory possible. Deviation from discipline within the ranks seems still as dangerous to the cause —and to some extent is so—as when the battle was on. In the largest view, all that is repellent in such affairs derives from the fact of *crisis;* and crisis may be defined as a state of social conflict so intense that everything one does can be made to appear a matter of life and death. If we desire to remove from politics that moral ruthlessness that distinguished Calvin and Knox and Cromwell and (more recently) Stalin, we must first prevent intensity of crisis. The future comes with the same degree of violence which is used against it. It were better, obviously, that no such violence were used.

Calvin was born at Noyon, near Paris, in 1509. His antecedents are interesting, as symptomatic of the new order. The father, Gérard Calvin, came of a family whose members had long been bargemen on the river Oise. He himself, avoiding this profession in favor of an ecclesiastical career, earned with entire merit a series of resounding titles: *Notaire apostolique, Procureur fiscal du Comté, Scribe en Cour d'Église, Secrétaire de l'Évêché, et Promoteur du Chapitre.*[3] John, the second son, was at first destined to the priesthood, but escaped (at Gérard's own suggestion) into law. He was thus far a youth of the Erasmian sort: genial among friends, elegant in taste and in Latinity, a true Renaissance savant. Yet there was that about him that earned him the nickname of "The Accusative Case."

3) *Cambridge Modern History,* Vol. II, pp. 349–50.

During the year 1533, a change came over Calvin: he received his mission in life, "supported," as he later said, "and sanctioned by a call from God."[4] He was now suspect of heresy and liable to punishment, and in 1534 he found refuge at the Swiss city of Basel. There, next year, he published the definitive theological treatise of all Protestantism, the *Christianae Religionis Institutio,* "Institutes of the Christian Religion." There is no equal to this work by one so young, unless it be Hume's *Treatise of Human Nature* (1739), which appeared when its author was twenty-eight. Calvin had got the body and elements of Protestantism clear, codified, and complete at the age of twenty-six. He was one of those geniuses who put an end to things by making further work unnecessary.

We may admire the performance without liking the content. Let us not presently labor those grim and odious doctrines, whose majestic, cosmological shape teeters on a hair between horror and absurdity: the powerlessness of men to do good, their native inclination to do evil, their arbitrary assignment to heaven or hell by an almighty God, who, in either choice and in both choices, effects his own incalculable glory. "When his light is removed"—so runs the *Institutio*—"nothing remains but darkness and blindness; when his Spirit is taken away, our hearts harden into stone; when his guidance ceases, we are turned from the straight path."[5] But the wicked are not alone those blinded, hardened, misled by the simple withdrawal of light. Some of the wicked, God has deliberately made wicked, to his greater glory: "He directs their councils and excites their wills, in the direction which he has decided upon, through the agency of Satan, the minister of his wrath."[6]

Calvin has here passed beyond Augustine, whose more modest view was that, although men's good acts must be attributed to God, their sins must be attributed to themselves. With Calvin, God is architect and creator of good and evil alike. He stands to us in the relation of a playwright to his play: the characters say and do whatever He makes them say and do. As an account of human life, this may well be hideous; but it must be confessed that it is magnificent theater.

It is really no refutation of this metaphysics to say that the theory

4) "Letter to Cardinal James Sadolet," excerpted in Fosdick, *Great Voices of the Reformation,* p. 204.
5) Book II, Chapter 4. Bettenson's translation, *Documents,* p. 301.
6) Ibid., p. 302.

has never been consecrated by action. What sane man ever does squeeze out into practice the full liquid of his theory? Predestination asserts that all the important questions were settled long ago, and that human planning is, in any case, *une chiquenaude de Dieu*— the flick of God's middle finger. Why should we ponder, when it is not we who decide? Why should we labor, when it is not we who effect?

To such questions there can be no answers, if predestination is really the case. But the lack of answers in no way inhibited the activity of Calvin himself or of any Calvinist who has ever lived. Quite to the contrary, the doctrine of predestination increased the ardor of militancy and the vigor of struggle, until it came to pass that, wherever that doctrine went in Europe, a body of men, in theory powerless, laid kings prostrate and taught to ruling classes the lessons of historical doom. When all was over and the thrones were down and the priesthood was humbled before the universal priesthood of all believers, these "errant saints,"[7] faithful to doctrine, observed very coolly that it had not been their doing at all, but God's.

If, dropping metaphor away, we let the term "God" be synonymous with the term "history," we shall find that predestination makes rather more sense than we had anticipated. "Men make their own history," says Marx in a famous passage, "but they do not make it just as they please; they do not make it under circumstances chosen by themselves, but under circumstances directly found, given and transmitted from the past."[8] Among the "found circumstances" is the structure of existing society, which, if it contains a basic disloca-

---

7) The phrase is Samuel Butler's, in "Hudibras," a satirical poem of the seventeenth century. Butler is here teasing Presbyterians for being "saints errant" as other men had been "knights errant." Also there is the pun on "errant." The whole passage is worth quoting, because Butler is so profoundly aware that orthodoxy is in fact "enforced opinion":

> For he was of that stubborn crew
> Of errant saints, whom all men grant
> To be the true church militant;
> Such as do build their faith upon
> The holy text of pike and gun;
> Decide all controversies by
> Infallible artillery;
> And prove their doctrines orthodox
> By apostolic blows and knocks. . . .

8) *The Eighteenth Brumaire of Louis Bonaparte*, Part I.

tion, provides the motive and the dynamic for change. At the same time it molds and limits what the change can be, for even if the change is revolutionary, part of its nature will derive from the system it overthrew. In some parts of the world feudal forms (like monarchy) still adorn the exercise of capitalist power, and the survival of religion attests in itself the difficulty of breaking with the past.

In those epochs when the tide of events moves brilliantly forward from old and corrupt institutions toward new and for the moment clean, the agents of the change feel themselves sustained and helped and even hurried by a power which may seem to them mysterious except that each man knows it is not his own. What it really is, of course, is the total effort, the accumulated drive, of the members of society; and this may, quite reasonably, be called "history." It is other than each agent, it is far more powerful than each agent; it is, indeed, powerful enough to be decisive, and one need not be surprised if some people wish to call it "God." "Calvin," says Tawney in a pregnant paragraph, "did for the bourgeoisie of the sixteenth century what Marx did for the proletariat of the nineteenth. . . . The doctrine of predestination satisfied the same hunger for an assurance that the forces of the universe are on the side of the elect as was to be assuaged in a different age by the theory of historical materialism."[9]

Further, it may well be the case that, as Engels thought, the sixteenth-century merchants found predestination to be no bad description of economic enterprise. "In the commercial world of competition success or failure does not depend upon a man's activity or cleverness, but upon circumstances uncontrollable by him. It is not of him that willeth or of him that runneth, but of the mercy of unknown superior economic powers."[1] Think of Antonio in *The Merchant of Venice,* whose argosies were reported lost and who was himself therefore deemed ruined, and you will see an economic reading for the old adage, "Man proposes, but God disposes." When the disposition turned out favorably, as in the end it did with Antonio, few would be the merchants who could resist inferring that they were among the elect.

In 1536, Calvin came to Geneva, a merchant city, very homogeneous in life and population. It had recently abolished Catholicism and

9) Op. cit., p. 112.
1) Friedrich Engels, *On Historical Materialism.*

expelled the reigning bishop. Calvin's eminence was now as plain as his precocity, and he was at once recruited into government. God's kingdom was now to be God's republic, and God's law was to be enforced, in vast detail, by the magistrates. The citizens, who had just rid themselves of one tyranny, did not take kindly to Calvin's first efforts. A man was pilloried for playing cards. A bride having appeared in too glittering finery, her dressmaker, her mother, and her two bridesmaids were arrested. An adulterous couple were whipped through the streets by the hangman, and then banished. After two years of this, the Genevans banished Calvin.

They called him back in 1541. From then until his death in 1564, amid incredible labors and scarcely any sleep,[2] he wrought the great theocracy, the rule of God on earth, so much imitated and so much despised. Geneva became a city as of glass, in which the smallest action was watched, recorded, reproached if necessary, and if necessary punished. You could not smile during a church service nor sleep during a sermon. You could not play at dice. You could not sing a worldly song or dance upon a Sunday. You could not name your son Claude when the magistrates wanted you to name him Abraham.

And of course there were heresies—new heresies, newly defined. And of course there were victims. Between 1542 and 1546, when the theocracy was first flourishing, there were fifty-eight executions— among them, it seems incredible to say, the beheading of a child for striking its parents. The Genevan total, over a period of sixty years, was one hundred fifty heretics burned at the stake. Small enough by comparison what what the bigots of reaction had done, but palpable, palpable.

The great encounter, in heresy newly defined, was between Calvin and a physician-scholar named Servetus. Calvin's duplicity in the affair is perhaps not beyond doubt, but it is believed by more than one scholar. Servetus, a Spaniard, held views tending toward the pantheism that did in fact crown and summarize Renaissance philosophy. As a denial of trinitarian doctrine, this was of course heretical in Catholic eyes. Calvin himself was not very sound on the Trinity, but Servetus's view was still more to the left. Some element

2) "I have not time," he wrote, "to look out of my house at the blessed sun, and if things continue thus I shall forget what sort of appearance it has." *Encyclopaedia Britannica,* eleventh edition, Vol. V, p. 74.

of personal antagonism also intervened. It appears that Calvin slyly denounced Servetus to the Catholic Inquisition. Servetus, then at Lyon, fled from France toward Italy, and, for reasons beyond conjecture, passed through Geneva on the way. He got no farther. Calvin pounced, almost as if he had lured him there. On October 27, 1553, Servetus joined the immense company of martyrs burned at the stake. Calvin said he had wished to be more merciful: he had favored beheading.

Violence begets violence, and violence is intrinsically evil. The holocausts effected by reactionaries will explain Calvin, but they will justify him no more than partially. What could possibly justify the beheading of that child? The essential truth was uttered in those years by the libertarian Castellio, who wrote, in Servetus's defense, a tract called *Concerning Heretics*. Castellio said, quite simply, "Christ would be a Moloch, if he required that men be offered and burnt alive."[3]

We may commend this saying to all the rulers of earth, of laggard views or hopeful. There have been few to heed it in the past. Perhaps there will be more in the future. If so, the earth, which has so often shuddered, may at long last permanently exult.

3) Quoted by Fosdick, *Great Voices of the Reformation*, p. 198.

HERESY AS A CAREER[1]

Then I, poor worm, thus trampled on, begin to turn again . . .

[MARC ANTONIO DE DOMINIS, CONCERNING HIMSELF]

Oₙₑ of the characteristic events in a contest of social systems is a certain shifting of allegiance. Individual members change sides: some go from the old order to the new, some from the new to the old. Loyal adherents are likely to regard these people as renegades, whichever the side that happens to be left. Those who have been deserted are angry; those who have been joined are suspicious. Changing sides is a spectacular act, even when performed by trivial personalities. It may be (and usually is) clothed with the loftiest of moral principles, but it makes everybody feel insecure.

This insecurity arises from the fact that the motives prompting the change are unavoidably obscure. It requires rather too much innocence of mind to suppose that the alleged motives are the actual ones. The actual ones, indeed, are in all probability hidden from the agent himself, who, nevertheless, offers page after page of fondly candid self-revelation. No one, it may be thought, would say such things about himself unless those things were true. And yet the most melancholy sacrifice of reputation can be made without the smallest accuracy in respect of fact. Or, if there be some small accuracy, the account as a whole will have been falsified by the very motive,

1) This interlude reproduces, in large part, the text of an essay I published in the *Promethean Review*, New York, Vol. I, no. 4, pp. 30–35. It is reproduced here by permission of the editors.

hidden from the convert, which had produced the conversion itself.

All this is so far the case, that it is even possible for heresy to be made into a career. It can happen (and, I rather think, does often happen) that a man whose ambition is frustrated within one organization seeks achievement in another and a contrary organization. The very change itself hurls him high among his new associates, who can say nothing more vivid of themselves than that they had always thought what he now thinks. At the same time, human motives are very mixed, and it is illuminating to perceive how thoughts and hopes and wishes are strung out along the passage of a career.

Therefore I shall tell the story of a renegade who lived and wrote and worked his renegacies many long years ago. He was a very renegade renegade, since he changed sides not once but twice, and might have changed more if other organizations had been available. This man was very able and variously gifted. He knew a good deal of the mathematics and physics of his day, and Newton believed him to have given the first accurate account of the nature of the rainbow.[2] He knew much Latin, and had command of its style. Beyond all this he was an administrator, and highly placed too, so that his changes of side echoed through Europe like the tread of a smallish giant. He was important enough to cause chagrin among those he deserted and delight among those he joined: a man one would like to have, or get, or, having got, retain, if only such felicities could be permanent!

Marc Antonio de Dominis, the chief personage of this story (for he was not, I should think, a hero), was born in or about the year 1560, on the island of Arbe, off the Dalmatian coast and near the very center of Venetian influence. It was in Dalmatia, likewise, that he became Bishop of Segnia and Archbishop of Spalato (the modern Split). Thus, when in 1605 Pope Paul V, pursuing a quarrel with the Seignory, placed Venice under interdict, de Dominis found cause to doubt the validity of papal power. His suspicions on this point had been already awakened by an annual payment of five hundred crowns that Paul exacted from his diocese, and had begun to compose themselves into an *opus magnum,* ultimately issued in three volumes, the *De Republica Ecclesiastica.*

During these years, there was in Venice an English ambassador,

2) This honor goes, as we have seen, to Roger Bacon: see *supra,* p. 215.

Sir Henry Wotton, who had with him a private chaplain, William Bedell, later a bishop in Ireland. These two not only gave de Dominis an alternative ideology but proposed also an alternative career. They assured him that if he went to England, King James I would give him a more than merely verbal welcome.

And so it happened that, early in 1616, de Dominis left Venice (secretly, some say), stayed for a time in Germany, and came at last to England. The welcome did not fail: he was speedily made Dean of Windsor, and then was presented to the living of West Ilsley, in Berkshire. Here he soon caused some stir by seeking flaws in the tenants' leases, so as to increase his revenues. For, as Canon Perry reports in the Dictionary of National Biography, our personage was, in the opinion of his contemporaries, "corpulent, irascible, pretentious, and exceedingly avaricious."

When a man changes sides in a big way, he is usually at some pains to explain his action; and when he is an important man, or a man who can be made to seem important, he can get the explanation published. The account does not differ greatly from age to age: when he goes from past to future, he talks about abuses suffered and ignorance escaped; when he goes from future to past, he talks about error and sin. In the forward movement he brags; in the backward he grovels.

These ideological shifts belong, no doubt, to the pathology of science and the science of pathology, but they have, perhaps, an eerie charm, rather like a shudder of ghosts among fossils. De Dominis' first apologia was what one could expect, passionate, emancipated, and turgid as its title:

> A declaration of the reasons which moved Marcus Antonius de Dominis, Archbishop of Spalato or Salones, Primate of Dalmatia and Croatia, to depart from the Romish religion and his countrey. Written by himself in Latine, and now for the popular Use translated.[3]

What had the prosperous convert to say for himself? Well, first of all, in the years of his ignorance, "while he wrangled with the truth, to overcome it, he was taken captive of it." Anyone could see

---

3) This little brochure is reprinted in *A Collection of Scarce and Valuable Tracts,* edited by Somers (London; 1748), Vol. 4, pp. 561–75.

that it was not career as such that attracted him: he was already an archbishop. "Therefore neither the Counsels of Men, nor the undaunted Affection, nor worldlie Necessitie, nor Event; neither ainie miserable accident, which useth to ranverse Men, and their estate, moved me to depart."[4] It was the pure and pious love of truth: "The Cause of Christ is in hand, which calleth me to itselfe."

But if he thus issued from the portals of Mother Church, he took care also to leave the door ajar. No hard feelings, he seems to say: "This my departing from my Countrey. . . . I will that it want all Suspicion of Schisme; for I flee from Errours, I flee from Abuses: Yet will I never sever myselfe from the Love which I owe to the holy Catholic Church, and to all and everyone who communicate with her."[5] It seems as though, in these contests, there is a third side— the side of making the most of the others.

So the new-made Anglican labored, reaping his revenues, writing his *Ecclesiastical Republic*. Beneath his analysis papal supremacy vanished: Christ had indeed given sovereignty to Peter, and Peter had been the first Christian bishop at Rome, but Peter had bequeathed sovereignty to *all* Christian bishops, not merely to that succession which had culminated in Paul V. Paul might perhaps have quailed before the argument; but, before he had time to quail, he died.

This happened in January, 1621. The next pope, Gregory XV, was, wonderful to say, a kinsman of de Dominis. The door, left silently ajar, seemed now to open, and sounds of welcome to be heard from within. The Cause of Christ beckoned elsewhere, and, through the Spanish ambassador, de Dominis undertook secret negotiations for a return to Rome. The terms were very flattering: pardon and a handsome salary. Something of the sort seems to have been arranged; at any rate, I have no doubt that de Dominis tried and that Gregory was willing. Counsinship apart, a recanting convert is almost as valuable to the one side as the convert himself was to the other.

The problem was, how to get out of England after so brief, though so lucrative, a sojourn there. De Dominis now risked adding James's displeasure to that of the Inquisition. And then there was

4) Ibid., p. 564. I cannot forbear reproducing the translator's delicious spelling and punctuation.
5) Ibid., p. 573.

the money, his newly gathered wealth. A solution as easy as ingenious came to him at once: he would store the money in trunks, lodge the trunks with a departing ambassador, and so get the money out under diplomatic immunity.

But getting himself out of England was much less easy. He had to have James's permission in order to leave. What would be the grounds, the ideological device? Well, he had always believed in the ultimate unity of Christ's Church. Anglican theory and Roman theory were different versions of one and the same thing, not irreconcilable. In fact he would reconcile them, and that would be why he was going to Rome.

Moreover, there was the British weather. "Besides all this," he wrote to James, "the diseases and inconveniences of old age growing upon me, and the sharpness of the cold air of this countrey, and the great want I feele amongst strangers of some friends and kinsfolkes, which might take more diligent and exact care of me, make my longer stay in this climate very offensive to my body."[6]

These genial arguments impressed James—to the point of rage. He sent the Bishop of Durham and other ecclesiastics to put a few questions. The replies were neither candid nor convincing, but they removed any sensible reason for keeping such a man in the country. The interview closed in a shower of assurances: "Before God and Jesus Christ," cried de Dominis, "I will always acknowledge from my heart, and profess openly, that the Church of England is a true and orthodox Church of Christ; and if I ever say or think otherwise of it, let all men report me to be a very knave."[7] Then he slipped away, unopposed, into Belgium.

There, while awaiting Gregory's permission to return, he composed the inevitable second explanation: *Consilium Reditus,* or, "My Motives for renouncing the Protestant Religion." It contained, among many other marvels, a view of the Church of England very unlike the one he had proferred the Bishop of Durham: "For, since the Church of Rome . . . is properly . . . the only Catholic, or Universal, Church of Christ . . . so does it, for this reason, follow, that, since the Church of England is cut off from this communion, it cannot . . . possess any claim to be considered as the *House of God* or the *Body*

6) H. Newland, *The Life and Contemporaneous Church History of Antonio de Dominis,* (London and Oxford; 1859), p. 193.
7) Ibid., p. 198.

of Jesus Christ, nor, therefore, properly speaking, as any Church at all."[8]

How then explain his conversion to that Church which was no Church? Well, it had been pride, the reckless use of his own rebellious judgment. "There is no disorder so common, nor indeed so natural, as for men, when once they are engaged in error or sunk in vice, to invent excuses for their errors and apologies for their crimes. . . . That such has been my case, I now with candour own it. I own it, and I weep for the misfortune."[9] We have heard the accents, and even the language, since.

So then he had been proud, angry, insolent, malicious, calumnious, and he had written abominable books. What in those books had he used by way of argument? Well, he had expatiated upon the corruptions of Rome, the *Index Expurgatorius,* the likeness of the Reformed Churches to primitive Christianity, and the doubtful grounds of papal sovereignty. All these arguments he now repudiated, along with the books themselves. And, lo, halfway through the repudiation, here is the man beginning to talk about "our" doctrines and "our" beliefs as if he had been uninterruptedly a defender of the faith.

Thus, in a cloud of self-abasement, de Dominis returned to Rome. There was a *coup de théâtre:* Gregory suddenly died. His successor, Urban VIII, had, like nearly everyone else, no reason to love de Dominis, and turned him over to the Inquisition. Now questioning began in earnest; this was no polite interview with English bishops. Indeed, de Dominis was quite beyond the saving power of recantation. But, strange to say, the old man (he was now sixty-four), thus set upon, held his ground. Within that labyrinth of careerism and conniving there still lived the analyst of the rainbow, the man who really did believe. And so the inquisitors had no trouble eliciting a series of assertions identical with those of the *De Republica Ecclesiastica.*

They threw him into prison, and there in a few months he died. Legal proceedings continued, however, against the corpse which was all that was left of Marc Antonio de Dominis. This was condemned to punishment and publicly burned in the Campo dei Fiore, the Field of Flowers, where many a heretic had suffered alive.

8) I take this passage from an edition of the *Consilium* printed in London without editorial designation, in 1827, p. 19. Italics in the text.
9) Ibid., p. 2.

The moral? Well, I fancy it is at least that changing sides, using heresy as a career, is by no means as profitable as contending parties like to make it seem. De Dominis ruined his own value by so much instability of allegiance: the Anglicans lost by winning him, and the Catholics, in recovering him, gained what they did not want. All three were betrayed, and in like measure, by their common antics; and the pattern, pathetically absurd, reproduces itself into our own time. The joy that is said to be felt in heaven over one sinner that repenteth is not, after all, an organizational joy. Perhaps it is because careerist sinners have less repentance than sin.

And yet I would not leave de Dominis a mere failure in diplomacy. There was a true man in him, and that man was a scientist. As we shall see from all the succeeding chapters, de Dominis was more of a heretic than he knew.

Science as Heresy

THE LANGUAGE we speak and are born to derives its eloquence from the tradition of its users, their struggles and triumphs, their agonies and joys. The wisdom of such a folk, greater than the wisdom of all but a few of the members, lodges in the language, and establishes there not seldom an ironic commentary upon events. If, for example, we say that a man takes things "philosophically," we mean (what no philosopher primarily means) that he accepts trouble and even disaster without being crushed. And if we say that a man goes about his work "religiously," we mean (what no theologian primarily means) that he is honest in his intentions and earnest about carrying them out.

The first of these linguistic oddities records the enormous attraction of stoicism as an ideal: the head bloodied but unbowed. The second records what will remain, I dare say, the permanent effect of religion upon culture: the sense that there are some things which demand to be taken seriously, with a view to rectification or achievement. Religion has always been a kind of communion with ultimate values, and the solemnity of communion remains even when the values have been altered out of recognition. It is possible to entertain religious feelings toward the physical universe, toward biological evolution, and toward human history; and it is even possible to do all this without involving any sort of god or any miraculous power whatever. In short, science can be a religion—that is to say, a thing to be taken seriously.

You may judge from protests now arising within your mind that, in so speaking, I have propounded a paradox. It is quite true: the bond between science and religion is a unity connecting opposites. Historically, science has been the antithesis of religion, and religion has been toward science a devout and energetic foe. Despite the great armistice that Kant proposed,[1] intending a permanent peace, every scientific generalization down to but not including relativity has been attacked by the churches as subversive of their doctrines. Undoubtedly these doctrines did negate various articles of faith. Thus if the earth is spherical, it is not "flat"; if the sun is the center of the solar system, the earth is not that center; if the earth rotates upon an axis, the earth is not motionless; if human beings developed from earlier organic species, they do not derive from a divinely created Adam.

Further, if the nature of the world remains in any degree undiscovered, and if existing descriptions of it have still to be refined, then what men have in the past said about the world is rather less important than organizations suppose. Certainly it would no longer be authoritative. And if it turns out that, by means of a method explicitly statable, any investigator can know what descriptions are true and what false, then there is scarcely any value in appeals to human and personal authority: councils, popes, fathers, and scriptures have no more relevance to knowledge than makers of myths and sowers of dreams.

The whole purpose of science is to find and to assert what actually is the case. The verb "to find" is, I suppose, a metaphor—and not as accurate a metaphor as one could wish. Finding the nature of the world is not quite like finding a penny: one ordinarily does much more than merely happen upon it. But in the metaphor there remains a signification which I should not care to lose: the signification, namely, that there exists a world to be found. That world is prior to all descriptions of it, and does not need those descriptions in order to exist. For if existence depended upon description, one could produce any state of affairs whatever by simply expressing it in language. One would only have to say, "I am rich," and one would be rich; or, "I am healthy," and one would be healthy.

1) "The objective reality [of a Supreme Being] cannot indeed be proved, but also it cannot be disproved, by merely speculative reason." *Critique of Pure Reason,* Transcendental Dialectic, III, §7. Kemp Smith's translation, p. 531.

This happy ease would be calamitous for brokers and physicians (who would, however, have the same resource), but it is in any event quite impossible. There is not a description in the whole wide world, however vivid or convincing, which can alter the thing described as that thing is at the moment of description. You may *say* that a certain cat is coal-black, when in fact it is tawny; it is tawny nevertheless. You may say that a certain society is free, when in fact it is enslaved; it is enslaved nevertheless. You may say that the earth lies motionless, when in fact it rotates; nevertheless it moves.

The only time when existence depends in any way upon description is when human beings produce effects according to a plan—when, for example, a bridge comes to be by virtue of the engineer's design (a sort of preliminary description). But even on these occasions men intervene into states of affairs which do not need to be described in order to exist. Thus, generally speaking, the universe and its contents exist quite independently of description. Some of the contents, indeed, exist without being described at all, and some exist despite false and even fantastic descriptions. It is likewise the case that some descriptions refer to things that never have existed,[2] others to things that do not exist, and still others to things of which the existence is quite impossible.

Existence does not depend upon description; rather, description depends, for accuracy and even for possibility, upon existence. If description is to occur at all, there must be people (i.e., users of a language) to do the describing, and there must be things to be described. A description will be accurate if it "corresponds" with fact—that is to say, if what the description asserts to be the case actually *is* the case. This condition of truth-finding is basic and irremovable. Modern philosophy is full of attempts to circumvent it, but every such attempt ends by making existence dependent on description—a view which is the logical presupposition of every lunatic on earth. Lunatics, that is to say, unable to adapt to the world as the world is, describe it as being a sort of world they can adapt to; and thus they become, in their own fantasies, prophets or conquerors not yet recognized but soon to be acclaimed.

Such folk we are accustomed to sequester, but in modern philosophy they have roamed free. They even bear distinguished names.

2) This fact is, of course, the terror of historians, and I myself fear that some examples of it may be found in this book.

One cause, perhaps the chief, is the power of social organizations. If survival is (as it appears to be) the aim of every organization, if unity and devotion in the membership are necessary to that survival, and if a certain description of the world is essential to that unity, then what is chiefly required of the description will not be correspondence with fact but persuasiveness to the membership. Organizations thus feel the same need to distort reality which lunatics privately feel; they feel it, indeed, rather more strongly than lunatics. The history and practice of organizational lying would alone suffice to make this clear. For, in organizational lying, the moral deterrent has been removed: the liar effects his lie (so it seems), not from self-interest, but from loyalty to the group. There is even a kind of self-sacrifice about it: the organizational liar surrenders his integrity to the common "good."

Lunatics deceive themselves, but they do not do it consciously, and so do not lie. The same unconscious self-deception can occur, and does habitually occur, within organized groups. The common ideology, accumulated from the past and petrified by repetition, presents toward new knowledge that stubborn surface which rocks present to waves. Waves can of course wear down rocks, and history wears down ideology, but time with the one is geological and with the other epochal. With what astonishment did the Renaissance mind discover that the world could be known and controlled and enjoyed without the smallest use of Christian eschatology! The discovery was as vast as it was astounding, but it had taken fifteen hundred years.

If, like the old Gnostics, we suppose our world to have been created by a careless or inefficient deity, we might have a reason why human organizations resist what their members most need, the description of things as things actually are. The arrangements, whatever their source, are sufficiently absurd, but I am afraid that they are thus far unavoidable. The kind of accurate description which science seeks requires some things which only organizations can supply: thousands of trained observers working together, and a vast technology of experiment. But it also requires some things which organizations supply reluctantly or not at all: an eagerness for new information, and a willingness to revise or discard inherited doctrines as these prove erroneous. In scientific procedure, decision and hesitancy maintain an exquisite balance, so that the truth is seized when it is known but is not pretended to when it is not known. The future safety of mankind depends upon how far human organizations can be got to imitate and approach this balance. They are not yet very near it, and the more desperately they engage in power politics, the farther they recede. But until major contestants understand, scientifically, what Mr. Jefferson called "the course of human events," mistakes will tend to be disasters.

The posture a leadership assumes when it is defending doctrine is exactly *not* the posture that scientists assume when they are describing what is in fact the case. Therefore if, as we have said, orthodoxy is what the leadership defends, science must tend to be always and everywhere heretical. There is nothing to suggest that science will ever be complete; hence novelty and revision will always be pressing in. If, pressing in, they are driven off by a series of organizational monoliths, the effect must be that human institutions, losing their hold on reality, fall into desuetude and decay. Even our race may perish because it could never organize itself fitly to receive the knowledge it was otherwise quite capable of possessing.

Men can control the course of events only to the extent that they understand it. They can be sure of survival and prosperity only to the extent that control puts the world in their power. Scholastic philosophy, though by no means as barren as its critics suggest, had never given control over nature because it never quite became a science. Its description of the world was far too general, too vacuous of concrete detail, too full of error, and above all too dependent upon Aristotle. The sort of observation of the world, and experiment with it, which we should call scientific, though attempted by Roger Bacon, really began with the Renaissance. The vastness of possible results was soon evident, and by the year 1637 Descartes was able to say in tones of triumph, "In place of that speculative philosophy taught in the schools, there is another directly useful in practice, by which . . . we may be able to make ourselves lords and possessors of nature."[3]

3) *Discourse on Method*, Part VI. My translation, which borrows Veitch's fine rendering of *maîtres* as "lords." The whole passage deserves quotation: ". . . *et qu'au lieu de cette philosophie spéculative qu'on enseigne dans les écoles, on en peut trouver une pratique, par laquelle, connaissant la force et les actions du feu, de l'eau, de l'air, des astres, des cieux et de tous les autres corps qui nous environnent, aussi distinctement que nous connaissons les divers métiers de nos artisans, nous les pourrions employer en même façon à tous les usages auxquels ils sont propres, et ainsi nous rendre comme maîtres et possesseurs*

Lords and possessors of nature! The need to be both is now more imperative than ever. Lords and possessors we astonishingly are of physical nature, and astonishingly are not when it comes to using what we know about history, society, and the human self. This failure to use, which may also be a certain lack of knowledge, explains why our mastery over physical nature tends toward destruction as much as toward our happiness. Yet the Cartesian hope remains supreme, and precisely in those terms in which he stated it. Organizations, particularly political organizations, must now meet and satisfy the terms of this hope, or they and their members and perhaps the whole human race are doomed. The common ruin will be the ruin of all organizations whatever, and capitalists who risk it, and socialists who risk it, are as vacant of essential knowledge as if they lay, darkling and limp, within the womb.

The extremity to which science has driven organizations, so that they must scramble for some sort of contact with it or perish, shows why the chief intellectual events of the past four hundred years have been so shattering. The Christian Church, for more than a millennium, had turned the unifying of belief into an exquisite and irresistible art. The members accepted doctrine, not because they could perceive that doctrine corresponded with fact, but because some authoritative person or authoritative group of persons had asserted doctrine to be true. The criterion of truth, therefore, was somebody's "say-so." Behind the say-so lurked, by no means invisibly, the inquisitorial process, the prison, and the stake. Truth, in short, was to be determined by power.

Now, it happens that, although political power can do very many things, one thing it cannot possibly do is to determine truth. It can, for example, prevent people from *saying* that the earth rotates, but it cannot prevent the earth from rotating. Consequently it cannot prevent the sentence, "The earth rotates," from corresponding with fact, from being true. Sooner or later, this trueness, this correspondence with fact, must win its way into even the most terrified consciousness. Despite authority and strength, everything tends to become *known*. And over the process by which truth is determined

---

de la nature." It is important to realize that the word "philosophy" signified all human knowledge whatever, until (by the early nineteenth century) the sciences had set up as separate disciplines. After that, "philosophy" signified only those subjects which the sciences had not yet appropriated.

authority has no control at all. The ruler has not lived, does not live, will never live, who can make a sentence correspond with fact by asserting that it does so.

How is the truth of a sentence confirmed? By a *method,* by rules of procedure in inquiry and observation. There is still some doubt, or at any rate there is dispute, what this method precisely is. But that it is a method there is no doubt at all. Now, the nature of a method is that anyone who understands it can use it. Moreover, the method has sufficient ease for anyone not an idiot or a moron to possess it. Consequently scientific method has entailed a democratization of truth: given the method, truth becomes immediately accessible to everybody. On the most important of all questions, therefore, the hierarchical structure of organizations is simply irrelevant. It may happen that the leaders know more about some things, but the members have only to make use of the method and they will become as knowledgeable as the leaders. It is perhaps vulgar, but it is entirely accurate, to describe Descartes' *Discourse on Method* as a "do-it-yourself kit." He intended that every man should know how to distinguish true sentences from false ones, and thus he became, I suppose, as dangerous to organizations as any honest man is likely to be.

One meaure of the change from the Middle Ages to our own day is this: ideology was once perpetually on trial before organizations, and now organizations are perpetually on trial before that special ideology which is science. Trial by science is a clear and candid form of trial by reality, which organizations must in any case undergo. Effects of the candor and clarity are, however, plain to be seen. Organizational lying and organizational myth are much more difficult nowadays, though there is a "science" of how to do them, and they shatter much more readily upon the presentation of fact.

No matter what the social order may be, it has grown ever more dangerous for an organization to let its doctrines wander away from science. For the first time in history, advantage now lies with the correctors of doctrine, with the scientists and philosophers. After forty centuries of wrestling, it is orthodoxy that now has its back upon the mat. This result, with its attendant fluidity in social relations, the authoritarians of the sixteenth and seventeenth centuries accurately foresaw. On the nineteenth of November, 1669, the great Bossuet delivered a funeral oration upon Henriette-Marie, the widow of Charles I of England. In it he prophetically described the results of the Reformation, the future as the future has developed into our own day:

> Everyman [said the Eagle of Meaux] constituted himself a tribunal wherein he was the arbiter of his own belief. . . . Hence it was very predictable that, there being no further limit upon licence, sects would infinitely multiply, and stubbornness would be invincible. . . . God, in order to punish the irreligious waverings of these folk, abandoned them to the intemperance of their mad curiosity. . . . It is not at all astonishing that they thereupon lost respect for majesty and for the laws, nor that they became factious, rebellious, and intransigent. You unnerve religion when you meddle with it, when you deprive it of a certain gravity which alone can hold populations in check.

This is how the process looked to a loyal genius of the Church. Yet an historian of the mid-twentieth century could not more accurately describe the historical development by which science (the union of private judgment with public observation) effected the democratization of truth.

I I

WE HAVE NOW to examine what may be called the effect of science upon the *style* of human discourse. If we compare our contemporary view of the world with the medieval view, we shall observe that we are much more interested in the contents of the physical universe than in gods, angels, or demons, whereas medieval men were more interested in gods, angels, and demons than in the physical universe. Likewise we are concerned to make the most of our brief lives as human animals, whereas medieval men regarded life as a rather painful prelude to eternity. It thus seems fair to say that the great transformation of thought has been a passage from "otherworldliness" to "this-worldliness" (we are still so far embarrassed that we lack a good noun for it)—or, as theologians might say, from religion to secularism.

But this account of the change is not subtle enough. The medieval preoccupation with supernatural personages was a preoccupation with personages that in all probability did not, and do not, exist. In such beliefs, therefore, there would be (as there necessarily is in false beliefs) some dislocation from reality—the sort you would have if you relied entirely upon Santa Claus to supply your Christmas presents. A non-existent being cannot produce any effects. The dislocation, however, was by no means total: human affairs were conducted under this ideology not very well but well enough for survival. It is evident that the ideology had some correspondence with fact, although it did not have the complete correspondence it was thought to have.

What was the correspondence? Well, consider: if you say your lady's cheeks are roses, her lips cherries, her teeth pearls, you are stating what is in fact not the case. Her cheeks are not roses (else you might be embracing a bush); her lips are not cherries (else you might be embracing a tree); her teeth are not pearls (else you might be kissing an oyster). But your reply will be that this was not at all what you really said. What you really said was that the cheeks were pink, the lips red, the teeth glistening white, and the ensemble irresistibly attractive. The lady herself would accept the correspondence of this description with fact, for it is part of her sweet Aristotelian essence to recognize when she is being adored.

Linguistically, you achieved your conquest and your ambiguity by omitting a verbal sequence that would have made all plain: the clause, "as if they were." The cheeks are as if they were roses; the lips as if they were cherries; the teeth as if they were pearls. Omission of the crucial words somehow heightens the emotional effect, perhaps because it requires more alertness in him who reads or hears.[4] Now, just as metaphor did not dislocate you from the lady (who, being wise in language as in all things else, received you the more graciously), so metaphor did not dislocate the believing Christian from the world he lived in. When he took the metaphors literally, when he behaved *as if* certain things were the case, he was not painfully out of accord with objective fact, and he was, above all, institutionally comfortable. But when this same believing Christian wanted also to produce and sell a great many commodities, his wealth accumulating with the volume sold, then inadequate descriptions of reality became to him at first painful and at last intolerable.

Now, as we know, one form of metaphor—of comparison implied but not overtly stated—is personification. What you are saying, in

4) Metaphors still cause trouble, even in discourse where they are to be expected. I remember a sophomore's crying out, after I had explained (and thus impoverished) a sonnet of Shakespeare, "Why didn't he say so?"

such circumstances, is that the universe, or some part of it, or some event within it, is *as if it were* a planned result, connected with something like human purpose. Personification uses the image "God" when ultimates are being signified, and a precise rendering would be, "The Church's (or the Pope's) commands as to beliefs and conduct are as if they were divine," or, "The commands of conscience are as if they were divine." The meaning, vividly expressed in the image "God," evokes in concrete behavior the posture of obedience: the bended knee, the bowed head, the gesture of assent. It also evokes, subjectively, fear and the feeling of guilt, such as, taken together, constitute a terrible, piercing awareness that pain is about to be inflicted and that the infliction is deserved. When "God" signifies organizational power, the instruments of pain are all too palpable: ostracism, public shame, prison, death. When "God" signifies conscience, the instruments of pain are yet more various, since, thereafter, every sort of frustration can be interpreted as punishment. The worshiper fears from the world what he once feared from his parents.

In this, of course, he is deluded. He has mistaken a metaphor for a literal description of fact, and he is like a man who would expect to find oysters as the source of his lady's teeth. But the personification which has thus deluded him has put him in harmony with organizations quite as much as it has severed him from reality. There will thus be fewer shocks to jar him into an awareness of error. The comforts of illusion are largely institutional, and that is why it takes so long for men in the mass to confront, clearly and distinctly, the actual world.

One of the things that metaphor does in the language is to fuse together fact and value, to point out a certain state of affairs and at the same time express approval or disapproval of it. There may be metaphors that do not do this, but I have not been able to think of any. At all events, it was characteristic of human thought before the scientific era that it mingled descriptions of fact with judgments of value so closely that it sometimes tried to infer the one from the other. Thus, for example, Aristotle said, and the medievals repeated after him, that the planets move in circular orbits because the circle is the perfect geometrical figure and therefore the only one "fit" for planets to move in.

Argumentation like this now seems incomparably naïve. It would not seem so, however, if science had not patiently and courageously sloughed off metaphorical discourse as inadequate to the description of reality. It is true that metaphor still lingers in science: I have heard geneticists talk about "coded information" being carried by the genes. But scientific speech tries to be as literal and as void of metaphor as it can. In this effort it has been supremely helped by mathematics, a language which (so far as I know) contains no metaphors at all.

Accordingly, I should prefer not to say (or at least not only to say) that the modern scientific point of view replaced concern for a supernatural order with concern for the natural order. There never has been a supernatural order for anyone to be concerned about. Consequently, everyone's concern has in fact been with the natural order, regardless what people may have supposed. It seems more accurate to say that the natural order became clearer and more subject to human control in proportion as men discovered how to speak of it in literal language. Such a language could direct attention immediately to fact, without imagery, without moral or esthetic evaluation, and without concern for organizational authority.

Detailed acquaintance with the real world has therefore imposed a prodigious discipline. The great men who made that acquaintance possible have suffered defamation, as indifferent to goodness, to beauty, and to holiness. They have sought refuge in solitude and exile; they have known prison and death. But, without them, we would now be as unable to understand the world as we still are to effect our happiness within it.

I I I

ON MAY 24, 1543, Nicholaus Koppernigk, known to us as Copernicus, lay upon his deathbed at Frauenberg in Poland. He was seventy years old; he was a canon at the cathedral; he had been physician to bishops and to lesser folk; and in an age of geniuses he was the genius of the age. While he lay thus, a newly printed copy of his masterpiece was brought to him: it was the *De Revolutionibus Orbium Coelestium*. His first sight of the book was almost his last sight of anything upon earth: "he had lost his memory and mental vigor many days before, and he saw his completed work only at his last breath upon the day that he died."[5]

So wrote Bishop Giese, Copernicus's staunch friend, to the true

5) Giese to Rheticus, quoted by Angus Armitage, *The World of Copernicus* (New York: Mentor Books; 1958), p. 102.

disciple Rheticus.[6] This young man, then twenty-five years old, deserves a fame he has not adequately received. For he was the one who persuaded Copernicus to publish, who carried the manuscript to Nuremberg and there gave it over to Johann Petrejus for printing. The whole adventure had been risky. Rheticus was a Lutheran, a professor of mathematics at (of all places) Wittenberg, and a kind of protégé of Melanchthon. To reach Copernicus, he had to enter Catholic territory, where Protestants were habitually persecuted.

Copernicus, for his part, was made suspect by having numerous Protestant friends. It was, thought the orthodox darkly, what might be expected of such a man. The rumor had run for some time that Copernicus believed the sun to be the center of the planetary system, and a man who fostered so egregious a heresy would be likely to consort with Protestants. The fact that Protestants also regarded the heliocentric view as heretical, and were on this question even more bigoted than Catholics, made no difference. Copernicus was always a loyal member of the Church, an ornament to it indeed on its own terms. Nevertheless he had made himself a dangerous man. With nothing more than naked vision (the telescope did not yet exist), a quadrant, an instrument of his own making called the triquetrum, and a magisterial mind, he established (or, rather, recovered) the science of astronomy. This information, of decisive import, he had from time to time informally discussed, but publication he had put off for fear of consequences. Rheticus, the young and brilliant enthusiast, proved irresistible. There is nothing like a sight of the future in human form to stir a man out of the cautiousness of age.

The appeal of Christian doctrine has always been its concern with human destiny. No doubt, according to doctrine, God is all-powerful, all-wise, all-good; no doubt he rules like a patriarch, commands like an emperor, reigns like a king; no doubt he has his seraph-choirs, his warrior-angels,

> Chariots, and flaming arms, and fiery steeds,
> Reflecting blaze on blaze . . .

Imagination has given him every attribute of honor, even love. And yet what was the heart of all this cosmic drama? It was, it is, the salvation of *man*. The earth might be, in fancy, God's footstool, but

6) Rheticus's real name was Georg Joachim. Since he came from the Austrian Tirol, an area the Romans had once called Rhaetia, he took "Rheticus" as his scholarly name.

on it lived the objects of his greatest interest, the objects therefore of supreme interest, human beings. These creatures of his hand God withheld until the sixth, climactic day of creation; then he surveyed all he had done, "and, behold, it was very good."

Thus, as we see, it is a habit of thought as old as Genesis—and older still—to make inferences about the physical universe from what seem to be the values of morality. By this logic, the center of value in the universe would be also the cosmological center, and the central orb would be as fixed and changeless as any moral principle. The view seemed empirically confirmed by the illusion which earthbound observers tend to have: that their position is motionless while everything else moves. This motionlessness is so far from being the case that the various speeds in which an earthbound observer is in fact involved are almost incredible:

> In the United States [says Mr. Fred Hoyle, a Cambridge astronomer] you have a speed of about 700 miles an hour round the polar axis of the Earth. You are rushing with the Earth at about 70,000 miles an hour along its pathway round the Sun. . . . On top of all this you have the huge speed of nearly 1,000,000 miles an hour due to your motion around the Galaxy.[7]

But this is not all: the galaxy itself is moving at a rate of *several* million miles an hour.[8] Such is, in part, the New Cosmology. Hoyle suggests that if one could present these new insights and conjectures to Sir Isaac Newton, he would of course at once understand them —and be shattered.

If Newton would be shattered, what about Kepler, Galileo, Copernius? What about their enemies and persecutors? About Luther, who said, "This fool [Copernicus] wishes to revise the entire science of astronomy; but sacred Scripture tells us that Joshua commanded the sun to stand still, and not the earth"? About Calvin, who wrote, "Who will venture to place the authority of Copernicus above that of the Holy Spirit?" About Cardinal Bellarmine (1542–1621), who declared that this "pretended discovery vitiates the whole Christian plan of salvation"?[9]

7) *The Nature of the Universe,* (New York: Harper & Brothers; 1950), p. 56.
8) Ibid., p. 116.
9) These three quotations will be found in Andrew Dickson White, *A History of the Warfare of Science with Theology in Christendom* (New York: Appleton-Century-Crofts; 1936), Vol. I, pp. 126, 127, 134.

Now, Bellarmine was one of the most formidable of inquisitors because one of the most learned. He has made himself immortal by an argument that justified the burning of young heretics on the ground that the longer they lived, the more damnation they would acquire. But when he asserted that Copernicus's novelty would vitiate the Christian plan of salvation, he spoke no more than the truth. Inquisitors are wrong about many things, and are wholly wrong about values, but they are almost never wrong about tendencies. They can foretell the future of an idea as a dog foretells the future of a scent: they have a nose for it.

By itself, Copernicus's theory was a rectification on behalf of mathematical elegance: it explained the facts with far fewer assumptions. Galileo, having invented the telescope, was able to show that the theory corresponded with the data. Next, Kepler showed that the planetary orbits were elliptical rather than circular, and that a simple arithmetical rule relates the size of the orbit to the time a planet takes to go round it. The discoverers knew their discoveries to be as important as convincing; yet such things could always be thought of as corrections. Kepler, indeed, a truly religious man, considered that the sun-earth-moon relationship bodied forth the Trinity. Why then, all the stir?

One sees why, by reading Mr. Hoyle or any other astronomer of today. The Copernican view, perfected in Newton, did at least, and impressively, maintain order in the cosmos. The stars moved with the assured solemnity of a religious procession, and God could be thought no less existent for having given over their movement to gravitation. So much stability suggested that the cosmos, from planet to gnat, was a machine of exquisite balance and harmony:

> And if each system in gradation roll,
> Alike essential to th' amazing whole,
> The least confusion but in one, not all
> That system only, but the Whole must fall.

All this is gone from the New Cosmology. Instead of a celestial *horlogerie,* where the divine artificer, having made all clocks and set them going, observes with satisfaction their inerrant mechanics, we have now a devil's smithy of explosions, vaporizations, condensations, tunnelings through gases, hurryings and collisions in interstellar space—the whole immense fusillade being kept up (according to one theory) by "continuous creation."[1] The cosmos as bombardment is a long way from the cosmos as procession. Supernatural personages could still be conceived as observers of the procession or even as participants in it, but it is much less edifying to think of God as the supreme artillerist. Moreover, the future explorers of space will find no divinities; and, though a thing not found in one place may yet exist somewhere else, the always disappointed search is bound to tire. In the end, all that will have happened doctrinally is that a metaphor has been discovered to be a metaphor, but one cannot expect that organizations whose unity depends on taking the metaphor literally will be pleased with the revelation.

In the years between Copernicus and Galileo, there was one man who, on wings of the rational imagination, got part way toward our new cosmology: Giordano Bruno. He had not the mathematics to sustain him, but he had that imperial fancy which sustains mathematicians. The persuasive Copernican view, together with the boundless Platonic vision recovered in the Renaissance, made him bold in conjecture and confident that reason would uphold him wherever he might soar. It seemed to him that orthodoxy had much constricted the nature and potency of God, by failing to draw those inferences which the definition of so grand a Creator would seem to imply. Infinity must produce infinity:

I hold the universe to be infinite, as being the effect of infinite power and goodness, of which any finite world would have been unworthy. Hence I have declared infinite worlds to exist beside this our Earth; I hold with Pythagoras that the earth is a star like all the others which are infinite, and that all these numberless worlds are a whole in infinite space, which is the true universe. . . . I place in this universe a universal providence whereby each thing grows and moves according to its nature; and I understand it two ways, one the way in which the soul is present in the body, all in all and in each part; the other way is the ineffable one in which God is present in all, not as a soul, but in a way which cannot be explained.[2]

1) Hoyle, op. cit., pp. 123ff. The fascinating idea of continuous creation does seem to rid us of two (out of four) Kantian antinomies, and to solve the ancient puzzle about creation *ex nihilo*.
2) Excerpted in Giorgio de Santillana, *The Age of Adventure* (New York: Mentor Books; 1956), pp. 249–50.

If, like Copernicus, Bruno had drawn this conjecture from mathematics, we would acclaim him as a scientist, and we would salute his result, not as conjecture, but as discovery. We are, I suppose, right to withhold the acclaim and the salutation. Yet Bruno leaped well beyond the accuracy of his scientist-colleagues, and made his leap, remarkable to say, from the traditional theology itself—which is, I think, clear proof that metaphor is veiled knowledge, and that the Church, though fatally preoccupied with certain forms of words, did not wholly dislodge man's grasp upon reality. It would now seem strange to argue that there are infinite worlds because there is an infinite Creator, but there *are* infinite worlds (or something very like them) nevertheless. And into the idea of an infinite Creator, the idea of "continuous creation," though never held by Bruno, very snugly fits.

It was a stage in the transition from metaphor to literalness that God as a personage presiding over the cosmos shrank into God as a spirit pervading the cosmos or even identical with it. This view is called pantheism, and it is heretical in terms of Christian, Judaic, and Mohammedan doctrine. The shrinkage squeezes out all that was paternal or patriarchal in the original idea, and also a good deal that was personal. Nevertheless pantheism, in spite of (and perhaps because of) being heretical, has had an enormous vogue. The American transcendentalists of the nineteenth century were pantheists, and they added to this offense an abhorrence of chattel slavery. Spinoza was, in some sort, a pantheist, and Wordsworth after him. Coleridge reports a ludicrous incident in the 1790's, when the British government, suspecting him of Jacobin sympathies, sent a spy to listen in on conversations between himself and a friend:

> He had repeatedly hid himself, he said, for hours together behind a bank at the sea-side (our favorite seat), and overheard our conversation. At first he fancied we were aware of our danger; for he often heard me talk of one *Spy Nozy,* which he was inclined to interpret of himself, and of a remarkable feature belonging to him; but he was speedily convinced that it was the name of a man who had made a book and lived long ago.[3]

The churches, Catholic and Protestant alike, have steadily equated

3) *Biographia Literaria,* Chapter X. This spy, like the visitor from Porlock, may have issued from Coleridge's imagination, but at least we have some evidence how Coleridge pronounced the name "Spinoza."

pantheism with atheism, perhaps because a "world-soul" will not adequately serve as a source of institutional authority. But further, history has made it plain that pantheism, though asserting and even adoring a god, is the first stage of descent on a toboggan, which slides with ever-increasing speed from the medieval and trinitarian view toward the modern and scientific.

Bruno's pantheism was his chief ideological offense, but also he was of a temperament likely to seem offensive. No organization could hold him; he was footloose in habit of life and habit of mind. Born at Nola, near Naples, in 1548, he entered the Dominican order at fifteen and left it at twenty-eight, having accumulated indiscretions which included a defense of the Arian heresy. These were enough to cause institution of a process against him, and he escaped first to Rome and then to Geneva. For a brief time Calvin's theocracy seemed to him libertarian, but there was soon trouble, and Bruno passed through France into England. There he found an intelligentsia much more to his taste. He entered the circle of wits around Sir Philip Sidney, and he has left a delightful account of their exploits and conversations in his *Ash-Wednesday* dialogue, the *Cena delle Ceneri*.

Bruno had in fact escaped beyond Catholicism and Protestantism into the full secular bloom of the Renaissance. His approach to philosophy was neither religious nor scientific, but literary. There is no extensive argumentation; the insights fall as they may. The subjects are often courtly: love finds expatiation, and sonnets intersperse the far from realistic dialogue.[4] The tone not seldom is sad, and the sadness is by no means always conventionally assumed. Bruno, who sought a considerable independence, well knew the penalties for seeking it. Some of his lines are prophetic of his fate:

> *Impotente a suttrarmi, roco e lasso,*
> *Io cedo al mio destino, e non più tento*
> *Di far vani ripari a la mia morte.*
> *Facciami pur d'ogni altra vita casso,*
> *E non più tarde l'ultimo tormento,*
> *Che m'ha prescritto la mia fera sorte.*[5]

4) It would be interesting to know why Plato alone among all the writers in this form has been able to be dramatically convincing.
5) This is the sestet of a *sonetto caudato* which Bruno placed in the *Eroici Furori*, Part II, Dialogue 1. Giordano Bruno, *Opere Italiane* (Bari: Laterza;

If he had consciously sought the fate which befell him, there would have been no need for him to act otherwise than he did. Italy was dangerous ground for him; yet, to the consternation of his friends, he returned there in 1592, at the invitation of a noble family of Venice.[6] Within a short time he was embroiled with the Venetian Inquisition, which extracted from him something like a disavowal of heresy. Despite this, and despite the Venetian habit of non-cooperation with Rome, Bruno was turned over, in 1593, to the Roman Inquisition. There had been secret negotiations to this end, their nature unclear.

Until the year 1600, Bruno languished in the inquisitorial dungeons, while the usual interrogations occurred and he gathered his strength for a final stand upon the pantheistic hypothesis. At last the powers pronounced his doom. The story is that Bruno replied, very levelly and not inaccurately, "You are perhaps more afraid to pronounce this sentence than I am to hear it." They burned him in the Field of Flowers on the seventeenth of February, 1600. Bruno turned his face away from the crucifix which was thrust through the flames for him to kiss. The Age of Science had begun.

Bruno was the first of the martyrs for science in modern times, and he was the last of the great incinerated victims of the Church. Martyrdoms there continued to be, but with Bruno's death coercive power at last abandoned the faggot and the stake. Knowledge is so estimable a thing in itself and so necessary to human well-being that it tends to shield its possessors from fatal attack.

Inquisitors, being politicians, are rather more prompt to learn

---

1927), Vol. II, p. 460. Volume II of this edition contains the *Dialoghi Morali*. I offer the following translation:

> I cannot flee. Hoarse with complaint and weary,
> I yield to my full fate, and therefore seek not
> Useless defense against the death impending.
> Let it deliver me from all life dreary;
> Let the last torment in its coming take not
> Delay: it brings my savage, fated ending.

6) Acidalius, writing to Forgacz, January 21, 1592: "Giordano Bruno, whom you knew at Wittenberg, the Nolan, is said to be living just now among you at Padua. Is it really so? What sort of man is this that he dares enter Italy, which he left an exile, as he himself used to confess?" Quoted in J. Lewis McIntyre, *Giordano Bruno* (London, Macmillan and Company; 1903), p. 68. The noble family was the Mocenigo, which gave several doges to Venice.

than, in view of their ultimate purposes, we ordinarily give them credit for. Their treatment of Galileo in the next generation, though foolish and cruel, drew back from the ultimate barbarity. He suffered no worse than imprisonment and house arrest. Moreover, his inquisitors showed some spirit of compromise, admittedly faint but nonetheless discernible. They were willing to accept the earth's rotation as an hypothesis, provided Galileo would say it was not essential to faith. The old genius, who maneuvered very cannily through ideological politics, would never quite accept nor quite refuse the compromise. The earth's rotation was not a hypothesis but a fact, and not a superficial fact but a fundamental one. At the same time, his recantation abolished any ground for the death penalty.

His posture was thus less heroic than Bruno's, but it was rather more astute, more aware of the political possibilities. Martyrdom is no doubt a noble act, and has more than once been necessary to human salvation. But it is possible for men to be made drunk with it, and thus to lose reason. Galileo's discovery—not less important than his discovery of the earth's rotation—was that one could now propagate science without ultimate personal disaster, and that a little suffering together with a little statesmanship would see one through.

I V

GALILEO'S LAST CONTEST occurred in 1633. At that very moment, the intellectual father of the modern age, René Descartes, was preparing for the press a treatise entitled *The World*. The content was answerable to the title: they were not afraid of large subjects in those days. The treatise, however, accepted the earth's rotation, and Descartes, who had already taken up residence in Holland on behalf of safety, withdrew the treatise so soon as Galileo's troubles were known. It appeared posthumously in 1664, somewhat disguised as the *Traité de l'Homme*.

Descartes was an altogether new phenomenon in philosophy, and indeed he has not been matched since. A great name, surely, a towering intellect; but the impression gains upon one that he was also something else, something quite unexpectable, a cavalier. He had the dash and the adroitness; his writing is learned and profound, but what it unmistakably is, is prose of the best society. Descartes wrote, not for specialists, but for every intelligent man alive.

He was born, a pleasant legend tells us, in a hayfield near La

Haye in the Touraine, in 1596. This story, if true, proves, not poverty, but only the mother's failure to get home in time. In point of fact, the parents seem to have possessed considerable landed property. They were able to send René to the Jesuit college at La Flèche, which a family relative then administered. Descartes liked the teachers much better than the curriculum: his opinion of the subjects he studied stands for all to see in the devastating critique which adorns Part I of the *Discourse on Method:*

> ... as soon as my age permitted me to pass from under the control of my instructors, I entirely abandoned the study of letters, and resolved no longer to seek any other science than the knowledge of myself, or of the great book of the world. I spent the remainder of my youth in travelling, in visiting courts and armies, in holding intercourse with men of different dispositions and ranks, in collecting varied experience. . . .[7]

By way of reading the great book of the world, he undertook the career of professional soldier—in 1618, under Maurice of Nassau, a Protestant; in 1619, under Maximilian of Bavaria, a Catholic.[8] It was the beginning of the Thirty Years' War. One of the advantages of soldiering in those days was that during the long winters, when campaigning was impossible, you got boarded and lodged at the employer's expense. It was just the thing for a meditative mind, and may have been what attracted Descartes into the profession. At any rate, when winter set in in 1619, he found himself at Ulm, on the Danube, lodged *dans un poêle.* The phrase has a pleasant ambiguity. Presumably it means a room heated by one of those vast porcelain stoves that still exist in the area, but it may mean that the philosopher spent much of his time on top of the stove itself, as people did, seeking warmth.

In any event, he was snug for meditation, and during that winter

7) *Discourse,* Part I, next to last paragraph. Veitch's translation.
8) According to a recent writer, M. Samuel S. de Sacy, Descartes never received from anyone, even in the army, pay, wages, or salary—*Descartes par lui-même,* (Paris: Éditions du Seuil; 1956), p. 186. I find this hard to believe: it seems extremely probable that Queen Christina must have financed his visit and services in Sweden, and I should think that he must have accepted pay as a professional soldier. But it appears that, in the main, he lived (very comfortably) on the income from the sale of his landed property, the proceeds of which he invested in Dutch banks.

(he says) he worked out the methodology by which a man might expect to rid himself of error and to possess truth. During the night of November tenth to eleventh, there came three dreams—two of anxiety and one of prophecy. *Quod sectabor iter?* asked insistently the prophetic dream, "What path shall I pursue?" And the answer was, the Sciences, the Sciences encyclopedically. Descartes awoke, not knowing sleep from waking, but inspired with the sense of definitive vocation. It had been a spiritual crisis, like the one Pascal was to have on the night of November 23, 1654.

The twenty-year sojourn in Holland (rather peripatetic it was, even there) began in 1628. Safe from inquisition but by no means safe from reactionary abuse,[9] he pursued various scientific inquiries, of which the chief achievement was his working out of coordinate geometry. Like all scientists in those non-specialist days, when everything waited to be discovered, he dabbled in many subjects: there were contributions to optics, and extensive but inconclusive anatomizings of bovine embryos, which he procured from various slaughterhouses. These efforts in biology were by no means idle, for they occurred about the time when Harvey discovered the circulation of the blood.

The naturalist tenor of scientific inquiry, its avoidance of metaphor and supernatural explanations, is very evident in Descartes, and sometimes charmingly so. For example, Chanut, the French Ambassador to Sweden, who arranged Descartes's later (and fatal) visit there, put to him once, by letter, the following query: "What are the causes which frequently induce us to love one person rather than another before we know anything about merit?" To which Descartes replied (June 6, 1647) with strict behavioristic theory:

The objects which touch our senses act through the nerves upon various parts of the brain, and there produce (as it were) certain creases [*plis*], which turn smooth again [*se défont*] when the object ceases to act. But the part where the creases were made remains susceptible of being creased again in the same manner by a similar object. For example, when I was a lad, I loved a girl of

9) Cartesianism was outlawed at the University of Utrecht in 1642 and at the University of Leyden in 1647—despite the fact that Holland was the most "liberal" country in Europe. On both occasions the French Ambassador intervened on Descartes' behalf. In the eyes of the Calvinist Dutch, Descartes was a Pelagian, as anyone would have to be who proposed to make his fellow men "lords and possessors of nature."

my own age, who was a little cross-eyed [*un peu louche*]. Accordingly, the impression produced by sight in my brain, when I looked at her unfocussing eyes [*ses yeux égarés*], was so intimately joined with all else that moved me to love her that a long time afterward, whenever I saw cross-eyed girls, I was more inclined to love them than to love others, precisely because they had this defect.[1]

That cross-eyed girl may well have been a charmer. One would like to know more about her, if only because philosophers are by and large not noted for prowess in love. Descartes has left no report concerning the eyes of Helena Jans, the Dutch housemaid who bore him his daughter Francine, but he did say that Francine was conceived on Sunday the fifteenth of October, 1634. Descartes was always a man of clear and distinct ideas.

In 1637 appeared the *Discourse on Method*,[2] which announced the modern age. Other Cartesian works need to be read if one wishes to know about Descartes; the *Discourse* needs to be read if one wishes to know about one's own world—or, indeed, about anything at all. The *Discourse* is one of the wonders of human intelligence, and not least among its many marvels is its supreme political tact. It is a masterpiece of revolutionary insinuation. In essence, it revealed the fact (long, long concealed) that organizational authority, however loftily described, cannot by fiat or pronouncement *cause* a sentence to be either true or false. No other idea can be more subversive. Yet Descartes, using the style of the familiar essay, laid down this doctrine so blandly and reasonably that ruling authorities could do nothing about the author, although they knew perfectly well what was going on.

How seductively the work begins! We are told (what is surely not the case) that "good sense is the best-shared thing in the world,"[3] and for this assertion, patently false, the reason is given that everyone appears to be satisfied with the amount of good sense that he has.

1) Quoted by de Sacy, op. cit., p. 118. My translation.
2) Originally entitled "Discours *sur* la Méthode," then altered to "Discours *de* la Méthode." Apparently Descartes thought "concerning" more accurate than "on." But in English the "on" has stuck.
3) *Discourse*, the very first sentence: *Le bon sens est la chose du monde la mieux partagée: car chacun pense en être si bien pourvu que ceux même qui sont les plus difficiles à contenter en toute autre chose n'ont point coutume d'en désirer plus qu'ils en ont."*

This combination of direct satire in the premise and ironic exaggeration in the conclusion permits Descartes to insinuate what he was after all the time—namely, that most people are really quite capable of understanding the world and of describing it accurately. In other words, truth is no monopoly of governments. One will go far to find a greater truth more skillfully surrounded with decoys.

Well, now—so the ironic argument proceeds—men of good sense, confronted with the same world, would naturally give it the same description. How comes it, then, that the descriptions disagree? The reason is that, although men have the same good sense and the same world, they do not all have the same method of inquiry. Particularly, they do not have the one definitive method that will distinguish true assertions from false. This method the author, though not an unusually intelligent man, has, to his great good fortune, stumbled upon.[4] He would like to share the information, not as advice, but as autobiography.[5]

The sly cavalier! Was this any way to treat the lords of human institutions: not to come solemnly toward martyrdom, but to walk nimbly, like David toward Goliath, bearing a mere slingshot and pebbles hardened with the facts of life? The contest was wildly unequal: the rulers of earth did not stand a chance. The little philosopher, alone amid Philistines, drove all adversaries from the field. He drives them yet. As recently as twenty years ago, Abel Bonnard, Minister of National Education in Pétain's fascist government at Vichy, declared:

> Among all the idols we must tear down, there is none we more urgently need to get rid of than this Descartes, whom people have wished to represent as the ultimate representative of French genius. He must be tossed out the window.[6]

4) Ibid.: *"Pour moi je n'ai jamais présumé que mon esprit fût en rien plus parfait que ceux du commun. . . . Mais je ne craindrai pas de dire que je pense avoir eu beaucoup d'heur de m'être rencontré dès ma jeunesse en certains chemins qui m'ont conduit à des considérations et des maximes dont j'ai formé une Méthode. . . ."*
5) Ibid.: *"Ainsi mon dessein n'est pas d'enseigner ici la méthode que chacun doit suivre pour bien conduire sa raison, mais seulement de faire voir en quelle sort j'ai tâché de conduire la mienne."* O lovely "seulement," fastidious "only"!
6) Quoted by Marcelle Barjonet, Preface to an edition of the *Discours* (Paris: Editions Sociales; 1950), p. 30. I have tried to preserve in translation the illiterate fascist vulgarity of the original, which goes like this: *"Parmi toutes les*

But one cannot, at so late a date, decree the overthrow of a man who knew, among the great facts of life, the method by which facts are known. Control over events is not granted to the ignorant, and even reactionaries feel the need of more knowledge than they desire others to possess. If those rulers most hostile to science need nevertheless some degree of scientific acumen, the four Cartesian rules of method are as generally useful as they are generally valid.

The first rule has to do with caution and clarity. We are not to be hasty in judgment—that is to say, we are not to assert any sentence as true until its meaning, its reference to reality, is quite clear. Sentences can be made unclear by their syntax or their vocabulary.[7] Metaphor tends to produce both kinds of unclarity at once: omission of the phrase "as if" syntactically conceals the fact that a comparison is intended, and the words which carry a freight of imagery may blur the intended reference to the world. Amendment of the syntax, definition of the vocabulary, and a disciplined restraint to literal language will enable us to determine what meaning corresponds with fact and is therefore true.

We recognize clarity in a sentence by a kind of intuition, which is, however, led to by our previous experience with language. Descartes seems to have thought, a little too hopefully, that the recognition of truth is intuitive also, that any true sentence wears its truth (so to say) on its face and thus is "evidently" true.[8] Like all advanced thinkers of that age, he was impressed by Euclidean geometry, in which the illusion of self-evidence does occur. But the remaining three rules show that Descartes did not underestimate the importance of demonstration in determining truth. The world being interrelated, and no circumstance occurring in isolation, the sentences which accurately describe the world are interrelated also. They are connected by

---

idoles qu'il nous importe d'abattre, il n'en est aucune dont il soit plus urgent de nous débarrasser que de ce Descartes qu'on a voulu représenter comme le représentant définitif du génie Français: il faut le faire passer par la fenêtre."
7) For example, the sentence "This is a comfortable old ladies' home" may mean (1) "This is a comfortable home for old ladies," or (2) "This is a comfortable old home for ladies," or (3) "This is a home for ladies who are old and comfortable." The obscurity is syntactical. " 'Twas brillig" is a sentence obscured by vocabulary.
8) *Discourse*, Part II: *"Le premier [règle] était de ne recevoir aucune chose pour vraie que je ne la connusse évidemment être telle. . . ."* The controlling word is "évidemment."

a logic which itself records the immemorial human experience of how things go together. It is therefore often (indeed, usually) possible to infer that such and such is the case, from the fact that certain other things are the case.[9]

This possibility of truth by inference Descartes elaborates in two rules, complementary to each other, of analysis and synthesis: we are to divide every complex phenomenon into its constituent parts, and then to reassemble those parts according to their pattern. The ultimate aim of science will thus be to construct an enormous system of sentences descriptive of the actual world.[1] This system would be human knowledge in totality. With such an aim, the fourth Cartesian rule crowns all the others: nothing is to be omitted from survey; the evidence is to be offered complete.[2] This rule, the rule of comprehensiveness, outlaws a favorite device of apologists—namely, to leave unmentioned just those facts which would yield conclusions opposite to the ones desired. Further, it defines the reason why science must be always developing. All human survey is unavoidably incomplete, and hence some relevant data escape attention. As these become known to later observers, the existing description has to be revised—an event which signally happened to Newtonian physics in our own century.

No doubt the Cartesian rules need some revising in the light of later criticism. For myself, however, I think their author knew most of what is necessary to be known about scientific method. The chief defect appears to be the lack of a standard for determining fact, for distinguishing between existing things and things merely supposed or imagined. Rather, the rules appear to describe what a scientist would do with data already assumed to derive from existing things. The lack is certainly serious, but it is only fair to say that no one as yet has repaired it.

However this may be, the Cartesian revolution is plain enough. Method has replaced official pronouncement as the means of deter-

9) E.g., if your house is to the west of George's, and George's is to the west of mine, then your house is to the west of mine.

1) This aim, the goal of all logic until recent times, has been much disturbed by Goedel's demonstration that in any formal system there are theorems such that if they are true, they cannot be inferred from the postulates, while if they can be inferred from the postulates, they cannot be known to be true.

2) *Discourse*, loc. cit.: "*Et le dernier, de faire partout des dénombrements si entiers et des revues si générales, que je fusse assuré de ne rien omettre.*"

mining truth. Those favorite Cartesian adjectives "clear" and "distinct" prescribe literal language, not metaphor, as the speech of science. Every man is to be able to know the world, just as (in the maxim attributed to Lenin) every kitchen maid is to learn how to run the government. "Democracy" is an ambiguous word and much abused, but it surely signifies at least some activity of the world's people in the conduct of their common affairs. Ignorance and the self-distrust attendant upon ignorance are alike paralyzing. It follows by logic, and has in fact followed by history, that democracy has grown with the growth of science; and the presumption is that, without science, democracy would be impossible.

In the light of these vivid changes, one can see why Descartes' most famous doctrine appeared to his contemporaries so perfect and so liberating: the *Cogito, ergo sum:* the "I think, therefore I am." In point of fact, it is a strange and perplexing doctrine, by no means as clear and as cogent as it seems. It it not free of presupposition and therefore of doubt, and the pronoun "I," the reference to a human person, has been smuggled in. It looks like an argument, a piece of deductive reasoning in the form that Aristotle would have called "enthymeme," but three centuries of Cartesian commentary have failed to show whether it really is an argument or not. Finally, alas, the conclusion, the thing proved, the "I am," is poverty-stricken. What can one make of the fact (assuming it to be a fact) that one exists? Some comfort, doubtless, but very little knowledge of the world.

The fact historically is, however, that to contemporaries this doctrine appeared the perfection of science. Descartes had preluded to it with a little drama of skepticism. You were to assume the posture of doubting everything. You were to let assertions present themselves with such demonstration as they could, and you were to dismiss them as inadequate until one should at last appear which was logically irresistible. You were to be the judge, and reason to be your code of judgment.

Were you not thus lifted far above mere following and mere membership? Your leaders—popes, councils, cardinals—had now to prove, where before they had only pronounced. The one realm, science, where human liberty is inalienable was now yours to occupy; and while you sat upon these mountaintops, free and visionary as an eagle, you suddenly perceived, in a double ecstasy of logic and intuition, that in order to doubt all authorities, together with all the assertions issuing therefrom, you had first to exist. Never mind that the argument secretly assumed there was a *you*. It seemed clear; it seemed cogent; and it did in fact shatter chains.

The effect upon Europe was enormous, rather like the sliding of a glacier into the sea. Everything frozen began to melt, everything motionless to move. *Cogito, ergo sum* had a revelatory self-evidence like that of lightning: organizational authority could add nothing to its truth and could take nothing away. You could credit this doctrine without the smallest concern for membership in any social body whatever. You needed no help, lure, or pressure toward belief, other than your own bare, naked reason. You were at last fully emancipated. You were intellectually on your own.

Descartes had now become a famous man. For the next hundred years, the question every young thinker asked himself was not whether he would be a Catholic or a Protestant, but whether he would be a Cartesian. If he decided not to be a Cartesian, he consigned himself thereby to second rank, or less, where there was more safety and eventual oblivion. Nevertheless, the time had passed when an advanced thinker would have risks only and no rewards. In 1647, the French government, perhaps liking Descartes better because he stayed in Holland, granted him a yearly pension of three thousand *livres*—which, however, he seems to have declined. His fame had impressed Queen Christina of Sweden, that most erudite of *femmes savantes,* who invited him to her court. Thither he went in September of 1649. By February 1650 he was dead. He had lectured the Queen on science and philosophy every frigid morning at the icy hour of five o'clock. It was by far too much for the respiratory system.

A contest ensued for possession of the corpse, the Queen desiring to keep it in Sweden, Ambassador Chanut desiring to return it to France. The Queen, not unnaturally, won, and Descartes was interred in a cemetery reserved for orphans, foreigners, religious nonconformists, and children who died before the age of reason.[3] A later ambassador had more success. In 1666, the Cartesian remains began their voyage homeward. But the coffin had been opened at departure and again during the voyage, and idolaters and collectors plundered the bones as if they had been (as perhaps they were) the relics of

3) de Sacy, op. cit., p. 171.

a saint. The skull stayed in Sweden, whence it came to France in 1822 as a gift to the scientist Cuvier. It is now on exhibit in the Musée de l'Homme, flanked on one side by primitive monstrosities and on the other by the skull of a solitary criminal, Cartouche.

Such of Descartes as was left was first buried in the Abbey of Sainte Geneviève. In revolutionary times, *An II,* the Convention ordered the transfer of what it called *le corps de ce philosophe* to the Panthéon. The order was somehow never executed. In 1819, Descartes's tomb, more cenotaph than grave, came definitively to be in the Church of Saint Germain des Prés. There at least his memory lingers, with Dom Bernard de Montfaucon, a Benedictine savant, on his right, and Mabillon, the medieval historian, on his left. As M. de Sacy says: *"le voilà bien gardé."*

CHAPTER

12

The Intellectual Love of God

T HE HOLLAND that served Descartes as a second motherland and offered John Locke a refuge between 1684 and 1689, was the most nearly tolerant country in Europe. The riches of mercantile capitalism flooded in, and, with them, ideas gathered along the trade routes. Sellers do not ordinarily inquire into the beliefs of buyers; in the simplicity of pure barter, it suffices that the buyer is able to pay. Jews have seldom scrupled to trade with *goyim,* even when risking persecution; and Christians have been eager to establish economic relations, chiefly exploitative, with members of every religion upon earth.

This Holland, which was strong enough to vie with England for commercial supremacy, was the Holland of Rembrandt and Vermeer, of Ruysdael's landscapes and de Hooch's tidy interiors, of sound fat bourgeois crowding to be painted with equal prominence and complaining that, in Rembrandt's view, artistry required some to be in shadow and others in light. It was a country of printing presses that supplied to Europe books unpublishable elsewhere, of gazettes and journals, of learned societies and celebrated universities, of a multitude of sects—Mennonites, Socinians, Remonstrants— against which the official Dutch Calvinism struggled in vain. The Pilgrim Fathers had their sojourn in Leyden before 1617, and breathed no freer air until they reached a land inhabited only by aborigines.

Yet tolerance, in Holland, was the sort that issues from a balance of conflicting forces rather than from a sympathetic appreciation of other people's ideas—a tolerance, that is to say, more rudimentary and therefore more basic. All the social virtues we admire have arisen from the fact that their opposites were, for certain prolonged periods, impracticable. The competing organizations within Holland had no means of suppressing one another, and, moreover, suppression, if achieved, was likely to entail a diminution of profit. Every organization endures what it cannot alter; then, if time enough be granted, endurance settles into habit and at the last adorns itself with morality.

The turmoil within Holland was, in point of fact, noisy and continual. Spinoza (our present heretic) has left a vivid account of it in a treatise which he published anonymously and which was burned (to no avail) by the public executioner:

> I have often marveled [he wrote] that men who boast of professing the Christian religion (which is to say, love, gladness, peace, self-control, and sincerity toward all) should quarrel with such rancor and daily use such hatred toward one another, that these traits identify them more than their professed faith. Things have in fact gone so far that one can recognize a Christian, a Turk, a Jew, or a pagan only by his dress and general appearance, by his attending this or that place of worship, by his embracing this or that opinion or taking oaths according to a special formula. In all other respects their manner of life is the same.[1]

How did it happen that all these folk resembled one another in iniquity quite as much as they differed in religion? Spinoza touched the heart of the matter: it was because

> ... the ministries of the Church are regarded as positions of prestige and its offices as sources of income [*beneficia*]. In fact, the popular idea of religion consists entirely in a respect for clerics. Accordingly, every fellow, however worthless, began to want to be a clergyman. The wish to propagate holy religion degenerated into sordid avarice and careerism, and the churches became a kind of theater, where orators rather than ecclesiastical savants were to be heard. None of these cared in the least about instructing peo-

---

1) This passage and the two following derive (in my translation) from the *Tractatus Theologico-Politicus* (1670), the "Treatise on Theology and Politics." The title itself shows how well Spinoza understood the fact that religion is a form of politics. The quotations are from the Preface.

ple, but only about getting themselves admired, slandering opponents, and propounding such novelties and oddities as would
make the listener gape.

Such circumstances were not congenial to the diffusion of truth,
and indeed tended to debase the very faculty by which truth is apprehended. This result Spinoza considered the worst of all:

Piety (good God!) and religion now consist in preposterous mysteries. People who utterly despise reason, who spurn and shun the
human intellect as naturally corrupt, are considered, most out-
rageously, to possess divine light. Truly, if they had one spark of
it, they would not rave so arrogantly; rather, they would learn to
worship God with something more like wisdom, and would be as
notable among their fellows for love as they now are for hatred.

It is plain that Spinoza knew what is essentially to be known
about the effect of organizations, and of careers within organizations,
upon the behavior of intellectuals. There was every reason for him
to know it: he had felt its savagery upon his own flesh and spirit. He
had confronted the choice that organizations characteristically set
before thinkers: career with conformity, or dissent with loss. To
career he had preferred veracity, and he had accepted reprisals rather
than falsify what he knew to be the case.

Spinoza was born, in 1632, into a Jewish family at Amsterdam,
whose ancestors had fled the Inquisition in Spain. His father Michaël
was a well-to-do merchant, probably an importer of colonial products.
The young Spinoza worked in the business while studying for the
rabbinate, and continued to be associated with it after the father's
death in 1654. He had thus two powerful influences upon him: one
economic, the business; the other economic and social, the rabbinical
career. And both of these had much to do with his being able to
marry and raise children.

It is said that Spinoza showed himself an excellent businessman[2]
—a trait which seems as odd as Descartes's having been a cavalier.
Yet Spinoza was always a perfectionist, and it is improbable that he
would have done badly anything he undertook. Certainly he became
a prodigious scholar. Having first exhausted the savants of his own
tradition, he found himself, like every other young man, facing

2) E.g., by Roland Callois, *Spinoza: Oeuvres Complètes* (Paris: Bibliothèque
de la Pléiade; 1954), p. 50.

Descartes. This liberating light, the radiance of pure reason, decided his philosophy and his fate. "Men whom reason guides," he wrote with epigrammatic eloquence, "want nothing for themselves which they do not want for all other men, and consequently are just, faithful, and honorable."[3] Yet if men whom reason guides are guided into heresy, they will probably have to accept a good deal less than other men get.

Spinoza's passage into heresy is the more striking because it was almost entirely intellectual. One looks in vain for signs in him of the rebellious boy, the nay-sayer avenging hurts of childhood. Quite to the contrary, he was an affectionate, sociable person, loved by many friends. This same love he still evokes from all who, reading him, ponder what they read. So far from indulging his heresy as a satisfaction of secret motives, Spinoza was at enormous pains to prove its rational necessity, its authentic truth as a description of the world. And just as Descartes showed, in the *Discourse on Method,* how philosophizing goes on in the midst of politics, so Spinoza showed, twenty-three years later in the *De Emendatione Intellectus,*[4] how philosophizing goes on in the midst of personal crisis.

What, then, was the view which made Spinoza a heretic, and what was its rational necessity? The view remains a prime example —and, for modern thought, *the* prime example—of unseating a metaphor. Looking back, we can see, as Spinoza's contemporaries could not, that the process had begun four hundred years earlier in the labors of the scholastics, who had tried to state Christian doctrine in as literal a language as they could command or as the doctrine itself would permit. Their partial success explains the guarded and skeptical view which the hierarchy took of their achievements.

In the course of this effort, the scholastics accumulated a series of definitions of the term "God," and, when all was done, they had left that term somewhere—about halfway—between metaphor and

3) *Ethics,* Part IV, Proposition XVIII, Scholium: ". . . *ex quibus sequitur, homines, qui Ratione gubernantur . . . nihil sibi appetere, quod reliquis hominibus non cupiant, atque adeo eosdem justos, fidos, atque honestos esse."* My translation.

4) A recent translator has, with amusing accuracy, rendered this title as "How to Improve Your Mind"—thus placing Spinoza among the authors of "How-to" books. I think Spinoza would be delighted. The usual translation, far more heavy-footed, is "On the Improvement of the Understanding."

literal statement. They had defined God as a being that needs nothing else in order to exist, or as a being which possesses all possible attributes (i.e., everything that can be said can be said about God), or as a being whose very nature implies existence.

We may now perform a simple experiment. We may ask, what being is there that needs nothing else in order to exist? The answer is, quite obviously, the Universe. Or what being is there of which all possible assertions can be made? The answer is, no less obviously, the Universe. And what being is there of which the very nature implies that it exists? The Universe, of course, the Universe. Thus the message of scholasticism lay open to be seized by the simplest of logical devices, equivalence: God and the Universe are identical.

Such was the inference which Spinoza drew, by Cartesian methods, from scholastic and from Jewish philosophy. The inference was surely valid, and, moreover, it had that geometrical self-evidence ("things equal to the same thing are equal to each other") which the seventeenth century so much admired. The scholastics had begun the depersonalization of God the moment they described him as a perfect being, but so great had been the power of tradition that the shock was immense when Spinoza laid bare the inevitable result. The result, indeed, had escaped Descartes entirely.

Now, as we have seen, all Western religions regard pantheism as heretical. Judaism needs a personal God to validate the Law, Christianity needs a personal God to validate the Church's authority, and Mohammedanism needs a personal Allah to validate Mohammed's prophetic mission. Thus, in the vicissitudes of ideology, God's being a person has become extremely important to organizational unity. It would be true (though certainly vague) to say that the Jews got their law, the churches their authority, and the Mohammedans their prophet, from the Universe. But such derivations are politically unimpressive; they simply will not evoke the desired loyalty and obedience.

Formal philosophizing of the scholastic sort is so distant from life and confined to so few persons that the ensuing disturbances would not in themselves be serious. It is very possible that, if Spinoza had done no more than this, nobody would have troubled him. He did, however, a great deal more. He specifically derided anthropomorphism (the idea that God is like a human person, only grander);

he flatly denied miracles; and he insisted on regarding the Scriptures, Jewish or Christian, as ancient documents written by men and open to the kind of analysis you would give the works of Hesiod or Herodotus. These views appear, expressed with much fire, in the *Tractatus* and the *Ethics*, which were written well after his excommunication. But I think we must suppose that he propounded these same views, with very similar fire, in the years before that.

Now, if you tell an ecclesiastical body that it cannot distinguish itself by miracle, and if to this you add a suggestion that writings allegedly sacred were but the work of Palestinian herdsmen, you are saying—what? The simple truth, no doubt, and something ideologically startling. But, more than this, you are telling the ecclesiastical body that its title to power rests upon nothing but human history—that is to say, upon sand. There are not many bodies, ecclesiastical or other, which will reward the veracity of your assertion.

The peril in which these views placed Spinoza was compounded by the fact that they were likewise unacceptable to Christians. He was thus exposed to the odious politics by which a minority defends itself in the midst of a hostile majority. The synagogue at Amsterdam feared the charge, which would doubtless have been forthcoming, that it harbored a heretic dangerous to the whole Dutch nation. The pattern has been repeated often enough—most lamentably by the Judenrat under the Nazis. Accordingly, at Amsterdam, the synagogue, in order to prove itself guiltless of "subversion," undertook to punish a "subversive" within its own ranks. Apparently, in such crises, it is impossible to act with any sense of history. The victim just happened to be the noblest philosopher of the modern age and one of the noblest men the Judaic tradition has ever produced. But minorities are frequently so slavish that they will do the evil work of their masters and patiently accept the guilt.

There had occurred, in the year 1647, when Spinoza was fifteen years old, a sad ceremony of flagellation, which the later excommunicate himself perhaps witnessed. A certain Uriel da Costa, unstable by temperament, was made yet more so by circumstance. He was Jewish by origin, Christian by education, a convert then to Judaism, a renegade next to Christianity, and at last a returned convert to Judaism.[5]

5) I follow here the account in Callois, op. cit., p. 50. There is a different version in Sir Frederick Pollock, *Spinoza* (London: Kegan Paul; 1880), pp. 8–10.

With all this indecisiveness were mixed some notions of a later age: da Costa grew materialist enough to deny the immortality of the soul. The final reconciliation with Judaism (if such it can be called) involved his submitting to thirty-nine lashes, publicly administered. His previous excommunication had involved his lying at the synagogue door, to be stepped over by members of the congregation. After the thirty-nine restorative lashes, da Costa went home, wrote during some days a tract against his persecutors, and then shot himself.

When his turn came in 1656, Spinoza, like any sensible man, absented himself from such antics: no one was ever to step over him. Nor would he give ear to the words of excommunication, bare empty pomposity of organization talk. For thus the pronunciamento ran: having joined the judgment of angels with that of saints, having got also the consent of God and of the holy congregation, and all this formidable alignment having occurred "in front of the Holy Scrolls with the six hundred and thirteen precepts which are written thereon," not to mention Joshua's excommunication of Jericho and Elisha's curse upon the boys, it was now proposed to extend all curses upon "Baruch de Espinoza," so that he should be cursed by day and by night, lying down and rising up, going out and coming in. "We order," said the pronunciamento, getting down to brass tacks, "that nobody should communicate with him orally, or show him any favor, or stay with him under the same roof, or within four ells of him, or read anything composed or written by him."[6]

Human records, I dare say, do not contain a sillier document. How were these petty hierarchs, who had nothing but power, to put curses upon an honest man? Ostracize him they certainly could, impoverish him and keep people cautiously surveying the prescribed distance of six ells. But how could they alter science, integrity, virtue by an exhalation of words? They were bound to be ridiculous, and have in fact become so. In any contest with morality, organizations are doomed. The world's tragedy lies in the fact that organizations do not yet know this.

6) Text quoted by Walter Nigg, *The Heretics* (New York; Alfred Knopf; 1962), p. 352. The grisly episode of Elisha and the boys will be found in II Kings, 2: 23–24—"On his way to Bethel, as he [Elisha] was walking up the road, some small boys from the town mocked him, crying, "Walk up, baldhead!" When he looked round and saw them, he cursed them in the name of the Eternal; two she-bears came out of the wood and mangled forty-two of the boys." Moffat.

Between 1656 and 1660 Spinoza more or less dropped from sight. There is no authentic knowledge of his activities. Possibly he went to live with his friend Van den Enden, with whose daughter he was once, according to a pleasant legend, in love. The girl, however, who was none of the prettiest, yielded to a rival suitor, more knowing or more affluent, upon presentation of an irresistible necklace. There is nothing incredible in this story, but it has won very little credence. The difficulty lies in crediting Spinoza's taste for such a girl or her taste for such a rival. Yet the story, if true, would be very humanizing. It would reveal a grateful fallibility in a man otherwise alarmingly habituated to being right.

In 1660, Spinoza took residence at Rijnsburg, a village near Leyden, which had become the resort of dissenters cast out of Amsterdam. There, with the penalties of dissent fresh upon him, he wrote the *De Emendatione,* a work of veiled autobiography, which shows in its opening pages how hard the decision had been. Three things in life, says Spinoza, attract everyone: wealth, prestige, and the pleasures of sense.[7] The power of organizations, as usually exerted, lies precisely in granting these goods or withholding them. Yet the clash between organizational demands and the personal integrity of members puts the fundamental question: How valuable, after all, are these values which everybody wants?

Upon further study, these values appear rather less valuable than had been supposed. For one thing, they are a source of instability: if you have wealth, prestige, and the pleasures of sense, you are made discontented by wanting more; and if you lose them, "there arises the greatest sadness."[8] Values that thus beget alternate hope and fear lack the attribute that highest value must have—namely, the giving of calm. And so, wrote Spinoza,

> When experience had taught me that all the usual events of social life are vain and futile, when I perceived that the things which seemed threatening were in themselves neither good nor bad except as the mind was moved to judge them so, I decided to inquire whether there is any genuine good, directly obtainable, which might impress the mind to the exclusion of all else;

7) *De Emendatione Intellectus,* first paragraph: *"divitias scilicet, honorem, atque libidinem." Libido* is too general a term to be translated by the phrase "sexual love," but I think Spinoza had this primarily in mind.
8) Ibid.: *". . . tum summa oritur tristitia."*

whether, that is to say, there is anything which, being found and grasped, would yield me a happiness constant and complete.[9]

He found that there is: the being one's true self, the acceptance of the real world with all its laws and forces, and the describing of these with comprehensive accuracy. Such manner of life, an exercise of the thinker's social function, would be a value limitless and everlasting. "Love toward a thing eternal and infinite," he wrote, with almost unbearable sublimity, "feeds the mind upon joy only, is free from all sadness, and is therefore to be greatly desired and mightily sought."[1]

Did he attain this happiness? He says that he did. Once he had seized the essential insight, serenity stole in upon him, fitfully at first, then oftener, until at last it settled there, never to depart.[2] In 1665, he wrote his friend de Blyenbergh, "I enjoy life, and try to spend it not in sorrow and sighing, but in peace, joy, and cheerfulness, ascending from time to time a step higher."[3] Allusions to serenity are frequent in his correspondence, and serenity is in fact the great theme of his masterpiece, the *Ethics*.

Yet, when all is said, perhaps he did protest too much.[4] There is no doubt that the serenity displayed seemed remarkable to his friends, nor that in some large and noble measure he really did possess it. Yet, despite all this, one can see in Spinoza from time to time the anger that every righteous man feels when he has been abused. It flames out, for example, in the attack on the clergy, which we have quoted; in the great polemic against anthropomorphism, in the Appendix to Part I of the *Ethics,* which attributes this error to "man's insatiable cruelty and avarice"; in a whole series of passages

---

9) Ibid., first sentence. My translation.
1) Ibid., paragraph 3; *"Sed amor erga rem aeternam et infinitam sola laetitia pascit animum, ipsaque omnis tristitiae est expers; quod valde est desiderandum, totisque viribus quaerendum."* My translation.
2) Ibid., paragraph 4: *"Et quamvis in initio haec intervalla essent rara, et per admodum exiguum temporis spatium durarent, postquam tamen verum bonum magis ac magis mihi innotuit, intervalla ista frequentiora et longiora fuerunt . . ."*
3) *Epistola* XXI. Elwes' translation.
4) As, perhaps, did Montesquieu in one of his *Pensées*: *"Je n'ai presque jamais eu de chagrin, encore moins d'ennui. Je m'éveille le matin avec une joie secrète; je vois la lumière avec une espèce de ravissement, et tout le reste du jour je suis content . . ."*

defending freedom of thought. "What greater evil can there be for a republic," he cries out in *Tractatus,* Chapter XX, "than that honorable men be thrust into exile like criminals, because they hold dissenting views and know not how to conceal them?"

There was a final flash of all this in 1675, when Spinoza answered an impudent letter from a former disciple, converted suddenly to Catholicism. The disciple wrote from Florence to say that Spinoza was doing the devil's work, was surely damned, but could yet by a timely repentance be saved. "You ask me," wrote Spinoza stiffly, "how I know that my philosophy is the best. . . . I don't presume to have found the best philosophy, but I know that I understand the true one."[5] Having impaled the graceless youth upon a disturbing but highly perspicacious distinction between the "best" and the "true," Spinoza invited him to demonstrate "mathematically" the authority of the Church.

Moreover, there were his occasional forays into politics. Between 1650 and 1672, the de Witt brothers governed Holland—John de Witt as Grand Pensionary, and Cornelius as Admiral. They were good liberals in the early bourgeois style, they admired talent, and they made friends with Spinoza, who more than shared their ideas.[6] The brothers were murdered by a mob in 1672, in disorders consequent upon the French invasion. Spinoza prepared a placard entitled *Ultimi Barbarorum,* "The Latest Barbarians," in which he denounced the mob, and which he proposed posting upon a wall in the center of town. His friend and landlord, the painter Van Spick, barely intercepted him, or Spinoza might have joined the brothers in their violent and calamitous end.

Such generous outbursts show what fires burned within the central calm. Spinoza was, like Socrates, a man of strong feelings, which with much effort he brought under rational control. Part V of the *Ethics,* which celebrates "the power of the mind over the emotions," is autobiography philosophized. It is also the profoundest account of the subject before Freud, whose work it in part anticipates. There we are told, in an astonishing passage (Proposition XX, Scholium), that the mind's power over the emotions consists in five things: in

5) *Epistola* LXXVI: ". . . *meque rogas, quomodo sciam, meam Philosophiam optimam esse inter alias omnes . . . ego non praesumo, me optimum invenisse Philosophiam, sed veram me intelligere scio.*" My translation.
6) John de Witt gave Spinoza a pension of 200 florins (Callois, op. cit., p. 52).

recognizing the emotions to be emotions; in studying them as psychological phenomena; in allowing time for the emotions whose sources we understand to prevail over those whose sources we do not understand; in the naturally superior power of those feelings which attach to general truths about the universe; and in the fact that the emotions can be given a rational and systematic account over their whole range.

Each of these rules enjoins the use of knowledge in one or other of its forms, and it is clear that a new redeemer—science—is henceforth to save mankind. Just as Descartes showed that men could possess truth without the authority of organizations, so Spinoza showed that science, which is truth possessed, could resolve the main problems of human appetite and human government. The *Ethics,* despite the straitjacket of its geometrical form and the obsolescence of its vocabulary, is a work of much dramatic suspense. Spinoza develops the tension little by little, from the calmest conceivable account of the universe, of mind, of the emotions, of society, and of a man's involvement in all these, until, awestruck and alarmed, we wonder whether, amid so formidable a constellation of powers, there can be blessedness or virtue or even simple decency. And then the triumphant Fifth Part shows how and why these can exist. The argument is persuasive, as philosophical arguments go; but the definitive proof is, with flawless modesty, never mentioned—that the author himself had actually done the thing described. Was he not, by singularly happy foresight, named Baruch, the Blessed One?

The redemptive power of knowledge was a favorite idea of the seventeenth century and a great contribution to the intellectual advance of our race. It lies open for all to see in the most celebrated epigram of that age, by Spinoza's contemporary, Pascal:

Man is only a reed, the feeblest of all things, but he is a reed that can think. The universe need not marshal all its power to crush him: he can be destroyed by a drop of water, a drift of mist. Yet though the whole universe were to crush him, man would still be nobler than the destroying power. He knows that he dies, but the universe in no way knows the advantage it has over him.

Thus all our dignity consists in thought. By that we must rise, not by space or by time. Let us therefore labor to think rightly. *Voilà le principe de la morale.*[7]

7) *Pensées: Grandeur de l'Homme.* My translation.

This moral principle was Spinoza's also, who worked out its application in detail. There is something liberating about knowledge as such, even before knowledge has translated itself into technology for the control of events. Just by having knowledge, a man is lifted out of mere passivity into a state and posture of control. He becomes what Spinoza called the "adequate cause" of his own actions, which thereafter record his conscious intent and deliberate planning, not a "push-button" response to stimulus. The danger in the emotions is their tendency toward compulsiveness: they may throw a man into ecstasy or panic, and make impossible that self-determination of behavior which is his virtue and his good. But knowledge, if it cannot remove emotions entirely, can at least reduce them until they form, as Spinoza quaintly says, *minimam mentis partem,* a very small part of the mind.[8]

Now, it takes a special kind and level of knowledge to do this. As a good Cartesian, Spinoza was not impressed by the immediate deliverances of sense experience. Confronted, say, with Locke's assertion that "if I myself see a man walk on the ice, it is past probability, it is knowledge,"[9] Spinoza would perhaps reply, "Well, and what then? It is much more knowledgeable knowledge to know that ice of a certain thickness will bear bodies of a certain weight." That is to say, sense experience yields single occasions, particular instances, but science seeks *generalizations* about the world. The data of sense are fragmentary, partial, or (to use Spinoza's word) "mutilated." Knowledge, at its summit, would be the kind of knowledge obtainable under Descartes' fourth rule: it would be universal, comprehensive, and complete. You would be past the stage of not seeing the forest for the trees or the trees for the forest; you would be seeing trees and forest, the trees *in* the forest, as a clearly articulated system.

Now, of course, no one man, or even the race collectively, can comprehend the universe and all its parts in a single moment of intuition. Apparently, however, Spinoza thought it possible to do so, and thought, moreover, that he had come near to doing it. Approximations, nevertheless, there can be. One has only to recall how the great generalizations of Darwin, Mendel, Marx, Freud, and Einstein have organized and elucidated vast accumulations of fact. Bring to

8) *Ethics,* V, XX, Scholium.
9) *Essay on the Human Understanding,* Book IV, Chapter XV, §5.

your mind some occasion when a part of the world, then under your study, fell suddenly into order and coherence, so that you could feel you knew the whole thing, and you will understand what Spinoza meant. Bring back also the feelings that went with this achievement, and you will understand what Spinoza meant by *beatitudo,* the sense of being blest.

This summit of knowledge Spinoza called *scientia intuitiva:* the awareness of system and members without loss of clarity in either. And he thought that a special kind of feeling attended this awareness—a feeling of triumph, not of loss; of affirmation, not denial; of love, and not hostility. Such feeling, gathering around such knowledge, would constitute a settled happiness; and, in his pantheistic manner, Spinoza was able to call it *amor intellectualis Dei,* the intellectual love of God. Thus it transpired that the universe, in its entirety, could be the object of emotions which had been supposed to attach exclusively to a personal God or to a God who was three persons in one.

It was a thorough heresy, of which the thoroughness is not yet exhausted. For it showed that morality can dwell with science and in fact needs science to dwell in. We have not yet made the residence secure, partly because the sciences, like prodigal sons, have wasted their substance these three hundred years in riotous living. Our goal, however, remains what Spinoza said it was, and our path to it the path he cleared. He could have called his masterpiece by any of a dozen names, for it discusses every subject under the sun. Yet he called it the *Ethics,* and in that choice of title, six letters long, lies much of the wisdom of this world.

In 1673, Fabritius, a professor at the Academy (as it then was) of Heidelberg, wrote Spinoza, on behalf of the Elector Palatine, offering him a chair of philosophy. "You will nowhere find," said Fabritius, "a prince more well-disposed toward superior intellects, and he ranks you among these. You will have the greatest liberty of philosophizing—a liberty which the Prince is confident you will not abuse by troubling the established religion."[1] But Spinoza well knew the range of such "greatest liberty." He declined the offer, and replied, with faint but perceptible irony, "I do not know what limits there would be likely to be on this freedom of philosophizing, and I would not want to give even the appearance of a wish to trouble

1) *Epistola* XLVII. My translation.

the established religion. Indeed, quarrels of that sort arise less from religious zeal than from various human passions or love of debate, wherein everything usually gets distorted and denounced, even if rightly said."[2]

So he clung to his scholar's attic in the Hague,[3] grinding lenses for telescopes by way of livelihood, and aggravating, in the dust of those lenses, his tubercular malaise. There was the entire frugality of diet, the morning glass of wine, the evening chat with the landlord. In 1676 he had visits from Leibniz, the great mathematician and courtier, who, less brave than brilliant, afterward maintained he had never been there. One would like to have heard those conversations, between a man who would conceal no truth and a man who would do no more than utter many.

Meanwhile, the lungs growing weaker, Spinoza visibly approached his end. It came when he was not yet forty-five, on Sunday the twenty-first of February, 1677, at about three o'clock in the afternoon. He had lain down in his attic to sleep, and slept into eternity— that infinite scheme of things which had never been absent from his sight. He was buried in a grave of many bodies, and there he still lies, as perhaps he would have wished, a rarity amid the commonplace. For his hold on reality was always firm, he allowed himself no hyperbole, and the last words of the *Ethics* tell us that "all excellent things are as difficult as they are rare."

I I

BESIDE THIS EPIGRAM—weary and sad, yet in its way content—we may set another last sentence, which closes a work twenty-six years older, Hobbes' celebrated political treatise, the *Leviathan:* "Such Truth, as opposeth no man's profit, nor pleasure, is to all men welcome." How true this also is, how rich in acquaintance with the deceits of exploitative society, how amiably cynical! Hobbes was, by self-description, a timorous man, but he knew whither timidity leads—to one of the failings of universities, which he described as "the frequency of insignificant speech."[4] His hope was that each

2) *Epistola* XLVIII. My translation.
3) The house still stands, though once there was a rumor it had been torn down by the Nazis in their morbid anti-Semitic rage. Beside it stands (what would amuse Spinoza) a tavern which bears the legend SPINOZA BAR.
4) *Leviathan,* Part I, Chapter I, last sentence. "Insignificant" = "empty of meaning."

reader would accept as much of *Leviathan* as profit and pleasure permitted.

It is perhaps a thinnish hope, when one writes on politics or any other sort of social question. For, as we know, organizations resist truths that are disadvantageous to them, and so, within their lesser spheres, do individual men. Hobbes wrote during a great English crisis, the Civil War, and he rationalized royal sovereignty at a moment when many Englishmen hoped that kings would disappear forever.

Yet it was the sign of a less persecuting age that *Leviathan* caused Hobbes scarcely more trouble than would confirm its own veracity. The book was born a classic, and still offers its readers a rare medicinal bath for the washing away of illusion. Men, says *Leviathan*, are creatures of self-interest, are in a kind of war with one another, and yet seek peace on behalf of safety. The only path to peace they have found lies in getting themselves governed, in submitting to authority. From this need of authority Hobbes inferred the right of kings to rule. And so it turned out that royal sovereignty, once supposed to have been a grant from heaven, was but a panic-gift from anarchists seeking safety.

One sees the truth of this account in the very exaggerations of its caricature. Hobbes meant the doctrine seriously, but nothing could confine his circumambient wit. He is the English Machiavelli, more commonsensical though not more veracious, and less shocking because more amused. Wit sweetens much the bitterness of fact, and we can see why Anthony à Wood, who did not like Hobbes (nor, indeed, anyone else), described him, with pleasant spelling, as "an enimy to Universities, school-divinity, Arostotle, presbyterians, metaphysics," and also as "a person of verie acute parts, quick apprehension to the last, ready to answer whatsoever is proposed, and would understand what you meane before you are at the end of half your discourse."[5]

Hobbes was born in 1588, the year of the Spanish Armada, and indeed his birth was said to have been hastened by his mother's fright at the Armada's approach. His long life of ninety years enclosed the epoch when, for Englishmen, it was most dangerous to be

5) *The Life and Times of Anthony à Wood,* abridged from Andrew Clark's edition, World's Classics Series (Oxford: Oxford University Press; 1961), pp. 242–43. Wood's name at birth was simply Anthony; the "à" was an affectation of his later years as antiquarian at Oxford.

alive. In 1649, the monarchy fell with the execution of Charles I, and rose again in 1660, never to regain its absolute form. Prelacy (which is to say, the political sovereignty of bishops) vanished with Laud's death at the block. For a time the bishops, like the king, vanished also. Cromwell's Protectorate, a monarchy without a king, established mercantile capitalism as the basic economy, which the feudal aristocrats, even in their half victory of the Restoration, could not budge. Indeed, some of them had already passed over into trade.

It had been the bloody labor of a decade of civil war, and the men who waged it for Parliament on the revolutionary side were clothed in doctrines as strong and hard as their steel, yet softened too with the love that rises between dedication and a cause. When Bunyan's Mr. Valiant-for-Truth was summoned across the river of death, he paused on its edge to declare the faith of all first-generation revolutionaries:

> My sword I give to him that shall succeed me in my pilgrimage, and my courage and skill to him that can get it. My marks and scars I carry with me to be a witness for me, that I have fought his battles who now will be my Rewarder.

"So," adds Bunyan, "he passed over, and the trumpets sounded for him on the other side."[6]

The revolutionaries supporting Cromwell were by no means unanimous: there were Presbyterians, Independents, Fifth-Monarchy men[7]—all doctrinally at odds, but united against Charles I. Oliver himself distilled the essence of their unity, which lay in devotion to the Good Old Cause as being in fact God's cause upon earth. A true humility accompanied this devotion, and Oliver, though inescapably dictatorial, remained skeptical of his own or anyone else's use of power. The night before he died, in 1658, he was heard in his bed-chamber to pray, "Teach those who look too much upon Thy instruments to depend more upon Thyself. Pardon such as desire to trample upon the dust of a poor worm, for they are Thy people too. And

---

6) *The Pilgrim's Progress,* Part II. I take this sentence to be, for rhythm and economy, the loveliest sentence in the language.

7) A form of premillenarianism. In this view, there had been in history four monarchies: the Assyrian, the Persian, the Macedonian, and the Roman. Of these, three were gone and the fourth was going. It would be succeeded by a fifth monarchy, the reign of Christ on earth.

pardon the folly of this short prayer, even for Jesus Christ's sake, and give us a good night, if it be thy pleasure."[8]

Cromwell, his Ironsides, the parliamentarians, and all who carried to victory the Good Old Cause, were of course heretics most entire. They compounded their heresy by physically destroying the man, Charles I, who bore sovereignty in the old and "orthodox" order. For the age of middle-class revolutions had begun, and from that time on the orthodox were as like to lose their heads as the heretics. When the revolution entered upon a pause, and a certain aristocratic reaction set in, the leading regicides were vengefully executed, and England came near to losing the head that had not yet composed *Paradise Lost*. Milton himself remained imperturbable, true to the historical forecast he had made two months before the Restoration: "I trust I shall have spoken persuasion to abundance of sensible and ingenuous men; to some perhaps whom God may raise of these stones to become children of reviving liberty."[9] History (which is "God" without the metaphor) did so raise them, and there have been children of reviving liberty ever since.

While all these events were going forward, Hobbes, the cautious if not the timorous man, absented himself from England. That marvelous anecdotalist, John Aubrey, whose first extensive piece was on Hobbes, reports the great man's own account of the matter:

> He told me that bishop Manwaring (of St. David's) preached *his doctrine;* for which, among others, he was sent prisoner to the Tower. Then thought Mr. Hobbes, 'tis time now for me to shift for myself, and so withdrew into France, and resided at Paris.[1]

There he became mathematical tutor to the Prince of Wales, later Charles II, who had retired thither after the battle of Worcester, and there he presented him with a manuscript copy of *Leviathan,* "engrossed in velume in a marvellous fair hand."

The greatest perhaps of English philosophers, Hobbes was always

8) This touching and oft-quoted prayer will be found, e.g., in Sir Charles Frith, *Oliver Cromwell,* World's Classics Series (Oxford: Oxford University Press; 1958), p. 435.
9) *The Ready and Easy Way to establish a Free Commonwealth.* Milton wrote this tract in a vain effort to rally the people against the return of monarchy.
1) *Brief Lives,* Anthony Powell's edition (New York: Charles Scribner's Sons; 1949), p. 243. Italics Aubrey's.

averse from organizational struggles. In him the tension is unusually clear between a wish to say what actually is the case and a wish to temper the resulting conclusions, so as not to become a target of power. It is a favorite tactic of advanced intellectuals, but it has its special risk—the risk of offending all parties. In basic philosophy Hobbes was materialist, and thought of the world as composed of particles in motion. He professed, to be sure, belief in God and in the tenets of Anglican orthodoxy, but I cannot think he held those views with anything like the fervor that informs the leading doctrines of *Leviathan.* Indeed, the attack on Catholicism in Part IV ("The Kingdom of Darknesse") can be read as an attack on religion as such. The adversaries who charged atheism upon him had ground for their complaint.

Thus Hobbes' philosophy was far too radical for the Stuart side, although Charles II, who had for religion the fidelity he had for his mistresses, remained friendly to Hobbes and brought him often to court. But during the Parisian exile the air grew hot, and Hobbes was moved to return home. Dissent, it would appear, was safer under Cromwell than amid the angry exiles—although, to the victorious revolutionaries, his strange mélange of monarchism and skepticism was repellent in the extreme. Beside all this, he was too painfully accurate about human motives, and too candid in stating them, not to be generally troublesome. One learns from Hobbes never to entertain extravagant political hopes.

Yet, during ninety years, the risks never proved losses, and Hobbes lived into his ancient age an admired person whom everyone wished to answer and nobody could. Aubrey shows him to us an old man, bald but bareheaded within doors, who "never took cold in his head, but . . . the greatest trouble was to keepe-off the flies from pitching on the baldnes."[2] He had always been temperate "both as to wine and women," but on the few occasions (about one each year) when he did drink, he drank to excess, "to have the benefitt of vomiting, which he did easily; by which benefit neither his witt was disturbt longer than he was spuing nor his stomach oppressed."[3] And we have at the end a picture of the sage, always sharp but never quite venerable, shutting his doors at night, retiring to bed where no one could hear, and singing pricksong—"not that he had a very good

2) Ibid., p. 250.
3) Ibid., p. 252.

voice, but for his health's sake: he did beleeve it did his lunges good, and conduced much to prolong his life."[4]

Hobbes was a man skillful in escape. Yet one must also observe that escape was a thing the political circumstances now permitted. In truth, the English had acquired a knowledge they still possess, alone among the nations of the earth: that thinkers are not dangerous, even in dissent, and that their social effect can always be put off to a later time and to more convenient handling. Every other people, so far as I know, suspects its thinkers of necromantic powers, able to seduce the young with logic and the old with eloquence. But from Hobbes to Shaw, the British establishment has endured tremendous intellectual shocks without the smallest risk of becoming republican in government or socialist in economy. As for Mr. John Milton, he suffered a very brief arrest, and was let off upon "paying his fees [i.e., the costs]"—which fees, being denounced by his friends as excessive, were thereupon reduced.

I do not know how the English have managed to confine intellectual ferment within the intellectual world, but I fancy that a persistent tolerance has had much to do with it. On the whole, a man is much more content with what is if he is allowed to speak boldly about what ought to be. This is in itself a social good, which confers yet other benefits: the community can, in its slow discursive way, ponder the notions and perhaps even effectuate some of them. At any rate, toleration was the great social discovery, by the Dutch and English, in the seventeenth century. In 1690, we find John Locke asserting it with an eloquence that the subsequent libertarian years have never surpassed:

> We should do well to commiserate our mutual ignorance, and endeavour to remove it in all the gentle and fair ways of information, and not instantly treat others ill as obstinate and perverse because they will not renounce their own and receive our opinions, or at least those we would force upon them, when it is more than probable that we are no less obstinate in not embracing some of

4) Ibid., p. 253. Pricksong was so named from the manner of inscribing the musical notation: Mr. Pepys records (May 7, 1668), "I did get him [Bannister, the musician] to prick me down the notes of the Echo in 'The Tempest,' which pleases me mightily." Hobbes' book of pricksong was that of Henry Lawes, Court Musician under Charles I, the man who invited Milton to write the masque "Comus" and supplied the music for it.

theirs. For where is the man that has uncontestable evidence of the truth of all that he holds or of the falsehood of all he condemns; or can say, that he has examined to the bottom all his own or other men's opinions? The necessity of believing without knowledge, nay, often upon very slight grounds, in this fleeting state of action and blindness we are in, should make us more busy and careful to inform ourselves than constrain others.[5]

In those days, trade was the parent of tolerance, not only because trade was indifferent to ideology but because trade involved, subtly and almost inattentively, an exchange of ideas. The great voyages of discovery, beginning with Columbus, brought back, along with the gold and silver, reports of most extraordinary customs, values, habits of social life. The explorers first, and then the ever more frequent traders, were astonished at what they found in regions remote then and (some of them) remote still. It was discovered, for example, that the inhabitants of Patagonia had no theological notions whatever, that many other peoples were in the same case, that in some societies men were venerated for vice or insanity, that among the Saracens holy men could be observed sitting stark naked upon hillocks of sand, and that these same holy men cohabited not only with women and boys but also with asses and mules. "The saints who are canonized among the Turks," wrote Locke sardonically, "lead lives which one cannot with modesty relate."[6]

After this manner, comparative sociology did more damage to Christian doctrine than philosophic criticism or the well-known failure of Christians to match doctrine with behavior. It showed that what had been deemed catholic (i.e., universal) was in point of fact parochial. When so many other peoples lived by radically different standards, what certainty could there be that Christian norms were correct? Locke, and perhaps Hobbes also, did believe those norms to be correct; nevertheless, the norms had lost their gleaming self-evidence, their awesome cogency *a priori*. It was no longer possible to think that they had been imprinted upon the mind, at birth, as "innate ideas," along with the three fundamental laws of logic.[7] As

5) *Essay on the Human Understanding,* Book IV, Chapter XVI, § 4.
6) Ibid., Book I, Chapter III, § 9. Locke quoted, in the chastity of its original Latin, the *Peregrinations* of one Baumgarten. The previous examples were all cited by Locke, loc. cit., and I, IV, § 8.
7) The law of identity (*A* is *A*), the law of contradiction (a sentence cannot be true and false at one and the same time), and the law of excluded middle (a

for Christian "anthropology," the myth of Adam and his fall, that could scarcely survive the flood of anthropological evidence. It has survived, of course, and its survival shows what organizations can do in the face of science.

Locke's personal life was as adventurous as Hobbes'; but he, alone among philosophers, had the good fortune of appearing at precisely the right moment and on precisely the right side. He was the first and greatest of the Whig intellectuals, the founder of our liberal tradition; and not the least of his indirect achievements are the Declaration of Independence and the Constitution of the United States. His liberalism was, to be sure, not limitless: he did not propose extending tolerance to Roman Catholics on the one hand or to atheists on the other. He was the sublime Centrist, hostile to extremes but hospitable to all who would gather beneath the main tent.

The historical Locke, born in the same year as Spinoza (1632), was a man of many talents and of even more interests. We must think of him as a lecturer in Greek, a reader in rhetoric, and Censor of Moral Philosophy, all at Christ Church College, Oxford. These subjects he abandoned, in 1664, for the study of medicine, and it was as physician that he entered the household of Lord Ashley, later the first Earl of Shaftesbury. There, it is said, he once used a draining tube in a successful operation upon the Earl. He helped procure a wife for the Earl's son, and attended as obstetrician at the birth of the Third Earl, who, with great propriety, grew up to be a philosopher.

The First Earl, a man small in stature and fertile in stratagem, did perhaps correspond with Dryden's celebrated description:

> A fiery soul, which working out its way,
> Fretted the pigmy body to decay . . .[8]

A certain immediacy of failure dogged all his efforts, which, posthumously, were crowned with spectacular success. The failures, indeed,

---

sentence must be, at any one time, either true or false). Book I of Locke's *Essay* is given over to a devastating attack upon the doctrine of innate ideas—an attack so successful that few read it nowadays, though it is a stupendous achievement of logic and eloquence. The immediate victim was Lord Herbert of Cherbury and his book *De Veritate*.

8) *"Absalom and Achitophel,"* ll. 156–57. Dryden is, along with Aristophanes, one of the few examples of a witty reactionary.

issued from no lack of skill, but from the obstinacy of circumstance. Shaftesbury aimed at protecting and extending the new-won dominance of the merchant class and, more generally, the liberties of the subject against the prerogatives of the crown. Charles II sought to recover these prerogatives even to the absolutism that his "martyred" father had professed. This absolutism was to have been buttressed, in the medieval manner, by a return to Romanism, and Charles seems to have been secretly (or at least not publicly) a member of the Catholic Church.

The dead hand of the past is, however, dead. As reactionaries cannot prevent the future, so they cannot recover the past. By 1667, when Charles had been restored only seven years, Mr. Pepys confided to his immortal diary the following observation:

> It is strange how everybody do now-a-days reflect upon Oliver, and commend him, what brave things he did, and made all the neighbor princes fear him; while here a prince, come in with all the love and prayers and good liking of his people . . . hath lost all so soon, that it is a miracle what way a man could devise to lose so much in so little time.

In the event, Charles quietly gave up his absolutist ambitions, and settled into a constitutional monarch. Not so his brother James, the heir to the throne—since, by a strange circumstance, to which feudal politics was vulnerable, Charles's frequent paternity was confined to illegitimate connections. It chanced that one of these connections, with a lady named Lucy Walters, produced a son of fair competence and unusual charm, a son never legitimated but given aristocratic rank as Duke of Monmouth.

Since James was a hopeless reactionary, Shaftesbury's scheme was to get Monmouth legitimated and declared successor to the throne. It was rather too devious a path to power, and it ended in Shaftesbury's disconsolate death in exile and in Monmouth's execution under James. But in the following of this path, intrigues proliferated so tortuously and so secretly that they cannot yet be charted or described. There seems no doubt, however, that in these intrigues Locke was somewhat involved. He was, of course, by no means as famous then as he later became; and, from his nest at Christ Church, he could operate almost unobserved.

Of observation, however, there was some. A fellow of his college, and a political opponent, has left letters which show that Locke aroused suspicion, without revealing a single fact:

> March 14, 1681. John Locke lives a very cunning and unintelligible life here, being two days in town and three days out; and no one knows where he goes or when he returns. Certainly there is some Whig intrigue amanaging. . . .
> March 19, 1681. Where J. L. goes, I cannot by any means learn, all his voyages being so cunningly contrived. . . . I fancy there are projects afoot.[9]

Shaftesbury went to the Tower in 1681 for high treason, was acquitted amid public rejoicing, escaped to Holland in 1683, and there died. Locke now felt himself without political defense, and quietly followed his patron's path into Holland. There he lived until 1690, Number 14 (for a time) on a list of "undesirable aliens," but stricken off it when the Dutch observed him to be engaged in nothing more dangerous than the *Essay on the Human Understanding*. In its way, however, this book was the most "dangerous" of the seventeenth century: it brought into existence the climate of opinion that we call "modern" and that has thrust the medieval view behind it forever.

Charles II died in 1685, with a touching tribute to two mistresses and a no less touching jest about taking "such an unconscionable time" to die. Within three years thereafter, James's truculent folly effected all the results for which Shaftesbury and Locke and the Whigs had labored. James's attempt to reconstitute the past (against the earnest advice, it ought to be said, of the Pope and the hierarchy) brought the future into existence quickly and bloodlessly. The Dutch prince, William of Orange, had married James's daughter Mary. Their religious beliefs were Protestant, their economic sympathies commercial. On invitation of James's opponents, who now included almost the whole population, they landed with an army at Torquay in Devonshire, in 1688. William's banner bore the device, *Pro Religione Protestante, Pro Libero Parliamento*.

Not a shot was fired nor a sword raised. James's army, gathered at Salisbury, melted away before the genial dawn. On November fifteenth, for example, the Second Earl of Clarendon (son of the

---

9) Quoted by D. J. O'Connor, *John Locke* (London: Penguin Books; 1952), p. 18.

great historian) learned that *his* son, Lord Cornbury, had defected to William. "O God," he wrote, "that my son should be a rebel! The Lord in his mercy look upon me, and enable me to support myself under this most grievous calamity!" On November thirtieth he followed his son into William's camp.[1]

Politics, particularly revolutionary politics, does strange things with traditional loyalties and predictable behavior. "The revolution," says Temperley, "was initiated by the great nobles, effected by the aid of a foreign ruler and a composite army, and consummated by a constitutional settlement made by country gentlemen in the House of Commons." One would not have expected great nobles to oppose a king, nor a foreign prince to be welcome, nor country gentlemen to side with mercantilism; but James, by threatening all these groups, had united them. Their alliance and its triumphant effect proved, what reactionaries never know, that in human history the past is past forever.

Locke returned from Holland in 1690, and immediately published, like salvos of artillery, his two works of greatest fame: the *Essay on the Human Understanding* and the *Essay concerning the True Original, Extent and End of Civil Government*. To this latter he had supplied, a year before, a sort of introduction in the form of a polemical treatise, *Concerning False Principles*. Therein he attacked the ideas of a Sir Robert Filmer, with such effect indeed that for more than two centuries thereafter Filmer survived solely as the target of Locke's attack.

For our present purpose, we must take Filmer rather more seriously, because his one notable work, the *Patriarcha,* written during the Civil War, had so much damaged the medieval view while trying to recover it. Filmer was not concerned with the divine institution of papal power—that was irrelevant to domestic politics—but with the divine right of kings, particularly as this right appertained to the Stuart monarch Charles I. Filmer's argument made its appeal to reason, not revelation, and was a quasi-scientific compound of fanciful history and antique jurisprudence. It assumed as true the Adammyth and the patriarchal-feudal right of primogeniture. God created Adam monarch of the world. There was, to be sure, a difficulty here, since Adam, alone in the world, had nobody to govern: he had

1) *Cambridge Modern History,* Volume V, pp. 255–56. The next quotation is from p. 256.

to beget his own subjects. Conceivably this would explain the copulative labors of later kings; yet a title to rule, when there is no one to rule over, is surely empty.

With a sedulous care that now seems ill rewarded, Filmer undertook to show how, generation by generation, Adam's sovereignty had passed, with exquisite accuracy, into the hands of the then reigning European monarchs. By inference, therefore, the English revolutionaries, in overthrowing Charles, were violating God's design—an inference that those same revolutionaries, being God's closet companions, perfectly knew to be false. Some defects in Filmer's derivation were indeed conspicuous. All went reasonably well until Noah and his flood, which, it will be remembered, left only such persons upon earth as had been accepted into the ark. It appeared, from Genesis 9: 8–18, that God thereupon distributed world sovereignty among Noah's three sons. What then became of the right of primogeniture? Why had Shem to share with his brothers, particularly when Ham proved indelicate?[2]

Filmer's difficulty was that if Noah, under God's guidance, divided sovereignty into three, then God had canceled the right of primogeniture, while if God had maintained the right of primogeniture, then the division had been solely Noah's idea and therefore man-made. Locke pounced upon the dilemma, and from it drew a charter of liberty for the modern age: "If it [primogeniture] be not a Divine right, it is only human, depending on the will of man, and so where human institution gives it not, the first-born has no right at all above his brother, and men may put government into what hands and under what form they please."[3]

Men may put government into what hands and under what form they please! This is the maxim of all revolutionaries, and Locke had derived it, with at least a show of logic, from the most reactionary work then popular. One may imagine the joy of those revolutionaries, newly supreme, to perceive that the hostile ideology had passed into their power even as the state itself had done. Fourscore and seven years later, Mr. Jefferson wrote, and Mr. Hancock was first to sign, a document which asserted, *inter alia,* "that whenever any Form of Government becomes destructive of these ends [Life, Liberty, and

2) The Freudian ground of the story of Ham, who "saw the nakedness of his father," is sufficiently plain.

3) *Concerning False Principles,* § 140.

the pursuit of Happiness], it is the Right of the People to alter or abolish it, and to institute new Government, laying its foundations on such principles and organizing its powers in such forms, as to them shall seem most likely to effect their Safety and Happiness."

Men may put government into what hands and under what form they please! What more complete humanization of politics can there be? The sweep of Locke's broom was cosmic, though terrestrial; and all the agencies of supernature, invoked alike by tyrants and rebels of the past, withdrew within that landscape of imagination which had ever been their true and only home. As for poor Sir Robert, his theologizing of politics ended in a science of social change. His metaphor fell from him like a garment destroyed, and the naked body of politics, more admirable because more real, showed forth the sinews of a better world.

Now, there are various ways of removing metaphors, depending on what one regards as the criterion of literal speech. We have seen that rationalists like Descartes and Spinoza took the language of mathematics and logic as ideally literal. But another way is to take as literal the language that describes whatever is *immediately* observable by our senses. Locke's sight of the man walking on the ice is a fine example of this empiricist criterion. Further, the empiricist criterion can claim, and does claim, an added advantage: it appears, at least, to be connected with real existence. Anything whatever can be put through logical and mathematical processes—imaginary entities as well as actual ones. But if you see a man walking on the ice, there is just that man and he is doing what he is doing.

Immediacy is an impressive criterion, though it has its difficulties. There is a story, from the early nineteenth century, of a lawyer's "proving" the impossibility of steam locomotives, in the presence of George Stephenson, who had invented them. Stephenson's remark was, "Of all the powers in nature, the greatest is the gift of gab!" In other words, if you have built a locomotive and seen it work, no amount of argumentation can prove the contrary.

On this criterion of immediacy Locke undertook to found a theory of knowledge. He was well aware of the hazards, and also he held (or at any rate stated) very nearly every other view that the problem permitted. He was a chatty, discursive philosopher, and his most endearing trait appears in the fact that inconsistency gave him no pain. He did not organize the world like Spinoza, nor shrink it like his successor Berkeley; but, with a blithe candor, he talked about all of it, with perfect acknowledgment of all points of view. He was, within himself and within the great *Essay,* the summation of all that came after him. The philosopher who does not know the *Essay* from cover to cover is no philosopher, and is scarcely, indeed, a citizen of the modern world.

The man on the ice, the entity immediately present to observation by the senses! It is very plain that this can never be the lot of any supernatural personage whatever. "Angels of all sorts," wrote Locke, with irony so delicate that one cannot know it to be intentional, "are naturally beyond our discovery."[4] From the reactionary side, Dryden had admitted as much:

> God thus asserted: man is to believe
> Beyond what Sense and Reason can conceive . . .[5]

If the sentences we most surely know to be true are those that issue from our sensory observation of the world, and if, in the course of that observation, we never come upon angels or divinities or (as Locke said) "intelligences whereof it is more likely there are more orders than of corporeal substances," then all our knowledge of supernature, if knowledge it can be called, is derivative. And always we shall be dogged with the suspicion that entities which we can never observe with our senses are entities which probably do not exist.

Thus by sense experience, as by logic and mathematics, the theological view of the world, dominant in Europe since the brief outburst of Ionian materialism in the sixth century B.C., stood fully revealed at last as poetry mistaken for science. Thereafter the rational man, with due observance of morality, would content himself with literal descriptions of the universe, and in that contentment find "the intellectual love of God."

This posture of the devoted scientist, though excellent Spinozism, is perhaps more advanced than anything Locke himself achieved, for all his shriveling of myth. He remained personally a theist, not a pantheist or a materialist—although he did suggest what Spinoza

4) *Essay,* IV, III, § 27.
5) *"The Hind and the Panther,"* Part I, ll. 118–19.

denied: that matter might be capable of thought.[6] But the weaknesses of human cognition, its brevities and biases, darkened from time to time his otherwise robust hope. In these moods, a little lamenting the "twilight of probability" in which we live our lives, he touched again, as with a distant hand, the old familiar metaphor:

Therefore, as God has set some things in broad daylight, as he has given us some certain knowledge, though limited to a few things in comparison, probably as a taste of what intellectual creatures are capable of, to excite in us a desire and endeavour after a better state; so, in the greatest part of our concernment, he has afforded us only the twilight, as I may so say, of probability, suitable, I presume, to that state of mediocrity and probationership he has been pleased to place us in here; wherein, to check our over-confidence and presumption, we might, by every day's experience, be made sensible of our short-sightedness and liableness to error; the sense whereof might be a constant admonition to us to spend the days of this our pilgrimage with industry and care in the search and following of that way which might lead us to a state of greater perfection; it being highly rational to think, even were revelation silent in the case, that as men employ those talents God has given them here, they shall accordingly receive their rewards at the close of the day, when their sun shall set, and night shall put an end to their labors.[7]

A metaphor, swollen by sea rhythms to an ocean's breadth. And yet I suppose that in the year 1690 there was no other way to express man's present insufficiency together with his future historical hope.

6) *Essay*, IV, III, § 6: "I see no contradiction in it, that the first eternal thinking Being should, if he pleased, give to certain systems of created senseless matter, put together as he thinks fit, some degrees of sense, perception, and thought."
7) Ibid., IV, XIV, § 2.

CHAPTER

13

The Dark Closet and the Enlightened Mind

MR. JOHN LOCKE, whose appeal to immediate sense experience as the norm of knowledge had so devastating an effect upon the medieval view, regarded experience with much simplicity. It required, he thought, only sensations and a receptacle to contain them. He thought this, at any rate, when he was obeying the scientist's urge to break compounds into their elements and to explain them by means of the fewest possible assumptions. Thus he wrote, "Methinks the understanding is not much unlike a closet wholly shut from light, with only some little opening left to let in external visible resemblances or ideas of things without: would the pictures coming into such a dark room but stay there, and lie so orderly as to be found upon occasion, it would very much resemble the understanding of a man in reference to all objects of sight, and the ideas of them."[1]

Perhaps Locke drew this image from the experiment by which Newton had demonstrated white light to be a mixture of colors. In any case, the image wonderfully reveals how shrunken the idea of human nature had suddenly become. Instead of an immortal soul whose salvation the entire cosmos was organized to achieve, instead of a spiritual entity of passion, intellect, and will, instead of a degenerated scion of God's original, we have—a dark closet! The loss of all this grandeur and of content issued from a cheerful use of

1) *Essay,* II, XI, § 17.

Ockham's Razor, the law (as philosophers used to call it) of parsimony.[2] This "law," which has no basis in logic but perhaps a good deal in esthetics, suggests that an explanation becomes more credible in proportion as it rests on fewer assumptions. Locke proposed to elucidate the nature and possibility of science by assuming just three things: that there are objects (some of which have sense organs); that objects give rise to sensations by acting on the sense organs; and that there are consciousnesses ("dark closets") for the sensations to be in. Once there, they would go through some kind of sorting process, either by their own activity or the mind's (Locke is not sure which), and they would find themselves arranged in general classes and under general laws.

The puzzles which this theory produced have addled all subsequent philosophy, and are still the theme of extraordinary labors. If what one really knows is just the immediate sense datum (the given color patch, or touch texture, or timbre of sound), how can one know that there is an object it came from or a generalization it goes toward? Pasteur would be limited to his own observed rabbits, and Mendel to his own observed peas, without a more extensive generalization to be had out of either. In short, the philosophy which escorted science into the world contained some notions which would make science impossible.

Yet, in the glory of its advent, Locke's philosophy had an inviolable charm—rather more potent, indeed, than the Cartesian *cogito* had once possessed. Locke, it seemed, had examined human consciousness with the cool simplicity of a detached observer, precisely as Harvey had done with the bloodstream, Boyle with gases, and Newton with light. All these triumphs had been independent of organizational doctrine, and their rational persuasiveness gained from an entire absence of partisanship. The joy that attended these events issued not only from seeming to discover what was the case; it issued also from a release from the coils of established ideology. In human nature you had, not an entity tainted with Adam's sin, paralyzed in guilt and awaiting atonement; you had, rather, a dark closet awaiting light from the world, a blank tablet awaiting the

2) Named after William of Ockham, the British scholastic philosopher, who died in or about the year 1349. The "razor" lops off unnecessary postulates, as in fact Copernicus did with Ptolemy's astronomy.

impress of experience, a bland susceptible tissue that wisdom (or unwisdom) might shape as it pleased.

That there was joy amounting to jubiliation we cannot doubt. Voltaire himself has expressed it to us in the thirteenth of the *Lettres Philosophiques,* which, as he entitled it, is *sur M. Locke.* There he ran through the history of philosophical definitions of the soul, scattering satire equally upon the great Greeks and the great scholastics, and not much sparing *notre Descartes.* But, arriving at Locke, he abandoned satire, and exclaimed:

> After so many thinkers had written romances about the soul, there came a sage who modestly wrote its history. Locke has revealed to man the nature of human reason as an excellent anatomist explains the parts [*ressorts*] of the human body. He uses, throughout, the torch of Physics. He sometimes is bold enough to speak affirmatively, but he is also bold enough to doubt. . . .

This Lockean doubt was not Cartesian doubt, not doubt used in search of self-evidence. It was the more usual scientific doubt, which supervenes when we have momentarily got to the end of our knowledge. Strange to say, this sort of doubt is exhilarating, partly because it gives us reason for not believing all we are told, and partly because it defines areas where we can learn. The young Voltaire, who, like the old Voltaire, was rebelliously in love with doubt, found in Locke that union of science and skepticism which introduced a new age, his own age, an age which (we may hope) will be always new.

The *Lettres Philosophiques* (also known as *Lettres Anglaises*) are an incomparably brilliant account of English thought during the hundred years between James I and Queen Anne—a model of how to write the history of philosophy. Not less instructive are the circumstances that produced this masterpiece. Voltaire had been twice in the Bastille—in 1717, when he was twenty-three, and again in 1725— once for publishing attacks on the Regent and once for a quarrel with the Chevalier de Rohan. The Chevalier, as an aristocrat, could invoke such penalties against a commoner. After the second imprisonment, Voltaire passed over into England in a kind of exile, until 1729. There he met various eminent intellectuals (Congreve, for example), and examined, like a superlative journalist, various characteristic English institutions.

The result was a propagandist work of the first order, which described, not only what English culture was in itself, but more especially what English culture meant for the progress of Europe. England was then, and long remained, the most advanced nation, with the greatest achievements in science, in economics, in governmental forms, and in the use of toleration. Voltaire had no trouble contrasting these excellences with whatever was laggard in French society. There were, for example, the Quakers, amiable and just, who would make no gesture of inferiority and would not even take their hats off in the presence of the king. These religious radicals had founded a colony in the new world, Pennsylvania, had there made with the natives the only treaty "not sworn to by oaths and not broken," and had achieved, in a very short while, "a government without priests, a population without arms, and neighbors without jealousy."[3]

The proliferation of sects in England was in itself an achievement in progress: "An Englishman, like a free man, goes to heaven by the path he prefers."[4] It was true that in order to have complete political rights and opportunities, you had to belong to the Church of England, *l'Église par excellence*. It was also true that the Church of England had retained many parts of the Catholic ritual, especially that of "paying strict attention to the collecting of dues." Nevertheless, the Church, being national, had become secularized and was to that extent free of nonsense: the English, or at any rate the Whigs, "prefer their bishops to draw their authority from Parliament rather than from the Apostles."

There were also the Presbyterians, much too dour for Voltaire's taste, who made Sunday into a time of desperate gloom, while "the rest of the nation goes to church, to the public-house, and to the brothel."[5] And there were the Unitarians, followers of the old Arian heresy, who denied the trinitarian conception of God and who "reason more geometrically than we do."[6] Thus religiously, in England of those days, a man could take his choice, within certain

3) *Quatrième Lettre*. Pennsylvanians may be surprised to learn that, according to Voltaire, their state lies *au sud de Maryland*.
4) *Cinquième Lettre*. The next two quotations are also from this letter.
5) *Sixième Lettre*.
6) *Septième Lettre*. "More geometrically" means, as we Cartesians know, "more rationally."

limits and certain penalties. How had these wonders come to pass? By means of a new religion, commerce:

> Go into the London stock exchange, a place more respectable than many courts. There you see representatives of all nations, gathered on behalf of usefulness to mankind. There the Jew, the Moham-medan, the Christian deal with one another as if they belonged to the same religion, and call a man infidel only when he is bank-rupt. There the Presbyterian trusts the Anabaptist, and the Angli-can accepts the promises of the Quaker. After leaving these free and peaceful gatherings, some go to the synagogue, others to drink. . . . If there were in England only one religion, despotism would be a threat; if there were two, they would cut each other's throat. But there are thirty, and all are content.[7]

It is plain that Voltaire, forty years old when the *Lettres* appeared, knew exactly what was the case. The French people, who had a single monarch and a single church, who, despite their own com-mercial successes, were still entangled in the web of feudal economy, were invited to contemplate a country where commerce was supreme, where the monarchy was constitutional, and where almost all re-ligions were acceptable. It will surprise no one that the *Lettres* were condemned by French authorities as "likely to inspire the most dangerous licence toward religion and the civil peace," and that they were torn up and burned by the public executioner.

But these authoritarian antics had now become silly. For, when all was said, who and what produced the *Lettres Philosophiques?* Voltaire, of course; but, in a Spinozistic sense, he was not the *causa adaequata.* If he had not gone to England, he could not have written that book; and, in order to get him to England, there was needed the insolence of the aristocrat de Rohan, the walls of the Bastille, and the tradition of cooling off by exile. In short, there was needed the whole apparatus of reactionary coercion. This apparatus, for cen-turies irresistible, now inflicted wounds upon itself, and the more it sought to prevent enlightenment, the more brightly it caused the sun to shine. Twelve years after the publication of the *Lettres,* Voltaire became, by order of Louis XV, historiographer of France.

I I

THE BOURBON MONARCHY in France claimed absolute power, but, like all other human organizations, could not of course possess it.

7) *Sixième Lettre.* My translation.

A creation of Richelieu's out of the anarchy among feudal lords, a weak edifice at first, which tottered beneath the tempest of the Fronde, it acquired the apparent solidity of a monolith during the reign of Louis XIV. This appearance was carefully cultivated and as carefully publicized, but it concealed much shrewd and flexible maneuvering. The throne maintained itself by balancing aristocrats against merchants, city against countryside, religious factions against other religious factions, and (under Louis XV and Madame de Pompadour) religion itself against the Enlightenment.

Louis XIV, through his brilliant minister Colbert, had deliberately strengthened the commercial class—politically, as a counterweight to the aristocracy; economically, as essential to the nation's wealth. Colbert lured skilled artisans from all over Europe, despite the fact that some nations made it a capital offense for artisans to migrate. There followed naval construction and colonizing efforts in India and the New World. By the early eighteenth century, France was in substance a modern nation, though not yet free from the trammels of its past. In England, the merchants had recruited part of the aristocracy into their own ranks. In France, merchants and aristocrats still confronted each other as rivals, indeed as enemies. The *annus mirabilis* 1789 was still to come.

It had been a great age—one of the four great ages (so Voltaire thought)—and its peculiar majesty lay in the fact that, under its beneficent care, "human reason in general perfected itself."[8] It was not alone a burst of intellectual genius; the government itself took interest in science and culture. Richelieu had founded the Académie Française in 1634,[9] partly to establish his influence upon culture;

8) *Le Siècle de Louis XIV*, Introduction. The other three great ages, according to Voltaire, were Greece under Pericles and Alexander, Rome under Caesar and Augustus, and Italy during the Renaissance.

9) The Académie Française developed from an informal coterie of intellectuals, and received from Richelieu, along with its official status, the task of regularizing French grammar, usage, and spelling. It still exists amid its fame. Like the Nobel awards, however, it is as notable for the hacks it has admitted and the talents it has ignored as for the geniuses who have adorned it. In 1855, Arsène Houssaye, the eminent historian, wrote a *History of the Forty-First Seat* (there are forty in the Académie), in which he listed satirically all the great writers who had never belonged. A jest of the present age, inspired perhaps by envy, is that the members are *les illustres inconnus,* the illustrious unknowns.

Colbert had reconstituted the Royal Academy of Painting and Sculpture in 1664, and had founded the Academy of Sciences in 1666. The public recognition that savants were socially important shifted prestige from clerics to secular intellectuals, and expressed a truly modern wish for the rapid development of all culture and all science whatever.

Meanwhile, as Voltaire said, "the Church, founded to teach morality, often gave itself over to politics and human passions." It suffered, in France, the same antagonisms as in England, but without the same losses; always the political circumstances allowed a compromise. The Church in France was Catholic but Gallican: nationalism guided it, the King kept his control over the appointment of bishops, and ultramontane clerics had a difficult time. A quasi-Protestant movement, which went by the name of Jansenism, was readily limited and at last suppressed. The openly Protestant party, the Hugenots,[1] were driven into death or recantation or exile after the Edict of Nantes was revoked in 1685. And behind the heretics of religion there rose the yet more alarming heretics of secular thought: forerunners, prophets, and sages of the Enlightenment.

The great reign had closed in a gloom of folly and defeat. The King's conscience, suddenly sensitive, roused ecclesiastical factions to struggle for its possession. More terrestrially, the English Marlborough stood supreme upon the battlefield. At last, in 1715, when Louis XIV lay dying after a reign of seventy-two years, there occurred a solemn and pathetic scene. The heir to the throne was his great-grandson, two intervening generations having been wiped out by smallpox. The great-grandson, five years old, was introduced into the death chamber to hear advice that, one must suppose, he could scarcely comprehend. The dying king said to the little fellow, who sat attentively upon the royal bed, "I have been too fond of war; do not copy me in that!"[2] This advice still waits for a ruler to adopt it.

After the rigors of conquest and construction, ease of enjoyment. The boy-king had as Regent during his minority the Duc d'Orléans,

---

1) From *eidgenossen*, "comrades of the oath." This bigoted persecution almost undid Colbert's labors, for the Hugenots were precisely the best and most industrious artisans in France.

2) "*J'ai trop aimé la guerre.*" Voltaire gives the speech (op. cit., Chapter XXVIII), of which he had seen the original record as historiographer of France.

a man of pleasant intelligence and relaxed morals, whom Louis XIV had once described as *un fanfaron de crimes*.[3] Under the headship (for I suppose one cannot call it leadership) of this amiable sinner, a kind of holiday set in. "Cupid dethroned Minerva," says M. Charles Kunstler, "and Mars gave place to Venus."[4] The new mode, more intimate and personal, may be seen in the paintings of Watteau, along with his piercing melancholy, which shows how little the new mode sufficed. Yet people cannot stay forever at the height of great events, and upper classes, which always have the means of enjoyment, can stay there less than others. Versailles had been, and remained, a place of monumental parade and stifling etiquette. In winter the palace was so cold that sauces froze upon the royal platters; and the fireplaces, all improperly constructed, gave forth smoke in such clouds that, traversing those vast halls, you could pass a friend without recognition.[5] It was time to live in smaller rooms, with books and friends and sweethearts of one's own choosing.

Amid this relaxation, which lasted long after the Regent was dead, ideas passed from under the old clerical monopoly into the salon and the drawing room, where ladies and gentlemen, now gathering out of wish rather than obligation, treated them as airily as virtue. The Regent had not principles enough to be a bigot, and men who fear no punishment fear no thoughts. Thus philosophy, as Descartes had intended, acclimated itself in high society; and for the next seventy years the court, the *salonnières,* and even some of the clergy went on refining, with exquisite clarity and wit, the doctrines that became their ruin.

Philosophy a familiar part of life! Here, for example, is Casanova at the bedside of Mlle. Vézian, in Paris in 1753. He is twenty-eight, she sixteen. "I'm glad," says he, "to see you on the way to becoming a philosopher." "What does one do to become that?" "One thinks." "For long?" "All one's life." "One never stops thinking, then?" "Never." And so they speculate about pleasure and the necessity of

3) "A boaster in offenses"—i.e., a man who parades his violations of the moral code. The great memorialist Saint-Simon, a loyal friend of the Duke, nevertheless observed of this description, "It was like drawing the man with a single stroke, in the most just and perfect likeness."
4) *La Vie Quotidienne sous Louis XV* (Paris: Hachette; 1953), p. 14.
5) See G. Lenotre (Théodore Gosselin), *L'Envers de Versailles,* in *Versailles au temps des Rois* (Paris: Grasset; 1934).

having no doctrinal illusions. And then—"What a philosophy lesson!" writes Casanova. "It seemed to us so sweet, and our happiness was so perfect, that when dawn came, we were still in each other's arms, and only on separating did we observe that the door had stayed open all night."[6]

Freedom of romance is hospitable to freedom of thought. Saint-Évremond, the great *esprit fort* of the seventeenth century, had already said as much in describing his imaginary general, the Maréchal d'Hoquincourt, who "loved war best of all, Mme. de Montbazon next to war, and philosophy next to Mme. de Montbazon." In the mid-eighteenth century it was said again, dispiritedly, by the Abbé Galiani, wittiest of all those wicked abbés: "The women of our time love with the head, not with the heart." Cynics like Galiani appear in all ages, but only in some are they recognized to express the general view. "One has wisdom and resignation," said Galiani, "to the extent that one has suffered. Philosophy is not the result of reason but of habituation. At most it is a kind of fear, and sometimes it is a rationalized despair." Or, as he elsewhere said, more simply, "If virtue doesn't make us happy, what the devil use is it?"[7]

Holidays grow more tedious as they grow more long: if one cannot always be working, one equally cannot always be idle. The aristocracy knew itself to be socially useless and even suspected itself to be doomed. Religion had long failed it, and it now had too much philosophy to attempt religion again. Philosophy, all too plainly aligned with commerce, held little comfort. Life seemed to have been a strange, charming, futile game; but even the futility was charming. That classicism which was so unclassical, that romance which was not yet romanticism! Those days of sleep and nights of conversation, those amours wherein the purpose was not to love but to conquer or ensnare, those exquisite jests which played with lan-

6) *Mémoires,* Bibliothèque de la Pléiade (Paris: Librairie Gallimard; 1958), Vol. I, pp. 690 and 692. My translation.
7) I take these three quotations from Karl Toth, *Woman and Rococo in France,* (Philadelphia: J. B. Lippincott Company; 1931), pp. 303, 234, 308. This book, wonderfully well translated and illustrated and produced, has the oddity that its quasi-fascist ideas about women and nations would be justly mocked by the people who adorn its pages. Toth gives the quotations in the original French; the translations are mine.

guage and did not fail of wisdom! They were all part of the new age, its elegant surface; they produced for those who could possess them, what has never since reappeared, *la douceur de vivre*.[8]

"Ah," said the actress Sophie Arnould, remembering at forty her romance with the Comte de Lauraguais at eighteen, "those were the good times. I was so unhappy."[9]

It is singular how completely the governing class deserted doctrines that had, historically, protected its rule, and how rapidly contamination spread throughout the whole society. The Church defended doctrine with all its considerable power, but the passage toward religious skepticism was almost uninterrupted. Occasional clerical victories were swallowed up in the irresistible tide. For instance, in 1678, a very remarkable man named Richard Simon, a member of the Oratoire at Paris, where Cartesian doctrines stubbornly survived, published a *Critical History of the Old Testament*. There he asserted, what his almost unique acquaintance with Oriental languages allowed him to surmise, that Moses could not possibly have written the Pentateuch, and that the Old Testament derived, not from divine inspiration, but from the genius of an entire people. Bossuet read the book on Holy Thursday, seized the edition, had all but two copies destroyed, and went on to crush Simon beneath a weight of genuine, if calamitous, eloquence.

The result was that the science of Biblical criticism did not rise again in France until the nineteenth century. Yet for all that, skepticism, increasingly armed with satire, walked far and wide. Bayle, in his Dictionary (1697), in an article on Pyrrho, the old Greek skeptic, observed that "Pyrrhonism is dangerous with respect to that divine science [theology], but it is not very dangerous with respect to Natural Philosophy or the state."[1] Bayle allowed skepticism this much range because he himself was a skeptic; and he went on to

8) Talleyrand's famous phrase and one of his few candid, heartfelt utterances. If we had in English a word which simultaneously meant "sweetness," "softness," and "elegance," we could translate the word *"douceur."*

9) Dussane, *Sophie Arnould* (Paris: Albin Michel; 1938), p. 50. This marvelous little book, by an actress of the Comédie Française, reveals Sophie as only a member of that tradition can.

1) Translation by Beller and Lee, *Selections from Bayle's Dictionary* (Princeton: Princeton University Press; 1952), p. 204. Bayle's Dictionary was one of the first attempts at an encyclopedia. "Natural Philosophy" = "the physical sciences."

suggest, with deadly delicacy, that religion had little to fear from skepticism because of the "ignorance" of men and their "natural inclination to be peremptory." The association thus suggested, between ignorance and dogmatism on the one hand and Christian belief on the other, did as much, I suppose, as direct argumentation ever did to promote unbelief. For what reasonable man will entertain notions that mark him, or appear to mark him, either an ignoramus or a bigot?

Certainly not the eighteenth-century intelligentsia. These folk grew well accustomed to taking metaphor as poetry and fable as theater. This growing up, this joyous passage from childhood to maturity, had left in total collapse one doctrine that the Church—unwisely, it would seem—had chosen to regard as essential: the possibility and actuality of miracles. There cannot have been a position feebler to defend, for if a miracle is not an impossibility, it is no miracle, but only a rarity. Moreover, the seventeenth-century thinkers had done their work so well that, afterward, miracles could be dismissed with an epigram. We will look at two examples, one from within the Church, and one from the salons.

In the year 1640, there had appeared a vast theological work, the *Augustinus,* by Cornelius Jansen, who, as Bishop of Ypres, had died three years before. As the title suggests, Jansen devoutly held Augustine's views on the depravity of human nature and the need of divine grace for even the smallest righteous exercise of human will. These views, as we know, put salvation out of the Church's power to confer, by lodging it directly with God alone. The views were consequently heretical and were harried by the Jesuits, who enforced everything laid down by the Council of Trent.[2] Jansen and his friends were so far aware of danger that, in their letters to one another, they made use of code. There were three or four code names apiece for Jansen himself, for his associate Saint-Cyran, for Augustine; code names also for the watchful Jesuits, and even for the crucial subject of discourse, the doctrine of grace. This they called

3) The Council held, rather reasonably indeed, that men can voluntarily "coöperate" with divine grace. The following proposition was therefore anathematized: "That the free will of man, moved and aroused by God, does not coöperate at all by responding to the awakening call of God. . . ." Bettenson, *Documents,* p. 369.

Pilmot or *Cumar,* or, in slightly raffish moments, *Mme. de Pilmot*
and *Mme. de Cumar.*[3]

In 1653, Pope Innocent X condemned five propositions said to be
in the *Augustinus.* There was a pause while Jansen's disciple Arnauld
(*le grand Arnauld*) argued that the five propositions, though admittedly heretical, were not to be found there. The succeeding pope,
Alexander VII, had merely to say that his predecessor had condemned them in the sense intended by Jansen. But Arnauld was
indefatigable: once, when his friends besought him to take some
rest for health's sake, he replied, "Rest? We have all eternity to rest
in!" His prodigious labors not only sustained the unequal strife but
gathered the two chief luminaries of the age, Pascal and Racine, into
the coterie of "solitaries" around the suburban convent of Port-
Royal. There, on behalf of Jansenism, Pascal wrote the incomparable
Lettres Provinciales, in which a sublime wit and an invincible intellect were exercised upon concepts that cannot be made clear.

Under the circumstances, Arnauld could only be an unsuccessful
Fabius. Port-Royal was razed by decree of Louis XIV in 1711; its
graves were violated, its nuns dispersed. The blow seemed wildly
disproportionate to its object: "the equivalent," as Sainte-Beuve says,
"of a coup d'état, which struck twenty-two women, of whom the
youngest was fifty years old and some were eighty and more."[4] But
in fact the blow fell upon a whole movement, already degenerating
from theology into mysticism. In 1713 the celebrated bull *Unigenitus*
denounced one hundred and one propositions in a Jansenist work
then forty-two years old, Père Quesnel's *Moral Reflections on the
New Testament,* as "false, captious, . . . impious, blasphemous, suspect of heresy, and savoring of heresy."[5] *Unigenitus* carried the
papacy far into French politics and with such force that the clergy
was cleft in twain for and against it. The Cardinal de Noailles, on

3) J. Orcibal, *Les Origines du Jansénisme* (Paris: J. Vrin; 1947), Vol. I, p. 617.
Jansen knew that he risked his career and perhaps his liberty and life. "This
study [of Saint Augustine]," he wrote, "has made me quite lose my ambition
for a chair at the University [of Ypres], since I must either stay silent or take
the risks of talking, and my conscience will not let me betray the known
truth." Ibid., pp. 69–70.
4) *Port-Royal,* Book VI, Chapter XIII. This magisterial work is perhaps the
classical account of a human institution in the midst of struggle.
5) Quoted by Saignac and Saint-Léger, *Louis XIV* (Paris: Presses Universitaires de France; 1949), p. 638.

his deathbed, signed two documents, "one of which accepted the Bull, while the other rejected it."[6]

Quesnel's heresy had been that of lifting private and mystical insight into a rule of faith; thus the judgment of the members was made superior to the judgment of their leaders. Effects were not slow to follow from this romantic anarchism, and their neurotic extravagance showed how painful and frustrating the struggle had been. Like all Protestant movements, Jansenism had its base among artisans and *petits bourgeois*, as expressing their industriousness and thrift. Its failures therefore heightened the discontent of a class whose members felt themselves worthy but deprived.

It happened that on the first of May, 1727, there died a Jansenist deacon, François de Pâris. He was buried in the cemetery of the Church of Saint-Médard, which lies at the foot of the rue Mouffetard, one of the oldest, most picturesque streets in Paris. This tomb at once became the scene of doubtful cures and indubitable manias. Pilgrims to the site went into convulsions, and chanted, groaned and rolled about. At last, in 1732, these spectacles reached a level of orgy in which males undertook the flagellation of females, who wholeheartedly consented to suffer. Sheer decency compelled the government to intervene. The cemetery was closed, and the grave of the deacon has since disappeared. But some wag, anonymous and immortal, affixed to the cemetery gate a placard that ran:

> God is forbid, by the King's grace,
> To work more miracles in this place.[7]

The example from the salons can be more briefly told. It is Madame du Deffand's celebrated *mot* concerning Saint Denis, the patron saint of France. A cardinal remarked, during one of her soirées, that Saint Denis, after having been beheaded, picked up his head and carried it away. This, said the cardinal, was well known, but it was less well known that the saint had walked, carrying his head, from Montmartre to the Church of Saint Denis, six miles off. "Ah, Monseigneur," said Madame du Deffand, thrusting to the heart

6) The Viscount St. Cyres, in *Cambridge Modern History*, Vol. V, p. 90.
7) The original text was: *De par le Roi, défense à Dieu/De faire miracle en ce lieu.*

with a popular adage, "in that sort of case, it's the first step that counts."[8]

Thus, at long last, theology had to pay for its primal mistake, the failure (once innocent, but now seen to be absurd) to distinguish metaphor from fact. One had only to assemble within a single brief compass all the metaphors connected, for example, with the Trinity, and it would be manifest at once that they could not possibly be statements of fact. Nothing more suited to Voltaire's talent can be imagined. Accordingly, there appeared, in 1768, a little brochure of his, entitled *The Banishment of the Jesuits from China*.[9] In it Voltaire conjures up the spectacle of a Jesuit missionary, Frère Rigolet (the name suggests the word for "joker"), trying to explain Christianity to the Emperor of China. A small part of the dialogue goes like this:

RIGOLET: . . . God changed himself into a dove, to beget a child upon the wife of a carpenter, and this child was God himself.

EMPEROR: But there we have two gods by actual count: a carpenter and a dove.

RIGOLET: Undoubtedly, Sire; but there is also a third god, who is the father of those two, and whom we always portray with a majestic beard. This is the god who ordered the dove to beget a child upon the carpenter's wife, of whom was born the carpenter-god. But basically these three gods are only one. The father engendered the son before he was in the world, the son was thereupon engendered by the dove, and the dove proceeded from the father and the son. But you can see very clearly that the dove which proceeded, the carpenter who was born of the dove, and the father who engendered the son of the dove, can be only one God, and that a man who will not believe this story ought to be burned in this world and the next.

EMPEROR: That is as clear as day. A God born in a stable, seventeen hundred and twenty-three years ago, between an ox and an ass, another God in a dovecote, a third God from whom the other two came and who is not older

---

8) I retell this story after Lytton Strachey's version in his essay on Madame du Deffand, *Biographical Essays* (London: Chatto and Windus; 1948), p. 176.
9) They had been banished from France in 1762, amid public rejoicing.

than they despite his white beard, a virgin mother—
nothing can be simpler or more sensible.[1]

It was the ruin of a whole theology. It was also the less pleasant ruin of a lovely work of art.

I I I

THESE TRIUMPHS of reason were largely negative and had to do with the stripping away of illusions. In mid-century, however, the Enlightenment produced its first positive achievement, the *Encyclopédie* of Diderot and D'Alembert. No other intellectual event in history displays at once so much patience under labor and courage under harassment. Mingled with these remarkable virtues was a political skill of the first order, so that the project, though twice suppressed and always collapsing, rose irresistibly to its grand result: seventeen volumes of text and eleven volumes of engravings. When this was done, the French (indeed, the European) bourgeoisie could look at its work, as God at His creation, and find it good.

The intent was to set forth, briefly but adequately, and in as many volumes as might be required, all human knowledge on all subjects of interest. The editors valued theory, but not at the expense of practice. Indeed, those volumes of marvelous plates, which visually explain a vast number of techniques, show how much emphasis fell upon the practical. This emphasis, which had some of its origin in freemasonry, perhaps did most to save the project. The Encyclopedia became indispensable, the living monument of man's wish "to see everything and guess at nothing."[2]

The aim and amplitude of the project threw reactionaries into instant alarm. For if there came to be a public repository of *knowledge* (however interspersed with error), the old myths, the tedious doctrines laden with illusion, would drop away forever. A whole social class, the merchants and the artisans, would draw from that repository constant strength and understanding, refining their skills as they learned to know the world. A shift in power might well follow, as in fact it did; and the old ideologists would confront, not merely an enlightened intelligentsia, but an enlightened people.

1) *Dialogues Philosophiques,* edited by Raymond Naves (Paris: Garnier Frères; 1939), pp. 222–23. My translation.
2) D'Alembert's phrase, *Encyclopédie, Discours Préliminaire, Deuxième Partie:* "*. . . tout voir et ne rien supposer.*"

The chief reactionary spokesmen were, as always, the Jesuits. They had already produced their own encyclopedia, the *Dictionnaire de Trévoux;* and in their magazine, the *Journal de Trévoux,* they kept up a steady fire of defamation and incitement. The Encyclopedists returned the fire from within their great collaborative work. Diderot, explicating the verb *pardonner,* remarked, "Some men, who produced a silly work which imbecile editors botched further, have never been able to *pardon* us for having planned a better one. These enemies to all good have subjected us to every kind of persecution. We have seen our honor, our fortune, our liberty, our life endangered within a few months' time. They would have *pardoned* us a crime; they could not *pardon* us a good deed."[3] And in the article entitled "Offense," Diderot took his own work as example: "The light of truth gives particular *offense* to certain men who are accustomed to darkness. Offering them light is like introducing a ray of sunshine into a nest of owls: it only hurts their eyes and makes them squawk."[4] This deep thrust Diderot covered with a gently cynical epigram: "To live happily, one must *offend* nobody, and be *offended* at nothing. This, however, is very difficult, for the first requires too much attentiveness, and the second too much insensibility."

Thus the *Encyclopédie* bore within its own text the flame and smoke of battle. It attempted, indeed, but could not maintain, the sobriety and calm that distinguish, a little tediously, our modern encyclopedias. Chances abounded in the subject matter to strike the enemy, and, where these were absent, there was always the passion for improving things. The public mind was to be set right on the nature of experimental science, on the sources of political authority, on the theory of taxation, and on the charms of representative government.[5] Similar disturbances would perhaps occur in our day, if the Britannica were to be revised from a Marxist point of view.

At its beginning, however, the project was very modest. A certain Parisian printer, André-François LeBreton, had the idea of publish-

---

3) Excerpted in J. Lough, *The Encyclopédie of Diderot and D'Alembert* (Cambridge: Cambridge University Press; 1954), p. 171. My translation. Italics are in the original as indicating a use of the word under discussion.

4) Ibid., p. 170. This image, and almost the same language, is used in the article *"Aigle."*

5) See respectively the following articles: *"Experimental"* by D'Alembert, *"Autorité Publique"* by Diderot, *"Impôt"* by the Chevalier de Jaucourt, and *"Représentants"* by Baron d'Holbach.

ing a French translation of Ephraim Chambers' *Cyclopedia or Universal Dictionary of the Arts and Sciences,* which had appeared in 1728. To this end he joined with an Englishman named Mills and a German named Sellius, but the association collapsed in fisticuffs, when LeBreton punched Mills in the stomach and twice cracked him over the head with a cane.[6]

In October of 1745, LeBreton acquired three new associates, all booksellers, who in their turn presented to him a brilliant young man, thirty-two years old, Denis Diderot. Under Diderot's soaring imagination the whole project changed. Instead of a mere translation from the English, the proposed encyclopedia was to be a national monument, a work primarily of French genius. Diderot already knew most of the intellectuals, who gathered once a week at Madame du Deffand's, there to celebrate the clarities of enlightenment. All these would respond as patriots and men of reason—with, as it turned out, one immortal enemy of reason, to whom were assigned the articles on music, Jean-Jacques Rousseau.

The booksellers had chosen wisely: Diderot was precisely the man. Yet if they had foreseen all the perils of the project, they might have preferred a man less bold and less bohemian. The mistake, we may well believe, would have been fatal: the *Encyclopédie* would scarcely have excelled the *Dictionnaire de Trévoux.* It chanced that Diderot's daring was profoundly modified by a gift for politics, and his bohemianism by a sort of principled personal charm. Since he was, of all men, most obviously free from malice, he could not without absurdity be suspected of evil intent; since his ideas were both benign and arresting, he persuaded where others could only protest. Such the Chancellor d'Aguessau found him, when he came to ask the government's consent to the project. But d'Aguessau took care to appoint censors for the articles on theology, metaphysics, and politics.

Diderot was, as perhaps a son should always be, loyal and rebellious toward his father. The old man, Didier, was a cutler at Langres, a specialist in surgical instruments, who amassed, with sober industry, a small fortune. Denis was intended for the priesthood, a vocation for which he was singularly unfitted. He escaped to Paris, where he lived precariously on a tutor's wages, got himself one or two mis-

6) Pierre Grosclaude, *Un Audacieux Message: l'Encyclopédie* (Paris: Nouvelles Editions Latines; 1951), p. 25. Thus Mills testified at a judicial hearing.

tresses, and married a mild virago.[7] During the 1740s he produced a series of anonymous works, all of them known by the police to be his, by reason of two spies, the printer's wife and the curé of his parish. The police, indeed, have left, in their abundant records, the public (or at least the official) image of almost every great man of the time. What they had to say about Diderot was that he was *un garçon plein d'esprit, mais extrêmement dangereux:* "a very bright fellow but extremely dangerous."[8]

Two of these anonymous works are notable because they were criticisms (cautious, to be sure) of Church and State. The *Pensées Philosophiques* (1746) proposed a sort of popular religion, free of organizational connections. God was greater than any church or creed. *Élargissez Dieu!* cried Diderot, using the verb for a release of prisoners: "Let God out!"[9] And the second work, *Les Bijoux Indiscrets* (1748), a novel in the gently erotic style then fashionable, wherein certain jewels spoke out the wearer's inner thoughts, seemed to be, and probably was, a satire upon king and court.

Meanwhile, during the decade, the War of the Austrian Succession—a moment within the long contest between France and England for commercial supremacy—drew to its discouraging close. It had been as expensive as fruitless, and the government, casting about for new sources of revenue, decided at last to tax the clergy. The tax was eventually withdrawn, after such howls as come only from men who are pious and privileged. But the times remained uneasy, the populace was restive, and the government began curbing intellectuals by frequent use of *lettres de cachet.*[1] This genial device, less terrible though not less terrifying than the old habits of inquisition, deserves some comment.

In theory, the French king was father of the French family, and, on patriarchal principles, his will was absolute. Other parents could appeal to him, and he would put refractory children in the Bastille. Thus, for example, the young Duc de Fronsac was shut up for "insufficiently loving his wife," and a greengrocer, the widow

7) Madame Diderot was twice arrested for quarreling in public.
8) This highly accurate description will be found in Diderot's *"fiche"* or police record, compiled on January 1, 1748. *Nouvelles Acquisitions Françaises,* No. 10781.
9) § XXVI.
1) I.e., letters issued under the king's seal.

Bernard, was able to immure her forty-year-old daughter in the women's prison of La Salpetrière. Insensibly the practice enlarged itself. On March 3, 1733, the young Comtesse d'Uzès had her valet jailed, by *lettre de cachet,* for amorous assault. She had summoned him to curl her hair the previous evening; her open peignoir laid bare objects of irresistible enchantment. "Faith," wrote the valet later, "the flesh of a Christian is feeble, and I found that out on the spot."[2] Happily, the Comtesse, recovering wisdom, had the victim freed.

By such custom it came to pass that, on the twenty-third of July, 1749, Louis XV, at Compiègne, signed a *lettre de cachet* which ran as follows:

> M. le Marquis du Châtelet: This letter instructs you to receive into my Château of Vincennes le Sieur Diderot, and to hold him there until some new order on my part. Further, I pray that God may have you, M. le Marquis du Châtelet, in his holy keeping.[3]

Charming, this piety with which imprisonment was conferred. Behold, then, our philosopher-encyclopedist, our Socrates-Diderot (as Voltaire called him), stretched shattered and weeping upon his cot in the old medieval donjon at Vincennes. After a week of anxiety, he came forth to answer questions by Berryer, Lieutenant of Police. "Did you write such-and-such, or such-and-such?" Berryer, more popularly known as Beurrier ("Butter Dish"), was quite aware that Diderot had in fact written them all. Diderot, partly in hope of protecting the printer and partly in naïve ignorance of police skill, denied authorship of any. Berryer, looking into these guileless prevarications as into a pool of clearest water, remanded him to his stony cell, and set about waiting for what time should accomplish.

Time—something less than a month of it—produced a letter from Diderot to Berryer, addressing him as "my worthy protector" and admitting authorship of three of the books, "intemperances of intellect which escaped me."[4] He still denied the others. It was not all that Berryer wanted, but it deserved some reward. Diderot was released from the medieval keep and lodged in the pleasant buildings that LeVau had designed for Mazarin. He had freedom to roam the

2) Quoted by G. Lenotre, *Ordres du Roi,* in op. cit., p. 197.
3) I have made this translation from a photostat of the original *lettre.*
4) *Nouvelles Acquisitions Françaises,* No. 1311, fol. 18.

park and to receive friends. Rousseau, walking thither one day, read, as he walked, the *Mercure de France* and saw in it the announcement of an essay contest upon the question "Whether the revival of the arts and sciences has contributed to the purification of morals." What, he asked Diderot, if a man were to write an essay saying no? Diderot, whose views were precisely contrary, told him to go ahead. The consequent literary explosion broke open a new age. For Rousseau's essay, wherein he attributed to the arts and sciences the whole depravity of civilized man, won the prize and prepared a revolution.

One day in mid-September, Madame Diderot brought to Vincennes a long letter from Denis's father, the honest cutler of Langres. Denis had written him from prison, sparing no tears over the sadness of fate and asking money for the family's support. The reply, full of quaint spellings, had a kind of grandeur: the nobility of a father whose disapproving doubts of a scapegrace son were profoundly modified by paternal love. Old Didier thought that the King was surely right, that the police had perhaps acted properly, and that Denis might thus be led to write "some Christian work in your own style." And then, with an adorable sense of climax: "Such a work will draw down the blessings of heaven and keep you in my good graces."[5] He enclosed a draft upon a Paris banker for one hundred fifty *livres,* and signed himself for what in truth he was, "Your affectionate father, Diderot."

Meanwhile, the syndicate of publishers had all along been busy. They had invested eighty thousand *livres* in the project, and this they stood to lose if the editor remained absent. Within a week of Diderot's arrest, they were petitioning for the release of the prisoner —"the one man," as they said in a risky metaphor, "who holds the key."[6] Their pressure was soon decisive. The government had wished only to cool Diderot off and to show its own power. This intent achieved, there came, at the beginning of November, a second *lettre de cachet*—for the same kind of document that got you in could get

5) Quoted by André Billy, *Vie de Diderot* (Paris: Flammarion; 1932), p. 94. In Vincennes, Diderot had the daily maintenance allowance set for the average tradesman, four *livres.* Cardinals and princes of the blood got 50; marshals of France, peers, dukes, and bishops, 36; ministers of state, 24; and so on down the hierarchy. Ibid., p. 83. "Everybody" went to the Bastille.
6) *Supplique des libraires associés au Comte d'Argenson,* Archives de la Bastille, No. 11671.

you out—ending Diderot's imprisonment. He jolted homeward in a hackney coach, laden with bundles, packets, and portfolios—all memoranda and manuscripts of the *Encyclopédie*. Except for that month in the "stone-box" (as Didier had called it), Diderot had pursued his tasks as editor; and the government, which wished to favor learning while spanking savants, had allowed him the necessary materials.

Nineteen months later, the first volume appeared. It contained D'Alembert's magisterial preface, a definitive statement of all that the Enlightenment believed, well worthy Raynal's eulogy in *Les Nouvelles Littéraires* (June 28, 1751): ". . . one of the most philosophical, important, luminous, precise, compact pieces we have in our language, and one of the best written." Starting with the Lockean maxim that all knowledge originates in sensations, D'Alembert proceeded to demonstrate the interconnection (*filiation*) of the sciences and their importance for practical techniques, wherein lay their true social value. "Contempt for the mechanical arts," he wrote, "seems to have affected even their inventors. The names of these benefactors of mankind are almost unknown, whereas the destroyers of the race—that is to say, the conquerors—are known to everyone. Yet it is perhaps among the artisans that one must look for sagacity, patience, and resourcefulness."[7] Encyclopedists did not side with the ruling class.

Volume I covered A to AZYMITES. In those articles the Encyclopedist faith was not slow to appear. "Adorer" (by Diderot) asserted that "the manner of *adoring* the true God ought never to be separated from reason, because God is the creator of reason and wished men to use it even with regard to himself." "Agnus Scythicus" (also by Diderot), discussing a mythical plant of Asia, dwells at length upon the credibility of testimony, with obvious implications for miracles asserted by the Church. "Aigle" (Diderot again), observing that the Romans believed the eagle to be Jupiter's bird, points out that credulity leads to superstition; then gracefully and cautiously concludes, "A hundred times happy is the people to whom religion offers only true things for belief. . . . Such is our religion, wherein philosophy need but follow its own rationality to reach our altars."

"Ame" ("Soul") shows how closely bound the soul is to the body, and refers the reader to later articles on the brain and cerebellum.

7) *Discours Préliminaire, Première Partie.*

"Athéisme" (by the Abbé Yvon) is carefully orthodox, but brings the whole argument down by acknowledging the political uses of religion: "Atheism publicly professed is punishable by natural law, because religion is the only effective guarantee of the power of the sovereign." "Autorité Publique" (Diderot) asserts that government derives its just powers from the consent of the governed.

Interspersed with these and other articles were certain culinary discussions—for Diderot was, as you might expect of a Frenchman, a gastronome. "Abricot" gives us recipes for apricot marmalade and apricot paste, both plundered from a cookbook by Chomel. But neither these household hints nor a careful orthodoxy in articles most likely to be suspect could conceal the heretical and even "subversive" tenor of the work. As public controversy grew, the *Nouvelles Littéraires* became less laudatory. Derogatory verses circulated in print (as the custom was), and Diderot was made to say, in one of them, "I know everything and believe nothing."[8] The *Journal de Trévoux* screamed month by month, alleging (quite truly) that Diderot had plagiarized some of the *Dictionnaire's* articles—some, indeed, of its own plagiarizings. And Jean-François Boyer, former tutor to the Dauphin and present chaplain to the Dauphine, interested the King in the inferences to be drawn from the doctrine of government by consent.

When, in October of 1751, the second volume (B to CEZIMBRA) appeared, the crisis was at hand. It took an unexpected and even trivial form, but it was, upon the whole, the most revealing philosophical event of the eighteenth century. It was the affair of the Abbé de Prades.

I V[9]

ON NOVEMBER 18, 1751, a young bachelor of theology appeared before the Sorbonne to be examined upon a doctoral dissertation. He

8) Grosclaude, op. cit., p. 53. The quatrain follows:
  Je suis bon encyclopédiste,
  Je connais le mal et le bien,
  Je suis Diderot à la piste;
  Je connais tout et ne crois rien!
9) Most of this section has appeared as part of my essay, "The Ordeal of the Abbé de Prades," in the magazine *Mainstream*, Vol. 12, no. 5. It is reproduced here by kind permission of the editors.

was (so the police described him) "tall, thin, dark, with long hair and a pockmarked face: an intelligent fellow, lively and a little mad."[1] He had dedicated his dissertation to *Jerusalem Coelesti,* the Heavenly Jerusalem; and, in a Latin which the Jesuit Father Brotier described as "a swollen tumor,"[2] he had undertaken to answer the question, "What being was it God breathed the breath of life upon?" Or, in other words, what is human nature?

The Sorbonne was in those days the Faculty of Theology, and called itself therefore the Sacred Faculty. It listened, questioned, approved, and made a doctor of the bachelor, the young Abbé de Prades. But some months later, after several intervenient and agonized sessions, it denounced the candidate and revoked the degree. It had found in the dissertation, a little belatedly and under official goading, ten propositions which it declared to be "false, rash, harmful to Catholic theologians . . . erroneous, blasphemous, materialistic, dangerous to society and the public peace . . ." and many things more.

Then the blows fell fast: a denunciatory charge from the Archbishop of Paris, a prelate unusually prolific in this kind; a charge from de Prades's own bishop, Monseigneur de Montauban, lamenting that "one of our diocesans has betrayed his God, his religion, his country, and his bishop"; a Pastoral Instruction from Caylus, the Jansenist Bishop of Auxerre, pointing out the candidate's "well-known associations with the authors of the Encyclopedia." And there was also the warrant issued by the Parlement of Paris, on February 11, 1752, for de Prades's arrest.

By this time, however, the Abbé was safely sequestered upon the estate of the Marquis d'Argenson. Thence he proceeded to Holland, and from Holland, under Voltaire's sponsorship, to Prussia, where Frederick the Great protected such thinkers as troubled other governments than his own. Meanwhile the turmoil in Paris brought about the first suspension of the *Encyclopédie.*

During the early months of exile, de Prades composed an apologia in three volumes, the third of which was written by Diderot. The other volumes set forth with much dignity and candor the surprised

---

1) De Prades's *"fiche"* is in the Bibliothèque Nationale, *Nouvelles Acquisitions Françaises,* No. 10783.

2) *Examen de l'apologie de M. l'abbé de Prades* (1753), p. 5. Quoted in Franco Venturi, *La Jeunesse de Diderot,* translated from Italian into French by Juliette Bertrand (Paris: Skira; n.d.), p. 200.

pain, the outraged innocence, of a philosopher assailed by rogues. Was it his fault, for example, that his supervisor, having approved the dissertation without reading it, thereupon called loudly for its condemnation? Or that the Jesuits, seeing a chance to smite the *philosophes,* were "first and noisiest precisely because they were not offended"?[3] Or that the Jansenists could strike Jesuits, *philosophes,* and the Sorbonne too?

The Sorbonne, for its part, was profoundly embarrassed. It had been, from the thirteenth century, a kind of tribunal where the great doctrines of Christendom were heard and argued, confirmed or over-thrown. Some occasions, indeed, had been tempestuous: of one of these an eyewitness said that the great hall resembled a forest shaken in violent storm, the crash of branches mingling with the howls of savage beasts.

With the poor pockmarked Abbé, the Sorbonne had exceptional reason to howl, for it had listened to heresies without recognizing them to be such, and it had awarded the young heretic a doctoral degree. The cause, cried the Sacred Faculty, was not our sloth but his cleverness. "Impiety no longer restricts itself to invading private homes; it has tried to slip into the very sanctuary of religion, there to take revenge if haply it may spread some drop or other of its poison."[4]

How was it possible for de Prades to write heresy, and the Sorbonne to hear it, all of them unaware? Simply that, with a kind of innocence, they examined the question on its own merits, apart from any organizational demands. It is a tendency to which thinkers are prone, because it is what they really should always be doing. In organizational life, however, when this sort of thing happens, the leaders may remind the thinkers, a little sharply, which side their bread is buttered on. De Prades and the Sorbonne alike were infected with the Lockean philosophy, and, more remotely, with the Cartesian. They would have continued so, if Christophe de Beaumont, the Archbishop of Paris, had not intervened.

What were de Prades's ten heresies? I give here, in condensed form, what I take to be their sense; the original Latin text, with an English translation, appears in the Appendix.

3) This is Diderot's jest, in Volume III of the *Apologie de M. l'Abbé de Prades.*
4) *Censure de la Faculté de Théologie de Paris contre une Thèse appelée Majeure Ordinaire* (1752).

(1) That human knowledge originates in sensation.

(2) That men formed society in order to satisfy their private self-interest, and that they got the idea of virtue from suffering one another's vices.

(3) That true religion is simply a higher development of ethics.

(4) That it is characteristic of a religion to be boastful of miracles, oracles, and martyrs.

(5) That the testimony of witnesses tells more about the witnesses than about the facts, and that its value must be estimated by observing the conflict of human interests on a large scale.

(6) That the systems of chronology discernible in the Pentateuch are probably not from Moses.

(7) That Moses based the moral economy on merely temporal rewards and punishments.

(8) That the cogency of miracles as proofs of a divine Creator have been much weakened by the obscurities of the scholastics.

(9) That the cures worked by Jesus very much resemble those of Esculapius.

(10) That the reasonings of the Church Fathers are subject to the usual tests of logic.

If we take Catholic theology as orthodox, there can be no doubt that these ten assertions are one and all heretical. They show the powerful influence of Descartes, Hobbes, and Locke, and they show it in a series of specific questions around which controversy raged. In essence, they all assume (and, by assuming, hint) that supernatural things are poetry and not science, and that the Church has no more claim to authority than any other historical organization. Let us then examine the derivation, for it is a prime example of philosophy's effect upon organizational strife.

The Cartesian ideal of knowledge is a system of sentences entirely free from contradiction and following from one or more sentences self-evidently true. The Lockean ideal is an immediate, direct awareness of the things being described. Each of these ideals conflicts with the supernatural; together, they probably extinguish it.

If, for example, the Cartesian test is supreme, then tests by authority or by mystical insight are less valid. It follows that we shall want to examine critically, and not accept obediently, what the Fathers, and the Schoolmen, and especially the witnesses of miracles have had to say. Thus wishing, we arrive at once at Numbers 5, 8, and 10 of the Abbé's heresies.

Again: in the very idea of miracles there is a contradiction which logic must either outlaw or be outlawed by. No event can be a miracle unless it is an event which is impossible, and in an effort to show that the impossible can happen, logic must either destroy the notion or destroy itself. If we undertake to save logic, then the definition of miracles slides away from the strictly impossible toward the unusual and rare. In this view, the cures worked by Jesus look like those of Esculapius (Number 9). For that matter, magic in prophecy and performance, a little comparison shows, is something every religion brags about (Number 4).

But suppose we desert logic, being unable to control it, and defiantly assert that there are miraculous events anyway, and that they originate in the supernatural. The result is not happier. For how do we know whether any given event is the work of God or Satan? Tertullian, indeed, had held that Satan, being "God's ape," can imitate everything God does. "Demons do harm," said this Father in a passage de Prades was condemned for quoting, "then they suggest remedies, and, having ceased harming, are thought to have been cured." It is very artful of them, and it renders permanently doubtful whether, if there *are* events of supernatural origin, they have the supernatural origin that one wants.

De Prades, at any rate, had tried to strike out one of the alternatives by saying that Satan is bound by natural law and hence cannot work miracles. But the Church needed Satan to account for the miracles of its competitors. Moreover, as a matter of ideology, if Satan is bound by natural law, then Satan is very likely not supernatural. The once transcendental source of evil sinks downward toward the natural world, dragging, it seems, the source of goodness after it. Ethics is on the point of being acclimated in space and time —which is where de Prades placed it in Heresies 2 and 3. No wonder that the Sacred Faculty, its memory spurred by superiors, asserted such views to be "subversive of the foundations of the Christian religion."

So far the Cartesian revolution. The Lockean lies in a belief, once inflammatory, that the truly known is the immediately sensed. Now, all that is immediately sensed is sensed in space and time. No ingenuity of science, no refinement of laboratory, no cloud chamber or cyclotron, has been able, or, it seems, will be able, to present to our view a single one of the celebrated supernatural entities. It follows that our knowledge (if such it be) of things supernatural is derivative from our knowledge of things natural. The last is made first: instead of theology's supplying the postulates for science, science supplies the postulates for theology. And rather lamely, too.

What then becomes of the good old Soul, with its inborn knowledge of God, immortality, right reason, and right conduct? Where upon that blank tablet or within that dark closet can one find the stain of Adam's sin? If, as de Prades said, our knowledge "sprouts from sensations like branches from a tree trunk," does not ethics become mere sociology, and theology mere comparative religion—that is to say, the anthropological analysis of legend and ritual? The conclusions follow, and they are Heresies 2, 3, 6, and 7.

> In speaking of the creation of man [wrote the testy Bishop of Auxerre] according to the Scriptures and orthodox doctrine, one could not avoid mentioning the gift of grace, the justice and love of God . . . man's disobedience, its consequences, the remedy, the matter of the Incarnation. . . . What Christian ought not to want these basic truths recalled to his mind?

I do not know about the "ought," but it is historically the case that in the pellucid void of empiricist consciousness all these lovely wonders were lost.

Upon de Prades's first heretical sentence the Sacred Faculty pronounced the damning words *materialismo faventes,* "inclining toward materialism." And the Sacred Faculty was not mistaken: "sensations" are the pitiful rubbish of Father Adam's soul. Doubtless they are themselves supernatural entities, concealing (from empiricists, anyway) events in the brain and nervous system. But the veil of sense is the seventh and last of Salome's veils. When that is gone, you may look with joy or with horror, but you will be seeing the world as it is.

This was the way that science went, the way on which de Prades set his brief, adventurous steps. In the great contests between mind and government men do what they can and as they can. The little Abbé, when he sacrificed a doctorate to freedom, did perhaps enough for one lifetime. He seems, at any rate, to have decided so, for in 1754 he recanted his "errors," saying he had not enough life left in which to atone. His work on the Truth of Religion, with a preface (so Diderot proposed) reciting his calamities, was never written. He sank into a canonry at Glogau, then into an archdeaconship; and he left a translation of Tacitus, which has been lost.

He is [wrote Voltaire when the Abbé first reached Potsdam] the drollest heresiarch ever excommunicated. He is gay, he is amiable, he laughs at his misfortune. If men like Arius, Huss, Luther, and Calvin had had his temperament, the Conciliar Fathers, instead of burning them, would have taken them by the hand and danced round with them in a ring.[5]

But in 1759, when the recantation and the case were cold, Diderot, the brave, the never-yielding, had a different thing to say of Jean-Martin de Prades:

What a detestable man! Unfortunately there are many like him.[6]

And, unfortunately, there are.

V

ON FEBRUARY 7, 1752, Louis XV withdrew the privilege he had granted for publication of the Encyclopedia, because of what he called its tendency to "destroy the royal authority, set up the spirit of independence and revolt, and, under obscure and equivocal language, to raise the foundations of error, of corruption of morals, of irreligion, and of unbelief."[7] The misfortunes of the Abbé de Prades (who had contributed to Volume II the article "Certitude") seemed to have involved the whole project in ruin. Yet, during the next two years, the number of subscribers to the Encyclopedia rose from two thousand to three thousand, and the third and fourth volumes appeared. A strange turn of events, which showed the fluidity of French politics and an ebb of power among the *infâmes*.[8]

It happened that, in those years, all printed material lay under the administration of a wise and honest man, Malesherbes, who had pondered the question of censorship from a liberal point of view. Once, when D'Alembert asked him to suppress certain remarks of

5) Letter of August 19, 1752. Quoted by Venturi, op. cit., p. 227.
6) Letter to Sophie Volland, July 15, 1759.
7) Quoted by Grosclaude, op. cit., p. 68.
8) Voltaire's celebrated name for the reactionary religious party (= "scoundrels," approximately).

Fréron, one of the most vocal adversaries, he replied, by letter, "I distinguish sharply between what I don't like or even what I personally disapprove and what I ought to prevent as an official of the government. My principles are that literary criticism is in general permissible, and that every piece of criticism which is solely concerned with the work criticized, and in which the author is judged solely according to his work, is literary criticism."[9]

He declined, therefore, to suppress Fréron's articles, but he also saved the Encyclopedia. When, following the revocation of privilege, he was ordered to confiscate all the relevant material, so that the editors could not use it, he quietly told Diderot, "Send everything to me; no one will look for it here."[1] And so, for some months, the Encyclopedia slumbered in Malesherbes's own offices.

If Diderot's political skill lay in an adroit boldness of attack, Malesherbes's lay in an administrator's calculation of the possibilities. The two skills modified each other most advantageously. Encyclopedist tactics were always slightly unscrupulous. For example, it appears that the first censors read in manuscript the articles assigned them, and that, afterward, the articles appeared in print in their original form, just as if there had been no censors at all. Also the editors had the habit of sending articles to censors other than the ones appointed for those particular subjects. Malesherbes perceived that this much unreliability would terminate the project. He therefore required that thenceforth the *printed* text be initialed by the appropriate censor.

Meanwhile the King himself grew favorable again, under the influence of Madame de Pompadour, who detested the bigots. This much-maligned lady, by no means a mere mistress and still less *une grande amoureuse,* whose brother gave to France some of the early benefits of city planning, was in fact a partisan of the Enlightenment. Her relations with the King, piously winked at and as piously denounced, introduced much social vision into governmental policy. It was as if history used every means to move forward. Perhaps, at

---

9) Grosclaude, op. cit., p. 75: *"Mais je mets une grande différence entre ce qui me déplaît et même ce que je désapprouve comme particulier, et ce que je dois empêcher comme homme public. Mes principes sont qu'en général, la critique littéraire est permise et que toute critique qui n'a pour object que le livre critiqué, et dans laquelle l'auteur n'est jugé que d'après son ouvrage, est critique littéraire."*

1) This story is told by Diderot's daughter, Madame Angélique Vandeul, in her *Mémoires.*

her death, she expressed the truest estimate of the old order, its repetitious mechanics, its indifference to people. For, while she sat dying (it was too painful to lie down), the priest who had given her absolution fidgeted, fidgeted, wishing to be gone. "One moment, Father," said Madame de Pompadour, "and we'll go out together."

By the year 1757, six volumes had appeared, and the number of subscribers had risen to four thousand. Then lightning struck again. In January, a man named Damiens tried to assassinate the King. He seems to have been alone in the enterprise, and he died for it, amid horrible tortures, in a public execution. Nevertheless the bigots, whose only arm was defamation, tried to connect Damiens's act with the doctrines of the Encyclopedists. The libels redoubled, and Moreau, librarian to the Queen, wrote two fanciful pieces, by no means devoid of wit, in which he depicted the Encyclopedists as a savage tribe, named Cacouacs, living on the forty-eighth parallel. The name stuck, and for some months the Encyclopedists, who had been everything else under the sun, found themselves savages.

In November, the seventh volume (FOANG to GYTHIUM) appeared. Within this compass fell D'Alembert's article on the city of Geneva. Now, Geneva was, of course, a Protestant city, the seat of what had been Calvin's ecclesiastical republic. D'Alembert, enraptured by his subject, grew, as he wrote, at first incautious and at last indiscreet. The lake was lovely, the city splendid, the citizens brave and self-reliant—and the clergy! Well, the clergy had modest incomes and desired no more; their morals were exemplary, their relations with one another amiable. They tended, indeed, to be Socinian,[2] and thus to regard Jesus Christ as a man rather than a God. Worship was simple and economical, there being no candles, no ornaments, no images.[3] D'Alembert thought this rather a loss to art. He also thought that the singing and the hymn texts might be improved, and he lamented the prohibition of theaters and plays.

Nevertheless, it was quite plain that he intended to compare

2) From Sozzini (1539–1604), an Italian rationalist theologian.
3) This was a favorite theme both of Protestantism and of the Enlightenment —namely, the expensiveness of Catholicism. Diderot, in the article "Pain Bénit" (the Holy Wafer), calculated all the candles burned and all the wafers swallowed in France of a Sunday, and suggested that the money thus spent could do a great deal for the poor.

French Catholicism unfavorably with Genevan Protestantism, and French morals with Genevan morals. He summed up his joy in a peroration:

> We shall perhaps devote insufficiently large articles to very great monarchies. To the philosopher, however, the republic of the bees is as interesting as the history of vast empires, and it may be that only in small states can one find the model of a perfect political administration. If religion forbids us to think that Genevans have effectively worked out their happiness in the other world, reason obliges us to think that they are supremely happy in this.

The effect was prodigious and wildly divisive. The Genevan clergy fell upon D'Alembert for calling them Socinian (which indeed they were not). Rousseau, a native of Geneva and a stubborn patriot, thundered at him for complaining about the prohibition of theaters![4] Plays corrupt morals, said Rousseau in his best savoyard-vicar style, and stormed out of the Encyclopedia. The *infâmes,* for their part, were hot with rage, for D'Alembert, with historical accuracy, had described them as more laggard than the Protestants, who were, in their turn, more laggard than the men of the Enlightenment. Thus D'Alembert, who had thus far not been personally attacked at all, found himself assailed by comrades, friends, and enemies all at once.

Now, D'Alembert was an intellectual of purest ray serene: he was earnest, honest, humane, and timid. He had the fatal weakness of intellectuals, a love of present reputation, which consists almost entirely in a wish not to be spoken ill of. Suddenly everybody was speaking ill of him. It was too much. He resigned. And thus he missed sharing the ultimate victory—exactly as he missed winning Mademoiselle de l'Espinasse, whom he loved from a near distance for many years. That febrile and passionate lady, who died in the blaze of two consecutive romances, gave him nothing but the legacy of her correspondence, wherein he discovered, for the first time, that she had all along loved someone else.

The frenzies aroused by Volume VII brought a second withdrawal of privilege by the government. Diderot was now alone as editor, and the printers were further committed financially, since they owed the subscribers either the forbidden volumes or a return of money. In this extremity, two capitalistic events saved everything:

4) In the *Lettre sur les Spectacles.*

the printers were able to win some respite for the adjustment of their business affairs, and the Jesuits were expelled from France.

A certain Jesuit, Père Lavalette, had established a business in Martinique, which prospered for a time but collapsed when the British captured some of its ships and cargo. The firm owed money to bankers in Marseilles, who thereupon (in 1762) sued the Society of Jesus for recovery. The Society defended itself, characteristically, with technicalities: it said that Père Lavalette had been excluded from the Order. This specious defense not only failed before the Parlement of Paris, but unloosed the accumulated wrath of a century. Jansenists now took revenge for the bull *Unigenitus* and for years of devotional life half underground. Merchants and artisans fell upon their chief ideological foe, and the King, willing to be rid of a potent pressure group, declared, in 1764, that "the Society should no longer exist in France."[5]

These events Diderot celebrated in his Encyclopedia article "Jésuite," with explanations so cogent that modern historians can repeat them without acknowledgment.[6] It was, in truth, the fall of a redoubtable enemy, and no power remained that could prevent the Encyclopedia. The last ten volumes of text appeared in 1765, the eleven volumes of plates between 1762 and 1772. Enlightenment shone down on Europe, never to be dimmed until the rise of fascism; and Diderot was left to smile at the little odious adversaries and at the friends who had fallen away.

There was, however, a final sting. Just before the last ten volumes simultaneously appeared, Diderot discovered that the printer, Le-Breton, had slyly expurgated large portions of the text. He had, for example, removed from Diderot's article on the Saracens the following statement (oblique but not unclear) of the Enlightenment's whole essence:

5) A decree of the Parlement of Paris had already suppressed the Society, August 6, 1762. The royal edict of 1764 was a sort of confirmation. Thus some historians date the suppression as of 1762, and others as of 1764.

6) E.g., Philippe Sagnac, *La Fin de l'Ancien Régime* (Paris: Presses Universitaires de France; 1947), p. 121. Diderot had said, among other things, that "there was no one left among them [the Jesuits] of any great talent: no more poets, philosophers, orators, scholars, writers of merit. Accordingly, the Society was despised." Sagnac says, "The Jesuits no longer had great preachers, illustrious writers, celebrated savants; for some time previously, their influence upon society was on the decline."

It is a general observation that religion declines as philosophy grows. You may reach what conclusions you like either against the usefulness of philosophy or the truth of religion; but I can tell you that the more philosophers there are in Constantinople, the fewer pilgrims there will be to Mecca.

"You have driven a dagger into my heart," wrote Diderot to LeBreton, "and the sight of you can only drive it deeper."[7] Nevertheless, he saw him because he had to see him, and only refused Madame LeBreton's invitations to dine. Diderot sacrificed everything for the project, even revenge.

The proof sheets still exist, and may be seen, with LeBreton's great crosses in black ink. The offended text still speaks to us. But, more than that by far, the doctrines thus pusillanimously excised have become, among ideas, our nearest brethren: salvation by science, government by the citizens, liberty for slaves and colonial peoples, therapy for evildoers, and peace for the world. What else should we expect of a work that gathered all knowledge, of value and of fact?

Those twenty years of risk and labor: we must not suppose they were without their joys. On the contrary, a heaven for intellectuals lay healingly beside their embattled hell. No dying class in history has so much embraced the future as the French aristocracy did. Diderot could visit the d'Épinay household at La Chevrette, or the d'Holbach household at Grandval. The conversation would be of the best; there would be jokes and even pranks, affection would be everywhere, and you would meet a marvelous middle-aged she-dragon like d'Holbach's mother-in-law, Madame d'Aine.[8] A short volume could be made of her exploits, but we will let this instance suffice. Diderot describes it in a letter to Sophie Volland, written from Grandval, October 20, 1760:

That evening we had all gone to bed. We had talked a great deal of the fire at M. de Bagueville's. Madame d'Aine remembered, after she was in bed, that she had left an enormous log burning in the fireplace of the salon. Perhaps the screen had not been put in front of it, and then the log might roll out onto the floor, as had already happened on one occasion. She grew alarmed, and since

7) Letter of November 12, 1764.
8) He liked her so well that, when his wife died, he married another of her daughters.

she never gave orders for anything she could do herself, she got up, put on her slippers, and left her room in nightgown and wrapper, a little night-lamp in her hand.

She was going down the staircase at the very moment when M. le Roy, who habitually sat late and had been reading in the salon, came up it. They saw each other. Madame d'Aine darted off. M. le Roy followed her, caught up with her, grabbed her by the waist, and began kissing her. She cried out, "Help! Help!" but the kisses of her ravisher kept her from speaking distinctly. Nevertheless she was heard to say, "Help, sons-in-law! If he makes me a child, so much the worse for you!"

Doors opened; people ran through the hallway, and found only Madame d'Aine much mussed up, looking for her nightcap and slippers in the darkness—for her lamp had fallen over and gone out, and our friend had shut himself up in his own room. I left them in the hallway, laughing like the Homeric gods until two o'clock in the morning.

Success is politics, and politics is people. With such people, how could the Encyclopedia fail?

One day in 1765, Mr. David Hume, the celebrated philosopher, then Secretary at the British Embassy in Paris, dined at Baron d'Holbach's table and was seated next to him. Hume was a radical without commitment (that is to say, no radical at all); he protected himself from ultimate boldness by interposing a timely skepticism. Hume was certainly not a Christian of any sort, nor a deist believing in God as a first cause or *primum mobile*. Yet he was also no atheist, and was content to say that, since we do not know whether we know anything, we do not know whether we know there is a God. This being his view, at one point in the conversation he remarked—a little condescendingly, one feels—that he had never met an atheist and did not think there were any. Said d'Holbach, "Count how many of us there are at table." Hume counted eighteen. "Well," said the Baron, "I'm happy to be able to show you fifteen atheists straight off. The other three don't know what to think about it."[9]

Such, in their hearts and minds, were the men who shaped our modern thought, who finally disentangled metaphor from fact and

9) Diderot was present and described the scene in a letter to Sophie Volland, October 6, 1765.

showed that we can remedy present evils in our present world. Years later, Hegel, lecturing on the history of philosophy, said that there was in them "a certitude of rational truth which defies the world of received ideas and is sure of its destruction." And Hegel, in his turn, had a disciple who founded a new heresy, productive of yet other heresies, to shake the modern world.

The last, and most awesome, of the *philosophes* was Karl Marx.

CHAPTER

14

Movement, Life, and Dialectics

A PHILOSOPHIC WORK of the year 1781 defined, with prophetic power, the limits of the French Enlightenment. It was written by a German, whose grandfather was a Scot—though this singular fact had nothing to do with the case. The author, then fifty-seven years old, was Immanuel Kant. The work was the *Critique of Pure Reason*.

The book is not without its obscurities, but there is nothing obscure about its final sentence. Having passed, during several hundred pages, through the growth (not to say the undergrowth) of his new Critical Philosophy, Kant suggests that the reader may now judge "whether, if he is willing to help make the path a highway, it may not be possible to attain, before the end of the present century, what many centuries have failed to attain: to satisfy human reason in respect of those matters with which it has hitherto busied itself in vain."[1]

"Before the end of the present century": a resolution of all philosophical problems within nineteen years! One marvels at a confidence so bold in a man so modest. There is not a philosopher alive who would dare make such a claim. The enterprise, Kant said, would need a little help, a bit of doing; but, given the help and the doing, it might ... it would ... it surely would settle everything. Incredible!

1) *Kritik der Reinen Vernunft*, Transzendentale Methodenlehre, Die Geschichte der reinen Vernunft. My translation.

And yet, although we are not conscious of having solved the problems of philosophy, the particular resolution that Kant had in mind
did as a matter of historical fact come to pass—in rather more than
those nineteen years. It was the great truce between science and
theology.

Kant had absorbed British empiricism in a shattering digestive
exercise. David Hume, if he had not died in 1776, would have entertained a smile, though not more than a smile, at the sight of an
empiricist Teuton. Yet the Lockean view, now endowed (perhaps,
indeed, burdened) with skeptical refinements, had penetrated beyond
France, where it had subverted all notions, into the cultural wilderness of Prussia along the chill and fogbound reaches of the Baltic
Sea. There Kant lived in Koenigsberg, Professor of Logic and Metaphysics at the university; and there, about the year 1771, he suffered
the shock, not much softened by translation, of reading Hume. The
shock was the same the whole century had suffered, but Hume had
increased it by showing that, if empiricism destroyed theology, it
destroyed science too.

Kant proposed to save both science and theology. His vast theoretical construction, implacably subtle and impressively serene, had the
contradictory effects of a brake and a spur. The Enlightenment,
whatever its professions, desired to get rid of theology altogether.
Kant stopped it short of that goal. At the same time, he restored to
philosophy the sense that men really can know the world. And one
of the things which men could know was that they could *not* know
anything theological.

Such was the foundation of the great truce. The scientists would
have to say that nothing they knew made theology absurd. The
theologians would have to say that, since they did not really know
anything, they knew nothing which made science impossible. It was
a truce, as one sees, between winners and losers, for the absence of
conflict thus ratified lay in the assertion that, although scientists
don't know everything, theologians don't know anything.

It will not be supposed that the theologians of Kant's time were
delighted with that Critical Philosophy which was to settle all problems within nineteen years. On the contrary, they called Kant "the
all-destroyer." A certain Professor Ulrich, of Jena, once closed a
lecture (he gave six every day) with the cry, "Kant, I will be a thorn
in your flesh! Kantians, I'll be a plague on you! Hercules does what

he promises!"[2] But Hercules was an ass if he thought he could do the impossible.

He was not alone in the effort. For another century, theologians broke lances with Darwinism, with the higher criticism of the Bible, and in general with that materialism which is endemic to science. Always, however, it was *their* lances that were broken. Darwinism and the higher criticism remained invulnerable, and genetic theory issued from the investigations of a Moravian monk. So the great truce came to be; and I think you will find that if you ask a scientist about theology, he will usually say, "That's none of my business," and if you ask a theologian about science, he will say, "That's none of mine." The stupendous metaphysical message of the *Critique of Pure Reason* has become a canon of public relations. Perhaps it is also the harbinger of yet other agreements that will give us a more peaceful world.

From time to time we have observed the fact that a thinker who simply thinks, forgetful of organizational needs, discovers more than he intends. When, toward the year 1790, Kant was completing his edifice of theory by dealing with problems of esthetics, he let fall a footnote which, unknown to himself, led into the nineteenth century. "It has been held questionable," he wrote, "that the divisions I have made in pure philosophy always turn out in threes. But this lies in the very nature of the case."[3]

It happened that, in point of fact, Kant's divisions sometimes turned out in fours—as, for example, the table of categories, the paralogisms, and the antinomies in the *Critique of Pure Reason.* Moreover, Kant was unusually clumsy at dividing up a subject—his "architectonic," as he called it. These aberrations, however, make rather more striking his recognition of "threes" and of a need to justify them. The justification seemed to him to lie in the fact that, whenever you talk scientifically, you talk about a certain entity, about a set of conditions which produced that entity, and about a relation between the entity and the set of conditions.[4] Thus you get your separate parts, and they are three.

2) Karl Vorländer, *Immanuel Kant, der Mann und das Werk,* (Leipsig: Meinen; 1924), Vol. I, p. 411: "*Kant, ich werde Dein Stachel, Kantianer, ich werde Eure Pestilenz sein. Was Herkules verspricht, wird er auch halten.*" My translation.
3) *Kritik der Urteilskraft, Einleitung,* IX, n2. My translation.
4) Ibid., loc. cit.

Now, I have no doubt that philosophy (or any other form of discourse not plainly mathematical) is better off without undue use of arithmetic. There is nothing peculiarly potent about the number three, and a philosopher who desires tripartite divisions at any cost will find that the cost is high. For in achieving such divisions, he will have crammed his material or stretched it until the natural shape is lost. This, I dare say, is what Kant's critics thought he was doing.

Nevertheless, there remained, and remains, a certain allure. The whole effort of science is to describe events—that is to say, things happening in time—and time, though familiar even to the point of lamentation, has a very odd structure indeed. It is made up of negations: maturity cancels youth, and old age cancels maturity. Every moment of time "negates" its predecessor in the sense that it makes its predecessor no longer actual—and, in the given illustration, no longer possible. Thus any temporal process is internally discontinuous: it is a series of "leaps." Equally, however, it is also continuous, or it would not be the one particular process which it undoubtedly is: the life, say, of George Washington would not be George Washington's life. The logic of time is a logic in which contradiction is, to the horror of logicians, a fundamental law. For time is both continuous and discontinuous, and if it were not both, it would not be time.

Recognition of this paradox is very old, at least as old as Parmenides and the year 500 B.C. Parmenides' response was to pronounce time an illusion, and in this view various other philosophers have followed him. But such a result too radically denies the constant sense—the daily, hourly sense—we have of living and acting. No man can conduct his affairs upon the supposition that "in reality" nothing is happening. At the same time, one does not readily believe that the world is irrational. One is therefore led to suspect that there is a logic, ampler than Aristotle had imagined, which more adequately expresses the general pattern of change. This logic, conceivably, is the dialectical.

Perhaps we may pause over the two words "logic" and "dialectical," because the one is undoubtedly thorny and the other may seem ambiguous. For myself, I am willing to think of the content of logic as being a series of generalizations about the universe—generalizations which have so high a degree of probability that they can be taken as rules of human discourse. If, for example, the sentence p implies the sentence q, and the sentence q implies the sentence r, then, so the traditional logic tells us (and tells us rightly), *p* implies *r*. It seems to me that this is the case, not because language is the way it is, but because the universe is the way it is. But equally, I do not, for myself, feel that an absolute absoluteness is necessary; probability and expectation will do as well. Thus I would be willing to say that the laws of logic (if that is what they are), or the rules, or the assertions, give us a reliable expectation that we can conduct our discourse in such a way as to describe the world accurately. Obviously, a logic which is to do this will have to take account of time.

For reasons which are speculative and perhaps not very flattering, dialectical logic has long been the stepchild, or black sheep, of the philosophical family. The thorny adjective itself comes from a Greek word that meant disputation, the countering of assertions with their opposites. In Plato's use this is all that "dialectical" meant. But assertions are ordinarily about real or imagined states of affairs, and if assertions can conflict, so also can the states of affairs. Contrariety of this sort is, indeed, universally the case; and its range extends from simple opposition, in which various entities modify one another, to extreme opposition, in which one entity makes the rest impossible.

This notion goes back to Parmenides' great rival, Heraclitus— and beyond. Yet it never had a detailed exposition until Hegel gave it one during the first three decades of the nineteenth century. That exposition has since become classical, and, like other classics, has its mysteries. Nevertheless, Hegel well knew what he was after. Though, with singular perversity, he drew the portrait of a sublimely static universe, he was all the while talking about time and change. "Wherever there is movement," he wrote in the *Shorter Logic,* "wherever there is life, wherever anything is carried into effect in the actual world, there Dialectic is at work."[5] This striking idea, that change could be made rational in logic as calculus had made it rational in mathematics, prepared all thinkers for the acceptance of quite extraordinary truths. It became possible to think that contrary things do not necessarily present a choice of either/or, but may be harmonized as parts of a process or as aspects of an underlying unity not yet perceived. Once this idea had become an expectation, men were able to think that existing species of animals had developed from other species, and even to describe the manner of development.

5) *The Logic of Hegel,* translated by William Wallace (Oxford: Oxford University Press; 1892), p. 148.

Much more recently, it has been possible to state in a single mathematical formula the unity of what I suppose are the two oldest opposites in human thought: matter and energy. Thus, $E = mc^2$.

In short, dialectical logic, though it has not yet attained anything like the refinement of the logic that descends from Aristotle, does nevertheless describe the point of view, the expectations about reality, which enabled Darwin to produce his theory of evolution, Marx his theory of social development, and Einstein the physics which in doctrine and application has so much astonished us all. It happened, indeed, that Hegel knew very little science. Yet the great thing about thinkers, the thing about great thinkers, is that they can seize ideas which float, as one may say, in the air, waiting to be seized. Hegel took his notion of dialectics from observing the development of philosophical doctrines; and, after him, observers, by using the principle of development, could explicate whatever subjects they wished.

I I

BEFORE WE REACH THE HERESIES of Darwin and Marx, which have so terribly vexed the modern age, there are two earlier heretics, both Englishmen, who require notice. The first of these is instructive for many reasons: he was heretical on behalf of reaction, he was heretical on intellectual grounds only, and he was himself transparently honest. A reactionary who is pure in heart is perhaps the greatest of human rarities. The life of John Henry Cardinal Newman is itself sufficient proof that in history anything can happen.

If a man of our time were to try to think himself back into antiquity, the effort would be scarcely greater than that of thinking himself into England of the 1830's. It would be blocked by a series of notions—indeed, a whole *Weltanschauung*—which intervening and rebellious generations have drenched with distaste. Nobody now, like Dr. Arnold of Rugby, would grow alarmed at learning that "Unitarianism is becoming very prevalent in Boston":[6] it would take something secular like communism (not very prevalent in Boston) to produce that sort of effect. Nobody now would be likely to compare, as Dr. Arnold did, the ruins of Pompeii with those of Sodom

6) Quoted by Lytton Strachey, *Eminent Victorians,* (London: Chatto and Windus; 1948), p. 207.

and Gomorrah, and to think that "one is not authorized to ascribe so solemn a character to the destruction of Pompeii."[7]

None of our basic concepts is any longer theological, not even in ethics. A man may wonder what is best to do, or even what is right to do, without once asking the dread question, "What is God's will?" But the early Victorians and their immediate predecessors lived "as ever in my great Taskmaster's eye." For them the legends of Palestinian antiquity had immediate and imperious relevance, and they felt that God (the Hebraic God, indeed) spoke to them as clearly and as sternly as ever he had on Sinai or in the burning bush. They themselves were rebels, against the slumbers of the eighteenth-century church; but their revolt cast them back toward Puritanism rather than forward to science. You will get some sense of the extraordinary fact, if you consider that Dr. Arnold was chosen Headmaster of Rugby because he was thought "advanced," and that his pedagogy rested on the view that "Rather than have physical science the principal thing in my son's mind, I would gladly have him think that the sun went round the earth."[8]

By the year 1833, the Church of England showed the entire effect of being a church and of being national. It had been founded, under Henry VIII, with an ideology skillfully devised so that Englishmen might be Anglicans without much disturbing the beliefs they had held as Catholics. The one profound change had been the substitution of the king's supremacy for the pope's. Otherwise little was altered: the sacraments retained their supernatural efficacy, and the bishops continued to derive their ultimate authority (in doctrine at least) from the ancient apostolic succession.

But nations are a secular phenomenon, and within their ideologies lie, sinking or swelling, all notions that the age permits. A national church, therefore, can scarcely avoid a certain laxity, if not in the doctrine itself, then at any rate in attention to the doctrine. The Anglican Church possessed, as its core of belief, the Thirty-nine Articles, and these sufficed to exclude various groups which dissented from them. But, for the mass of members, the Articles had little meaning and less interest, even when they had to be subscribed to on ceremonial occasions like matriculation at Oxford or Cambridge.

Moreover, during the eighteenth century a gross and sleepy indo-

7) Ibid., p. 213.
8) Ibid., p. 202; letter to Dr. Greenhill, May 9, 1836.

lence stole over the Church. Bishop Butler and Archdeacon Paley had successfully summoned physical nature to the evidential support of Christianity (if not of the Articles), and theological issues assumed the same resolved calm that Newtonian theory had long achieved. The mind, it seemed, had little more to do; meanwhile, there was fox hunting with the squire and the pleasures of table and company. Gibbon describes the clerics at Magdalene as "steeped in port and prejudice," and, with the contempt which the Enlightenment had for the Middle Ages, delighted to call them "monks."[9]

Now, within a great mass, however sleepy and sundered from belief, it was odds that one man, or several, would arise who took the Thirty-nine Articles at their face value, brushed off as irrelevant the convolutions of Tudor diplomacy, and judged candor to require that the doctrine mean precisely what it said. Such men would be intellectuals in the purest form, to whose vision all compromise is insincerity and all politics corruption. Accordingly, during the 1820's, a brilliant and rather fevered coterie gathered in Oxford: John Keble, Hurrell Froude, W. G. Ward, and John Henry Newman. Keble's Assize Sermon of 1833, "On National Apostasy," began (or so Newman always thought) the Oxford Movement. A few weeks later appeared the first of the *Tracts for the Times,* written by Newman, which called upon the Anglican clergy to defy the liberal tendencies of the age (the Reform Bill had just become law), and to regard once more "the real ground on which our authority is built—OUR APOSTOLICAL DESCENT."[1]

The intellectual posture thus taken was the backward look which Vincent of Lerins had established as orthodox, in 434 A.D.[2] In this direction of sight, all roads visibly led back to Rome. Authority by descent and continuity of doctrine alike must undo the labors of the English Reformation, close the institutional schism, and bring the Anglican Church once more into communion with Rome. At first, however, the Tractarians either did not notice or did not confess such implications. They desired to free the Church from control (or even influence) by Whig politicians, and to restore, as against the democratic impulse of history, the divine glories of government by

9) *Autobiography,* World's Classics Series (Oxford University Press), p. 85.
1) A. V. Ward, editor, *Tracts and Pamphlets,* World's Classics Series (Oxford: Oxford University Press; 1927), p. 503. The capitalization is Newman's.
2) See *supra,* Interlude: On Nets and Fishes.

subordination. Newman, indeed, so much hated all that came from the French Revolution that, touching at Algiers on a recuperative cruise in 1832, he could not bear to look at the tricolor flying from a ship in the harbor.[3] In the year 1964, we are peculiarly fitted to judge how reactionary this hatred was. For the tricolor that Newman could not look at was at that moment the emblem, not of a republic, but of the "bourgeois" monarchy of Louis Philippe; and the ship that flew it was in Algeria at the beginning of a long, bloody, and bitter colonial occupation, which ended only while this book was being written.

Newman and his associates desired and enjoyed what Chesterton wonderfully calls "the exalted excitement of consistency."[4] The following of ideas along the straight strong line of logic, independent of application or of social milieu, is one of the headiest of pleasures and, to intellectuals, irresistible. Newman's passage along the straight strong line was much assisted by the fact that, philosophically, he never could, and never did, distinguish accurately between metaphor and fact. His marvelous candor, matched with a no less marvelous clarity of style, makes plain exactly that mode of thought which it had been the Enlightenment's purpose to abolish forever. Consider, for example, this remarkable passage from Chapter I of the *Apologia*:

I considered them [angels] as the real causes of motion, light, and life, and of those elementary principles of the physical universe, which, when offered in their developments to our senses, suggest to us the notion of cause and effect, and of what are called the laws of nature. This doctrine I have drawn out in my Sermon for Michaelmas day, written in 1831. I say of the Angels, "Every breath of air and ray of light and heat, every beautiful prospect, is, as it were, the skirts of their garments, the waving of the robes of those whose faces see God."

Now, in the lovely sentence which he quotes from himself (surely knowing it to be lovely), the "as it were" shows some awareness that he was talking poetry. But the first sentence shows that he also thought he was talking fact. He really did believe the world to be moved by wholly supernatural powers: he had angels about him everywhere, and over them in salutary government the archangels

3) *Apologia pro Vita Sua,* Chapter I.
4) *The Victorian Age in Literature,* Home University Library (New York: Henry Holt and Company; 1913), p. 44.

and the triune God. Yet, if we take up any book of science in our own day, we shall discover no supernatural powers whatever, nor do we find, so far as I am aware, any scientist disposed to think that nuclear fission is a revolt among angels.

Indeed, the light that Newman's career sheds about our central problem is so bright as to be astounding. Nobody is any longer surprised at what happens when a radical gets entangled with an organization on behalf of social advance; but when an honest reactionary (save the mark!) gets similarly entangled on behalf of a retreat into antiquity, then we see, as perhaps we cannot otherwise see, what organizational politics really are. Leaders, if they do not dislike change, dislike at any rate certain directions of change; and, in the 1830's, the Church of England wished to move neither toward disestablishment nor toward Rome.

The ultimate irony of Newman's career, however, lies in the treatment he received after he had come to his journey's end, the Roman Church itself. His conversion, which occurred in 1845, he faithfully described as "like coming into port after a rough sea," and he added, "My happiness on that score remains to this day [1865] without interruption."[5] No doubt he so thought, but it cannot have been the case. The Church was then ruled by Pius IX, one of the most conservative of popes, who, in the *Syllabus of Errors* (1864), anathematized every doctrine that has enlightened the modern world, and, following the Vatican Council of 1870, pronounced himself, his predecessors, and his successors infallible on matters of faith and morals. Two thousand years of strife and politics had taught the Church the dangers of doctrinal speculation divorced from pragmatical utility. What was to be done with a convert whom logic, and logic alone, had brought into the fold? He was to be watched and somewhat sequestered, given status adequate to his fame but such also as to prevent any further journeyings along the lines of logic.

Moreover, Newman had in the English branch of the Catholic Church a rival, Henry Edward Manning, also a convert, who, upon conversion, shortly became Archbishop of Westminster and then Cardinal. Manning's religious interests were far more in administration than in doctrine; he was in fact a careerist of enormous skill. Juxtaposed with a convert who was Roman Catholic solely because he believed the doctrine, Manning felt threatened, and so disposed

5) *Apologia,* Chapter V.

affairs that Newman remained shut up in his oratory at Birmingham, emerging only on futile projects in journalism and education. As Monsignor Talbot, Manning's confederate among the papal secretaries, wrote, "Dr. Newman is more English than the English. His spirit must be crushed."[6]

Yet, in truth, nothing could be less English than naked logic, than bare remorseless inference. Before Newman those islands had never known, nor since him have they ever seen, philosophical naïvety—a thrust of intellect inattentive to political need. The habit of arguing with an eye upon affairs, if remarkably British, is also widely human. The sad fact is that in no organization on earth would Newman have been at home.

The life of pure reason has thus its tragedies. It is pleasant, however, to know that in Newman it had also a crown. For Newman too became a cardinal, when he was very old and there remained few years in which he might be dangerous. He had never shirked struggle; he had never abandoned principle; he had overwhelmed adversaries with an irresistible candor; and he descends to us, in his poems and in the great *Apologia,* as a sweet and lovable man. "O Lord," he wrote in one of the most famous of English prayers, "support us all the day long, until the shadows lengthen, and the evening comes, and the busy world is hushed, and the fever of life is over, and our work is done. Then in thy mercy grant us a safe lodging, and a holy rest, and peace at the last." Perhaps—how should one not believe it? —these things were so.

Our second heretic among the English churchmen differs in every possible way except in purity of heart. So far from living and working at the center of ecclesiastical events, he was a colonial bishop—of Natal, in South Africa. He had been born into a poor family of Cornwall, had been educated through the generosity of relatives, had, while teaching at Harrow, lost most of his little property in a fire, and had in the end paid off his debts from the royalties upon two textbooks in mathematics. He was John William Colenso.

Set down in Natal for the conversion of the Zulus, he discovered his proposed converts to be friendly but full of common sense. Under his instruction they studied, among other things, the Pentateuch, and their questions, unwarped by childhood indoctrination, turned up fables in the narrative. Colenso soon perceived that the Pentateuch

6) Quoted by Strachey, op. cit., p. 91.

was decidely other than it appeared to be or had been held to be. It related feats that were as mythical as they were impossible. Colenso concluded that when, for example, twelve thousand Israelites were said to have destroyed two hundred thousand Midianites, the hideous slaughter "had happily only been carried out on paper."[7]

Colenso was not a man to convert Africans, or anyone else, to nonsense. "My heart answered in the words of the prophet, 'Shall a man speak lies in the name of the Lord?' I determined not to do so."[8] He did, in fact, even better: he undertook to enlighten his own coreligionists, a task of much greater difficulty. In 1862, he published *The Pentateuch and the Book of Joshua Critically Examined,* wherein, with much success, he disentangled history from legend, showed the Mosaic Law to have been comparatively late, and made plain that part of the text was propaganda on behalf of the priests.

The scandal was prodigious. On both sides of the Atlantic, Anglican churchmen raged against the new interpretation. They would in no point doubt the literal inerrancy of Scripture, even when confronted, as Colenso confronted them, with the hare in Leviticus 11: 6 "that cheweth the cud." The cud-chewing hare, said Colenso, must be an error. Not so, cried the offended clergy; if Scripture speaks of a cud-chewing hare, then there is, or was, a cud-chewing hare. It may seem absurd to risk the divine veracity upon what must have been a copyist's error, but the frenzies of organizational fidelity are often boundless. A wag of that time wrote,

> The bishops all have sworn to shed their blood
> To prove 'tis true the hare doth chew the cud.
> O bishops, doctors, and divines, beware—
> Weak is the faith that hangs upon a hair![9]

Now, it happened that Colenso's scientific disposition extended also into what might be called practical anthropology. He had the wisdom to desire leaving the Zulu civilization intact to follow the laws of its own development—a policy which, if it had been followed,

7) Quoted by Andrew Dickson White, *A History of the Warfare Between Science and Theology* (New York: D. Appleton-Century Co.; 1936), Vol. II, p. 350. The Midianite story is in Numbers 31. It is worth noting that Colenso learned the Zulu language, produced a dictionary and a grammar of it, and translated the New Testament into it.
8) Quoted, ibid., loc. cit.
9) Quoted, ibid., II, 351n.

would have saved the Zulus from being the sweated laborers they have since become. More specifically, Colenso was willing to tolerate polygamy among the converts, to the pious horror of his fellow bishops in South Africa. He had, moreover, in a commentary on Romans, denied the doctrine of eternal damnation. The charm of this extraordinary doctrine (if charm it be) fascinated the Victorians, who poured into it their immense, ungratified angers.[1] Indeed, if the wicked are not to be eternally damned, what is one to do with one's enemies? Thus, all told, Colenso sided with the colonial peoples, with the higher criticism, and with the merciful exercise of divine judgment.

Accordingly, in December, 1863, the bishops in South Africa deposed Colenso from office. The Bishop of Cape Town, Robert Gray, went further and excommunicated him. All this was highly irregular. The courts in England threw out the excommunication and deposition. They also threw out a proposal to deprive Colenso of his salary. These decisive efforts having failed, the Reverend John Keble was heard to murmur a lament that excommunication had ceased to be popular; and the Bishop of Oxford, Samuel Wilberforce, regretted "the devotion of the English people to law in matters of this sort."[2] We shall shortly meet this bishop again, in the affair of Darwin and *The Origin of Species*.

The courts, however, could not much abate the winds of defamation. Every important Victorian joined in blast or counterblast. Mr. Gladstone himself led in the attack, the great Prime Minister, a man who thought it a duty to have strong opinions on all subjects. Mr. Matthew Arnold, son of Thomas, joined the assault in *Macmillan's Magazine*, complaining that Colenso ought to have taken as his model—Spinoza's *Tractatus!* This blunder, by the ablest of Victorian critics, is almost incredible: Spinoza in that very *Tractatus* had made himself the father of the higher criticism. We are left in breathless supposition that organizational allegiance will warp anything. For, as between Colenso and Spinoza, the sole advantage that Spinoza can have possessed was that of not belonging to the Church of England.

1) An epitaph upon Baron Westbury, Lord High Chancellor of England, who had acquitted two clergymen similarly charged, concludes with the remark that he "dismissed Hell with costs, and took away from orthodox members of the Church of England their last hope of everlasting damnation" Ibid., II, 348n.
2) Quoted, ibid., II, 352.

Things fell out finally into calm, but the pattern of their falling out is instructive. The enlightened found themselves frozen in the various stations to which God had thus far called them. Arthur Stanley, Dean of Westminster, Colenso's ablest supporter, remained Dean of Westminster—a result that illustrates the British habit of making gifted and safe men bishops, and gifted and unsafe men deans. Thirlwall, Bishop of St. David's, another defender, never advanced beyond his impoverished diocese in Wales. But this fate, mild enough in itself, had a certain good fortune denied to other prelates. The enlightened remained enlightened; the others went on, in the Darwinian controversy, to make asses of themselves. Alone among the regulars, the Archbishops of Canterbury achieved some balance between truth and doctrine. Tait had been conspicuously fair in the Colenso controversy, and his successor, Benson, when a similar dispute broke out in 1889, let fall the saving if not redemptive question, "May not the Holy Spirit make use of myth and legend?"[3]

Colenso went back to Natal, a partial victor. There he continued to labor, with commentary and exegesis, for the enlightenment of his fellow men. There he continued to defend the native Zulus against the tyranny of the Boers. Colenso died in 1883, and that tyranny still prevails. It is, however, near its final doom, and of that doom Colenso will, in the end, prove to have been one of the architects. It is a striking fact that the higher criticism of the Bible and the liberation of colonial peoples should have been thus joined. He who explicates Scripture must set the world free.

I I I

SOMETIME during the sixth century B.C., Anaximander of Miletus, the old Ionian philosopher, made the striking conjecture that men are descended from fish. It was, I believe, the earliest known use of the evolutionary hypothesis, and we do not know what data Anaximander was generalizing upon. A dweller along the Aegean would be well acquainted with fish, and perhaps Anaximander had seen gill clefts in a human embryo. We do know, however, that he professed the dialectical logic—the view that things modify one another, "opposites" acting upon "opposites." The conclusion seems almost irresistible that a good scientific guess, made in an epoch when such guesses were rare, owed something to accuracy in the basic philosophical point of view.

3) Ibid., Vol. II, p. 359.

In the subsequent contests of thought, however, the dialectical logic lost supremacy. In human discourse there undoubtedly is a need that every term shall maintain one identical meaning throughout any stretch of argument, and this need grew, under Plato's rapturous praise, into a *Credo in unum Deum* for secular philosophy. Thus the logic of disputation triumphed over the logic of change. It was felt, accordingly, that, since the meaning of the term "fish" and the meaning of the term "man" unalterably differed, there could be no genetic connections between the species which the terms signified.

After Genesis became for Christians a holy book, and Plato a holy poet (or as much so as a man irremediably pagan could be), the doctrine grew fixed that God had not only created all animals "after their kind,"[4] but had established in every kind a firm immutability. The phyla, genera, species were therefore disparate, united only by occasional logical inclusion and by the alleged cosmic fact that God had created them all. God, it will appear, was a Platonist in cosmology and an Aristotelian in logic.

From our present vantage point, we see things rather differently and rather better. Terms, no doubt, ought to have precise meanings —that is, "clear and distinct" references to the world—and no term can, without perilous ambiguity, have two or more meanings at once. Nevertheless, there also is in any one term a unity of meaning that is the history of its usage, of the changes in its various meanings as these were altered by growth in knowledge or by mere social circumstance. It is quite possible to define, say, the term "man" in such a way as to express the best information now available, but it is most unlikely that the definition thus established will suit scientists of the twenty-fifth century. These scientists, however, will be able to recognize our present meaning as part of the historical unity of the term. If Plato had been willing (as he was not) to admit "becoming" into his world of forms, he would have captured science and preserved permanence too.

Thus the novelties of biology and sociology, breaking in upon European culture about a hundred years ago, required for their acceptance a profound change in very old habits of thought. This change was, as we have seen, well prepared by Hegel—by Goethe also in some measure—but it made only slow and quiet progress until

4) Genesis 1: 21.

the controversies surrounding Darwin and Marx. Events once more took the Christian Church, in almost all its segments, as the target of absurdity; but, in this, events were somewhat unfair. The clergy did indeed, with a fine abandon, appear as dunces. The true dunce, however, was an ancient logic that had crept through ideology as through an ill-kept house, leaving dust and cobweb as the normal state of things.

One of the values of empiricism is its distrust of generalizations. Facts, to be sure, it loves—whatever those remarkable entities are, which seem so immediate and certain, and are so mediate and doubtful. Generalizations it rather fears, unless the generalizations happen to be its own. Yet there is invincible good sense in letting the evidence accumulate at whatever pace is necessary, until the sheer mass of it does indeed support a conclusion. For this to happen there needs to be a human observer accurate in detail, patient in accumulation, steadfast in inference, and, at the end, comprehensive of view. Such an observer has what Bagehot called "the alluvial mind;"[5] facts silt down upon it, and there establish the definitive shape. Just such observers were Darwin and Marx. I fancy that neither the theory of biological evolution nor the theory of socialist revolution would have gained so rapidly, against such resolute organizational resistance, without the power of data serried and massed. The double notion that species and social systems are alike immutable has yielded, in both its parts, to a remorseless explication of change.

The circumstances surrounding Darwin and his triumphant book, *The Origin of Species,* are even more instructive than the book itself. No doubt biological science gained enormously by attributing species to a common natural origin and by showing that variations within species could be the beginning of new types. It was a splendid display of identity and difference locked in an archetypal embrace. Yet the effect of the theory upon things outside itself was rather more impressive. So vast was the range of this generalization that supernature was expelled from most of the territory left it by the Enlightenment.[6] For if the human race had derived from apes, and all vertebrates from some reptilian monster that crawled out of water

---

5) Quoted by William Irvine, *Apes, Angels, and Victorians* (New York: Meridian Books; 1959), p. 48.

6) Even Mrs. Darwin wrote, rather sadly, of her husband's "putting God farther off." Irvine, ibid., p. 199.

to test the primeval slime, why, then a connection between men and God was much more remote than Scripture had led one to believe.

Moreover—and this was capital—although Darwinism was in its way a look backward, it definitively ended the backward look of Vincent of Lerins. Doctrinal credibility and organizational authority do not persuasively descend from apes; orthodoxy seems not confirmed by dinosaurs. Suddenly—too, too suddenly—Christ's charge to Peter and all the canonized genius of the Church lay overwhelmed by rocks and fossils, the odd behavior of barnacles, the marvelous irritability of orchids, and the busy fertile journeyings of bees.

Now, there is something inspiriting in the notion that, say, a Daughter of the American Revolution would, if she pursued genealogy far enough, discover herself to be the daughter of an arboreal ape. I have for some time thought that much is lost by abbreviating one's ancestry. What is inspiriting, however, is not so much the origin itself as the distance one has come from it. The heart of modern ethics will not be found in a search for conformity with the past, but in a search for—nay, a rush after—the perfection that lies before us, graspable though it may be missed. Eight years before the *Origin of Species,* Tennyson, not in our time much valued as a thinker, had already achieved the appropriate rectification of theology, replacing the backward look with the forward look!

> Ring in the valiant man and free,
>   The larger heart, the kindlier hand;
> Ring out the darkness of the land,
>   Ring in the Christ that is to be.[7]

The Christ that is to be! The whole modern view is in that line, and one must disregard the verbal limitation to Christian lore and poetry. Every nation that comes into independence, and every citizen thereof, feels the future as a place of achievement and the past as something risen from. Upon this view, perfection is seen to lie, not in an ancestral Adam, but in the works and beauty of our progeny. It was, I suppose, no part of Darwin's scientific intent to effect this reversal of values. Yet the reversal occurred most beneficially, and the occurrence shows, what some philosophers cannot yet perceive, how closely science and ethics are intertwined.

Despite all this, however, the preparation for Darwinism (a

7) "In Memoriam," CVI.

preparation as old as Darwin's grandfather Erasmus) somehow failed to prepare. The theory of evolution, which Darwin cunningly presented as forced by the facts upon a reluctant observer, seemed like an assault upon the British Establishment. The *Origin* appeared in 1859, and year by year thereafter the clamor of opposition grew. Darwin, for his part, had a convenient neurosis, which, in periods of strife, upset his stomach and left him bedridden in his country house at Down. The sanest strategy could not have been more suitable. Oracles fall silent when attacked, and because they do so, we know that they are oracles. Into Darwin's thick silence enemies thrust their fists as flies their feet in flypaper, and were left helpless to wither and decay. Meanwhile the oracle quietly marshaled friends and allies to conduct all public disputation.

The events that sent Darwin to bed sent Thomas Henry Huxley to the lecture platform. "At that time," he wrote in his little *Autobiography,* "I disliked public speaking, and had a firm conviction that I should break down every time I opened my mouth." That is as it may have been. At any rate, nothing cures like victory, and on Saturday the thirtieth of June, 1860, Huxley became for the rest of his life apostle of evolution and pedagogue to the English people. He had a victim that day—precisely the right sort of victim —Samuel Wilberforce, Bishop of Oxford, whose obvious careerism, thinly coated with charm, had earned him the nickname of "Soapy Sam."

The British Association for the Advancement of Science (known in our day as the "British Aas") was meeting at Oxford, and Darwinism, though not on the program, was in the air. Huxley had gone down to protect it, and had, on June twenty-ninth, politely pulverized Sir Richard Owen, a then celebrated anatomist. Next day, the anti-evolution forces brought out Soapy Sam, who had spent the intervening hours getting coached by Owen. The Bishop, however, remained impenetrably ignorant, and Owen irremediably wrong. History was about to teach once more the lesson that hierarchs are loath to learn, this time with ridicule.

Soapy was at his most genial. Coruscations of wit and misrepresentations of data sped, with equal velocity, from his mouth. The seated clergy chuckled, the listening ladies smiled. He rose into his peroration, and, turning toward Huxley, "begged to know, was it through his grandfather or his grandmother that he claimed descent from a monkey."[8] At that moment Huxley muttered to his next neighbor on the platform, "The Lord hath delivered him into my hand."

It was so indeed, although in this regard Soapy had left little for the Lord to do. Huxley, called upon to speak, laid bare in a few sentences the Bishop's ignorance and the true content of Darwinian theory. Then, joining his peroration to the Bishop's, he said he would not be ashamed to have apes in his ancestry but would be ashamed "to be connected with a man who used great gifts to obscure the truth."[9]

Huxley afterward called this "letting himself go." It was a great moment certainly, and the English-speaking world, at any rate, has long considered it a moment of emancipation. From then on, science was to be supreme, subjecting all princes and powers to the sovereign test of fact, and punishing their disobedience with painful torments of absurdity.

Yet the lengthening controversy allowed every man a word, however silly that word might prove to be. The politicians, less cautious then than they now are, gave forth their views—of course, on the erroneous side. Mr. Gladstone was heard to complain that God had been relieved of the labor of creation; and Mr. Disraeli, who did not often risk bathos, risked it thus:

What is the question now placed before society with a glib assurance the most astounding? The question is this—Is man an ape or an angel? My Lord, I am on the side of the angels.[1]

In his old age, when the fires of righteous combat still glowed within him, Huxley demolished all this arrogance with a single remark. "I am inclined to think," he growled, "that the practice of the methods of political leaders destroys their intelligence for all serious purposes."[2]

The shock of Darwinism upon the British Establishment, however, effected much more than a wrecking of theology. It shook the Victorians into an awareness of their own social conditions. Darwin

8) Quoted by Irvine, op. cit., p. 6.
9) Ibid., p. 7.
1) In a speech at Oxford in 1864. Professor Irvine has drawn from this passage the title of his witty and admirable book.
2) Quoted by Irvine, ibid., pp. 356–57.

had said that, throughout the worlds of flora and fauna, species and the members of species are engaged in a vast struggle for survival. Animals, birds, insects eat one another; plants compete for possession of soil. Those best suited to the demands of environment survive; those less well suited perish. It is "nature red in tooth and claw," and, moreover, some of the qualities that make for survival are, it is plain, not very edifying.

No doubt all inferences from animal biology to human sociology are invalid, and "Social Darwinism" (which Darwin himself did not hold) is now as dead as any fossil. But the Victorians, who lived in the heyday of competitive capitalism, with heights of wealth and depths of poverty, with defeated competitors falling daily from height to depth, suddenly saw themselves as beasts in the primordial jungle. "Darwin did not know," wrote Engels in his *Dialectics of Nature,* "what a bitter satire he wrote on mankind and especially on his fellow countrymen when he proved that free competition, the struggle for existence, which the economists praise as the greatest historical achievement, is the normal state of the *animal kingdom.*"[3] And Lord Russell has said, perhaps unaware that he was repeating a Marxist, that Darwinism was "an extension to the animal and vegetable world of laissez faire economics."[4]

The complete historical fact is much more astonishing. It was not only that Darwin's idea found extension into sociology; Darwin had actually *got* the idea from sociology—indeed, from one of the gloomiest of social thinkers, the Reverend Thomas Robert Malthus. Here is Darwin's own account of the derivation:

> In October 1838, that is, fifteen months after I had begun my systematic inquiry, I happened to read for amusement Malthus on *Population,* and being well prepared to appreciate the struggle for existence which everywhere goes on from long-continued observation of the habits of animals and plants, it at once struck me that under these circumstances favourable variations would tend to be preserved, and unfavourable ones to be destroyed. The result of this would be the formation of new species. Here, then, I had at last got a theory by which to work. . . .[5]

3) Engels' italics.
4) *Religion and Science* (Oxford: Oxford University Press; 1935), pp. 72–73.
5) *Autobiography,* edited by Nora Barlow, (New York: Harcourt, Brace, and Company; 1958), p. 120.

Malthus had published in 1798 his *Essay on the Principle of Population As It Affects the Future Improvement of Society*. Rather to his surprise, he found himself famous. He had "proved," with an appeal to science and none to theology, that the existing distribution of property need not be disturbed, because even if one disturbed it beneficently, the human struggle for survival would in due course restore it. The British ruling class was delighted to learn that it governed and prospered by natural selection as well as by divine right. Malthus, for his part, took a gruesome pleasure in describing human behavior in times of scarcity:

> The temptations to evil are too strong for human nature to resist. The corn is plucked up before it is ripe, or secreted in unfair proportions; and the whole black train of vices that belong to falsehood are immediately generated. Provisions no longer flow in for the support of a mother with a large family. The children are sickly from insufficient food. The rosy flush of health gives place to the pallid cheek and hollow eye of misery. Benevolence, yet lingering in a few bosoms, makes some faint expiring struggles, till at length self-love resumes his wonted empire, and lords it triumphant over the world.[6]

Applied to human society, this doctrine is pessimistic rubbish, precisely because men are *men*. Applied, however, to those parts of animate nature where ethics is either rudimentary or non-existent, it did give a clue to the mode and path of development. There is a lesson in this: one seldom can know in advance the destiny of an idea. If the British government had been tempted (as it was not) to suppress Malthusian doctrine on moral grounds—grounds that were surely not wanting—there might well have been a long delay in the production of evolutionary theory. Governments therefore do well to keep in the air as many ideas as possible, to be used when scientifically suitable, to be let fall as they prove absurd. It is perhaps the supreme lesson that heretics can teach. They have been teaching it a long time, and now possibly . . . possibly . . . the lesson is beginning to be learned.

As we have seen, in modern times the careers of heretics tend to have happy endings. Darwin was soon a very great man. Honors and children crowded upon him, and in 1877 Cambridge University

6) Excerpted from the *Essay*, in D. O. Wagner, *Social Reformers* (New York: The Macmillan Company; 1939), p. 76.

conferred an honorary LL.D. At the ceremony, where Darwin made one of his rare appearances in public, the undergraduates strung a line across the auditorium and dangled from it a monkey image and a large beribboned ring, which symbolized (so Mrs. Darwin thought) the missing link.[7] Afterward, Darwin dined alone with Mrs. Darwin; he had sent Huxley to represent him at the official banquet.

The solitude at Down, the illnesses that conveniently filled his leisure hours, left time for an enormous productivity. Darwin observed, with the sharpest of eyes, his flowers and insects, and wrote and wrote. He feared he wrote badly, and out of the royalties from *The Descent of Man* he paid his daughter Henrietta thirty pounds for improving its style. Yet his distaste for his own prose was as neurotically misconceived as his distaste for Shakespeare's poetry. It was no mere scribbler who wrote, "Great is the power of steady misrepresentation," and who then went on to say, "The history of science shows that fortunately this power does not long endure."[8]

The great man was already legendary when he died, on the nineteenth of April, 1882. He was buried in Westminster Abbey— an event that the Reverend Dr. Laing (known to history solely for this comment) regarded as "proof that England is no longer a Christian country."[9] Great, one may say, is the vitality of organizations, that they can survive the idiocies of their own intellectuals.

The path of ideology, though torn with struggle, has been quite plain. Protestantism affirmed that men can and should make up their own minds. The Enlightenment affirmed that, if they did so, they would find the world open to science and responsive to human control. Darwin showed that control over nature could be regarded as the highest form of adaptation. And Marx? Marx showed that man's control over nature needs completion by a similar control over his own society. To that concept we now turn.

I V

ON AN EVENING in early July, 1850, Herr Wilhelm Liebknecht, twenty-four years old, a refugee from south Germany, found himself at a massive mahogany table in a London home. "In a moment,"

7) Irvine, op. cit., pp. 218–19.
8) *Origin of Species,* Conclusion.
9) White, op. cit., Vol. I, p. 83.

he later wrote, "the beer arrived and we sat down, I on one side of the table, Marx and Engels opposite me."[1]

The beer led to a cross-examination, in which the young man's political judgment was carefully explored. Suddenly the conversation turned to natural science. Marx had lately seen, exhibited on Regent Street, the model of an electric locomotive that would pull a railroad train. Steam, then, was to yield to electricity, and there would be untold consequences. Only two years before, Liebknecht's table companions had asserted, in a document since very famous, that "the bourgeoisie cannot exist without revolutionizing the means of production, and thereby the relations of production, and thereby the whole relations of society."[2]

It was broad daylight when Liebknecht left. They had sat up all night. Liebknecht went to his lodgings, tried to sleep, could not sleep, and, next moment, was off to Regent Street to see the electric train.

This was the beginning of Liebknecht's higher education. Marx drove him hard: into Spanish for the reading of *Don Quixote,* into other literatures, into philology, where the brothers Grimm presided—and, of course, into economics. This last meant daily trips to the British Museum and the new reading room, where Marx exultantly scanned the "blue books," the Parliamentary reports on all phases of English society. "Learn! Learn!" cried the inexorable master. And thus, while other refugees dreamed vaguely of revolutions to begin next day, "we sat," wrote Liebknecht, "in the British Museum and endeavored to educate ourselves."[3]

It was an age of revolutions—a prototype, on a smaller scale, of our own. All over Europe, in 1848, the settlement arranged at the Congress of Vienna (1815) came undone, and Metternich, its guiding spirit, had himself to flee from Vienna. Populations which had paid with blood for the Napoleonic wars and with starvation for the establishment of industry now sought decisive influence upon affairs. The first months of 1848 were filled with uprisings: Sicily (January 12), Paris (February 24), Vienna (March 12), Berlin (March 18), Milan (March 18), Venice (March 22). In England, the Chartists

---

1) *Reminiscences of Marx,* excerpted in *Karl Marx: Selected Works* (Moscow: 1935), Vol. I, p. 103.
2) *Communist Manifesto,* Part I.
3) *Reminiscences,* in op. cit., Vol. I, p. 109.

rose to their greatest power, but the revolution, though expected, did not occur.

Chartism was a workers' movement on behalf of political representation, particularly in Parliament. Its first petition, issued in 1839, made three demands: universal suffrage, the secret ballot, and annual elections to Parliament. When the petition, signed by millions, finally reached the House of Commons in 1842, Mr. Macaulay (not yet Baron), speaking against it, pointed out with perfect candor his reasons for opposition:

> In every constituent body throughout the empire the working class will, if we grant the prayer of this petition, be an irresistible majority. In every constituent body capital will be placed at the feet of labor; knowledge will be born down by ignorance; and is it possible to doubt what the result must be?[4]

The legislative representatives of the ruling classes were franker in those days. The majority, said Macaulay, were not to be allowed a chance at government, because, if they governed, they would dominate the propertied minority: "knowledge would be borne down by ignorance." How these same matters seemed to the victimized majority was eloquently put, in 1846, by one of the Chartist leaders, George Julian Harney:

> In all countries the men who grow the wheat live on potatoes. The men who rear the cattle do not taste flesh food. The men who cultivate the vine have only the dregs of its noble juice. The men who make the clothing are in rags. The men who build the houses live in hovels. The men who create every necessity, comfort and luxury, are steeped in misery. Working men of all nations, are not your grievances, your wrongs, the same? Is not your good cause, then, one and the same also? We may differ as to the means, or different circumstances may render different means necessary, but the great end—the veritable emancipation of the human race—must be the one aim and end of all.[5]

In the struggles of those years, and particularly in the various revolts of 1848, the two classes of capital and labor (so Macaulay

4) *Speeches by Lord Macaulay,* selected by G. M. Young, World's Classics Series (Oxford University Press), p. 195.
5) Speech to the German Democratic Society for the Education of the Working Classes, excerpted in Max Morris, *From Cobbett to the Chartists,* (London: Lawrence and Wishart; 1948), p. 247.

called them) made common cause against the remnants of aristocratic rule; but they were at the same time in conflict with each
other, for reasons that Harney made abundantly clear. Capital was,
however, victorious in all those struggles, and Baron Macaulay died,
in 1859, without ever seeing knowledge borne down by ignorance.

For a time, however, the opposite result appeared possible and
even probable. Engels, writing years later in 1895, remarked that
there had seemed to be "every prospect of turning the revolution of
the minority into the revolution of the majority." He was obliged
to add, "History has proved us, and all who thought like us, wrong."[6]
Nevertheless, an observer in those years could not escape perceiving
that there was a strife of classes in society, and that the contending
classes were capital and labor. Macaulay had seen this, and so had his
fellow members of the House of Commons, who defeated the
Chartist petition by 287 votes to 49.

These two classes seemed fundamental to society, because they
had to do with the production of goods. The strife between them
seemed equally fundamental, because it disturbed everything else.
Indeed, the events of 1848 had shown that the laboring class "cannot
stir, cannot raise itself up, without the whole superincumbent strata
of official society being sprung into the air." So Marx wrote in Part
I of the *Manifesto,* and proceeded throughout his later works to
describe in detail the structure, interaction, and political history of
the two classes. In brief, his description was this:

In a capitalist economy, the capitalists own the factories and the
land, and control the use of them. The workers possess chiefly their
ability to work, their "labor power." This they sell to the capitalists
in return for wages, but in working the machines and tilling the
land they produce more "value" than is returned to them. In other
words, profit (the goal of all capitalist enterprise) equals price minus
costs (among which are the workers' wages).

From these relations it follows that the members of society tend
not to have sufficient purchasing power to buy all that is produced.
Production periodically slows down, and people find themselves
poor for having produced "too much." Capital goes abroad, seeking
more profitable investment; basic exploitation shifts from home
populations to colonial populations; and wars begin among the
capitalist powers for a redistribution of markets and colonies. Con-

6) Introduction to Marx's *Class Struggles in France,* in op. cit., Vol. II, p. 176.

spicuous social waste becomes suddenly useful. Farmers are paid *not* to produce, surplus crops are stored at the taxpayer's expense, and armaments (obsolescent and sometimes obsolete as soon as produced) become an important prop of the domestic economy. Some of these events are too late in time for Marx to have described or even to have foreseen; but they nevertheless follow from the basic theory.

Thus, in Marx's view, capitalism is a society which can produce but not distribute—or, in his customary language, a society in which the productive forces constantly struggle against the relationships of production. He concluded that if the strife between capitalists and workers were definitively resolved in the workers' favor, there would come into existence a "classless society"—that is, a society without antagonistic classes—which could distribute and use everything it produced. Such a society would be at peace within itself, and from that peace there could be expected to develop new skills, new accomplishments, and a new sort of human being. For Marx's humanism, taken directly from the Enlightenment, never deserted him, and he purposed nothing less than the terrestrial redemption of mankind.

Marx, indeed, with a scholar's accuracy and candor, acknowledged the specific sources of his ideas: Hegel in philosophy and various middle-class thinkers in economics—including Benjamin Franklin, whom he praised for having given "the first sensible analysis of exchange value as labor-time."[7] His own contribution to social theory he severely limited to three assertions: that the existence of antagonistic classes belongs only to certain historical epochs (i.e., is not a permanent fact); that the working class can, by taking and using political power, amend the social order; and that, when this has been done, society will be thereafter free of acute antagonisms and able to solve its problems in a peaceful rational way.[8]

7) In *A Contribution to the Critique of Political Economy,* translated by N. I. Stone (Chicago: Charles H. Kerr and Company; 1904), p. 62. Marx here refers to Franklin's essay, "A Modest Inquiry into the Nature and Necessity of a Paper Currency" (1721). If this date is correct, Franklin would have been only fifteen years old.

8) See the letter to Joseph Wedemeyer, March 5, 1852: "What I did that was new was to prove: (1) that the *existence of classes* is only bound up with *particular, historic phases in the development of production;* (2) that the class struggle necessarily leads to the *dictatorship of the proletariat;* (3) that this dictatorship itself only constitutes the transition to the *abolition of all classes*

It is the second of these assertions that, in the capitalist view, makes Marxism the heresy of the age. Marx himself, as a great thinker, the capitalists have long accepted; they are now accepting even Lenin—apparently on the doubtful premise that the dead are no longer dangerous. But things are different with the theory itself. Any assertion that economic and political power is to be taken from those who presently possess it is the very heart and blood of heresy. Capitalist governments, therefore, have surrounded the doctrine of "the dictatorship of the proletariat" with an enormous and redundant mass of punitive legislation. For the doctrine plainly states what capitalists must ultimately fear—namely, their permanent political nullity.

That Marx produced and believed this doctrine there can be no doubt. He would have overwhelmed with laughter all subsequent attempts (and there have been many) to make him "respectable." In private life, no one can have been more Victorian: there was the Marx who romped with his children, who allowed his grandson, Jean Longuet, to make him into an omnibus "horsedrawn" by Engels and Liebknecht[9]—the Marx who was sensitive, sedate, and uxorious. But when it came to the struggles of men against their masters, the old lion roared to such effect that it will be many a day before the sound of it is gone.

And so we can see why any man who now discusses Marxism—in the United States of America especially, but *mutatis mutandis* elsewhere—will feel all the pains and joys to which embattled doctrine is subject. Such pains and joys we have thus far in this book been able to apprehend only in imagination, but we now grow aware of a complex of acutely puzzled emotions identical with those that once stirred Arius and Athanasius, Pelagius and Augustine, Abelard and Bernard of Clairvaux, Jeanne d'Arc and Cauchon, Servetus and Calvin, Diderot and the *infâmes*. Our feelings are perhaps intenser than theirs because our risks are greater. The present struggle between orthodoxy and heresy, whichever view is held to be the one or the other, may end in the annihilation of mankind.

It is fair to say that Marx never thought of the "dictatorship of

---

and to a *classless society."* The italics are Marx's, and the passage will be found, excerpted, in *Selected Works* (Moscow: Cooperative Publishing Society of Foreign Workers in the U.S.S.R.; 1935), Vol. I, p. 377.
9) Liebnecht, *Reminiscences,* in op. cit., Vol. I, p. 120.

the proletariat" as supervening upon a democracy. He thought of it as supervening upon another dictatorship, that of the capitalists. Marx was, and his followers have steadily been, extremely skeptical how democratic the forms of political democracy really are. The doubt has, for that matter, been shared. In 1821, Sydney Smith, a witty clergyman with an eye for politics, remarked, "Of all the ingenious instruments of despotism I must commend a popular assembly, where the majority are paid and hired, and a few bold and able men by their brave Speeches make the people believe they are free."[1]

In Marx's view, the "dictatorship of the proletariat" was to be a dictatorship vis-à-vis the capitalists and a democracy for everybody else. It was, in fact, to train the whole population in the art of self-government. More than this, it was to prepare for itself a kind of historical suicide by ending the need of all government whatever. As Engels wrote in *Anti-Dühring*, "In proportion as anarchy in social production vanishes, the political authority of the state also dies away. Man, at last the master of his own form of social organization becomes at the same time the lord over nature, master of himself—free."[2]

The first historical appearance of a workers' government was the Paris Commune of March to May, 1871. It arose according to what has since become a pattern—namely, the tendency of capitalist nations to produce socialism by conducting wars among themselves. The Commune sprang from the defeat of France by Prussia in alliance with other German states. Forty-six years later, the First World War produced socialism throughout Russia, and thirty-two years after that, the Second World War produced socialism in China and the Balkan countries. Capitalist nations, it may be thought, have a desperate need for peace.

The Commune was destroyed by a provisional government under Thiers (the "monstrous gnome," as Marx called him), with the aid of French prisoners of war released by Bismarck for the purpose. The slaughter in Paris was immense, and the *Mur des Fédérés* in the cemetery of Père Lachaise, where the last Communards were shot, remains a shrine for socialists. That bloody week, which ended on

---

1) Letter to Lady Grey, in *Selected Letters of Sydney Smith,* edited by Nowell C. Smith, World's Classics Series (Oxford University Press, 1956), pp. 147–48.
2) *Karl Marx: Selected Works,* as cited before, Vol. I, p. 188.

Whitsunday, broke resistance but not the spirit of resistance. The struggle, wrote Marx in the greatest of political eulogies, "cannot be stamped out with any amount of carnage. To stamp it out, governments would have to stamp out the despotism of capital over labor—the condition of their own parasitical existence."[3] And Eugène Pottier, the French worker-poet, a Communard who escaped first to England and then to the United States, expressed in celebrated lines the indestructibility of his hope:

> Debout! les damnés de la terre!
> Debout! les forçats de la faim!
> La raison tonne en son cratère,
> C'est l'éruption de la fin.

The next *éruption* occurred toward the close of what had been the bloodiest of all wars and in the country most shattered by that war. The vast Russian Empire was still feudal in political structure and agricultural in basic economy. The Czarist government was overthrown in February, 1917, and the succeeding government, which never grew to be more than provisional, vanished in the socialist revolution of November seventh. This time the revolution stuck. Counter-revolutionary armies failed to dislodge it, though at one time troops from fourteen foreign nations were "unofficially" on Soviet soil.

Thus the "dictatorship of the proletariat" established itself amid just those conditions most likely to increase dictatorship and decrease democracy. The nation had yet to build a modern industrial system. It was surrounded with enemies who threatened to return to the assault. It was infiltrated with those enemies' agents. And it contained among its own leaders the largest body of quarreling ideologues ever assembled since the French Revolution. The possibility and the fact of the "purges" cannot be understood unless it is realized that, amid continuing dangers and emergencies, dissenters could be suspected, guilty or not, of connivance with real and powerful foes.

Lenin, while he lived, was able to control the ideologues by persuasion, by a triumphant gift for showing the true constellation of forces and the consequently suitable policy. But Lenin died in 1924, and there remained no voice comparably rational and authoritative. The revolution had thus far gained only the opportunity to build

3) *The Civil War in France,* op. cit., Vol. II, p. 525.

socialism. Proposals for how to build it began to be lost in a confusion of tongues. More fundamentally yet, there was the question
whether you could have socialism anywhere unless you first had it
everywhere. If not, then the major task would be world revolution.

On this question, what may be called "applied Marxism" produced its first orthodoxy and heresy. Stalin's notion of socialism in
one country triumphed and became "orthodox"—that is to say, it
marshaled the Party organization, and ultimately the country, behind
it. Trotsky's preference for world revolution failed, and became
"heretical." As is usual in these cases, even the scientific writing of
history is for a long time influenced by the original victory and
defeat. The supporters of Stalin's view can say that they did in fact
build socialism, and that it subsequently spread to one billion of
the earth's inhabitants. The supporters of Trotsky's view are condemned to a series of counterfactual statements (as philosophers call
them) in the form, "If such-and-such had been done, such-and-such
would have happened." And for counterfactual statements, of
course, there can be little empirical proof.

The victor in this struggle, as in other struggles against other
"heresies," did for applied Marxism what Athanasius did for the
early Church. Stalin imposed upon Babel a settled policy, enforced
it, and made it stick. In the days of 1917, a close observer (Sukhanov)
described him as "a grey blur, floating dimly across the scene and
leaving no trace."[4] During the 1920's, that gray blur became extremely distinct; some will say that it became an *éminence grise*.
A self-contradictory character—"an emancipator," as Professor Carr
says, "and a tyrant"—he has left the socialist world attracted and
repelled at the same time. The capitalists, of course, had no such
problem: they were repelled all the while.

They were repelled, indeed, in both senses of the word: they
were horrified by the advent of socialism, and beaten off when they
attacked it. Whatever else may be said of Stalin, it is historically the
case that under his leadership socialism was in fact established and
the country which established it grew to be the second power in the
world.

These various events have produced throughout the world the
present pattern of orthodoxy and heresy. The economic source of

4) Edward Hallett Carr, *A History of Soviet Russia* (New York: The Macmillan Company; 1958), Vol. I, p. 176.

the pattern is much more visible now than it was wont to be in the past. Ever since socialism passed from theory into fact, men have been able to compare the results of production for use with the results of production for profit. It has become evident that production grows more readily when it is for use than when it is for profit, and that use-economies can absorb without dislocation all that technology affords. The day when socialist production begins to exceed capitalist production will see much alteration in men's minds of what is to be believed.

Meanwhile, in what is called by a geographical convenience "the West," socialism remains the great punishable heresy. How long it will remain so I cannot say. Its ideals and advantages seem not much dimmed by abusive description or even by the crimes committed in its name. Its appeal to new countries is obvious: they have no other means of setting up independent economies. Finally, it has evoked, in curious but extensive ways, imitation by the capitalist states themselves. Reactionaries are not wrong to speak of "creeping socialism." They are only wrong to regret it.

I think every socialist laments the fact that questions of orthodoxy and heresy survived so painfully into socialism itself. The hope had always been that, when you got rid of class struggles, you would no longer punish people for their ideas. The sad fact is, however, that police power, no matter what it defends, brings on these evils. May one think nevertheless that these evils will cease and that socialism itself will end them? Perhaps. Stalin, it appears, is now condemned for a too narrow dogmatism too ruthlessly enforced. There may be hope in the condemnation. For, from the moment it becomes heretical to determine orthodoxy, the peoples of the world have begun to be saved.

CHAPTER

1 5

Spacious Skies

In the fall of 1892, when Mr. Harrison was contesting the Presidency with Mr. Cleveland, my great-grandfather David Dunham, a farmer of Bedminster, New Jersey, said to my father, then a young graduate from Princeton, "It doesn't matter who wins, Harry; they are both Presbyterians."

There cannot be a more comic simplification of politics; yet the history of the United States of America gave that remark a certain persuasiveness in 1892. Calvinists had founded the country, had begun the building of it with their courage and labor, had helped lift it into nationhood, and had shared (though with much splintering[1]) the struggle against chattel slavery. A great deal of what the country was—indeed, of what the country is—came from Calvinist ideals: the resolution, always embattled and never lost, that righteousness must prevail. One could have confidence in this tradition, and, while national affairs were conducted within it, one could feel content.

Yet I suppose that the year 1892 was almost the last in which persuasiveness might prevail over comedy. In 1884, James G. Blaine, the Republican presidential candidate, had lost the election because one of his supporters, the Reverend Mr. Samuel D. Burchard, had said (Blaine being on the platform) that the Democratic Party stood for "Rum, Romanism, and Rebellion."[2] Burchard put rather too

1) E.g., the Presbyterian Church split into northern and southern branches.
2) Speech of October 29, 1884.

much hope in alliteration and in Calvinism. The Democratic Party had indeed been associated with chattel slavery and was presently associated with what used to be called the "liquor interests." It was, further, supported by an increasing population of Catholics, whose votes, thus wantonly alienated, gave the presidency to Grover Cleveland.

In this result there was the shrewd, sure sense that Americans frequently display for immediate issues. The Reverend Mr. Burchard's "Rum, Romanism, and Rebellion," if indeed it was anything more than campaign oratory, was bigotry. Yet two of its three components had been, in their time, chief obstacles to progress: human society had found it necessary to break the political power of Rome and to abolish chattel slavery. Moreover, a case can always be made against rum. But an attack upon evils already removed or limited could only mask a far less reputable intent. The Reverend Mr. Burchard was attempting to gather votes out of fear of an immigrant minority, which, being neither native nor Protestant, could be suspected of dark designs.

Thus near to bigotry do libertarian notions lie. It is true very generally among mankind, but it is peculiarly true of the American tradition. This tradition has always moved between two polar opposites: the Bill of Rights and the witch hunt, the court of justice and the lynching bee. For all their celebrated pragmatism, Americans seldom do anything by halves. Epoch by epoch, they will be found either demolishing tyranny or demolishing dissent. Both these things, in fact, they have done, and do now do, upon one and the same theoretical ground: whether they are dispossessing a slave owner or putting a socialist in jail, it is all on behalf of liberty. Americans are pragmatic toward theory, not toward practice, and if they find that one doctrine will serve precisely opposite ends, they see no reason to be unthrifty of ratiocination.

I I

THE UNITED STATES OF AMERICA lies between two oceans, which were its moat and guard until technology reduced them to rivulets. The country stretches, topographically splendid, from the rocky soil of New England and the rich arable soil of the Middle Atlantic and Southern States, across the Appalachians, into a vast and fruitful basin, where at a certain point the trees drop away and nothing intervenes between a man and the sky. Then come deserts and greater mountains, and beyond them a thin coastal tract of adventure and fertility, almost all the inhabitants of which have been born somewhere else.

Every inch of this soil has been trod and farmed and made bountiful by heretics. Heretics have climbed these mountains, sailed these lakes and rivers, mined these veins. Every blade of wheat, every ear of corn, every head of cattle, every commodity issuing from that most conformist of all systems, the assembly line, has been touched in one way or another by heretics. If there be (as indeed I doubt) an American who is not a heretic, then at least he is descended from one, and he cannot pursue the dismal round of orthodoxy without denying his ancestors.

It all began (if we omit the earlier touch upon Virginia) in the bleakest of these regions, where the new arrivals were baffled to find a habitable site, and where the aborigines, lately stricken with pestilence, had little to offer but communicable disease. More than half the Pilgrims died during the winter of 1620 to 1621; the rest, fit upon Darwinian principles, survived to begin a nation.

These people, known to themselves as Saints and to the English public as Separatists, had reached that stage of organizational discontent in which members, seeing no hope of purity in official doctrine, decide to form a new organization of their own. They rejected ritual and sacrament, and cast off with loathing all notion of a clergy set apart as consecrated by a laying on of hands. Their own worship was in fact shared by all the members, and tailors, tapsters, cobblers rose to expound Scripture according to an inner and private light. In time, at Plymouth, they acquired a ministry, being moved by the love of good sermons such as extempore utterance could not supply. But they nicely balanced social need against the supreme fact (for so they conceived it) that every man was to be his own master. They were a sensible folk, and, though they found one or two "witches," they (unlike the Puritans) killed none.[3]

The Separatists, part of the left wing of those days, were plainly heretics, since they had reached the stage of schism. Oppressed in England, they had gone to Holland in 1608; there, though sheltered, they found themselves and their children aging under labor or

3) Cf. George F. Willison, *The Pilgrim Reader* (New York: Doubleday and Company; 1953), p. 430.

drawn, amid that prosperous society, "into extravagant and dangerous courses."[4] They thereupon determined to seek the new world,
as it then was, and their wish chanced to agree with that of certain
merchant adventurers who foresaw a profit in colonizing.

The Saints left Delfthaven in July of 1620, bound for England,
where they were to pick up forty "Strangers," employees of the
merchant adventurers. It was an anguished parting, for the little
congregation, close-knit by Christian love, was being permanently
sundered. The Pilgrims, setting out for unknown lands and unknown perils, had nothing to rest upon but faith and charity and
hope. These proved, in the event, enough.

> So they left that goodly and pleasant city [wrote Bradford] which
> had been their resting place near twelve years. But they knew
> they were pilgrims and looked not much on those things, but
> lifted up their eyes to the heavens, their dearest country, and
> quieted their spirits.[5]

Then, having changed vessels at Plymouth, they came in the
Mayflower to the northern tip of Cape Cod, four months after they
had left Holland. It was the onset of winter, and "all things stood
upon them with a weatherbeaten face."[6] There was, moreover, a
singular social contretemps. The one hundred four emigrants had
contracted for settlement in Virginia. They had missed by many
miles even the generous boundaries then ascribed to Virginia, and
consequently the contract was no longer binding. The passengers
suddenly found themselves reduced to the state of nature, devoid of
all constituted authority. In jurisprudence they were what men had
not been since the earliest organization of society: individual persons
without legally established government.

This remarkable fact struck home as the *Mayflower* (how lovely
a name for so icy a circumstance!) lay within the waters of Cape
Cod. There began to be what Bradford called "discontented and
mutinous speeches,"[7] issuing from the Strangers, who represented
the commercial as distinguished from the religious interest: "that
when they came ashore, they would use their own liberty." But not

4) Ibid., p. 46. This is William Bradford's account of the matter. *Of Plimouth
Plantation.*
5) Ibid., p. 76.
6) *Ibid.,* pp. 94–95. Bradford.
7) Ibid., p. 99.

for such an issue had the Saints sailed that tempestuous sea, nor daily
sung from the Ainsworth Psalter such verses as

> He that walks perfect, justice works
> And in his heart speaks truth.
> That slandereth not with his tongue;
> None ill to his friend dooth.[8]

Accordingly, the Saints assembled the entire ship's company for
the ratification of a compact, the Mayflower Compact, in which "we
. . . covenant and combine ourselves together into a civil body politic
for our better ordering and preservation . . . and by virtue hereof to
enact, constitute, and frame such just and equal laws, ordinances, acts,
constitutions, and offices, from time to time, as shall be thought most
meet and convenient for the general good of the Colony, unto which
we promise all due submission and obedience."[9] Thus the Pilgrim
Fathers performed the sort of act which, thirty-one years later Hobbes
in *Leviathan* and seventy years later Locke in the *Essays on Government,* described as the true origin of all civil society.

The Colony, with its institutions, survived and even prospered,
and to this day Americans feel privileged (indeed, almost consecrated) if they can trace descent from one of the *Mayflower*
passengers.[1] Yet, despite their remarkable valor and achievement,
the Saints had rather less influence upon subsequent history than their
rivals, the Puritans, who settled the area around Massachusetts Bay.
These came for a like reason, religious liberty, but, politically speaking, they were not so far to the left. As their name suggests, they
proposed to remain within the Church of England and to purify it
—an extremely hopeful intent, seeing that, often as the thing has
been tried, it has never been effected. Yet it left the Puritans short of
being schismatics, which the Saints, with their separatism, were.

During the decade of 1630 to 1640, some twenty thousand emigrants, mostly Puritan, settled in New England. Politically, they

8) A version of Psalm 15. A fine recording (now out of print) of these Pilgrims' hymns was issued by the Haydn Society, Boston, 1953.
9) This text has been often reprinted—e.g., in Willison, op. cit., p. 100, and
Bernard Smith, *The Democratic Spirit* (New York: Alfred A. Knopf; 1941),
p. 4.
1) My own *Mayflower* ancestor, John Howland, a servant in the household of
John Carver, fell overboard during the voyage and was rescued from the
waves with a boat hook. Willison, op. cit., p. 93.

were refugees from the archiepiscopal tyranny of Laud; economically, they were artisans and enterprisers in search of opportunity. No doubt it is true to say that they had been driven out for stubborn rebelliousness of mind. Yet the case also was that, in the eyes of the English government and of the Anglican Church, colonizing was a shrewd and not unmerciful means of getting rid of dissenters. Being gone, they would no longer trouble the domestic arrangements, while at the same time they might be expected to yield some future profit in trade. Governments have a great advantage when they can frustrate dissenters without killing them, and I dare say that the colonial system has in this manner done much, during three hundred years, to temper the asperity of British politics.

Arrived in Massachusetts, the Puritans at once enacted all those ecclesiastical reforms which they had been impotent to produce in England. Sacerdotalism, the idea of a consecrated clergy with special rights and powers, had, as we know, been long obnoxious[2]—made so by the vice and rapacity of clerics themselves. The Puritans annulled all such status and the theory which justified it, and proposed that ministers be merely first among equals. As the Quakers had refused to doff their hats in the presence of any king, so the Puritans refused to kneel in the presence of God. They stood up to pray, and thus addressed their Maker as children mature. They married before a magistrate, not a minister, and they buried their dead without utterance of prayer. In all this conduct, there was the self-respect and thrift of artisans and men of business, whose rise toward power cast ritual aside and left ceremony to the decaying lords. As Bancroft says, "The institutions of chivalry were subverted by the gradually increasing weight and knowledge and opulence of the industrious classes; the Puritans, rallying upon these classes, planted in their hearts the undying principles of democratic liberty."[3]

In all respects but one, the Puritans established a legal code which was, for that time, extremely merciful: it is notable indeed that they did not prescribe capital punishment for crimes against property. Yet the one exception to the rule of mercy has, in the view of descendants, sufficiently tarnished their fame. Like most Protestants —like most revolutionaries in the early heat of revolution—they

2) Supra, Chapter 8.
3) George Bancroft, *History of the United States of America* (New York: D. Appleton and Company; 1890), Vol. I, p. 322.

exaggerated the importance of ideology. Faith justifies, Luther had said, and Calvin after him; works (that is to say, actions) do not. Or, to turn theological language into philosophical: a right theory as to fact and morals is sufficient to the good life.

This theory the Puritans believed themselves to possess; and, just as they had defended it with rebellious zeal against the Anglican hierarchy, so they defended it with legal violence against men of yet more democratic mind than themselves. There ensued, rather briefly, that singular contest between "law" and "grace" in which, to say truth, the eminent Reformers had been from the very beginning entangled. Infallible Scripture had given men an infallible law; it had also, in the Pauline passages, asserted that there is such a thing as irresistible grace (the talent for right choices), and that he on whom grace irresistibly descends may do without law altogether. The persons persuaded of this latter view were called Antinomians—which is to say, "opposed to law"—and, like Anne Hutchinson, trusted to personal righteousness rather than the social law, whenever the two seemed to be in conflict.

The contests that now ensued within the Puritan domain turned, with Protestant accuracy, upon faith rather than works. Not Anne Hutchinson, nor Roger Williams, nor the Reverend John Wheelwright, nor, afterward, Mary Dyer, William Robinson, Marmaduke Stevenson, William Laddra (all Quakers) had committed any actionable offense other than the public expression of more or less antinomian ideas. Yet, of these, Anne Hutchinson and Roger Williams were banished, and the rest were hanged. There was a grisly scene on October 27, 1659, on Boston Common, when Mary Dyer, having watched Robinson and Stevenson strangled upon an elm tree, mounted the ladder—and was suddenly reprieved.[4] She was pardoned and refused to be pardoned; she was escorted fifteen miles on horseback into banishment; then she returned—such was the strength of inner light—and perished on the gallows, June 1, 1660. The sacrifice was as effective as gallant, for, after her, only one other Quaker (Laddra) was ever hanged. Somewhat before, in 1643, Anne Hutchinson, having settled in Long Island, was there massacred by Indians, along with all but one of her eight children. A tragic and, as one may think, an irrelevant end to that beautiful, brave, and

4) Bertram Lippincott, *Indians, Privateers, and High Society* (Philadelphia: J. B. Lippincott Company; 1961), p. 75.

fecund woman. She has a highway named after her now, and it seems not quite enough.

Anne's martyrdom attests, no doubt, Indian resentment of the colonists' rapacity. The martyrdom of the others attests the distortions of Protestantism. So soon as "faith" was elevated above "works," coercion was bound to settle upon just that area where it is necessarily intrusive: personal integrity. This was precisely the realm which the Inquisition assailed and sought to conquer, and its possession by the person or by authority defines the difference between free man and slave. For, after all, theory gets at least part of its verification in practice, and, in practice, even gets part of its ultimate meaning. From theory alone, there are no very certain inferences what practice will in fact be. The old Whigs of England, *circa* 1830, whose philosophical eminence rested upon the mistakes (well pondered) of the Puritans, made the ground of liberty clear:

> To punish a man [wrote Macaulay] because he has committed a crime, or because he is believed, though unjustly, to have committed a crime, is not persecution. To punish a man, because we infer from the nature of some doctrine which he holds, or from the conduct of other persons who hold the same doctrines with him, that he will commit a crime, is persecution, and is, in every case, foolish and wicked.[5]

There can be little doubt that this is indeed the case, and, if doubt remain, it must perish before Macaulay's ultimate rebuke: "Man, in short, is so inconsistent a creature that it is impossible to reason from his belief to his conduct, or from one part of his belief to another."[6] Thence derives the liberal insight that penalties are to fall upon the overt act, not upon some inward thought which may—or, equally, may not—be prelude to it.

In our early history, the man most persuaded of this truth was Roger Williams, who took, indeed, a rather loftier view of the case than will be found among the more pragmatic Whigs. Private conscience, in Williams' view, was sacred and inviolable; God had intended, and had permitted, its self-directed use, free from all compulsion. "It is the will and command of God that (since the coming of his Son the Lord Jesus) a permission of the most

5) "Essay on Hallam," in *Critical and Historical Essays,* Everyman's Library (London: J. M. Dent and Sons; 1920), Vol. I, p. 7.
6) Ibid., p. 8.

Paganish, Jewish, Turkish, or Antichristian consciences and worships to be granted to all men in all nations and countries: and they are only to be fought against with that sword which is only (in soul matters) able to conquer: to wit, the sword of God's spirit, the word of God."[7] In short, in matters of belief ("soul matters"—lovely phrase!) persuasion is valid, force is not.

The remarkable thing about Roger Williams is that he did in fact found just such a commonwealth, Rhode Island, which for many years held to the principle, though it has long since abandoned so amiably anarchist a view. Banished from Massachusetts, ill received in Plymouth and Salem, Williams took title to a tract some seventy miles west of Cape Cod, on the basis of an Indian deed. This procedure, highly irregular in respect of English law, was characteristic. For Williams believed that the land belonged to its original inhabitants and that consequently the colonists were interlopers. On this higher—and certainly anti-imperialist jurisprudence—he accepted nothing that the Indians did not willingly grant. Thus he settled himself and his colony, all of like mind, at a place the Indians called Seekonk, which he renamed Providence, "in a sense of God's merciful providence unto me in my distress."[8]

Thither came dissenters from the authoritarian neighborhoods, chief among them Quakers in great numbers. The aggressive peaceableness of these folk soon made them dominant in the colony, and Williams, though not compromising the principle of free conscience, began to assert its more polemical side. The eminent Quaker George Fox, on tour of the New World in 1672, escaped, by a timely departure, debate with him; but two disciples, Stubbs and Edmondson, were less lucky. One day Williams took boat, rowed the twenty-one miles to Newport, and on the morrow, from nine in the morning to six in the afternoon, visited upon those adversaries the wonders of his rhetoric. There were giants in the land then, but at least, in those special precincts, violence had become purely verbal. In his published commentary upon the affair, Williams described Fox, in a metaphor obscure to me, as an old cow with a kettle on her head.[9]

Thus, even in the most libertarian of colonies, there was some-

---

7) From *The Bloody Tenent* [Tenet] *of Persecution for Cause of Conscience,* excerpted in Bernard Smith, op. cit., p. 6.
8) Often quoted, e.g., in Lippincott, op. cit., p. 34, and on maps issued by the American Automobile Association.
9) Lippincott, op. cit., p. 48.

thing less than peace. Peace would have involved some general agreement in doctrine, and the New England settlers were ideologues who regarded agreement as a surrender of personal sovereignty. This trait remains—modified, to be sure, but not lost—as part of an American's image of himself. He is sure he is right, even if he is in fact only quoting the daily newspaper, and, even more than being sure he is right, he is sure other people are wrong. He has an abiding faith in the power of righteousness and of abusive rhetoric. Alas that, abusive or commendatory, rhetoric will not alter in the slightest degree the intransigeance of objective fact!

The peculiar circumstance that thoughts rather than acts were the primary subject of quarrel produced, in the year 1692, the most shocking episode in American history: the trial and execution of "witches" in Salem. Behind this dreadful and absurd event lay centuries of ignorant speculation mixed with the dim inveterate malice that ignorance ordinarily breeds. We have thus far treated the description of things "supernatural" rather genially, as metaphor masking a kind of science. We must now observe that it had also a gross and ugly aspect, which masked not science but hate. Odious as have been the persecutions of the righteous, far more odious have been the persecutions of the lowly, the aged, the sick, and the insane. The righteous at least were lucid, and to that extent could defend themselves. But the wretches whom society itself had stricken and enfeebled—what could they do against militant authority?

For these cruelties, however, a long tradition had accumulated. The politics of this tradition issued from the fear which insecure and exploitative rulers have of the inward thoughts and silent commentary of the multitudes they rule. Perhaps no word or act appears to remind the rulers what the multitude really thinks; nevertheless the rulers suspect some magical converse leading to revolt. Indeed, in our own time and place, supposedly scientific and free, there are educational administrators who really do believe that a teacher can stand before a class and, without mentioning the name of Marx or any of his doctrines, convey to students a knowledge of communism and a desire for it.

Thus there is still, and for many centuries has been, a myth of social forces that are destructive and supernatural. The simple figure of speech, personification, which enabled any and all happenings to be connected with intent, easily allowed destructive happenings to be connected with malicious intent. But whose intent was it that was malicious? Satan's, no doubt, ultimately; but Satan had also his angels and collaborators among men, whose own malicious intent was joined with his.

In Christian doctrine, to be sure, God is the ultimate cause of all that happens, whether for good or evil. The Church has long outlawed Manichean theory, which regarded events as a contest between good and evil forces equally matched. Nevertheless, there runs through Christianity a current of belief, now submerged and almost lost, in a supernatural and evil personage whom God could destroy but for some reason does not. This belief, a kind of poetry of ugliness, records in its twisted way certain quite authentic facts. In the first place, there really is a latent rebelliousness among masses of the governed; and, in the second place, there was in old time a vast amount of quasi-religious myth upon which Christianity with its elaborated doctrine supervened. This popular religion could be suppressed but not extirpated, and it survived, rather vigorously, as a rival creed and ritual that became a kind of satiric commentary upon the Christian churches themselves.

Thus there was the worship of Satan rather than of God, the Black Mass instead of *Missa Solemnis;* there were demons instead of angels, witches instead of saints, a sexuality permissive and perverse, and occult contacts with less attractive animals like goats, toads, frogs. Angels traveled by wings; witches by broomstick. At a distance, or nearby, angels and saints conferred their mercies; at a distance, or nearby, witches imposed all sorts of human loss. Beauty of outward form (in fact or in vision) was the recognizable sign of a saint; ugliness was that of a witch. Accordingly, any old woman in whose eyes shone the agony and anger of a miserable life could be denounced as a witch, and all her woes, innocently suffered, could be crowned by death at gallows or stake.

From the twelfth century through the eighteenth,[1] scores of thousands of these wretches perished by execution. They were, almost all of them, helpless, hapless folk, whom a rational society would have put in homes for the aged or asylums for the insane. Or, what

---

1) The last trial for witchcraft in England was in 1712; the last executions for it were, in Scotland 1722, Spain 1782, Germany (at Posen) 1793, Peru 1888. Estimates of the total deaths vary from 100,000 to several millions. *Encyclopaedia Britannica,* eleventh edition, Vol. XXVIII, p. 757.

is worst, they were sane, good people, upon whom the charge of witchcraft had been maliciously laid.

A vast and odious theory developed concerning the identification and punishment of witches, and was codified about the year 1500 in the *Malleus Maleficarum* ("Hammer of Witches") by Jacob Sprenger, a learned maniac. Since one of his maxims was that any person is a witch who cannot be coerced into confessing witchcraft, it will be seen that defendants had very little defense; and since punishment derived from the most inhumane text to be found in Scripture,[2] the resolute defendant was plainly doomed. Even as late as 1886, a theological work of marvelous erudition and consistency asserts that demons "hinder man's temporal and eternal welfare—sometimes by exercising a certain control over natural phenomena, but more commonly by subjecting man's soul to temptation;" further, that "possession [i.e., by demons] is distinguished from bodily or mental disease," and that it is "impossible to interpret the narratives of demoniac possession as popular descriptions of abnormal physical or mental conditions."[3]

If an intelligent man could entertain such nonsense toward the end of the nineteenth century, we need not be surprised that some of our ancestors acted upon it toward the end of the seventeenth. Even so, the outburst at Salem, so violent, so brief, so quickly repented, was by these very characteristics shown to be exceptional. Essentially, perhaps, it displayed the emotional stress of building a new society in remote and dangerous surroundings. Yet within the general hysteria moved more familiar wishes, familiarly evil: the wish to acquire property, to protect power already possessed, to satisfy grudges, to seem important despite mediocrity. These lusts will be found in every witch hunt, old or contemporary; and they constitute the whole purpose, though not the whole environment, of persecution.

The Reverend Mr. Samuel Parris, pastor of the church at Salem and a quarrelsome cleric, maintained with his flock a vigorous controversy, which, by end of the year 1691, had reached its height. He had within his household a daughter Elizabeth, aged nine, and a

---

2) Exodus 22:18—"Thou shalt not suffer a witch to live." Or, as Moffat has it, "You shall not allow a sorceress to live." This injunction was probably laid down by the priesthood to discourage competition, especially by females, in "spiritual" affairs.

3) Augustus Hopkins Strong, *Systematic Theology* (New York: A. C. Armstrong and Son; 1893), p. 228.

niece Abigail Williams, aged eleven. There was also a chum of these two—Anne Putnam, aged twelve. Mr. Parris had a hostile mind, if there ever was one, and it is not difficult to guess that the daughter and niece responded with hostility—deflecting it, however, from the father, as pious children should do.

Within the household also were a Negro servant, Tituba, and her husband, John the Indian. Tituba had come from Barbados in the West Indies, full of necromantic lore, to which John the Indian added something of his own. What else was lacking, the girls readily supplied from the writings of Cotton Mather, a Boston clergyman and son of a president of Harvard College.

The three girls, who had certain other young accomplices, had no notion of practicing witchcraft; rather, they had the far more ingenious notion of pretending to be attacked by witches. They had learned the necessary behavior, which, indeed, was of the simplest: moans, convulsions, cries of being bewitched. Their histrionic skill was considerable, and grew with success. What remains astounding is that this malicious play-acting was ever taken as ground for legal charges and as sufficient evidence for conviction. Throughout the affair, however, may be seen the political acumen of the odious Parris and Mather's absurd demonological speculations.

The girls first denounced Tituba, who, in panic, confessed herself a witch. This splendid success led the movement out-of-doors. The first public victim was one Sarah Good, "a forlorn, friendless, and forsaken creature, broken down by wretchedness of condition and ill repute."[4] She was easily convicted, and persecution spread. The victims perished as the children howled. When October of 1692 arrived, nineteen persons had died upon the gallows, one had been pressed to death by weights,[5] fifty-five had been tortured into confession, one hundred fifty were awaiting trial, and two hundred more were denounced or under suspicion.[6] The Reverend Mr. Parris had used the hysteria adroitly, for among the hanged were his rival for the pastorate, the Reverend George Burroughs, and various opponents within the congregation. Yet I think we must not suppose

4) Charles W. Upham, *Salem Witchcraft,* (New York: Frederick Ungar), Vol. II, p. 13.
5) This was the celebrated Giles Corey, who would not at all answer the question, "Are you now or have you ever been a witch?" A laconic old man, all he said during his long and horrible execution was, "More weight!"
6) Bancroft, op. cit., Vol. II, p. 65.

Parris to have been a coldly calculating assassin. His moral blindness was more dense: he really did believe that opposition to himself and subservience to Satan were one and the same thing.

As for Mather, he was a bright man numbed by stupidity. He had an interest in natural science, wrote rather well upon it, and even advocated vaccination against smallpox.[7] Yet he approved the witch trials, attended on horseback at least one of the hangings, wrote up the whole affair in *The Wonders of the Invisible World,* and went on to plan a similar, though never effectuated, persecution in Boston. *Tantum religio potuit suadere malorum!*

After eight months, the horror vanished before a mixed response of guilt and common sense. The body proved stronger than its ague. Parris, dismissed from his pastorate, sank toward poverty. The Reverend Mr. Noyes, who had joyfully cried at one execution, "There hang eight firebrands of hell!" gave himself over to repentance and good works. Anne Putnam, upon confessing in 1706 that she had been "deluded by Satan,"[8] was received into communion. Families of the victims were paid, in 1711, the trifling total sum of five hundred seventy-eight pounds, twelve shillings.[9] And Cotton Mather, that errant, evil genius, failed of election to the presidency of Harvard College in November of 1724. He had spent the previous first of July, "our insipid, ill-contrived anniversary which we call the Commencement," praying that that office "may not be foolishly thrown away."[1] Obviously it was so thrown, and the egregious Mather, who to the end of his life steadfastly supposed himself a fountain of good for all, never at any time conceived how it could be that men should hate him.

Libertarians, bigots, heroes, scoundrels, sages, fools—in America we have had, and do now have, them all.

I I I

THE AFFAIR AT SALEM, which arose, ideologically, from an abuse of metaphor, became in time a metaphor itself. During subsequent

7) Richard B. Morris, *Encyclopedia of American History* (New York: Harper and Brothers; 1953), p. 541.
8) Quoted in Upham, op. cit., where the whole text of the "confession" appears. "Satan" will serve as an excuse if not as an adversary.
9) Ibid., Vol. II, p. 480.
1) Ibid., Vol. II, p. 505.

centuries into the present day, Americans have grown accustomed to
describe as "witch hunts" all organized attacks on people for their
opinions. This practice reveals a basic decency, a reluctance to harm
fellow citizens, which the inhabitants of Salem did in the end display. In order to display it, they had to rise above a good deal of
what they believed to be the case. Very few of them doubted the
existence of witches. Yet the community withdrew in horror from
the consequences of believing in witchcraft, and, after a time, the
belief itself dropped away.

Within a hundred years the people of the colonies were back in
their old role of active dissent and were defending with force of
arms the nationalist heresy. The brilliant scheme by which the outcasts of England—dissenters, convicts, ne'er-do-wells—were to become, in their exile, sources of profit to the mother country, collapsed
so soon as those same dissenters, convicts, and ne'er-do-wells built
an economy they could defend. Their war of national liberation,
1775–83, inaugurated an epoch of world history which may perhaps
be described as "running the British out." That epoch, now almost
consummated, seems to be followed, with singular but not inex-
plicable irony, by an epoch of "running the Americans out." For if
the colonists of 1775, from New England south through Georgia,
wished to be free of all government but their own, that wish is now
shared and acted upon by every people on earth. Mr. Longfellow's
moral has now a worldwide application, that

> In the hour of darkness and peril and need,
> The people will waken and listen to hear
> The hurrying hoof-beats of that steed,
> And the midnight message of Paul Revere.

A student of heresy, approaching the American scene from past
events in Europe and the Mediterranean, will be struck by the fact
that, though it is reputable in America to be a heretic, it is not always
safe to be one. The urge for a diversity of views is much modified by
a fear of what those views may be. The fear is, in part, genuinely
patriotic—an alarm lest the nation be imperiled in the world. It is
also fear touching the possible loss of property and privilege (not
necessarily those of caste or class) won with much labor in the
nation's history. Despite a revolutionary past that established independence and abolished chattel slavery, Americans are "by nature"

(lovely Aristotelian phrase!) no less conservative than other folk. Given certain pressures, they will exaggerate the conservatism, just as, given other pressures, they will exaggerate rebelliousness. The divided colonial self is warmly present in them: they will appear at times unanimously libertarian, at times unanimously authoritarian, and at times, to the perplexity of all observers, unanimously both.

Our student of heresy, approaching America from Europe, will notice a second phenomenon, which is the apparent imitativeness of American thought. During three hundred fifty years, not a single idea which could be called by the unforgiveable adjective "epoch-making" has originated upon these shores—not even that curious anti-theory which goes by the name of pragmatism.[2] We have produced no Luther, no Locke, no Darwin, no Marx. This fact has somewhat embarrassed American intellectuals, as suggesting a prolonged infancy.

I think it need not do so. No one makes an epoch until the epoch is ready to be made, and no one turns up a great idea unless he happens to stand, with all the light of past knowledge, at the exact place and moment of discovery. Moreover, the concepts borrowed by Americans have generally been adequate to the need, and were held, not as mere expedient borrowings, but as profound personal convictions. After this manner, Calvin served the Puritans and Pilgrims, Locke the warriors for independence, and a cluster of European philosophers the Abolitionist movement. These events, indeed, are rather less astonishing that the fact that the ideas of Karl Marx, a German working as an exile in England, should have found fulfillment on Russian and Chinese soil.

Between any new great concept and its application to practice lie subtle degrees of inference, which, if properly traversed, lay bare the mode and accuracy of use. General concepts can, of course, be misapplied, and, when the concept is new and great, the novelty and the prestige incite to hurried application. The discovery Hobbes and Locke drove home, that human society was a human contrivance rather than a divine establishment, and that it could be rearranged according to human wishes, made men immediately aware that their grievances had practicable remedies. It could not, however, without

2) Pragmatism had an unexpected, if highly reputable source, in Immanuel Kant. Its "Americanness" lies in the fact that the philosophers of every other country rejected it.

intervening inferences, prescribe the mode of remedy. American colonists of, say, the year 1765 knew from the Quartering Act and the Stamp Act that they were being asked to support troops for their own repression. Locke's theory confirmed the fact that this was as unnecessary as it was absurd. But what were the colonists to do?

Fortunately for their labors and for the nation that has issued therefrom, the colonists had leaders who understood practical politics as well as Lockean theory. The great second paragraph of the Declaration, a union of sociology and jurisprudence, describes with wonderful exactitude the conditions in which basic change can occur:

> Prudence, indeed, will dictate that Governments long established should not be changed for light and transient causes and accordingly all experience hath shewn, that mankind are more disposed to suffer, while evils are sufferable, than to right themselves by abolishing the forms to which they are accustomed.

Thus the Lockean insight that men could, on occasion, justifiably alter their form of government was seen to be modified by the sociological fact that such alteration cannot be effective unless the mass of the people desires it. No *putsch* or "palace revolution" will suffice, and all movements that are not mass movements must fail.

The colonial leaders therefore waited until, in the view of almost everyone, evils were no longer sufferable. The mercantile classes of New England, New York, and Pennsylvania found their trade intercepted and their profits reduced. The planters of Maryland, Virginia, and the Carolinas were never out of debt to bankers and businessmen in England. The robber's pinch, which it is the whole purpose of an imperialist system to maintain, nipped and stung throughout the colonies.

The final response was profoundly and characteristically American: a movement embracing all sorts of contrary classes and interests —merchants, slave owners, artisans, professionals (like the clergy), and independent farmers. The military leader and public hero of the war was George Washington, a Virginia planter of far from radical views. It appears to be characteristic, and may even be fated, that in American politics, social advance, though always prompted by leftists, is never led by them, but is led by some centrist personage around whom the whole people can rally.

On the night of the eighteenth to nineteenth of April, 1775, certain farmers of the land around Boston, roused from sleep to defend "illegal" stores of powder and shot, gathered on Lexington Common and (some hours later) at Concord Bridge. They were encountering well-trained infantry, symbol and arm of the ruling power. At Lexington, events proceeded in the proper eighteenth-century fashion: the British lined up and fired, and among the sixty opposing farmers a few heroes fell. But at Concord, resistance became effective. During the long march back to Boston, the British infantry was treated to the arts of guerrilla warfare, and, when all was over, His Majesty's forces lay at Boston in a state of siege.

Certain small events of that day suggest themselves as revealing or prophetic. British soldiers, stopping at a farmhouse near Concord, asked food and offered to pay for it. The housewife, a Mrs. Barrett, answered with a wonderful blend of firmness, magnanimity, and Calvinism, "We are commanded to feed our enemy, if he hunger."[3] And she accepted no pay.

Two British soldiers died in the skirmish at Concord Bridge. Their tomb, now part of the general shrine, bears a quatrain beginning,

> They came three thousand miles and died
> To keep the past upon its throne . . .

But keeping the past upon its throne is precisely what no one can do. The mortuary legend of those two British soldiers, who doubtless wished to be anywhere else than where they were, survives as admonition to all who descend from either the victors or the vanquished at Concord Bridge.

The same sense of the practical which put off revolution until there could be inner unity also informed the leaders' conduct of foreign affairs. France was then the most powerful conservative country in Europe, ruled in the feudal manner which Locke had theoretically made out of date. In respect of political principles, there could be nothing but hostility between the American revolutionary government and the French monarchical system; yet the two had, as it chanced, a common, if temporary, enemy. Thus Franklin was able to achieve the alliance which brought the war to its end. If the Founding Fathers had been purists, unwilling to touch the decaying power of the past, they might not have brought off their victory.

3) Bancroft, op. cit., Vol. IV, p. 158. See Romans 12:20.

But Americans, as one sees, are never purists, except on some few lamentable occasions when they are engaged in being impure. The War of Independence was a great international event—the first, but not the last, libertarian offering to come from these shores. The nation thus established stood for some years alone in the world, an ideal for radicals, a target for reactionaries. The French Revolution modeled itself upon the American, and the Holy Alliance gathered to undo the work of both. In the 1840's and '50's, visitors to the United States (like Mrs. Trollope and Mr. Dickens) returned with gleeful stories of vice and failure, just as visitors to the socialist world now do. Yet the Republic stood, unassailable across its oceans and abundant in its land. There was room for its own dissenters, who had merely to remove to the frontier.[4] There was also room for European dissenters: German socialists escaping Friedrich Wilhelm or Bismarck, Irish farmers escaping famine, Jews from various nations escaping pogroms—the "huddled masses yearning to breathe free."

The great ideas of the Revolution were ideas of the Enlightenment, and they modified, though they did not extinguish, the Calvinist heritage. This heritage, indeed, had enjoyed a kind of Renaissance during the first half of the eighteenth century. A highly emotional religious revival, known as the Great Awakening, had swept over New England, and thousands of people underwent that strange catharsis in which a conviction of hopeless sin is somehow transformed into nobler personal integrity. In these events Jonathan Edwards participated—the ablest philosopher of the age, the ablest that America has produced.

Edwards has had the ill luck to be remembered for his least credible assertions, and I can recall from my boyhood my father's citing, with a smile, the celebrated sermon *Sinners in the Hands of an Angry God:* "The God that holds you over the pit of hell, much as one holds a spider, or some loathsome insect over the fire, abhors you, and is dreadfully provoked."[5] But the *Freedom of the Will* (1754) is a magisterial work, by no means wholly orthodox, unequaled in American philosophy and unsurpassed elsewhere for rigor

4) The "frontier" lay, rather oddly, toward the geographical center of the country, the last area to be settled and organized into states. This process continued into the twentieth century.

5) Excerpted, e.g., in Clarence H. Faust and Thomas H. Johnson, *Jonathan Edwards, Representative Selections* (New York: Hill and Wang; 1962), p. 164.

of argument and precision of concepts. One gets a sense of the philo-sophic mission in those days when one reflects that Edwards was sent into western Massachusetts as missionary to the Indians, and that it was among them he wrote his treatises.

The passions of the Great Awakening spent themselves, and had in any case seemed repellent to soberer citizens. Charles Chauncy, pastor of the old First Church in Boston, observed that "an enlight-ened mind, and not raised affections, ought always to be the guide of those who call themselves men; and this, in the affairs of religion, as well as other things."[6] Here spoke the quiet, moderating voice of the Enlightenment. Yet this voice, though quiet, was not silent in aspiration. It also uttered ideals: the advance of knowledge, the death of superstition, the worship of God as a universal Creator, the love of virtue and of mankind. These seemed, indeed, the ultimate aims of the American Revolution, attested not only by political leaders but by at least some of the warriors themselves. Thus Ethan Allen, leader of the Green Mountain Boys, wrote, immediately upon the war's end, a little treatise entitled *Reason the Only Oracle of Man*.

I am persuaded [said he] that if mankind would dare to exercise their reason as freely on those divine topics, as they do in the common concerns of life, they would, in a great measure, rid themselves of their blindness and superstition, gain more exalted ideas of God . . . make better members of society, and acquire many incentives to the practice of morality, which is the last and greatest perfection that human nature is capable of.[7]

That was a dawn indeed in which to be alive! There was a God in heaven: "Nature's God," as Mr. Jefferson called him in the Declaration with the assent of all the signers, the deist's God, rational in his own nature, acting rationally, and therefore able, along with all his works, to be understood. Tom Paine, the tireless revolution-ary, who had written the war's most eloquent message from Valley Forge,[8] and who had gone on to assist in the French Revolution,

6) From *Seasonable Thoughts on the State of Religion in New England* (1743), quoted, Ibid., p. xx.
7) Section I. Never had preposition been more magnificently used to end a sentence with.
8) *The American Crisis*, first sentence: "These are the times that try men's souls: the summer soldier and the sunshine patriot will, in this crisis, shrink from the service of his country; but he that stands it *now*, deserves the love and thanks of men and women."

produced, in *The Age of Reason,* an attack upon all organized religion from a deistic point of view. Miracles vanished before his argumentation, and his analysis of the Bible, remarkable for its time, reached the level of the higher criticism somewhat before that level was definitively set. But Paine attacked ideas with a view to attacking institutions which he regarded as obnoxious. Institutions do not easily forgive. As a consequence, though Ethan Allen survives as an acknowledged hero, Paine survives as rather too radical to be admired. A statue of him (so I am told) sleeps in the cellars of the Philadelphia City Hall, and cannot be brought forth, lest the sight of it rouse Philadelphians to rash and dangerous activity.

I V

A MARVELOUS HOPE issues from successful revolutions, when, in those revolutions, men once subject have mastered their own destiny. On the fifth of July, 1814, possibly in an aftermath of celebrating the Fourth, Mr. Jefferson wrote to Mr. John Adams—one former President to another—"Our post-revolutionary youth are born under happier stars than you and I were. They acquire all their learning in their mother's womb, and bring it forth into the world ready-made." The words were genially satiric. The young, in their new-found freedom, were rejecting the past (as happens with them always, free or not), and Mr. Jefferson went on to hope that nevertheless "our successors will turn their attention to the advantages of education." They did so—with what effect we are still puzzled to perceive. For the hope once roseate upon our Revolution is now weary and pale. The grace of knowledge and the wonder of new things are closed upon us like ancient books, and we have no love toward learning, only a tremulous fear that, if we do not gather knowledge, the Russians surely will.

A love of learning and a fear of not learning are quite different things; they are as self-confidence to self-distrust, and as wisdom to puerility. Such sad negatives, however, the young Republic scarcely knew. Problems it had in abundance, and perhaps it relied rather too much upon what men might individually accomplish. Yet if a breeze were again to stir among us with Lowell's music,

> They are slaves who dare not be
> In the right with two or three,

we should perhaps be lifted to certain heights we stood upon a hundred years ago.

So closely bound are men with their society that the epochs when individual persons feel victorious and fulfilled are also the epochs when society itself has been advancing.[9] Whenever any form of exploitation is ended, the world takes on a new and nobler aspect, rather like a landscape in flower. With us, the zest of being independent fed and grew upon successive triumphs: a written Constitution, a peopling of the land, and the charming innovation of representative government. We twentieth-century folk, who find representative government so little representative, may recover the freshness of that hope in John Pierpont's lines upon the ballot:

> A weapon that comes down as still
> As snowflakes fall upon the sod;
> But executes a freeman's will,
> As lightning does the will of God.[1]

Yet the country contained a subject population, which even the Constitution itself declared was to be regarded as three fifths of a person per person.[2] This subject population was the Negro slaves, held mostly in the South, but held also, in far smaller numbers, in the North.[3] The rise of such an institution was originally quite unforeseen. The first Negroes—to the number of twenty—came to Virginia in 1619 as "bound servants," that is, persons who had agreed to work for an employer for a term of years.[4] An act of 1661, in Virginia, "assumed" that at least some Negroes were servants for

9) The converse also seems true: that, when society is in decline, men feel individually unfree and unvictorious.

1) Excerpted in Edmund Clarence Stedman, *An American Anthology* (Boston: (Houghton, Mifflin and Company; 1900), p. 34. Pierpont (1785–1866) entered the Unitarian ministry in 1819, and resigned his charge in 1845, an Abolitionist defeated by a conservative congregation. He volunteered as an army chaplain during the Civil War, but proved too infirm to serve.

2) Article I, Section 2, ¶ 3 (superseded by the Fourteenth Amendment, 1868). Members of the House of Representatives were to be apportioned to each state according to its population, and, in estimating the population, slaves were to count as three fifths their actual number.

3) As of the year 1790, New York had 29,264 Negro slaves, New Jersey 11,423, Delaware 8887, Pennsylvania 3707, Connecticut 2648, Rhode Island 958, and New Hampshire 157. Richard B. Morris, op. cit., p. 513.

4) Ibid., p. 512.

life. The assumption grew into a law of almost universal application (there were, in 1790, fifty-nine thousand, five hundred fifty-seven free Negroes). Status as Negro (and hence as slave) was held to follow from the status of the *mother*. Hence, no doubt, issued the tabu, still violently defended, against unions of Negro males with white females, while at the same time unions of white males and Negro females were not only permitted but widely indulged.

The moral absurdity of such an institution in such a Republic was sufficiently clear. For how were the "natural" rights of life and liberty and the pursuit of happiness to be reconciled with the existence of a class that had no rights at all and hardly any happiness? To the extent that the Republic tolerated slavery, it denied its own ideals; but also, to the extent that it did not tolerate slavery, it estranged the Southern states and weakened the national union. To this dilemma, for a time, various *ad hoc* solutions were attempted. Mr. Jefferson, himself a slave owner, proposed, in 1776, repatriation of the Negroes in Africa. A movement developed for the purpose, which in 1821 purchased a site at Monrovia and there established what remains Liberia. Congress, in 1808, prohibited the importation of slaves; yet the trade continued illegally, and it has been conjectured that no less than a quarter of a million slaves were thus "bootlegged" up to 1860.[5]

Morality, to be effective on a social scale, needs economic incentive. It happened that the Republic was becoming, and did in fact become, an industrial society. Industry needs wage workers, people who can be hired and fired as production for the market makes necessary. The slave owners were stuck with their slaves for life, unless they could sell them to other slave owners, who would in turn be stuck. This "being stuck" was sometimes fairly painful, and the slave owners often felt themselves a generous and much abused class of men. Moreover, the industrialists needed high tariffs to protect the domestic market, and these same tariffs much increased the costs of the slave owners while diminishing their foreign markets in cotton and tobacco.

There ensued, in time, the question of what the Republic was to be: a modern industrial system from ocean to ocean, or a system primarily agricultural and organized according to relations that had not existed since the Roman Empire. There could be no doubt that

5) Ibid., p. 514.

progress required the industrial system; and, by a happy coincidence, ethics, repudiating slavery, required the industrial system also. Thus that same union of virtue and profit which had, in the War of Independence, set us free from England, set us, in our Civil War, free from at least a legally sanctioned enslavement of man by man.

From this struggle there issued (as is characteristic of the nineteenth century) two sorts of heresies—a reactionary and a radical. It is fair to say that, until the Emancipation Proclamation, Abolitionists were heretics of the radical sort. They were, indeed, treated as such, as the murder of Elijah Lovejoy (1837) and the steady persecution of William Lloyd Garrison show. After the Proclamation, the *ci-devant* slave owners were heretics, and the relatively tolerant treatment they received shows the benevolence that middle classes have always felt for defeated reactionaries.

As such contests move toward resolution, thinkers observe, ever more attentively, the effect of organizations upon doctrine. A political debate is never a scientific discussion; it is a parade of dogma. "If I know your sect," cried Emerson in the essay on self-reliance, "I anticipate your argument." And he went on:

> I hear a preacher announce for his text and topic the expediency of one of the institutions of his church. Do I not know beforehand that not possibly can he say a new and spontaneous word? Do I not know that, with all this ostentation of examining the grounds of the institution, he will do no such thing? Do I not know that he is pledged to himself not to look but at one side—the permitted side, not as a man, but as a parish minister? He is a retained attorney, and these airs of the bench are the emptiest affectation.[6]

Such indeed is the ill that lies at the heart of organizations: they tend to conduct intellectual affairs in a manner least likely to encounter truth. Argument rebuts argument, and system system, and, though all men are warmer, none is wiser for the effort. In this sort of ratiocination (if such it can be called) there is something mechanical, something machine-tooled indeed, which defeats the purpose of human mind. When one contemplates these laborious arguments, laboriously self-serving, one may wish to be Thoreau in his cabin at Walden Pond, muttering, "There never will be a really free and enlightened State until the State comes to recognize the individual

6) *Essays: First Series* (Boston: Houghton, Mifflin and Company; 1890), p. 50.

as a higher and independent power, from which all its own power and authority are derived, and treats him accordingly."[7]

Yet if organizations sometimes make themselves repellent to thinkers and thus drive them toward heresy, it remains the case (as we know) that organizations are the chief means of getting things done. The passage of heresy into schism (i.e., into organized opposition) is an acknowledgment of this fact by the heretics themselves. Consequently Thoreau's genial anarchism has had almost no social effect other than to create more or less noble postures among his disciples. Indeed, Thoreau let the doctrine degenerate so far as to say, "There is but little virtue in the action of masses of men"[8] —a statement both snobbish and profoundly false.

In any case, discontent with organizational ideology needs for its satisfaction a great deal more than a simple "I don't agree, and I'm an honest man." Ultimately it needs social action, but, short of that, it surely needs an alternative ideology. Ordinarily, as we have often observed, it chooses one from among the ideologies available. Now, it happened that Lockean theory, which had truly liberated mankind from feudal ideas, disclosed within itself a singular and attractive pragmatism. All knowledge, Locke had said, originates from sensation: environmental forces are decisive for what we know, or value, or believe. From this followed an inference—more, perhaps, than Locke intended but not more than commercial society wished—that ethics is merely a statistical compilation of human preferences, and political principles merely the accumulated practice of the race. On this view, one could not say that slavery is morally wrong and politically unjust, but only that some people prefer it and practice it while others do not. Locke's theory had passed from revolution toward a defense of status quo—where, indeed, it has remained ever since.

Against this sodden acceptance of what is, an Abolitionist like Theodore Parker seized as his weapon the German transcendentalism which had been imported into England by Coleridge and Carlyle and had thence passed into the United States. The "innate principles" which Locke had expelled from the mind were restored to it, and conscience was held to be in possession of the knowledge of right and wrong, regardless what sense experience might show to be the

7) From the celebrated essay *Civil Disobedience*. Thoreau meant, of course, that men are important as persons, not as property holders.
8) Ibid.

opinions, habits, and practices of human kind. If Locke's view reduced ethics to sociology, Parker's ennobled sociology into ethics:

The problem of transcendental philosophy is no less than this, to revise the experience of mankind and try its teachings by the nature of mankind; to test ethics by conscience, science by reason; to try the creeds of the churches; the constitutions of the states by the constitution of the universe; to reverse what is wrong, supply what is wanting, and command the just. To do this in a nation like ours, blinded still by the sensational philosophy, devoted chiefly to material interests, its politics guided by the madness of party more than sober reason; to do this in a race like the Anglo-Saxon, which has an obstinate leaning to a sensational philosophy, which loves facts of experience, not ideas of consciousness, . . . is no light work. . . .[9]

It will appear that thinkers are either too impatient or too docile to serve the needs of organizational change. Happily there was, at the time of our Civil War, a mind of the very first rank and an immensely able administrator, the sweetest spirit ever to occupy the presidency, Abraham Lincoln. If one were to point out an occasion when a development of ideas perfectly matched a social advance, one could well point to *him*. That such a man should, amid the crudity of events, hold any office is remarkable; that he should have held the highest office is astonishing.

His approach to events was extremely empirical. He brought a theory to events, of course, as every man must; but the theory was very general, and predetermined nothing. It was rather like a lamp, to illumine things already there. The temper of his speech was modest and equable, and his principles were always secure. He regarded power as a burden and its use as a duty seldom to be served without pain. He had a kind of non-denominational religion, and his references to God are among the few that can be read without suspicion of hypocrisy. Philosophically, he was Lockean and transcendentalist: events had taught him the need to be both. He was, that is to say, a philosopher-statesman after the Platonic ideal, but in so American a style that I doubt if Plato would have recognized him.

9) *Transcendentalism,* excerpted in Walter G. Muelder and Lawrence Sears, *The Development of American Philosophy* (Boston: Houghton Mifflin Company; 1940), p. 138. Parker was once indicted for obstructing the Fugitive Slave Law.

The heart of the marvel is that Lincoln, though head of a great organization in a momentous time, was eminently *not* a mere organization man. He led the Republican Party, but not with partisanship; he led the North, but for the sake of the nation; he restored the Union, but on behalf of mankind. Yet such is the dialectic of these circumstances that he could not surpass the organization man without at the same time being one. He saved the nation *because* he represented the North; he served mankind *because* he saved the nation. He remains, I would judge, the model of a political administrator. To the extent that future administrators resemble him, the long contest between orthodoxy and heresy will be resolved.

In this light, it is instructive to juxtapose the First and Second Inaugural Addresses. Both have the same precision and modesty, the same sustaining hope. But the Second Inaugural is far richer and deeper, with a quiet joy of having touched, after four bitter years, the essential truths. He has discovered[1] that slavery was, after all, the cause of the War, and that economics moves thus tumultuously beneath politics. He has discovered[2] that history is the modification of every man's will by all the other wills, and that therefore results are likely to be "fundamental and astounding." He has discovered[3] that progress occurs even through strife, and that events can turn out as if (what he himself never doubted) there were a righteous God to ordain them. And precisely because history does permit—perhaps even demand—astounding human betterment, he is able to offer, in the famous peroration, charity for all and "a just and lasting peace among ourselves, and with all nations."

Philosophers who wish to settle the interrelation of fact with value, of science with ethics, may study the life and works of Abraham Lincoln, where they will see (as I think nowhere else) value rising from fact and returning to it as guide of achievement. And for the sake of tragic contrast, they may also study the fate of a no less noble spirit, John Brown, who missed the time by only six years but missed the historical circumstance almost totally.

As for ourselves, who are Americans, we shall find in Lincoln the union we earnestly seek between theory and practice, between

1) ¶ 3.
2) ¶ 4.
3) ¶ 5.

thought and administration; and thus learn to temper our native anarchism with love, and our imposed conformity with freedom.

V

DURING THE HUNDRED YEARS since our Civil War, heresy in the United States has narrowed to questions arising from the relationships between capital and labor—that is to say, between a group of persons who own and administer the land and the factories and another group of persons who are merely employed there. To be sure, prosecutions for heresy have occurred within the churches, but these have had no importance except to the victims. The public can no longer be roused over theological refinements, and the Scopes trial of 1925, in which a young biologist was convicted of teaching Darwinism in a high school in Tennessee, was a pathetic comedy devoid of serious interest.

To find heresy, one must always look where the jailings are, and the killings, and the other inflicted losses. These will be found in a series of events in which the forces of capital and of labor met in severe and sometimes sanguinary contests: the railroad strikes of 1877, the Haymarket bombing of 1886, the Homestead lockout of 1892, the Pullman strike of 1894, the steel strike of 1919, the unemployed demonstrations of the early 1930's, the general strike in San Francisco in 1934, when for three days the workers held *de facto* administration of the city's affairs. That is to say, there runs through American history of the last ninety years an intermittent armed conflict which was a conflict of social classes. As Thomas Scott, President of the Pennsylvania Railroad in the 1880's, put it, "Give the workingmen and strikers gun-bullet food for a few days, and you will observe how they will take this sort of bread."[4]

Since the main instruments of power lay with the capitalists (as indeed they still lie), the ability to determine heresy lay there also. It followed that punishable opinions were, in the main, those which advocated the interests of labor as against those of capital. Such opinions were of two sorts: those which favored certain immediate gains for labor (higher wages, the eight-hour day, collective bargaining) and those which advocated, more or less in the Marxian manner, that labor should displace capital as the chief economic and

4) Quoted by Aleine Austin, *The Labor Story* (New York: Coward-McCann, Inc.; 1949), p. 103.

political power in the nation and that it should proceed to construct a socialist society, in which the products of all men's work should be available for all men's use.

Heresies of the first sort were intermittently heretical, as the struggles themselves were intermittent. Heresies of the second sort would be constantly heretical so long as capital ruled. They would be, like the late medieval challenges to the sovereignty of the Pope, "ultimate" heresies, outrages not to be surpassed for outrage, the sin against the Holy Ghost.

To be sure, none of all these heresies has ever, I think, been called by the name "heresy." The use of that word would awaken all the skepticism and resistance which grew rock-strong out of human experience with the churches. Other terms have seemed more suitable to isolate the dissenter from his fellows: "un-American," "unpatriotic," "subversive." The capitalists, having "secularized" everything else, have revealed the fact that heresy was all along a secular phenomenon: it always had to do with, and only with, resistance to political power on this planet.

Essentially, then, for the United States of the last eighty years, all anti-capitalist doctrines have been heretical, and all heresy has been anti-capitalism. It may perhaps appear that the struggles over women's suffrage (not without violence they were, too) touched upon a different issue. And so they did, in respect of winning for half the adult population an important political right. Yet the resistance to women's suffrage turned upon the question how far the votes of female citizens would complicate the problems of the governing class. When it was shrewdly guessed that no great change would occur, the Nineteenth Amendment became law. There was a slight budging of the bureaucracy, who had to count more votes; but the first president whom the female suffrage helped elect was Warren Gamaliel Harding.

To the industrialization of the country the entrepreneurs contributed much ingenuity and the workers much toil. Industrialization always requires present sacrifices, since the labor of it goes into producing, not goods for immediate consumption, but goods that will later produce goods for immediate consumption. In England of, say, 1800 to 1840, these sacrifices fell, with singular cruelty, upon children, whose early labors meant an early death. In America of the late nineteenth century, the sacrifices fell upon the workers generally, of whom women and children, as well as adult males, were a part. The "iron law of wages" seemed universally to prevail, and wages supplied no more than bare subsistence together with the chance of propagating more workers. This low purchasing power in the multitudes, joined with an increasing productivity, gave rise to the familiar crises of "overproduction"—the *crises pléthoriques,* as Fourier once called them. Then workers had to bear the debility and starvation attendant upon being unemployed.

The workers' response was to form brotherhoods, like the National Trade Union (1866–1872), the Knights of Labor (1878–1893), the American Federation of Labor (founded in 1886). These had a tendency to disappear or to turn conservative (which is a living form of disappearance). At the same time there developed political parties expressive of labor's aspiration toward socialism. Marxist thought had come to America, in at least a primitive form, with the German refugees of 1848, and one of Marx's close friends, Joseph Wedemeyer, was a colonel in the Union Army during the Civil War. Marx himself, it seems extraordinary to say, served at one time as foreign correspondent for the New York *Tribune.*

The American workers, like the American capitalists, took their basic ideas from abroad; that is to say, they accepted an already existing heritage. Also like the capitalists, they reworked the ideas in American terms. The man who did this most successfully was Eugene Victor Debs (1855–1926), by far the ablest, most eloquent socialist the country has ever produced. Indeed, the words that once rang with the glory of his own voice are still warm upon the printed page. "The cross is bending," he said to the court on September 14, 1918, "the cross is bending, the midnight is passing, and joy cometh with the morning."[5]

Debs, I have no doubt, was the supreme American heretic of the last hundred years. Not only did he hold anti-capitalist ideas, but he passed into "schism" by leading an organized movement for transformation of the social order. He ran for the presidency on the Socialist ticket five separate times, and during some of those campaigns he

5) He was being sentenced to ten years' imprisonment for violation of the Espionage Act, more specifically for having advocated resistance to the draft during the First World War. He was released from Atlanta Penitentiary, by order of President Harding, on Christmas Day, 1921. The five dollars given him by the government as a newly released prisoner he gave in turn to the defense of Sacco and Vanzetti.

toured the country on a train called the "Red Special." He proved an attractive candidate: in 1912, he polled six per cent of the popular vote (897,011), and he polled 919,799 votes in 1921 while a prisoner at Atlanta.[6] This last was a remarkable campaign: Harding won without leaving his "front porch" in Marion, Ohio; Debs ran splendidly from his cell; and Cox, who toured the country, was overpowered.

Furthermore, Debs brought to the socialist movement a love of people and a strong sense of his own manhood. Far too often heretics have neither of these, and perhaps it is the case that a man must have the one in order to have the other. "Anybody can be nobody," said Debs, "but it takes a man to be somebody."[7] There is no difficulty finding where he got this strength, for, while he was in Cook County Jail during the Pullman Strike of 1894, there came to him a telegram as follows:

> STAND BY YOUR PRINCIPLES REGARDLESS OF CONSEQUENCES.
> YOUR FATHER AND MOTHER.[8]

Observing so much inward security of mind and purpose, one can credit as wholly devoid of hypocrisy Debs' repeated description of himself as less than the least of men. He meant that he intended to serve everyone except "the bosses," that he was brother to all the victims of society. When he left Woodstock Jail in November, 1895 —he had been imprisoned for contempt of court—the inmates addressed to him a resolution, of which these words are part:

> We, the undersigned, inmates of Woodstock Jail, desire to convey to you our heartfelt thanks and gratitude for the many acts of kindness and sympathy shown us by you during your incarceration in this institution.

> We selfishly regret your departure from here into the outer world and scenes of labor. Your presence here has been to us what an

6) These voting figures are taken from Richard B. Morris, op. cit., pp. 273 and 331.
7) From the famous speech at Canton, Ohio, June 16, 1918, on the basis of which he was prosecuted. Quoted in David Karsner, *Debs,* (New York: Boni and Liveright; 1919), p. 235.
8) Quoted in *Debs: His Writings and Speeches,* The Appeal to Reason (Kansas: Girard; p. 66.

oasis in a desert is to the tired and weary traveler, or a ray of sunshine showing thro' a rift in the clouds. . . ."[9]

Such a man must necessarily escape the corrosive left wing curse (observable also in sixteenth-century Protestantism) of being doctrinaire and sectarian. Under his treatment the almost scholastic vocabulary of Marx disappeared in familiar Americanisms, and the mighty doctrines rose in simplicity, almost in nakedness. "They [the capitalists]," he told the railway workers in 1906, "fleece and pluck; you furnish the wool and feathers."[1] Or, "Stand up and see how long a shadow you cast in the sunlight." How much more genial, and indeed more accurate, an expression than the lumbering, ominous phrase "dictatorship of the proletariat"!

Debs built a great movement, which afterward dissipated itself into fragments so small that even government agents can scarcely find them. The heretics who hoped for socialism survive as whipping boys in precisely the one country in the world where socialism, if effected, would produce within a brief time the abundance and peace it always promised.

Victory, for the moment, lies with present orthodoxy, and is complete. Orthodoxy has made Americans ignorant of the socialist intent and hostile to it, at the very moment in history when a billion people have entered upon socialist life. It has made a very large population reject certain benefits which that population would, if left to ponder the matter, desire. It has drowned the workers in a poppied sleep, "and all that mighty heart is lying still." I think that this is a political feat of the very first order, and, for skill and effect, it has few equals in history.

Yet perhaps the triumph is in the nature of a pause. Back in 1852, the old thunderer, musing upon the strange behavior of workingmen, observed:

> Bourgeois revolutions, like those of the eighteenth century, storm more swiftly from success to success . . . Proletarian revolutions, on the other hand, like those of the nineteenth century, criticize themselves constantly, interrupt themselves continually in their own course, come back to the apparently accomplished in order to begin it afresh, deride with unmerciful thoroughness the in-

9) Quoted, ibid.
1) Ibid., p. 220. The next quotation is from p. 465.

adequacies, weaknesses and paltrinesses of their first attempts, seem to throw down their adversary only in order that he may draw new strength from the earth and rise again more gigantic before them, recoil ever and anon from the indefinite prodigiousness of their own aims, until the situation has been created which makes all turning back impossible, and the conditions themselves cry out: *Hic Rhodus, hic salta!*[2]

Perhaps one can already discern what the spur will be: automation. From an employer's point of view, automation offers the irresistibly attractive prospect of reducing costs by reducing the number of paid workers. But, in the mid-twentieth century, workers are much more prompt than once they were to decline the want and idleness thus thrust upon them. Moreover there are now in the world societies which can accept technological advances without this sort of dislocation: they socialize leisure as well as work. Successful solutions are contagious, and I would doubt that propagandist skill, powerful though it is, can halt the spread of the relevant knowledge.

There is also what may be called the morality of Americans—a very real and influential thing, which allows departure from its principles only in confrontation with an adversary presumed to be ruthless. Our libertarian tradition, Calvinist or Jeffersonian, makes most of us extremely uncomfortable in any oppressive role. We do not like to think that our present prosperity (if such it be) is founded upon the poverty of peoples in South America, in Asia, and in Africa. It is of course so founded, and realization of the fact will tend to alter a good deal that Americans think about the world. When they discover that they can abandon the oppressive role by reconstituting their own society, they will, I fancy, undertake the appropriate changes.

Americans are not a martial people, though no one would regard them as timid or reticent. They cannot be summoned to conflict by illusions of being a master race or even of having a "manifest destiny." They always need to think that somehow they are helping the world. Yet, despite their decided preference for peace, their economy is now maintained by military expenditures paid from taxation, while at the same time housewives solicit contributions, home by home, for research into heart disease and muscular dystrophy. A society

2) Karl Marx, *The Eighteenth Brumaire of Louis Bonaparte,* Part I. *Hic Rhodus,* etc.—"This is Rhodes; you've got to dance here!"

reveals its motives by what it insists upon and what it leaves to improvisation. When Americans grow fully aware that their society is thus organizing itself for death rather than life, the torpor of recent years may well vanish as sleep vanishes from the waking eye.

In the modern age, social change is far too potent to be long resisted. It is, however, no *rational* part of heresy to wish that changes in our social structure be other than those which the American people, in their developing wisdom, shall desire. If, as present heretics are like to think, that wisdom is momentarily numb, its existence and its recovery into life must nevertheless be trusted. Undoubtedly it has existed and has carried us far. It expresses itself in general maxims rather than in elaborated theory, and the maxims are at work even when the people seems to sleep.

Moreover the maxims lie, not only among our great men, but among our lesser and least, so that we know them to be popularly held and therefore popularly to be acted upon. In the year 1743, for example, a certain Ebenezer Wales, of the Province of Massachusetts Bay, "a man laborious in his calling, which was the labor of the hand," wrote certain Counsels to his children, of whom he had, all told, twenty. Among the Counsels was this:

> There is a rational pleasure in love and peace. To keep the love of another who is on the contrary side of our interest, gives us the best advantage to convince him if he be in the wrong. And if we are in the wrong, we are the more likely to be convinced by him, and you should be more pleased to get the truth established, than to get the mastery, or your supposed interest or opinion vindicated.[3]

What Ebenezer Wales desired was an end to all contests between orthodoxy and heresy, and a solution of problems by reason and not by violence. It may perhaps be the case that this desire is the most heretical of all. Yet, if Americans were to accomplish so great a feat, they would be most faithful to their ancestors and at the same time most advanced among the nations of the world.

3) From a genealogical tract, *The Redington and Wales Families,* edited by Joseph Granville Leach (Boston: Press of David Clapp and Son; 1909), p. 69.

Hope and Fulfillment

As I wrote the preceding pages, the belief grew upon me that no reader ought to be asked to traverse so many words in order to reach a melancholy conclusion. The political history of ideas has not been cheerful, and this tale of manifold imprisonments and executions has made me wonder whether such events, which seem always to have been, must always be. Readers will perhaps find the inference tempting, but it is precisely the one which I wish not to draw. Indeed, if the inference were necessary, the chief purpose of this book would be lost. For my hope is that, having thus observed the anatomy of intellectual conflict, we may learn to mitigate conflict itself.

It is not, however, a hope which rises out of history with such power that its fulfillment seems inevitable. Rather, it is a hope which remains after discouragement. The sight of human violence and folly, repeated so often for so many years, never quite kills the faith that what is rational in men will one day discipline what is merely hostile. And there are signs, there are signs. Wherever scientific method and the behavior conformable to it have prevailed, discussion has replaced conflict, and reason strife. Ah, if politics were only like that!

In the year 1909, Thomas Hardy, being asked to state his general view of human affairs, replied thus:

We call our age an age of Freedom. Yet Freedom, under her incubus of armaments, territorial ambitions smugly disguised as patriotism, superstitions, conventions of every sort, is of such stunted proportions in this her so-called time, that the human race is likely to be extinct before Freedom arrives at maturity.[1]

One does not usually think of Hardy as a man of profound political insight, but these words, read in 1963 or after, suffice to raise him to the status of a seer.

It is evident that we have, immediately before us and pressing hard upon us, a problem greater than any this book describes. Intellectual tolerance is no doubt essential to the sane conduct of human affairs, but the survival of mankind is essential to any conduct of human affairs whatever. Unless our progeny live on in their multitudes, there will have come either an end to all things human or an odious life, unknown even to our most primitive ancestors, in which a few degenerated hunters stalk radioactive game. In either event, there would not be socialism or capitalism or feudalism or any other of the systems wherein men have contrived to live, not very peaceably, with one another.

Yet in "defense" of at least two of these systems—socialism and capitalism—men now invoke a force which is quite capable of destroying all. If I understand correctly what the leaders of the capitalist world and the leaders of the socialist world say, amid the repeated pieties of organization talk, there are circumstances, entirely possible, in which the one system would conduct nuclear warfare against the other, with the certainty that both would be destroyed. In that event, we should all die, allegedly on behalf of assertions by Marx or by Jefferson, neither of whom had any intentions of the sort. What survivor, treading the blackened crust of earth, would then meditate those ghastly inferences, so helpless in logic and so fatal in effect, which the pursuit of happiness and the withering away of the state had been deemed to require?

To the strife of social systems we must add also the strife of nations. Nationhood has now a history of some five hundred years. Because those years were filled alternately with warfare and construction, nationhood has come to be the mode in which men are most passionately organized. Nineteenth-century socialists, to be sure, were hopefully international, and Marx in the *Manifesto* (an

1) Florence Emily Hardy, *The Life of Thomas Hardy* (New York: St. Martin's Press; 1962), p. 347. According to some scholars, this book is actually autobiography.

inspirational work and therefore hyperbolical amid its science) expressed a belief that "the workingmen have no country." It has turned out, in the years since, that, whether or not the workingmen have had a country, they have generally thought they had, and have thought also that their country was the one they lived in. Nationalism split the socialist movement during the First World War, and the socialist states which have arisen since the Second World War appear to feel their nationalism as strongly as their socialism.

Thus in our world there are two sorts of conflict, and both sorts have throughout the past tended to proceed *à outrance*. That is to say, whenever these conflicts reached a critical stage, the contending parties attempted a settlement by all the violence they could command. But all the violence which can now be commanded is more than enough to extinguish life on this planet. Our difficulty therefore is that we live amid conflicts which, if they proceed as they always have proceeded, will surely be our doom. It is rational to hope, however, that they will not so proceed, and it is even rational to believe that they may not.

This belief and its rationality have philosophical grounds which derive, it seems ironic to say, from that pale but stinging skeptic, David Hume. Hume showed that predictions about the future generally rest upon an expectation that the future will resemble the past. If, now, we inquire what reason there is for expecting the future to resemble the past, the sole answer appears to be that past futures have regularly done so. In such an argument, however, the conclusion has been used to prove itself, and into this sad *petitio* the inference subsides.

We have therefore no necessitarian ground for expecting events to repeat themselves, and perhaps all such expectation is, as Hume said, a matter not of logic but of habit. The genuine fact seems, however, rather stronger than this. It is fair to say that, in our experience of past futures and past pasts, very many events in those futures turned out to be quite different from anything previously known. Our present peril of nuclear annihilation is itself a striking example of novelty, of a circumstance which has never before existed and which in most previous ages could not even have been conceived.

If, a hundred years ago, it would have been erroneous to predict that men would never learn to control atomic energy, it may well be erroneous now to predict that men will never learn to limit the severity of their struggles. Possibly they will fail to learn, or, learning, fail to limit. But none of this is fated. Our political choices, though strongly influenced by appetite and social structure, are yet in some measure spontaneous and free. We can preserve our race if we wish to, despite the fact that governments use their populations like flails to smite one another and smite the world.

I I

PERHAPS we may say, in broadest terms, that what endangers mankind is the unevenness of its own development. Our knowledge of physical nature is extensive, and our use of that knowledge spectacular. We have allowed ourselves to know rather less about society and human nature—subjects which are always liable to propagandist distortion. Yet, after the labors of Freud and Marx, we can no longer profess ignorance. Essential knowledge of society and of human nature now exists, and obviously exists. What we have thus far not shown is sufficient willingness to use this knowledge for the general good.

During thousands of years, organizations have developed habits for dealing with one another. These habits are now largely out of date, as belonging to a pre-nuclear age. They constrict improvement, and they may indeed be the death of us all. Habits, of course, are difficult to shed; and politicians, long hardened to the use of violence in all its forms, do not readily perceive how little is the good that violence can now confer. Yet in the play of circumstance, habits are always getting broken and replaced. It is very usual for an advance of knowledge in one area to produce advance in others. Our descendants in the twenty-first century, if we allow them to exist, will probably possess a psychology and a sociology equal to their physics, together with a rational use of all.

Those will be happy times, the great perils having passed. Meanwhile, short of that felicity, though not indeed remote from it, we may ponder the means of approach. More particularly, we may ask whether this present journey through the politics of philosophical thought gives useful information as to what we may expect or ought to do. I think that it does. The information is of two sorts: one which concerns the whole development of thought, and one which concerns the behavior of organizations.

It is, of course, not easy to generalize about the history of philosophy. That tumultuous sea, where wave has clashed with wave, bears on its surface no very clear pattern. It has had, however, a direction and a tide. From its origins into our own times, philosophy has been a struggle about a poem—a poem which celebrated things imaginary in the midst of things real. This "poem" has included all the mythologies, religions, and transcendental philosophies of men, for these have all the common trait of using figurative speech and not literal.

The poem's purpose has been to present as real a great many things which were not real, thus to compensate for inadequacies in human beings, in their social arrangements, and in their relations with the physical world. Thus man's old weakness before the strength of nature could be repaid by an allegory to the effect that nature was under the control of a power, or powers, friendly or at any rate willing to be propitiated. His rebelliousness could be repressed by joining governmental authority with divine authority, and his conscience made firm by worship of supernatural personages who embodied moral ideals.

The poem was reworked in various forms: we have glanced at the Greek and Egyptian versions, and have dwelt upon the Christian at some length. For a long time the poem was for the most part not recognized to be poetry. Only a few materialists like Epicurus and the great Ionians were able to set it aside in favor of science. Yet it was always probable that, sooner or later, philosophers would be driven out of metaphor into literal language, and out of dreams into an exact survey of the actual world. This event happened, as we know, during the seventeenth century A.D., when European society came under the leadership of commercial magnates whose prime need was to describe the physical world without error and without imagery.

Until this moment, philosophy had been struggling to incorporate the poem into something like a scientific account of the world. After this moment, philosophy struggled to expel the poem, to make everyone see that the poem was a poem and no more. There would have been not much greater difficulty in this than there is in classroom exegesis, except for the fact that the poem had settled into the ideologies of various organizations, which defended by force its erroneous pretensions to science. There followed at last the Kantian truce between science and theology, which, though strongly hinting that the poem was only a poem, allowed people to take it literally if they wished.

Astounding results have followed this separation of poetry from science. The human race has rapidly acquired the powers, if not the dignity, which it once ascribed to gods. Almost every hope which the old poem so beautifully sang is now attainable by human ingenuity—an ingenuity which began to grow in skill and power the moment the poem was recognized to be such. Science has come, if not with the intent then at any rate with the means, that we may have life and have it more abundantly. The entire population of earth can now be fed and clothed and housed, and most lives liberated from the perils of disease. Indeed, as medical knowledge increases, we move toward a kind of physical immortality, and this corruptible puts on incorruption in a mode more earthly than Saint Paul's.

Even our darkness shows forth the same strength. At least two men in the world, mere human beings, have the power to extinguish all life and bring our history to an end. They thus possess an attribute once ascribed to deity. They are level now with Zeus and Jahweh, Moloch and Baal. One cannot tell which of these they most resemble, and in that doubt lies much of the anguish of the age. Yet it seems that, if our earth remains habitable, the lowly will in time inherit it. In the resolution of this choice between democracy and oblivion it will be discovered which side the gods were on.

If abandonment of the old poem thus gave remarkable power to men, it also gave remarkable confusion. So soon as those metaphors were seen to be metaphors, it was plain that a literal description lay somewhere else. But where? The search became, what it has not ceased to be, a scramble. During the nineteenth century and the twentieth, philosophies multiplied. They were all concerned with the awesome touch of science upon human affairs. If they could not (as indeed they could not) abate its pressure, they could at least try to describe the extent of the pressure itself.

How various the views began to be may be seen, rather comically, in Pius IX's *Syllabus Errorum* of 1864.[2] This document undertook to outlaw all notions then current which declined to read the old metaphors as the Roman Church required. The notions thus pronounced heretical were placed under ten headings, but to no avail. Classification could not organize their infinite variety. They had little logical relation among themselves, and were united chiefly in what they

2) The text will be found complete in Anne Fremantle, *The Papal Encyclicals,* pp. 143–152. It is excerpted in Bettenson, *Documents,* pp. 381–83.

were against. Yet from even so much disunion orthodoxy had nothing to hope. Philosophers had become explorers of new places and could not listen to orders from home.

Many the theories, many the schools: all sorts of Hegelianisms —right, center, left; all sorts of Idealisms, Hegel's being only one; all sorts of Realisms—the Naïve, the Cambridge, the Critical, and the New; Vitalisms *versus* Mechanisms, flame against steel; Pragmatisms so manifold and anarchic that no pragmatist has ever yet defined the term—although the late Professor Lovejoy convinced himself that there were such definitions and that the definitions numbered exactly thirteen.[3] Now, a multitude of choices gives a lively sense of freedom. Thus liberation from orthodoxy was confirmed and extended by the abundance itself of views that a man might hold with reason and even with good sense. Since all these views were intellectually reputable, if also conflicting, disagreement among philosophers became at first an expectation and at last something like a duty.

This welter of thinking surged around many problems. Did one, for example, really know anything? If so, how did one know it, and how did one know that one knew it? Did this knowledge refer to a world independent of the knower, or were the knower, the knowledge, and the world in some lofty and transcendental sense identical with one another? Was change but the surface look of an immutable universe, or, if change was itself primordial, did it proceed with mechanical regularity or with shocks and explosions as in fireworks and in life? Was the universe friendly to human hopes, or indifferent to them, or conspiratorially bent on their defeat? Was man animal or angel, mortal or immortal? And could a man make up his own mind, or did his genes and his environment do that for him?

All these problems, it is clear, are quite genuine and will long be with us. Every mistake suggests the problem of knowledge, every difficult choice the problem of fate. An age that has seen vast man-made horrors cannot avoid pondering human nature and history, and each individual person, solitary amid tremendous forces, must ask what chance there is that things will in the end go well. All previous expectations—the reasoned, accumulated guesses of a century—are now in doubt, for if the issue of events is annihilation, our problems and their remedies will have disappeared.

3) Arthur O. Lovejoy, *The Thirteen Pragmatisms, Journal of Philosophy,* Vol. V, pp. 29–39. The date of this celebrated article is January 18, 1908.

One can understand how the Enlightenment broke philosophy into fragments. It is less obvious, however, why Western philosophers have remained so long content with the fragmentation. Probably every one of the diverse views has some contact with reality, and is to that extent true—a state of affairs which has invited much eclecticism. Yet every one of the diverse views is also visibly partial and incomplete. For example, the realists, in order to maintain that the universe exists independently of being known, reduced scientific activity to the dimensions of a searchlight, and thus could give no account of scientific activity itself. Their rivals the idealists, intent on showing that thinking makes a difference, caused the external world to be swallowed up in some sort of "mind"—God's, the universe's, or our own. Determinists threw free will out altogether; indeterminists abolished the reign of law. Eclectic philosophers, shopping around for views they could accept, were limited in their choices by a love of bare consistency—whereas the main task is to see how opposites go together to make up the world.

Why the extremism, each view defending itself so desperately against every other? There must have been many reasons: rebelliousness, pride of personal commitment ("It's my very own idea!"), sectarian loyalties, the slam-bang competitiveness of commercial society, and the shrewd refusal of that society ever to formulate a detailed ideology of its own. Yet I have the impression that this love of the fragment, this feeling that disagreement is somehow preferable to unanimity, issues from the great wound which the Middle Ages left. The scholastic philosophers had differed among themselves, but they had differed only in their interpretations of one and the same world view, that of orthodox Christianity. These were lesser disagreements, but, even so, perilous. The world view itself was enforced by police power. Within it, safety and comradeship; without, danger and loneliness. Rebels were bound to seek, and did in fact achieve, a state of affairs in which safety, diversity, and comradeship were possible all together.

Thus philosophers of the past hundred years have, upon the whole, regarded intellectual systems with profound distaste. They expect the sciences to be systematic, but they wish philosophy to be fluid, sinuous, and even improvisational. They believe any philosophical system to be in error just because it is a system. They believe, further, that it threatens them with suffocation by doctrine and sometimes with economic or political coercion. All such forms of threat reopen the old wound, and, as it bleeds afresh, men seek once more the healing balm of diversity. If one visibly speaks for oneself, even though in error, one is at any rate not a mere organizational hack.

This love of personal spontaneity, this spirit of criticism and experiment, spread beyond science and philosophy into the fine arts. In painting, the Impressionist movement, developing after 1870, studied the play of light upon objects as that play occurs in nature rather than in the studio. There followed analysis of the spatial constitution of objects and at last, what we now have, the analysis of space as such. What began as an escape from "orthodoxy" as the academies and salons defined it has ended in an exhaustive (and perhaps exhausting) search through the possibilities of the medium. The other arts have been similarly searched: we now have the anti-novel and *la musique concrète*. There has never been in history so loud and long a shaking of all the media which used to house our masterpieces.

Suddenly, after 1917, this foaming tide of experimental analysis began to encounter a series of rocks. The new socialist countries, as they arose, asserted for the arts two purposes which elsewhere had disappeared beneath experimentation: enjoyment by a large public, and commentary upon human affairs. These purposes, unexceptionable in themselves, were natural enough in societies engaged upon resolving their inner conflicts and in fitting themselves to produce abundance for all. Moreover, revolutions tend to have, or to elaborate, extensive philosophies, and in Marxism the socialist world has a philosophy almost complete.

This sudden burst of homogeneity in thought and culture has horrified the Western intelligentsia as much as the fall of capitalism has horrified the Western bourgeoisie—and with somewhat more excuse. Philosophy and the arts do grow sterile in proportion as they cease to experiment and to criticize; their services to mankind rest always upon an awareness of possibilities to be explored. Yet, remarkable to say, the philosophy which most accepts this fact is Marx's dialectical materialism. For the word "materialism" simply means that there's a world out there, and "dialectical" means that the world out there is full of change and surprises, which have, however, an intelligible pattern.

This view, supposing it to be generally acted upon, yields interesting results for the long contest between orthodoxy and heresy. If the world is more than an invention of our minds, if it has a discoverable nature of its own and in that nature has novelty, then all descriptions of it are incomplete and subject to revision, not only because we may err about what is or what has been but also because what will be does not yet exist. Accordingly, there cannot be a body of doctrine which is at one and the same time changeless and true. But orthodoxy, as we know, is the effort of organizations to keep doctrine changeless or nearly so. It therefore is doomed to a loss of truth, which is, in its turn, a loss of contact with reality. In this manner, orthodoxy imperils the very organizations it serves.

Many philosophies have protested against orthodoxy, but the twofold doctrine of materialism and dialectics is, so far as I know, the only one which explains, from its own basic assertions, why orthodoxy (and, by consequence, heresy) ought to cease. It may be that this is the best and noblest of Marx's gifts to mankind. The world is perhaps not yet ready to receive it, because sharpness in conflict begets dogmatism in organizations. Yet the gift is there, set forth in quaint philosophical language of the nineteenth century, to be seized when struggles are milder or even, perhaps, while they run their present course. For I think that any population which convincingly showed it could do without orthodoxy in the midst of conflict would speedily win praise and emulation from mankind.

I I I

AFTER DESCARTES had shown that scientific method rather than hierarchical status put men in possession of truth, after the Enlightenment showed that science was a means of salvation, there came to pass the circumstance which still prevails and grows: vast knowledge shared by very many men. This knowledge gets fragmented in the sharing, and is sharpened or dulled by the men who have it. Moreover, its very vastness and complexity make the interrelations within it difficult to trace and right applications of it difficult to prepare. The organizing of knowledge, and the use of it in practice, have proved more baffling than the Enlightenment supposed.

Consider, for example, the four theories which everybody now regards as the intellectual foundation of our age: Darwinism, Marxism, Freudian psychology, and Einsteinian physics. All these laid bare, in their different ways, certain facts of the greatest importance for human destiny. They were plainly advances in knowledge and thus true offspring of the Enlightenment. Yet, severally and collectively, they show barriers as well as paths to our salvation. Science does not save quite as easily as had been hoped.

Each of the theories, after its appearance, set off bursts of philosophical exaggeration, some very optimistic, some very pessimistic. It was held, for example, that biological evolution would produce the perfect man, that social evolution would produce the perfect society, that all problems would prove solvable on the psychiatrist's couch. Pessimistically, it was held that human improvement must await biological changes, or that it must be attended with historical catastrophe, or that it never can quite triumph over aggressive egoism. These two sets of exaggerations devour each other. They share a common and concealed assumption, surely doubtful and probably false, that human behavior cannot control the forces which affect our destiny.

Setting these exaggerations aside, we are still left perplexed in the midst of so much data. Darwin, I fancy, will trouble us little, since leaps of biological evolution are not among our pressing problems. Einstein, however, has unsettled the old notion of causality, on which all science seemed to depend, and has vastly increased our social problems by giving us access to atomic energy. And Marx and Freud? Well, together they bring us toward the heart of the matter.

Events of the past fifty years seem to have confirmed Marx's belief that the "contradictions of capitalism" would give rise to socialism. A billion people are now socialist, and they became so in order to solve certain problems which capitalism had set. The success of this prediction tends to strengthen other predictions of Marx: that there can be a society of abundance and an end to coercive government. However, the continuing play of power politics *after* socialism leaves unresolved the Freudian doubt whether improved social relations can discipline the primitive aggressiveness in men.

The opposition, so far as there is any, between Marx and Freud is an opposition between what we know about historical tendencies and what we know about personal motivations. We had better modify this knowledge by an awareness also of what we do not know. There is as yet no society of abundance in the Marxist sense, and consequently we cannot observe its effect upon human motivation.

We simply do not know how people will behave in that kind of society, and we cannot be absolutely sure that they will be able to create it. They may; they may not. Nothing of this sort is predetermined, apart from human activity. We ourselves are even now determining the future, not by knowing what it will be but by conceiving what it can be. As the result of our labors, a great deal more will be known, a hundred years hence, about the effect of society upon men and of men upon society.

Thus it is by massive historical action that we give answers to the problems philosophy has set. These answers will generally be more rational in proportion as they are not coerced; and coercion, being an organizational affair, will diminish as there are fewer or less violent shocks among organizations and within them. At the present moment, organizations are rather too small and too quarrelsome; indeed, they are quarrelsome because they are too small, and they remain small because they are too quarrelsome. They suppose among themselves (with some accuracy) all sorts of rivalries and contrary interests, and these they so far exaggerate that loyalty to the organization and its interests becomes the highest ethic of which the members are thought to be capable. It is now evident that this narrow parochial view will do little more than provide high moral grounds for the destruction of mankind.

Since organizations share the general wish for survival, perhaps they will act, or can be made to act, accordingly. I think there are already some signs of this. The various postwar crises have thus far been adjusted without catastrophe, and, despite threats and imprecations, governments seem willing so to adjust them. There may develop a habit of solving problems short of annihilation, and, as practice strengthens this habit, we may pass, squawking, posturing, and bullying, into a future peace. The rights of man were established in just this way. They are not less grand and valuable for all that. No doubt a sane society would grant rights and peace at once, but less sane societies can be brought to grant them in the course of doing something else.

Coercion having fallen away, there would be left merely differences of opinion, and these would diminish as problems are solved. The love of diversity prospers when it serves a political need, but no sane man cultivates disagreement on matters that are known. In 1959 I talked with Professor Fedoseyev, head of the Institute of

Philosophy in Moscow, about the range of views among Soviet philosophers. "We all agree," he said, "that there is an independent external world, but from that point on disagreement sets in; we don't yet know enough." This seemed to me a reasonable—one might almost say, a natural—state of affairs: disagreement when knowledge is lacking; agreement when knowledge is possessed. It was the Enlightenment's hope that knowledge would unite mankind. I share that hope, though violent men abound and have knowledge which is perilous.

It will be seen, therefore, that I do not share the existentialist pessimism which advocates surrender before attempt. We know our future to be uncertain, but more than this we do not know. Where nothing is certain, nothing is doomed, and accordingly we may explore with some confidence certain very attractive possibilities: an abundant life, a peaceful world, all blessings shared with all men. If such tasks seem above our powers, why, so seemed the tasks of every age to the people of it. They grew, however, equal to their tasks—and so can we. While friends are warm and grandsons are glorious, I cannot think the growth will fail. For we are to become (it will be remembered) "lords and possessors of nature"—lords also and possessors of ourselves.

THE TEN "HERETICAL" PROPOSITIONS OF THE ABBÉ DE PRADES

[I give the propositions first in de Prades's original Latin and then in my translation. I have collated the Latin with de Prades's rendering of it into French—renderings that are sometimes extremely free. Presumably, however, de Prades knew what he meant to say. Each proposition is followed by the Sorbonne's comment, except in one case where none was offered.]

1. *Homo cuius ideae rudes adhuc et informes sese produnt per sensationes, ergo ex sensationibus, ceu rami ex trunco omnes eius cognitiones pullulant. . . . Pronum est inquerere sedulo quae natura sit principii in nobis cogitantis. . . . Mens ignea terrenae foecis nihil habet . . .*
Man, whose ideas in their raw and unformed state are produced through sensations—all his knowledge sprouts therefore from sensations like branches from a tree trunk. . . . It is natural to inquire what the nature of the thinking principle in us may be. . . . An ardent mind has no earthly dross . . .
(*Materialismo faventes.* Inclining to materialism.)

2. *Nos incumbit necessitas ea seligendi potissimum objecta quae in nostram vergant utilitatem. . . . Hinc origo Societatis, cuius vincula magis ac magis stringere debemus, ut ex ea quam plurimam in nos derivemus utilitatem. . . . Cum quodlibet Societatis membrum, omnem ac totam utilitatem in se velit convertere. . . . Omnes ac singuli nati cum eodem jure, non idem sortientur*

commodum. Jus ergo tam rationi consonum obmutescet ante jus illud inaequalitatis Barbarum, quod vocant aequius, quia validius. Hinc origo legum civilium. . . . Hinc origo legum politicarum. . . . Quo saevior est Tyrannis cui vis imbecillitatem submittet, eo magis indocilis est jugum pati, haud ignara, sibi rationem contra vim ipsam militare. Hinc injusti notiones, proindeque boni et mali moralis. Hinc etiam lex naturalis. . . . Malum quod in nobis humana procreant vitia, nobis ingenerat ideam virtutem illis oppositarum. . . . Hinc vis licita tantum, ubi nullus Judex, legesque proculantur. . . .
We are under the necessity of choosing chiefly those things which are useful to us personally. . . . This is why society came into existence, and we need to tighten its bonds more and more, so that we can get the greatest benefit from it. . . . Since every member of society tries to monopolize its advantages. . . . Everyone is born with the same right, but not everyone gets the same advantages. The right conformable to reason falls silent before that savage right of inequality which means (as they say) "the stronger, the juster." This is why there are civil laws. . . . This is why there are laws of states. . . . The crueler the tyranny to which weakness is forcibly subjected, the more restively does weakness bear the yoke, well aware that reason fights on its side against mere force. This is how there came to be notions of injustice and hence of moral good and evil. This is, further, the source of natural law. . . . The evil which human vices produce in us engenders the idea of exactly contrary virtues. . . . This is why force is permitted only in circumstances where there is no judge and the laws have been trampled down.
(*Societati et publicae tranquillitati perniciosas, Boni Malique morales notiones et Legis naturalis originem perperam et falso assignantes.* Dangerous to society and the public peace, wrongly and falsely assigning the moral concepts of Good and Evil and the origin of natural law.)

3. *Maxime distinguendum inter Religionem supernaturalem et Religionem revelatam. . . . omnes religiones (si unam excipias veram) praestat sane Theismus; illae si quidem a veritate degeneres, Lexque naturalis in Theismo non est decolor. Vel ipsa vera Religio revelata nec est nec esse potest alia a Lege naturali magis evoluta . . .*

We must distinguish sharply between supernatural religion and revealed religion. . . . Theism far surpasses all the religions which claim to be revealed (excepting, of course, the one true one). However much these others have failed of truth, in Theism the natural law remains unblemished. Moreover, true revealed religion is, and can be, nothing but the natural law in a higher stage of development . . .

(*In ruinam Religionis supernaturalis assertas.* Asserted to the ruin of supernatural religion.)

4. *Quaenam porro sit illa Religio quam fidem suae revelationis custodem Deus instituit? Scaturiunt hinc inde Religiones, Polytheismus, Mahumetismus, Judaismus, uno verbo Christianismus. . . . Sua quaeque Religio nimis ambitiose Miracula ostentat, suos Martyres. . . .*

What, then, may be that religion which God has established as the guardian of his revelation? There are many religions: Polytheism, Mohammedanism, Judaism, and, in short, Christianity. . . . Every religion somewhat overzealously displays its miracles, its martyrs.

(*Blasphema.* Blasphemous.)

5. *Non in uno quidem duobusve ac tribus testibus veritatem comperiemus, nec in concursu plurium testium seorsim interrogatorum. Hacce methodo singulorum testium explores probitatem, quae tibi probabiliter tantum cognita nusquam dabit nisi probabilem facti cognitionem. Ut ergo summam attingas certitudem in se indivisam, nec ex distractis hinc et inde probabilitatibus ortam, illam metiore diversa studiorum combinatione. Tunc enim manus tuae veritatem contrectabunt, ubi numerus testium tibi aperiet campum satis amplum, in quo sibi invicem occurant varia hominum studia, variaeque professiones inter se praelientur. . . . Facta sint effectus mere naturales an supernaturales nil interest, utrique iisdem circumscribuntur cancellis.*

One, two, or three witnesses do not suffice for the demonstration of truth, nor does the agreement of several witnesses separately questioned. You can test the reliability of individual witnesses by this method; but since the reliability is itself merely probable, it cannot yield you more than probable knowledge of the fact. If, therefore, you would reach complete certainty, not divided nor derived from a scattering of probabilities, you must judge it by a somewhat different combination of studies. For your hands will grasp truth the moment that the number of witnesses opens an area large enough for you to see the various interests and assertions of men in common struggle. . . . It does not matter whether the events are natural results or supernatural. Both kinds are bound within the same limits.

(No comment in the Censure.)

6. *Moses coeteris Historicis audientior hanc epocham [Creationis] determinare non dubitavit. . . . In fastis Hebraeorum se nobis offerunt tres Chronologiae pro vario Scriptuarum textu: libenter ego crediderim nullam ex his tribus a Mose Chronologiam proficisci, sed tria tantum esse Systemata praepostere adornata, et in ipsam Mosis Historiam alienis manibus inferta. . . .*

Moses, more daring than other historians, had no hesitation about fixing the limits of this epoch [Creation]. . . . Three chronologies appear in the records of the Hebrews according to the varying text of the Scriptures. I am quite willing to believe that none of the three comes from Moses, but rather that they are later inventions, supplied in reverse, and imported by foreign hands into the genuine Mosaic account.

(*Integritati et Auctoritati Librorum Mosis adversas.* Contrary to the integrity and authority of the books of Moses.)

7. *Oeconomia Mosaica in Poenis tantum ac Praemiis temporalibus sancita. . . . Cum nativus sensus indicat bona tantum temporalia, consequens est ad ea Mosem unice respexisse. . . . Legem itaque Mosaicam habemus Divinitus sancitam, sed quia positam in Poenis tantum ac Praemiis temporalibus, ideo non aeternum duraturam. . . .*

The Mosaic economy was based on temporal rewards and punishments only. . . . Since the original sense [of the terms of the Covenant] refers solely to temporal goods, the inference is that Moses had these exclusively in view. . . . Accordingly, we hold the Mosaic law to have been divinely established; nevertheless, because it rests on temporal rewards and punishments, it cannot eternally last.

(*Dignitati Legis antiquae, et Dei cum Populo Judaico foedus ineuntis bonitati detrahentes.* Detracting from the dignity of the ancient law and from the goodness of God in His covenant with the Jewish people.)

8. *Naturam eorum [miraculorum] ex se claram ac lucidam mille tricis et ambagibus plures [Scholastici] implicuerunt, suisque argumentis id effecerunt, ut nullam amplius habent vim vox Dei per miracula suam hominibus voluntatem attestantis.*

The nature of miracles is plain and clear in itself, but many scholastics have wrapped it round with a thousand shifts and circumlocutions, and by their arguments they have brought things to such a pass that the voice of God, in the very act of displaying his intentions for mankind by miracles, has no further force.

(*Fundamenta Religionis Christianae subvertentes.* Subversive of the foundations of the Christian religion.)

9. Laedunt demones, *inquit Tertullianus,* dehinc remedia praecipiunt, et postquam desinunt laedere, curasse creduntur. *Ergo omnes morborum curationes a Christo peractae, si seorsum sumantur a prophetiis, quae in eas aliquid divini refundunt, aequivoca sunt miracula, utpote illarum haberent vultum et habitum in aliquibus curationes ab Esculapio factae . . .*

"Demons do harm," says Tertullian; "then they prescribe remedies, and, having ceased injuring, are thought to have been cured." Accordingly, all Christ's healings, if they are considered apart from the prophecies which restore to them something of the divine, are doubtful miracles—particularly since they strongly resemble the cures of Esculapius . . .

(*Veritati et divinitati miraculorum Christi non sine impietate derogantes.* Derogating, not without impiety, from the truth and divinity of Christ's miracles.)

10. *Fidem omnimodam merentur [Patres] ubi Traditionem suo aevo vigentem commemorant; ast ubi in subsidium Traditionis veniunt eorum ratiocinia, jam tum ratione eorum momenta ponderentur. Non numerum Scholasticorum, sed rationes perpendo.*

The Church Fathers are completely credible when they are relating a tradition which flourished in their own time. But when they bring argument to the aid of tradition, then argument must be judged by reason. I do not number the Scholastics; I weigh their arguments.

(*Temerarias, in Theologos Catholicos injuriosas.* Rash, harmful to Catholic theologians.)

BIBLIOGRAPHICAL
ESSAY

I SUPPOSE that everything a man writes derives in some manner from his entire reading, especially if he be a scholar, whose primary and professional task it is to read. Amid all this reading, moreover, books of indirect relevance to the main theme have sometimes as much importance as books of direct relevance. Hence a bibliography which undertook to give all the sources of a particular book would be large indeed. Comment upon some of the sources, however, will be useful, for they draw the reader into areas he may delight to explore. This sort of comment I now undertake for the bibliographical sources of *Heroes and Heretics*.

First, the great histories. There are several masterpieces in this genre: the works of Herodotus, Thucydides, Tacitus; Gibbon's magisterial *Decline and Fall of the Roman Empire*; Michelet's *Histoire de France*; Carlyle's *French Revolution*; histories of England by Hume, Macaulay,[1] Froude, and (perhaps) John Richard Green; and, I would be willing to add, Bancroft's *History of the United States*. These works have the

1. Macaulay wrote, in a letter dated March 8, 1849: "At last I have attained true glory. As I walked through Fleet Street the day before yesterday, I saw a copy of Hume at a bookseller's window with the following label: 'Only 2 pounds, two shillings. Hume's History of England in eight volumes, highly valuable as an introduction to Macaulay.' I laughed so convulsively that other people who were staring at the books took me for a poor domented gentleman. Alas for poor David!" (Sir George Otto Trevelyan: *Life and Letters of Lord Macaulay* [Oxford University Press: World's Classics Series; 1932], Vol. II, p. 190).

singular property of being undamaged by their own mistakes. They have a grandeur, a respect for humanity, a moral elegance, that saves all. Philosophy has not been so fortunate in its historians. By a tradition now long established and difficult to breach, historians of philosophy content themselves with the chronological recording of ideas, and nothing more personal appears than the names of the men who thought them. What thus results is "a spectral ballet of bloodless categories"—formidable, to be sure, somewhat tedious, and more than a little inaccurate because divorced from life. Within these limits, Windelband's *History of Philosophy* (translated by James H. Tufts; New York: The Macmillan Co.; Second Edition, 1921), a work of the 1880's, remains particularly valuable for its excellent organization. Windelband traced the largest philosophical concepts through various epochs of history, and was thus able to reveal, though abstractly, their development. For the play of a first-rate mind upon the work of predecessors, Bertrand Russell's *History of Western Philosophy* (New York: Simon and Schuster; 1945) is admirably stimulating, and gains from the fact that it contains rather more Russell than history of philosophy.

But the best men to read are, of course, the philosophers themselves. The notion that they need commentary is, in some part, a hoax of the commentators. It is difficult to see how a philosopher can have been a great philosopher without knowing his own mind, and if he knew that, he needs no commentator to point out the contents. Yet a sad penalty attaches itself to greatness: the more eminent the philosopher, the more probable it is that commentators, into the latest age, will have imported into him their own favorite ideas.

Thus the wise reader will want to know what Plato actually did write in the dialogues, or Augustine in the *Confessions* and in *The City of God*. A reader who is not at ease in Greek or Latin will have to rely on translators, and these differ, not so much in ability, as in the culture and scholarship prevailing when they worked. Most of us know Plato through Jowett's translation—a great *English* classic, which reveals Plato the poet rather more than Plato the philosopher. For the *Republic,* I have long preferred the translation by Davies and Vaughn (London: Macmillan and Co., Golden Treasury Series; 1852 and often reprinted), but there is an excellent recent one by W. H. D. Rouse, *Great Dialogues of Plato* (New York: Mentor Books MD167; 1956). Shelley's incomplete translation of the *Symposium* has the charm of being Shelley's, and there is a lovely Victorian translation of the *Phaedrus* by J. Wright. These two will be found in the Everyman's Library volume, *Five Dialogues of Plato* (New York: E. P. Dutton and Co.; 1924).

Our knowledge of Socrates comes from Xenophon's *Memorabilia,*

Aristophanes' satirical play *The Clouds,* and, above all, from those dialogues of Plato which contain much biography. Of these, the *Apology,* the *Crito,* and the *Phaedo* are most important, for they give in detail the circumstances of Socrates' trial and death. It is possible to offer reasons for doubting the Platonic portrait, but I think it is not possible really to doubt it; the account is much too convincing. *Socrates: the Man and His Thought,* an admirable little book by the late Professor A. E. Taylor (New York: Doubleday Anchor Books; 1952), reworks this account in terms of modern scholarship.

On the philosophers before Socrates' time, the reigning work in English was, during many years, John Burnet's *Early Greek Philosophy* (London: A. and C. Black; Fourth Edition, 1930). It has now been displaced by *The Presocratic Philosophers,* by G. S. Kirk and J. E. Raven (Cambridge University Press, 1957), which brings to the subject a more recent and hence more extensive scholarship. On the Greeks generally, a large corpus of splendid commentary exists; no other subject has been more lavishly adorned with erudition. Among these myriad works, Lowes Dickinson's *The Greek View of Life* (various editions) remains a small masterpiece, and Kitto's *The Greeks* (in the Penguin Series) allows Kitto's Toryism to show very pleasantly.

The life of Jesus, the Bible, and the problems relating to both, however, are matters of much greater difficulty. A vast literature surrounds all these, such as only a scholar devoted to the subject can adequately know. I confess at once a limited acquaintance. My belief that the historical Jesus was leader of an insurrectionary movement comes directly from Archibald Robertson's *The Origins of Christianity* (New York: International Publishers; 1954), a book (so it seems to me) of most impressive proof. The interpretation is, however, by no means new. It appeared as early as 1838, in Charles Hennell's *Enquiry Concerning the Origins of Christianity,* the book that made George Eliot a skeptic and set her to translating Strauss's *Leben Jesu.* The same view appeared in Kautsky's *Ursprung des Christenthums* 1908), recently translated by Henry Mins under the title *Foundations of Christianity* (New York: S. A. Russell; 1953).

This interpretation is, quite plainly, attractive to men of radical mind, and is ordinarily not held by scholars who separate erudition from politics. However, the chance of bias against the view is perhaps as great as the chance of bias for it. If the reader finds my account extreme, he may undertake to correct it with the aid of various scholarly books: Rudolph Bultmann, *Jesus and the Word,* translated by Louise Pettibone Smith and Erminie Huntress Lantero (New York: Charles Scribner's Sons; 1958); Morton S. Enslin, *The Prophet from Nazareth* (New York: McGraw-Hill; 1961); E. J. Goodspeed, *A Life of Jesu* (New York:

Harper; 1950); John Knox, *Christ the Lord* (Chicago: Willett, Clarke and Co.; 1945). Two accounts of the subject from the Roman Catholic point of view are: Jules Lebreton, *The Life and Teaching of Jesus Christ Our Lord* (New York: The Macmillan Co.; 1950), and Henry Daniel-Rops, *Jesus and His Times* (New York: E. P. Dutton and Co.; 1954). Canon B. H. Streeter's *The Four Gospels* (New York: The Macmillan Co.; 1925) is perhaps the best scholarly account in English of the textual problems in the Gospels.

As for the Bible itself, perfect clarity (or approximations to it) must be sought in the work of the latest translators. Goodspeed is clear but pedestrian; Moffatt is clear and elegant. The New Testament, in *The New English Bible,* published (1961) by the University Presses of both Oxford and Cambridge, is the work of collaborators who are left nameless. It seems to me to be, on the whole, the best translation thus far. The original Greek of the New Testament is of very modest literary quality, and the NEB translators have matched it with comparable English. A reader of the NEB, therefore, will get approximately the same impression of the text as an ancient reader got, say, in the third century A.D. The King James Bible (the Authorized Version) of course stands alone. It is even more an English classic than is Jowett's Plato. The splendor of its speech arose directly from the struggles of our ancestors toward nationhood and cultural independence. I know no Hebrew and remember not much Greek, but I suspect that, as literature, the King James Bible surpasses its original. It is, however, often unclear and sometimes inaccurate, and the enormous inspiration it yields comes from terrestrial history rather than from transcendental doctrine.

An admirable source book on church history is Henry Bettenson's *Documents of the Christian Church* (Oxford University Press, 1949—new edition, 1963). This small, compact volume gives, in English translation, all the historical materials required for an understanding of the subject. For the history of doctrine, the standard work is still Harnack's *Dogmengeschichte,* which appeared in English translation, 1896–99, under the title *History of Dogma* (London, Williams and Norgate). There is a recent reprint in paperback in four volumes (New York: Dover; 1961). The writings of the Church Fathers, in the original tongues, are collected in an enormous fleet of volumes which constitute Migne's *Patrologia.* A digest, with useful commentary, will be found in Johannes Quasten's *Patrology,* now appearing, volume by volume, from Spectrum Publishers at Antwerp. Bettenson has done a useful anthology entitled *The Early Christian Fathers* (Oxford University Press, 1956), and Anne Fremantle has edited, with her customary skill, *A Treasury of Early Christianity* (New York: Mentor Books MT285; 1960). F. A. Wright's *Fathers of the Church* (London: George Routledge and Sons;

1928) has fewer but more complete selections, with a most enlightening introductory essay. Bishop Lightfoot's *The Apostolic Fathers* (London: Macmillan and Co.; 1898) gives the original text and English translation of the essential treatises in early Christianity. Some readers may wish to consult, in the Loeb Classical Library, Irenaeus's *Adversus Haereticos,* and to enjoy in that same series the energetic polemics of the great Tertullian.

Many of these books relate also to the struggles of the Church against its own heresies. On the Trinitarian controversy I would doubt that Cardinal Newman's *Arians of the Fourth Century* (London: Longmans; 1833) can be surpassed; its Athanasian bias is amply balanced by Newman's own luminous and candid mind. There are several extensive collections of the Nicene and Post-Nicene Fathers, any of which will adequately serve. Augustine can be read in various editions and translations, of which Monsignor Ryan's translation of the *Confessions* (New York: Doubleday Image Books; 1960) and Marcus Dods's of *The City of God* (New York: Random House, Modern Library; 1950) are particularly good. Augustine's smaller treatises will be of most interest to theologians, but they will repay reading as the works of a magnificent mind. *The Cambridge Medieval History,* Volume I, has abundant material, particularly from Alice Gardiner, on the ideological conflicts of the fifth century. The classic work defining heresy is Vincent of Lerins' *Commonitorium,* written in A.D. 434 (translated by Rudolph Morris, J. U. D., in *Fathers of the Church*; New York: Fathers of the Church Inc.; 1949). I have drawn from Vincent much of the concept of heresy which I expound in this book.

On the Middle Ages, three works seem to me exceptionally useful: Henry Adams's *Mont-Saint-Michel and Chartres* (New York: Mentor Books MT 317; 1961), C. H. Haskins's *The Renaissance of the Twelfth Century* (New York: Meridian Books; 1957), and G. G. Coulton's *Medieval Panorama* (New York: The Macmillan Co.; 1945). The Adams book, an enchanting piece of American scholarship, seems to express what life really felt like to medieval folk. The Coulton portrays that life in rich concrete detail, and the Haskins matches the urbanity of its subject with its own urbanity of style. Abelard is best reached through his autobiography, the *Historia Calamitatum* (Texte Critique edited by J. Monfrin; Paris: J. Vrin; 1959); there is an English translation by H. A. Bellows under the title of *The Story of My Misfortunes* (St. Paul, Minnesota: T. A. Boyd; 1922). Interesting selections from Abelard's writings, translated into French, appear in Maurice de Gondillac's *Oeuvres choisies d'Abélard* (Paris: Aubier; 1945). English readers will find Abelard and the other great Scholastics translated and excerpted in Professor McKeon's standard anthology, *Selections from*

Medieval Philosophy (New York: Charles Scribner's Sons; 1930). *The Portable Medieval Reader,* edited by J. B. Ross and Mary McLaughlin (New York: The Viking Press; 1949), provides excellent source material for the period, and *The Oxford Book of Medieval Latin Verse,* edited by F. J. E. Raby (Oxford University Press, 1959), will delight all those who can read it. Henry C. Lea's classic, *The Inquisition of the Middle Ages,* now abridged into one volume by Margaret Nicholson (New York: The Macmillan Co.; 1961), remains the authoritative account of that odious institution.

G. W. Greenaway's *Arnold of Brescia* (Cambridge University Press, 1931) and H. B. Workman's *John Wyclif* (Oxford University Press, 1926) are excellent biographies. The late Middle Ages, with all their corruptions and hopes of reform, stand eloquently revealed in two works of the period: Langland's *The Vision of Piers Plowman* and Chaucer's *Canterbury Tales* (the Prologue especially). The *Tales* may be read in various editions, some of which have a modernized text. The most poetic rendering of *Piers* into modern English is, strange to say, the prose translation by J. F. Goodridge (Baltimore: Penguin Classics L 87; 1959). Froude's *Lectures on the Council of Trent* (New York: Charles Scribner's Sons; 1896), a work well worthy of that admirable historian, describes the defensive politics of the Roman Church confronted with the Reformation. On the development of the English Bible, C. C. Butterworth's *The Literary Lineage of the King James Bible* (Philadelphia: The University of Pennsylvania Press; 1941) deserves more note than it appears to have. James Baikie's *The English Bible and Its Story* (London: Seely, Service and Co.; 1928) is useful, but, distressingly, its sources are not documented. Two other books in the Penguin Library give admirable accounts of medieval times in England: Doris May Stanton's *English Society in the Early Middle Ages* (Baltimore: Penguin Books, Pelican A252; 1951) and A. R. Myers's *England in the Late Middle Ages* (Harmondsworth: Penguin Books Ltd., Pelican A234; 1952).

A year or so ago there appeared in England a book about the books that have been written about Joan of Arc. There are, it appears, some three thousand of these—a fact which must humble anyone who writes about Joan. Of the three thousand, I have, for my own part, read perhaps six, but I doubt that my view of the case would be changed by reading the rest. Joan's character is very clear in the record of her trial— a record almost stenographic. It has been recently reprinted, along with the later proceedings of rehabilitation, in Raymond Oursel's *Les Procès de Jeanne d'Arc* (Paris: Editions Denoël; 1959).

The most useful recent anthology of writings of the Reformers is *Great Voices of the Reformation,* edited by Harry Emerson Fosdick (New York: Random House, Modern Library; 1954). A reader who adds to this volume another in the same series, *The Wisdom of Catholicism* (edited by A. C. Pegis; New York: Random House; 1955), will have before him the whole range of Christian speculation about man and the cosmos. Froude's *Life and Letters of Erasmus* (New York: Charles Scribner's Sons; 1894) and *Short Studies on Great Subjects* (Oxford University Press: World's Classics Series; 1924) offer absorbing accounts of Erasmus and Luther and the struggles between them. The celebrated (and classic) work on the economic origins of the Reformation is, of course, R. H. Tawney's *Religion and the Rise of Capitalism* (New York: Harcourt, Brace and Co.; 1926), a model of scholarly analysis and literary style. This book changed the thinking of my generation; it continues, I hope, to do the same for younger folk, who can now possess it in an inexpensive paperback edition (New York: New American Library; 1947). A wonderfully clear and compendious digest of orthodox Catholic doctrine, which also specifies the traditional heresies in some detail, is Gervais Dumeige's *La Foi Catholique* (Paris: Editions de l'Orante; 1961).

The "modern" philosophers have been so called to distinguish them from the medieval. It is a distinction they themselves made every effort to establish. Their works may be read, for the most part, with ease and with joy: we are still so nearly their children that, in order to reach them, we do not make the imaginative leap that is needed to take us into the Middle Ages or antiquity. English prose has few works finer than Hobbes's *Leviathan* and Locke's *Essay,* or French prose than Descartes's *Discours de la Méthode* and Pascal's *Pensées.* Bossuet, a great stylist and an honest conservative, reveals the political implications of orthodoxy—as bishops alone can know them, but as bishops seldom venture to state them (*Oraisons Funèbres, L'Histoire des variations des Eglises protestantes, Avertissements au Protestants*).

Among modern philosophers, Spinoza, Kant, and Hegel really do need commentators—all three because of their vocabularies, and Hegel because of his startling (but very fruitful) dialectical method. Hegel is himself one of the most stimulating historians of philosophy, as the first six chapters of the Shorter Logic show (*The Logic of Hegel,* translated by William Wallace, Oxford University Press, 1892). Despite all difficulty, these men demand direct acquaintance, and the reader who labors over them will be well repaid. If small doses seem preferable, I would suggest Joseph Ratner's *The Philosophy of Spinoza* (New York: Random House, Modern Library; 1927), which gives skillfully arranged selections from translations by Elwes and White, and abolishes the baffling geometrical form. Kant wrote a popularization (or such it was intended to be) of his main theory in a small work which he proudly entitled *Prolegomena to Any Future Metaphysic.* This is now available in the Mahaffey-Carus translation, revised and edited by L. W. Beck (New York: The Little Library of the Liberal Arts; 1950), and offers a not quite permissible escape from the *Critique of Pure Reason*. I know of no self-simplification by Hegel, but his writings may be pleasantly sampled in *Hegel: Selections*, edited by J. Loewenberg (New York: Charles Scribner's Sons; 1929), and in *The Philosophy of Hegel*, edited by Carl J. Friedrich (New York: Random House, Modern Library; 1953). Readers will ordinarily find that the easiest approach to Hegel is through his *Philosophy of History*. Two excellent anthologies in The Modern Library, taken together, provide all excerpts the average reader will need from philosophers of the seventeenth and eighteenth centuries: *The English Philosophers from Bacon to Mill*, edited by E. A. Burtt (New York: Random House; 1939), and *The European Philosophers from Descartes to Kant*, edited by Monroe Beardsley (New York: Random House; 1960).

On the French Enlightenment, a vast literature, vastly entertaining, exists in the French language, in which of course it is best studied. André Billy's *Vie de Diderot* (Paris: Flammarion; 1932) is a novelized biography, but so near to true biography as to escape the faults of novelization. Pierre Grosclaude's *Un Audacieux Message: l'Encyclopédie* (Paris: Nouvelles Editions Latines; 1951) tells, with admirable terseness, the story of the great Encyclopedia. Professor J. Lough offers selections from the Encyclopedia in *The Encyclopédie of Diderot and D'Alembert* (Cambridge University Press, 1954), and has edited also *Diderot: Selected Philosophical Writings* (Cambridge University Press, 1953), both volumes containing the original French text. An anthology of Diderot's writings in English translation has been published in paperback by International Publishers, of New York. Diderot's letters to his mistress Sophie Volland give an incomparable picture of an intellectual's life in those days of *la douceur de vivre*; they may be read in the two volumes of *Lettres à Sophie Volland*, edited by André Babelon (Paris: Gallimard; 1938). There are several anthologies of Voltaire in English, but the best is probably *The Portable Voltaire* (New York, The Viking Press), which contains his marvelous account of British culture and philosophy in the *Lettres Anglaises*. E. A. Beller and M. duP. Lee have edited *Selections from Bayle's Dictionary* (Princeton University Press, 1952), and have thus made available in English the writings of one of the founders of the Enlightenment. For what the French call *la petite histoire* (history personal and anecdotal), the essays of G. Lenotre, whose real name was Théodore Gosselin (d. 1934), are altogether unrivalled. There are several volumes of these essays, but perhaps I may direct the reader especially to *Versailles au temps des Rois* (Paris: Grasset; 1934). For *la grande histoire*, I may suggest *Louis XIV* by Sagnac and Saint-Léger,

La Prépondérance Anglaise by Pierre Muret, and *La Fin de l'Ancien Régime* by Philippe Sagnac; these are Volumes X to XII in the series *Peuples et Civilizations,* published in Paris in 1947 by the Presses Universitaires de France.

For insight into the Victorian Age, Lytton Strachey's *Eminent Victorians* (London: Chatto and Windus; 1948) remains, to my mind, unsurpassed. Cardinal Newman is best understood through his own *Apologia Pro Vita Sua,* of which there are several editions—a work which shows how candor can crush calumny. Darwin's view of himself is endearingly set forth in the little *Autobiography,* edited by Nora Barnes (New York: Harcourt Brace and Company; 1958); his *Origin of Species* and *Descent of Man* are published within one volume in The Modern Library (New York: Random House; no date). Chesterton's *The Victorian Age in Literature* (New York: Henry Holt and Co.; 1913) is a delightful work of its kind, which may sustain the author's almost vanished reputation. A recent book, *Apes, Angels and Victorians,* by William Irvine (New York: Meridian Books; 1959), a charming account of the struggles of Darwin and Huxley, has the sole and strange defect of being perhaps too constantly witty. The supreme work on the long contest between religion and science is, however, Andrew Dickson White's *History of the Warfare of Science with Theology* (New York: D. Appleton-Century Co.; 1936, two volumes). It was first published in 1896, when its author was president emeritus of Cornell University; it has recently been republished by George Braziller. The zest of White's attack on obscurantism, his freedom from the bias and timidity which ordinarily afflict a college administrator, are beyond praise and (I fear) beyond imitation.

Marxism must be sought primarily in Marx himself—in the mature Marx, not the young Marx (as some people have lately been saying). His philosophical observations are in the nature of *obiter dicta,* scattered throughout his writings: for example, the Preface to *Capital,* and the *Theses on Feuerbach.* Engels assumed the task of explicating dialectical materialism, and his account of it will be found in *Historical Materialism, Ludwig Feuerbach,* and the *Anti-Dühring* (a celebrated polemic against an unlucky German professor). The heart of Marxist doctrine lies, of course, in the *Manifesto of the Communist Party* (1848), a joint work of Marx and Engels, which they themselves later said (1872) should always be read in the light of changing times. Most readers interested in the subject will read Volume I of *Capital,* if not the remaining two. I may say, for my own part, that I regard Marx's *Eighteenth Brumaire of Louis Bonaparte* as the most splendid of all his performances, for there he shows with incomparable skill the interplay of theory and practice, of general trends and particular occasions, of things economic, social, and political. All these works, with the exception of *Capital*, will be found complete (or nearly so) in *Karl Marx: Selected Works*, edited by Clemence Dutt (Moscow: Cooperative Publishing Society of Foreign Workers in the U.S.S.R.; 1935, two volumes). A recent paperback anthology, smaller and more readily obtainable, is *Marx and Engels: Basic Writings on Politics and Philosophy*, ably edited by Lewis S. Feuer (New York: Doubleday Anchor Books A185; 1959).

For events in the history of the United States, Richard B. Morris's *Encyclopedia of American History* (New York: Harper and Brothers; 1953) is admirably organized and rich in detail. Contemporary records of the Pilgrim Fathers, especially selections from Bradford's wonderful journal, will be found in G. F. Willison's anthology, *The Pilgrim Reader* (New York: Doubleday and Co.; 1953). Bertram Lippincott's *Indians, Privateers, and High Society* (Philadelphia: J. B. Lippincott Co.; 1961), though not formal in its historical writing, has captivating material about New England in colonial times. Bernard Smith's *The Democratic Spirit* (New York: Alfred A. Knopf; 1940) anthologizes the whole range of the libertarian tradition in the United States. Jonathan Edwards, the ablest of American philosophers, is admirably presented in *Jonathan Edwards: Representative Selections*, edited by C. H. Faust and T. H. Johnson (New York: Hill and Wang, American Century Series; 1962). *The Life and Writings of Abraham Lincoln*, edited by Philip Van Doren Stern (New York: Random House, Modern Library; 1940), lets its selections reveal the growth of that remarkable mind, in which rectitude and mercy met together for the salvation of the country. An excellent anthology of American philosophical writing is *The Development of American Philosophy*, edited by W. G. Muelder and L. Sears (Boston: Houghton Mifflin Co.; 1940). Aleine Austin's *The Labor Story* (New York: Coward-McCann; 1949) is an informative account of the labor movement in the United States. There is an anthology of Eugene Debs's writings and speeches, published without date but within his lifetime, at Girard, Kansas—a somewhat random and unorganized work (the better, indeed, for being unorganized) which conveys with a certain immediacy the hopes and the zeal of that noble spirit.

Such, then, are some of the books which have helped me toward knowledge and understanding. Among them are a few which gave not only knowledge but inspiration. No writer can ever feel that he has read enough; there must always be the fear of knowledge overlooked or wisdom lost. But readers may be more comfortable: they may read or not read, they may open or close books where and when they wish. It is a fundamental right of man, and no government has as yet entirely cancelled it.

INDEX

A NOTE ON THE TYPE

THIS BOOK is set in Granjon, a type named in compliment to Robert Granjon, type-cutter and printer—Antwerp, Lyons, Rome, Paris—active from 1523 to 1590. The boldest and most original designer of his time, he was one of the first to practice the trade of type-founder apart from that of printer. This type face was designed by George W. Jones, who based his drawings on a type used by Claude Garamond (1510–61) in his beautiful French books, and more closely resembles Garamond's own than do any of the various modern types that bear his name.

Composed, printed, and bound by
The Haddon Craftsmen, Inc., Scranton, Pa.
Typography and binding design by
GUY FLEMING

CONNECTICUT COLLEGE LIBRARY
109 D918
Heroes heretics;

3 1839 001168271

dc

DATE DUE

JUL 1 0 '64			
NO 2 0 64			
DEC 3 1964 DEPT.			
SEP 2 5 1968 CARREL			
GAYLORD			PRINTED IN U.S.A.